FROM RATIONALISM TO IRRATIONALITY

THE DECLINE OF THE WESTERN MIND FROM THE RENAISSANCE TO THE PRESENT

C. GREGG SINGER

Presbyterian and Reformed Publishing Company
Phillipsburg, New Jersey 08865
1979

PRINTED IN THE UNITED STATES OF AMERICA

ISBN: 0-87552-428-1

PRESBYTERIAN AND REFORMED PUBLISHING CO.
PHILLIPSBURG, NEW JERSEY
1979

Dedication

Even as the fall of Rome has challenged many of the greatest minds of the West to find a satisfactory explanation for this apparently catastrophic event in human history, so has the decline of the Western mind during the past century offered a similar challenge to the scholarship of our own era. Many efforts have been made to explain the emergence of the political, social, economic, and cultural decline which has become so very obvious during the second half of the twentieth century. Many of them have not been unproductive, and they have shed some light on this perplexing question. But only a very few of the scholars have attempted to interpret the present intellectual crisis which is engulfing the West in terms of a consistent biblical theism.

This work is written in the light of the conviction that the basic epistemological and apologetical principles so ably set forth by Cornelius Van Til, who for 45 years served as the professor of apologetics at the Westminster Theological Seminary in Philadelphia, offer the key to the proper solution of this tremendously important question. It is the purpose of this author to apply these basic principles to the history of Western thought in the hope that such an approach will serve to give an understanding of what has been taking place in Western culture. He gladly acknowledges his great indebtedness to this stalwart and brilliant defender of the historic Christian faith, whose great scholarship is equalled only by his Christian humility and kindly spirit.

Once again I gladly admit my tremendous debt to my good wife Marjorie, who has consistently inspired me in my chosen profession and who has also so patiently typed the manuscript for this book.

C. Gregg Singer

Contents

Introduction

That the Western mind is sick unto death and that Western culture and the civilization to which it gave birth are in serious danger of collapse are facts that have become so evident that few observers are prepared to dispute this conclusion and argue for their vitality. Many historians and students of Western culture have taken note of this decline and have attempted to offer various explanations of this phenomenon. Oswald Spengler in his *Decline of the West,* Arnold Toynbee in his *Study of History,* and Pitirim Sorokin in his *Crisis of Our Age* have offered their differing diagnoses of the illness which has the Western mind in its grip. Arnold Toynbee, while admitting that Western civilization is on the brink of destruction, made a desperate effort to offer hope for the possibility of the recovery of the West. On the other hand, Spengler was frankly pessimistic and insisted that historical determinism had doomed the West and there was no possible remedy for the fatal illness from which it was suffering.

In quite a different vein of thought, John Hallowell in his *Main Currents in Modern Political Thought* tackled the problem and offered a curative prescription for the West, but he also left the impression with his readers that he had little hope that the West was willing to pay the price which the cure demanded. The price, according to Hallowell, involves the renunciation of the humanism inherited from the Renaissance and a return to the biblical view of government. Hallowell was very frank to say that if the West would not be willing to pay this price, then it must be willing to pay another price, and this price would be the emergence of a new wave of totalitarianism among the governments of the Western world. Although Hallowell's work is largely concerned with the development of modern political thought, the author, with great insight, portrayed the decline of political philosophy in the West to the progressive denial of the biblical view of government and the resultant development of a political philosophy which was both secular and naturalistic in character.

Hallowell's basic thesis is that modern political thought reflects the basic irrationality which has achieved an increasingly dominant position in Western philosophy since the Renaissance, and this basic irrationality gained a dominant role in the intellectual world of the nineteenth century with the appearance of Hume, Kant, and Hegel, and this dominance necessarily resulted in a political philosophy which culminated in the appearance of modern totalitarianism.

This basic irrationality in Western thought has engaged the attention of many scholars in recent years, secular and Christian, and it has received excellent treatment in two recent volumes, *The Emergence of Modern Humanism,* and *The Ordeal of Modern Liberalism,* by Wilson Coates and Hayden White. These authors, making no pretense of writing from a theistic point of view, deal with the issue of growing irrationalism on a wider scale than does Hallowell, but on the other hand, they do not pay as much attention to the political implications. In general, however, they are in agreement with Hallowell that modern liberalism, whether it be political, social, or economic, is suffering from the effects of its own inner contradictions which have led it into the prison house of an irrationalism from which there is no escape. On the other hand, these authors apparently see no solution to the dilemma which they have so graphically and painstakingly depicted. While they freely admit the dangers of materialism and existentialism, they do not suggest that the remedy for that ordeal is a return to Christian theism.

The basic premise of this study is that this flight from a rational interpretation of all reality (i.e., the view that the world, man, and history have meaning and purpose in distinction to the more narrow view of the term as it is used in the history of philosophy) is the logical and necessary consequence of the importation of classical philosophy into the mainstream of European thought during the Renaissance. The thesis of this work, then, is that the rationalism adopted by the humanists of the Renaissance from classical culture brought with it the irrationalism inherent in Greek and Roman thought and that this classical world and life view has gained the mastery of the modern mind. As a result, Western thought of the twentieth century has been brought to the nadir of despair and frustration with the appearance of existentialism and its devastating impact on Western culture. The history of Western thought since the Renaissance vividly supports the accuracy of what Charles Pinckney wrote to his Charleston constituents nearly two hundred years ago: "We may think wrongly upon right principles, but we must forever do so upon wrong ones, for how can the stream flow pure when the source of truth is polluted?" The seeds of irrationalism were buried in the soil of the Renaissance philosophy and soon began to germinate in the friendly soil of seventeenth-century Europe. Both the

Renaissance and the Reformation, each in its own way, had so shaken the strength of the Roman Catholic Church, even in nominally Catholic countries, that the church was virtually powerless to prevent the growth of philosophical systems which were basically contrary to its theology. In those countries where the Reformation held sway, philosophers who did not accept the theology of the Reformers found themselves in possession of a new freedom from restraint on the part of either church or state, which allowed them to develop their own systems of thought with little or no reference to any creedal or theological position.

Although this philosophical development was inspired by the rebirth of classical thought with its insistence that man is the measure of all things, it soon began to look elsewhere for its basic presuppositions, and in the Enlightenment it found a new standard of measurment which, made available by the scientific revolution, had its culmination in the work of Sir Isaac Newton. By the end of the seventeenth century, science and the scientific method, along with mathematics, had replaced the classical mind as the source and the measure of all truth. Man's scientific achievements and the scientific interpretation of the world of nature became the new deity before which the European mind of the latter seventeenth and eighteenth centuries bowed in abject adoration, as this new deity was now being mediated to man through a new high priesthood composed of scientists and mathematicians.

Thus the eighteenth and nineteenth centuries constitute the age of worship of science, as modern man found in his new understanding and mastery of the natural world a new frame of reference, and he substituted science for the God of the Bible, whom he no longer worshiped. This departure from even the deistic concept of nature brought with it a new wave of irrationalism in Western thought, signalized by the appearance of Kantian idealism in Europe, Romanticism in England, and Transcendentalism in this country. Kantian irrationalism became the great matrix which has given birth to the many strains of thought during the nineteenth and twentieth centuries. It was but a short intellectual hop from Kant and Hegel to Marx and Darwin. By 1900, modern liberalism was in the grip of the Great Ordeal, an ordeal which has culminated in the triumph of existentialism over much of the Western mind and which has brought in its wake a devastating loss of consciousness of meaning and purpose in life and the possibility of a productive intellectual and cultural activity.

In the twentieth century, the irrationalism of the Renaissance has been devoured by its own offspring, the irrationalism of our day. The Renaissance may be dead as a historical phenomenon, but it has killed its own offspring in the deluge of irrationalism which has engulfed modern thought.

This is the essence of the ordeal which confronts liberalism today, and for which it has no answer. In embracing the various facets of Renaissance thought, it created its own ordeal. Thus, the solution to the dilemma demands that liberalism repudiate the intellectual heritage which it claims as its own.

The author makes no claim to originality in writing an intellectual history of the West in the light of this thesis. He owes a great debt to Cornelius Van Til, long time professor of Christian apologetics at the Westminster Theological Seminary in Philadelphia, with whom he had the great privilege of study for two summers for the purpose of producing this book. He approaches this task with a great sense of his own unworthiness, but also with the burning conviction that the basic principles of Dr. Van Til's system of apologetics should have a far wider treatment and application than it has thus far received. These principles make it possible to understand the various threads of thought which have entered into the vast stream of ideas which we call the modern Western mind.

But this development of Western thought with its intricacies and inherently contradictory currents offers no built-in interpretation of its own unfolding. Modern scholarship with its liberal predilections may well recognize that ordeal which liberalism faces today, but this liberalism offers no clues as to the origin and meaning of this ordeal and leaves the liberal scholar by the outcome of the humanistic philosophy which has claimed his loyalty. He is thus confronted with questions which he cannot answer. How can the denial of all meaning and purpose be the fruit of a philosophy which in its early stages confidently set out on its quest for truth in the light of the conviction that the mind of man is fully capable of discovering all truth, purpose, and meaning in human existence? How can rationalism issue forth in irrationalism? How can the concepts of freedom which the twentieth century inherited from the Renaissance and the Enlightenment produce the political totalitarianism of our day? How can the eighteenth-century dream of a heavenly utopia on earth and the nineteenth-century confidence in the inherent goodness and perfectibility of man be dashed to pieces on the rocks of present-day reality? How could the almost unlimited optimism of the eighteenth and nineteenth centuries in the future of Western civilization be so easily turned to despair and doubt that this civilization can survive beyond the end of the present century?

That these questions demand answers and that modern liberalism has been utterly unable to provide any basis for the understanding of the present dilemma of Western culture is all too obvious. Liberalism—intellectual, political, social, and economic—has produced the ordeal which it confronts and for which it has no answer.

It is the basic conviction of this writer that the dilemma can be answered. However, the answer cannot be found in the liberalism which is the cause of the ordeal. The answer can and must be found in a consistent Christian theism which looks to a consistent and well-rounded biblical doctrine for its frame of reference. It is furthermore the conviction of this author that the answer to the problems of contemporary culture can and must be found in historic Calvinism and in the apologetics and epistemology which underlie this theology as it has been so faithfully and profoundly set forth by Van Til.

Chapter 1

Rationalism and Irrationalism In Classical and Medieval Thought

Irrationalism and anti-intellectualism are not the peculiar properties and attributes of modern thought. Neither did they suddenly emerge in the Western mind during the Renaissance, even though at first glance this might seem to be the case, for it is certainly true that the philosophers of that era were much bolder in the formulation of their conviction in the autonomy of human reason than were the scholars of the Middle Ages.

At the same time it must be admitted that the irrationalism which lurked beneath the mighty endeavors of Thomas Aquinas and his fellow scholastic thinkers was not supported with either the same purpose or boldness which became characteristic of the thinking of so many Renaissance humanists. However much we may disagree with Scholasticism and its endeavors to find a synthesis with Greek thought, particularly with that of Aristotle, it cannot be denied that with very few exceptions, if any, these medieval scholars all held to the unique authority of Scriptures and to many basic Christian doctrines. Their tendency to ascribe varying degrees of autonomy to the human mind and will were not the fruit of unbelief but of the attempt to achieve a synthesis between Augustine and the heritage which he left them on the one hand, and the philosophy of Aristotle on the other. Medieval irrationalism was more the result of a failure to understand that Aristotle and Augustine could not be reconciled, rather than of the desire to overthrow his theological legacy. It is not too much to say that Aristotle, particularly for the Scholastics, held a fatal fascination which ultimately undermined the foundations of what seemed to be a magnificent medieval theological and philosophical cathedral, a kind of Chartres or Notre Dame for the human mind.

If we are to find the seeds of the irrationalism which now pervades both modern philosophy and theology, we must go back beyond even the Middle Ages and look into the basic presuppositions of classical thought. We must retrace our steps in our investigation of the history of Western thought and come to terms with the basic presuppositions of the philosophies of Parmenides, Plato, and Aristotle. For it is in Greek thought that the seeds were sown which have persisted throughout the whole of the intellectual development of the West and which have been a continual challenge to orthodox Christianity.

The seeds of this irrationalism are common to all the varieties of Greek philosophy.[1] All Greek philosophers held to the autonomy of man and his rational powers. Man is autonomous, and because he is autonomous his philosophy is quite capable of explaining the universe and his role in that universe. In the light of this same assumption, the Greek mind, to the extent which it felt the necessity of belief in a God of some kind, also exulted in its ability and right to fashion the kind of deity or divinity which suited its purposes.

In the same way, Greek thought constructed its metaphysical, logical, ethical, and political systems. Man was the center of all truth and the final arbiter of his meaning and destiny.

However much the various schools of Greek thought may seem to differ, or actually differ, in their metaphysical and epistemological presuppositions, these differences pale into insignificance in comparison with those basic assumptions which they all held in common. And because they held these basic presuppositions in common, these various schools of philosophy all held the truth of God in error, as the Apostle Paul clearly indicates in the early chapters of his Epistle to the Romans. Because they were committed to these principles, they were also committed to a rationalism which had as its inescapable corollary the principle of irrationalism.

For the purposes of this study we need only to refer to Parmenides, Plato, and Aristotle, for in their philosophies we see these basic presuppositions at work producing highly developed philosophies which, although seeming to advance man's understanding of the universe and of himself, deal with questions for which they had no answers and provided a legacy of the belief in the autonomy of the human mind and will which from their days until our own has consistently led philosophy into false and dangerous answers for the great issues of life and ultimately has plunged it into a vast quagmire of existentialist disillusionment and despair.

The principle of the autonomy of human reason became very visible in the thinking of Parmenides (b. *c.* 515 B.C.). A member of the Eleatic school of thought, he was regarded as a great, if not the greatest, pre-

1. It is not necessary that we consider all the various schools of Greek thought for the purposes of this study. It is sufficient to point out that no matter how the schools differ, they held certain basic assumptions in common, as noted above.

Socratic thinker. It was his intent to turn philosophy from speculation about the cosmos to the examination of ideas. He did not deny the Monism of the Milesian school, and neither did he assume that reality was merely some form of logical existence. However, he adopted the method of logical rather than physical explanation of all reality. He thus came to the conclusion that being is thought. He argued that only that can exist which is subject to the laws of human logic.[2] He assumed that the ultimate reach of human logic is the limit of all possible reality or existence. For Parmenides, being was an eternal, self-complete, motionless, solid body, beyond or apart from which there is pure nothingness.[3]

Parmenides thus asserted the ideal of the identification of the human with the divine mind. This conclusion brought with it the further implication that there is no divine mind which stands above the human mind. This is a purely rationalistic and deterministic position which stands opposed to all Christian truth.

God's being is what man thinks Him to be, and yet, at the same time, this god of Parmenides is the ideal in which the Parmenidean requirement of the adequacy of thought with being is regarded as finding its expression. The god of Parmenides is obviously a product of the autonomous human mind, but Parmenides also insisted that this god was beyond the thought of any man. In essence he is pure form and also a limit. It is obvious that this view of God involves a hopeless contradiction which cannot be resolved by any rationalistic approach, for it is thoroughly irrational.

This irrationalism is an inescapable aspect of the basic assumptions of Parmenides. Parmenides assumed that if man is to have unity in his thinking, then he must be able to penetrate the whole of reality, using the laws of thought. In such a position there was absolutely no room for any distinction between the Creator and the creature. Thus the autonomy which Parmenides claimed for human reason became its prison house, and the rationality which he assumed brought with it a necessary irrationality and determinism as an inescapable aspect of this monistic approach to the nature of reality. To follow Parmenides is to lose the free will of man by its absorption into an eternal, immutable law.[4]

Thus the assumption of Parmenides that the mind of man is autonomous and that he can by the law of contradiction determine what can and what

2. Cornelius Van Til, *A Christian Theory of Knowledge* (Nutley, N. J.: Presbyterian and Reformed, 1969), p. 171.

3. A. K. Rogers, *A Student's History of Philosophy* (New York: Macmillan, 1949), p. 30.

4. Van Til, "The Scale of Being," unpublished manuscript, vol. 2, pt. 2, p. 50.

cannot exist results in the negation of human freedom and the very autonomy upon which Parmenides built his system.

As an answer to Parmenides, Heraclitus offered a dubious solution. In his desire to avoid the Parmenidean principle of a static reality in which there is no change, Heraclitus simply denied that permanence existed and declared that change or movement governs the universe. His efforts to maintain the concept of human autonomy and freedom of the will were no more successful than that of Parmenides. If Parmenides allowed the free will of man to be absorbed into an eternal immutable and impersonal law, Heraclitus (563–470? B.C.) permitted them to be absorbed into the "bottomless cauldron of chance." This concept of chance is as irrational as the determinism which Parmenides offered. In neither system was there any room for a personal sovereign God of the Scriptures. In both cases their rationalism was necessarily accompanied by an inescapable irrationalism and the contradiction involved in these correlatives not only plagued Greek thought, but continued to produce the heroic efforts of St. Thomas Aquinas to find a synthesis between the philosophy of Aristotle on the one hand and Augustine on the other.

Modern philosophy, with its proud announcement of its independence from the Scriptures and the God revealed therein, is no less the prisoner of this irreconcilable dilemma than its Greek antecedents.

Unmindful of the fact that because of their basic assumptions there was no answer to their dilemma, the philosophers of Greece continued their efforts to solve the riddles which were so perplexing to them. Undaunted by the failures of their predecessors, philosophers of the Golden Era of Greek thought persisted in their efforts to find a solution to the problem of the nature of reality which would safeguard the autonomy of the human mind and the freedom of man's will on the one hand, and which would not doom man to a perpetual uncertainty as to the answers to the great questions with which they were dealing.

Plato (427–347 B.C).

In the works of Plato we find what many historians and philosophers consider the most important achievements in the realm of Greek thought. For many he is the greatest of all idealist philosophers, if not the greatest of all Western thinkers. We might thus expect to find in his works a solution to the problems which his predecessors had failed to solve, if solutions could be found. Many of the early fathers of the Christian church were convinced that of all pagan thinkers he came the nearest to Christianity, and some were even inclined to regard him as a Christian. Nevertheless, only disappointment is in store for those who expect to find in the works of Plato satisfactory answers to great philosophical questions, for this great philosopher was caught in the same web which has enslaved all non-Christian thought from the Greeks to the existentialists. This web is unbelief and a blindness which has caused all thinkers who reject Christianity to hold the truth in error.

No less than his predecessors did Plato proceed from the assumptions which had beset them in every effort to discover the nature of reality and man's place in it. Van Til rightly observes that "even in the best and highest of Greek systems of thought it is the autonomous man who takes himself to be the source and standard of truth, of goodness and beauty."[5] This autonomous man by the very nature of the case created for himself a god who could not possibly be for him the sum of all truth and the ultimate source of all knowledge and light.

Plato in his use of theological analysis of experience was thus forced to conclude that reality is comprised of two ultimate principles, one, the Good, and the other, the Evil. But this was a most unsatisfactory conclusion and one with which Plato could not live. To overcome this difficulty, Plato therefore simply postulated the idea of unity and goodness and being as above all dualism. Van Til thus concludes: "The god who would get him out of his intellectual dualism is a god that must be wholly unknowable."[6] This must necessarily follow from his position, for if this god is unknown, he then must be part of the dualism that he was designed to overcome. The dilemma is therefore not only unresolved, but actually heightened, for any light that comes from such a god as this must first be projected into him by man himself.

In Plato's philosophy there is no Creator God at all and most certainly not in the biblical sense. His system makes no provision for a god of any kind. Admittedly, in his *Timaeus* he speaks of a god who acts, but this is only a metaphor. It is only a secondary principle, a purely irrational principle which must serve as a supplement to the idea of an ultimate and timeless and unknowable nothingness which is denominated *one* and *good*.[7]

From such assumptions as these arise many difficulties in Platonic thought which could only strengthen the irrationalist trend already evident in Greek thought. In Platonic thought the ethical is identical with the ontological. Thus the ideal is the only real or fully real world. It must therefore follow that to the extent that man possesses any reality, it must be the

5. Van Til, *Christianity in Conflict,* vol. 1, pt. 2, p. 82.
6. Ibid.
7. Ibid.

result of his participation in the Ideal world and ultimately in the Ideal of the Good. It thus must also follow that man is evil to the extent that he is separated from the Good or God. But this Good or this God is an impersonal being or entity. An important question emerges at this stage in Plato's thought. How can the good have residence in an impersonal being or god, and if it does have such a residence, how can it transmit itself or be transmitted from such an impersonal source into men? Plato's identification of the ethical with the ontological reality thus yields an irrationalism in the ethical realm as well as the metaphysical.

Plato's ethical system was imbedded in a very serious morass. The only God whom Plato knew or acknowledged was a god which possessed no rational or moral nature. This dilemma raised the problem of the nature of a moral law which would give substance to any ethical system. Van Til was quite correct when he wrote that Plato's highest law, his absolute universal, is a purely empty form, and he is equally correct when he insists that this form is actually correlative to the idea of pure contingency. Of necessity, when Plato spoke on ethical issues, he had become a relativist, because he absorbed pure contingency into his pure absolute. Thus Plato's whole system is basically irrational.[8]

Plato's difficulties arise from the fact that the god he presents is a far cry from the God of the Scriptures. The Scriptures present a holy God who is at the same time the holy and sovereign Law Giver. He is the triune God who is the Creator of both heaven and earth. He is the Redeemer of His people and the Judge of all men. He is presented in the Scriptures of the Old and New Testaments as the standard for all the thoughts of mankind. Because He is the sovereign Creator, He is also the source of all law. Plato's view of law is as far removed from this biblical teaching as is his view of God. Plato set forth an impersonal law which was independent of, and therefore necessarily above, the Law Giver. Ultimately this law was the creation of the autonomous man which would yield its fruit of irrationalism in the ethical and political aspects of Plato's system. Many scholars who have so much admired Platonic philosophy have conveniently forgotten that the political system which he described in his *Laws* was not the democracy they wanted to find in Greek history, but a thinly veiled absolutism which they did not want to find. The concept of the autonomous man which underlay the whole of Platonic philosophy when applied to political questions has frequently, if not always, been the source of some form of absolutist or totalitarian government. The doctrine of human

8. *Christianity in Conflict,* vol. 2, pt. 1, p. 4.

autonomy has been a continuing dilemma in the history of Western political thought. Political philosophers who have lauded this humanistic concept have never been able to ward off its irrational effects in the life of those peoples and nations who have sought to erect governments in the light of this basic premise. Political philosophies and systems which are grounded on the doctrine of the autonomous man bring forth governments which claim for themselves that autonomy which their subjects have claimed as their own innate prerogative.

Greek Thought After Plato

If Plato was not unaware of some of the major difficulties involved in his philosophy, his successors were even more aware of the problems which he had bequeathed to them and the various unanswered questions which confronted them in their quest for philosophical certainty. The inability of Plato to offer satisfactory solutions to the great problems of philosophy was not for them an indication that the questions were insoluble, but rather did these unanswered questions serve as an inspiration for the achievement of a better method of solution. There was no doubt that the autonomous mind of man was equal to the occasion. Yet Plato had offered a formidable challenge to these successors for which, apart from the Scriptures, there could be no answer. We have seen that for Plato the Idea of the Good was the summit of the hierarchy of being and as such was his God. At the same time this Idea of the Good stood in sharp contrast to the material world, but he also considered it to be the source of its origin and nature. The problem was further complicated by Plato's tendency to regard matter as evil in contrast with the Ideal of the Good. Thus the question comes to be this: How can the Ideal Good be the source of a material world which is evil? And at this point another question must emerge. Why should Plato's Good or God even desire to produce a world? But the question in this form implies a degree of personality in the "Ideal of the Good," which most students of Greek thought agree that Plato did not assume.

Aristotle set himself to the task of providing answers to some of the basic issues which Plato had raised. However, in accepting the major assumptions of his predecessor, Aristotle could not rise above the limitations of his master. The concept of the autonomous mind haunted his every effort and beset him at every point. Van Til rightly observes that the efforts of Aristotle at developing a satisfactory epistemology occupy a place between Parmenides and Kant. It can hardly be denied that in his earlier writings Plato was basically Parmenidean, but that he somewhat changed his position in his later dialogues in which he changed his thinking to the extent that what he called non-being in these earlier works he later called otherness.[9] Aristotle continued this epistemological development and substituted the concept of potential being for Plato's *Otherness*.

By such an innovation Aristotle felt that he had placed man's ability to have knowledge of change and changing things on a higher level than that found in Plato. Aristotle thus argued that real knowledge is of universals only. But this raises an important question. How then are we to have a demonstrative knowledge of material change?

Aristotle's solution to this question raises the spectre of the inherent irrationalism in his whole position. "The more demonstration becomes particular the more it sinks into an indeterminate manifold, while universal demonstration tends to the simple and the determinate. But objects so far as they are an indeterminate manifold are unintelligible, so far as they are determinate, intelligible. . . ."[10]

At this point an interesting contradiction appears in Aristotle's whole theory of knowledge. He was concerned with establishing a theory of knowledge in which the process of learning by experience would be made intelligible. But if we follow the logic involved in the above quotation, we see that scientific knowledge is not possible through the act of perfection. Van Til summarizes his attempts to improve upon Plato with the observation that it was actually an attempt to combine an abstract principle of unity with an equally abstract principle of diversity, and that he still retained the Parmenidean view that reality can only be that which man declares it to be.[11] Van Til further observes that, in his efforts to carry through this Parmenidean principle, Aristotle really held that "all reality is amenable to the logical exhaustive manipulation by man without falling into the obvious consequence of this position, namely that therefore there is no knowledge of space-time facts."[12] But to accomplish this aim Aristotle had to appeal to intuition or faith, but even more, to a faith in pure contingency as somehow furnishing the basis for the validity of logical demonstration. The only way that Aristotle had of telling us that abstract universals and abstract particulars are somehow related is by insisting that we must believe that they are related.[13]

9. *Christianity in Conflict,* vol. 2, pt. 1, p. 9.

10. *The Student's Oxford Aristotle,* vol. I, Logic (Oxford University Press, 1942), *Analytica Posterioria,* p. 71.

11. *Christianity in Conflict,* vol. 2, pt. 1, p. 10.

12. Ibid.

13. Ibid.

Thus we are asked to believe that our contingency and pure formal rationality are somehow united in our human experience. It is refreshing to hear Aristotle admit: "It is hard to be sure whether one knows or not."[14]

Such an uncertainty was the logical result of the impasse which he faced. For him there was no answer to the dilemma. His so-called "moderate realism" demanded the use of the law of non-contradiction for a knowledge of the nature of ultimate reality. Van Til has pointed out the difficulty in the quest for a knowledge of the nature of ultimate reality. However, this law presupposes multiplicity, and Van Til rightly observes that without multiplicity there is no necessity for the application of this law. But since multiplicity presupposes unity, the law of non-contradiction cannot be applied in the realm of pure chance or flux."[15]

Aristotle found his solution to the dilemma by insisting that the same thing can, without contradiction, be both one and many only if we use the notions of potentiality and actuality. This was only an apparent solution to the problem. In his valiant efforts to explain change through the introduction of potentiality and actuality along with the concept of analogy, Aristotle failed to solve the basic issue. He was well aware that the law of non-contradiction was not truly self-evident, but was actually presupposed in his system.

In his system he was ultimately forced to combine the Heraclitean principle of flux with the Parmenidean principle of the locked universe. Thus, for Aristotle being was inherently analogical, and therefore it is neither exclusively changeless nor exclusively changing.

The end of his effort was failure, and Van Til has well emphasized the important principle that "when apostate man finds that his purely rationalistic ideal of knowledge—complete adequation of thought and being—leads to the loss of his own identity, then, in desperation, he turns to the idea of pure irrationalism. He asserts that no one knows ultimate reality in any way. To claim to know ultimate reality or even to know anything about it is, we are told, to bring this ultimate reality down into the realm of flux.[16]

It is for this reason that the apostate man, whether he follows Plato, Aristotal, or Kant, must seesaw back and forth between pure rationalism on the one hand and a pure irrationalism on the other. The fulcrum for this dialectical procedure is, of course, the would-be-autonomous man. When man refuses to see himself as a creature of the God revealed in the

14. *The Student's Oxford Aristotle,* vol. I. Logic, 1942, *Analytica Posteriora,* p. 76.
15. *Christianity in Conflict,* vol. 2, pt. 1, p. 11.
16. Ibid., p. 12.

Scriptures and a sinner saved by Jesus Christ, he will continue to follow this erratic pattern, looking first to rationalism and then turning to irrationalism.

Both Plato and Aristotle struggled with the problem of how it is possible to have the world of timeless reality brought into a significant relationship to the world of time. Both philosophers sought the answer to this problem in their study of the soul. Plato sought to give form (the Soul) and matter a degree of independent existence from each other, while Aristotle stressed the correlativity between form and matter. In neither system do we find a satisfactory answer to the problem of the relationship between timeless reality on the one hand and the world of change on the other. The efforts of Greek thought to find a solution to the problem were doomed to defeat. They could not know themselves as men because they did not know the living God in whose image they were created.

Van Til once again has summarized the magnificent failure of Greek philosophy in its assault on the basic problems of human life.

> Thus we have the form-matter scheme of the Greeks. Form stands for the abstract, non-personal thought thinking itself. Matter stands for the idea of pure contingency. Pure form cannot think and has no power. To be sure Aristotle's God is said to be pure Act. But how can empty form be act? Aristotle's God is active either generally or in relation to the world. On the other hand, pure matter is not active either. It is said to be active, i.e., moving. But pure matter must contain no action at all, for action leads to differentiation and differentiation would take away the *purity* of *pure* form. Thus *pure* form and *pure* matter are merely ideas or ideals with which the autonomous man seeks to make of his environment something that will be amenable to his self-centered evil purposes of making himself his own creator and redeemer. For if man's environment were what the "Greek spirit" by its form-matter scheme made it out to be then man is truly "free" in the way that Satan in paradise said he would be free only if he declared his independence of God. Greek mythology, Greek poetry and Greek philosophy all betrayed this same spirit of defiance of the living God. While seeking for truth, they were always more basically suppressing the truth. The idea of "Greek theism" is, therefore, a misnomer. The Greek spirit made its contribution—a great contribution—to the coming kingdom of Christ, but it did so in spite of itself—as an incendiary on a boat is made to scrub its deck. The Greek spirit is the spirit of humanism.[17]

It is doubtful that in all of the voluminous literature on this subject there can be found a better summarization of the Greek dilemma and a more profound insight into its nature. Lacking a personal God, lacking a

17. Ibid., p. 22.

doctrine of creation, lacking any sense of sin or the need of personal redemption, the Greek spirit drifted from one form of irrationalism to another, never achieving the truth it sought or any solution to the problems which vexed it.

Later Greek thinkers and systems of thought were no more successful than their predecessors in their philosophical endeavors and for the same reasons. They sought the truth in unbelief and rebellion against the sovereign God revealed in the Scriptures, and what glimpses of truth they did receive, they received through His common grace. And in receiving it they beheld it in unbelief. Sophists, Epicureans, Gnostics, and Stoics were all engaged in their respective versions of irrationalism as correlatives of their particular form of rationalism.

Christianity and Classical Thought

The emergence of the Christian church and its theology for the first time made available to the classical world the possibility of a truly theistic approach to the great philosophical issues which had claimed the attention of both Greek and Roman philosophers for centuries. But if classical paganism remained unaware of this possibility, the early fathers of the Christian church only slowly grasped the cultural significance of the gospel to which they were now giving their allegiance. The truths of the Scriptures were to their minds huge boulders of granite from which a theistic approach to problems of human thought must be quarried. The very fact that classical thought offered such a challenge to the church greatly aided the development of a theological approach to these questions. But the development of a systematic theology capable of supporting a truly biblical theism did not come quickly or easily to the church fathers. Too many of them had been brought to a belief in Christianity when they had already been immersed in the pagan humanism of either the Greek or the Roman world, and they did not easily shed their heritage in which they had been so thoroughly trained.

The very grandeur of the biblical revelation demanded a consecrated scholarship which would devote itself to the task of forcing the biblical reply to the questions which humanism can never answer. This task would command the attention of many generations of Christian scholars, and the faltering steps of the early apologists must be viewed in this light. Only gradually did they begin to see the answers in the clear light of the gospel. If the full light of the gospel message did not dawn upon these early scholars in all of its grandeur, neither did the attractions of Greek thought cease to have a fascination for them after they became believers in Christ. Even as they were facing steadfastly toward Jerusalem, the temptation to cast a fleeting glance back toward Athens was rather frequently too strong to be resisted.

Thus only gradually did the early fathers shake off the humanistic outlook which clouded their thinking in regard to the relationship that should exist between their classical past and their Christian present. But this problem was not the unique possession of the church of the first four centuries. Humanism has been the persistent enemy of Christian theism throughout its history, and the church has had to do battle with its ancient enemy as it has assumed many garbs and appearances down through the centuries.

In the early days of this conflict, the fathers assumed three well-defined attitudes or approaches to the problem. The first of these was that which characterized the church in the East, and particularly that group of scholars who have been known as the Alexandrians.[18]

Justin Martyr, Clement of Alexandria, and Origen (185–254), the leading members of this school, were all heavily influenced by their own classical training and believed that Christianity was the perfect philosophy and therefore the completion of the philosophies of Plato and Aristotle.

They believed that a synthesis between Christianity and philosophy was not only possible but highly desirable. Justin Martyr (100–165) felt that the best teaching of the Greeks had either been derived from the Old Testament or it had been achieved by reason with divine aid, and thus was a special gift from God. He felt that it was a serious error to emphasize a latent antagonism between faith and reason and thus to overlook the divine element in all of human history and intellectual endeavor. Thus for Justin Martyr Christianity was the completion and not the contradiction of philosophy. The only difference between the content of the gospel and that of Greek philosophy was the degree of truth which they contained. The Christian church had the whole Word of God through the incarnation, while philosophy had only a partial relation of divine truth.

The tendency to exalt Greek philosophy at the expense of the uniqueness of biblical revelation was even more pronounced in the works of Clement of Alexandria (150–226). He was born in Athens and, like Justin Martyr, he had also been a philosopher before his conversion. He professed to find in the Scriptures the completion of his quest for higher truth, for which he had long been searching and had not been able to find in the philosophy of his day.

---

18. Because they had gathered at Alexandria in Egypt, a famous center of learning.

In his *Stromateis* he held that Christianity was the perfect gnosis. In this major apologetic work he made the attempt to achieve a synthesis between faith and reason, between Christianity and Gnosticism. He insisted that Christianity was a divine gift to the Greeks and was for them a preparation for the coming of Jesus Christ. As the law of Moses was a schoolmaster to bring the Jews to Christ, so was philosophy a schoolmaster to bring the Greeks to Him. For Clement the gospel was not so much a fresh departure in the quest of knowledge as it was a meeting point for two converging lines of intellectual and spiritual progress. Clement willingly admitted that this body of philosophical truth as it was rationally comprehended must be supplemented by the revealed truth found in the Scriptures alone. At the same time he also insisted that although all truth is one, one portion of it is to be found in reason (philosophy) and another in revelation. It was the duty of the Christian to neglect neither.

Underlying his views on the nature and purpose of philosophy was his conception of the nature of faith. For Clement as well as for Origen, philosophy was the light of reason which the Logos has imparted to mankind: it is thus the preparation for the higher light which shines in the gospel. Through Greek philosophy the soul was prepared for the reception of faith, on which truth builds the edifice of knowledge. Philosophy for Clement was thus the means by which the real nature of Christianity was disclosed to the thinking man. For both Clement and Origen Christianity was a higher philosophy, and Christ towered above Plato and Zeno because He overcame their polytheism.

But how could they claim that to overcome polytheism is good unless it has been divinely revealed that monotheism is the only true view of God, and this view must come by revelation?

It is obvious that the Alexandrian school was seeking a synthesis between the gospel on the one hand and Greek thought on the other. Clement and Origen were seeking to develop a Christian doctrine and apologetical system which would incorporate what they felt were the truths of classical thought into the body of Christian doctrine.

The result was a Christian system strongly impregnated with Gnosticism. Clement clearly taught that saving faith must precede knowledge, but knowledge is superior to faith in the sense that it makes possible the achievement of a higher level of insight into the Christian life and truth.

The logical result of this synergistic approach to the relationship of Christianity and classical culture introduced a rather high degree of irrationalism as a correlative of the rationalism with which the Alexandrians approached the study of the Scriptures and the formation of a doctrinal system. Not only did Clement and Origen deny the absolute uniqueness of the biblical revelation, but they seriously modified such biblical truths as the fall, total depravity, the incarnation, and the atonement. Christ the Teacher was exalted at the expense of Christ the Saviour.

Their tendency to regard sin as simply a lack of knowledge rather than as a fatal defect reaching into every aspect of man's personality had as its correlative the belief that man retained, even after the fall, an important degree of his autonomy. There was in their thinking a heritage from their classical background; a belief in the autonomy of the will and a natural ability on the part of the autonomous man to build his character on what good remained in his own person. Origen made this very clear in his advice to his readers to use the natural good in them with Christianity as an end to seek from Greek philosophy what could be used as a preparation for Christianity.

From the Alexandrian apologists and many of the other early fathers there thus came into the stream of Christian thought a body of Greek thought.

This synthesis of Greek and Christian thought was inevitably tainted with the irrationalism involved in Greek rationalism. To the extent that the resulting theology denied the total depravity of fallen man and the slavery of the human will, while exalting his residual goodness and freedom, it rested upon a foundation which could only prove to be at best a flimsy foundation for the formation of a systematic theology which was truly biblical in all of its aspects. This irrationalism would continue to haunt the church throughout the Middle Ages, except to the extent to which Augustine would cleanse its theology of its Platonic and Aristotelian legacy.

In the West, Tertullian was so thoroughly aware of the danger which the syncretism of the Alexandrians posed for the church that he cried out in alarm: "What has Jerusalem to do with Athens?" But Tertullian was himself too well trained in his pagan culture to be able to offer a satisfactory answer to the dilemma confronting the church in its efforts to speak to the unbelieving world. His plea to break off all cultural intercourse with classical culture was hardly a solution which was compatible with the biblical imperative to preach the gospel to all men.

Augustine

Augustine has been called the "Father of Fathers and Doctor of Doctors," and "is of the past, present, and future," and Stanislaus J. Grabowsky goes on to say that "the intellectual attainments of the ages preceding him converge in him; religious knowledge sweeping down on succeeding generations diverge from him. He imbibed the culture of the ancients; he nourished the souls of the Middle Ages; he sheds light for the mind of modern man."[19] Windelband, the great historian of philosophy, declared that Augustine was the only true teacher of the Middle Ages. "Herewith was given, in pregnant unity, the system which became the basis of the scientific training of the European peoples, and in this form the Romanic and Germanic peoples entered upon the inheritance of the Greeks."[20] We must grant the greatness of the man. It is true that his emotional and intellectual appropriation of Christianity was more comprehensive and profound than any scholar who followed him for many centuries.

The question emerges: How accurate are these vivid statements in regard to the greatness of this church father? Windelband and other historians of philosophy feel that he in some way was the actual founder of modern philosophy as he somehow transcended both the Middle Ages and the Reformation. Christian thinkers such as A.D.R. Polman, Cornelius Van Til, and even John Calvin take a quite different view of Augustine and herald him as the theologian of sovereign grace who, in the light of his mature theology, made possible a well-developed, if not fully developed, biblical theism, which in turn enabled the Christian church to interpret all culture—classical, medieval, and modern—in the light of the biblical revelation.

Augustine did not at once become what his admirers claim for him as the great theologian of the early church. He did not at once come to that full understanding of the Christian faith which he had so long despised. The maturity which marks his later writings was not easily achieved, but was the product of his many years of study of the Word of God and his gradual surrender of his classical background and his sojourns into the various heretical cults of the day.

His early writings give evidence that he was truly seeking the depths of the truth in the Scriptures, even though he was still greatly influenced by neo-Platonic concepts. It is in the writings of this early period of his Christian experience that Windelband, Harnack, and others find the Augustine who is the forerunner of modern thought. Only gradually did he become the Augustine to whom Calvin and other Reformers looked and in whom they found their authoritative inspiration for their own doctrinal development.

---

19. Stanislaus J. Grabowsky, *The Church: An Introduction to the Theology of St. Augustine* (London, 1957), p. vii.

20. Windelband, *A History of Philosophy* (New York: Harper and Row, 1957), p. 266.

The true Augustine, the great defender of the faith, comes to light in his later writings, for in them he lays a greater stress on the doctrines of sovereign grace and thus escapes almost all of the enslavement to Plato which beset his early theological quest. In these later works he comes to grips with the meaning of his commitment to the Lord Jesus Christ. The growth in his thinking is easily discerned in his *On the Trinity*. After declaring that he wanted to guard against the "sophistries of those who disdain to begin with faith and who are deceived by a crude and diverse love of reason," he went on to assert that those who submit to the Scriptures will find in the doctrine of the Trinity the one and only true God.[21] Augustine has now come a long way in his quest for truth, and he has found it in the Scriptures, because they alone reveal the triune God who sovereignly controls the whole of human history. And at the center of this history is Christ the Redeemer. Philosophy no longer had any charm for him or claim of loyalty from him. He confessed that the pagan thinkers had "utterly failed in searching out the succession of more lengthened ages, and in finding any goal of that course down which, as down a river, the human race is sailing, and the transition thence of each to an appropriate end."[22]

Not only was he now aware of the failure of those philosophers in whom he had formerly placed his trust, but he was now also aware of why they had failed so desperately in their quest for certain knowledge. "Therefore neither concerning the succession of the ages nor concerning the resurrection of the dead, ought we to consult those philosophers who had understood as much as they could the eternity of the Creator in whom we live and move, and have our being. Since, knowing God through those things which are made, they have not glorified Him as God, neither were thankful; but professing themselves wise, they became fools."[23]

The spiritual and intellectual development of Augustine which is clearly seen in his *De Trinitate* and other writings comes to its fullness in his *De Civitate Dei*. As his understanding of the uniqueness and grandeur of the Scriptures developed, so did his theological insights, and in this work we clearly discern the emergence of a Christian theism. He leads us to the conclusion that the whole interpretation of every fact of the universe must be seen in the light of the revelation of the triune God as that revelation is given to man in the Scriptures.

This Augustine is now ready to set forth the outline of a biblical ap-

21. Augustine, *On the Trinity,* bk. I:I; bk. I:II.
22. Ibid., bk. IV:XVI.
23. Whitney J. Oates, ed., *Basic Writings of St. Augustine,* 2 vols. (Westminster, Md.: Random House, 1948), vol. 2, p. 748.

proach to the interpretation of history. In this great work he views the whole of history as the story of a continuing conflict between the City of God on the one hand and the City of Man (Civitas Terrena) on the other. This conflict will continue until Jesus Christ returns on this earth as the Victor, and history will come to an end with the establishment of the eternal kingdom of Christ. Rejecting both fate and fortune and emphasizing the doctrine of divine providence, Augustine offered a biblical approach to the understanding of the ancient world, interpreting the history of both Greece and Rome in a far better manner than either the Greeks or the Romans could explain their own past. And in so doing he set aside the rationalistic approach of the classical mind to the meaning of human history and replaced it with one which was essentially theistic in character and yet in which some elements of Platonism survived. Even in the *City of God* Augustine had not yet been able to shake off some remnants of his early training.[24]

And yet, we must also gladly admit that Augustine pointed the way to the theological summit ascended by John Calvin and the theism which flowed from it, and Van Til summarizes his accomplishment in masterful fashion.

> Surely then the believer who would really follow Augustine must make every thought captive to the obedience of Christ. This must be done in the field of philosophy and in the field of science as well as in the field of theology. And one cannot be fully subject to the Word of God in Christ unless he is subject to the same Word of Christ in all of his thinking. The whole personality of man, in every aspect of its expression, must submit itself to the revelation of God. There must be no more working up of philosophy in terms of the autonomy of man. There must be no more working in the laboratory in the interests of the development of science in terms of the autonomy of man. There must be no more natural theology which serves as a first story to the second story of a revealed theology. There must be no more appeal to the independent significance of the course of history, even in the interest of proving that Christianity is "true." There must be a frank admission that the basic view of man and of his work as created, redeemed and directed by the triune God is taken from the Scriptures as the final and finished revelation of God in Christ to sinners.[25]

More than any Christian scholar before him Augustine pointed the way to a truly Christian theistic vew of reality and summoned those who would follow him to develop even more fully his theology in all of its aspects. He announced to the classical pagan world that man cannot confer mean-

24. See Van Til, *Christianity in Conflict,* pt. III, pp. 146-151.
25. Ibid., pp. 167-168.

ing upon either the universe or his own life and that he is not autonomous in any aspect of his personality or life, but must be subject to the God revealed in the Bible, through Jesus Christ, the Redeemer of men. In the grandeur of his accomplishments and in the loftiness of his purposes Augustine set for his heirs during the Middle Ages a standard which was for them a challenge calling them to even greater heights of biblical insights. But by its very nature it proved to be a challenge and an accomplishment which they seldom equalled and never exceeded. Not until the Reformation would Augustinianism once again become the basic theology which would call forth an even greater penetration of the biblical message and a more consistent theology and well-developed theistic interpretation of all reality. In short, Augustine laid the foundation of philosophy which would be based upon a biblical theism rather than on the classical concept of the autonomous mind. This theism is most clearly set forth in his *De Civitate Dei,* which constituted a revolutionary break with all classical interpretations of human history. In this great treatment of the meaning of history he saw history as a revelation of God having its meaning from the sovereign God of the Scriptures who is the Creator of finite reality and who directs history toward its ultimate goal—the final revelation of the glorious triumph of Jesus Christ at His second coming. In his grasp of the biblical teaching that grace and election are the very essence and mystery of history he gave to the church not only an interpretation of history as such, but of all human cultural endeavor, which was a veritable mountain peak of biblical insight to serve as a guide for those who would follow him.

The Medieval Mind: The Thomistic Synthesis

The Augustinian theology with its appropriate supporting apologetical system proved to be a lofty summit of biblical understanding which the scholars of the Middle Ages found exceedingly difficult to uphold. The grandeur of the spectrum of biblical thought in the later Augustine proved to be one of those lofty summits of theological insight which his successors could not scale.

There were several reasons involved in this failure. The first lay in the theology itself. Augustine's emphasis upon the sovereignty of God, the total depravity of the human will, and the inability of man to be saved apart from the operations of sovereign grace in his heart were as offensive to the medieval as they are to the modern mind. The closer a theological system approaches to the biblical norm, the more difficult it becomes for the church to maintain it inviolate. This is the testimony of the history of the church through the ages.

Augustinianism was thus exposed to attack for this if for no other reason, and even in his own lifetime the bishop of Hippo witnessed these attacks and was called upon to give support to the doctrines which had so gripped his own heart and soul.

In the second place, through Boethius and other early scholars who transmitted classical culture to the Middle Ages, the logic and a few ethical treatises of Aristotle were widely spread. The tremendous appeal which Aristotle exercised in the early Middle Ages prepared the way for the acceptance of the whole of his philosophy, the *New Organon,* when it made its way into Europe from Spain late in the twelfth century and from the Eastern Empire with the capture of Constantinople in 1204 by the Fourth Crusade.

Once again the church fell victim to the charm and fascination of Greek thought in its Aristotelian form, and once again its scholars sought to fashion a new apologetic which would rest upon a synthesis of Augustine and Aristotle rather than upon some adaptation of Platonism with the Christian revelation. Once again irrationalism as an inescapable correlative of Greek rationalism became the handmaiden of Christian theology. The resulting Thomistic synthesis, although it was in appearance a medieval cathedral of the mind, rested upon very fragile foundations, and the theism of Augustine was replaced by a syncretistic apologetic whose theology allowed the unbelief of the Greek mind to have an undue influence in the molding of Western thought in the thirteenth, fourteenth, and fifteenth centuries.

The victory of Aristotelianism in the medieval church of the West was a turning point in its theological development as well as of the philosophical development of the Western mind. It represented a serious threat to the Augustinian heritage and even to the authority of the Scriptures. He presented a challenge which could not be ignored, and Thomas Aquinas was thoroughly aware of the gravity of the advent of this new Aristotle.

There were four avenues of approach open to the scholars of the thirteenth century: (1) They could have maintained the Augustinian heritage in its pristine purity. This would have been difficult because of the fascination which Aristotle held for the Scholastic mind. (2) They could have maintained an Augustinianism in the manner and spirit of Bonaventura, and some few scholars chose this solution to the problem. (3) Others, like Siger of Brabant, accepted Averrohism and the resulting pantheism and surrendered the Augustinian legacy. The fourth avenue of approach was to accept the strictly natural and physical doctrines of Aristotle and work out a synthesis between them and Christian thought. This was the path chosen by Thomas Aquinas and Albertus Magnus and their numerous followers. Their purpose in this was to make Aristotle an ally rather than an enemy of the church.

But this Thomistic solution was faced with many pitfalls, and, try as he would, Aquinas was not able to avoid the dangers involved in this synergistic approach to theology and philosophy. He assumed that there is a common ground on which Christians and unbelievers may meet. Thus by the superior use of logic and with the aid of revelation the Christian thinker may prove the existence of God to the unbeliever. In both his *Summa Theologica* and *Summa Contra Gentiles* he made the Aristotelian arguments for the existence of God his springboard for his apologetics and theology. The assumption that reason can prove the existence of God was a controlling factor in all of his thinking. He thus relied on natural theology as a kind of handmaiden to both his philosophy and theology.

In this it was his purpose to show the "reasonableness" of Christian truth to the natural man. He wished to demonstrate that many truths revealed in the Scriptures are obtainable through the use of natural reason, and even those truths which are not obtainable by reason are not contrary to it.

> Some truths about God exceed all the ability of human reason. Such is the truth that God is triune. But there are some truths which the natural reason also is able to reach. Such are that God exists, that he is one and the like. In fact, such truths about God have been proved demonstrably by the philosophers guided by the light of natural reason.[26]

Thomas followed Aristotle rather than Plato in holding to the primary substance as being individual as well as specific. In his argument for the existence of God he admitted that, while this existence is self-evident to God, it is not self-evident to us since we do not know the essence of God. In his effort to escape the consequences of the Parmenidean rationalism he was led into other consequences equally serious and damaging to the very Christian position he was endeavoring to protect. Nevertheless, he began both of his great *Summae* with this basic assumption.

> Because what it is to be God is not evident to us, the proposition is not self evident to us, and needs to be made evident. This is done by means of things which, though less evident in themselves, are nevertheless more evident to us by means, namely, of God's effects.[27]

26. St. Thomas Aquinas, *Summa Contra Gentiles,* tr. Anton C. Pegis, (Garden City: Hanover House, 1955), vol. 1, p. 63, I; 32.

27. St. Thomas Aquinas, *Summa Theologica,* gen. ed. Thomas Gilby, O.P. (New York: McGraw-Hill, 1964), p. 7 (1 a 2).

According to St. Thomas, in sharp distinction to Augustine, all knowledge must begin in the senses, and thus human knowledge, to this extent, must be empirical.

Although St. Thomas rejected the Parmenidean rationalism, he did not escape the difficulties involved in Greek thought. His acceptance of basic Aristotelian principles to a great extent negated his escape from the dilemma of Parmenides. He passed from the irrationalism of Parmenides to that which underlay Aristotle's principle of individuation. The problem assumed a new form for St. Thomas, since he did insist upon the doctrine of creation. His acceptance of this position should have led him to a rejection of Aristotle's principle of individuation and its attendant irrationalism. He took the Christian doctrine of creation for granted, and it thus became his purpose to prove this doctrine by an appeal to "reason." He even went so far as to assume that those who do not think of man as created by God have used their reason correctly in essentials.

In all of this he assumed that there is a neutral area in which the Christian and the unbeliever find a common meeting place. Thus in his frequent assertions that human knowledge is derived from the senses, if he had been consistent with his basic approach, he should have assumed with Aristotle that there is a non-rational, wholly contingent principle of individuation.[28]

But those who reject the biblical principle of equivocism must hold to a principle which is irrational, and this is the kind of a principle of equivocism which Aquinas constantly employs.

At this point Van Til brings to the forefront the basic issue which constantly confronted St. Thomas in his reliance upon Aristotelian principles in his apologetics. For St. Thomas the fact that our knowledge as human beings is derived from the senses means that such knowledge lacks universality and must therefore be uncertain. Thus to the extent that our senses are involved our knowledge must be defective.

Van Til rightly holds that such a view is wholly inconsistent with the biblical doctrine of creation and providence. "If God has made all things and if he controls all things by his plan, then knowledge from sensation is no less certain and true than knowledge obtained more directly by intellection proper."[29] Van Til also rightly observes that the whole approach of St. Thomas implies that man does know the relations and even the essence of created things without referring them in any way to their Creator and Governor. "It is quite in accord with his basic principle of theology as well

28. Van Til, *A Christian Theory of Knowledge,* p. 172.
29. Ibid.

as in accord with his basic principle of apologetics that he should assume this."[30]

Van Til's analysis of the intrinsic relationship between Thomistic theology and philosophy is of extreme importance in his total approach to Thomism. He rightly argues that if one holds to the idea of human autonomy to such an extent that he thinks man can resist the plan of God, by the same token he sets aside the all-comprehensiveness of that plan and has to some extent, at least, introduced the non-Christian concept of individuality as being what it is by chance and the equally non-Christian principle of universality as existing above both God and man.

In summary of his analysis of St. Thomas, Van Til points to the fact that Thomas Aquinas assumed that he had the right to argue from effect to cause without first inquiring into the difference in meaning between the biblical conception of cause and the idea of cause when it is used by non-Christians such as Aristotle. It is this uncritical and erroneous assumption which not only vitiates the entire Thomistic argument for the existence of God which he borrowed from Aristotle, but also vitiates his approach to every other theological and philosophical issue. Aristotle's God was an impersonal being and not the Creator of the world. For Aristotle God was the prime mover. His god was neither self-conscious nor personal. He was an "It." Aristotle's god was the result of Aristotle's assumption of human ultimacy and autonomy. Involved in this assumption was the further assumption that rationality was inherent in any reality that enveloped both gods and mankind.

The dilemma which St. Thomas faced at this point was insurmountable for him and must continue to be insurmountable for all those philosophers and theologians who would seek to create some kind of a synthesis between Christian and Aristotelian or Platonic thought. The dilemma emerged for St. Thomas because he was a Christian theologian, and as such he accepted certain basic presuppositions concerning the nature of God and insisted that God is His own essence and that in Him essence and existence are identical. But on the basis of his epistemology St. Thomas could not accept such a presupposition. We cannot relate the essence and existence of God unless we start with the assumption that they are related. We cannot know anything about a thing unless we presuppose that all things we know have intelligible relations to each other as a result of God's providence.

But St. Thomas overlooked this critical issue and on the one hand as-

30. Ibid., p. 173.

sumed the abstract Parmenidean rationalism even while, on the other he rejected it. In his philosopsy he accepted it, but in his theology he rejected it. The method adopted by St. Thomas logically should have led him to the conclusion that God is both wholly determinable by and also wholly indeterminable by man. But as a Christian he could not accept this rationalistic conclusion. We must then conclude that the idea of Scripture as the Word of the self-contained God of Christianity cannot be accepted if the principles of Thomas are true. If these principles are true, there is no necessity for Scripture in the Protestant sense of the term. For man is not a sinner in the sense that he is spiritually blind to truth. The principles of the natural man, even when they are inherently destructive of the Christian position, are nonetheless assumed to be such that man can by means of them know the truth about reality.[31]

From the foregoing it is evident that the dual role which St. Thomas chose for himself, that of a philosopher looking to Aristotle on the one hand and that of a theologian looking to Augustine on the other, resulted in a dualism of nature and grace, and of revelation and reason, of a natural theology based upon Aristotelian principles. This dualism was an unstable synthesis which attempted to bring about a union of the irrationalism inherent in Greek thought with the biblical interpretation of reality found in the Scriptures and formulated for the church by St. Augustine. These two systems of thought could not long abide within the stately edifice of the medieval church without being the cause of serious intellectual and theological tension. Any synthesis between Augustine and Aristotle was only superficial at best, and the underlying differences and contradictions could not be reconciled. If St. Thomas failed to recognize this truth, his successors at Paris and other medieval centers of theology and philosophy soon came to recognize the insuperable difficulties inherent in Thomism as a philosophy and a theology and sought to find a solution to the problem. Nominalists like William of Occam, Duns Scotus, and Roger Bacon devoted their intellectual energies to meeting the challenge which St. Thomas had bequeathed to them. They rightly saw that if St. Thomas was correct in his insistence that man can know certain facts about God without the aid of divine revelation, then logically Aquinas was on very shaky ground when he limited the ability of the natural man to achieve his knowledge of the supernatural through the use of his rational powers and natural revelation. Equally questionable for this was his basic assumption that the truths discovered by reason would be in agreement with those revealed

31. Ibid., p. 174.

in the Scriptures. It became very difficult for them to continue to believe in transubstantiation as an article of faith when their philosophical presuppositions spoke so strongly against the possibility of such a miracle. Under such conditions, how could the integrity of the faith of the church be maintained?

Both Augustine and St. Thomas had insisted upon the indivisibility of truth. All truth had its origin in God. Augustine had further insisted that basically all truth known by man is through a revelation from God, whereas for St. Thomas both reason and revelation were methods by which he might attain a knowledge of God. Even though Thomas never accorded to reason the role in the quest for truth which he reserved for revelation, the logical implication of his epistemology was to create the impression that there were actually two kinds or areas of truth—theological and philosophical. The post-Thomists, in an effort to protect the integrity of the Roman Catholic theology as it had developed by 1300, came to accept the idea that truth was divisible into two realms or areas—the philosophical and the theological—and that they did not have to be in agreement. These post-Thomistic nominalists then found it convenient to avow their belief in transubstantiation as a tenet of their theology, but to question it philosophically. That this was an irrational position which seriously threatened the entire structure of Catholic theology hardly needs to be demonstrated. The medieval tradition had strenuously insisted on the unity and universality of truth. But by the fourteenth century this basic presupposition of the church was being threatened by those who were interested in maintaining the purity of the faith. It was a strange defense and would soon open up a Pandora's box of philosophical and theological conflict. This conflict would, on the one hand, issue forth in the Renaissance and its accompanying humanism and, on the other, it would produce the Reformation. With the Renaissance there would be a rebirth of classical thought which would bring back into the mainstream of European thought the irrationalism of Greek philosophy and which in turn would bring back the seeds of decay which had destroyed classical culture and its civilization and which would, if not checked, bring about a similar destruction to the culture of the Renaissance. The Renaissance humanists were so captivated by the grandeur which they thought was Greece and Rome that they failed to realize that in rejecting Christianity in favor of Plato they were paving the way for the ultimate collapse of that Western civilization which was being born during the era known as the Renaissance.

Chapter 2

The Renaissance: Promise of Hope or Harbinger of Doom?

Accepting almost without question the exalted opinion in which the humanists of the Renaissance looked upon their own achievements, historians have been very content until quite recently to accept the evaluation which the Renaissance scholars placed upon their accomplishments. They repeatedly claimed that they had brought light in the place of darkness, that darkness which the medieval church had imposed on the human mind for a thousand years in the name of theology. They claimed that they had broken the shackles of dogma and had freed the mind of man to walk forward in the light of his own reason and to discover the truth which had been neglected and almost forgotten since the fall of the Roman Empire. A new age had dawned for Europe, and these Renaissance humanists were thoroughly aware of their own achievements and what they portended for the future.

Suddenly, through the efforts of Petrach and his many followers in both Italy and northern Europe, these ecclesiastically imposed shackles were shattered by the fresh sunlight of a reawakened classical spirit which swept over the European mind and stirred it as it had not been stirred since the Golden Age of Imperial Rome. At least, this was the conviction the Renaissance humanists held of the importance of their achievements.

The scholars of the fourteenth and fifteenth centuries were fully convinced that their work in freeing the mind of Europe from what they regarded as the intolerable shackles of medieval dogma marked a new era in the history of Western culture and that their achievements were truly the sunrise of a new day, marking a distinct break with Europe's past and heralding the inauguration of a new era of freedom and intellectual achievements. References to this optimistic concept of humanistic activity are quite frequent in the various writers of that period. But such references are not the whole story. One has but to read the literature of the Renaissance to be impressed with the fact that it breathes this new spirit of an optimistic belief in progress. If these writers were convinced of nothing else, they were completely assured that their achievements were imperishable and that the mind of Europe would walk in their dazzling light as it had not been able to walk for at least a millennium.

This uncritical appraisal of the Renaissance can no longer be accepted without serious modification. Later humanist historians and literary scholars accepted uncritically this evaluation which the leaders of the Renaissance placed upon their own achievements. In the same way, they also appropriated the Renaissance view of the Middle Ages. The result of this failure to apply those standards of critical investigation which these historians used in their approach to other eras of history resulted in a serious distortion of their understanding of both the Middle Ages and the Renaissance, a distortion which lingered on in historiography well into the twentieth century, and traces of its influence can still be detected not only in college textbooks but in general histories of the period as well. Some historians still look back to the glories of the Renaissance with intense devotion, and yet one can also detect in contemporary authors a gnawing awareness that somehow the rich promises of that period in European history have not been fulfilled in the development of the West since the close of that era.

Only slowly and painfully have historians and literary critics awakened to the painful recognition that the glories of the Renaissance were but transient in many respects, and that beneath the surface and the glitter of its accomplishments there lurked the dry rot of intellectual decay. Those scholars who have held the Renaissance in such high regard have seldom paused to consider a very important question. If this classical culture which the Renaissance revived was as truly magnificent as the humanists believed it to be, why did it collapse and bring an end to the classical civilization to which it had given birth? Those scholars who have admired the Renaissance for reviving classical culture never seem to relate the collapse of the ancient world to any inherent weaknesses in its intellectual foundations. In fact, they tended to reject much of Edward Gibbon's evaluation of the causes of the fall of Rome, although some of them were inclined to accept his judgment that Christianity was the fundamental cause for the fall of Rome.

The historical and literary scholarship which has tended to exonerate classical culture from any involvement in the collapse of ancient civilization was itself greatly influenced by the basic metaphysical and epistemological presuppositions of Greek and Roman thought, and was thus psychologically almost incapable of examining the relationship between classical thought and the decline of the Roman Empire. Still less were these scholars able to contemplate the possibility that any revival of classical culture might have a similar effect upon the European civilization of their own day. Renaissance scholarship which so feverishly reclaimed classical scholarship and philosophy for its own day was serenely oblivious of the fact that it was importing into the mainstream of European thought the seeds of decay, and that these seeds were the anti-intellectualism and irrationalism inherent in Greek and Roman thought. They were equally oblivious of the fact that this philosophy which they were so zealously reclaiming had brought about the downfall of the classical cultural edifice. Theirs was an imposing superstructure, but it rested upon foundations incapable of giving sustaining meaning and purpose to it. It inevitably lacked that permanence which only Christian theism could give.

But humanism was a conscious negation of the Christian theism inherent in Augustinianism. Thus the historians and their colleagues in other disciplines who looked with longing eyes to the grandeur of Athens and Rome spurned the emerging culture which had begun to take root in the soil of European thought and which reached a high level in the theological contributions of Augustine. They overlooked the fact that very early in the Christian era the most productive forms of scholarly endeavor had shifted from the ranks of paganism and had moved over into a new breed of scholars who were openly Christian and who thus sought to create a new world and life view based on the Scriptures rather than on classical thought.

Why was this the case? Why were the laborious efforts of a thousand years threatened with such swift destruction? These questions along with their answers point directly to the conflicting developments in late medieval thought which led to the emergence of the Renaissance on the one hand, and to the Reformation on the other. All epistemological dualism rests upon assumptions which by their very nature are ultimately irrational and anti-intellectual in spite of the grandeur of their superstructures as imposing cathedrals of the mind. This basic weakness in the Thomistic synthesis rose to the surface among his successors within fifty years after his death and set the stage for the appearance of humanism and its rejection of revelation as the source of truth. Sometimes the assumption that the human mind is autonomous was openly acknowledged, but more often it was tacitly adopted. The very nature of humanism, whether it be that of the Renaissance or that of the twentieth-century variety, necessarily involves the rejection of any concept of revealed truth. All truth must somehow originate within the mind of man or his sensate experiences. Man must be the measure of all things and the source of all truth. In short, for the humanists, man is to be the ultimate interpreter of the meaning of his own experience in history.

However, the apparent attractiveness of this theory of knowledge with its outright appeal to human pride scarcely concealed a deadly trap. If man is the measure of all things, is it man in his collective judgment, or is it each individual man who becomes the measure? In theory, the answer would seem to lie in some sort of collective judgment, perhaps of the elite of any society. But in practice this has not been and could not be the case. In practice there is no such thing as collective man or his collective judgment, short of a totalitarian regime which imposes a collective judgment on a nation. Thus man in his collective capacity cannot be the measure of all things and the source of all truth.

This approach to the problem of the nature of truth issues forth into another problem: Which man, or which group of men, becomes the final source of knowledge in political affairs, in ecclesiastical affairs, or in social and economic life? The history of the intellectual life of the Western world from the Renaissance to the present day is largely concerned with the various efforts to find an answer to this continuing problem. The concept that man is the measure of all truth is essentially anarchistic in its implications, with the implication that, ultimately, each man becomes his own norm for the evaluation of reality. Thus this democratic approach to knowledge, which has come to its own in contemporary thought, is a logical and almost necessary result of the Renaissance. But the very anarchy of this approach has yielded strange fruit in the rise of the totalitarian state of the twentieth century, a state in which one leader, as in Germany or Italy, or a small group of leaders, as in Russia, have decided for the rest of the people of those nations what truth is and how it is to be applied in all areas of life. Thus, in Germany there was Nazi truth, a Nazi political truth, a Nazi economic truth, a Nazi social truth, a Nazi religious truth, to which all institutions had to subscribe or be banished. Likewise in Russia there was and continues to be a communist version of truth in political, economic, social, and religious affairs which derives its authority from dialectical materialism. This totalitarian appraisal of truth is a logical fruit of the inherent anarchy of the Renaissance epistemology, and was a determined effort to overcome this humanly created anarchy with a humanly instituted totalitarianism.

But this inherent totalitarianism did not manifest itself immediately in European history, except in the petty city states of Italy. Before it would become the order of the day in the major nations of Europe, rationalism must first appear and then yield its sceptre to the empiricism of the Enlightenment, which in turn would be replaced by Kantian idealism, the dialectical logic of Hegel and Marx, and ultimately by the anarchy of the existentialist philosophy of the twentieth century. The faith in reason which characterized the Renaissance thus, over a course of five or six centuries, would ultimately yield as its fruit the irrationality of Jean Paul Sartre and his many followers in philosophy and even theology.

However, the irrationality inherent in the Renaissance revival of rationalism was not apparent to the scholarship of that era. We can argue that it should have been and that no student of the classical era could possibly be oblivious to the lessons which were so clearly etched in the history of the fall of classical culture and the Roman Empire. But an unfounded optimism in the inherent capabilities of human reason to achieve all necessary truth has blinded many astute and learned minds and led them into deadly error as a result of their inability to read the lesson which history so clearly teaches. It was this blindness which allowed the humanists of the Renaissance to bring back into the mainstream of European thought the seeds of that irrationalism which had virtually destroyed classical culture.

The Renaissance: Its Character and Impact

Although many historians persist in painting the Renaissance in glorious hues which tend to conceal much of its true nature, they do so at the expense of historical accuracy and perhaps at the expense of their own professional integrity. It must be fully admitted that in some areas the work of the humanists was of great value. Certainly the new emphasis upon the study of Hebrew, Latin, and Greek and the recovery of classical and early Christian literature were very productive and of great value for understanding the ancient world. The recovery of the biblical languages was a tremendous benefit for the Reformers as they turned the New Learning to the task of reforming the church in its doctrines and life. With the Hebrew and Greek Scriptures and Augustine and the other early church fathers at their side, they were able to call the church back to what it ought to be. We must never come to the place in our interpretation of history that we cast aside the Renaissance as a totally negative era and of no value to the modern mind.

The inherent paganism of the humanism of this era is visible in the writings of Petrarch (1304–1374), often regarded as the Father of Italian Humanism. There is no doubt that he was the inspiration for many who followed him to pursue the cult of classical letters. But his influence was not confined to inspiring others. In his own work there is an evident willingness to accept classical paganism in place of the Christian gospel. In his *Scipio Africanus* he offered the civic virtue of republican Rome as a desirable alternative to what he considered to be a faulty Christian ethical system. He looked to Cicero and found in him a kindred spirit. As a result, he adopted as his own position the cult of beauty and a pure latinity of style, and declared that in the writings of Cicero and Seneca, two leading Roman Stoics, he found models for a well-developed human personality, by which he meant that in the Stoicism of the Roman mold he found a view of man more attractive to him than that view revealed in the Scriptures. However, it must not be thought that in coming to such a conclusion Petrarch surrendered all of his Christian heritage. He was much too wise to flaunt the authority of the church, which required at least an outward conformity to its standards. Petrarch maintained an outward adherence to Roman Catholic doctrine which was sufficiently persuasive to save him from any risk of a charge of heresy.

On the other hand, his effort to find a synthesis between Christianity on the one hand and the ethics of Stoicism on the other, was doomed to failure. These two world and life views proceeded from very different assumptions, and there was no possibility of finding a common ground on which the humanists of the Renaissance could build a permanent intellectual edifice which looked to both Jerusalem and Athens for its inspiration and support. As a result, many of Petrarch's immediate followers in the humanist camp were less dedicated to finding such a common ground and were much less persuaded of the necessity of maintaining the appearance of the acceptance of Christian morality and doctrine. Their drift into unbelief with its almost inevitable trend toward an irrational rationalism or an irrationalism superficially rational soon became very evident. Petrarch was thus the father of a cultural and philosophical development which within a century would go far beyond anything he had ever dreamed of or would desire.

His humanism almost inevitably led to an intellectual relativism which would one day issue forth in an intellectual anarchy. Since man is the measure of all things and hence a truth itself, almost immediately this question arose: Which man? And for many humanists, even in the fifteenth century, there could be but one answer to this question. Each man must be his own measure and thus become the final authority in answer to the question of the meaning of reality. Each man not only can, but must, judge all things in the light of his own predilections. The ultimate conclusion of such a position must be intellectual and moral anarchy.

This pattern of anarchistic individualism soon began to unfold, even in the day of Petrarch. Ethical as well as aesthetic individualism found an enthusiastic defender in Giovanni Francesco Poggio Braccolini (1380–1459), who openly flaunted his cynical view of life, his libertine ethics, and unabashed paganism before his fellow humanists. The trend toward an essentially irrational rationalism was somewhat concealed in the work of Lorenzo Valla (1407–1457), although his reverence for what he believed to be the inherent ability of the human mind to achieve all needed truth always lurked just beneath the surface of his many-faceted literary endeavors. Even his efforts to restore Latin to its original purity were not so much the result of his interest in philology as they were the product of his conviction that the recovery of pure Latin would somehow aid in bringing about a revival of classical culture in Italy. Under the impetus of this same conviction, he edited his *Commentary on the New Testament* in 1447 in the expectation that the recovery of the Greek language would aid in the revival of the church.

The real bent of his mind, however, is more clearly seen in his other works: *On Pleasure, On Free Will,* and *On the Monastic Profession.* These works were dedicated to the recovery of the classical view of life with its emphasis upon the Greek view of the freedom of the will and the pursuit of pleasure as a goal of life. Under the guise of recovering the classical view of life, Lorenzo was actually attacking the medieval concept of life and was actually encouraging a return to classical culture as a kind of antidote to the biblical view of God, man, sin, and redemption. In these negations of Christianity lay the seeds of a later full-grown irrationalism and anti-intellectualism which, when nurtured by the thinking of five centuries, would finally issue forth in the existential nihilism of our own era.

Leon Battista Alberti (1404–1472), scholar and artist and a contemporary of Lorenzo Valla, held to a similar view of classical thought. In Stoicism he found the philosophy for which he had been seeking—a philosophy which he believed would make it possible for him to live in a responsible manner without being obliged to believe in either heaven or hell. He insisted that it is the great and noble task of man to develop his virtue, his inner potentiality for greatness. Immortality for Alberti was the reward for having achieved a good name on earth, and this good name is the result of how a man lives his life in this world. However, he defined life as a continual struggle within each individual between the animal and the human self. This willingness to define man as something less than human, a being with both a human and an animal potentiality, was obviously a further departure from the biblical view of man than even Lorenzo Valla had been willing to take. While this view of Alberti was probably not representative of Italian humanism as a whole, and was most certainly not the pattern of humanist thought in northern Europe, it was nevertheless an early indication of the logical result of the surrender of the biblical view of man as having been created in the image of God. If man is not what the Scriptures declare him to be, then man will seek to define himself, but in such a way that he will be willing to degrade himself in order to escape from what the humanists believed to be the shackles of the biblical view. The ultimate in the degradation of man is seen in both Marxian thought and existentialism.

Although Machiavelli and Marsilio Ficino (1433–1499) might be regarded as representatives of the most divergent kinds of response to the challenge presented by the new learning to Italian scholarship in the last quarter of the fifteenth and the early years of the sixteenth centuries, they both represent the trends inherent in humanism away from the biblical standards, and each of these scholars in his own way took another step toward the abyss of humanistic anarchy. Machiavelli, far more widely known than Ficino because of his relationship with the de Medici family and his *Prince,* openly announced his break with the Christian view of the state and rejected Christian ethics. But it is doubtful that his assumptions and conclusions were any more dangerous to Christianity than were those of Ficino. The political thought of Machiavelli will be treated elsewhere. Ficino presents an interesting response to the challenge of the classical revival and its potential impact on Christianity. He assumed the possibility of achieving a synthesis between Christianity and classical culture almost parallel to that of Justin Martyr and Clement of Alexandria in the early centuries of the Christian era.

Attracting the attention of Cosimo de Medici, Ficino became the head of the Platonic Academy which had been founded in Florence in 1462. Obsessed with the idea of achieving the great synthesis between Greek and Christian thought, Ficino looked to Plato as a kind of second Moses, an Athenian Moses, who was to play the role of a schoolmaster to bring the Greeks to Christ even as Moses had been used in the Old Testament for the same purpose. But Ficino looked at Plato through the mysticism of Plotinus, and holding this mystical approach to philosophy and religion, he looked upon the world as a battleground, the scene of a great conflict between the forces of the spirit and those of darkness.

Although Ficino was probably not a dominant figure in the intellectual development of Renaissance Europe, he nevertheless represented the trend to the irrational in his zeal for finding a common ground between human reason and divine revelation. No more in him than in the other humanists of that era was there any recognition of the sovereignty of God or of the fact that man was created in the image of that sovereign God. Thus we look in vain for any awareness of the implications of the fall of man and the doctrine of original sin and their impact on human personality. Ficino proceeded on the assumption that the will of man is free and that the fall in no way impaired either man's original freedom of the will or the ability of reason to achieve a knowledge of God. Ficino erected his synthesis without any real understanding of the inherent incompatibility between historic Christian doctrine on the one hand and Greek thought on the other, and therefore reinforced the trend toward the debasement of rationalism into the irrational.

Biblical Theism the Answer to Humanistic Irrationalism

The drift of the humanism of the Renaissance toward irrationality was checked by the powerful influences of the Reformation when it appeared in Europe during the sixteenth century. The work begun by Martin Luther for the reformation of the church culminated in the appearance of Calvin's *Institutes of the Christian Religion* in 1536. Building upon Augustine, Anselm, and other theologians, Calvin provided the Christian church with a theology which was truly biblical, and in so doing he offered to the Europe of his day and to all succeeding generations the framework for a biblical world and life view. Calvin thus provided a sound biblical theism as an enduring foundation which Christian scholarship would use to give both meaning and purpose to the cultural endeavors of modern man. In place of the irrationality inherent in humanism, Calvin gave to the emerging modern world the theological means for interpreting all reality in the light of the biblical revelation, thus helping to insure a truly rational (meaningful) insight into every aspect of created reality.

Calvinism provided such a foundation because it rested upon a sound systematic theology which was based upon and presented the whole counsel of God. The whole thrust of Calvinism is the assurance that the life of man has meaning and purpose not of his own making, but given to him by the very God who created the universe and man in His own image.

Calvin first dealt with the problem of epistemology and, discarding all reliance upon both Aristotle and Plato, he offered the solution to the vexing problem of human knowledge in terms of the revelation of God made available to man in the Scriptures. It may not be amiss to note that epistemology has become the most profoundly disturbing issue confronting the modern mind, simply because contemporary philosophy has rejected this biblical solution and has sought answers from various other sources, all of which have led to the despairing conclusion that man simply cannot know reality and that there is no ultimate truth that can be known.

Calvin offered the solution in his affirmation that God had created man to know a world which He had made to be known, that man had an intellectual mandate as God's vice-regent to investigate every aspect of created reality in such a way that he would think God's thoughts after Him. God gave to man the rational power to know a world that was subject to this rational power. But this solution of the epistemological problem did not stop at this point. Calvin further affirmed that man knows God by the very same act by which he knows himself.[1] Thus our consciousness of ourselves and of God is indelibly written upon our minds by the fact that we bear the image of God. Our consciousness of ourselves and of external reality is not the product of any empirical experience with the external world but results from the act of creation. Consciousness is not the product of our external environment, as the irrational schools of modern psychology and sociology would hold, but rests upon the indelible knowledge we have of God.

Man's knowledge of God since the fall, however, would be very limited and misleading and totally insufficient for his redemption if he had no other source than that which was supplied to him by the fact that he had been created in the image of God and which was available to him through nature. The fall into sin made man totally incapable of either thinking the thoughts of God after Him or doing His will. This inability is the essence of man's total depravity. By the fall he became totally depraved in every aspect of his nature and was thus unable to fulfill his high mission of obeying and glorifying God. Not only did the fall drive man from that first estate in which he had been created, but it also brought with it drastic changes in the natural world, so that man could no longer correctly understand creation or use it as God would have him administer it. The fall, then, was catastrophic in its results, both in regard to Adam and his posterity and in regard to the world in which the posterity would have to live. Both man and nature must henceforth bear the marks of the fall.

The spiritual blindness into which the human race was plunged by reason of Adam's first transgression drove man to find his own meaning and goals for his life on earth—goals and a meaning which he derived from either his reason or his sense experience. Inevitably this question led him to conclusions which were quite contrary to the meaning and goals which God in creation had bestowed upon man. Because they were contrary to the will of God, they were inherently irrational in that they were false interpretations of the meaning of human life and of all reality. By the fall man became a covenant-breaker, and as a covenant-breaker he has ever

1. Calvin, *Institutes of the Christian Religion,* bk. I:I.

since sought to interpret his life on earth in terms of his own creation. Throughout this book this is the meaning which will be given to such terms as "irrational" and "irrationalism." These terms will not be used to imply that man is not basically rational, as the term may be used in psychology or psychiatry.

Irrationality in the sense in which it is used in this study simply means that man remains under his creation mandate to think God's thoughts after Him and to find the meaning of all aspects of created reality, but because of the fall he is unable to fulfill the terms of this mandate. Still conscious that the world is to be known and that he is to understand himself and his role in this world, man constantly endeavors to fulfill this mandate on his own terms, interpreting God and the world according to his own insights, which have been blighted by sin. Unable to find that meaning which God has given to His creation, man has created his own presuppositions, which can only lead him to conclusions which are erroneous and sinful, because they do not honor God as the Creator and Ruler of all life. Man as a covenant-breaker cannot free himself from the requirements of the covenant, and the history of humanism is the continuing account of man's constant endeavors to create purpose and meaning for human existence in terms of his belief that he is the measure of all truth.

From the era of Plato and Aristotle to the world of the twentieth century, philosophy has been man's attempt to answer questions which can only be answered in terms of the biblical revelation. This is why one prominent historian of philosophy has well said that the history of philosophy is the history of never-changing questions and ever-changing answers. This indictment of philosophy does not, of course, mean that there may not be a Christian philosophy or that the Christian scholar should not devote himself to the understanding of philosophical thought. Indeed, just the reverse is true. The well-trained Christian scholar must always be aware of the history of man's unending and yet unavailing effort to achieve his own answers to the great questions of life without any resort to divine revelation. Furthermore, the Christian theologian must ever be alert to the constant threat which philosophy poses to Christian doctrine, and this very alertness must also be the motivation which will lead Christian scholars to a necessary understanding of those philosophical systems which are basically humanistic, naturalistic, and materialistic in their essence, and thus contrary to biblical Christianity at every point.

A second basic thesis of this study is that Calvinism offers the best defense against the attraction of all non-Christian philosophical systems. The only enduring remedy for the irrationality inherent in the humanism of the

Renaissance is to be found, then, in those scholars who were part of the Calvinist Reformation.[2]

In the first place, in his insistence on the complete infallibility and authority of the Scriptures as the only rule of faith and practice, Calvin not only gave to the church a basis for its authority and doctrine, but also provided a theistic foundation to meet the challenge of the humanism of the Renaissance. In his insistence that the Scriptures are divine in their origin and not dependent on the sanction of any ecclesiastical institution, but dependent entirely upon the operation of the Holy Spirit, who not only infallibly inspired the human authors but who also continues to enlighten the minds of men so that they may understand and appropriate the Word of God, Calvin provided the one possible solution to the epistemological problem. The restoration of the Scriptures to their original place of authority in the life of the church was a contribution the value of which is almost beyond calculation. No longer would man be regarded as the source and measure of truth, for the mind of man must now be brought into subjection to the Word of God. In this way the disintegrating synthesis of St. Thomas was set aside and banished from the thinking of the church. For Calvin and his associates, the prime duty of man was to search the Scriptures in order to know what he must believe concerning God, and what duty God requires of him. Once the doctrine of religious authority was settled by these Reformers, they could erect on the foundation of the authoritative Word of God a theology which reflected their desire to present the whole counsel of God in its purity. Once the epistemological question was settled in terms of the complete infallibility of the Scriptures, then the Reformers were in a position to erect on this basic presupposition their theology, and from this theology there naturally and logically flowed a world and life view which came to its fruition in Calvinism.

In making available to the Christian church a systematic theology, Calvin answered many of the basic questions which were perplexing both the mind of the church and the mind of secular scholarship. The foundations of his solution were to be found in his view of Scripture as the only infallible rule of faith and practice, and upon the depravity into which the race fell as a result of the fall. However, by insisting upon man's total depravity and his resulting inability to carry out God's will and to fulfill any aspect of the creation mandate, Calvin turned the searchlight of the Scriptures not only

2. This statement is not intended to imply that such a defense is not to be found in Luther or is even lacking entirely in St. Thomas Aquinas. Rather does it mean that Calvinism as a systematic interpretation of the whole counsel of God provided a fully developed biblical theism for the advancement of a true Christian scholarship.

upon man's desperate moral and intellectual condition, but in doing so he set forth with monumental clarity the one remedy for the dilemma of human sin. Calvin's tremendous insight into the biblical doctrine of redemption involving election, effectual calling, justification by faith, regeneration, and sanctification brought to fallen man the realization that by redemption in Jesus Christ he could once again begin to fulfill in some manner the terms of the mandate given to him at creation. Calvin's doctrine of redemption, as no other can, presents the remedy for the irrationality implicit in the rationalism of the Renaissance.

This Reformed doctrine of redemption applies the fruits of salvation to every area of human life and means that once again the believer in Christ is enabled to think to some degree the thoughts of God after Him and to interpret both himself and the world in which he lives in the light of the new life which he has in Jesus Christ. Thus the Reformed theology provided the basis of a biblical *Weltunschauung*. Thus the man who truly believes in Jesus Christ commits himself to much else besides, to a view of God, creation, man, sin, history, and all the cultural activities of the human race, and in this view he finds the correct interpretation and the motivating power to think God's thoughts and to do His will after Him.

Roman Catholic Theism

Standing between the world and life view of the Reformers and that of Renaissance humanism, Roman Catholic theology offered a theistic approach to the problems of culture based upon Thomism. At the Council of Trent, the Thomistic theology of the High Middle Ages received an official sanction of which it had been previously deprived.[3] This Thomism was a Christian theology derived from the early ecumenical creeds, from Augustine and other early fathers. But it also depended upon Aristotle as his philosophy had been understood and brought into the life of the medieval church by Thomas Aquinas and his associates. The decrees of the Council of Trent had as their purpose the maintenance of the Thomistic synthesis as the official theological position of the Roman Church. It was designed to bring a very clear demarcation between the Roman Church as such and the Reformation on the one hand, and between it and the humanism of the Renaissance on the other. This official doctrinal position

3. This Thomistic synthesis was the result of the efforts of Thomas Aquinas to incorporate certain elements of the Aristotelian philosophy with the theology of St. Augustine. This synthesis began to collapse within fifty years of the death of St. Thomas, in the hands of William of Occam, Gabriel Biel, and Duns Scotus.

was also intended to be the foundation for a culture which would be distinctly Catholic in its content and outlook.

Thus since 1563 three distinct cultures have been striving to gain possession of the Western mind. Although the Roman Catholic position, as it was affirmed by the Council of Trent, differed markedly at certain basic points from the theologies of Lutheranism and Calvinism, it was nevertheless much closer to the Reformation than it was to the humanism of the Renaissance. But because it was a synthesis of Augustine and Aristotle, it did not find itself in harmony with the religious or cultural implications of the Reformation, and it thus remained a distinct theological and cultural movement from 1563 to the present day, or at least until 1962.[4]

This Thomistic synthesis, by its very nature, was and remained an unstable theology. There was no real possibility of an enduring reconciliation between Aristotle and Augustine, and the Thomistic theology contained at its very center a constant tension between the paganism of Aristotle and the theism of Augustine which produced an inner compulsion toward disintegration, a compulsion which could be overcome only by a very strong papacy armed with the appropriate powers to ward off this theological catastrophe. For four hundred years the vastly increased spiritual power of the papacy proved to be generally adequate for the task assigned to it in safeguarding the orthodoxy of the church's theology.[5]

The growth of humanism and its various intellectual and philosophical offspring took place in virtually every country of Europe to varying degrees of success, with the result that three powerful intellectual movements found themselves in continuing conflict, and they became involved in a continuous struggle to gain the mastery of the European mind. Although the successors of the Council of Trent on the one hand and those who led the churches of the Reformation on the other to a great extent continued the religious conflicts of the sixteenth century, they were gradually forced to recognize the fact that humanism was an opponent with which they both must reckon. However important the differences between the Roman Church and its Protestant opponents were and even continue to be, these

4. The selection of the year 1962 may seem to be an arbitrary date. It is certainly not true that the Roman Catholic doctrinal system ceased to be a dominant force in the life of the church within the span of that year. But at the same time it is also true that Vatican II marked the beginning of sweeping doctrinal and ecclesiastical changes in the life of the church which opened the doors to serious departures in the life of the church which made possible doctrinal inroads which in time would certainly erode Thomism as the official theology of the church.

5. In France, a façade of orthodoxy covered serious departures from Roman Catholic thought and practice. In Germany a serious revolt against papal claims led to the formation of the Old Catholic Church.

differences are rather insignificant in contrast to the lethal nature of the humanistic threat to Christianity in general and to the very concept of a culture based on theistic presuppositions.

With the appearance of the Enlightenment, humanism under the guise of naturalism with its unquestioning reliance upon the empirical epistemology and the scientific methodology, gained the upper hand in Europe, and also secured a firm foothold in American thought during the eighteenth century with the rise of the democratic philosophy as it was stated by Jefferson in the Declaration of Independence. This democratic philosophy soon made itself felt in American political, economic, and social life in much the same way as it had in Europe. However, during the nineteenth century it was never able to gain the mastery over the American mind to the same extent which it had captured the European. Nevertheless, it made drastic inroads into American constitutional, political, social, and religious thought, and with the rise of the common man it became an important influence in the life of the nation.

The history of the Western mind from the period of the Renaissance and the Reformation is thus the history of the rise of rationalism, empiricism, the German idealism of Kant and Hegel, Marxism, naturalism, and, ultimately, existentialism. This is the intellectual genealogy of the decline of the Western mind which has now come to a virtual end with the almost universal destruction of belief in a rational, purposeful universe and in man as a rational creature. The abyss has been reached, and the irrationalism inherent in the Renaissance has come to full bloom in both communism and existentialism. The nadir of intellectual despair is upon the mind of the West and has brought chaos in its wake.

Chapter 3

The Renaissance and Reformation: Irrationalism versus Theistic Rationalism

Descartes

With the advent of Descartes (1596–1659) on the philosophical scene during the first half of the seventeenth century, modern thought shook off any vestiges of those theological restraints which, to a degree at least, restrained the inclinations of his predecessors to declare their independence of both Roman Catholic and Protestant doctrines in their quest for a satisfying philosophical scheme. Descartes was imbued with the determination to rid philosophy of its previous accretions which had obscured previous attempts to define a new basis of certainty in man himself and to provide for intellectual activity a new foundation which would not admit of any doubt or uncertainty.[1]

In his quest for certainty, however, he came to doubt the reliability of the testimony of his own senses as well as of the traditionally accepted first principles or axioms. Although it was not his intention to be skeptical, it is obvious that in his dictum, *Cogito ergo sum,* or his *Dubito ergo sum,* he was well on the way toward such a skepticism. Descartes completely repudiated the Thomistic insistence that all knowledge begins with sense experience. But he was also in revolt against all previous philosophical systems, particularly was he against all previous epistemological assumptions. He had come to the conclusion that all former systems were in error in regard to their first principles and that it was his duty in making a fresh start to sweep away all the accumulated debris bequeathed by his predecessors.

This revolt was the result of his settled conviction that the greatest need in philosophy was the formulation of an accurate and fruitful method of investigation. He thus began his search for certainty with the study of

1. It should be observed that Descartes did not openly deny the Roman Catholic doctrine in which he had been trained by the Jesuits. He simply ignored it, and gave it no place in his philosophical speculations. Yet he always insisted that he was a loyal Roman Catholic.

mathematics and found in this discipline the methodology for which he had been seeking. "If I can find a first principle, clear and distinct, all things can be deduced therefrom with more or less clarity." Using this approach to make metaphysics an exact science, he outlined for himself the following procedure:

(1) Never accept anything as true "which I did not clearly know to be such; that is to say, carefully to avoid precipitancy and prejudice, and to comprise nothing more in my judgement than what was presented to my mind so clearly and distinctly as to exclude all ground of doubt."

(2) "The second rule was to divide every difficulty which I should examine into as many parts as possible, or as might be required for solving it."

(3) "To conduct my thoughts in such order that, by commencing with objects the simplest and surest to know, I might ascend by little and little, and, as it were step by step, to the knowledge of the more complex; assigning in thought a certain order to those objects which in their own nature do not stand in relation of antecedence and sequence."

(4) "In every case to make an enumeration so complete, and reviews so general, that I might be assured that nothing was omitted."[2]

Descartes' methodology relied on intuition rather than sensation as the source of knowledge. Like axioms in geometry, for Descartes, clear and distinct ideas are apprehended by the mind intuitively and render a clarity to ideas which cannot possibly be obtained through the senses. The source of these clear ideas is innate, even though they are not present in the mind at birth. The facility for acquiring these ideas, however, is an innate possession of the mind from the moment of birth.

But these innate ideas must be carefully nurtured. Descartes insisted that they must be carefully distinguished from the so-called adventitious ideas gained from sensation and from the fictitious ideas which have their origin in the imagination. Included in his list of innate ideas were the axioms of mathematics, the laws of thought, the belief in one's own existence, and the belief that causes have as much reality as their effects, and all of these innate ideas are very valuable in the acquisition of truth.

Having laid the foundation of truth and certainty in innate ideas as he defined them, Descartes was then ready to attack some of the basic issues in the area of methaphysics, particularly the problem of existence. How do we prove our own existence? His solution to this problem was to doubt

2. Descartes, *Discourse on Method,* ed. Norman Cantor and Peter L. Klein, Seventeenth Century Rationalism (Waltham, Mass., 1969), pp. 113-114.

everything that can be doubted. The end of this procedure is to even doubt one's own existence, but he was forced to the conclusion that doubting one's own existence involves the admission that he is doubting and therefore that he was existing. To doubt implies the existence of the doubter. So his original "Cogito ergo sum" became "Dubito ergo sum." In answer to the perennial philosophical issue: "Who am I?" Descartes gave the answer: "A thing which thinks, doubts, understands, wills, imagines, and feels." Thoughts imply a thinker, and a thinker must be a soul, a spiritual entity.

Having proved his own existence to his own satisfaction, Descartes was then ready to tackle another question which has haunted the minds of philosophers down through the ages. Does God exist and, if so, how can His existence be proved beyond any reasonable doubt? Descartes was convinced that his methodology was equal to this occasion and provided all necessary truth.

His argument was essentially this. We can claim truth for anything which is as distinctly given as our own being. It is distinct and clear that I am not the author of my own existence or experience. Therefore a being more perfect and more complete than I must exist in order to guarantee the reality of my own existence. Taking this argument to its next step, Descartes argued that since our existence must have a sufficient cause, and since that sufficient cause cannot be found in us, it must, therefore, be found in God. Our existence demands the existence of God.[3]

Descartes then revised the traditional form of the ontological argument for God as it had been advanced by Augustine and Anselm to fit into his rationalistic mold. Both Augustine and Anselm had begun their argument with their stated belief in a perfect being, the God revealed in the Scriptures, but Descartes interpreted Anselm to mean that the existence of God depends upon our idea of a perfect being. For Anselm it was not that that God exists because our minds conceive of Him, but rather our minds conceive of Him as the perfect being because He exists independently of man and man exists because of Him as the Creator. According to both Augustine and Anselm, the true foundation of our faith in God is not the result of our conception of Him as the perfect being, but rather that God reveals Himself to us.

Descartes then advanced to his next position in the statement of his metaphysics. He held that reality is composed of only three substances: God, who is the only perfect substance, Mind (Thought), and Matter. But Mind and Matter need the concurrence of God to exist. From this

3. Ibid., pp. 128-152.

metaphysical assumption he then proceeded to draw this argument: "I know that I exist, therefore God exists and the existence of God guarantees the corporeal world also."

Van Til's observations at this point are most appropriate when he states that with Descartes modern man frankly and openly asserted the claim that he knew himself whether or not God existed.[4] In his insistence on human autonomy and that man may know himself without knowing God, Descartes is rightly called the father of modern philosophy, for he set in motion a trend in thought which has characterized Western philosophy from his day until our own. The audacity of this position has become so commonplace that it has long since lost its ability to arouse the apprehension in nominally Christian circles which it once was able to excite. Nevertheless, it must never be forgotten that Descartes asserted the sovereignty of man in strident tones as it had never been asserted in philosophical circles in Christendom since the advent of Christian scholarship.

In his reliance upon the inherent reliability and even infallibility of human reason as the source of truth, he raised more problems than he was able to solve and bequeathed them to his rationalist successors. Perhaps one of the most important of these was the problem of interactionism (the relationship existing between mind and matter), which continued to haunt philosophy even until today. Pantheism and deism represent two different and equally unbiblical approaches as a solution to this issue. An equally important legacy from Descartes in the eyes of many philosophers is the epistemological problem which he bequeathed to his successors. This is the problem of the relationship between thought and experience. How can the mind of man, separated as it is according to Descartes, from the outside world and other minds by the sense organs, come into contact with reality? Descartes offered an answer to this question which failed to satisfy many thinkers. He insisted that only that which can be thought exists. And in this dubious explanation his rationalism had as its correlative a thoroughgoing irrationalism.

In his concept of evil and the free will of man, Descartes departed from the biblical position and held to an essentially Greek concept of ethical freedom. For him human evil was the result of human imperfection, an imperfection which is the result of man's finite nature, and thus he can and does err. Evil results from the failure of the will and the impulses of man to operate within the area of understanding, and of the intellect or mind of man.

---

4. Van Til, *A Christian Theory of Knowledge,* p. 152.

Nevertheless, in spite of his finite limitations, man is naturally inclined to follow the good, even as his reason is naturally directed toward the truth. Freedom of the will is not an impossibility for man to achieve, for it becomes truly free when man arrives at a clear and distinct understanding of the true and the good. When men follow the dictates of nature given to them by God, they are then in perfect freedom.

But a very serious difficulty emerges at this point. There is in his view of nature a mechanistic element which is totally devoid of any theological character. This mechanistic element by its very nature must rule out any possibility of the operations of divine Providence as the controlling force in both nature and human actions. This virtual denial of Providence in the world of nature and human affairs destroys the possibility of any meaningful view of freedom. Thus the freedom which Descartes ascribed to the human will turns out to be no freedom at all, but simply a kind of Stoic acceptance of the inevitable.

In his vain efforts to set forth a doctrine of human autonomy he replaced the subjection of man to the will of a personal and sovereign God with a completely impersonal law of nature which cannot have provision for meaning and purpose in life or any degree of moral responsibility on the part of man, who is the captive of this impersonal force. Thus in his ethical as well as in his metaphysical concepts Descartes rested his position upon an irrationalism which in due season would bring forth its fruits of determinism in the political, economic, and social philosophies which emerged in Europe and America in the latter eighteenth and nineteenth centuries and which bore their ultimate fruit in the totalitarian views of government and society which have become so dominant in our own day.

It is quite obvious that Descartes was anti-theistic in his thinking, even though at some points he seemed to allow a place for the supernatural in his system. But the biblical doctrine of God was carefully excluded as a presupposition for his thinking. Yet we must admit that in one sense Descartes was quite logical in excluding the God revealed in the Scriptures as a basic presupposition in his thinking. The god of Descartes was essentially a product of his own imagination and autonomous reason and actually depended upon this rationalism for his existence. For Descartes to give such a god a prominent place in his thinking would have been to deny his own rationalism, for this god was neither the creator nor the sustainer of the universe and was not a personal being who could command the worship which the God of the Bible requires.

There can be no doubt that the lack of meaning and purpose so clearly seen in Descartes is an invitation to irrationalism in the name of rationalism, but it is unlikely that Descartes was aware of the invitation which he issued to his successors—to draw the logical consequences from his position. In spite of his desire to break with all previous philosophy, he was still sufficiently under the influence of Scholasticism to avoid the implications of his logic, and he was also sufficiently loyal to the church to openly flaunt its theology. Yet it is also true that his successors found a powerful stimulus in his thought to carry them much further along the road to irrationalism. In his *Cartesianism,* J. H. Mahoney made some very pertinent observations. "Taking away from us all the finding of sense and reason there seems to remain for Descartes nothing but his own consciousness."[5] He then raised some very pertinent questions. "Will he be able to start a train of knowledge from it as from a solid rock? Will he be able to keep us from sliding down the roof toward a stream-of-consciousness philosophy like that of William James and his followers? We trow not. Descartes failed to rebuild what he had so ruthlessly destroyed by his methodical doubt. He thought that he could make a fresh beginning for philosophy by starting from his Cogito Ergo Sum."[6] But in his endeavors to attain a fresh start to the knowledge of God and of the world he failed. He did not fail because he rejected the Thomistic or Scholastic view of man and God. He failed because he rejected the very plain teachings of the Scriptures in regard to God, the nature of man, and the source of man's knowledge of God and of himself.

The successors of Descartes wrestled with the unsolved questions which permeated his efforts to answer the persistent questions of philosophy in terms of the autonomy and sufficiency of human reason, but to no avail. The failure of Arnold Geulincx to unravel the basic issues took the Cartesian system further toward its ultimate irrationalism. His efforts to find a meaningful connection between body and soul led him to conclude that the soul cannot possibly be the cause of any effect or change wrought upon the body, nor can any external matter, not even our own bodies, be the cause of any change which takes place in the human soul. In effect, Geulincx denied that there are any secondary causes at work in the world which may influence man. This attempt by Geulincx to ovecome the dualism in the philosophy of Descartes is known as Occasionalism. It represents a very serious departure from the biblical position and makes God the direct cause of sin. His denial of secondary causes also easily led to pantheism.

This tendency toward pantheism became more apparent in the efforts

5. J. H. Mahoney, *Cartesianism,* pp. 39-40.
6. Ibid., p. 47.

of Malebranche to correct both Descartes and Geulincx, and further accelerated the inherent irrationalism in Descartes along the path which had brought the rationalism of the seventeenth century into disrepute.

Spinoza (1632–1677)

For some, Spinoza is the most important of the rationalist philosophers of the post-Renaissance era. Although he was in agreement with Descartes on many issues, he was also quite conscious that his predecessor had failed to deal in an adequate manner with some basic issues. His methodology was quite similar to that of Descartes, but he used it to arrive at quite different conclusions. He agreed with the basic Cartesian conception of the nature of true philosophic knowledge. Only clear and distinct ideas are true, and error has its origin in confused ideas. He also agreed that knowledge or reasoning proceeds in a chain of propositions such as that which is used in geometry. In this respect he was a stricter rationalist than Descartes. He insisted that the highest degree of certainty is to be found in intuition, and thus the most certain kind of knowledge which man may possess is not the certainty of one's own existence but the immediate knowledge of God Himself. The mind may achieve this immediate knowledge of God because the mind of man is actually a part of the mind of God.

In his metaphysics, Spinoza postulated three fundamental concepts. The first was substance, by which he meant "that which exists in itself and is conceived by itself—the ultimately real." The second was the attribute, by which he meant, "that which the intellect perceives as constituting the essence of the substance, the essential quality of the real." The third concept was mode, or modifications of the subject, by which he meant "that which exists in and is conceived by something else than itself, the essential modification of the real."

Having thus stated or defined his metaphysical presuppositions, Spinoza then moved to the problem of God. In reply to the question, "Who is God?," Spinoza proceeded to define Him in terms which met the demands of his own metaphysical presuppositions. He proceeded to define his god as the self-caused, self-existent, free and eternal substance, an existent thing which requires nothing but itself to exist. It is quite evident that this god which Spinoza presented is most certainly not the God of Scripture. It is not the eternal, living God who created the world, revealed Himself to the prophets of the Old Covenant, and who ultimately and supremely revealed Himself in Jesus Christ in the New Covenant. He is impersonal and not personal, and is strictly the creation of Spinoza's own autonomous reason.

That this is the case becomes increasingly clear from a study of his arguments for the existence of this god. Although Spinoza resorts to the ontological argument, it is a far cry from the position of Augustine and of Anselm. Spinoza's god is the captive of his intellect, and his very existence depends on Spinoza's willingness to grant him that degree of existence which is not forbidden to him by any logical contradictions involved in Spinoza's logic. At best, he is a finite substance and has no sovereignty or other attributes which in any way differentiate him from those very human beings on whose autonomous reason he is dependent for his existence.

Spinoza's third argument for the existence of his god is no more convincing. Since we have not produced ourselves, nor are produced by others, only an infinite being can be the ground and cause of our own existence. This must be the case since an infinite being must necessarily have infinite powers and could thus produce and maintain his own existence. Spinoza does nothing to advance his cause when he insists that this conception of God involves no logical contradictions; thus what is not impossible must exist. There are very obvious and very serious objections to these arguments which Spinoza advanced, and therefore they speak out against his rationalism as a whole, since his pantheism is both a philosophical and a theological presupposition. In the first place, the idea of the perfect does not imply its existence. A universe of finite beings infinitely extended in time and space does not in any way prove the existence of Spinoza's god. Equally unimpressive is his argument which is based upon the attributes of God. His insistence that God as an infinite being must possess an infinite number of attributes is simply a logical proposition and is in no way related to the scriptural view of God. But he weakened his own argument by claiming that man can know only two of this infinite number of attributes, namely, thought and extension. At this point Spinoza differed from Descartes in that these attributes were not derived but were the essential and underived characteristics of God.

In this manner Spinoza felt that he had been able to solve the problem of the relationship of mind and matter. For Spinoza, God was both mental and material at the same time, and the one attribute does not affect the other. In this way his universal parallelism was an answer to both interactionism and occasionalism. Spinoza had constructed an answer in which the mental and the material were a twofold aspect of the same reality. But was it an answer? How could it be a satisfactory answer to the unsolved problems found in Descartes and his immediate successors?

This pantheism raised more questions than it could possibly solve, one of the most pressing of which is the problem of individuation. How can the many arise from the one? More particularly, how can an infinite and impersonal substance known as god to Spinoza be the cause of personal beings known as men? Spinoza was not unaware of the problem, and he framed an answer which for him seemed to be satisfactory. He defined god as the *Natura naturans,* one essential nature bringing separate things or entities into existence, not as the Creator, but as the immanent cause or logical ground and substance of all that which exists. The result of this process is *Natura naturata,* which Spinoza defined as things or reality as we know them.

Spinoza's remedy for the problem of individuation was no more satisfactory than that of his predecessors, and in some ways even less convincing. How can pantheism in any way explain individuation? Once again we are faced with the fact that the rationalist effort to overcome the difficulties involved in its basic assumption was not only a failure but actually led philosophy into an even deeper quagmire of irrationalism. Spinoza's pantheism demanded an impersonal god who has no desire or love or holiness or any other attributes inherent in the God of Scripture. Spinoza argued that the god in his system had no need of emotions simply because such perfection does not need them, and for the same reason he had neither reason nor intelligence in the human sense. In Spinoza's theology of philosophy there was no room for any teleology, and therefore Spinoza could only beckon man to believe in a finite god who was the creation of his own philosophical speculation, a substance devoid of both purpose and meaning.

The determinism which permeated Spinoza's philosophy struck a vital blow at any possibility of a meaningful doctrine of human freedom. His parallelism left no room for freedom in a metaphysical sense, since every event must take place with a mathematical necessity. Spinoza was willing to grant to his god a certain kind of freedom, holding that this god was free in the sense that he was not under constraint but under necessity. He defined freedom not as being indeterminism, but as the opposite of bondage. He further regarded bondage as slavery to the passions, to emotions, and to confused ideas. In this sense Spinoza's god could be free since he was not a slave of passions, emotions, or confused thinking. To be more accurate, the impersonal god of Spinoza has no passions or emotions and is therefore completely free.

In a similar fashion Spinoza argued that human freedom consists in that clear knowledge by which we can come to accept the universe of mathematical necessity. To be truly free is to accept with equanimity that which is mathematically determined and therefore inevitable. Spinoza tried to make this concept of freedom more palatable by referring to it as the contemplation of every event under the aspect of eternity. To understand reality in this light is to be free. But such an interpretation of freedom is obviously fatalism and clearly contrary to the whole biblical concept of freedom. It is irrationalism dressed in the phraseology of liberty. In his *Ethics* Spinoza clearly set forth this view of freedom which was encased in fatalism. All final causes are only figments of the human imagination and do not exist in reality. Man regards himself as free simply because he is conscious of his wishes and appetites, but he does not understand their causes. Man is truly free when he acts in the light of clear and distinct ideas and not on the basis of passions and emotions. Rationality is that end or goal which gives freedom its meaning and reason, a kind of intuitive knowledge by which he attains his ends or goals.

Spinoza developed this concept of freedom in order to provide what he felt was a sound basis for his ethics. He regarded as the good for man that which promotes the preservation of his being as rational. Thus virtue for Spinoza was the degree of perfection achieved by a man to the extent to which he is a rational being. Thus the supreme good for man is the intellectual love of God.

His doctrine of evil paralleled his concept of the good. For him evil could not be native to the intellect since the intellect belonged to the attribute of thought, but neither can it be located in the will since the will and the intellect are not distinct faculties. Rather did Spinoza look on evil as an outside interference with the normal and natural processes of reason, and these outside interferences had, according to him, their origin in the operation of the senses, for the sensible images lead to confusions of various kinds because of the nature of the environmental influences to which they are subject. In such a manner Spinoza defined anger as a response to interruptions from external causes, while error for him was misplaced truth, by which Spinoza meant a lack of correlation between an idea and its physical counterpart. Evil can be corrected by a knowledge of the absolute truth of thought and extension. But science can aid in this process by finding a solution for any seeming discrepancy between the real situation and what Spinoza defined as the seeming situation.

The social philosophy of Spinoza is of great importance since its basis was the hedonism and naturalism of Hobbes. In his hedonism Spinoza laid down three fundamental considerations. The first was that a thing is good and pleasurable simply because men desire it. But why is this the case? Spinoza's answer to this question was quite in keeping with his fundamental philosophy. Since there is a desire for perfection in an all-around development in every man, each man ought to consider his well-being rationally, and by this he also meant that every man should strive for a well-ordered society. It can hardly be denied that Spinoza was thoroughly humanistic in his ethical presuppositions, and that the resulting system is a far cry from biblical standards. It represents the efforts of the natural man to create his own ethical standards and to clothe his basic hedonism with a veneer of social acceptability in his insistence that in the development of his well-being, every man should strive for a society in which all other men may also achieve their all-around development.

Inevitably in his views of the state Spinoza also departed from the biblical position. He agreed with Thomas Hobbes that the state and government are necessary for the realization of acceptable social conduct by its citizens, but he differed from Hobbes in asserting that a government cannot enforce its prerogatives unless it acts in the best interests of its subjects. But the best interests which Spinoza had in view were not those to be found in the Scriptures. They were simply an extension of the basic hedonism which underlay his whole ethical system; and the resulting government would be some type of a democracy in which the best interests of the majority would become the standard of what was best for all.

In our final appraisal of Spinoza we must admit that he and Descartes held many basic presuppositions in common, and, although there were some very significant differences between them in their respective systems, these difference were overshadowed by common problems and weaknesses. The pantheism of Spinoza was no more satisfactory than was the dualism of Descartes as a solution to the basic metaphysical issues inherent in their rationalism. If the dualism of Descartes led through deism to atheism, so the pantheism of Spinoza ultimately led to the same conclusion. Thus neither Descartes nor Spinoza had a satisfactory explanation for the problem of individuation and the problem of the one and the many, for this problem is insoluble from the point of view of philosophy. The only solution can be found in a firm belief in the biblical doctrine of the Trinity.

In conclusion, we must conclude that the rationalism of Spinoza was essentially as irrational as that of Descartes. Descartes had held that mechanism was supreme in the organic world of nature, but he reduced mechanism to extension and added another substance (thought or mind) in order to explain the self-consciousness of man. For Spinoza there was but one substance of which thought and extension were the attributes. In departing from Descartes at this point, Spinoza was convinced that he had saved the concept of the fundamental unity of all things, which had been so shattered by the dualism of Descartes. But in his efforts to save the unity of reality he failed to provide any suitable explanation for individuality, reduced human freedom to a meaningless term, and removed teleology from human life and history. Lurking just beneath the surface of the grand scheme of Spinoza's pantheistic rationalism there appears the irrationalism which must accompany the efforts of all unbelievers to explain man apart from the Scriptures.

Leibniz

Gottfried Wilhelm Leibniz (1646–1716), the most important seventeenth-century representative of the rationalistic school of thought, continued the efforts of his predecessors to achieve truth through reason alone. Extremely versatile in his intellectual interests, he pursued mathematics, linguistics, and theology. As a mathematician he developed both integral and differential calculus and found time to invent a calculating machine. As a linguist he was one of the first proponents of a universal language for the purpose of uniting mankind into one harmonious community. As a theologian, he endeavored to defend the doctrine of the Trinity by reason and sought to reconcile Roman Catholics and Protestants in an ecumenical fellowship. After the failure of this project he devoted his energy to formulating a common theology which would unite Calvinists and Lutherans.

The rationalism of Leibniz differed decidedly from that of Descartes and even more so from that of Spinoza. He was dissatisfied with what he regarded as the meager results of the efforts of both of his predecessors and felt that there must be a new solution to the continuing issues of philosophy. In his *New Essay on Human Understanding* he did much to prepare the way for the revolution which took place in philosophy in Kant, and he would certainly have felt at home in the intellectual world of the twentieth century, because of his views on the relativity of space and time and his keen interest in symbolic logic.

Like both Spinoza and Descartes, he was imbued with what seemed to be the infallibility of the science of mathematics, and he also sought to build a system of metaphysics which would be based upon the logical implications of mathematics and physics. Impressed by the idea of continuity in the infinite mathematical series, he came to the conclusion that the fundamental essence of all reality is force or energy, and that it was the essence of both matter and motion. He defined space as the arrangement of those things which coexist, while time is the arrangement of those things which succeed one another. The self-sustaining essence which Spinoza called substance became force for Leibniz, but for Leibniz was not merely a single entity but many, and thus Leibniz held to a pluralistic idealism rather than to the monist position of Spinoza. Leibniz held that monads are the centers of force and he defined monads as those unique individualistic forces which constitute the whole of reality. He further insisted that in every monad there is a self-representation of life and that these monads differ qualitatively to the degree to which they represent to themselves the universe. Leibniz thus presented a scheme of reality consisting of a gradation of monads in which God was the primitive or original unity of whom other monads are the created products or fulgerations. This position lies somewhere between the Gnostic conception of reality and the view of creation by divine fiat. In order to safeguard this system against the very obvious danger of an atomistic anarchy, Leibniz decreed the existence of a pre-established harmony among the many monads which constituted his reality. This pre-established harmony simply meant that all monads must mirror the same world, and they differ only in the distinction of their perceptions of this world. By such an invention Leibniz felt that he had been able to offer a solution to the problem of interaction between mind and body, since God had created all the monads with an identical content. For Leibniz God was the great clock maker who had produced two clocks with perfect mechanical connections (a view very similar to that of Descartes), and he further insisted that these clocks were so perfectly connected that they alway keep perfect time. We may say that Leibniz presented a modified theism. He acknowledged the sovereignty of God and human responsibility as well, but he also held that God ordained all things according to His foreknowledge. However, at the same time, he also held that each spirit makes its own choice according to its own nature and is therefore morally responsible. But these spirits do not make their decisions apart from sufficient reasons in their own nature. Essentially Leibniz held to a Thomistic conception of nature and grace. He defined liberty as the ability to accept and carry out those determinations imposed upon us by our nature. True liberty is found only in God, who is the supreme and perfect monad. On the other hand, man vacillates in his decisions and actions because of attitudes which arise within him from the unconscious to the conscious. At this point Leibniz obviously foreshadowed Freud.

Leibniz's attempt to create a theistic interpretation of reality fell far short of the goal which he had in mind. In asserting that God knows all truth, both eternal and contingent, he betrayed his own cause. In holding that God's knowledge of all truth, includes all possibilities of existence and that these possibilities are limited by those which God selects, he seriously limited the sovereignty and foreknowledge of God upon which he had built his case. In the biblical view there can be no contingent truth in the mind of God, and the sovereign God of the Scriptures is never in the position of selecting possibilities in His government of creation.

The admission that the system developed by Leibniz was the last vigorous effort to reconcile the ideal and real worlds must not blind us to the fact that in many ways his was a fantastic philosophy. Although it contained biblical ingredients, nevertheless, at the same time, this philosophy was a curious composite of theistic references and non-theistic concepts. Its rationalism was also accompanied by the usual correlative of irrationalism. In holding that God created the world out of His own substance rather than out of nothing, Leibniz based his case on a conception of creation which was definitely anti-theistic.

Rationalism: A Conclusion

With the failure of Leibniz to offer satisfactory solutions to the serious problems which he had inherited from Descartes and Spinoza, European rationalism had run its course. It was out of tune with the scientific temper which characterized the emerging Age of the Enlightenment. In spite of his devotion to mathematics as an exact science, neither Descartes nor Spinoza nor Leibniz allowed any room in his system for the emerging spirit of scientific investigation, and the philosophy of Leibniz was definitely hostile to the scientific methodology. His reliance on innate ideas ruled out the inductive approach to the formulation of knowledge, which was coming into prominence with the scientific revolution then underway.

The Enlightenment and Empiricism

By 1660 a strong reaction had developed against rationalism as a satisfactory attempt to explain the universe and man's role in it. Rationalism was being proclaimed a failure. Its efforts had ended in confusion, and its basic presuppositions ran sharply counter to the growing feeling that empiricism offered more promise for the understanding of philosophical issues. The conviction was also growing that man should begin his philosophical quest with the world in which he lived, with the things in hand rather than with a vast universe which he only faintly understood. This new spirit was quite evident in Alexander Pope's famous *Essay on Man,* in which he laid down the dictum: "Know thyself, presume not God to scan. The proper study of mankind is man." The Enlightenment may be regarded as having its beginning with the appearance of Locke's *Essay on Human Understanding,* and it may be regarded as coming to its end with the appearance of Kant's *Critique of Pure Reason* in 1781. Although Cartesian rationalism still interested philosophers after 1690, it no longer claimed their loyalty, and criticism of it became the prevailing tendency.

The Enlightenment marked the emergence of a new spirit in European thought, and many students of the intellectual history of the West look upon this era as marking the final triumph of the humanistic philosophy of the Renaissance over both the Reformation on the one hand and the Thomistic system of the Roman Catholic Church on the other. This triumph was certainly not too apparent in 1690, but it was a very impressive reality by the time of the French Revolution.

This triumph of the Renaissance, however, in the Enlightenment does not mean that it was also the triumph of the classical humanism or Platonic philosophy which had motivated and inspired the humanists of the earlier era. No longer was classical man the model for the mind of the Enlightenment. No longer was classical man the source of all truth and the measure of all things. Rather was it the man of the eighteenth century who would in a very real sense evaluate himself in the light of his own scientific achievements. The essence of this new philosophy was humanistic, to be sure, but it was now naturalistic rather than classical in its outlook.

The mind of the Enlightenment now had found a new source of authority in a new deity which it had created for itself, and this new deity was natural law. Its prophets were Copernicus, Galileo, Kepler, Newton, and others. In fact, the scientist had now become the new high priest, and the test tube, the microscope, the telescope, and mathematics were the sources for this new revelation. Its new temples were to be the emerging scientific laboratories with their various experiments, for natural law had now become the new infallible rule of faith and practice which would bring its ardent worshipers into a millennial era based on the achievements of the high priests, who would diligently consult natural law for the proper guidance of European society.

It was an age of an almost unbounded optimism. Throwing off the shackles of Christianity on the one hand and the influence of a dead classical past on the other, the mind of the Enlightenment looked to natural law as its infallible source of authority; in short, its new god; and revelation would now come through the application of the scientific method rather than through the study of an infallible book, the holy Scriptures.

The Enlightenment very easily discarded all those Christian doctrines and previous philosophical systems which in any way contradicted the content of this new revelation, of this new knowledge which man would gain of the world and of himself, through the scientific approach and methodology. The high priests of this new religion with an absolute assurance informed the Europe of the eighteenth century that man was inherently good and ridiculed the biblical insistence that man is totally depraved and inherently evil. The Enlightenment also insisted that what seemed to be evil in man was nothing more than a lack of knowledge, and that through proper education men, who are inherently good, can be improved and even perfected. This doctrine of human perfectibility had as its logical conclusion the perfectibility of the whole human race, and the achievement of a millennial era of a thoroughly secular character. Perhaps nowhere in the literature of this era do we find a more forceful expression of this confidence in human progress than in the words of Condorcet:

> Everything tells us that we are approaching the era of one of the grand revolutions of the human race. What can better enlighten us as to what to expect, what can be a more sure guide to us amidst its commotions than the picture of the revolutions that have preceded and prepared the way for it? The present state of knowledge assures us that it will be happy. In fine may it not be expected that the human race will be ameliorated by new discoveries in the sciences and the arts, and, as an unavoidable consequence in the means of individual and general prosperity; by farther progress in the principles of conduct, the moral practice, and lastly by the improvements in our faculties, moral, intellectual and physical, which may be the result of either of the improvements of the instruments of our natural organization? . . . Do not all the observations in fine, which we propose to develop prove that the moral goodness of man, the necessary consequence of his organization is, like all his other faculties, susceptible of an indefinite improvement? And that nature has connected by a chain which cannot be broken, truth, happiness and virtue.[7]

To the modern mind of the second half of the twentieth century, such an assurance of a golden age to be achieved by new discoveries in science may be almost inexplicable, but for the Enlightenment to question such a possibility was tantamount to heresy. With this introduction we may now begin to examine the development of European thought during the eighteenth century and come to an understanding of its ultimate outcome in a blind optimism stated so clearly in the midst of the French Revolution, the greatest upheaval which Europe had yet known and which would become the source of even greater revolutionary catastrophes during the nineteenth and twentieth centuries.

John Locke

Locke became the most influential philosophical spokesman for the

---

7. Condorcet, *Outline of an Historical View of the Progress of the Human Mind* (London, 1798).

new age which was dawning for Europe toward the close of the seventeenth century. He was one of the first to realize the implications of the Newtonian system and to use it as the basis of a new *Weltanschauung* in the light of which he hoped to rewrite the philosophy, the political, social, and economic thought of Europe, and its educational practices as well. He was even convinced that the scientific methodology could be used to offer an irrefutable defense of Christianity.[8] He thus sought to erect a new philosophy which looked to the empirical epistemology rather than to the rationalistic principles of Descartes. He categorically rejected the traditional concept of innate ideas as a source of knowledge and insisted that all ideas originate in the operations of the senses on the mind. He denied that conscience and basic moral principles are innate in man, even the idea of God Himself. Locke did not deny the existence of God and immortality, but he was quite sure that these beliefs could not be substantiated through innate ideas.

Locke insisted that the minds of infants at birth are a *tabula rasa,* devoid of all content, but not of power.

> Every man being conscious to himself what he thinks, and that which his mind is applied about, whilst thinking, being the ideas that are there, it is past doubt, that men have in their minds several ideas, such as those expressed by the words, Whiteness, Hardness, Sweetness, Thinking, Motion, Man, Elephant, Army, Drunkenness, and others. It is in the first place then to be inquired, how he comes by them. I know it is a received doctrine, that men have native ideas, and original characters, stamped upon their minds, in their very first being. This opinion I have, at large, examined already; and, I suppose, what I have said, in the foregoing book, will be much more easily admitted, when I have shown, whence the understanding may get all the ideas it has, and by what ways and degrees they may come into the mind; for which I shall appeal to every one's own observation and experience.
>
> Let us then suppose the mind to be, as we say, white paper, void of all characters, without any ideas; how comes it to be furnished? Whence comes it by that vast store which the busy and boundless fancy of man has painted on it, with an almost endless variety? Whence has it all the materials of reason and knowledge? To this I answer, in one word, from experience; in that all our knowledge is founded, and from that it ultimately derives itself. Our observation employed either about external sensible objects, or about the internal operations of our minds, perceived and reflected on by ourselves, is that which supplies our understandings with all the materials of thinking. These two are the

8. Locke's most important works are the following: *Two Treatises on Government* (1690), *Essay on Human Understanding* (1690), *The Reasonableness of Christianity* (1695).

> fountains of knowledge, from whence all the ideas we have, or can naturally have, do spring.
>
> First, Our senses, conversant about particular sensible objects, do convey into the mind several distinct perceptions of things, according to those various ways wherein those objects do affect them: and thus we come by those ideas we have, of Yellow, White, Heat, Cold, Soft, Hard, Bitter, Sweet, and all those which we call sensible qualities; which when I say the senses convey into the mind, I mean, they from external objects convey into the mind what produces there those perceptions. This great source of most of the ideas we have, depending wholly upon our senses, and derived by them to the understanding, I call *sensation*.[9]

He insisted that once the mind has the material to work on, brought to it by the senses, it assumes an active role in obtaining genuine knowledge. He further taught that there are three types of simple ideas. The first of these he called sensation, since they arise from the operation of the senses on the mind. He found a second type of simple idea in what he called reflection, which he defined as the awareness of our own mental processes such as thinking, believing, and knowing. The third type of simple idea he called sensation and reflection, by which he meant such experiences as pain, pleasure, existence, and the succession of events in time.

He also assumed that the mind has the power to make complex ideas. It may do so by what he called combination. He held that the mind has the ability to combine several simple ideas into a compound idea, such as beauty, man, or misery. The second type he called relation, by which he meant the ability of the mind to place simple or complex ideas together and view them at once. His examples of this ability are father and mother and cause and effect. The third complex idea he called the power of abstraction, by which he meant that the mind abstracts an idea from accompanying ideas. An example of this would be whiteness.

> Secondly, The other fountain, from which experience furnisheth the understanding with ideas, is the perception of the operations of our own mind within us, as it is employed about the ideas it has got; which operations when the soul comes to reflect on and consider, do furnish the understanding with another set of ideas, which could not be had from things without; and such are Perception, Thinking, Doubting, Believing, Reasoning, Knowing, Willing, and all the different actings of our own minds; which we being conscious of and observing in ourselves, do from these receive into our understandings, as distinct ideas, as we do from bodies affecting our senses. This source of ideas every man has wholly in himself; and though it be not sense, as having

9. John Locke, *An Essay Concerning Human Understanding,* 21st ed. (London: 1805), pp. 144-145.

> nothing to do with external objects, yet it is very like it, and might properly enough be called internal sense. But as I call the other sensation, so I call this *reflection,* the ideas it affords being such only as the mind gets by reflecting on its own operations within itself. By reflection then, in the following part of this discourse, I would be understood to mean that notice which the mind takes of its own operations, and the manner of them; by reason whereof there come to be ideas of these operations in the understanding. These two, I say, viz., external material things, as the objects of sensation; and the operations of our own minds within, as the objects of reflection; are to me the only originals from whence all our ideas take their beginnings. The term operations here I use in a large sense, as comprehending not barely the actions of the mind about its ideas, but some sort of passions arising sometimes from them, such as is the satisfaction or uneasiness arising from any thought.
>
> The understanding seems to me not to have the least glimmering of any ideas, which it doth not receive from one of these two. External objects furnish the mind with the ideas of sensible qualities, which are all those different perceptions they produce in us; and the mind furnishes the understanding with ideas of its own operations.[10]

Building his system of thought on these basic and yet unprovable presuppositions, Locke refuted the existence of universals as independent realities as in the thought of Plato and as existing in particular entities as in Aristotle. He insisted that the only entities which exist by themselves are individual particular things or substances. In sensation and reflection these entities constitute the original source of human knowledge. But at this point Locke was forced to concede that there are degrees of knowledge. Our most certain knowledge is intuition, by which he meant our immediate apprehension of the agreement or disagreement of ideas such as the realization that white is not black and that a circle is not a triangle.

Demonstrative knowledge is less clear and is valid only when it is verified by intuition. The least dependable form of knowledge is that which comes to us through our senses. It can only assure us of the existence of the external world but cannot tell us anything of its nature.

But a very real problem appears in Locke's scheme at this point. If all we learn must come to us originally from the senses, and if this knowledge is the least certain form we possess, what is the test for the reliability of what we know? Is there such a test? For this question Locke had an answer: Our knowledge is reliable in so far as it concerns itself with the things experienced or demonstrated from experience. Thus there is no knowledge that is truly reliable.

10. Ibid., p. 145.

Locke's test of the reliability of knowledge placed serious restrictions on the extent of knowledge which we may obtain. His empiricism confined human knowledge to the nominal essence of objects but excluded any possibility of knowing their real essence. Our senses suggest the perceptions that are produced in us by external objects, but this experience cannot be verified. Locke defined nominal essences as those abstract, complex ideas to which men have annexed general names. But, on the other hand, he also maintained that we can have real knowledge and make universal propositions in the realms of mathematics and ethics. This Lockean empiricism leads to the conclusion that certainty is scarce, so scarce that our knowledge, except in the realms of mathematics and ethics, can only be based upon probability and the presumed agreement or disagreement of ideas, and not on propositions.

The question may well be asked: What place did revelation have in Locke's epistemology? In his writings as a whole he suggests that it is an object of faith and therefore offers less certainty than intuition or what Locke called demonstrated certainty. He also insisted that revelation may not run counter to intuitive knowledge. Thus we are to take on faith what cannot be known by the unaided intellect. God can ask our assent to truth, for He made truth reasonable. It may be asked at this point if there is any room for a belief in miracles in his system. Inconsistently, Locke held that the miracles recorded in the Scriptures can be regarded as true, for their apparent improbability is more than offset by the fact that they are contained in God's revelation to man. With reference to the existence of God, Locke also made an exception to his principle that nothing can be known of real existence except through the senses, for he insisted that the existence of God is based on absolutely demonstrative knowledge. To be thoroughly consistent, Locke should have based his argument for the existence of God on sensate knowledge, which can only provide the probability of His existence. But he held that God exists not merely as an idea, but as an independent being. In spite of these concessions to the Scriptures and the doctrine of God, Locke insisted that reason must be our last judge and guide in the quest for knowledge, and his ultimate defense of Christianity was based upon his assertion that he found that it was not contrary to reason. It is quite obvious that in demanding a religion that was not contrary to reason, he was a forerunner of the deists and Voltaire and the other skeptics of the eighteenth century who rejected Christianity because they declared it to be contrary to right reason.

Locke's empirical system is riddled with serious difficulty and Van Til is quite correct when he points out that irrationalism is as dominant a motif in the empirical tradition as it is in the rationalism which began with Descartes. In the first place, Locke's basic assumptions themselves were a contradiction to themselves. Using his empirical approach, it is utterly impossible to prove that the mind is a *tabula rasa* at birth. This assumption most certainly was not derived from sense experience on the part of Locke or anyone else. The assertion that all we learn must come to us through the senses is also unprovable. To say that we learn through the senses is an unverified assumption and it is utterly impossible to claim that all we learn we must learn through the senses. Yet upon this feeble foundation Locke proceeded to erect his philosophical structure, his metaphysics, psychological and political and educational systems.

The assumption that the mind has an innate power to form more complex and more reliable ideas was for Locke a convenient escape hatch in view of his admission that the ideas we derive from our senses are the least reliable. But this assumption likewise is one which cannot be verified by his empirical approach to knowledge.

Locke's system posed many dangers for the future of the intellectual development of the West, of which he seemed to be quite unaware. His denial of the doctrine of innate ideas in all of its forms led to a very serious problem with consciousness. His position led to the conclusion that human consciousness is the result of the contact of the mind with the material world through the senses. Viewed in this light, consciousness is not the result of the fact that the soul is God's image in man, but rather human consciousness is the result of the impact of the material world on the brain, which gives rise to this question: How can unconscious matter produce consciousness in the human mind through the senses? This question Locke left unanswered, but it has remained to haunt empiricists from his day on. Locke's position has logically and historically led to the various forms of determinism which have come to dominate contemporary psychology, sociology, political thought, and educational thought and practice. Man has become the pawn of those forces which he cannot control and before which he is powerless. Stripped of his image of God, man in the philosophy of Locke has ultimately become an animal, a more complex type of mechanism, to be sure, but a mechanism nevertheless, stripped of dignity and freedom, and yet a vehicle to be manipulated by his eager manipulators.

Seen in its true light, this aspect of Locke's system simply stated that the soul of man, if he should possess one, contains no innate knowledge of God or the principles of right and wrong. Thus the conscience of man is stimulated only by its contact with the world of sense, and this world of sense or of matter cannot possibly bring to the mind those sensations which lead to the formation of moral values.

Locke's denial of the biblical concept of the soul as the moral conscience given to him by God has led to the modern conclusion that since man does not have any innate ideas concerning morality and ethics, and since he is nothing more than a complex animal, he is therefore determined by his external environment in his ethical insights and actions and is therefore not morally responsible, since he is the slave of his environment. Morally as well as intellectually, he came to be regarded as beyond freedom and dignity.

Locke's Political Thought

Locke's empiricism became very important in modern political philosophy and development, where it has had an increasingly devastating influence, and in the twentieth century has led to the emergence of the totally irrational totalitarian regimes which have become the predominant form of government in our day.

Locke's application of his basic empirical assumptions to the problems of government has led to conclusions very different from those which he had in mind. Writing his *Two Treatises on Government* in 1690 for the purpose of defending the revolution of 1688–1689, which brought William and Mary to the throne of England, Locke endeavored to set forth a political philosophy which would anchor his democratic political thought on what he felt were the firm foundations of his empiricism. However, his insistence that nature has bestowed upon mankind certain basic and inalienable rights was an assumption quite contrary to his empiricism. His denial of conscience as an innate possession or quality makes it impossible for men to know that they possess the rights of life, liberty, and property. The very concept of a human right is moral in nature and has its basis of authority in the human conscience. It is thus impossible for men to know through the senses that they have these cherished human rights. Granted that it was far from Locke's intention to undermine or destroy this traditional English concept of personal rights, his empiricism removed from his political thought the necessary foundations on which a government could be built for the protection of these rights. His empiricism supported neither the idea that men have such rights nor that they are inalienable. Their inalienability must forever elude the realm of sensate knowledge.

It is thus no accident that the erosion of Locke's basic philosophy in the hands of his successors brought with it the collapse of his political thought and the denial of the very rights which he sought to protect. The transformation of Locke's political thought into the vehicle for the creation of the totalitarian state became very obvious in both Hegel and Marx.

The Decline of Empiricism

We have said that irrationalism was the dominant motif in empiricism as well as in rationalism.[11] Locke assumed that the facts of man's environment are simply there and that the mind of man is a *tabula rasa.* Locke's assertion that the mind has no innate ideas was soon followed by the insistence that it has no general ideas. The next step in this rendezvous with irrationality was the conclusion that ideas are only faint replicas of sensations. At this point all connection between things and ideas and between ideas among themselves was lost. Van Til was entirely correct when he wrote that "so far as this position was consistently developed it was calculated to destroy all intelligible human experience."[12]

The irrationalism inherent in Locke is the almost inescapable result of his rejection of the biblical world and life view. Christian theism declares that the knowability of the universe is guaranteed to man by the act of creation. God knows the facts before they are facts, and he created man as a knowing mind in a knowable world. Our knowledge is analogical, but it is just as real as God's knowledge of creation, for we are so created after God's own image. In this view, being is primary. The innateness of a knowing spirit and the reality of the world impinging on our minds through the activity of our senses gives us true knowledge. The knowability of man lies in the correspondence existing between the created world and his mind. In his neglect or denial of this fundamental biblical concept, Locke promoted the growth of irrationalism.

His errors strikingly illustrate the dangers inherent in the empirical approach to truth. The Christian thinker may properly use induction and deduction, analysis and synthesis, but he must always use them in the light of the great postulates of biblical theism. In Locke's view of revelation there was the absence of the realization of the authority of the revealed will and mind of God, and no understanding of the self-revealing God of the Scriptures.

But his system was not developed consistently, and it was on the basis of an inconsistently developed empiricism that succeeding thinkers could speak of having a probable knowledge of the facts of nature and history. Bishop Butler even attempted to defend the truth and acceptability of Christianity on the basis of such an empiricism. He argued that certainty was

11. Cornelius Van Til, *The Triumph of Grace,* vol. 1, p. 27.
12. Ibid.

not possible for man because it pertained to the realm of mathematics only.

Bishop Berkeley (1685–1753)

Bishop Berkeley is the second most important thinker in the development of empiricism. He accepted much of Locke. He held that knowledge is framed in terms of the ideas formed in the mind. He denied innate ideas and held that the only function or role which the mind has in the process of acquiring knowledge is the capacity to receive ideas from the senses and then to act in certain ways in regard to the ideas coming to it from the outside world of sense.

It would seem that Berkeley was a close disciple of Locke, but this is not the case. He was aware of the problems which Locke had raised and sought to develop certain trends in Locke's empiricism which Locke had not followed. Because of this he has frequently been called a subjective idealist.

In his *An Essay Toward a New Theory of Vision* (1709), he argued that experience as such must be distinguished from mere sensation. In this connection he argued that such ideas of "space, outness and things placed at a distance are not, strictly speaking, the object of sight," but rather "our judging objects perceived by the sight to be at any distance without the mind, is entirely the effect of experience."[13] In the same manner he held that the extension, figures, and motions perceived by sight are specifically distinct from the ideas of touch, called by the same names, "nor is there any such thing as one idea, or kind of idea, common to both senses." Berkeley concluded that experience must be distinguished from mere sensation and that the relationship thought to exist between the ideas of touch and sight is neither natural nor necessary, but is rather habitual and customary.

Berkeley has taken Locke one step further in the descent to skepticism. And Berkeley was not entirely unaware of the abyss toward which philosophy was heading, for in his later work, *The Theory of Vision or Visual Language, Vindicated and Explained* (1733), he tried to answer the problem by asserting that although the senses do not bring to us the necessity of any connection between the senses of sight and touch, there is such a necessary connection, and it was instituted by the Author of Nature. This answer differed sharply from that found in Locke, for Locke held that the idea of space comes to us from more than one sense (sight and touch). For Locke there was then no problem in conceiving space, and objects in space exist independently of any perception of them.

---

13. Bishop Berkeley, *An Essay Towards a New Theory of Vision,* par. I.

In his most important work, *Principles of Human Knowledge* (1710) Berkeley sought to provide an answer to the basic problems which he found in Locke, and his solution lay in a denial that there is no such thing as reality in matter. His solution is found in his assertion that to be is to be seen. Thus there is no independent reality of any kind. All is mental. To explain the possibility of knowledge, all that we need is mind and ideas. By this he meant that in perception we are aware of a combination of sense qualities along with a consciousness of our own existence as a thing distinct from our perception. Taking this logic one step further, he insisted that there is no evidence in either reason or the senses that external objects exist outside the mind. For Berkeley it followed that all ideas are passive; they cannot do anything or be the cause of anything. Hence extension, figure, and motion cannot be the cause of our ideas. How, then, do ideas originate? To this question Berkeley supplied the answer that the mind of the individual is active in that it can excite or arouse ideas, and illustrated this with his insistence that we have a notion or an idea of our own being.

But what about ideas which come to us through the senses? He insisted that such ideas are involuntary on the part of the minds of men. Such ideas are not produced by the mind, and neither is there any matter to produce them. Thus they cannot produce themselves. Berkeley's ultimate answer to this perplexing question in his system was that the activity of God is their cause. For the Christian thinker, this is a most unsatisfactory answer. In denying the reality of matter and the created world, Berkeley was arguing against the biblical doctrine of creation and was plunging philosophy more deeply into the morass of sheer irrationalism. Why and how would God be the active cause of ideas which come to us in an involuntary manner? His assumption that such ideas are the result of the activity of God has no real foundation in his system, and it fails to account for the problem why men have the senses as part of their own physical makeup, if there is no external world with which they may have contact.

At this point it is interesting and important to note that Berkeley's interest in developing his system was largely theological. In his philosophy he sought to give to orthodox Protestantism a solid apologetical foundation, and he insisted that the removal of matter from the world removed the basis for skepticism and made real knowledge possible. He further contended that his system overthrew atheism and made the existence of God absolutely sure.[14]

14. In his later thinking (*Siris*) he departed from the English empiricism and became Platonic and neo-Platonic in anticipation of the later concepts of Kant and Hegel.

In summary, we must say that Berkeley's basic error was his attempt to create a metaphysics in the area of general revelation in place of the God of special revelation. His efforts to create an impregnable defense for Christianity by assuming the existence of a common ground on which both the believer and the unbeliever could reason together ended in failure, and he once again illustrates the general principle that Christian theism cannot walk hand in hand with the principles of unbelief.

David Hume (1711–1776)

The degeneration of empiricism into sheer skepticism is clearly evident in the thought of Hume, for Hume's devastating attacks on the empirical epistemology stemmed from the fact that he was much more thorough in his empiricism than either Locke or Berkeley. He insisted that all knowledge originates in the senses, but he also admitted that the mind does have an ability to compare ideas through the use of memory and imagination, and has the ability to identify ideas which it receives at one time with those received at other times. In short, somewhat inconsistently to be sure, Hume did hold that the mind can conceive of certain types of relationships. It could understand relationships between ideas; it could have a concept of continuity by time and space, and it could recognize differences in number as found in mathematics.

In his metaphysics, however, his further development in the direction of irrationalism is clearly evident. He not only rejected all abstract ideas including the existence of material substances, but he went further than Berkeley in denying the existence of spiritual substances, and this denial included the concept of the self. He insisted that we ourselves constitute our own experience, for we can never, as it were, "catch ourselves without a perception." Hume's very consistency in following his empiricism brought him into a hopeless skepticism and he left unanswered that most important question as to the source and nature of human consciousness. How do we know that we ourselves are our own experience, and, in this frame of reference, how did Hume know that there is a "self" to catch? In Hume's philosophy the self must forever remain a most elusive concept. His emphatic denial of the existence of both spiritual and material substances raised the very important question of what the "self" is, and for this question Hume had no answer. In the development of his position, he simply assumed the self, for even his blatant skepticism would not permit him to doubt his own existence.

Hume's devastating attacks on the traditional theory of causation were probably his most important contribution to the decline of the empiricism he was expressing. It has been well said that Hume had very little to offer in the way of either a new theory of knowledge or a new body of knowledge. But it would also be unfair to conclude that Hume failed to make any contributions to philosophic thought. His success in showing that the Lockean position was untenable was in one sense an advance in that Hume offered a devastating attack on the basic empirical assumptions, and this basic attack reached its climax in his analysis of the problem of causation.

Hume divided all objects of knowledge into two kinds and held that the relation of ideas, their clearness and distinctness, is the test of all truth, since the contrary of a true proposition would be a logical contradiction.

What Hume called matters of fact represented his second kind of knowledge, by which he meant the facts of history, geography, and chemistry, in which the contrary of any proposition does not involve a logical contradiction. There is no logical contradiction in asserting that George III was king of England in 1776. Another example would be that H_2O is the chemical composition of water. But at the same time he held that these principles are gained through the concept of cause and effect.

Hume, having gone thus far, then went on to assert that these ideas are representative neither of objects nor of the content of the mind, by which he meant innate ideas. Therefore, knowledge stands for the essences arising from the comparison of ideas. This inevitably led him to the conclusion that all knowledge consists of varying degrees of probability. This insistence that all knowledge simply consists of various degrees of probability led Hume to deny the traditional concept of causation. He insisted that we cannot penetrate into the reason for what he called the conjunction of cause and effect, for this conjunction is of the nature of belief, rather than a mathematical proof. He concluded his argument with the admission that a cause may be followed by an assumed result or effect in a certain percentage of cases, and it is possible to calculate the ratio of probability. On the basis of such assumptions or definitions Hume then asserted that such commonly accepted postulates as causation and the uniformity of nature cannot be empirically demonstrated or proved. Nevertheless, he did admit that they were extremely useful hypotheses.

In his psychological approach to the problem of causation Hume considered what he felt were the three basic elements in the commonly accepted interpretation of this concept: contiguity, succession, and necessity. Admitting that the first two are to be found among our impressions, he denied that necessity is the result of the senses. Rather did he insist that our minds add necessity as the third ingredient to those impressions which are received by the senses. Thus necessity is not a quality or a relationship inherent in the impressions themselves. Thus the relationship between fire and heat is a habit of our minds devised to form a causal connection between these two impressions. In the same way we imagine that energy passes from one billiard ball to another, when in actuality we observe nothing of the kind. This logical application of the Lockean empiricism was a far cry from what Locke had in view in his own writings. Hume's devastating onslaught against Locke threatened to destroy the whole Newtonian conception of nature which Locke had fondly imagined he could use to build an entirely new world and life view founded upon the empirical approach to knowledge and the scientific methodology. But such concepts as cause and effect and the uniformity of nature in its laws were basic ingredients in this Lockean scheme, and now, if Hume were correct, they were only useful hypotheses at best, but were creations of the mind and could not be regarded as true.

As devastating as these attacks of Hume on these commonly cherished presuppositions were, his task was not yet done, for he did not confine his critical assault on the world around man. With a rigorous, if disconcerting, consistency he turned his attention to man himself. Having declared that we never perceive things as they really are in themselves, he went on to insist that man never really knows himself. At best we feign the identity of our perceptions of our reflection, and so we come to believe in the continuity of ourselves. Thus man has no more certainty of his own essence than he does of the world around him. Hume's dreary conclusion to his own train of thought was that knowledge is at most a belief, but it is neither necessary nor certain in an objective way.

Ethics

Hume was equally consistent in his application of his rigid empiricism to the field of ethics as he had been in his discussions of epistemology and metaphysics. Pleasure or pain accompany all our sense impressions, but emotion and our passions are subsequent to the appearance of ideas, and volition is then the result of our emotions and passions. Apparently realizing the ethical chaos which lay just ahead of him in this logical sequence, he called upon reason as the necessary guide to passion for the formation of a coherent organization of our impulses.

But how do our emotions arise in the light of this empirical approach to ethics? How does pleasure arise? Hume was not lacking for an answer to such questions. In a similar manner Hume described sympathy as a reaction arising from our observation of the reaction in others to the same extent that the same impressions originate in ourselves.

Hume's view of ethics was a far cry from, and a conscious repudiation of, the biblical view. It could hardly have been otherwise in view of his previous departures from the Scriptures in his epistemology and metaphysics. The extent of this departure becomes very evident in the various schools of ethical thought which emerged out of his position. His hedonism was probably its leading characteristic, but equally important, possibly, was the voluntarism which was also a part of his thought. He also gave an added impetus to the later utilitarianism, but he identified his concept of utility with that which brings pleasure. Inherent in his whole ethical outlook was an emphasis on free will, by which he meant that man has the power to act or not to act, according to the determination of the will. This conception of the freedom of the will was anchored in humanism, and Hume actually did not have a well-defined and meaningful doctrine of freedom in any sense of the word. His concept of freedom was not undergirded by any reference to the biblical views of God, man, or sin; and therefore was actually deterministic in its essence. His view of freedom therefore was essentially irrational and once again reveals the eroding effects of Lockean empiricism as it was brought to bear upon the biblical ethic.

Hume's social philosophy was a further illustration of the unstable nature of Locke's world and life view and how quickly it would crumble under the sledge-hammer blows of the very consistency of Hume's own interpretation of the Lockean philosophy. He held that the state, like language, had its origins in human instinct and human needs as these instincts were assisted by intelligent reflection. He completely rejected Locke's position that the state was the result of a social contract. Therefore the moral obligation of its citizens to render their political allegiance to this state, according to Hume, rested on its utility and its ability to promote the general welfare, and not on the concept of a social contract, which had played such an important role in Locke's political philosophy.

With the development of Hume's consistent empiricism, the grand edifice which Locke had sought to erect was fast crumbling apart. Like the rationalism for which it was supposed to be an answer, it fell apart because of the inherent anti-intellectualism and irrationalism which inevitably accompanied its underlying presuppositions. For the empiricist, man was supremely capable of achieving all necessary knowledge, for man was inherently good, and the proper use of right reason would lead him on to the conquest of truth. Like the rationalists, these eighteenth-century empiricists left little or no room for the God of Christianity in their thinking and proceeded to build their castles of philosophy without any real regard for the biblical doctrines of creation of both the world and man, the role of man in creation, the fall into sin, and the redemptive work of God in the person of Jesus Christ. With Hume it seemed that all of philosophic endeavor must come to a grinding halt, and we can well understand how Hume's logical development of the empirical methodology could so horrify Kant.

The empiricism of Hume, carried out to its logical conclusion, could lead only to positivism and to skepticism, both of which positions are totally incompatible with the basic postulates of Christian theism. This empiricism failed to give credit to the ability of the human mind to form concepts out of the raw material brought to it through the senses. It failed utterly to regard man as God's vice-regent on earth with a creative capacity to think the thoughts of God after Him and to do His will after Him. Hume's insistence that we can have no certainty, but only probability logically applied, would have meant the end of man's intellectual endeavors not only in philosophy but also in science and the other areas of intellectual and artistic activity. In Hume philosophy had reached the nadir of despair.

Chapter 4
The Enlightenment in Western Thought During the Eighteenth Century

Both rationalism and empiricism had exercised an influence upon the development of Western thought in both Europe and America during the eighteenth century which far transcended the boundaries of formal philosophy. The extension of the influence of philosophical speculation into virtually every area of intellectual activity had received a great impetus from the scientific formulations of Sir Isaac Newton and the work of John Locke. Newton had assumed that physical laws had a universal validity. Acting on this assumption, Locke and other philosophers endeavored to transform these Newtonian assumptions into a new frame of reference as a kind of guide for all of human thought. In the minds of his many eighteenth-century disciples Newton came to be the source and inspiration for a new world and life view which differed radically from that provided by the Reformers and also from that of the rationalists. Although Newton did not include theology in his scheme and did not subject it to the laws of nature, many, if not most, of his successors did not shrink from including it in the domain of natural law.[1]

In this way natural law became the order of the day, and thus there was born the Age of Enlightenment. In its fantastic faith in the infallibility of the scientific method, this new age created for itself a new trinity of reason, nature, and humanity and proceeded to worship this secularized or naturalized god with a devotion which would have been much more fitting for the worship of the God revealed in the Scriptures. The authors of *The Emergence of Modern Humanism* are quite correct in their insistence that the Enlightenment was the final step in the process of secularization which began in Western thought during the early Renaissance.[2] Equally acute is their observation that the Enlightenment marks the triumph of Newton and Locke over Descartes.

---

1. It had been Newton's attempt merely to free science from theological restraints.
2. Wilson Coates and Hayden White, *The Emergence of Modern Humanism* (New York, 1906).

Locke was convinced that it was now possible to use the laws of nature as they had been proclaimed by Newton for the purpose of determining those natural laws on which human society must be founded, and then to use this "humanized" natural law as the pattern on which a new social order would be created. Although the rejection of the biblical pattern for human society was implicit in these assumptions which Locke deduced from Newton, he never pushed them to their logical conclusions. In fact, Locke was quite ambivalent in his attitude toward Christianity at many points. His chief interest was the formulation of a natural theology, by which he meant a Christianity which would conform to the dictates of right reason. In his *Reasonableness of Christianity* (1695) and his *Discourse of Miracles* (1706) he set forth a Christianity which met his basic demand that it conform to right reason. Locke's demands which he placed upon a reasonable Christian faith were the belief in Jesus as the Messiah and the living of the good or the Christian life. He was vaguely aware that the human spirit needed something more than an empirical relationship with reality, and he felt that Christianity gave to his philosophy a supernatural reinforcement to that which natural reason asserted was true and good. He felt that revelation confirmed what the right use of reason made available to man.

Leslie Stephen may well have been right in his insistence that Locke was basically a rationalist in the sense that reason was the final court of appeal for the ascertaining of religious truth. There is no doubt that Locke argued that the ultimate test of the truthfulness of the Christian religion was its social utility, by which he meant its influence for the promotion of morality. Locke's efforts to combine a belief in the reasonableness of Christianity with his empirical epistemology were ultimately a failure. In fact, he was not truly consistent in this effort, for he admitted that the doctrine of the incarnation of Jesus Christ was beyond the reach of his empirical search for truth.

Under the sledge-hammer blows of Hume and Voltaire and their successors, the attacks on historic Christianity grew more and more bold, and natural law became the new religion, as we have seen. This natural law philosophy, which was based in part on a belief in the natural ordering of the physical world and on which was believed to be the basic character of man, became the new frame of reference for human intellectual inquiry and the pursuit of truth. In the light of the Newtonian physics, nature was now regarded as an orderly, stable mechanism governed by a set of universal, automatic, and immutable laws.

Emanating from this natural law philosophy, which permeated the mind of the eighteenth century to a far greater extent than is often realized, was a philosophy which was thoroughly secular in nature and which, therefore, set forth a secular concept of man and his social, political, and economic order. In place of the biblical view of the sovereignty of God in nature, it created a doctrine of a sovereign natural law. For the eighteenth century natural law became a sovereign entity in itself, not subject to the divine decrees of the God of the Scriptures, but an independent sovereignty over which God had no control, and to which He was even subject, although many deists were willing to admit that somehow or other He had created this natural law.

In much the same way the doctrine of natural rights, already seriously modified by John Locke, was subjected to further deterioration, and what moral foundations may have been left for them were being dissolved in the midst of the skepticism which enveloped the mind of Western Europe toward the end of the eighteenth century. Even the concept of human rights itself began to dissolve, and in his formulation of the Declaration of Independence Thomas Jefferson seriously weakened the concept of the right of private property by re-defining it as the right to pursue happiness. Inevitably the concept of the majesty of the law began to weaken. Montesquieu, in his *Spirit of the Laws* (1743), had insisted that the laws of any state or nation were not essentially the result of the capricious acts of legislative bodies, but reflected predetermined conditions which were independent of human control. "Law in the widest sense of its meaning consists of the necessary relations derived from the nature of things." He admitted that different nations have different laws, but he attributed such differences to varying environmental factors, and in his opinion the most important of these was climate.

This emancipation from Christianity did not bring with it the solution for all human problems which so many leaders of the Enlightenment had confidently expected to emanate from this new-found freedom from man's dependence upon a sovereign God. Their rejection of the biblical view of man and evil provided no answer for the problem of evil. Thus the age of the Enlightenment was forced to defend itself against impending chaos by creating a new religion, the religion of humanity, in which man would worship himself and his own noble achievements. If man is not inherently and essentially evil, then how can the persistence of evil be explained? This was the question which haunted the leaders of the Enlightenment, for they were very much aware of the fact that men who were inherently good lived in a society which was very wicked. Carl Becker, in his *Heavenly City of the Eighteenth Century Philosophers,* has provided a very provocative answer to this perplexing problem. "Thus was born the religion of humanity. For the love of God they substituted the love of humanity; for the vicarious atonement, the perfectibility of man through his own efforts; and for the hope of immortality in another world, the hope of living in the memory of future generations."[3]

Inherent in this optimism was the belief in a secularized millennium—that mankind could, and over a period of time would, create a millennial society on earth. Given his inherent goodness and his potential perfectibility, if only the right ingredients of knowledge were injected in him, the road to a social, economic, and political utopia lay right before him.

Natural Law, Determinism, and Freedom

Beneath this reliance of the Enlightenment on the Newtonian interpretation of natural law lay some very serious contradictions. If an unchanging natural law is the dominant force in control of human society and history, then how is progress possible, and if it is possible, how can it be measured? Since this natural law is not only deterministic in its nature, but also impersonal, how could it bring about moral improvement? How could an amoral natural law produce moral progress in human beings and their society? This was an unresolved question for those who clung to the optimistic illusions of the Enlightenment and who refused to accept the skepticism of a more logically consistent Hume.

Underlying the secular and naturalistic assumptions of the thought of the Enlightenment was a related and equally serious problem. In their political and economic thought the leaders of this era were passionately devoted to the pursuit of freedom, and yet they seemed to be completely unaware of this incompatibility between their quest for freedom on the one hand and their reliance upon natural law on the other. How can an impersonal and deterministic concept of law produce and sustain a meaningful concept of freedom? Blindly convinced that there was no problem involved in this contradiction, the leaders of the Enlightenment pushed boldly ahead in their quest for political and economic liberty. However, their failure to recognize the issues involved in this quest led not only to the disaster of the French Revolution but to the growth of the totalitarian political and economic philosophies which first appeared in Hegel and Marx during the nineteenth century and reached their culmination in the totalitarianism of the twentieth century.

John Hallowell, in his *Main Currents in Modern Political Thought,* has stated the issue very clearly. He insisted that the liberalism of the En-

---

3. Carl Becker, *The Heavenly City of the Eighteenth Century Philosophers* (New Haven: Yale University Press, 1932), p. 130.

lightenment was really an effort to bring about a compromise between two conflicting principles—the absolute value of human personality on the one hand and the eternal, universal law of nature on the other. He is also quite correct in his observation that in its appeal to the Christian conscience, liberalism was trying to achieve a compromise between these two principles. But when the Christian conscience is separated from the church and progressively divorced from revelation, it degenerates into a mere cult of sentiment and loses its value.[4]

The liberal effort to force a synthesis between these two irreconcilable principles, coming as it did in an age which was worshiping science, could only push the doctrine of the soul of man as the source of his personality further into the background and force it to yield to the growing conviction that this traditional doctrine of man had no validity in an age which was witnessing the growing popularity of philosophic materialism. In his *Natural History of the Soul* Lamettrie made this very clear.

> One must grant me only that organized matter is endowed with a principle of motion which alone differentiates it from matter that has no organization at all and that all animal life depends on the diversity of this organization.[5]

This unabashed naturalistic concept of man which denied the existence of his soul and reduced him to a mere form of animal life, was no isolated statement of this degrading view of man. In Holbach's *System of Nature* the same view of man again becomes evident, but here the moral and ethical implications are more clearly expressed. In broad outline Holbach is a precursor of Auguste Comte, and contemporary sociology and psychology. Asserting that there is no evil, no guilt or disorder in nature, and that all natural phenomena are necessary, Holbach insisted that there can be no freedom for man, for he is not only composed of atoms, but the atomic activity in his physical makeup propels him forward. Holbach also openly attacked theology and insisted that Christian theology has prohibited autonomous men from developing their political and social systems. "As the born enemy of experience, theology, the science of the supernatural, has been an insuperable obstacle to the progress of the natural sciences. Physics, natural history and anatomy were not allowed to see anything except through the malevolent eyes of superstition."[6] A similar train of thought

4. John Hallowell, *Main Currents in Modern Political Thought,* p. 158.
5. Lamettrie, *The Natural History of the Soul,* Collected Works (New York, 1970).
6. Baron Paul Holbach, *System of Nature,* ed. H. D. Robinson (New York, 1970), p. 311.

is found in Condillac's *Treatise on Sensations,* in which he not only insisted that the first activity of the mind is to grasp what the senses present to it, but also that a biological order determines the order of our ideas as they are formed by the mind.

The atheism of the philosophes was a strident note in much of their thinking and writing. The editors of the *Encyclopedia* took the offensive and openly declared war on religion, not only historic evangelical Christianity and Roman Catholic theology, but some of them hurled their thunderbolts against deism on the ground that it was too moderate.

Claude Helvetius (1715–1771) pushed the implications of Enlightenment thought even further toward their ultimate goal. In his *Of the Mind* (1758) he repudiated not only Christian theology, but Christian morality as well. Developing an ethical theory entirely consonant with his virtual atheism, he held that pain and pleasure are the predominant motives in the moral actions of men and insisted that acts are good or bad insofar as they aid the public welfare. On the other hand, he also taught that a favorable environment is necessary for the realization of this ethical goal, and thus he favored education as a means of encouraging the natural goodness of men. Not only education, but the state should be called upon to produce the necessary favorable environment. Particularly should the state be used to abolish false class distinctions and false codes of morals, particularly those found in Christianity.

Perhaps even more venomous in his attack on the church and the Scriptures was Baron Holbach (1723–1789), whose *State of Nature* (1770) was probably the eighteenth century's most impressive effort to set forth a fully developed theory of man and the universe. He attacked the very idea of God, calling it morbid and even abnormal. In his view religion in general and Christianity in particular were the result of fear and credulity. In many of his views he anticipated Marx. Not only did he insist that despotic rulers used religion for their own ulterior purposes, but he also held to a metaphysics which most certainly foreshadowed the later position of Marx. He taught that the world consists of nothing but matter and movement, for matter itself is alive and in constant motion. Nothing existed for Holbach apart from nature. There was no God in his thought, no soul in man, and no creation. Man, in his view, was totally determined by the laws of his physical being, and the faculties of his mind were rooted in the faculties of his body. All that man can do is to know these physical laws and conform to them. In short, man for Holbach was an animal, doomed to remain forever an animal. But in spite of his materialistic conception of man, he also insisted that the state should control education in order to mold future citizens.

His irrationalism, like that of Helvetius, stands in its stark nakedness for all to see. The God of creation was denied, and the eternality of matter assumed. Men were regarded as more complex pieces of mechanism, but mechanisms nevertheless. As such they were completely determined by their external environment and incapable of conceptual thought.

Yet, in spite of this impersonal conception of man, he was somehow to be improved, because of some indefinable quality within him which apparently defied the logical implications of his impersonality and allowed him to be improved and fitted as a good citizen of a state, which was a collection of impersonal men such as himself. The agency or institution through which he was to be made a better citizen was education. But just how and why education could bring this about were questions shrouded in mystery. Equally mysterious was the problem of how he should be made better. Now the answer that he would be better able to contribute to the public good was no answer at all, for the question of the public good was in itself a question which this deterministic view of man could not possibly answer. What was the public good to which he should contribute, and why and how could an impersonal entity known as man contribute to this "public good" when the philosophes had no answer as to what either the public or private good was. The determinism inherent in the philosophy of the philosophes precluded any meaningful conception of either good or evil and denied to man as they defined him any possibility of the moral freedom and responsibility which would sustain his efforts in the quest for the achievement of either a private or public good.

Although the question of freedom in its political context will be dealt with in a later discussion of the relationship between the philosophy of the eighteenth century and the French Revolution, it is pertinent to the examination of the philosophy of these eighteenth-century thinkers to note that they had no meaningful view of freedom in its social and political context because they had no meaningful view of man as a human being. Their quest for a secular utopia and millennial existence was without any ethical or moral foundation because it was erected on a foundation which was composed of only the sands of humanistic philosophy. In a universe completely subject to a naturalistic determinism, these Enlightenment thinkers steadfastly held that human society could and must be improved and that man was in possession of a freedom which would allow him to achieve such an improvement in a universe which made no provisions for the possession or exercise of such a freedom.

Equally tenuous and questionable was their view of progress. If man is an animal and nothing more, how can he be conscious of either the need for or the possibility of human progress? And in the light of what goals may it be achieved? Even more pointed is this question: If man is an animal, why does he have a compulsion to achieve progress? Why does he feel the need for bettering his society politically, socially, and economically?

Strictly speaking, the naturalistic determinism which underlay the thinking of these philosophes gave no occasion for raising such questions any more than it provided the answers for them. Naturalism as an impersonal force in the universe makes no provision for such concepts as meaning, goals, or progress for man, and yet man persists in his efforts to achieve these goals. Their philosophy was simply another variety of the irrationalism which became enthroned in European thought in the Renaissance and which gained a new foothold during the latter sixteenth and seventeenth centuries.

Thc unbeliever, although a covenant breaker and holding the truth in unbelief, cannot divest himself of the image of God within him, as shattered as it may be as a result of the Fall. He cannot rid himself of the innate knowledge of God, fight against it as he will. He will thus cling to such ideas as goals and purpose in life, the concept of a better society, and an ultimate triumph of good over evil. He has frequently secularized such concepts in the past and will doubtless continue to do so in the future, but even in these secularized forms he gives a muted witness to the fact that he possesses an indelible image of God within him and that he is not an animal, but a man. The philosophes, denying God and breaking their covenantal relationship with Him, continued to cling to the remnants of this relationship, and, refusing to recognize Him as God, they fell into the gross idolatry of the worship of their own minds. But in so doing they used their rational powers to create an irrational view of life in all of its aspects.

The logical and almost inevitable conclusion to the Enlightenment was the French Revolution, which began in 1789, ostensibly as a conservative reaction to the absolutism of the Bourbon regime in France. Although the thinking and work of the French National Assembly was unquestionably more conservative than that of the National Convention and the committees which operated under its authority, there can be little doubt that the seeds of the atheistic thought which underlay the more radical period of the revolution from 1792 on were also present in the thinking of the leadership of its first phase. The anatomy of revolutions is such that the opening of the conservative period gives way to the more radical and hence more irrational period, which in turn ushers in a new despotism. The philosophes had prepared the French mind for the upheaval which was to come and which would make this revolution the most catastrophic and even disastrous event in the history of modern Europe until the communist triumph in Russia and the coming of World War II—and these events have their origins in the disaster which overtook France in 1789 and soon spread the deadly poison of its philosophy over much of Europe and even into the United States.

This revolution has been heralded by liberals as the dawn of a new day not only for France, but for all of Western civilization. It has been heralded as the end of despotism and the birth of liberty, equality, and fraternity. And there can be no doubt that it has been the inspiration for the numerous revolutions which have overtaken France, Italy, Germany, Russia, and other European nations since that time. In fact, it is doubtful that there has been a revolution in either Europe, Asia, or the Western continents since 1789 which has not to varying degrees been influenced and guided by the French Revolution. The underlying philosophy which produced that revolution has been the dynamic contagion and source of revolutions ever since. And their basic principles have been those which the leaders of the later upheavals have eagerly claimed as their own.

In its essence the French Revolution was the first major politically organized rejection of the biblical view of government and revolt against a sovereign God in the history of the West.[7] Granted that the excesses of the Bourbon monarchy demanded correction, the basic philosophy of the movement was directed as much against Christianity and biblical theism as the foundation of national life as it was against the corruption and misuse of power by the Bourbon monarchs of eighteenth-century France.

The French Revolution was a product of the Enlightenment. It was the culmination of the philosophical currents set in motion by Descartes and which reached their ultimate development in the philosophes and in the political leadership of Abbé Sieyès, Mirabeau, Danton, and Robespierre.

The rallying cry of Liberty, Equality, and Fraternity had a tremendous appeal to the average Frenchman and to thousands of people in the other nations of Europe. It attracted the ears of many Americans who were prone to regard the struggle in France simply as an extension of their own recent conflict with England. But this artfully conceived slogan was deceptive and failed to convey its real meaning. It concealed the deadly

7. It is true that this same spirit was present in the thinking of some of the leaders of the American Revolution, notably Franklin and Jefferson, but other influences were also present which by 1787 had considerably modified the radicalism derived from the Enlightenment.

venom upon which it rested and the ultimate consequences of its adoption as a political program by any nation. The human rights or privileges which inspired this revolution were not possessions of the human spirit found in the Scriptures. They did not arise from any recognition of the duties which man owes to God, nor did they reflect any sense of the covenantal relationship necessarily existing between God and man as a result of the covenantal relationship between the Creator and His creatures as that relationship is set forth in both the Old and New Testaments. No, this doctrine which triggered this great European conflagration was a purely human invention announced in defiance of the God of Scriptures and set forth in the strident terms of an unabashed human autonomy which was atheistic or deistic in its character.

Thus the French Revolution was irrational in its underlying philosophy and antitheistic in its purposes. Hence it could not possibly achieve the political, social, or economic results which its architects claimed for it. Its very militancy provided for its own ultimate defeat. Its extreme actions provided for a reaction which would make the end result far worse than the monarchy against which it had originally been directed. The revolution was an act of utter defiance against a sovereign God. Conceived in the sin of irrationality, it could bring forth only a reign of death and absolutism in the country which spawned it.[8]

The French Revolution was the first modern expression of the philosophy of democracy which expressed so forcefully and grotesquely the doctrine of the sovereignty of man. Previous revolutions in the West had given voice to the desire for self-government and the curbing of an excessive monarchial absolutism, as in the case of the English Revolution under Cromwell, but these outbursts had generally been tempered with a sufficiently strong theistic frame of reference to keep the movement within bounds and allow it to maintain a semblance of sanity and rationality. But this was not the case with the French Revolution. It let loose the vials of irrationality upon the nations of Europe to such an extent that this position still has control of the European mind and is still bringing with it totalitarianism in the name of popular sovereignty.

At first glance, it would seem to be impossible for the Enlightenment, with its unbounded enthusiasm for the spread of human freedom and the

8. This is not to say that the church in France had not been guilty of flagrant abuses or that the Bourbon monarchy had not been corrupt or that the absolutism had not placed crushing burdens on segments of the French people. But it does mean that the philosophy of the French Revolution could not possibly lead to a proper solution of the political crisis then raging in France.

advancement of education, to result in modern totalitarianism. How could such a zeal for liberty produce the despotisms of the twentieth century? These questions seem to be contradictions in themselves. One is tempted to give a short answer and declare that the Enlightenment could not possibly have such a result, and that to ask these questions is to raise questions concerning nearly all the historiography which has dealt at length with the Revolution and its results. For this movement has been hailed as the progenitor of modern democracy, and the contemporary emphasis upon human rights—not only those popularized by Locke and the philosophers of the French Revolution, but also those which are more commonly associated with the advanced democratic ideals of the second half of the twentieth century.

In spite of the seeming impossibility of any kinship between the French Revolution and modern totalitarianism, such a kinship does exist, and it has been largely overlooked by liberal historians, who have shared the ideals of that upheaval and have fondly believed that it has been the copious fountain of all modern liberty. There was, however, a fatal weakness in the philosophy of the French Revolution, and it was not absent from the American War for Independence. And this weakness is the fact that the philosophy lying behind both movements was erected upon the sinking sands of the irrational empirical philosophy which was then in vogue. This philosophy had driven a wedge between the biblical view of man and his covenantal relationship with the sovereign God revealed in the Scriptures and the human rights which he was supposed to possess as conferred upon him by the Law of Nature. These rights, separated as they were from man's duties to God, were resting upon the flimsy foundations supplied by Natural Law as it was empirically observed and understood. Those political philosophers who followed Locke affirmed that revolution itself was sanctified, and the nineteenth and twentieth centuries have become the home of a continuous revolutionary process. But these revolutions have not brought liberty, but an abject submission to the various forms of totalitarianism which have the modern world in their grip. Democracy has become the vestibule through which dictators have entered upon the political scene and used it for their own purposes. The supposed opposites in political thought and practice have become companions in arms against mankind because of their common background in the irrationalism of the political philosophy of the Enlightenment. In his quest of a false freedom, modern man has become the prisoner of the darkness imposed upon him by the Enlightenment.

Montesquieu, in his *Spirit of Laws,* was aware of some of the possible effects which the Enlightenment could have on the history of Europe. He wrote, "The corruption of every government begins almost always with the destruction of its inner principles for a republic must rest on civic virtue if it is to endure."

> It is not fortune which rules the world. There are general intellectual, as well as physical causes active in every monarchy which bring about its rise, preservation or fall. All accidents are subject to these causes. . . . In short, it is the general pace of things which draws all particular events along with us.[9]

Voltaire, in spite of his skepticism, and in spite of his desire to free the writing of history from theology and from the domination of the concept of final causes at work in the historical process, nevertheless clung to the idea that history had meaning and could be used for the achievement of those purposes which the enlightened minds of men might choose to achieve. He looked upon history as a means and not an end in itself, namely as an instrument for the education of the human reason. While Voltaire greatly expanded the scope of historical writing in such works as *The Age of Louis XIV* and *History of Charles XII* by including social and intellectual aspects of the development of mankind, his own irrationalism prevented him from seeing the grandeur of the human drama and clouded his vision as to its real meaning. Thus in the hands of such of its own historians as Montesquieu, Voltaire, and David Hume the Enlightenment sought to overcome the limitations of its own dedication to empiricism and the determinism of natural law to find a note of progress in spite of a philosophical orientation which made no provision for such a concept.

And so, the Enlightenment had come to its end. Hemmed in on every side by its own limitations, its philosophy had come to disaster in the hands of David Hume, its religious insights had come to naught as they had been hardened by a cold and unsatisfying deism, and its political aspirations had been brought to destruction as it had seen its brightest hopes for the future government of human society dashed to pieces by the bloody French Revolution and the emerging absolutism of Napoleon.

The light which it had sought was turning to darkness, and the new world which it had envisioned was being destroyed by political upheaval and wars which could hardly be accommodated to the utopian visions of the eighteenth century. Even in the latter part of the eighteenth century a reaction was setting in. Its harbinger was Jean Jacques Rousseau, and it came to full bloom with the German idealism of Kant and Hegel. The ebb and flow of philosophy and all non-Christian thought caused men to tire

9. Baron Charles De Secondat Montesquieu, *The Spirit of Laws*, tr. Thomas Nugent (Chicago, 1962), p. 53.

of the coldness of deism and the reliance on natural law and to seek a warmer haven for their fondest aspirations. But this new era would prove to be no more satisfactory than the one it was replacing, and the great questions which had remained unanswered during the eighteenth century would find no more satisfactory answers in the age of German idealism. The unbelieving minds of the nineteenth century would continue to hold the truth in unbelief and error in the form of idealism, which would replace the former idols of the eighteenth-century mind.

The coldness and emotional drabness of the Natural Law philosophy and the general intellectual outlook which accompanied it made it most unlikely that the Enlightenment could continue its hold on the European mind for an extended period. The death-dealing blows of David Hume were not actually necessary to produce a reaction against empiricism, although his conclusions undoubtedly hastened a change in the direction of the currents of philosophical thought as Europe approached the arrival of the nineteenth century. As rationalism had run its course, so did the empiricism of Locke and his successors fail to satisfy modern man's quest for knowledge.

The reaction which set in took several different directions, but it became most evident in the philosophy of Jean Jacques Rousseau (1712–1778) and in the political thinking of Edmund Burke. What came to be known as the Romantic reaction against the natural law philosophy is seen in the political, social, and educational thought of Rousseau. Although this French thinker worked within the general framework of the natural rights philosophy, he gave this form of thought a romantic flavor which looked forward to the nineteenth century. He had a warmth and passion in his writing which were quite alien to the general trend of French thought of his day, even though he dealt with many of the problems which his contemporaries had been attacking. But, although he approached these issues with a different spirit, he could not escape the pitfalls which haunted the school of thought of which he was a member. In his *First Discourse,* which appeared in 1750, he insisted that civilization is only a form of decaying corruption, and this pessimism pervades much of his writing.

In his *Social Contract,* Rousseau blended his background in the Enlightenment with some insights which seem to be more a part of the nineteenth century and the Romantic era. He saw private property as the cause of all human inequality, and so reversed Locke's defense of private property and other human rights when he insisted that men gave up all their rights and handed them over to the state when they formed the social contract. In this he very definitely foreshadows Hegel. He insisted that the formation of the social contract marked the beginning of both humanity and history, for in this new state of political society which resulted from the social contract, man became both a moral and a political entity. Rejecting the individual rights of life, liberty, and property, Rousseau marked the beginning of a trend which would ultimately result in the formation of the totalitarian states of the present day. His most original contribution to political thought was his concept of the general will, which asserts itself through the means of the state. Although he insisted that direct representation in government was essential for the expression of the general will, nevertheless the majority vote on any issue by a legislative body was actually an expression of the general will of a nation and must be obeyed as such. Rousseau's insistence that the majority in framing this general will was actually speaking in behalf of the minority was obviously a difficult proposition to prove and defend, and actually constituted an abandonment of the social contract.

Equally dangerous to the biblical view of government as well as to the Enlightenment theories was his insistence that the organized state by its very nature cannot possibly have interests which run counter to the best interests of any citizen. Thus the state does not need to give guarantees for the maintenance of the natural rights of its citizens. This insistence that the state cannot pursue policies contrary to the welfare of its citizens and therefore does not need to give any guarantees is also in direct contradiction to his *Discourse on the Sciences and the Arts,* in which he gave voice to his basic assumption that man is naturally good and that his social institutions alone have rendered him evil. A critical issue emerges at this point: If the institutions which man has created are responsible for human evil, how then can Rousseau trust the state to always act in harmony with the best interests of its citizens? It would seem that a state which makes men evil could hardly be regarded as a trustworthy institution to act in the manner which Rousseau assumed it would.

His solution to the problem can hardly be regarded as satisfactory for anyone who is at all conversant with modern history. Rousseau insisted that if individuals should retain certain basic rights, there would then be no superior power to decide between them. His solution, then, was very simple in his own eyes. If the citizens of a country surrender all their rights, equality is maintained. His answer to the charge that he had surrendered the social compact lay in his insistence that this compact had actually created a public person which would act in the place of individuals. Thus individuals must conform to the general will. To put it briefly, men are forced to be free.

His conception of law is equally contrary to the Christian position, for the general will is actually the voice of the majority, and since man is good, it will always be right. But beneath Rousseau's intricate arguments and inconsistencies one important conclusion emerges. Right is what the majority declares it to be in the general will, and thus it can never be unjust.

There can be no doubt that Rousseau naturalized the basic Christian doctrines. In his whole philosophy nature assumes the role of grace in historic Christianity, and this grace is that grace which is found in the natural goodness of all men. Yet he was not blind to the need of the people for some kind of religious faith to give cohesion to the state, and for this purpose he proposed a kind of civil religion, which made the nation itself the center of all religious worship. He even went so far as to insist that citizens who would not accept this civil religion and adore the state should be banished. His plea for a civil religion came to reality during the French Revolution, when even the cathedral of Notre Dame was renamed the Temple of Reason.

Rousseau, as a child of the Enlightenment and yet at the same time as a prophet of Romanticism and idealism, embodied in his thought the irrationalism of the eighteenth century and bequeathed it to his successors. In his *Emile* he provided the foundations for the further invasion of irrationalism into educational thought and practice, and in his political writings he prepared the way for the further deterioration of political thought in the hands of Hegel and Marx to the totalitarianism of the present day. His autonomous man was to be forced to surrender his basic rights in order to be free, but this new freedom would be based upon the duties he would owe to a sovereign general will embodied in a dictatorship rather than in his obligations to the sovereign God revealed in the Scriptures.

Rejecting the sovereign God of creation and the authoritative revelation of Himself in Scripture, Rousseau proceeded to erect a god from his own imagination whom he could control through political manipulation, and he thus carried forward the retreat from biblical theism as the frame of reference for the life of modern man. In his educational theories he provided for a kind of program which would extend and popularize this naturalistic conception of life and which would ultimately create schools designed to manipulate the young people of these schools in such a way that they would accept this naturalistic philosophy and claim it as their own.

Edmund Burke and the Conservative Political Reaction

Edmund Burke (1729–1797) was very much disturbed by the direction which the political thought of the Enlightenment was taking in both France and England, and sought to provide a theistic answer to the revolutionary character of the Natural Rights school. In this attempt he was only partially successful. Although he was an avowed conservative and looked with horror on the excesses of the French Revolution, he was not entirely able to free himself from the empirical atmosphere of eighteenth-century England. Thus his conservatism, while certainly headed in the right direction and a great improvement over the French Revolutionary thinkers, was not adequately grounded in the Scriptures. This is not to say that he ignored the Scriptures or that he in any way denied the divine origins of government. Burke took some positive steps toward a biblical view of government by completely rejecting the social contract theory and insisting that God ordained the institution of political society. In his insistence that government is a product of the will of God he also taught that the will of God is the source of all true law. In all of these affirmations there is a very clear return to biblical theism and hence to a biblical rationality.

His conservative trend is also seen in his insistence that the representatives of the people not only have obligations to their constituents, but also to God. Perhaps it would not be too much to say that Burke was the last great voice in English political thought to call the attention of the people to their medieval heritage. In an effort to point out the errors and the dangers of the revolution then under way in France, he reminded the English people that the revolution of 1688–89 was the best possible reconciliation of the two principles of liberty and authority, and he argued in behalf of the tripartite theory of the division of the powers of government with the monarchy as represented by the king, parliament, and the courts, with each one of these branches of government having the power to check the others and to prevent excesses.

In his endorsement of reform he betrayed his devotion to some aspects of the Enlightenment. He made it very clear that he was not opposed to reform or to change, but the reforms and changes, to be valid, must grow out of the historical process. One eminent writer has suggested that, like the French philosophes, he placed too much faith in the redemptive power inherent in the historical process and thus laid the foundations for the nineteenth-century idealistic conception of history.

Chapter 5
Kant and German Idealism

The unbelief of the eighteenth-century mind appearing under the guise of the Age of the Enlightenment had come to its dreary conclusion with its temple of human knowledge lying prostrate in the dust from the impact of Hume's savage and deadly attacks levelled against its foundations. Once again unbelief had come to naught, and the thinkers of the eighteenth century who had struggled to suppress the truth of the living God were brought to confusion by the conclusions of their own efforts. The tragedy of their efforts, and irrationalism was the correlative of their rationalism, had finally produced in the French Revolution the greatest political catastrophe yet experienced by the Western world. Those who had sought to escape from the control of the sovereign God had now become the political prisoners of a despotic emperor. The Age of the Enlightenment was in shambles, religiously, philosophically, and politically. Neither the rationalism of the seventeenth century nor the empiricism which replaced it had been able to offer satisfactory answers to the perennial questions which had challenged philosophy through the ages. The questions remained, and thoughtful men were convinced not only that the questions must be answered, but that they could be, if only the right methods and the correct epistemology could be found and applied.

Out of this confusion, idealism arose as an attempt to rescue not only philosophy in the narrower sense of the word, but all of human intellectual endeavor, from Hume's devastating attacks. However, the emergence of Idealism by no means signalized a return to biblical theism. Although the philosophers of idealism were fully aware of the failure of the Enlightenment to offer satisfactory answers to the great questions confronting man, they were, at the same time, the children of the Enlightenment and too deeply imbedded in many of its presuppositions to free themselves from its entanglements. For them, the failure of their eighteenth-century predecessors was an invitation and a challenge to improve upon their methodology, but not to retreat from their basic presuppositions of the autonomy of man and the irrelevance of the Scriptures.

Immanuel Kant (1724–1804)

German idealism came into its own with the emergence of Immanuel Kant in the last quarter of the eighteenth century. Kant knew very little of the history of philosophy, and after his conversion from the German pietism in which he had been reared, he fell under the influence of the rationalism of Leibniz. He soon became discontented with Leibniz and fell under the influence of English empiricism. From Locke and Hume he came to the conclusion that knowledge originates in sense experience, but he also retained from Leibniz the belief that while the mind has no innate ideas, it possesses innate capacities that give form to the experience brought to it by the senses. However, about 1765 he began to see the implications of Hume's devastating attacks on Locke, and claimed that it was this understanding of Hume which aroused him from his dogmatic slumbers.

For Kant, then, this was the problem. How can the absolute certainty supplied by mathematics and physics be reconciled with the fact that our knowledge comes from sense experience? It was his hope to erect the foundations of a new rationalism which would be unassailable. Although he joined both Locke and Hume in the empirical approach, he also began with the assumption of the absolutely certain knowledge found in physics and mathematics for which he felt that neither Locke nor Hume could give a satisfactory account. In his effort to account for this certainty he assumed that the mind has three faculties: thought, willing, and feeling, and he devoted a critique to each of them: *The Critique of Pure Reason* (1781), *The Critique of Practical Reason* (1788), and *The Critique of Judgement* (1790). Differing from both the empiricists and the rationalists in his approach to the problem of knowledge, and yet clinging to elements found in both of these schools, Kant insisted that the true method is the transcendental or critical method, by which he meant a study of reason itself, an investigation of "pure reason" to see if its judgments have a universality beyond human experience itself, and yet are necessary and related to human experience. The logic involved in such judgments must be absolutely reliable, yet they must also be applicable to the world of things. Kant believed that thought, feeling, and willing are the fundamental forms of reason, and he placed the transcendental principles of reason in the realm of thought, the transcendental principles of morality in the will, the transcendental principles of beauty in the realm of feeling.

To achieve this task he formulated what he called his transcendental approach to the problem of knowledge, by which he meant that he was not interested in the contents of experience or in the forms or ways in which the mind reacts to the content of the external world. This knowledge is transcendental in the sense that it must occur in human experience under all circumstances.

To realize this goal Kant restructured the philosophical scheme of Wolff and other rationalists as well as the world of Hume and Locke, and offered a threefold division of the realm of human life and experience: the subjective states, the realm of things in themselves, and the realm of phenomena. But the realm of the subjective states was not, for Kant, a realm of knowledge. Rather for Kant was it the realm of the individual's self-consciousness, the realm of intuition, and the immediate apprehension of the individual's own ideas and sensations.

Kant, however, insisted that this subjective state is that arena in which the individual lives alone and which confers upon him his unique individuality. But at the same time Kant denied that this subjective consciousness lacks the capacity for knowledge.

Apart from the individual, Kant then divided reality into the noumenal and the phenomenal areas. He placed the realm of things in themselves in the noumenal area, which for Kant was both unknown and unknowable. At this point in his thinking a very serious problem emerges. If the noumenal realm is so far removed from man, how can he say that it exists? To say that this realm exists is to imply a certain degree of knowledge concerning it. Kant was not unaware of the dilemma which confronted him in his insistence that the noumenal exists, but his answer to this question is something less than satisfactory. Kant only increased his difficulties in this respect when he placed God, freedom, and immortality in the noumenal world. If they are in this noumenal world, how can man know that they exist, for if this world is unknown and unknowable, then God, freedom, and immortality must forever be unknown and unknowable by man.

What, then, is that realm in which man may acquire knowledge? Kant answered this question by asserting that men acquire their knowledge in the phenomenal world, or the world of sense experience. It is in this phenomenal world that Kant found the solution to his epistemological problem. Man's subjective state becomes conscious when it comes into contact through the senses with the world of physical reality. But Kant did not mean that the mind is simply passive in the acquisition of knowledge. It is not merely aware of sensations as they are brought to it, but rather does it have the power to synthesize these sensations, which brings meaning to what otherwise would be unrelated sense experiences. For Kant the sensations were merely the raw material and the basic content of knowledge. Reason, through its various forms, creates knowledge as such. Through the power of reason the mind "makes sense" out of the raw material which comes to it. This raw data is organized into a meaningful whole through what Kant regarded as the pure forms of time and space. Kant held that time and space are not empirical concepts and not innate ideas, but innate forms. For him, our ideas of time and space are the result of our own reflection, but not the properties of the things themselves. Kant also held that both time and space have an empirical reality which holds for all possible human experience. However, they also have a transcendental reality in that they are only subjective and do not apply to things in themselves. It was for this reason that Kant called his philosophy empirical realism or transcendentalism.

In his quest for an epistemology which would bring or guarantee certainty to our knowledge, Kant also used what he called transcendental logic, and he devoted the second part of his *Critique of Pure Reason* to its meaning and application. He defined his transcendental logic as the mechanism and operation of the understanding, but he actually divided his logic into two parts: the Transcendental Analytic and the Transcendental Dialectic. He defined the Transcendental Analytic as the search for the *a priori* structure of the understanding, that mechanism by which the mind makes a world out of the data brought to it through the senses. How can these categories of understanding and the sensible manifold be brought together? This was the question which confronted Kant and for which he was seeking an answer in his logic. He found what he felt was his answer in the transcendental activity of apprehension and the transcendental unity of apperception. For Kant, self-consciousness and the consciousness of the unified world are found together. He insisted that the processes of perception due to sensibility and the processes of knowing due to the categories of understanding are inseparably present in every experience. He summed up his position in the following: "Percepts without concepts are blind, concepts without percepts are empty."

Kant then proceeded to define his Transcendental Dialectic, calling it the transcendent use of transcendental logic, which he regarded as the attempt to use the concept and principles of understanding to solve the problem of things in themselves. This in turn involved Kant in a curious paradox. The mind continues to think, although it cannot know. By this he meant that in pure thinking reason becomes involved in a series of contradictory arguments. He placed pure reason on a level above understanding, by which the mind seeks to employ innate forms and categories where there is no sensuous experience to which to apply them. In spite of the fact that it cannot know, the mind is not satisfied merely to conceive of the existence of things in themselves, for it also seeks to conceive their nature. In other words, it seeks to understand the nature of the noumenal world and its content, in distinction from the phenomenal world. For Kant the value of Pure Reason reveals that there is a reality beyond experience and that the world of natural science cannot possibly be the ultimate reality. Thus pure reason clearly reveals the limitation of knowledge and points to the postulates of practical reason. It must not be assumed, however, that Kant was attacking the validity of the natural sciences and of the scientific methodology, but he did have serious objection to the insistence of the philosophical realists and materialists that scientific laws extend to ultimate reality.

For Kant the greatest illusion of all was the claim that by pure reason the existence of God can be demonstrated. Kant always regarded God as Ideal and insisted that the value of the Ideal of God is regulative, in that it discloses the possibility that it may be true. It was for this reason that Kant rejected the traditional arguments for God as they had been formulated by previous philosophers and theologians like Augustine, Anselm, and Thomas Aquinas. Evangelical Christians can very well agree with Kant's rejection of these so-called traditional proofs for the existence of God without in any way accepting his epistemological and logical arguments which brought him to this conclusion. On the other hand, they cannot, for this same reason, accept his own argument for the existence of God.

Kant dealt with the problem of the existence of God in his second great work, *The Critique of Practical Reason,* but he placed the concepts of God, freedom, and immortality in the realm of the noumenal, the realm of the unknown and the unknowable. It is obvious that this was hardly a basis for a certainty of belief in regard to these three great concepts. It is quite obvious that Kant was an uncompromising rationalist, and this rationalism had as its correlative a fatal irrationalism. Kant was endeavoring to remove ethics from any theological foundation without resorting to empiricism, and thus his only refuge was to find the basis of the moral life in what he called the Categorical Imperative, which was nothing else than the unconditional command of practical reason in action. He insisted that practical reason must acknowledge as a self-evident proposition that the good will is the only good as an end in itself, for it alone acts in a sense of duty without regard to the consequences. This good which the good will performs is self-imposed, self-legislated, and autonomous. This good will must act in order to be good in accordance with what Kant called the Categorical Imperative, to which he gave three formulations: (1) Act solely on that principle which you would be willing to have become a universal law of nature and on which every other person would also act. (2) Treat every human being you know, including yourself, as an end in himself and not as a means to the advantage of anyone else. (3) One should always act as if he were a member of the kingdom of ends in which one would be at the same time both sovereign and subject.

Within the context of his ethics, Kant gave grounds for a belief in God, freedom, and immortality, but he offered them as grounds only and not as proofs. His view of freedom was well summarized in his dictum: "Thou oughtest, therefore thou canst." In his view human actions, although empirically determined, rest upon things-in-themselves, that, is, upon the noumenal realm which lies beyond human knowledge. They are determined by men themselves, hence they feel responsible, and Kant insisted that this feeling is not an illusion. In a similar vein he discussed the idea of immortality. Moral good contains virtue and happiness. Because virtue and happiness are often in conflict because of the autonomy of the will of man, unlimited perfectibility must be possible. And this concept of the necessity of unlimited perfectibility demands immortality, since duty increased with its fulfillment. It is at this point that Kant brought his view of the existence of God into his discussion of ethical perfection. God, in his view, must be necessary as a guarantee of man's ability to achieve this perfection. It is only in the infinite mind that duty can come to completion, for it is not conditioned by forms of time and space. God Himself, however, according to Kant, must be subject to the moral law, but the law does not present itself to God as an obligation. For in Him there is no conflict between the transcendental and empirical selves as there is in man.

Kant: An Evaluation

Kant believed that in his *Critique of Pure Reason* he had brought about a revolution like that which had been wrought by Copernicus. Before Kant all philosophers had proceeded in their work on the assumption that our perceptions correspond to the external world. But Kant held that the world, to be known, must conform to the constitution of our minds. He even held that the laws of mathematics and physics owe their origin and validity to the structure of the human mind. Men, according to Kant, live in a world that is governed by laws that owe their constitution to the structure of the human mind.

In his philosophic quest Kant firmly believed that he had destroyed the materialism and the atheism of the late eighteenth-century thought to make room for faith. For him the ultimately real world was not the mechanical world of mathematics and physics. Although we cannot know what the real world is like, Kant insisted that we have a right to hope that our wills are free, our souls immortal, and that we shall know God. But these hopes are no more than postulates permeated by reason. We may hope that they are true on the grounds of moral obligation and aesthetic appreciation. But they were hopes only, at best, and were merely permitted by Kant's system of thought which offered no truth for their validity apart from his insistence that they were demanded by the categorical imperative.

Kant insisted that he had placed limits on the realm of science in order to make room for faith, but it is also true that he had no intention of making room for faith at the expense of science. On the contrary, by limiting science he intended to save it. In the last analysis, Van Til is quite correct in his observation that Kant saw no way of even saving science except by making room for faith. Kant's purpose becomes clear in his insistence that "only in man, and only in him as subject of morality, do we meet with unconditioned legislation in respect of purposes, which therefore alone renders him capable of being a final purpose, to which the whole of nature is teleologically subordinated."[1]

Dooyeweerd is quite correct when he insists that the humanistic freedom motive is the driving force behind the modern religion of human personality.[2] Van Til is equally astute in his observations of the humanistic conception of freedom. The concept insists that if man is to maintain his freedom, he only needs to declare himself independent of every law of God, but at the same time he must also declare his independence of any law of nature, even when he regards himself as the source of such a law.[3] Man must therefore stand in an essentially negative relation over against any concept or reality which appears to possess any form of universality. "God must be wholly hidden to man in nature. God must also be wholly hidden to him even in his own experience. If God were anywhere known by man, then man would no longer be free."[4]

At the same time modern man, under the influence of this humanistic view of freedom, seeks to dominate nature, but this human attempt to dominate nature spells out a determinism which tends to envelop man himself.

---

1. Kant, *Critique of Judgement,* trans. J. H. Bernard (London 1892), p. 361.
2. Herman Dooyeweerd, *A New Critique of Theoretical Thought,* 4 vols. (Phillipsburg, N. J.: Presbyterian and Reformed, 1969), vol. I, p. 190.
3. Cornelius Van Til, *Christianity and Barthianism* (Phillipsburg, N. J.: Presbyterian and Reformed, 1977), p. 244.
4. Ibid.

Van Til calls attention to the fact that in this dilemma there is a basic antinomy within the modern idea of free personality, and that the "modern personality finds itself in the situation that, having rejected God as its creator and Christ as its source of freedom, it has lost itself."[5]

The basic irrationalism in Kant's intricate and complex philosophical system is clearly seen in his efforts to create a concept of human freedom in which man would be subject to neither God nor nature. When Kant insisted that he was limiting science to make room for faith, he achieved his goal by developing the apostate idea of the autonomy of man with a far greater consistency than any previous philosopher. In his philosophical system God is neither the Creator of man nor the Law Giver to man. "God cannot reveal himself to man through nature or through man's own constitution as the image-bearer of God." Rejecting the whole biblical doctrine of God and creation, Kant developed a doctrine of freedom which was wholly negative in nature, and Van Til rightly saw that in order to have any relation with either God or nature in such a situation, man must project both God and nature, and Kant projected them both.

Kant basically held that man projects nature in the sense that man confers order upon nature through his own logical ability. The mind of man acts upon pure contingency, and its formalizing activity constructs from this raw stuff a universe that is subject to him.

But Kant also projected God in a somewhat different fashion. He insisted that the intellect of man can make no positive assertions about God since he cannot know God in the way in which he knows nature. "If man were to know God in the way he knows nature, then God would be an object of nature. As such he would not be God at all. To be truly God, he must be wholly other than nature."[6]

It is at this point that Van Til lays his finger on the basic dilemma in the whole Kantian system. Kant's god can be posited only by the practical reason. In this practical reason the will of man is central, and it deals with the questions of good and evil, even as the theoretical reason deals with the question of the true and the false. But in the Kantian system the realm of the practical reason is higher than that of theoretical reason. The realm of practical reason is the higher because the free man has placed it there, but this free man cannot know this higher realm.

The free man even postulates the idea of the ultimate supremacy of good over evil in this higher realm of practical reason. Van Til thus rightly

5. Ibid.
6. Ibid., p. 247.

concludes that the dualism between man and nature is ethical in its character; it is a dualism in which the will of man as act considers itself the ultimate source of the distinction between good and evil.

In this conclusion, which is actually basic to the Kantian system as a whole, Kant's irrationalism appears with full force in its ugly nakedness. Although Kant denied that man can know anything of the noumenal or super-sensible realm, he felt no hesitation about making negative statements about it. He insisted that the god whom he consigned to this realm could neither create man nor be his Law Giver. To believe in such a God would be contrary to the principles of theoretical reason. Thus Kant was really saying that only a certain kind of god can exist, and that god can make no demands on man. "It is a god against whom man could not sin, and therefore has not sinned. Accordingly man's radical evil is not so radical as to need atonement by any sacrifice provided by God himself. Salvation is a matter of character."[7]

Van Til expressed the dilemma with an indictment which must stand the test of time, for it is doubtful that it can be refuted by future scholars of any school of philosophical thought. "According to Kant, man's theoretical reason knows nature but not nature's God. But according to Kant's practical reason man postulates a God who has a purpose with nature. It is thus that pure rationalism and pure irrationalism are 'harmonized' and the primacy is given to morality and religion."[8]

But this solution which Kant offered is ultimately no solution at all to the problem of man. Kant's insistence that man is surrounded by raw stuff which is wholly pliable and lacks order creates a very serious dilemma. Van Til points up the difficulty very clearly when he insists that the very rawness of the stuff confronting the free man is actually a limitation on his freedom, and that this limitation is inherent in his nature. For this means that man has no self-awareness except in terms of his relationship to the content of his being that comes from this raw stuff. There is in man's personality both a formal and a material principle, and man's self-awareness is nothing for man "except in terms of the non-rational intuitions of space and time."[9] According to Kant, the world of man is composed of two factors, one wholly rational and the other wholly irrational, and Van Til brings us to the very heart of the Kantian dilemma when he points out that Kant made the two principles of his thought, pure rationality and pure irrationality, "correlative to one another in order to escape both the em-

7. Ibid., p. 248.
8. Ibid., p. 208.
9. Ibid., p. 270.

pirical and the rationalist thought of his days."[10] But this escape also brought Kant to the principle that the human self must be the unifying agency for pure rationality on the one hand and pure irrationality on the other.

In arriving at this conclusion Kant set forth his belief in the autonomy of man with startling clarity, and once again Van Til is eminently correct when he points out that it reveals the purely speculative and anti-Christian character of Kant's philosophy. Kant has made man the ultimate source of all law. Man, and not God, is to be considered as the ultimate and self-sufficient reality. "The idea of ultimate mystery is employed as a means of keeping God indeterminate and therefore subject to man. And nature must be made subject to the moral act of man lest some law of God might be mediated to man through it and man again should lose his freedom."[11]

The Impact of Kant on Religious Thought

Although Kant seems to have felt that in his division of reality into the noumenal and the phenomenal he left a meaningful role for both science and faith, we have seen that this is actually not the case. Not only did Kant subject the ordering of the phenomenal realm to the mind of man, but no less did he place his god under the control of the human mind. In the final analysis, all of reality must be viewed as the construct of Immanuel Kant.

Neither Kant's god nor Kant's phenomenal realm has any degree of reality, for Kant denied the God revealed in the Scriptures, the biblical doctrine of creation, and the biblical doctrine of man. In spite of Kant's heroic efforts to rescue philosophy and Western thought from the impasse which Hume had created for it, it was all in vain. Kant's impressive cathedral of idealism rested upon the flimsy foundations constructed from his rationalistic and empirical inheritance to which he had an additional ingredient of human self-awareness. His system was as humanistic as those of his predecessors. He had excluded the sovereign God of heaven and earth from any role in the affairs of man or nature, and in so doing he had removed any possibility of a doctrine of creation. Thus reality in its totality was without meaning or purpose, and man and his history were in the same dilemma.

If Kant made room for religion, as he claimed to have done, it most certainly could not be Christianity. The religion which resulted has been "at most a non-credal, super-credal, mystical sense of something that lies

10. Ibid.
11. Ibid., p. 285.

beyond the realm of science."[12] In this religion which has emerged from Kantian philosophy, not only is there no supernatural personal God, but there is no atoning Christ, no redemption, no Christian life, and no hope of and eternity in heaven and the final triumph of Jesus Christ at His second coming.

Thus Kantian philosophy has become the basis in one way or another for all heresies which have threatened and invaded both the Roman Catholic Church and the Protestant churches during the nineteenth and twentieth centuries. Kant and his successors in the school of German idealism introduced a new and more dangerous form of irrationalism into Christian theology, and in so doing prepared the way for the eventual entrance of existentialism not only into Western thought in general, but into Christian thought in particular. The history of nineteenth-century thought after Kant is largely the story of the devastating results of the infiltration of the principles of Kant into practically every aspect of the intellectual endeavors of the West.

The Successors of Kant: Fichte and Hegel

We can and should agree with the late Cornelius Jaarsma who, agreeing with Cornelius Van Til, declared that Kant was the most vicious and dangerous enemy of the Christian system of thought to have arisen in the modern era. His irrationalism, cloaked as it was with the garb of an appealing idealism and rationalism of a kind, was nevertheless devastating in its impact on Western philosophy and much of Christian theology. He had relegated such cherished biblical concepts as God, freedom, and immortality to the realm of the unknowable and made the mind of man the source of order in the empirically knowable universe. In his endeavors to eradicate the dangers which he rightly saw in Hume as the logical successor to Locke, he created new dangers and presented issues even more critical in their implications for Western thought than those which he had sought to eradicate from the current philosophical tides of his own day. His immediate successors, while aware of some of the problems which Kant had created, were deeply under his spell and labored within the framework of his idealism to provide an even more satisfactory answer to the questions to which Kant had addressed himself in his great *Critiques* and other works. So deeply were they influenced by Kant that they fell into his basic errors and claimed them as their own, and thus deepened the chasm between idealism and Christian theism, and hastened the growth of irrational-

12. Cornelius Van Til, *Immanuel Kant and Protestantism,* p. 16.

ism in every area of Western thought. When the reaction against Kantian thought did set in, it still was not able to free philosophy from some of the basic issues and their solutions which Kant had proposed.

In the meantime, German idealism swept German and French thought and took possession of the English mind in the form of English Romanticism, and appeared in this country as Transcendentalism. As a result, Kant gained a position of dominance not only in philosophy, but in theology as well, which spread the gospel of irrationalism throughout much of the Western world.

Kant's immediate successor, Johann Gottlieb Fichte (1762–1814), attacked the problems which Kant had raised, but never solved. If we are limited in our knowledge to the perception of phenomena only, how is it possible to imagine the existence of a noumenal world which transcends the phenomenal? Fichte was convinced that Kant had created a sharp dualism between the world of sense and understanding on the one hand, and the will as practical reason and understanding on the other.

To provide an answer for this all-important question, Fichte concluded that there must be a science of knowledge, the science of sciences, the *Wissenschaft* which should contain all the *a priori* principles from which all universal knowledge of every kind could be deduced. More rationalistic than Kant, he found the solution to the problem in consciousness. For him consciousness was the one active principle from which the whole universe is derived. The consciousness thus involved the principles of the ego and the non-ego. Fichte proceeded to define the absolute ego as all that needs to be posited outside of human experience as the source of the forms of our minds by which sensations are organized. At the same time he also regarded it as the source of our sensations themselves.

In his *Theory of Science* (1794) he held that the fundamental fact of consciousness is our awareness of our own existence and also the simultaneous awareness of other external selves. From this basic assumption he drew the conclusion that all consciousness is self-consciousness, and all knowledge is therefore a form of self-knowledge. Fichte identified the absolute ego as God and the non-ego as nature.

Fichte, according to many of his interpreters, held that perception is a tool of practical reason and that space and time are the creation of the will. He thus shifted the problem to his view of ethics. He regarded the world as in the process of becoming—a process in which the various moments are constituted by wills. In his *Vocation of Man* he regarded the world as an infinity of wills, but at the same time he insisted that the world is not a chaos, because the will submits itself to the moral imperatives of a general order. Thus for Fichte ethical conduct was essentially social in its origin and character. This led him to the conclusion that true freedom is not realized in individuals, but in the relationships existing between individuals. These relations in turn constitute the source of the natural and political rights of man. This in turn led him to the conclusion that the end or purpose of each human will is to communicate with other wills. He predicted that in history this general purpose would result in the unification of the human race. He held that the state is a guarantee of human freedom, but private freedom could not be regulated by the state. Nevertheless, the immediate stage of unification was the nation, and its field of operation was history itself.

This view of the function of the human will and the state led Fichte to develop a new form of logic—the dialectic, with its ensuing emphasis upon will as the motivating factor in both nature and history. By such reasoning Fichte became the prophet of that philosophy of nationalism which came to its fruition in Hegel. Thus Fichte's idealism, like that of Kant, sowed the seed of the totalitarian regimes of the twentieth century.

Fichte's principle of the continuity of consciousness has as its premise a one-layer reality. Fichte also reduced God to a process and this god acquired consciousness only in a willful, purposeful striving toward a goal. Thus in his system of thought there is no God of creation and redemption as He is revealed in the Scriptures. There is no sovereign God to give meaning and purpose to the world, for Fichte's god is struggling to find meaning as he strives to achieve a goal beyond himself. Fichte's god is a finite concept, strictly the logical necessity for the completion of Fichte's philosophy. In brief, every Christian doctrine is denied in the idealism which Fichte set forth, and it plunged the mind of Europe further into the depths of an irrationalism which would ultimately come to its conclusion in existentialism and communism. These two twentieth-century intellectual phenomena, however different and opposed they may seem, were actually hatched out of the same egg of German idealism. All that was needed to bring them into being was Hegel, and he soon appeared on the scene to restructure German idealism into a process philosophy which would give birth to many seemingly opposed movements in Western thought. Once again rationalism, partially masked as voluntarism, had as its inescapable correlative the deadly virus of irrationalism.

The Romantic Movement

The Romantic movement of the first half of the nineteenth century was largely a protest against the naturalism of the Age of the Enlightenment, and as a reaction it emphasized the emotional rather than the rational side of man. The Romanticists felt that the philosophy of the Age of the Enlightenment was an entirely inadequate vessel for the expression of the deepest longings of the human spirit. They even rejected the eighteenth-century conviction that the natural was the rational and that alone. For the leaders of the Romantic Era this was no longer the case. As we have noted, the reaction began in a rather tenuous way with Rousseau, but its flame was also fanned by Kant and Fichte. Rousseau had broken with the rigid eighteenth-century approach to natural law and had come to regard the feeling and personal experience as more important in life than abstract reasoning. Kant had given impetus to this reaction in his insistence that the outer world of experience is produced at least in part by our minds. Thus men are greater than the world which our minds call forth.

The Age of the Enlightenment had been characterized by at least three basic assumptions. The first was that there is an enduring rational order of eternal truth. The second followed from the first. Man can know this order of eternal truth through his mind. The third was the logical corollary—namely, that man has a will which is capable of acting in accordance with the truths which his mind has deduced from this order of eternal truth. Not only is man capable of applying them, but he must apply them to all that he does.

These assumptions came under sharp attack in the hands of the thinkers of the Romantic Era, and the general agreement which had characterized the Age of the Enlightenment disappeared after 1800. Not only was there a growing doubt about the existence of the eternal truths, but there was also an even greater uncertainty concerning the power of the human mind and will to apply them. The orderly universe of the eighteenth century had been badly fractured by the excesses of the French Revolution, and in a very real sense the Romantic Era was a reaction against the smug assurance of the previous age that men were truly rational and that they could apply the truths which they might find in the Natural Law.

In a reaction against the supremacy of Natural Law in eighteenth-century thought, all of the basic assumptions of that era were brought into question and, although the search for certainty continued unabated, it took a different direction or directions. The Romantic thinkers did not have any real agreement on a commonly accepted set of beliefes, but, following Kant, looked to intuition as their guide. They felt that Kant's emphasis upon intuition had made it possible for them to believe what they wanted to believe. The Romantic thinkers rejected the deistic notion that the universe was a vast piece of machinery and preferred to regard it as some kind of a living organism of which man was a part.

This trend of thought in turn gave birth to a resurgence of individualism, and new importance was attached to the individual personality. These early-nineteenth-century thinkers did not stop with their interest in human personality, for they sought to transfer this concept to an interpretation of the universe. But this search or interest brought them to a belief in some great force behind the universe, which might be call God, to which or to whom their religious aspirations might be directed. However, this god to whom they looked was by no means the God of Scripture who had created this universe. He was rather the soul of this universe, and the result was a revival of pantheism in place of the deism which had dominated so much of the religious thinking of the previous era. This transition from deism to pantheism was not as profound a change as it might seem to be. The Romantics were no closer to the biblical world and life view than were their predecessors. Tired of the coldness of the Natural Rights philosophy of the Enlightenment, they created for themselves a god who was part and parcel of the world as they viewed it. But the warmth which they managed to generate was not the product of a genuine revival of Christian thought. Rather was it a creation of their own famished souls.

This new philosophy or philosophies as they emerged in Germany gave rise to literary and cultural movements elsewhere. Goethe and Schiller represented it in German literature, while Beethoven and Wagner reflected its basic philosophy in the realm of music. In England Wordsworth, Scott, Coleridge, Byron, Shelley, and Keats created a school of literature which was largely motivated by German idealism, particularly by Kant and Fichte. In this country the Transcendental movement represented the same influences at work. Each in his own way, Emerson, Thoreau, Whittier, Lowell, Hawthorne, and Whitman translated German idealism into the American mode of thought, and the result was the Transcendentalist movement, which claimed the attention of the country during the first half of the nineteenth century. In may ways it had a similar impact upon the political, social, and religious thought of this country which had marked its arrival in Germany, France, and England.

All of these young artists and writers felt the spirit of infinity surging within them and to varying degrees looked to Kant, Fichte, or Schelling for their inspiration. But for most of them, the cry of Whitman was a more accurate description of their outlook: "All we need is Hegel."

The Romantic Movement in part was a continuation of the French Revolution, in that it looked to the autonomy of the human spirit as the source of human thought and activity. It was a continuation in the sense that it was an attempt to interpret the past in a new spirit. But it was also a reaction to the excesses of the French Revolution in that it held that we cannot break as completely with the past as was implied in the philosophy which produced that movement.

German idealism advanced to a more formal state in the hands of Friedrich Wilhelm Schelling (1775–1854), who became its leader at the University of Jena and was its formal interpreter. He was also the connecting link between Fichte and Hegel and, like them, his early training was in theology. In the early stages of his thinking he was deeply influenced by Fichte and sought the ultimate ground for certain knowledge in the ego. Thus he endeavored to deduce nature from the ego. Holding also to the liberty of the will, he regarded God as a necessary postulate for moral faith. He soon became more independent in his philosophy and contrasted mind and nature much more sharply than he had previously. This led him to the conclusion that knowledge must rest upon an agreement of the subject and the object, and that there must be a correspondence, a union of the ego (intelligence) and nature. With this came the admission that we may study intelligence first to show how objects proceed from it.

But Schelling was not content with this position, and he developed a third stage in his philosophy, in which the influence of Spinoza became dominant and he came to regard mind and matter as practically identical. Like Spinoza, Schelling faced a difficulty in answering the problem as to how Absolute Identity can be related to a world of diverse persons and things. It was the perennial problem of individuation, and idealism, like its predecessors, could find no solution, for, apart from the trinitarian God revealed in the Scriptures, there is none.

Toward the end of his life Schelling became more mystical and became quite neo-Platonic in his understanding of reality. But finally, under the influence of the Christian mystic Jacob Boehme, he came to see God as the primal absolute identity, subject to suffering and to growth. This mystical being, according to Schelling, participates in the advance of the world process through struggle. He viewed all religions as progressive stages in the revelation of God, and Christianity as the embodiment of the highest revelation yet known.

In his *Ethics* he held that freedom is self-determination. We think of things as we do, not as the result of an outer determination but by the very constitution of our minds. But this freedom of action in experience is opposed by the necessity inherent in our external environment and is overcome by an inner compulsion. It is quite obvious that this view of ethical freedom which Schelling presented is totally unknown to the biblical revelation and is really no freedom at all. The human self, under the domination of sin, cannot possibly be self-determining in the sense in which Schelling used this phrase, and the freedom which Schelling presented as the basis of his ethical and moral system is no freedom at all, but slavery—slavery to one's sinful self.

Not only was Schelling's view of freedom an illusion, but his idealistic philosophy was wholly inadequate to account for the individual consciousness in the finite world; indeed, it was totally unable to give any meaningful account of reality and evil. In summary, his position was thoroughly antitheistic in regard to God, the world, man, and evil. His idealism was accompanied by an irrationalism which, stemming from the philosophy of Kant, was bringing modern thought slowly but surely to its nadir of despair in the existentialism of the twentieth century.

George Frederick Wilhelm Hegel (1770–1831)

Hegel was undoubtedly the greatest of all German philosophers after Kant, and was probably the most rationalistic of all the German idealists. In the end he succeeded in presenting to the world what many thinkers came to regard as a more plausible and comprehensive system of idealism than his predecessors had developed. He was certainly more objective than Fichte and Schelling, and he was the most self-confident philosopher of all time. He was quite certain that he was adequately explaining the constitution of the universe, and it has been remarked that not even God Himself could keep secrets from Hegel. There are still those who feel that Hegel has given to modern man the most adequate statement of the universal philosophy. It must be admitted that his system is the most comprehensive philosophy to be developed in modern times.

Hegel's basic concern was to understand the world as it is and to explain everything logically. But he found Aristotle's logic most inadequate as a tool for the magnificent plan which he had in mind. Hegel held that the Aristotelian logic actually divided reality, and for this reason it was unable to give to it a meaningful interpretation. To achieve the task which he had set for himself, Hegel in his *The Phenomenology of Mind* (1807) set forth a new system of logic which would support his basic contention that reality is an organic whole, and this logic he called the dialectic. This dialectical logic provided Hegel with the tool which he felt was the necessary support for a philosophy of evolution, in terms of which he hoped to develop his whole system. Basically, this new logic rested on the assumption that reality grows with truth and that the world is a growing and living organism. For Hegel, thought in dialectical motion is the only reality. Only the real is rational, and only the rational is real.

Hegel's use of the dialectical logic was intimately related to his basic conception of metaphysics and ultimate reality. He developed what has since become known as the organic theory of truth and reality, by which he meant that the whole logically determines the character of each of its parts. Reality, or the Absolute, is an infinite whole, consisting of finite parts, each of which contributes to the whole and is determined by it. This Absolute is not something which existed prior to the world and then proceeded to create it, but it is the world in its unity and completeness. Thus there is no chronological, but only a logical priority. But what is the nature of the organic relationship within the Absolute? Hegel answered this question by insisting that one's conscious life at any time is a part of the whole and includes not only past experience, but the preparation for future experience. "I am my life taken as an organic whole. I am also interrelated biologically and socially. I am constituted by and also help to constitute other persons." The human race is related to our planet, which in turn is related to the universe. Thus every man is an organic part of the universe as a whole. The universe, which is the Absolute, has in us become conscious of itself and of its internal relationships.

To give full expression to his concept of reality, Hegel developed his dialectical method. In its simplest form he held that any thesis implies its antithesis, and these two are united in a higher synthesis in which the opposition between the two is sublated, by which term Hegel meant that both the thesis and the antithesis are reconciled in a larger unity.

For Hegel his rationalism which he expressed as "the real is rational and the rational is real" rested on the assumption that the Absolute or Absolute Idea is logic, in which thinking and being are identical. His pantheism is evident in his insistence that the Absolute is the world in its organic unity, and not the creator of it. Hegel's world was real, even though it was dependent upon the unity of the whole, and in this respect his pantheism was not the pantheism of the East, which regards the world as an illusion. The following diagram (next page) will help explain Hegel's concept of the Absolute Idea which embraces all reality.

Hegel firmly believed that human reason can disclose the nature and process of the ultimate reality and believed that the key to this discovery was in the use of the dialectical logic, for he assumed a pre-established harmony based on organic unity of all things. Building on these assumptions, he held that the Absolute Idea passes through a dialectic of many triads, each triad having its own thesis, antithesis, and synthesis. The most general triad begins with logic as its thesis, the most abstract as mere being,

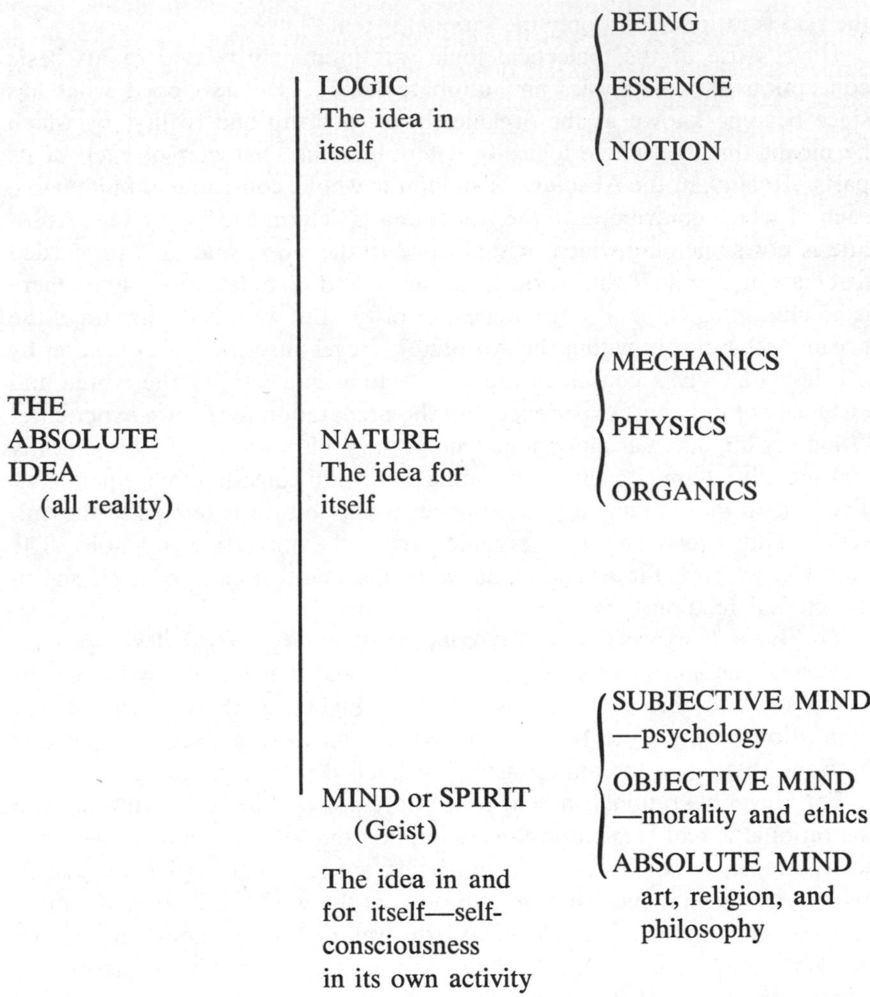

and continues through nature as its antithesis and terminates in a synthesis of Absolute Mind. In this most general triad, Hegel defined logic as the Absolute Idea in itself, before it becomes external nature. But Hegel's use of the word "before" has reference to a logical priority only, for he did not mean that the Absolute Idea once existed as the categories of the logic before it externalized itself in nature. Rather did he hold that the order of the categories represents a progression from abstractness to concreteness, for in his thinking all categories were co-eternal and each implied every other. It is well to note that Hegel's categories were not those of William James or the pragmatists. He denied that they were inventions of men derived from human consciousness, and held that they were genuinely objective realities, modes of divine and human and all rational thought—that they were *a priori* in human experience because they are inherent in the structure of the universe.

His basic triad, which he used to explain the development of the Absolute Idea and his categories, was that of Being. He defined Being as the most abstract aspect of any quality that is. It is the most abstract of all universals, for it is the least that can be affirmed about anything. The antithesis of Being is Not Being, and these two concepts are harmonized in Becoming, which Hegel defined as the passing of something over into what it previously was not.

Hegel regarded Being itself as the synthesis of a subordinate triad (quality, quantity, and measure). Hegel regarded quality as the synthesis of a more subordinate triad, and he held that quality and quantity as thesis and antithesis are sublated into measurement. Using his triadic system, following measurement we advance to a higher level into the inner structure of reality, which is knowable by reflection, and at this point we come to his most fundamental triad, which included Being as its thesis, Essence as its antithesis, and Notion as its synthesis. Using this same principle of logic, he developed his philosophy of mind, by which he meant the cultural activity and experience of mankind. Here once again we meet with a principle triad in which Hegel's thesis is what he called subjective mind, by which he meant the mental processes of individuals apart from society. This is really the realm of psychology. The antithesis was the objective mind, in which Hegel held that the human mind gains freedom, concreteness, and objectivity in social relationships. The synthesis in this triad Hegel found in what he called the Absolute Mind, and in this Hegel declared that man becomes conscious of himself and of the material and social worlds in which he lives. Through art, religion, and philosophy man comes to an appreciation of his divine origin and destiny as a manifestation of the Absolute Idea.

But more needs to be said in regard to the ingredients of this triad. His psychology or Subjective Mind certainly suggests that the soul is not a separate substance in interaction, but that consciousness is a synthesis or organization of bodily functions. Hegel's objective mind likewise was founded upon a principle triad, the thesis of which was law, viewed as an abstract right which Hegel defined as the claims which individuals have upon one another. Its antithesis was morality, in which individuals turn their thoughts inward to examine their own consciences. Hegel found the synthesis for this triad in ethics, which was social in nature, and inward consciences become objectified in social institutions as in the family and the state.

Some commentators on Hegel regard his treatment of ethics as the best section of his whole philosophy, and from one point of view there is some justification for this conclusion, but this in no way means that Christian theists may endorse it without some very serious reservations. Hegel advocated a social order in which ownership of property would become more general and better protected, but he offset this statement in regard to property with an insistence on the correctness of Kant's doctrine of the autonomy of the human will. But with the realization that there are serious pitfalls in this Kantian approach, he seemingly modified his own position. Although he insisted that we should always obey conscience, he admitted that conscience can be mistaken. Thus he also insisted that the rational knowledge of what is really good or bad arises from the convictions found in organized society, because the reasoned ethics of society are embodied in those instiutions which are the product of the wisdom of the ages, and therefore much more trustworthy than the conscience of the individual. This conclusion in regard to the greater importance of the ethical decisions of society as over against those of the individual led Hegel to place a great importance on the state as the ideal notion. He held that the state is more important than the individual. Admittedly, he did not in making this assertion have in mind the modern totalitarian regime, and in his own thinking he regarded the constitutional monarchy as he had seen it develop in Prussia as the fully developed state. But the total impact of his political thought in conjunction with his philosophy of history led directly to the emergence of modern totalitarian regimes. This whole problem will be treated much more fully when we come to his philosophy of history.

Hegel's treatment of Absolute Mind demands special attention, for he regarded it as the final culmination of the Absolute Idea, in which the whole of reality is appreciated in its organic unity and completeness. Absolute Mind, representing the highest achievements of the spirit, consisted of a triad of art, religion, and philosophy. Hegel defined art as absolute reality shown as beauty through the medium of the senses. The antithesis to art was religion, which he defined as the second highest achievement of the Spirit. For Hegel, religion was the absolute clothed in imagery, but he also insisted that religion is not a popular delusion, for in it are found actual revelations of the absolute, which express truth as accurately as the popular mind could grasp it. Thus he held that Christianity is the most adequate expression of the absolute that could be found in religion. And here again

Hegel set forth his triad in which God the Father served as the thesis, Logic; and God the Son became the antithesis as Nature. The synthesis Hegel located in God the Holy Spirit, and he defined this synthesis as Reality becoming self-conscious in the mind and present in the church.

Hegel insisted that the great value of Christianity lay in the fact that its representations corresponded to his own philosophy. It was for this reason that his philosophy appealed to many theologians who wished to be Hegelian and yet remain Christian in their theology. But Hegel regarded religion as subordinate to philosophy, even though he was convinced that through religion man does come into contact with the divine.

Philosophy, then, was the final synthesis in Hegel's system of thought, for in philosophy man discovers the Absolute in all stages of the dialectic. In philosophy man becomes rational and self-conscious, and appreciates his position in the universe. But at the same time the universe becomes conscious of itself in the cultural life of man.

Hegel's Philosophy of History and of the State

We must now give separate treatment and pay special attention to Hegel's philosophy of history and of the state, for it is this aspect of his thought which has had such widespread repercussions in the political life of modern man in both Europe and America.

His philosophy of history was an integral part of his general system of thought. We have seen that Hegel taught that through philosophy God reveals himself as an ideal system of thought. God is thought, and thought or mind is the one ultimate reality. This one ultimate reality grows, changes, and develops according to the dialectical method already described. Thus history also unfolds according to the same dialectical pattern. In his *Philosophy of History,* published in 1837, Hegel set forth what he felt was the great design of human existence, and it was his purpose to trace that law of development which he felt he could see running through the whole past life of the human race, and thus to discover the particular genius which each great world power has displayed and then to relate this to the comprehensive Idea which is immanent in the entire historical process.

For Hegel, then, history is the manifestation of Reason realizing itself as will. It is the dialectical unfolding of the will of God. But it is much more than that. It is the progress in the consciousness of rational freedom. In universal history, the spirit displays itself in its most concrete reality: it is the exhibition of spirit in the process of working out the knowledge of that which it is potentially. Reason in turn is the sovereign of the world, and history is the process of the working out of that which it is potentially.

For Hegel, this universal divine reason was not an abstraction but a vital principle, and as human beings follow the dictates of their reason, they participate in the realization of this vital principle in history. The one great aim of world history is the realization of the Idea of Spirit, but since the essence of spirit is freedom, the whole process of history is directed toward rendering this unconscious impulse a conscious one. Thus history is progress in the consciousness of rational freedom; it is the account of that discipline of the uncontrolled natural will which finally brings it into obedience to a universal principle, thus conferring subjective freedom.

Hegel saw several gradations in the development of this consciousness of freedom. He held that the East knew only that one man is free, while the Greek and Roman worlds knew that some men are free, but the German nation under the influence of Christianity was the first nation to attain the consciousness that man as man is free. Hegel defined the Eastern view as despotism, the Graeco-Roman concept as democracy, while the German consciousness that all men are free resulted in monarchy. In this way Hegel believed that he had succeeded in reconciling the subjective will of man with the objective order of the universe, and freedom with necessity. History thus uses the passions, instincts, and wills of man to fulfill purposes of which men are not conscious.

In Hegel's scheme the dialectical process replaced the sovereign God of the Scriptures because Hegel's god was not above history, but co-extensive with it. God is the Idea. Thus freedom for Hegel was simply the recognition of historical necessity as that necessity is revealed in terms of the dialectical process. God is revealed only in the historical process, for God is history and history is God, and both history and God are captives to Hegel's dialectical system. By this reasoning Hegel concluded that freedom is nothing more than the recognition of subjection to the determinism of this dialectical unfolding of the historical process.

It is at this point that Hegel's general philosophical system brings forth its fruit in his concept of the relationship among the state, history, and freedom. He argued that substantial freedom is the abstract undeveloped reason which is implicit in volition as it proceeds to develop itself from the state, for the state is the embodiment of rational freedom. It is the incarnation of the "spirit of the world," the divine idea existing on earth. Furthermore, it is the march of God on earth, and its basis is the power of reason actualizing itself as will.

Hegel's view of the relationship between God and the state and between the state and freedom is of tremendous importance in the development of modern political thought. It becomes apparent that Hegel's god was the captive of his dialectical system and could achieve a greater degree of "godness" or divinity only as he participated in the dialectical unfolding of the state. At the same time man could achieve a greater degree of self-consciousness and humanity only as he found it in the state.

It will be very difficult for scholars to deny that in this unique union which Hegel saw in God and the state and man there is evident the very lively germ of modern absolutism and totalitarianism. The state becomes the one agency in which both God and man achieve their personality. Apart from the state God is little or nothing, and apart form the state man is little or nothing. Thus the state literally becomes the unit or agent in the dialectical process which confers meaning upon man and his culture and confers upon him his freedom. But this freedom is the product of the evolutionary determinism involved in Hegel's dialectical process, and on this vine freedom withers by the very nature of the case. Hegel's basic rationalism has produced that irrationalism, that dialectical madness which in the forms of fascism and communism has so much of the contemporary world in its grip. His basic rationalism produced irrational political philosophies and systems which have destroyed freedom wherever they have gained power.

Freedom for man consists in his making his natural self conform to his thinking self. This freedom is realized in his submission to the law. Substantial freedom is the abstract undeveloped reason implicit in volition proceeding to develop itself in the state. But in this phase of its development personal insight is still lacking. This is the subjective reason which is realized only in the individual and which constitutes the reflection of the individual in his own conscience.

As subjective freedom arises, man descends from the contemplation of external reality into a contemplation within his own soul. This drawing back from the external world, according to Hegel, constitutes an antithesis of which one side is the Absolute Being, the divine, and the other is the human subject as an individual.

In that immediate unreflected consciousness which is the East these two are not yet distinguished from the individual, for the antithesis has not yet created a schism between absolute and objective spirit, and spirit is still immersed in Nature. In the East the unreflected consciousness, substantial, objective spiritual existence forms the basis to which the subjective will first sustains a relation in the form of faith, confidence, and obedience. In the political life of the East there is realized rational freedom developing itself without advancing to subjective freedom. This is the second main principle in human history. In Greece the principle of universality was impressed on the individual himself. Hegel saw this as the union of the moral with the subjective will by which he meant that the individual will of the subject adopted the conduct and habit imposed by justice and the laws. At this point the individual was in conscious unity with the Idea. Thus, for Hegel, the Greek spirit was a consciousness of the Spirit, but only in a limited form. The "natural" was transformed into an expression of eternal truth, but since the freedom of Spirit was still conditioned by some stimulus supplied by Nature, spirituality was not absolutely free and self-produced. In this stage the Idea was not yet seen in its essence, but was bound up with the real, as in a beautiful work of art. Because the Idea was thus too closely bound up with a particular material form, it was not recognized as purely spiritual and thus the Greek spirit did not prove to be enduring.

In the next phase or stage of development in the historical process, the Idea becomes separated, but only as an abstract universal. This stage is seen in the Roman state, which in Hegel's thinking represented the severe labors of the manhood of history. Here the state began to have an abstract existence of its own and to develop itself for a definite object, and thus Hegel held that in Rome we find that free universality, that abstract freedom, which, on the one hand, sets up an abstract state, a political constitution and power over concrete individuality, and which, on the other side, creates a personality in opposition to that universality. These two elements—political universality and the Abstract freedom of the individual—constituted Rome in this Hegelian philosophy of history. Hegel found that element of subjectivity in the Roman state which had been lacking in the Greek political system.

But while in the Roman era individuals had a share in the purpose of the state, it was not one which called their whole being into play. Free individuals were sacrificed to the demands of national purposes. The existence of an authoritative government such as that of the Roman Empire showed that human subjectivity in its proper form had not yet developed itself. In the heart the evil will was surrendered, but the will as human had not yet been penetrated by deity. The human will in the Roman system had been emancipated but only abstractly and not in its concrete reality, but the whole sequel of the historical process, according to Hegel, was occupied with the realization of this concrete freedom. Up to this point in human history, freedom has been annulled only in order to make way for infinite freedom, but this latter had not yet penetrated secular existence with its laws. In brief, speculative freedom had not yet attained validity as such.

But how is this goal achieved? Hegel found the answer that it is through

Christianity that the idea of God in its true conception gains consciousness. Here man finds himself comprehended in his own true nature, given in the specific conception of the Son. Man, infinite when regarded from himself, is yet at the same time the image of God and a fountain of infinity in himself. He is the object of his own existence and has in himself an infinite value and an eternal destiny.

Consequently, he has his true home in a supersensuous world, an infinite objectivity gained only by a rupture with mere natural existence and volition and by his labors to break their power over him. This is the state of religious self-consciousness, but Hegel insisted that in order to enter this sphere and display the active vitality of that religious life, humanity must be worthy of it, or become capable of it. These conditions which are the necessary corollary for the consideration that man is an Absolute self-consciousness are won through the instrumentality of the Christian religion for the secular state.

The first of these was his insistence that slavery is impossible under Christianity, and the second was that humanity has this sphere of free spirituality in and for itself, and that everything must proceed from it. What among the Greeks was a form of customary morality cannot maintain its position in the Christian world, for the unreflected morality of the Greek mind could not hold its ground against the principle of subjective freedom. Man in Christianity becomes conscious that he is a partaker of divine existence. But Hegel also held that during the Middle Ages the church and feudalism had combined to destroy freedom and to debase the world spirit. He viewed the Renaissance as a return to the spirit and a reaction against the transcendentalism of the Middle Ages. The Renaissance was thus the reassertion of man's self-consciousness. The Reformation, then, in Hegel's view of history was the next step in the dialectical process, developing from the Renaissance in man's march toward a greater degree of self-consciousness of his freedom.

For Hegel the basic problem in the historical process was the imbuing of the sphere of unreflected spiritual existence with the Idea of Spirit. Reason in general is the positive existence of Spirit, divine as well as human. For Hegel, the distinction between religion and the world was only this—that religion as such is reason in the soul and heart of man—that it is the Temple in which truth and freedom in God are presented to the conceptual faculty of man. On the other hand, the state, regulated by that same reason, is a Temple of human freedom concerned with the perception and volition of a reality whose purpose itself may be called divine. This freedom in the state is established and preserved by religion, since moral rectitude is only the realization of that which constitutes the fundamental principles of religion.

The process displayed in history is only the manifestation of religion as human reason—the production of the religious principle which dwells in the heart of man under secular freedom. In this principle Hegel believed that the discord which exists between the inner life of the heart of man and the world of actuality would be removed. To realize this, however, the emergence of the German nation was necessary, since Rome had not furnished Christianity with those conditions which were necessary for the attainment of this ideal.

Hegel believed that the German spirit furnished the conditions which Rome had not been able to furnish because the German spirit was the spirit of the new world. Hegel declared that its aim was the realization of Absolute Truth as the unlimited self-determination of freedom—by which he meant that freedom which has its own absolute form as its purport. The basis of this definition of freedom lay in Hegel's conviction that the supreme law of the universe must be recognized as being identical with the dictates of conscience. He further held that the destiny of the German people was to be the bearers of the Christian principle. It was not merely their destiny to possess the Idea of freedom as the substratum of their religious conception, but of producing it in a free and spontaneous development from their subjective self-consciousness. True and substantial freedom is thus obtained only in this fourth stage of world history—the German stage.

According to Hegel, the German world appeared superficially to be only a continuation of that of Rome, but this was a misreading of the Germany of the nineteenth century, for there lived in it an entirely new spirit through which the world would ultimately be regenerated. This is the Free Spirit, which reposes on itself—the absolute determinism of subjectivity. To this self-involved subjectivity the corresponding objectivity stands opposed as absolutely alien.

The antithesis which Hegel held to have evolved from these two principles was that of church and state. On the one side the church develops itself as the embodiment of Absolute Truth, for it is the consciousness of this truth, and at the same time it is the agency for rendering the individual harmonious with it. On the other side stands the secular consciousness which occupies the world of limitation. The state is based on emotional and social affections of mutual confidence and on subjectivity in general. Hegel saw Europeanism as the manifestation of the growth of each of these principles in the church and state, the final result of which would be the harmonizing influence of the antithesis.

In keeping with his dialectical concept of history, he further taught that there were three periods in the development of the German world up until his own day. The first period began with the appearance of the Germanic nations in the Roman Empire and endured until the age of Charlemagne.

The second period saw the development of the two sides of the antithesis, church and state, to independence and opposition, the church as a theocracy and the state as a feudal monarchy throughout the Middle Ages. For Hegel the era of Charles V marked the close of the second period in German history and the beginning of the third. This third period extended from the Reformation to Hegel's own day. In this third era the principle of the Free Spirit is made the banner of the world, and from it are evolved the universal axioms of reason and formal thought. This latter (formal thought) received its true material first with the Reformation through the revival of concrete consciousness of free spirit. From that date on thought began to gain a culture properly its own, for principles which were derived from it and which became the norm for the constitution of the state and political life were now increasingly consciously regulated by reason. But not until the advent of this third era was the freedom of spirit realized, for the German peoples were predestined to be the bearers of the Christian principle and to carry out the idea as the absolutely rational aim.

Involved in Hegel's conception of history was a similar view of the state. For Hegel the state was the embodiment of rational freedom and the incarnation of the spirit of the world. He regarded it as the Divine Idea existing on earth and the actuality of the ethical idea. For him it was not only mind on earth, but, furthermore, the very march of God on earth.

Its basis is to be found in the power of reason actualizing itself as will. This led Hegel to the conclusion that freedom is submission to the law, and since the state was for him the most nearly perfect embodiment of social morality, freedom then was defined as obedience to the moral will of the community. It includes, but also transcends, the purposes of individuals. Thus the individual conscience cannot possibly be the court of final appeal, as it was for Kant. Hegel held that the conscience of the community is much more likely to be right than that of the individual. Obviously Hegel rejected both the doctrine of natural rights and the social contract theory as to the origin of political society. In his view, human rights were commensurate with duties, but the duties were prescribed by the state rather than by God. Thus men have social rather than natural or divinely bestowed rights, which are prescribed by the state. For Hegel the state was the absolute power on earth and only history can judge its actions.

Since Hegel believed that nations are the unconscious tools and organs through which the world mind works, wars can only be a part of this whole process and are an aspect of reality which must be accepted. It does not follow that Hegel intended to exalt war; it was simply his purpose to explain and to justify it as a historical phenomenon. Since in any age there is only one nation that truly represents the *Zeitgeist* (the World Spirit), and since it must be dominant in that era, then war becomes a necessary instrument for the realization of the dominance of that nation. Thus war may be justified, if not exalted. Hegel clearly believed that the emergence of Europe and the dominance of Germany within Europe were the goal of history, and that a Christian Europe under German leadership was the maturity of history.

Hegel: An Evaluation

Since Hegel's view of history is so deeply embedded in his philosophical system, we can safely evaluate both aspects of his thought at the same time. Since his whole system was the construct of his own idealism, it was a rejection of the Christian revelation, all denials to the contrary notwithstanding, therefore it must be concluded that in him we are confronted with a highly developed form of irrationalism. He found no place for any biblical doctrine, and his system was frankly and openly pantheistic. The Christianity which he regarded with favor was a Christianity of his own making, and bore little or no resemblance to that system of doctrine revealed in the Scriptures.

In Hegel's philosophy God is a postulate of Hegel's own thinking and is the captive of his own dialectic logic. He is always becoming and never becomes a true God. In contrast to the God of the Bible, he is a pathetic and servile being held captive by human logic. Thus there is in the Hegelian system no absolute truth, but only the contradictory conception of absolute change.

Likewise, there is no doctrine of creation, for thought is the only reality. In spite of his valiant endeavor to explain the existence of nature and matter, they have no real place in his system. Without any origins, they have no destiny. Thus the material world has no real meaning or purpose. The same can be said for man, for he was not created in the image of God and, like God, he must always be a captive to the process of becoming. He is the captive of a process of always being engaged in the struggle to achieve through the state his humanity. But the state itself is also held captive by this deterministic force described as the dialectic. In spite of the brilliance and apparent profundity of his system, Hegel only drove philosophy and Western thought deeper into the abyss of that irrationalism which still grips the Western mind.

Hegel's impact on the philosophy of history has been equally devastating, not only because he plunged the study of history into the abyss of irrationalism, but also because his concept of history became so very influential in molding the future of the West from his own day until now. His insistence that history itself is the final court of appeal for its own past is still very much a part of contemporary thought. This view, however appealing it may appear, denies very clearly that God is the author of history through the act of creation and gives to it both its meaning and its purpose. The dialectical process by its very nature not only denies the sovereignty of God in human affairs, but confers upon history an evolutionary interpretation which is destructive of any serious effort to derive meaning from the stream of human events. Even for the liberal thinkers of our day, Hegel's conclusion that the emergence of Germany in the nineteenth century represented a new stage of historical maturity is something less than appealing and most decidedly not convincing.

Likewise, his insistence that history is its own judge denies that God is the ultimate court in which men and nations shall be judged, and such a conception has had disastrous consequences in modern history. If history is its own judge, then it cannot be judged, for it is subject to no superior authority. History, then, becomes an impersonal process, and it cannot judge itself, for it is not God. When Hegel identified God and the historical process, he deprived history of a moral directive, governor, and goal. A God who is part and parcel of the historical process and who is also in a state of dialectical evolutionary development from the unconscious to the conscious, can give to the stream of history neither a sense of destiny nor moral purpose. Those nations which are sincerely attached to this Hegelian view of the human past must logically display the tendencies inherent in his outlook.

Since Hegel viewed the historical process as the history of the Spirit, it became true for him that the most effective springs of historical action are the interests, passions, and the satisfaction of the selfish desires of men. In giving vent to these inner forces, men unknowingly fulfill a general purpose in history, and Hegel conceded this was true of such leaders as Julius Caesar and Napoleon. With an almost instinctive comprehension of such a destiny these men achieve what is intended for them, but what is intended is forced upon them by the irreversible tides of historical determinism, for men are the tools of a god who is itself the captive of this same historical process. Thus the irrationalism of Hegel's system of thought in its political results has given birth to the irrational totalitarianism of our day.

Chapter 6
The Successor of Hegel: The Impact of Hegelianism On Western Thought

It should not be surprising that Hegelianism gave birth to a wide variety of divergent philosophical systems. This rich productivity was almost the inescapable result of the breadth and depth of his system. His all-inclusive idealism had been intended to bring all reality within the scope of his dialectical system. Thus its very inclusiveness proved to be the inspiration for many different and even contradictory strains of thought, all of them tainted with the basic irrationalism which underlay his philosophy.

In the ceaseless ebb and flow of the tides of philosophical speculation, action and reaction have been the leading characteristics of its development. From Plato on into the twentieth century idealism has given way to empiricism and materialism, and they in turn have produced new waves of reaction in the form of a new idealism. Thus German idealism, as it was formulated by Kant and Hegel, once again manifested this continuing characteristic of the history of philosophy. Hegel's successors then fall into many schools of thought, but these divisions can be arranged into two groups; those who follow idealism to its ultimate conclusions on the one hand, and those who reacted against it and chose materialism as their alternative solution to the problems which Hegel had raised but not solved.

Arthur Schopenhauer (1788–1860)

Schopenhauer marks the beginning of the recent period of philosophy. In one sense he is a transitional thinker; in some respects he reflects both Kantian and Hegelian influences, but in his concept of the will he was somewhat post-Hegelian. His chief work, first published in 1819, was *The World as Will and Idea.* In this work he revealed his basic conceptions. In the first place, he was a thoroughgoing subjective idealist or mentalist. Basic to his thinking was his insistence that there can be no object without a subject, by which he meant that there is no material substratum that serves as a support or cause of ideas. At this point he was strongly pro-Berkeley and in opposition to Locke. For him all matter is merely the idea of the knowing subject. Secondly, he held to the principle of sufficient reason. With Kant, he believed that the single principle lying behind the *a priori* forms and categories of understanding is a sufficient reason for all things, which makes knowledge other than will possible. But the ultimate reality is will as the thing in itself, and this is known by the immediate intuition in reason or by introspection.

In his theory of knowledge Schopenhauer emphasized the importance and necessity of intuition, holding that perception can yield no real insight into the nature of the real world. Our real knowledge of the inner nature of reality arises from an intuitive insight into its nature, for this ultimate reality is will or the thing in itself, and it is known by this process of an immediate intuition in reason or by introspection, and not by ideas which come to the human mind through the senses.

For Schopenhauer, the whole world is will and so are we. The universal will (mind) individuates itself in people and other phenomena in the world in accordance with the principle of sufficient reason. This universal will, for Schopenhauer, was free, for it was not determined by anything except itself. On the other hand, the wills of separate individuals are derivatives and are therefore determined. In the world-will all men are identical, and this world-will exists only as idea in relation to the minds of men, while time and space are the principles of individuation.

According to Schopenhauer, the will affirms ideas which are unchanging, and they are the universals which include both genus and species—as man and men. It is the function of the universal will to individuate itself into particular ideas (*Vorstellungen*) or representatives.

Of particular importance in the philosophy of Schopenhauer was his aesthetics, and he gave to art both an ethical and a cognitive function. Its cognitive function lay in his belief that ideas are affirmed by the will and, therefore, they are eternal. They also stand between the will and changing individual things.

But knowledge is ordinarily subordinate to the will, and its function is to carry out the desires that proceed from it. Schopenhauer also held that it is in this aesthetic experience that man is able to abolish his subordination to the will and to contemplate ideas apart from the satisfaction of desires. At this point the distinction between the subject and the object disappears, and in this aesthetic experience man can have a much clearer understanding of the world than he is able to achieve from science. For Schopenhauer, art thus is the knowledge concerned with the underlying content of all things, ideas. This concept of art was well expressed by Lord Byron when he wrote: "Are not the mountains, waves and skies a part of me and my soul, as I of them?" Schopenhauer's conception of the ethical and religious function of art was as pantheistic as the cognitive function which he assigned to art. He proclaimed that the original sin of man was to have been born as a finite person, with all the egoism which that implies. Tracing the history of various types of moral conduct, he then came to the place in which he taught that men make their first real progress in ethics when each man realizes that his is not the only will in existence. When a man reaches this point, pure egoism is replaced by a new sense of justice and of what he called fellow-feeling. But the real advance is achieved when men come to realize that all of their desires are really the product of one underlying and all-embracing universal will. For this reason Schopenhauer admired Hinduism and held that it was much superior to Christianity. In other words, the highest state of ethics is achieved when we deny the will and extinguish our own self-consciousness and individuality. The highest state of ethical achievement, then, really centered in the idea that men should escape from this world and bring it to an end. This last stage of ethical development brought with it the effort to repress all desires, to practice celibacy and cultivate the contemplative life in the hope of entering a blissful state of existence—a kind of Nirvana.

The basic irrationality of Schopenhauer's position has been well recognized by both humanists and Christian thinkers, and many philosophers have clearly pointed out that his view of the nature of reality as it is to be brought to him by intuition makes a rational explanation of human experience impossible. We can only agree with those who have written that Schopenhauer's quest for a new certainty produced a greater uncertainty, and his frantic search for authority in his emphasis upon the will became in later philosophy another invitation to the emergence of political despotism. Once again the rationalism and voluntarism had as their inescapable corollary irrationalism, as the breach between idealism and Christian theism became wider and more pronounced.

The Mainstream of the Hegelian Legacy

Very soon after his death, Hegel's followers broke into two opposing camps of philosophy. One group, known as the right-wing Hegelians, contended that there was nothing in his system of thought which was basically incompatible with biblical Christianity in general and Lutheranism in particular. It may well be wondered how the members of this school of thought could be unaware of the incongruities which existed between Hegel's dialectical philosophy on the one hand and historic Christianity on the other, but they were apparently sublimely unaware of such differences.

The second group, known as the Young or left-wing Hegelians, frankly admitted that there was a radical difference between Hegelianism and the Scriptures, and decided in favor of Hegel. This latter group, which included in its membership David Strauss (1808–1874) and Bruno Baur (1809–1882), the radical biblical critics, became the more important of the two groups in the intellectual life of Europe, and had a tremendous impact on the development of theology in Germany and elsewhere in Europe and even in this country during the latter part of the nineteenth century. The positivistic tendencies of the left-wing Hegelians became very evident in the radical biblical criticism of both Strauss and Bauer. An even more radical member of this group was Ludwig Feuerbach, whose influence over Karl Marx became very pronounced. Feuerbach had come to the conviction that man had created God in man's own image, and this conception became a dominant part of Marx's own thinking.

It is important to note that Marx began his career as a philosopher, as a member of the Young or left-wing Hegelians and not as an economist, and that he derived much of his Hegelian background from Feuerbach. As early as 1844 Marx began to show the influence of Feuerbach in *The Holy Family,* in which he declared that the proletariat would be compelled to abolish itself and private property for the good of humanity. He furthermore combined the epistemology of Locke with his left-wing Hegelianism and insisted that all that man learns, he learns through his senses. He therefore concluded that "It is our business to order the empirical world in such a way that man shall have truly human experience." Self-interest for Marx was thus the guiding principle of morality. Borrowing again from Hegel, he taught that man becomes truly incarnate through the creation of a communist society, and not in the state, as Hegel had taught. For him man apart from society has no value. Society confers upon men their value and rights. But this process of the incarnation of man could only be achieved through the destruction of private property, and this must be achieved through revolution. It was but a short step from Hegel's insistence that man achieves his true identity in the state to the Marxian insistence that this same true identity is achieved through a communist society.

Marx laid the foundation for his dialectical materialism in *Theses on Feuerbach,* which appeared in 1845. Here the full bloom of his basic philosophy became apparent. In it he declared that reality is nothing but human sensuous activity. But not only was this concept not original with Marx, but Marx failed to realize that at no time had he discussed the problem of the relationship between mind and matter or offered a solution to this very vital philosophical problem. In fact, it can well be said that there is very little that is original with the Marxian philosophy. He borrowed his epistemology from Locke and the dialectical logic from Hegel, but he removed it out of its idealistic setting and placed it in a purely materialistic metaphysics. In contrast to Hegel, Marx insisted that development is not logical, not a rational order fulfilling itself throught the dialectical process, but a play or interaction of forces, of economic forces which manifest themselves in the struggle between the social classes throughout human history for the supremacy. Marx did borrow from Hegel, however, the important concept of a dynamic reality, not an abstract concept of thought or mind, but of matter itself as the only reality. But for him the dynamic reality was not an abstract concept of thought or mind; for Marx, matter in dialectic tension was the only reality.

Basic to the Marxian thought was his insistence that only human action is important. Yet at this very point Marx and his followers created an important and insurmountable contradiction in their system. The contradiction lies in the inescapable conclusion from their premise that motion is the mode of existence for matter. "There is no matter without motion." Lying behind this was the assumption that matter contains within itself the energy which is necessary for its own transformation. Inescapably the conclusion follows, then, that the universe is self-creating, self-sufficient, and self-perpetuating, having neither beginning nor end. For this inner energy which matter contains, Marx again looked to Hegel's doctrine of an immanent God, but he placed this Hegelian conception in a very different setting. Marx insisted that organic life is only a complex of material existence and nothing more than the science of the general laws of motion and the development of nature, human society, and thought. Inescapable in Marxian materialism is the insistence that thought itself is a natural process and nothing more. It acts upon and is acted upon by its natural environment. But it is impossible for man to transcend this natural environment, and human nature cannot possibly have any reality apart from this process within nature. If Marx had simply remained a left-wing Hegelian philosopher, he still would have been important, to a degree at least, as a thinker who contributed to the growth of irrationalism in European thought, for his philosophy is studded with insurmountable difficulties and logical inconsistencies. His insistence that mind is simply a part of the natural processes and a part of the dialectical process most certainly could not be affirmed in the light of the empirical epistemology which he borrowed from Locke. The whole Marxian system most certainly was not the result of the empirical process. The irrationalism inherent in Marxian philosophy is written large on every page that Marx ever wrote. That this is the case can hardly be denied.

But Marx was not merely a philosopher, writing for the benefit of a few admirers and students of the history of philosophy. Like Hegel, he became something far more than a philosopher, enunciating metaphysical and epistemological principles within university circles. Marxianism, like Hegelianism, became an important factor in directing the flow of modern history and political thought and practice. Like Hegel, Marx became an important part of the historical process. His philosophy of history and economic determinism have never been mere museum pieces or merely interesting relics from nineteenth-century thought, but they have entered into the very warp and woof of modern life and have conquered a large part of our globe.

Contemporary governments and economic institutions have been conquered by dialectical materialism, and modern totalitarianism in its communistic forms is the direct offspring of this German left-wing Hegelian thinker. Through Marx the irrationalism inherent in the Hegelian system of thought took on a more deadly hue and became not only a vital, but even a lethal, influence in the political and economic life of the twentieth century. In short, to an even greater extent than Hegel, Marx made history even while he was interpreting it.

Although in none of his writings did Marx give a unified treatment of his philosophy of history, it is quite possible to glean his basic concepts from his major writings. There we find the first statements of his case in the *Communist Manifesto* of 1848, in which he and Engels asserted their interpretation of history in terms of a continuous struggle between the classes. Basic to their position was the assumption that the methods by which goods are produced and exchanged lie at the heart of, and constitute the basis of, every social order. Thus the ultimate causes of all social changes are not to be found in the minds of men but in the changes which take place in the way goods are produced and exchanged. This fundamental concept, however, is a derivative of Marx's basic philosophy and his insistence that consciousness does not determine the existence of man, but rather does his social existence determine his social consciousness. From this basic assumption concerning the nature of man, Marx drew the conclusion that the mode by which the material means of life is produced conditions the whole process of the social, political, and intellectual life of the human race. In *The Communist Manifesto* this thesis was stated very briefly: "The history of all hitherto existing society is the history of class struggles."

In 1888, after the death of Marx, Engels expanded this basic theme in a preface. "That in every historical epoch, the prevailing mode of economic production and exchange and the social organization necessarily following from it, form the basis upon which is built and up from which alone can be explained the political and intellectual history of that epoch; that consequently the whole history of mankind . . . has been a history of class struggle, contests between exploiting and exploited, and the oppressed class—the proletariat—cannot attain its emancipation without at the same time and once and for all, emancipating society at large from exploitation, class distinctions and class struggles."[1]

On the baisis of this foundation Marx and Engels then applied the dialectical logic of Hegel to human history and attempted to show that beginning with a stage of primitive communism, and moving from it into feudalism the dialectic finally produced the age of capitalism, in which we now find ourselves. They then declared that society would pass through a fifth stage—socialism—which they regarded as a transitional development, and then with the triumph of the proletariat society would move into the communist era.

Engels held that the state is the product of society at a certain stage in its development and the state moderates the conflict existing between the classes by holding their mutual antagonisms in check. However, in fulfilling this function the state in turn becomes an instrument of class coercion. After the creation of the dictatorship by the proletariat, Marx and Engels taught that the state will wither away, for it will already have fulfilled its function with the emergence of the proletariat and the establishment of socialism as a necessary transition between capitalism and communism.

Marx: An Evaluation

The Marxian philosophy in general and his conception of history are open to very serious objection on logical grounds as well as from the point of view of Christian theism. In the first place, Marx's denial of absolute truth must by necessity negate his contention that communism is a true philosophy. For the same reason, if there be no absolute truth, there can be no absolute moral truth. Therefore, Marx's insistence that capitalism is bad and communism is good has no logical foundation. If all truth is relative, then his strictures on both capitalism and communism can at best

1. Friedrich Engels, *The Origins of the Family, Private Property and the State* (London, 1884), pp. 5-6. See also pp. 157-158.

be only relatively true. If there is no absolute truth, then of course there can be no absolutely true dialectical logic, for determinism cannot be true in any of its forms.

In the second place, Marx was guilty of imposing his dialectical determinism on the historical process without due regard for the available factual evidence. He overlooked the fact that not one of the great dialectical changes which he professed to see in the historical process was the result of any changes in the method by which goods were either produced or exchanged. The changes came later. There can be no doubt that this is a very serious weakness in the communist ideology, and is a very severe blow against the basic postulate of the Marxian view of history. It poses for all advocates of communism a serious question which never has been and cannot be successfully answered.

A third and equally devastating criticism against Marx's philosophy stems from his reliance on the empirical epistemology and the resulting pragmatic methodology. *The Communist Manifesto* is not a purely scientific statement of the case based upon empirical evidence of tangible facts. Not only is it a call to action, but it makes predictions and affirmations concerning the future which are totally incompatible with the empirical epistemology. Marx committed the same error in his prophetic utterances in *Das Kapital.* In the light of the empirical evidence available to him, he had no right to predicate future events such as his dictum that the rich grow richer and the poor grow poorer, or his insistence that capitalism will collapse and the proletariat will emerge triumphant. Because of the limits inherent in his empirical approach to his understanding of history, Marx had no right to predict coming revolutions. Within the framework of the Hegelian idealism, such predictions of the future might be defended, but not in terms of the Marxian epistemology.

For the same reason the reliance upon empiricism affords no room for moral judgments. The empirical epistemology cannot be used as a basis for the formulation of moral and ethical values. It can and must be said that the reliance which Marx placed upon the empirical approach to knowledge undermined his philosophy as a whole and therefore his views of history and economics.

The communist philosophy of Marx and his successors is encumbered by another very serious problem which is very seldom discussed, and this is to be found in the tension existing between his determinism on the one hand and his conception of freedom on the other. Marxian dialectical materialism is the most ruthless form of determinism yet found in the history of philosophy. In its denial of the biblical doctrines of God, man, and truth, it destroys the very essence of human freedom. Marx's view of man really condemns him to slavery—to a servitude to the forces of nature, over which he can have no control. This servitude or slavery to the dialectical forces in nature actually denies that man has any moral responsibility to anyone, including himself. In spite of its frequent demands for the protection of human rights, communism is in a trap of its own making, for without the doctrine of human responsibility to God, there can be no meaningful doctrine of human rights. Thus the communist philosophy of human rights is nothing more than a philosophical abstraction which crumbles to the dust as soon as a communist regime gains control of the government of any nation.

In summary, then, there is in Marxian thought a continuing, and yet insoluble, tension between a rigid determinism on the one hand and a pragmatism on the other. It is a kind of contest between the empiricism of Locke and the dialecticism of Hegel, as Marx attempted to bring them together in his dialectical materialism.

The Marxian view of history stands as an almost complete antithesis to Augustine's mature theological interpretation of history, for the whole Marxian philosophy is probably the final and most comprehensive negation of Christian theism, and yet it is ironic that even in his deep hatred of Christianity, Marx could not escape from Augustine, try as he would. In place of the Scriptures as the infallible rule of what men are to know and to believe about God, Marx offered his *Das Kapital* as their replacement for human life and conduct. In place of the sovereign God of Scriptures, Marx offered the impersonal forces of dialectical materialism as the sovereign before which men must bow. In place of the incarnation of the Son of God as the focal point of all history, Marx offered the incarnation of man as he finds it in his membership in a communist society. Instead of a redemption purchased by Christ on the cross, Marx offered a salvation wrought in the blind working of the dialectical process in matter. To replace the final judgment of a risen and glorified Christ after Armageddon, Marx could only provide hope in the final crisis and revolution which would destroy the bourgeois world and its culture. And in place of the biblical doctrine of a new heaven and a new earth, communism placed its hope in a classless society as a communist heaven on this present earth. Finally, in the place of an exalted and reigning Lord Jesus Christ, Marx offered an exalted and dominant proletariat society.

Although many scholars insist that Marx stood "Hegel on his head," he left the irrationalism of his philosophy intact. Indeed, it could be well argued that the irrationalism which lurks in every basic presupposition of the Marxian philosophy intensifies the irrationalism which enshrouded the Hegelian system. In both cases rationalism has as its correlative a basic irrationalism, and in both cases the freedom which these philosophies seem to offer brings with it not only an intellectual but a political, social, and economic slavery as well. The schism which Kant and Hegel opened between their respective versions of German idealism and Christianity was deepened and widened by the dialectical materialism which Marx offered as its substitute. Unlike Hegel, Marx openly denied Christianity and made no pretense of offering any possible reconciliation between his philosophy and the gospel of Jesus Christ. Declaring that religion is the opiate of the people, he waged open warfare against the Christian church in all of its forms.

Chapter 7

Darwinism, Social Darwinism, and Their Impact On Western Thought

Evolutionary philosophies had been in circulation among European intellectuals since the eighteenth century, and the philosophy of the Enlightenment very definitely regarded social evolution as one of the most important aspects of human history. Many of these eighteenth-century thinkers had confidently expected that a secular millennium was a very real possibility as a goal for the opening of the nineteenth century. In 1789 many liberals were confident that the French Revolution would mean the realization of their bright hopes for the achievement of such an era in Western history. Even the theories of biological and geological evolution were not unknown, even though they did not play an important role in the eighteenth-century outlook. In the writings of Lamarck (1744–1829) and Erasmus Darwin, the grandfather of Charles, we find early presentations of the theory of biological evolution, but these early statements of the theory did not receive too much attention, and it remained for Charles Darwin with his *The Origin of Species* in 1859 to gain a widespread hearing for this theory in both Europe and America.

Nevertheless, the belief that human society was evolving from one stage of development to higher stages was widely held. Not only was it an important aspect of the philosophy which helped bring about the French Revolution, but it was also a factor in the thinking which helped to produce the American War for Independence.[1] This optimistic view of human history underlay the revolutionary movements which broke out in Europe during the first half of the nineteenth century and which inspired the emergence of Jacksonian democracy in this country. In fact, this optimistic view of the potential meaning of nineteenth-century history became so closely identified with the democratic philosophy that progress and democracy became almost indistinguishable terms in the political thought of the day.

1. Thomas Jefferson confidently believed that the American Revolution, as well as the French, heralded a new order of the ages.

This optimism received a powerful stimulus from Hegel's conception of history as the unfolding of his dialectical system. It is also true that the Marxian view of history, dependent as it was on the Hegelian dialectical logic, seemed to promise unlimited progress as history moved forward inexorably toward the triumph of the proletariat. Both European and American non-Marxist socialist movements shared to varying degrees this Marxian optimism, even though they repudiated the means which Marx advocated for the realization of his utopia. However, all of these optimistic philosophies which had captured various segments of the Western mind during the latter part of the eighteenth and the first half of the nineteenth centuries lacked any scientific proofs or foundations. Rather were they the fruit and results of idealistic systems of philosophy in an age which was turning its back on Kant and Hegel and looking to the emerging interpretation of natural law which would offer a scientific basis for a philosophy of evolution which had sprung from philosophic idealism.

If by 1860 the eighteenth-century conception of the world as a vast machine had become orthodoxy, it was an orthodoxy which had undergone vast change, for the conception of natural law which had been popularized by Newton and his eighteenth-century disciples underwent vast changes during the nineteenth century. And even the work of Newton himself underwent revision. John Dalton (1766–1844) made significant revisions in Newton's version and interpretation of the atomic theory. The triumph of this reinterpretation of Newton was aided by other developments in the field of organic chemistry. Probably the first major departure from Newton's corpuscular theory of the structure of matter came in connection with the nature of light.

Nevertheless, these developments, which to varying degrees were departures from Newtonian orthodoxy, in no way reduced the belief of nineteenth-century intellectuals that the world was a vast machine. In fact, many of these developments intensified the widely held conviction that the world in which we live was a much more complex machine than Newton had ever dreamed.

Charles Darwin, in his *The Origin of Species* of 1859, laid the foundations in biology for a new orthodoxy in the area of science which, while looking back to Newton in one sense, gave to natural law an entirely new interpretation which neither Newton nor his immediate successors had foreseen, and which some of them might well have repudiated if they had come into contact with the Darwinian theory. Although Darwin worked in the area of biology, his theories were soon adapted to the whole realm of scientific endeavor and to nearly every other aspect of the intellectual life of the

West. This evolutionary interpretation soon became the foundation of a new *Weltanschauung* in much the same fashion that John Locke had used the Newtonian principles for the formulation of a new world and life view at the end of the seventeenth century.

This conquest of Western thought by Darwin was not accidental or unplanned, for Darwin himself compared himself with Newton. In his *The Origin of Species* Darwin had confined himself to the area of biology, but in his *Descent of Man* (1871) he broadened his approach and applied his evolutionary interpretations to the emergence of man, thus laying the foundation for the emergence of a world and life view which would be evolutionary in its nature and outlook.

In his interpretation of his evolutionary biology as well as in his conception of it he went far beyond such predecessors as Lyell in his *Principles of Geology* and Lamarck. Lamarck was much more theistic than Darwin, and Darwin used his evolutionary theories against what might be called theistic views of the evolutionary process. Darwin looked upon the natural world as a vast and complex mechanism without any goal or purpose. He thus reduced all life to the level of natural selection and the survival of the fittest.

There can be no legitimate doubt that Darwin was not only interested in the evolutionary hypothesis as a scientific explanation of the origins of life, but that he was also intent upon using this theory to discredit the biblical record of creation and, furthermore, to discredit the God presented in the Scriptures. In so doing, Darwin was guilty of misusing the scientific method to which he supposedly attached such loyalty.

Not only the Darwinian theory of evolution but other evolutionary theories as they had been advanced by Ulrici Halle in his *Gott und die Natur* (1844) and other European scholars almost inevitably led to atheism and materialism. This fact was clearly seen by Charles Hodge of Princeton Theological Seminary one hundred years ago, when he wrote that "Darwinism involves the denial of final causes; . . . it excludes all intelligent design in the production of the organs of plants and animals, and even in the production of the soul and body of man."[2]

It is a well-known fact that Darwin did not originate the theory of evolution, as we have already observed. In its earlier versions it did not arouse among intellectuals in either Europe or America that tremendous enthusiasm which greeted the appearance of *The Origin of Species* in

2. Charles Hodge, *What Is Darwinism?* (New York, 1874), p. 95. This work by the great professor of systematic theology remains today as one of the most acute and penetrating analyses that has ever been written of the whole Darwinian position.

1859. The question must arise: What was there in the Darwinian thesis which brought about this change in attitude? The answer is not difficult to find. All previous statements of the evolutionary hypothesis in various ways and in varying degrees admitted some form of purpose and design as an explanation of the theory. David Strauss, the nineteenth-century radical theologian, very openly paid a tribute to Darwin for eliminating from the process of evolution any remnants of the operation of a supernatural force.

> We philosophers and critical theologians have spoken well when we decreed the abolition of miracles; but our decree remained without effect, because we could not show them to be unnecessary, inasmuch as we were unable to indicate any natural force to take their place. Darwin had provided or indicated this natural force, this process of nature; he has opened the door through which a happier posterity may eject miracles forever.[3]

Hodge rightly concluded:

> The only way that is apparent for accounting for evolution being rejected in 1844, and for its becoming a popular doctrine in 1866, is, that it happens to suit a prevailing state of mind. It is a fact, so far as our limited knowledge extends, that no one is willing to acknowledge himself, not simply an evolutionist, but an evolutionist of the Darwinian school who is not either a materialist by profession, or a disciple of Herbert Spencer, or an advocate of the philosophy of Hume.[4]

Hodge, after carefully analyzing the Darwinian theory in all of its inconsistencies, gave forth the answer to the question which constituted the title of his book. He decreed that Darwinism as a theory was and is nothing less than atheism.[5] David Strauss, late in life, set forth the inexorable logic of the Darwinian hypothesis with startling clarity when he wrote:

> We demand for our universe the same piety which the devout man of old demanded for his God. In the enormous machine of the universe, amid the incessant whirl and hiss of its jagged iron wheels, amid the deafening crash of its ponderous stamps and hammers, in the midst of this whole terrific commotion, man, a helpless and defenseless creature, finds himself placed not secure for a moment that on an imprudent motion a wheel may not seize and rend him, or a hammer crush him to a powder. This sense of abandonment is at first something awful.[6]

---

3. David Strauss, *The Old Faith and the New* (New York, 1872), p. 177.
4. Hodge, *What Is Darwinism?*, p. 149.
5. Dr. Hodge was very careful to point out at this point that he did not mean to imply that all those who accepted Darwin's position were atheists, but he also implied that they did not understand the implications of the evolutionary hypothesis.
6. Quoted in ibid., p. 177.

The question then emerges: How do we explain the continuing popularity of the theory of evolution, not only in its Darwinian, but in its later forms? It certainly cannot be the result of any inherent attractiveness in the theory itself. That man descended from lower forms of life is not a belief in which he can take pride and in the light of which he should gloat. Neither can the popularity of the theory be explained in terms of its scientific correctness. The boldest and most erudite champions of this scientific theory have always been forced to concede that their own scientific methodology has utterly failed to provide the necessary evidence to establish the validity of the evolutionary hypothesis. Indeed, the evidence provided by contemporary science speaks out loudly against the validity of this theory, and many scientists contend that the second law of thermodynamics makes impossible any belief in the theory of evolution in any of its forms.[7]

If the theory is unattractive in its implications and scientifically unsound, why then has it had such an enduring popularity? One hundred years years ago Charles Hodge supplied the answer to this question. The enduring popularity of the evolutionary hypothesis does not lie in its attractiveness as a scientific explanation for the origins of life. As a scientific theory it leaves too many questions unanswered and creates more problems than it can solve. Its real popularity has always existed and continues to exist in its non-scientific implications. In the area of theology and biblical studies it was seized upon by left-wing theologians like David Strauss and Bruno Bauer as a useful weapon to use in their attacks on the infallibility and authority of the Scriptures. In the hands of communists and other revolutionary reformers, the Darwinian emphasis on the survival of the fittest was used to justify their revolutionary activities and their efforts to destroy the traditional theistic political and economic philosophies and institutions which stood in their way in their struggles to remake the political and social life of both Europe and America.

But if Darwinism could be used to give life and vitality to radical democratic revolutions, it could also be used to justify the emergence of super races, super classes within a race, and super men within a class, and the history of Europe from 1850 on even until our own day has been the continuing scene of the realization of the many social, economic, and political implications of the evolutionary philosophy. Perhaps no author has per-

7. The second law of thermodynamics is a formidable problem which has forced many non-Christian theistic evolutionists to abandon their position, not because of their theological or philosophical convictions, but because evolution cannot stand up against the implications of this law.

ceived these implications or presented them in such brilliant and penetrating manner as did Jacques Barzun in his *Darwin, Marx and Wagner.*[8] In this work Barzun has one basic theme—the emergence of mechanistic materialism in science, art, and the social sciences during the second half of the nineteenth century, and in this connection he wrote:

> Darwin, Marx and Wagner certainly do not represent absolute beginnings, but neither are they arbitrary starting points. If we take up the history of certain ideas—the idea of struggle for life, of economic interpretation in history, of nationalism in art—we find ourselves discussing Darwin, Marx and Wagner; but we also find ourselves embroiled in the present day problems of democratic freedom, autarky and cultural revolution.[9]

Barzun in the unfolding of his basic thesis insisted that the contributions of Darwin, Marx, and Wagner to the intellectual development of Europe during the second half of the nineteenth century actually formed a single stream of influence, which he called mechanical materialism. He justified his decision on the basis that all three of these men wandered outside of their respective disciplines. Darwin strayed into the areas of psychology and social sciences, while Marx, originally a philosopher, turned to history and sociology and attempted to create an economic system based upon dialectical materialism. Barzun describes Wagner as an artist-philosopher who claimed the cosmos as his own province.[10] Barzun further contended that if we make due allowance for some superficial differences among these three molders of contemporary thought,

> we find so many links uniting Darwinism, Marxism, and Wagnerism that the three doctrines can be seen as the crystalization of a whole century's beliefs. Each of the systems may be likened to a few facets of that crystal: at the core they are indistinguishable. Though the three authors worked independently and were acclaimed by their own age at different times, they expressed with astonishing unity one common thought; they showed in their lives, and even in their characters one common attitude; they imposed on their contemporaries one unified view of themselves. So much so, that it would be hard to find in the whole history of Western civilization a corresponding trio to share in the honors of a single epic with such perfect parallelism.[11]

Barzun found a common core of the materialism of these three architects of Western thought in evolution.

Barzun has rightly seen that evolution was not and could not be confined

8. Jacques Barzun, *Darwin, Marx and Wagner: Critique of a Heritage* (Boston: Peter Smith, 1946).

9. Ibid., p. vii.

10. Ibid., p. 10.

11. Ibid.

within the realm of scientific endeavor, and all the evidence points to the fact that its advocates never intended that it should be. Certainly in the hands of Darwin, Marx, and Wagner it was used as a means of reshaping the intellectual life of the West by turning it away from its historic basis in Christian theism to its new foundation in the theory of evolution. Thus the political, economic, social, educational, and aesthetic views of both Europe and America from their day on show the pervasive and destructive nature of this evolutionary conception of life which enthroned irrationalism in place of the biblical view of life and deified nature as it attempted to destroy the God of creation.

Although Darwin may have changed his mind late in life and repented of his earlier position, there can be no doubt that he was firmly convinced that the universe betrayed no evidence of any plan or purpose.[12] It was plainly and undeniably a fatalistic philosophy, which made its way into Western thought and eventually conquered the modern mind. Darwin insisted on this fatalism. In his *The Origin of Species* he made this very clear:

> Some have even imagined that natural selection induces variability, whereas it implies only the preservation of such variations as arise and are beneficial to the being under its conditions of life. No one objects to agriculturists speaking of the potent effects of man's selection; and in this case the individual differences given by nature, which man for some object selects, must of necessity first occur. Others have objected that the term selection implies conscious choice in the animals which become modified; . . . It has been said that I speak of natural selection as an active power or Deity; but who objects to an author speaking of the attraction of gravity as ruling the movements of the planets? Everyone knows what is meant and is implied by such a metaphorical expression; . . . So again it is difficult to avoid personifying the word Nature; but I mean by nature only the aggregate action and product of many natural laws, and by laws the sequence of events as ascertained by us.[13]

Barzun gave an admirable summary of what the advent of Darwinism has meant.

> The idea of development which made its way into every thinking mind in the first half of the nineteenth century was philosophical; it was a way of understanding things and it implied purpose. The evolution which triumphed with Darwin, Marx and Wagner in the second half of

12. It has been recently asserted that Darwin did have a change of heart in his later years and repented of these assertions and returned to the Christian faith. However, such a change has not in any way diminished the initial impact of Darwinism on Western thought.

13. Charles Darwin, *The Origin of Species* (New York, 1877), p. 63.

> the century was something that existed by itself. It was an absolute. Behind all changes and all actual things it operated as a cause. Darwinism yielded its basic laws and its name, when viewed historically it was progress. All events had physical origins; physical origins were discoverable by science; and the method of science alone could, by revealing the nature of things, make the mechanical sequence of the universe wholly benevolent to man. Fatalism and progress were as closely linked as the Heavenly Twins and like them invincible.[14]

One may take exception to certain emphases which Barzun has given; he may also doubt that the previously existing evolutionary thought had seized hold of every thinking mind. But there can be no doubt that he has correctly analyzed the drastic change which Darwin brought with it. The determinism and fatalism which were so closely woven into the fabric of Darwinian thought could not be and were not confined to the realm of scientific thought alone, for Darwinism itself within fifty years had come to permeate nearly the whole of Western thought. In alliance with Wagner, his doctrine of the survival of the fittest gave a specious form of rationality to the philosophy of government which resulted in Hitlerism and Nazi Germany. In alliance with Marx it gave birth to the equally vicious form of Russian communism which has become the enduring menace to Christianity and Western culture from 1917 on, and presumably it will continue to play this role throughout the remaining decades of the twentieth century.

Its rationalism, rooted and grounded in the concept of the absolute nature of change and the struggle to survive as Darwin claimed to have it operating in the world of nature, was essentially a new version of the irrationalism which has plagued the Western mind since the Renaissance, and it spawned a philosophy of intellectual, moral, and ethical relativity which accompanied the amazing development of a totalitarian absolutism in government during the twentieth century. At first glance, these twin developments of intellectual relativism on the one hand and political absolutism on the other seem to be so totally incongruous that they could not possibly have sprung from the same womb.

A closer examination of this seeming contradiction, however, will lead to a solution to the problem. Relativism in theology and morality must almost inevitably bring with it a political absolutism. No society can endure with relativism as its only absolute and the struggle to survive as its only rationale. The relativism to which Darwin gave birth by its very nature had to result in a political antidote to the anarchy inherent in its

---

14. Barzum, *Darwin, Marx and Wagner,* pp. 351-352.

nature. Without a rationalism thoroughly grounded in the biblical revelation, those who sought to overcome this anarchy in the social, economic, and political life of the West could only oppose one form of irrationalism with another derived from the same source. The relativity of all values which they professed to find in Darwin's Absolute made such a conclusion both easy and popular—at least for those who were able to survive in the struggle and become the "fit."

Thus the history of the economic thought and practice, as well as the political development of Europe and the United States from 1865 on until our own day, is the story of the unfolding of the effects of Darwinism. And its effects were no less evident in the history of philosophy, educational thought and practice, and even in the theology of the Christian church. No area of human interest has remained untouched or undamaged by the poisonous effects of Darwinism.[15] Indeed the history of Western thought from Darwin on is the history of the spread of this poison and the ensuing popularization of a new form of irrationalism which has sapped the stability and vitality of the modern mind to an alarming degree. Its lethal influence on Christian thought has been no less devastating in this country than in Europe. At the same time it has virtually paralyzed large segments of the secular mind throughout the world.

The question naturally arises as to why the theory of evolution should have gained such a widespread popularity not only among scholars in the various academic disciplines but in leaders of virtually every area of human activity. The answer to this lies in the fact that modern man had long been prepared for the acceptance of a biological theory because he had been exposed to a philosophy of evolution for over a century. The idea of some kind of human development was not new. It had been popularized by the philosophes and Hegel, as we have seen, and it had become an essential aspect of all political revolutionary activity in the nineteenth century and was not absent from the American political scene.

This philosophical preparation for Darwin, while important, was certainly not the whole story. Philosophy by itself could not have paved the way for the acceptance of evolution as a *Weltanschauung* if it had not had the powerful support of science itself. Darwinism was a part and an important part of the scientific outlook which came to be the dominant aspect of nineteenth-century thought. With Darwin, science came to the

---

15. It is interesting to note that even those historians who lament the effects of Darwinism on the West are very hesitant about raising any serious questions about the validity of the theory of evolution. Even less are they willing to call it the villain in the case.

aid of philosophy at a time when the older metaphysical concepts were yielding ground to the scientific outlook, and philosophers eagerly looked to science as a powerful ally in their conflict with the biblical concept of both God and man.

Underlying both nineteenth-century philosophy and scientific endeavor was the growing revolt against biblical theology and historic Christian thought, both Roman Catholic and Protestant. The biblical doctrines of a sovereign God, who had created man in His own image, the fall into sin with its corollary of total depravity, and the need of redemption through the atoning work of Christ upon the cross became increasingly foreign to the mind of the nineteenth century. This mind had been prepared and nurtured by philosophy and revolutionary activity to believe in the sufficiency of man to achieve his own redemption through the application of his own unlimited wisdom to the problems which confronted him. These historic Christian doctrines stood in the way of this unbounded optimism. As a result, the nineteenth-century intellectuals rebelled against what they felt were the chafing restraints of an outworn theology which was unsuited to the bright new day which science and technology were making available. Since science and technology had made progress well nigh inevitable, it was obvious that the Scriptures must be made either to conform to this progress or to be shunted aside in favor of a religion which could and would accommodate itself to the doctrines of the perfectibility of man and the inevitability of progress. Thus the appearance of scientific developments and the tremendous technological achievements of the nineteenth century cooperated in preparing the way for the widespread acceptance of evolution and an equally widespread rejection of historic Christianity.

The implications of the Darwinian thesis were easily and quickly recognized by both philosophers and theologians, and the lines of battle were quickly drawn both in Europe and in the the United States between the two parties to the conflict—those who favor evolution as the most satisfactory explanation of the origin of all forms of life on the one hand, and those who rejected it and clung to the biblical view.[16] As a result, irrationalism based upon the concepts developed from the evolutionary hypothesis gained a new foothold in the intellectual life of the Western world and gave a mighty impulse to the destructive currents which were slowly but surely eroding the strength and vigor of modern cultural activity.

16. There was also another group composed of those who sought to find grounds of accommodation between the two groups and who assumed a position known as theistic evolution. In the nineteenth century John Fiske became its leading exponent in this country.

And although the opening skirmishes of the war were fought during the last three decades of the nineteenth century, the war has continued unabated for over one hundred years and shows no signs of abating. Herbert Spencer (1820–1893) was one of the first to endeavor to use the theory of evolution to forge a whole new world and life view based upon a biological view of human nature.[17] His efforts to create such a synthetic philosophy appeared at first in his *Social Statics,* in which he proclaimed his conviction that the time had come to synthesize all knowledge, for it was now possible to arrive at a conception of evolution which applied universally—from the stars and the planets on the one hand, to government, art, and religion on the other. In 1860 he announced that it was his purpose to write a synthetic philosophy which would bring all scientific knowledge into a unified whole. Beginning this ambitious project in 1860, he worked on it for the next thirty-three years. He inaugurated his crusade with the revision of an earlier work, *Principles of Sociology,* which had first appeared in 1855, in which he attempted to present a biological view of human nature. But his *First Principles,* which appeared in 1864, set forth his basic philosophy. In it he announced that the ultimate nature of reality is unknowable and assigned this realm of the unknowable to the area of religion and held that the realm of the knowable lay in science. But at this point he paralleled the difficulties which Kant had faced. Declaring that the ultimate reality is unknowable, he proceeded to say a great deal about it. If it was and is as unknowable as Spencer would have us believe, we may then raise a legitimate question: How unknown is Spencer's unknowable?

Spencer unblushingly applied the principles of evolution to all finite phenomena, including human beings and their social organizations. His evolutionary principles almost irresistibly led Spencer to turn to utilitarianism in his ethical outlook. He declared that the biological laws which he found in the theory of evolution confirmed utilitarianism as the proper ethical outlook on the assumption that sensations producing pleasure arise from those acts which promote human survival. He also argued that as the concept of duty becomes more and more pleasurable, it will become progressively less disagreeable and will ultimately disappear.

When Spencer spoke of the laws of biology, he had in mind the law of the survival of the fittest and the transmission of acquired characteristics in and by the surviving individuals of any species.

---

17. It is important to observe that Spencer at this time was not familiar with Darwin but only Lamarck.

It is obvious to us that Spencer accepted in full the philosophical and social aspects of the evolutionary philosophy which he had acquired from Comte and Lamarck. Using this same approach to the broader sphere of human society he also held that the ultimate goal of any society was the achievement of peace and prosperity, and when this goal had been achieved the state would no longer be necessary. In short, the state was a kind of necessary evil which should have both limited functions and limited powers. In the interests of the broadest possible freedom for the individuals under its control, Spencer believed in an unfettered social and economic freedom as well as political freedom, and held to a conception of free enterprise in keeping with his utilitarian assumptions.

He had absolutely no faith in the power of the state as an institution to produce an ideal society such as he envisaged. In fact, he leveled his attacks against the liberal concept of social and economic reform through political means and held that true reform must come only through the operation of the law of the survival of the fittest. He did not even have any faith in the power of education to bring about reform. It has been argued that Spencer was not a true Darwinist, and in the narrower sense of the word this description is fairly correct. But it cannot be denied that he was an evolutionary philosopher. At the same time it is also true that he did not fit into the usual pattern of nineteenth-century liberalism. He had little regard for socialists, communists, and most liberals, regarding them as idealistic dreamers who were attempting the impossible. For Spencer progress could be achieved only as a result of changes brought about in the character of free individuals. In spite of this limitation on the possibility of progress, he held to a belief in its inevitability. This is not as illogical as it might seem at first glance, since he also held to a deterministic concept of the survival of the fittest, and this concept, for Spencer, was the key to progress.

It is at this very point, however, that the fundamental weakness of his position becomes very apparent. Irrationalism stalks him at every point in his philosophical outlook. It is contradictory to speak of freedom within the context of an evolutionary philosophy which is dominated by a theory of determinism. And this is exactly what Spencer did. Accepting determinism as his point of reference, he erected a theory of individual freedom and *laissez faire* on this foundation. His view of man was thus faulty. Man is the product of forces beyond his control and which have no sense of purpose or plan for him. Spencer denied the biblical view of God and creation and was thus forced to deny the biblical view of man. But having denied this biblical view of creation he nevertheless insisted upon a doctrine of freedom which could not be sustained by his evolutionary philosophy and which could find its true nature only in the Scriptures, Spencer was thus another link in the march from the rationalism of the Renaissance to the irrationalism of the twentieth century. In terms of the spread of the theory of evolution to the United States, he is an important figure in that he was the first to help popularize Social Darwinism, although it can be argued that he was not a true member of this school of thought. Nevertheless, he had a great influence on both William Graham Sumner and John Fiske, both of whom along with Lester Frank Ward applied Darwinian principles to the American political, economic, and social scene.

William Graham Sumner

William Graham Sumner was one of Spencer's first disciples in this country, and it is with him that the seeds of that irrationalism which had been so carefully nourished by his mentor in England were brought to the United States. However, Sumner was much more thoroughly Darwinian in his outlook than Spencer and had a much greater impact on the development of the American mind after 1865 than the latter had in England.

Sumner had been an Episcopalian rector in New Jersey, but resigned his pastorate to engage in graduate study abroad. Upon his return to this country he became a professor of political economy at Yale College, and in this chair he was able to exert a tremendous influence upon the thinking of future leaders in American business and industrial life. As a graduate student he had become convinced of the correctness of Darwinism, not only as an explanation of the biological process, but also as a new frame of reference in the light of which political and economic thought must be formulated.[18] He placed his greatest emphasis, as had Spencer, on the concept of the survival of the fittest, arriving at the conclusion that every aspect of human life is a struggle to survive and that liberty is a result of the continuous struggle to survive in which man must engage against the forces of nature. In 1879 he gave voice to his outlook:

> If we do not like the survival of the fittest, we have only one possible alternative, and that is the survival of the unfittest. The former is the law of civilization; the latter is the law of anti-civilization. We have our choice between the two, but a third plan, social desideratum—a plan for nourishing the unfittest and yet advancing civilization, no man will ever find.[19]

---

18. C. G. Singer, *A Theological Interpretation of American History* (Nutley, N. J.: Craig Press, 1975), p. 103.
19. William Graham Sumner, *Essays,* ed. A. G. Keller and M. B. Davie (New Haven, 1934); cited in Richard Hofstadter, *Social Darwinism in American Thought* Philadelphia, 1944), p. 43.

Implicit in this outlook is the assumption that man is not the product of divine creation, but that he is completely the product of blind evolutionary forces. Thus he has no control over his own destiny, but is swept along by natural and cultural forces over which he has no control and in the face of which he is helpless. The same holds true for the social order of which he is a part.

> The truth is that the social order is fixed by law of nature precisely analogous to those of the physical order. The most that man can do is by his ignorance and conceit to mar the operation of the social laws.[20]

Sumner was led to reject much of modern political, social, and economic thought and to construct a new ethics based upon assumptions which were completely naturalistic. In doing this he was quite logical. Since man is a pawn of nature, he is helpless in the face of natural forces, and his institutions must be erected in the light of this overwhelming fact. Basic to his ethics was the insistencc that the historic Christian conception of right and wrong could no longer be regarded as having any force in modern society.

> Nothing but might has ever made right, and if we include in might (as we ought) elections and the doctrines of the courts, noting but might makes right now. . . . If a thing has been done and is established by force (that is no force can reverse it), it is right in the only sense we can know and rights will follow from it which are not vitiated at all by the forces in it. There would be no security at all for rights if this were not so.[21]

This amazing statement is a very clear indication of the trend of evolutionary thought in this country. The admission that only might makes right is an echo of Machiavelli in the new dress of scientific determinism. This determinism, so rigidly stated by Sumner, nevertheless makes human rights relative and does away with the biblical concept of duty to God, which alone furnished a sound foundation for such rights. This relativism was not confined to his view of human rights, but permeated his entire ethical outlook. Not only were human rights placed in a precarious situation, but all human relationships were likewise to be interpreted in relationship to the pattern of evolutionary thought as interpreted by Sumner. At the same time, Sumner's whole philosophical outlook was pervaded by a dreary pessimism which could hardly make his economic and political philosophy attractive to any but those who were determined to be

---

20. William Graham Sumner, *The Challenge of the Facts and Other Essays* (New Haven: Yale University Press, 1914), pp. 55-56.
21. William Graham Sumner, *Folkways* (Boston, 1906), p. 65.

the fittest and thus survive in the continuous struggle to which they were doomed by the very nature of the evolutionary process. This pessimism was clearly set forth by Sumner himself in an essay which has received comparatively little attention.

> The great stream of time and earthly things will sweep on in spite of us. It bears with it now all the errors and follies of the past, the wreckage of all the philosophies, the fragments of all the civilizations, the wisdom of all the abandoned ethical systems, the debris of all the institutions and the penalties of all the mistakes. It is only in imagination that we stand by and look and criticize and plan to change it. Every one of us is a child of his age and cannot get out of it. It will swallow both us and our experiments. It will absorb the efforts at change and take them into itself as new but trivial components and the great movement of tradition and work will go on unchallenged by our fads and schemes. The things which will change it are the great discoveries and inventions, the new reactions inside the social organism, and the changes in the earth itself on account of the change in the cosmic forces. These causes will make it just what, incidentally to them, it ought to be. The men will be carried along with it and be made by it. The utmost they can do by their cleverness will be to note and record their course as they are now carried along, which is what we do now, and is that which leads us to the vain fancy that we can make or guide the movement. That is why it is the greatest folly of which men can be capable to sit down with a slate and pencil to plan out a new social world.[22]

Sumner was not unaware of the pessimistic conclusions to which his philosophy led him:

> I have lived through the best period of this country's history. The next generations are going to see war and social calamities. I am glad I do not have to live on into it.[23]

It is ironic that a philosophy which was designed to assert in incontrovertible terms the supremacy of man over God and nature, which was designed to afford additional scientific support for an optimistic philosophy of evolution, should produce such a hopeless pessimism. Liberty and purpose became its immediate victims as it reduced mankind to an abject slavery to a blind and relentless natural law which had neither meaning nor purpose in its operations. Thus once again the rationalism of an age of science had as its correlative an irrationalism demoralizing in its effects on those it was supposed to free from the slavery of subjection to the sovereign God revealed in the Scriptures.

---

22. Keller and Davie, *Essays,* p. 301.
23. A. G. Keller, *Reminiscences of William Graham Sumner* (1933), p. 109.

Lester Frank Ward (1841–1913)

The fatalism inherent in the approach of Sumner to the Darwinian world and life view was quite apparent to many of his contemporaries who rallied to the cause of the evolutionary theory with a firm determination to set forth its meaning in terms of a glowing optimism which promised a virtual secular millennium to those who would enroll in the cause under their banners.[24] The champion of this version of Darwinism was Lester Frank Ward.

The real objection to Spencer and Sumner lay in their use of the concept of the survival of the fittest, and Ward supplied an answer to this objection, an answer which he found in Darwin himself and thus in effect he used Darwin against Sumner's "Social Darwinism." Ward also relied on Darwin's evolutionary hypothesis, but he was repulsed by the idea of the survival of the fittest by Sumner's use of Darwin and thus turned to another aspect equally prominent in Darwin—the transmission of acquired characteristics. Ward admitted that in all of the lower forms of life environment was the determining factor in the evolutionary process, but he insisted that this was not the case with the emergence of man on the scene. Ward held that the mind of man could and should exercise a determining influence on his environment. Ward rebelled against what he felt was the negative approach to social and economic issues which Sumner had derived from Darwin, and instead used what he called the positive or dynamic approach to them. In his *Dynamic Sociology* and subsequent works he sought to prove that sociology offered the necessary positive approach. His basic thesis was that man is able to control the process of evolution and direct it toward those social goals which he could choose, and for the realization of which he could plan the necessary political program. Through his mind man can determine these goals.

> In this great struggle for survival brute force played a diminishing part and mind an increasing one. Low cunning and animal sagacity, though very prominent, were more and more supplanted by the more refined and subtle manifestations of the same psychic principle. This advance was greatly accelerated by the growth of institutions and the establishment of codes of conduct requisited to life in collectivity. The

---

24. The term "Social Darwinism" came to be largely restricted to those who followed Sumner's version of Darwin, but there is no real reason for such a restriction. The economic and social philosophy which Ward developed was as much Darwinian and social as the views of Sumner. It would seem that among historians and sociologists there has been a silent conspiracy to shield Ward from the reproach of the term and an effort to confer on his version a respectability which it most certainly does not deserve.

> rude animal methods were intolerable and by natural selection, if not otherwise, society discarded them.[25]

Much can and should be said concerning Ward's thinking at this point. In the first place it should be noted that his thesis is not logical. He simply assumed that man somehow or other developed the capacity to control his environment when all life beneath him had been controlled by it. There was and is no empirical evidence for such an assumption that man evolved in such a way as to bring about such an abrupt change in the relationship between him and his environment. How did he achieve such an ability? In what way is man so different from all lower forms of life that suddenly he acquired such a capacity to rise above his environment and subject it to the control of his mind? In this respect Ward was much less consistent than Sumner, but his optimism demanded such an inconsistency. But his very inconsistency raised questions which neither Ward nor other evolutionists could possibly answer.

It was necessary for Ward to interpret Darwin in such a way that he could create a dynamic sociology which would embody the doctrine of unlimited progress for the human race and then make available those methods by which a secular millennium could be achieved under the guidance of his "sociocrats." Using the principle of the transmission of acquired characteristics, Ward drew a blueprint for the scientific betterment of the race. It was actually a program by which the forces of evolution would be directed toward the realization of human happiness which, in the eyes of Ward, was man's chief end. Society was to utilize science for this purpose. In his writings he lavished upon science and its methodology a kind of praise which virtually deified it.

> Science is the great iconoclast. Our civilization depends wholly upon the discovery and application of a few profound principles, thought by a few great minds who hold the shallow babble of priests contempt and have no time to dabble in theology.[26]

For Ward, then, science was to be the salvation of society, and sociology was the queen of the sciences. He attributed all the evils in this nation to the existence of the competitive system, and he demanded its replacement by another system which he called collective achievement. In his insistence on group rather than on individual initiative for the achievement of human happiness he differed radically from Sumner and other utilitarians.

---

25. Lester F. Ward, *The Psychic Factors of Civilization* (Boston, 1893), pp. 156-157.
26. Ward, *Iconoclast,* August, 1870.

In the actual realms of politics Ward called for the establishment of a sociocracy in place of our government under the Constitution, by which he meant a government run by trained sociocrats, who were nothing more or less than sociologists who accepted the principles of Social Darwinism as interpreted by Ward. In this scheme legislation would not be the product of an elected Congress, but the result of legislative experiments carried out by sociologists, and under their trained leadership sociocracy would be the vehicle by which the various problems confronting the American society—disease, ignorance, poverty, and inequality—would yield to the magic touch of this new statesmanship. Ultimately the earth would be transformed into a secularized garden of Eden in which even labor would become pleasant.

The importance of Ward's work does not lie solely in the fact that he is rightly considered to be the father of American sociology. There can be no doubt that he gave a permanent direction to most later sociological thought in this country. If his influence had been largely confined to the realm of sociological theory, he would still be important. But this is not the case. Ward gave to sociology a much greater importance in his insistence that this discipline must enter into the political and economic life of the nation. His insistence that his version of Social Darwinism must replace political science and statesmanship operating under the Constitution gave to sociology an importance which it probably would not otherwise have obtained. While Sumner had a much greater impact upon the conduct of the American government and business activity during the latter part of the nineteenth and early part of the present century, Ward has had the more prolonged and greater influence upon American life. In his open advocacy of social betterment through governmental action he laid the foundations for the welfare state of our day, which had its beginning in the various programs of Franklin Roosevelt's New Deal. Because of the excesses committed by business during its era of adolescence, Ward was able to capture the fancy of many people who were greatly concerned with trend of our economic and social development and who looked on competition as it had been sanctified by a *laissez-faire* philosophy enumerated by Sumner and his followers, as the cause of many of the problems which the nation was facing. In their eyes Ward seemed to offer the one solution to the rampant and unbridled competition which they saw as the great enemy of the people. This remedy was the collectivist state dedicated to collectivist achievement. But this collectivist state offered by Ward was nothing more than a thinly disguised totalitarian regime. His insistence that the individual will find his true happiness only in this collectivistic state was only a little removed from the Hegelian doctrine that man is nothing apart from the state and that in the state he achieves his personality and derives his rights from it.

Ward's importance also stems from the fact that he openly claimed education as his ally in the realization of his social goals. At this point it is very clear that he was borrowing this idea from the *Communist Manifesto* of 1848. Both Marx and Ward clearly saw that a properly controlled system of public education was absolutely necessary for the creation of a collectivist society, for public education itself is a form of collectivism. In advocating such a system of public education Ward became the inspiration for John Dewey and a host of "progressive" educators, who joined his ranks in looking upon the public schools of this nation as the most effective weapon in their program for democratizing the United States, by which they actually meant the socializing, collectivizing, and communizing of the United States.

Ward was more hostile to evangelical Christianity than Sumner, and he openly broke with orthodox Christianity at every essential point. His attitude toward historic Christianity was one of actual hatred rather than contempt. He was equally opposed to all metaphysical theories and was very close to Marx in his acceptance of materialism. Materialism permeated every aspect of his system. Believing that man is the product of evolutionary forces, Ward was forced to deny the biblical account of creation and that man had been created in the image of God. In short, he rejected the supernatural as an explanation for finite reality and this rejection is very clearly seen in his explanation of the rise and function of human institutions and in his ethical and moral philosophy. He held that the family in its origin was simply an institution "for the more complete subjugation and enslavement of women and children. . . . The primitive family was an unnatural and autocratic excrescence upon society."[27] He thus very easily arrived at the conclusion that marriage, like the family, is a whited sepulchre. Just as easily he also declared that sexual satisfaction is a social necessity and morality is only the product of the rational faculty.[28] He gave a naturalistic explanation for the origin of all human institutions. In his thinking they fulfill a purpose imposed on them by the race; the idea that the family, the state, religion, and the church are ultimately divine in their origin and were given to man for the proper ordering of society by God was totally contrary to Ward's whole outlook on the human scene. The very clear implications of his writings is that such institutions as the family, mar-

---

27. Ward, *Pure Sociology* (New York, 1903), p. 353.
28. Ibid., p. 389.

riage, and the church would no longer be either necessary or even desirable, nor would they be allowed in a state which is under sociocratic control.

The inherent positivism and relativism in his ethical and moral outlook was brought vividly to the fore in his declaration that morality and religion were devices by which mankind had been lulled into a passive acceptance of the status quo. At this point in his thinking Ward clearly reflects Marxian influence. Having completely rejected the biblical view of ethical and moral life, he replaced it with one which was naturalistic and hedonistic in its tone. At the same time and for the same reason he denied the fundamental biblical distinction between good and evil and thus denied that man is evil.

> The fundamental assumption of the old ethics is that there is something essentially evil in human nature. Its whole purpose is to destroy this evil element. No other science is so wholly destructive. . . . But all true science is essentially constructive. Where, then, is the fundamental fallacy which must lurk somewhere in the current of moral philosophy? It lies in the very assumption of evil propensities. They underlie the social world and belong to the nature of man. They would never have been planted there if they had not been necessary to his development. They are evils only insofar as they conflict with individual or social interests. . . .[29]

In place of the destructive ethical teaching of the Scriptures, Ward proposed a new concept based on social science, which he felt was the only truly constructive science. If men would only accept this new ethics based on "social science," they would come to a new understanding of the purpose of life. They would understand that man's chief end is the satisfaction of his desire for happiness, and it is not to be found in our duty either to God or to our fellow men. On this Ward was very clear and equally insistent.

> The world labors under a brave and serious error. It has generally been supposed that our duties to our fellow men and to our Maker are more important than the mere acquisition of knowledge. . . . This position, however sound it may seem, is as false in logic as it is pernicious in effect. . . . Moral culture leads abstract sophistries and invalidity. Religious culture, to the exclusion of intellectual training, degenerates into morbid asceticism or bigoted fanaticism. Neither serves to accelerate in the smallest degree the onward march of civilization.[30]

29. Ward, *Glimpses* V, pp. 275-276.

30. From an unpublished address quoted in Samuel Chugerman, *Lester Frank Ward, the American Aristotle* (Durham, 1939), pp. 537-538.

In short, Ward taught an ethical hedonism; the aim of human life is happiness. Pleasure means life and pain means death. Pain and pleasure become the only real basis for moral judgments. The revealed will of God and His moral law had no place in Ward's philosophy. They cannot, for they are a part of a moral philosophy which the true understanding, according to Ward, will banish from the mind of man. Only dynamic sociology can provide the necessary insight for the truly educated man.

Ward's conquest of sociological thought in this country has been nothing less than a disaster. For sociologists of his school penetrated not only the major universities, but eventually the law schools and much of our jurisprudence. Sociologists have become an important aspect of the judicial equipment of a majority of jurists in the nation to such an extent that the traditional and Christian view of justice has become virtually extinct from our courtrooms. The transition began even during Marx's own lifetime, in the person of Oliver Wendell Holmes, Jr. In his *Common Law* he showed the beginning of the departure from the biblical view of the meaning and application of law.

> The life of the law has not been logic; it has been experience. The felt necessities of the time, the prevalent moral and political theories, intuitions of public policy avowed or unconscious, even the prejudices which the judges share with their fellow men, have a good deal more to do with the syllogism in determining the rules by which men should be governed. . . .
>
> The law embodies the story of a nation's development through many centuries, and that in order to know what it is, we must know what it has been, and what it tends to become. Much that was taken for granted has been laboriously fought for in past times; the substance of the law at any time corresponds fairly well with what was regarded as convenient by those making or interpreting it, but the form and the machinery and the degree to which it is able to work out desired results, depends much upon its past.[31]

Through William Graham Sumner and Lester Frank Ward, Darwinism made its way into American life, bringing with it a new and deadly form of irrationalism. It was thrice deadly because it apparently rested upon the infallible dictates supplied by the scientific methodology to which many intellectuals in this country were paying due homage by 1890. Because of the widespread acceptance of this outlook, irrationalism in the form of Darwinian rationalism spread into every sector of the American intellectual endeavor, bringing with it almost inevitable rejection of the Scriptures and

---

31. Oliver Wendell Holmes, Jr., *The Common Law* (Boston, 1881), pp. 1-2.

replacing them with the frame of reference which was studded with relativism, a relativism which is the inescapable companion of the rationalism inherent in evolutionary rationalism.[32]

The Impact of Darwin on European Thought

Althought Herbert Spencer was one of the first important European thinkers to pay any real attention to Darwin and to incorporate portions of his evolutionary theory into his philosophy, he was not the most important of those who looked to Darwin for support or inspiration. We have already noted the interest which Marx displayed in Darwin and Richard Wagner also. But it is not too much to say that the evolutionary hypothesis swept over European thought to an even greater degree than it had captured the American mind. In the United States, even though the biological and geological disciplines largely succumbed to Darwinism and even though it made inroads in the fields of political science, sociology, and economics, many scholars in these areas resisted the charm of the evolutionary philosophy and actively opposed it. It also met the strong and quite effective resistance among evangelical conservatives, particularly within Roman Catholic and Presbyterian and Lutheran circles.[33] In Europe as well as in England, it made much headway in the Protestant churches, largely because many of these churches secured their ministers from the universities, where the evolutionary theory was widely taught, almost to the exclusion of the biblical view of creation and the origin of man.

However, this apparent triumph of the principles of evolution in Western thought in both Europe and the United States had far-reaching consequences which were not foreseen and which brought in their wake various crises which caused a revolution against the application of these principles to problems which faced Western culture. The optimism which had first emerged with the uncritical acceptance of Darwinism faded as the theory gave birth to relativism in ethics and political, social, and economic practice, and gave rise to psychological views of man which raised grave doubts about the worth of the whole human endeavor. Scientists began to criticize the philosophers and social theorists who adopted Darwinism as their own, and philosophers on the other hand began to formulate theories of evolution which would not give rise to the embarrassing social and political consequences which they saw as inherent in the

32. The later influence of Darwinism on American thought will be dealt with in subsequent appropriate chapters.

33. It was also vigorously opposed by the Fundamentalist movement in and out of the mainline denominations.

Darwinian theory of evolution. Darwin was an embarrassment to them even as their formulation of his position became a source of embarrassment and indignation to the scientists who resented the rise of "Social Darwinism."

But Darwinism was apparently here to stay as the Western world rushed on toward its relativistic and nihilistic philosophies which have characterized the mind of the twentieth century. There was, however, an alternative —the return to orthodox Christianity. The problem lay in the fact that in the thinking of many, if not most, intellectuals, the evolutionary biology along with evolutionary geology had so shaken the integrity of the biblical account of creation and the origin of man that to once again adopt the biblical view was a confession of anti-intellectualism on the part of those scholars who would adopt this as their resolution of the various dilemmas which the theory of evolution had raised.

Since it is not the purpose of this study to give a detailed history of the intellectual development or decline of the West, it is not necessary to present the thinking of all philosophers of any era and particularly of the era which began about 1860. Rather will we concentrate upon those philosophers and scholars in the various disciplines who followed Darwinism and the other movements of the day to intensify the first toward an utter irrationalism under the guise of rationalism. Science had now been enlisted in the cause; it was to be the instrument by which Western man would further destroy the intellectual edifice which he had been rearing since the Renaissance and the Reformation. In the strenuous effort to destroy the biblical account of creation and trustworthy history, Western man would ultimately proclaim the death of God, but in this proclamation he would at the same time proclaim his own death as a rational being living with a purpose in view.

Chapter 8
The Impact of Evolutionary Theory On Western Thought After Darwin

It is not too much to say that within three decades after the appearance of *The Origin of Species* Darwinian thought in its several guises was the commonly accepted interpretation of the beginnings of life on earth. To an equal extent the evolutionary hypothesis also became the new frame of reference for the origin and function of all human institutions. Government, economic thought and practice, sociology, and education as well as philosophy and theology were all subjected to the demands and scrutiny of the evolutionary hypothesis. No area of human thought or activity was allowed to escape from this scrutiny. When scholars did not openly assert their fidelity to Darwinism, they nevertheless allowed it to guide their activities and conclusions. Darwinism became the order of the day. Scholarship which did not pay due obeisance to this new deity became suspect. The theory became thoroughly entrenched as scientific fact, and its truths could not be questioned. Permeating every area of academic and intellectual endeavor, it became the frame of reference for the Western mind.

As we enter upon our study of the growth of irrationalism in the second half of the nineteenth century and the first seven decades of the twentieth century, it becomes increasingly evident that it is no longer possible or desirable to study pure philosophy, as such, first and then investigate its impact on the political, social, and economic thought of the era. Rather it is necessary to consider the growth of irrationalism in its wider scope, in the area of political philosophy, economic and social thought, in psychology, religion, and in the arts. For all of these fields of intellectual and cultural activity are increasingly tainted with the virus of irrationality. Pure philosophy, as such, while it does not cease to exist, becomes increasingly rare as philosophers address themselves to the arena of the social sciences, the humanities, and the arts. As a result, philosophical literature is more and more concerned with the meaning of history, the proper economic and social relationships as seen through the eyes of evolution, the meaning of art and music in terms of this philosophy, and even educational thought and practice take on a new importance as they become part of this intellectual battleground and take part in the departure from the older, generally accepted, norms of thought and behavior and become part of the ever-shifting scene of evolutionary thought. This invasion by the evolutionary philosophy is not always easy to detect, since it took several different forms, but beneath the superficial differences the basic pattern becomes quite evident upon close investigation.

In France one of the first to betray its underlying theme was Adolph Taine (1828–1893). Seeking a science of culture, he looked to history as the source and foundation for such a culture. He regarded history as the account of the confluence of hereditary, social, and environmental forces as they acted on the primitive psychological qualities of various peoples throughout the various historical epochs. Although he was rigidly opposed to the whole Jacobin tradition, regarding it as the cause of the political instability which he found in the France of his day, he was not able to escape from the trap into which Jacobism had fallen. This trap was a view of man and history which was poisoned by the very same assumptions to which the radicals of the French Revolution had fallen victim. Denying in essence the Christian view of man, Taine held that man was the victim of forces outside of him, and thus human life, for Taine, could not be anything essentially different from that view which was at the root of the revolutionary philosophy which he hated vehemently. Dispossessed of the necessary ingredients which bequeath purpose and meaning to human life, Taine was ill-equipped to fight the battle he had entered. Irrationalism was as much a part of his philosophy as it was of Comte and the Jacobins.

In Jules Michelet (1798–1874) the evolutionary philosophy is even more prominent, although it took a somewhat different form. In his writings, notably in his *Introduction to Universal History* (1831), we see the incipient view of the historical process which would reach its zenith in Hitler, Mussolini, and Stalin, although he would have vehemently denied such a charge.

In this work Michelet viewed the whole of the historical process as a magnificent yet ceaseless struggle between spirit and matter. At the same time, it was a conflict between two irreconcilable principles of free will on the one hand and determinism on the other. In his view of history and the emergence of reality there was an interesting blending of Darwin and Hegel. In this evolutionary spiral of cultural progress, each of the European nations had a role to play in the realization of liberty. Even as Hegel had insisted that the Germans had a peculiar destiny in the unfolding of liberty, so did Michelet insist that the French had a similar role, but the French role was unique in that the French identified liberty with equality, at least since 1789.

Although by no means one of the most important figures in the intellectual history of nineteenth-century Europe, Michelet represents the trend in which European thought was moving, and for this reason he demands some attention. He built a lofty superstructure for the European cultural development, but failed to provide a necessary foundation. Lacking the biblical view of God and man, and failing to realize the meaning and impact of sin in man's cultural development, he set forth a view of liberty which was glaringly at fault. Since history, for him, was a ceaseless struggle between two contending and hopelessly irreconcilable principles of free will and fate, the kind of freedom which he found in the French Revolution was incapable of sustaining the kind of edifice which Michelet was presenting. The kind of freedom which is found in the unbiblical view of human equality is no freedom at all, but merely subjection to the tyranny of a faceless majority. At the same time, he mingled this doctrine, derived from the French Revolution, with the idea of a blind determinism which he found in Darwin. Although his views have not produced in France the kind of totalitarianism which appeared in Germany under Hitler, it can hardly be denied that Michelet was heading in that direction.[1]

The impact of Darwinism on philosophy and more specifically on political thought became even more evident in Michelet's German contemporary, Heinrich von Trietschke (1834–1896), who combined the various elements which characterized the thought of the idealists into a more comprehensive system. In Trietschke the future Nazi state is there to behold. What was somewhat varnished and even concealed in Michelet is evident in Trietschke without the polish with which Michelet coated his bitter pills. Trietschke argued that national unity must be created in Germany by sheer strength of will and even brute force if Prussia was to achieve its true destiny in nineteenth-century Europe. It can well be said that he deified the state, but the resulting god is hardly attractive or conducive to worship. Therefore force must be used to obtain worship of which it is not worthy, and without which it could not obtain such reverence or adoration. Absolutely convinced that Prussia must unify Germany, he became a most articulate spokesman for Chancellor Bismarck in the Reichstag from 1871 until 1884.

In the political thought of Trietschke, the outlines of a Hitlerian Germany are no longer faint, but are much easier to read. In his *Die Politik*

1. It should be observed that the French concept of liberty and equality have generally produced some form of a despotic government wherever they have been applied.

(1897–1898) he offered a justification for the kind of state which we first saw emerge in the thinking of Machiavelli. Since it is the function and role of the state to unify the people of a nation into a true *volk,* it is justified in using whatever means seem to be necessary to achieve such a goal. Among these means Trietschke specifically mentioned that of preaching and teaching the concept of racial purity. War also received his sanction, if not his blessing. In his thinking, waging war performed a double function: it at once is both the creation of a national unity and the expression of such a unity. Since he held that war will heal a nation that lacks a sense of national purpose and unity, war then becomes a positive good. Pursuing this line of ethical thought, Trietschke came to the conclusion, not unnaturally, that when the state is organized for the waging of war, it is by virtue of this fact achieving the highest form of moral community.

Lurking just beneath the surface of his ethical system is the Darwinian insistence upon the survival of the fittest, and to survive a nation or *volk* is justified in using any means which will achieve this goal. The irrationalism inherent in Hegel's political thought and view of history in Trietschke is combined with a reliance upon irrationalism involved in Darwinian scientific thought. As a result, the dominant strain of political philosophy in Germany from his day on until the rise of Hitler bears the mark of an intensified irrationalistic outlook on the nature of the state and history which has its culmination in the rise of the Nazi state in Germany, the Italy of Mussolini, and the communist regime of Stalin, Lenin, and their successors in modern Russia. However, the philosophy of Trietschke would not bear this fruit immediately. The political philosophy which first gained an active role in the German Empire under Bismarck would be "refined" by the contributions of Nietzsche and others before it would be able to capture the German people after World War I.

The emergence of irrationalism in political thought took another step forward to its fulfillment with Houston Stewart Chamberlain, the son-in-law of Richard Wagner, who in his *Foundations of the Nineteenth Century* inspired the Nazi movement in Germany. Chamberlain stripped the Darwinian dogma of whatever romantic veneer it may have received from Wagner and brought its basic implications clearly to the forefront. He was an important link in that rocky road which led from Darwin and Wagner to the ultimate in political irrationalism in the emergence of Hitler to power in 1933.

Friedrich Wilhelm Nietzsche (1844–1900)

Implicit in all of the thinkers thus far considered was a revolt against historic Christianity. Some concealed their repudiation in terms so general and non-specific that many in Europe and in this country were, at best, but faintly aware of the deeper revolution which was taking place in philosophic thought. Some were very explicit in their repudiation of the Christian position, but they were largely regarded in their own day as being outside of the mainstream of thought and somewhat eccentric, hardly representative of the more serious school of philosophic inquiry. But Nietzsche made it virtually impossible for those who harbored those comforting illusions to hold fast to such an optimism. He brought into full focus the naked implications lurking just beneath the surface of this drift in Western thought. Although Friedrich Wilhelm Nietzsche was descended from a long line of Lutheran ministers, the Christian legacy seemed to have little influence on his own intellectual development, and it soon passed from the picture completely. He was a student of Albert Ritschl, a colleague of Jacob Burckhardt at Basel, and for a time he was an admirer of Richard Wagner. In his early years, his so-called Romantic Era, he was greatly influenced by Schopenhauer.

Quite soon the charm which these apostles of irrationalism had for the young scholar was eradicated in his conclusion that they were not suited as vehicles for his own cultural and intellectual development and were no better suited for the great needs of the development of the German people. They were entirely inadequate for what he regarded as the one great age of German cultural development, the age of *Sturm* and *Drang*.

This growing dissatisfaction with these early influences in no way shook his basic addiction to irrationalism, and neither did it lead him back to his Lutheran heritage. Rather did it drive him to seek a new foundation for his own intellectual development. This search led him to renounce the culture of his own day. He even came to the conclusion that the culture which he found in the Germany of the latter part of the nineteenth century was not equal to that which characterized the nation one hundred years earlier. He attributed this decline in spirit to the triumph of the bourgeois with its emphasis on the mass man and the resulting triumph of cultural mediocrity on the one hand, enslaving and debasing in its impact, and of Christian morality on the other.

From this impasse Nietzsche could find only one escape, and that was a return to Greek culture, particularly to the Greek sense of tragedy. In this he professed to find a value of enduring worth. He despised what he felt was the Christian negation of life on this earth and its insistence that the real goal of mankind is an after life. In place of this debilitating ethic Nietzsche argued for the Greek concept of the hero, by which he meant the heroic resolve to create his own world in defiance of the gods. Nietzsche concluded that Goethe and Napoleon were the closest representatives of this Greek view of life in nineteenth-century Europe, but they left no enduring influence on the cultural development of Europe because of the rise of the bourgeois mass man. These themes constitute the essence of his earlier works, *The Birth of Tragedy* (1872) and *Untimely Thoughts* (1873–1878).

However, the culmination of his thought is found in *Thus Spake Zarathustra* (1883–1891), *Beyond Good and Evil* (1886), and *The Genealogy of Morals* (1887). In these works the basic themes of his mature thoughts are brought out with great vigor and clarity: the death of God and the resulting destruction of all values found in historic Christianity, the insistence on the recognition of the will to power as the basic principle of all life, the doctrine of eternal recurrence, and the ideal of the Superman.

In these basic themes Nietzsche is really the unabashed irrationalist, flaunting his convictions before the world and giving full vent to his repudiation of any Christian values. Some have valiantly argued that we must understand Nietzsche's frame of mind in his purposes in making these pronouncements. It is true that a writer must always be studied in this light, but the assumption that, if we study Nietzsche in such a context, we will by understanding come to an appreciation of, if not agreement with, his position must fall by the wayside, by the weight of its own inherent anti-intellectualism. When he speaks for himself, he leaves no doubt as to his purposes in writing as he did. In Nietzsche the floods of humanism let loose on Western Europe by the Renaissance have broken through the dams that had been able to hold them somewhat in check until his day. Since then they have been over-running European and American thought in a veritable deluge which is almost, if not completely, out of control. The rationalism of the early humanists has now become destructive irrationalism, so violent and devastating in its character that to express it is to do violence to its nihilism. The irrationalism of the later nineteenth century was now devouring the rationalism which gave it birth.

The style which Nietzsche employed in *Thus Spake Zarathustra* makes quoting him very difficult. The entire work is suffused with irrationalism and an accompanying nihilism. Explicit in his basic outlook is the denial of God as revealed in the Scriptures. He insisted that the history of mankind is the continuous story of the human attempt to create values, but these values have been false, even as his attempts to create a god.

> Once people did say God, when they looked out upon distant seas; now, however, have I taught you to say, Superman. God is a con-

> jecture: but I do not wish your conjecturing to reach beyond your creating will.
>
> Could ye create a God?—Then, I pray you, be silent about all Gods! But ye could well create the Superman. . . . God is a conjecture: but I should like your conjecturing restricted to the conceivable.
>
> Could ye conceive a God?—But let this mean Will to Truth unto you, that everything be transformed into the humanly conceivable, the humanly visible, the humanly sensible! Your own discernment shall ye follow out to the end! . . . But that I may reveal my heart entirely unto you, my friends; if there were Gods, how could I endure it to be no God! Therefore there are no Gods.[2]

However, this vacuum which Nietzsche created for himself and for those who could accept his nihilism, was in itself unsatisfactory. No more than nature could his philosophy (if it can be called that) tolerate such an emptiness and dreariness. In its place he became a creator of sorts, and so he could write:

> But so willeth it my creating Will, my fate. Or to tell you more if candidly: just such a fate—willeth my Will. . . . Willing emancipateth: that is the true doctrine of will and emancipation. . . . No longer willing and no longer valuing, and no longer creating! Ah, that that great debility may ever be far from me! And also in discerning do I feel only my will's procreating and evolving delight; and if there be innocence in my knowledge, it is because there is will to procreation in it. Away from God and Gods did this will allure me; what would there be to create if there were—Gods! But to man doth it ever impel me anew, my fervent creative will; thus impelleth it the hammer to the stone. Ah, ye men, within the stone slumbereth an image for me, the image of my visions! Ah, that it should slumber in the hardest, ugliest stone! Now rageth my hammer ruthlessly against its prison. From the stone fly the fragments: what's that to me? I will complete it: for a shadow came unto me—the stillest and lightest of all things once came unto me! The beauty of the superman came unto me as a shadow. Ah, my brethren! Of what account now are—the Gods to me![3]

While his study may leave much to be desired as he speaks in ambiguous and uncertain language, one thing is very clear: Nietzsche had replaced the God of Christianity with a god of his own creativity—the Superman.

The anti-intellectual aspects of Nietzsche's thought were neither accidental nor unknown to him. He boldly declared his basic convictions at this point:

---

2. Friedrich Nietzsche, *Thus Spake Zarathustra,* tr. Thomas Common, Modern Library edition (New York, n.d.), pp. 97, 98.

3. Ibid., pp. 99, 100.

> . . . I must tell myself the following: the largest part of conscious thinking must be considered an instinctual activity, even in the case of philosophical thinking. We must simply re-learn, as we have to re-learn about heredity and "inborn" qualities. As little as the act of birth is of consequence in the whole process and progress of heredity, so little is consciousness in any decisive sense opposed to instinct. Most of the conscious thinking of a philosopher is secretly guided by his instincts and forced along certain lines.[4]

Any lingering doubts about Nietzsche's intent should be banished by this frank declaration in regard to the meaning of thought. Thought is not conceptual in nature; it is not the result of a conscious effort to discern meaning in creation or human life. It is instinctive and void of any real meaningful content. Nietzsche took great pains to leave no doubt as to the meaning of his position at this point:

> No matter from what philosophic point of vantage one looks today . . . the fallaciousness of the world in which we think we live is the firmest and most certain sight that meets our eye.[5]

Neither did he shrink from bringing ethics and morality within the scope of his system. He placed them firmly within the scaffolding of his relativism.

> "My judgment is my judgment, to which hardly anyone else has a right," is what the philosopher of the future will say. One must get rid of the bad taste of wishing to agree with many others. "Good" is no longer in the mouth of my neighbor. And how could there be a "common good"! The expression contradicts itself: what can be common cannot have much value.[6]

In his *Beyond Good and Evil* Nietzsche used this negation of Christian morality as a prelude to his main assault on the traditional system of ethics which Europe had derived from the Scriptures and an unrelenting assault upon Christianity in general.

> To love mankind for God's sake has up to now been the most distinguished and far-fetched feeling that mankind has reached. That love for mankind, without some sanctifying reservation, is only one more stupidity and brutishness, that the impulse to such love must first get its proportion, its delicacy, its grain of salt and dash of ambergris from a higher impulse. . . .[7]

Declaring that all moralities are but a symbolic language of passion,

---

4. Friedrich Wilhelm Nietzsche, *Beyond Good and Evil,* tran. Marianne Cowan (Chicago: Regnery, 1955), p. 3.
5. Ibid., p. 40.
6. Ibid., p. 48.
7. Ibid., pp. 66-67.

Nietzsche insisted that they are at the same time a work of tyranny against nature and against "reason." Nevertheless, he also admitted that in these moralities, even in the Christian morality, which he called gruesome, there was some value—

> all this violence, arbitrariness, rigor, gruesomeness and anti-irrationality turned out to be the means for disciplining the European spirit into strength, ruthless inquisitiveness, and subtle flexibility.[8]

But this apparent value was offset by the harmful results of such a process of discipline.

To offset the danger, Nietzsche called for the emergence of "the philosopher of the future," declaring that the time for petty politics was over; the twentieth century will bring with it the struggle for world dominion, the compulsion to high politics.

Nietzsche was in reality seeking for an antidote to the poison which he rightly felt had emerged and spread over much of Europe as a result of the French Revolution. Looking with horror upon that movement and the socialism and communism which had issued forth from it, he was seeking for a remedy which would restore order and tranquility to Europe. However, his correct insight into the nature of the problem did not bring to him the answer to the problem. It could not be otherwise, for Nietzsche suffered from the same infection—the rejection of biblical Christianity.

He did not like the European culture of the day, but he had nothing to offer in the way of a solution. To decry and banish the Christian ethic from the scene was to intensify the very problem he was seeking to solve. To declare the death of God was to proclaim the inevitable death of all cultural achievements and to destroy the possibility of any cultural development in the future. To offset the mediocratization of man, which he had seen in the emergence of democracy and the herd, Nietzsche had nothing to offer but the will to power and the emergence of the superman. For this reason he did much to bring about the chaos which he foresaw to be the nightmare of the twentieth century.

We can appreciate Nietzsche's insights into the European mind of his own day and the tendencies which lay thinly concealed just below the veneer of its cultural achievements, but just as strongly must we insist that his rejection of historic Christianity gave an added impetus to the trend already in progress toward sheer nihilism in the intellectual life of the West and the inescapable emergence of totalitarianism as a furious but futile effort to escape from the political and social chaos which necessarily ac-

8. Ibid., p. 99.

companies such a philosophy. There is no more fitting epitaph for any analysis of the thought of Nietzsche than that penned by John Hallowell: "In Nietzsche the tortured soul of modern man is laid bare for all to see."[9] In the loss of Christian faith we see the death of a civilization, and Nietzsche's works are a literary casket in which Western man may behold his cultural self ready for burial.

However, it must not be supposed that Nietzsche stood alone in preparing for the final demise of Western man. Such a mighty event could not be brought about by an unstable mind such as his. This Western mind had been long in the making. There had been many contributors from Augustine through to the Reformers, who, building upon the foundations laid in the Scriptures, had diligently sought to erect an inellectual and cultural cathedral on those magnificent foundations. This structure would not, and could not, collapse overnight; it would require the systematic and prolonged efforts of many enemies of the faith to achieve this goal. The efforts of the eighteenth-century thinkers, in conjunction with those of the nineteenth, had made great headway in their determination to destroy the cultural products of Christian theism as it had been guiding the mind of Europe for over a thousand years. But the deists and the philosophers such as Kant, Hegel, Darwin, Marx, and Wagner had also made significant strides in this direction. Not even their advance toward irrationalism could be permanent or complete without the efforts of their successors in the areas of theology, psychology, sociology, and political and economic thought. It required a massive onslaught by all of these various academic disciplines to bring to fruition the efforts of these earlier apostles of anti-intellectualism and irrationalism. In due season these apostolic successors rose to meet the challenge of the hour. This is not to imply that philosophers, in the more restricted sense of the term, did not continue to hammer away at the foundations of certain knowledge—far from it. They were joined in these efforts by a new breed of scholars in these other disciplines who were equally zealous in producing a world and life view, a *Weltanschauung,* which would be thoroughly humanistic and naturalistic in its outlook and totally opposed to the norms of Scripture. Thus, we must turn our attention to these sources of irrationalism, for it was in the area of the "special sciences" that irrationalism made a new and significant impact upon Western life. No longer was it chiefly confined to the area of philosophical speculation with only occasional sorties into the political, eco-

9. John Hamilton Hallowell, *Main Currents in Modern Political Thought* (New York, 1963), p. 550.

nomic, and social realms. With a devastating and frightening rush it gained not only a foothold, but almost a sweeping victory in these other areas of intellectual activity which boded ill for the future of Western civilization.

John Stuart Mill (1806–1873)

Along with Herbert Spencer in England, John Stuart Mill reflects post-Darwinian emphases in his thought. It has well been said that Mill was much more than a philosopher; he was indeed a radical reformer, a thinker who translated his basic philosophy into channels for social, economic, and political activity. He is therefore a very important figure in the long journey which the Western mind has taken in the direction towards its ultimate decline and very possible demise.

Mill pursued philosophy as a proper field of study not for the sake of philosophy alone, but for thc application of such knowledge to the advancement of human welfare. In his thinking there could be no such purpose as philosophy for philosophy's sake. It was the pursuit of philosophy for the sake of humanity.

Mill was a utilitarian, a follower of Jeremy Bentham. Utilitarianism was a particular form of empirical thought which stressed the utility, the usefulness of philosophical knowledge in the improvement of the human condition. In turn, this meant in essence "the greatest happiness for the greatest number of people." In practice, for John Stuart Mill and for those in his school of thought in Victorian England, the practical application of this goal was to be realized in the reform of the English legal system, a new or improved theory of representation based on the major utilitarian premise, the channeling of economic theories into a systematic academic discipline, the abolition of all legal restraints upon trade and labor, and the substitution of a utilitarian doctrine of morality in place of the biblical ethic. Along with these major goals he also insisted upon a reform of the educational system of Victorian England into an instrument which would promote, rather than hinder, the achievement of his major aims. Mill regarded science and the scientific frame of reference as the necessary replacement for the earlier religious or Christian outlook. He was a follower of August Comte, but it is also true that he sought to soften or modify some of Comte's more revolutionary and radical demands and fit them into a frame of reference which would make them more acceptable to the English mind. As a pragmatist he was solidly in the English tradition springing from John Locke and had sought to adapt the principles of Comte to this tradition.

Basic to Mill's thinking was the assumption of human benevolence. This assumption, which denied the biblical doctrine of original sin and total depravity, placed a great deal of emphasis upon the innate goodness of man and held that when men sought their freedom and welfare they were at the same time promoting these for society as a whole. Thus Mill, along with other members of his school, placed great emphasis upon human liberty. It was for this reason that he demanded the abolition of restrictive laws on labor organizations. It is obvious that in holding to these assumptions Mill was not original, but was greatly influenced by Bentham, who in turn was deeply indebted to both John Locke and Hume. The essentially good man will use his freedom not only for his own improvement, but for that of society as a whole.

In his essay on utilitarianism, Mill launched a strong attack on all previous ethical systems. He insisted that both the intuitive and the inductive approaches were essentially the same as to the content of the systems they had erected. Their difference lay in the approach. He concluded that both schools held that morality must be deduced from certain basic principles to which they each gave allegiance. He indicted them for their failure to make out a list of those principles which must serve as the basis for the science of ethics.

In place of these faulty approaches to ethical and moral problems, Mill advanced his own ethical theory in his *Utility,* or *The Greatest Happiness Principle,* and defined it as that theory which holds that "actions are right in proportion as they tend to promote happiness, wrong as they tend to produce the reverse of happiness."[10]

Mill further defines happiness as pleasure and the absence of pain. Unhappiness, then, was the presence of pain and the privation of happiness. To the student of the history of philosophy this theory sounds strangely like that of the Epicureans, and Mill was not unaware of the strong resemblance. His reply to the charge was that he did not hold them faultless in drawing out their basic conclusions.

> But there is no known Epicurean theory of life which does not assign to pleasures of the intellect, of the feelings and of the imagination, and of the moral sentiments, a much higher value as pleasures than those of mere sensation.[11]

To further defend himself against the charges frequently hurled against this theory of pleasure, Mill replied that utilitarians, although they have

10. J. S. Mill, *Utilitarianism: Liberty and Representative Government* (New York, 1951), p. 3.
11. Ibid., p. 9.

fully proved their case, could have taken a higher ground.

> It is quite compatible with the principle of utility to recognize the fact, that some kinds of pleasure are more desirable than others. It would be absurd that while, in estimating all other things, quality is considered as well as quantity, the estimation of pleasures should be supposed to depend on quantity alone.[12]

Mill then went on to insist that he did not mean that a greater pleasure was greater because of its amount, but in respect to its quality, because it employs the higher faculties of mankind. Not only in the use of the term "higher faculties" did Mill betray the weakness of his own position, but he made further concessions to the traditional Christian outlook when he spoke of "lower" and "higher goods." Utilitarians, relying on the empirical approach of Locke and Bentham, could not with any degree of consistency make use of such a terminology, since the empirical epistemology cannot possibly yield any knowledge of either good or evil. His empiricism rested upon assumptions which were his by common grace, and he was using, as it were, God's own values, which did not have any place in his system. He had no right to use them, in view of the fact that he flouted his own unbelief in the teachings of Scripture. In fact, he openly denied the doctrine of original sin. In his discussion of utilitarianism he insisted that there was absolutely no reason why men should not, through the beneficent influence of culture, seek the higher things of life.

> Now there is absolutely no reason in the nature of things why an amount of mental culture sufficient to give an intelligent interest in these objects of contemplation should not be in the inheritance of everyone born in a civilized country. As little as there is an inherent necessity that any human being should be a selfish egotist, devoid of every feeling or care, but those which center in his own miserable individuality.[13]

Cultural evolution would come to the aid of what Mill had in mind. Of this he had no doubt.

Something far superior to this is sufficiently common, even now, to give ample earnest of what the human species may be made. His optimism concerning the happy future of the human race knew almost no bounds. He described it in terms which sound like a contemporary politician appealing for votes.

> Yet no one whose opinion deserves a moment's consideration can doubt that most of the great positive evils of the world are in them-

12. Ibid., pp. 10-11.
13. Ibid., p. 18.

> selves removeable, and will, if human affairs continue to improve, be in the end reduced within narrow limits. Poverty in any sense implying suffering may be completely extinguished by the wisdom of society, combined with the good sense and providence of individuals. . . . As for vicissitudes of fortune and other disappointments connected with worldly circumstances these are principally the effect either of gross imprudence, of ill-regulated desires, or of bad or imperfect social institutions.[14]

It is obvious that the main thrust of this whole outlook is humanistic in its origin and sanctions. But Mill did not dismiss the idea of a divine influence as being of no consequence. He was too Victorian to set forth such a conclusion. He did, however, greatly limit his role in human affairs and reduce it to a secondary role at best, even though he readily admitted a certain influence of religion on the moral life.

> With regard to the religious motive, if men believe, as most profess to do, in the goodness of God, those who think that conduciveness to the general happiness is the essence, or even only the criterion of good, must necessarily believe that it is also which God approves.[15]

However theistic this statement may sound, it is essentially humanistic. Mill is simply stating the case in religious terms. And the case is this: He is asking God to approve what most men feel to be right. In his thinking God is to be called upon as an ally to reinforce the decisions which man has already made. Mill gave expression to this humanistic assumption in language that was somewhat varnished, but the meaning is quite clear.

> The ultimate sanction therefore, of all morality (external motives apart), being a subjective feeling in our own minds, I see nothing embarrassing to those whose standard is utility, in the question, what is the sanction in that particular standard?[16]

In this position Mill not only asserted a rampant individualism in the creation of ethical and moral standards, but opened the door to sheer anarchy in political, economic, and social activity. Such was not his intent because he also believed in a moral consensus within society, but his logic was against him, and his utilitarianism fell into the hands of those who were much less influenced by the current Victorian mood then reigning in England and who were quite ready to put his logic into practice.

These dangerous trends inherent in Mill's utilitarianism were evident in his own social theory and practice. He was conscious of certain problems in his own philosophy and in the political life of Victorian England, and he treated one of the most important of these in his famous *Essay on Liberty.*

---

14. Ibid.
15. Ibid., p. 34.
16. Ibid., p. 35.

In this often quoted work, Mill admitted that the majority in any given society can become a tyranny and that individuals need protection against such a tyranny. Now we must admit the truth of such a contention. But it is at variance with the position which he set forth in his *Essay on Utilitarianism,* in which he upheld the theory of the benevolence of men in general and that this widespread benevolence would lead the great majority of men to seek that which was best for society at large. In his *Essay on Liberty,* in his Introduction, he laid down the principle which underlay his whole approach to human liberty:

> The principle that the sole end for which mankind are warranted individually or collectively, in interfering with the liberty of action of any of their number is self protection. That the only purpose for which power can be rightfully exercised over any member of a civilized community against his will, is to prevent harm to others. His own good, either physical or moral, is not a sufficient warrant. He cannot rightly be compelled to do or forbear because it will make him happier, because, in the opinion of others, to do so would not be wise or even right.[17]

In assuming such a position and definition of liberty Mill has seriously departed from the biblical norm and entered into the broad plain of empirical morality. It is a view of liberty which took no account of sin against either the public or an individual. To define liberty in this restricted and unbiblical sense could only result in the ultimate destruction of the liberty he was seeking to preserve.

To Mill such an ultimate consequence of his position was unthinkable, not in the sense that he was unaware of such a remote possibility, but in the sense that he felt that his evolutionary optimism would prevent such a catastrophe.

> As mankind improves, the number of doctrines which are no longer disputed or doubted will be constantly on the increase; and the well-being of mankind may almost be measured by the number and greatness of such truths which have reached the point of being uncontested.[18]

Obviously in such a millennial state as Mill here described, this approaching universal agreement on great and greater number of truths could not lead to anything but harmonious society in which neither anarchy on the one hand, nor tyranny on the other, would prevail.

It is also obvious that this entire discussion by Mill overlooked essential Christian doctrines on man's duty to God and to himself, the sinful condition of the race, and offers in place of these basic Christian beliefs a humanistic view of the nature of man and the ability of education to remove those obstacles to the achievement of that kind of society of which

17. Ibid., pp. 95-96.

18. Ibid., p. 137.

he dreamed and which he believed to be very possible.

Mill was guilty of adapting for his own purposes those Christian ethical concepts which his epistemology banished from the scene. He was also guilty of using the biblical ethic in an illegal and illogical manner to adorn his humanism with a goal which it could not possibly achieve in the light of its presuppositions. Thus, once again, we see that rationalism in its empirical form, has as its correlative an irrationalism which is studded with contradictions of his own making and for which Mill had no satisfactory or convincing answer.

The inadequacies of Mill's ethical position become even more painfully evident when we see him as he would apply them to the social conditions of his day. In his discussion of the application of his general position he leads the reader through a maze of doubtful and even contradictory solutions. Trying to safeguard society from actions which he deemed to be harmful to its best interests, Mill struggled with the question of how to locate this protection of society within his framework of the supreme task of protecting individual liberty. Here, we are led into a series of propositions in regard to the correctness of governmental action in defense of society and of the liberty of the individual, which are both an invitation to social and economic anarchy on the one hand, and an invitation to extreme governmental action on the other, far beyond that permitted by the Scriptures. In short, we have in John Stuart Mill a blueprint, even though its outlines be faint and blurred at times, of a modern socialistic totalitarianism such as that which has most of Western Europe and Great Britain in its grip and now threatens to overthrow what is left of the American Constitution and tradition of Christian liberty. The very threat or realization of that kind of anarchy which Mill invited constitutes an invitation for a severe reaction by which society seeks to protect itself against the anarchy and licentiousness inherent in the kind of social and economic philosophy which has its roots in the thinking of Mill.

The history of Europe in the twentieth century is largely the story of the ebb and flow of its political life between these two extremes, with little possibility of the recovery of its Christian heritage of political, social, and economic thought. For the political and economic thought of Europe since the day of Mill has become largely the account of the triumph of revolutionary thought into every area of Western intellectual activity.

The Concept of Liberty in Europe During the Nineteenth Century

This is a most important consideration for the understanding of the social, economic, and political trends in contemporary Europe and the

United States. The whole problem of liberty cannot be understood apart from its philosophical context. The doctrine of liberty underwent a tremendous change after the French Revolution. This change has penetrated deeply into twentieth-century thought and affected the political, economic, and social development of the West down to this day.

Although liberty or freedom is basically a theological concept and is deeply imbedded in the biblical doctrine of God and man, it has, nevertheless, been the continuing concern of philosophers who have endeavored to state a satisfactory definition in terms other than those found in the Scriptures. The biblical doctrine of freedom has always been, and will continue to be, repugnant to the unbelieving mind and anathema to secular humanism. It is for this very reason that we in this volume must devote some attention to one of the most glorious aspects of the Christian faith and, when rightly understood, one of the most important constituent parts of the life of the human mind.

As a result of the impact of the French Revolution, the older definitions of liberty gave way to new concepts, which were forged on the anvils of evolutionary thought and activity and by those philosophers who, for the most part, were intent on banishing the Scriptures and the God of the Scriptures from the human scene. It is for this reason that the upheaval in France from 1789 to 1815 not only shattered the old political regimes and gave birth to the modern European states, but at the same time bestowed on freedom a new meaning commonly bandied back and forth under the slogan "liberty, equality, and fraternity."

This popular slogan, containing the seeds of the destruction of liberty and equality, could only mean the destruction of liberty, even as it was understood by the leaders of the French Revolution and their contemporaries in both Europe and America. Whatever understanding of the term "liberty" may have lingered on during the eighteenth century, it could not survive the continued misuse of it by both philosophers and the militant revolutionists who brought a series of tumultous upheavals to the first fifty years of nineteenth-century Europe and which were in turn superseded by a half century of warfare and political reconstruction. The appearance of a new type of nationalism boded ill for both the peace of Europe and the frail tree of liberty which had managed somehow to survive the revolutionary movements of the first half of the century and the wars of the second half.

The Background of the Concept of Liberty or Freedom

The concept of freedom or liberty was by no means the invention of the philosophy of the seventeenth and eighteenth centuries. It did not spring forth from the philosophic systems of the rationalists or the empiricists like John Locke. Its roots were much more deeply imbedded in the intellectual soil of Europe than the leaders of the eighteenth-century revolutions dared to admit. The European doctrine of freedom had its roots in Christianity rather than in the classical thought of Greece and Rome. It did not wither on the vine during the Middle Ages, as the advocates of the Natural Rights school of thought and the Enlightenment fondly believed, but it had an amazing strength, as many of the students of the history of the Middle Ages have strikingly proved beyond dispute. Indeed, the basic ingredients of English constitutionalism and common law were deeply imbedded in the structure of feudalism. These seeds of liberty were given new nourishment and encouragement by the theological developments of the Reformation. John Calvin and Martin Luther gave this doctrine a theological foundation which has enabled it to survive the constant attacks of the naturalists and secularists over the past four centuries.

However firm these foundations undoubtedly were, they were not sufficiently strong to ward off the erosion which resulted from the ceaseless tidal waves of humanistic onslaughts. As the nineteenth century wore on, the results of the humanistic and naturalistic opposition to the biblical doctrine of freedom became increasingly evident.

At first glance, it would seem almost impossible for the staunch defense of liberty as it had been set forth by such writers as Locke and his followers, in both Europe and the United States, to fail and for their conception of liberty to beget contemporary tyranny. An understanding of the philosophical developments after Locke as they have been traced in the preceding chapters offers the background for such an understanding. But they do not discuss liberty as such, nor do they attempt to delineate its decline as a result of these philosophical movements.

Ruggerio was quite correct when he insisted that Reason and her radical admirers of the latter part of the eighteenth century offered a new path for the supporters of freedom to follow, a new path which appeared much more satisfactory in their eyes because it called for the "rational reconstruction of the state in accordance with the indefeasible demands of the individual." In effect this liberal view of freedom which emerged as a result of the rise of the Natural Law philosophy became democratic in its political emphasis and Ruggerio suggested that this trend became quite evident in Rousseau in his Social Contract theory.[19] There is certainly this emphasis

19. Guido De Ruggerio, *History of European Liberalism*, p. 61.

in Rousseau's Social Contract theory, but at the same time there are in his political thought the seeds of totalitarianism or at least, a democratic absolutism. His introduction of the concept of the general will was not only a rather significant departure from Locke, but an equally important step toward a democratic despotism, and the resulting liberty was of very questionable worth. Even more than Locke, Rousseau denied any biblical standards for human individual conduct and for the guidance of political activity. As a result, there is in Rousseau's political philosophy an irrationalism which appeared as the necessary correlative of his rationalism.

For this reason it remains true, however, that although Rousseau may have proclaimed his devotion to liberty and human rights, the basic assumptions on which he built his political philosophy seriously undermined not only the biblical, but also the Lockean view of freedom. His general will could, by no stretch of the imagination, be a satisfactory replacement for the sovereign will of the God of the Scriptures. The freedom which Rousseau offered to his day was both a faint and a ghastly caricature of that doctrine found in the Scriptures.

For both the eighteenth and the nineteenth centuries the biblical view of freedom, as it had been forged by Calvin and his colleagues, was very distasteful. The Enlightenment view of liberty was founded on the doctrine of the natural law. Against this view the Reformers had championed the view of the servitude of the will to a sovereign God as the only source of true freedom for man. Beginning with Descartes, this view began to recede into the background of European thought, and by the time of the Enlightenment it had very little hold on the intellectuals of that day.

Locke and his followers claimed the inviolability of human personality as the essence of true freedom, and this concept furnished the basis for Kantian and post-Kantian definitions of human freedom. The Lockean reliance on natural rights as a basis for freedom provided a very unstable foundation for the preservation of human rights, and Ruggerio is quite correct in his insistence that the eighteenth-century view of property as a natural right logically led to a denial of this right. Communism was equally logical when Marx and his followers, using Locke's epistemology, turned Locke against himself.[20]

The radicals of the French Revolution had already used Locke for this purpose when they sequestered the property of those conservatives who opposed their frantic efforts to bring in a new order. Ruggerio also performs a very valuable service when he sets forth the logic of the French *Declara-*

20. Ibid., p. 27.

tion of the Rights of Man and shows it actually contained the germ of three revolutions: the liberal, the democratic, and the social revolutions which ushered in socialistic and communistic regimes.[21]

Locke's empirical epistemology actually destroyed any possibility of a meaningful defense of human rights because it rested upon the negation of any innate ideas, including the conscience. Without an *a priori* recognition of his duty to God, man has no real consciousness of his rights and no philosophical defense to use in their behalf against the onslaughts which the radicals of the French Revolution, their successors, and Karl Marx used against them. Locke's empiricism was the Achilles heel of the whole philosophy of natural rights and the rights of human freedom. The consistent failure of non-biblical libertarianism, from Burke on, to offer an effective defense of human freedom should be sufficiently convincing of the folly of such efforts.

As a result of the impact of Descartes, deism, and Locke on historic Christian orthodoxy, the doctrine of liberty or freedom as it emerged in the hands of the leaders of both the American and French Revolutions was in a precarious condition. Deeply tinged with the irrationalism inherent in the philosophy of Natural Rights, it lacked sufficient theological vigor to sustain itself against the attacks which it met during the nineteenth and twentieth centuries. Weakened by the inherent contradictions within this political philosophy and the relativism which it must logically engender in the thinking of those who accept it, freedom has become the vanishing human right over the past two centuries and with it the rights to life and property and, in a curious way, the right to marriage. This right has not been denied to those who wish to enter into such a union, but it is no longer really deemed necessary. The increasing use of divorce to release people from the marriage vows is in essence a denial of the meaning of the institution as even Locke viewed it.

We have seen that Kant directed a masterful assault against the empirical tradition as it emerged from the attacks of Hume, but Kant was unable to save human freedom from that determinism which had undermined it in the Natural Rights framework. Kant placed freedom in the unknowable realm of the noumenal. He made it very clear that in his view individual actions were determined by the impersonal forces at work in the determination of all of human history, and thus there could be no true freedom for man in the world in which he lived. In his brief treatise on universal history, Kant insisted that human actions are determined by Nature rather than by the laws or by the will of God. Yet in spite of this openly avowed

21. Ibid., p. 69.

determinism, Kant at the same time defined human freedom as the right and ability of man to make his own laws according to his own nature. Man, for Kant, had achieved an inward theology which assumed the complete sovereignty of man to fashion his own historical destiny. Man, determined by the laws of nature in the phenomenal world, is somehow free to order his own historical development. This is the same impasse which haunted Kant at every step in the development of his philosophy and which ultimately reduced his rationalism into a maze of irrationalism.

Although the concept of liberalism and freedom developed along different lines in Europe during the nineteenth century, these differing patterns converged along remarkably similar lines in the twentieth century. Essentially by 1800 the problem was the same in all of the major nations of Europe: how to find a reconciliation between the extreme individualism of Locke and the advocates of natural law, and the needs of society. In England liberalism moved more or less steadily toward collectivism and giving to the state a greater role in the regulation of industry while, at the same time through the Reform Acts beginning in 1832, it extended to the people a greater share in the electoral process. Much the same pattern emerged in France. However, the revolutionary process was used in 1830 and 1848 to achieve similar goals. Saint Simon turned to socialistic collectivism in an effort to escape from the effects of an untrammeled and undisciplined individualism which he felt was threatening French society. His utopia would come through the agency of a state democratically controlled. In such a democratic absolutism individualism would somehow be preserved and liberty maintained. On the other hand, Fourier, equally fervent in his quest for a utopia, distrusted the state and chose other means for the achievement of his goal. The quest for freedom in both France and England left the prized human possession in dire jeopardy by the end of the first half of the twentieth century in both of the countries. Democracy proved to be an unfaithful vehicle for the preservation of liberty.

In Germany there was a different intellectual development, a somewhat different development of a philosophy of freedom in the nineteenth century after Kant, but the Kantian influence was clearly evident in the later development and an absolutism of a different kind emerged, partly as a result of the earlier development, both philosophical and political, in eighteenth century Germany, and partly because of the continuing impact of the irrationalism inherent in Kantian thought. As a result, neither German political conservatism nor German philosophical and theological liberals were able to safeguard the doctrine of liberty as it had been preached by Kant, Fichte, and Hegel.

Kant based his view of the role of the state on his distinction between pure and practical reason, and assigned the state to the realm of practical reason. Accordingly, he was able to draw a further distinction between legality and morality and assigned to the state the area of legality, but denied that it had anything to do with morality, which he had placed in the area of the noumenal. This solution, of course, in turn created a serious problem. If the state had nothing to do with morals, which is only the concern of the individual conscience, how can either the state or society survive if the individual conscience is the arbiter of moral problems. The German idealists, and their counterparts in other countries, felt that they had solved the issue by introducing the nation as the limit between their individualism on the one hand, and the state as an organ of government and law, on the other. Thus, in Germany this liberalism was made into a vehicle for the expression of a national interest or destiny which, in turn destroyed the essence of liberty as liberals had long understood it.

For Hegel the state became the expression of rationality; it is the world become spirit. It is freedom in the fullness of its realization; this is true because, at the same time, it is the incarnation of reason and liberty. Because the state is the incarnation of reason, it is possessed of a divine character which allowed Hegel's state to absorb the church. He insisted that this must be the case since the state has a more perfect form than the church. In a somewhat paradoxical discussion Hegel also held that the state understands that the freedom of the church is essential to its achievement of a fuller rationality.

In a very interesting discussion of European concepts in the nineteenth century, Ruggerio offered a very valuable insight, which actually betrays the very development of which he is speaking. He insisted that liberty is necessarily a formal concept to prevent liberties from degenerating into privileges and monopolies, but, at the same time, liberties are necessary for the continued existence of liberty. These liberties provide the content for the formal concept of liberty without which it is empty and meaningless.[22]

Although an advocate of democracy and liberalism, Ruggerio is no blind follower of this twentieth century. He was quite conscious of the fact that the liberal state is prone to change its character as the worship of the state as an institution. He professed to see the seed of such a danger in Rousseau's political thought. But the real foundation for this development is very evident in Hegel. Ruggerio was also acutely aware of the in-

22. Ibid., p. 349.

herent dangers in Rousseau's general will, and he went so far as to write that the "democratic state is the result of depriving people of their rights conferring those rights upon a general, indivisible sovereign people—the will of the numerical majority."[23] Thus a dangerous tyranny is created in which both the majority and the minority become its victims. Ruggerio, with penetrating insight, comes to the conclusion that such a liberal state ultimately creates slavery of the soul as well as of the body. The result is a modern totalitarian regime in which the state as such is worshiped. The state thus becomes a man-made god of some kind and assumes a species of divinity. To refuse to bow before this humanly created divinity becomes, in turn, a political heresy or treason punishable by exile or death, according to the whims of those in power.

We need to look at the history of Germany, Russia, and Italy in the twentieth century to see examples of this development. We also need to remember that this country is not exempt, and the liberalism which has taken over since 1933 has become a religion of sorts which seeks to crowd Christianity out from the courts, the schools, and the public life and replace it with a civil religion instead, in which the state would become a kind of god or democracy, and as an abstraction would be worshiped as it is found in a centralized bureaucratic federal machine.

Darwinian Liberty

It must not be assumed that the only danger to true freedom in our day has arisen from the insidious attacks of German idealism as against the Christian view. The continuous philosophical onslaught has undeniably exacted great toll on the political and economic and social freedom of Western man. Nevertheless, the emergence of mechanistic views of nature found in Lamarck, Comte, and the French materialists of the latter part of the nineteenth century has added passionate fury to such attacks. It is even doubtfult that they, along with the idealists, could have achieved such a victory in Western thought if it had not been for Darwin, who popularized the preceding evolutionary scientists and, at the same time, gave added strength to the evolutionary philosophy of Hegel and his successors. Such biological theories as the unconscious transmission of acquired characteristics, and the survival of the fittest, rest upon a deterministic view of nature and natural law. Although some have claimed that Darwin himself was not a determinist, the weight of evidence is against such a position, and it seems to be well established that Darwin began his voyage on the *Beagle*

---

23. Ibid., p. 375.

to find the necessary evidence to reenforce a deterministic view of the processes of biological evolution.[24] There can be no doubt that, whatever purpose Darwin may have had in mind, determinism as the dominant principle in nature received his blessing and became the standard orthodox interpretation of his theory. The very fact that John Fiske, and other scholars, found it necessary to combat this widely held interpretation should be sufficient evidence that Darwinism was believed to rule out any divine role in the unfolding of the process of evolution. It is also interesting to note that orthodox evolutionists ridiculed these efforts to give evolution a theistic frame of reference.[25]

Professor James Hyslop of Columbia University voiced the inherent contradiction most succinctly in an article written over seventy years ago, and it is as true today as it was then. Contending that the theory of evolution did not justify the assumption of an intelligent background and purpose behind the universe, he wrote:

> The struggle of modern philosophy to make its peace with both orthodoxy and skepticism is one of the most amazing and one of the most amusing and at the same time one of the most irritating and exasperating events in the history of thought. The agnostic who is trying to appropriate the language of the orthodox party and at the same time to repudiate his ideas is simply inviting the accusation either of insincerity or of ignorance of his problem.[26]

The later development of evolution as a frame of reference for Western thought, as a *Weltanschauung,* clearly reveals the fact that determinism was its essential characteristic. Although Spencer in England and William Graham Sumner and his allies in America tried to find a rational basis for freedom in their interpretation of Darwin, there can be little doubt that Marx in Germany and Lester Frank Ward and his numerous successors in America were the correct interpreters of the Darwinian thesis and made political collectivism the correct expression of Darwin's position.

Determinism, whether it be of the idealistic philosophical version, or whether it has its origins in a deterministic concept of nature, can only be irrational in its nature and bring with it irrational consequences when it is applied to the political, social, economic, or cultural life of man. This

---

24. Perhaps the best treatment of this aspect of Darwin is found in *What Is Evolution?,* by Charles Hodge.

25. It was also opposed by many evangelicals and orthodox scholars in Protestant circles and by the Papal Court in the Roman Catholic Church on the ground that a theistic approach could not change the basic antagonism and supernaturalistic character and purpose of the evolutionary hypothesis.

26. James Hyslop, *Literary Digest* XXIX (September 24, 1904), p. 389.

irrationalism must deny to man any meaning of purpose in human life even as determinism denies these to nature itself. Thus, freedom is banished from the human scene as evolutionary determinism is enthroned as the new deity before which men are called to worship. In this worship they are promised that they will be freed from those old theological beliefs which imposed upon their minds the shackles of a theological obstructionism from which modern science has freed them. What degree of freedom might have been left to modern man by nineteenth-century philosophers has been almost destroyed by the widespread acceptance of the evolutionary hypothesis in the name of freedom.

The immediate effects of Darwinism in the United States had not been confined to the realm of the biological sciences, but, as we have seen, quickly infected other areas of study: theology, psychology, and the social sciences. Political economy was the first of these to be invaded, and sociology appeared on the scene as a result of the writings of Lester Frank Ward. In the same way it can be said that economics, as a separate discipline, had its beginnings with William Graham Sumner. However, a new school of economic thought developed under the leadership of John Bates Clark, Richard T. Ely, and Simon N. Patten, which was much closer to Ward in its outlook than to Sumner. Sociology and economics became the area in which Darwinism would be applied to American business and social life. Under the guise of rationalism and social improvement, a strident social irrationalism gained a foothold in American thought under the leadership of these Darwinians.

William James (1842–1910) *and the New Psychology*

Although William James is generally included within the orbit of American empirical thinkers, his pragmatism was of a very special breed or variety. James preferred to call his system "radical empiricism" and preferred to restrict the term "pragmatism" to the methodological approach which he used in his approach to psychology and philosophy. In his most interesting Preface to his *The Meaning of Truth* he wrote: "Radical empiricism consists first of a postulate, next of a statement of fact, and finally of generalized conclusion."[27]

At the age of thirty, in 1873, he had been appointed to teach physiology at Harvard Medical School, but he soon became interested in physiological psychology. As a result of this transformation of his interests, he set up

27. William James, *Pragmatism . . . With Four Related Essays Selected From the Meaning of Truth* (New York, 1943).

one of the first, if not the first, physiological laboratories in this country. In 1890 he published his *Principles of Psychology,* a book on which he had begun in 1878. In this work James showed an amazing awareness of the achievements and weaknesses of European psychologists, as well as those of his American predecessors, until his own day. This historical survey gave an unusual importance to this book. Its greatest impact lay in the fact that it was the most fully developed evolutionary psychology which had yet appeared. In presenting such an interpretation James made a radical break with the traditional approach and replaced it with a new concept, in which he viewed the human mind as a functional instrument of adaptation to its environment. James regarded mind as a process rather than as a thing. Thinking was a process, a function of the brain. He held that when the brain acts, thought occurs. Thinking, for him, was thus a biological functioning of the brain. As breathing is the biological function of the lungs, so is thinking the biological function of the brain.

It is obvious that James repudiated entirely the traditional separation of mind and matter and the dualism which had characterized much of the psychological and philosophical development before him. At the same time, his insistence that mind is not a substance but an activity struck damaging, if not lethal, blows against the empirical tradition which had started with John Locke. In short, James adopted the theory of evolution much more fully than most of the other psychologists and philosophers of his day and held that the brain, or mind, was also a product of this process.

James, in one sense, continued the devastating attack which Hume had launched against Locke a century before. Denying that the mind was a *tabula rasa,* he insisted that it was a passive instrument which received the idea brought to it by the senses and was armed with the power to combine these simple ideas into complex ideas through concepts in mechanical laws of association.

In place of Locke's view of human consciousness, James substituted what he preferred to call the stream of consciousness. He denied that sense experience consists of a separate sensation which is somehow imbedded in a faculty called consciousness, as Locke believed.

He further held that the human consciousness selects certain sense impressions for particular attention out of myriad experiences which come to it. The mind can and does pick and choose these according to its interests and dismisses the rest of them as being unworthy of such interest. James thus regarded the mind not only as a product of evolution, but as a part of the evolutionary process itself in that it is an active instrument of human adaptation and survival. But at this point he became quite contradictory and insisted that this mind, in selecting and rejecting certain stimuli, is also teleological in its activities and is able to choose the means by which it will attain its goals.

At this point James opened himself to the same charges which can be, and have been, leveled against all varieties of empiricism. How do sensations, arising in an impersonal and materialistic world, convey any concept of purpose, and how is the mind thus able to formulate purposes and choose appropriate goals for their achievement? We have seen that the empirical approach to knowledge logically forbids any knowledge of the future and any possibility of a knowledge of goals, since they lie beyond the ability of the senses to comprehend or formulate them.

James is largely known for his pragmatic concept of truth and a corollary of his whole position known as the "will to believe." James located truth in his pragmatic frame of reference and defined it as "the attitude of looking away from first things, principles, categories, supposed necessities; and of looking towards last things, fruits, consequences, facts."[28]

For James, then, ideas are to be regarded as true if they can be assimilated and validated by men. "Truth happens to an idea. It becomes true. It is made true by events."[29]

It is evident that for James truth was closely related to the usefulness of an idea—to its "pragmatic value." For him an idea was "useful because it is true and true because it is useful." Such a view of truth should lead to intellectual and social anarchy. Certainly this would be the logical conclusion to his dictum that only as truth has some agreeable consequence, or consequences, in the experience of an individual, does the idea have truth value. The objections to this are almost too evident to need any treatment. It is obvious that what is agreeable to one individual is not to another and may indeed be most objectionable to him. This applies not only in the realm of pleasure, but equally forcefully in the realms of duty and moral obligation. Inevitably this variety of truth resulting from individual experiences leads to conflicting truths, and truth itself, as a concept, vanishes into the area of relativity.

It would seem that James was not entirely unaware of such a possibility and sought to overcome it, to a degree at least, in his famous concept of "the will to believe." According to James, those ideas which agree with the evidence are true or verified; those that are contrary to the evidence, are, by the same token, to be regarded as false. But there is a third cate-

28. Ibid., pp. 54-55.
29. Ibid., p. 201.

gory of ideas, according to James, those that lack sufficient evidence to be regarded as true, and yet there is not sufficient evidence to declare them false. It is at this point that the "will to believe" comes into the picture.

In such cases we have a right to accept them as true if they seem likely to be useful to us. This is simply an extension of utilitarian philosophy to the realm of religion, and it was on this basis that he justified varieties of religious beliefs. The ultimate basis for believing in Christianity, or any other religion, was thus the prospect that for the particular believer such a faith would be fruitful and meaningful. His *Varieties of Religious Experiences* grew out of this application of the will to believe to the area of religion.

Summary

William James was basically a humanist and naturalist in his approach to philosophical, psychological, and religious problems. His utilitarianism is the logical deduction from his basic assumption of the sovereignty of the human will. Man, for him, must be the ultimate judge of what is good and useful, or what is bad, using as the basis for such a judgment the effects of any action on his own welfare.

His approach to knowledge and truth through pragmatism is simply another application of his basic assumption of the autonomy of the human personality. His "will to believe," far from being a defense of the Christian faith, is little more than an invitation to religious anarchy, even as his utilitarianism is an invitation to moral anarchy. In short, his entire philosophy (and psychology) is humanistic and irrational. Grounded in Darwin's scientific methodology, James laid the foundation for the further disintegration of American thought. His destructive influences were peculiarly notable in the field of psychology, where his influence has been much more extensively felt than in the field of philosophy.[30] Seeking to promote the autonomy of the human will by freeing man from the shackles of what he felt was an outmoded evangelical orthodoxy into the alleged freedom to be found in the determinism inherent in Darwinism was his aim. Once again, in his efforts to free man from submission to the will of a sovereign, allwise God, mankind was being asked to bind itself in abject slavery to the fatalism inherent in a subjection to the blind forces of natural law.

In both religion and psychology James did much to prepare the way for the further decline of American thought into the agonies of the twen-

30. James never regarded himself as a philosopher and vainly endeavored to keep philosophy out of his psychology system. James did hold to a philosophy in spite of his efforts to keep the two disciplines separate.

tieth century. In psychology Dewey and his group, and in our own day Skinner and his group, can claim a kinship with James, even though James might vigorously deny it.

Likewise, in educational psychology Dewey also rises to haunt James, as do myriad others in the field of education. In like manner, James prepared the way for the peculiar reception given to Freud when he appeared in this country. The dreary road which James opened up has claimed thousands of devotees, even though it is a blind alley leading to intellectual despair and moral anarchy. He banished God from the American scene in philosophy and psychology and opened up the possibility of the American religious pluralism which has enervated the witness and activity of the organized church in the twentieth century.

Although the relationship between the psychology and philosophy of William James and the contemporary decline of constitutional government and law in this country might seem to be, at first glance, either non-existent or very remote, this is not the case. In terms of years, the relationship is over the span of a century, but in terms of the germ of ideas which are in his system, the relationship between his pragmatism and utilitarianism and the contemporary idea that "everyone should do his own thing" is quite close. American society has felt it necessary to create its own safeguards against the anarchistic implications of this kind of ethical thought. Without choosing to return to the biblical view of man and law, it has sought a corrective in the very philosophy which has produced the crisis. Such a solution is no corrective in any sense of the word.

The twentieth century has endeavored to overcome the defects of an anarchistic political, social, and economic philosophy by turning to a political absolutism. This political absolutism is also based on the premise that man is autonomous and not under the restraints of the moral law of the Scriptures. The repudiation of biblical theism brings with it a fearful price which the nineteenth century is exacting from our own.

The intellectual crisis is upon us, and for it modern man has no answer. The twentieth century is now aware of this crisis, but lacks the necessary awareness that its remedies are, by their own nature, bound to be failures and to intensify the very problems which they are intended to correct.

Chapter 9
Transitional Thinkers — Part One

The twentieth century is reaping the harvest of irrationalism and despair which the thinkers of the two previous centuries sowed. Signs of impending crisis were clearly visible with the attacks which Hume launched against Locke, in the emergence of the Kantian idealism, the Hegelian Absolutism and its offspring in Marxian thought. The latter part of the nineteenth century nurtured the anti-intellectualism and irrationalism inherent in the various systems of philosophy which had arisen as the offspring of Descartes and Locke.

Even though impending intellectual collapse was visible, there were very few thinkers who were able to comprehend it or (if they did understand) were willing to give voice to their fears. The last decades of the nineteenth century were characterized by an optimism which is almost beyond the ability of the average man to understand today. The thinkers of our day have been so prejudiced by this unthinking optimism that they have turned into an equally fruitless despair and pessimism. Both of these retreats are the logical outcome of the rejection of the biblical view of God and man and the Christian view of the meaning of human life.

The entrance of the Western mind into the twentieth century did not bring with it an immediate collapse. The heritage of sound biblical theism was still too much a part of the picture to allow for any such descent into the arms of an unrestrained irrationalism. This legacy was too deeply rooted in the European and American past to yield easily to its foes, even though they abounded on every hand. It must not be thought that theistic orthodoxy was lacking in defenders. This was certainly not the case. For them the cause was not lost, and they quickly rallied to the cry of mighty battle as it had been sounded by the followers of Darwin, Marx, Wagner, and Nietzsche. In this country, even though the voice of James and his associates was less strident, it was no less inherently hostile in its attacks on the Christian legacy, and the defenders of the faith arose to accept the challenge of the new intellectual currents which were gaining strength in the colleges, the universities, and even the leading seminaries of the North.[1]

1. For a discussion of this important aspect of American intellectual development,

The battle was intensified after 1900 by a group of scholars in various disciplines who had been thoroughly trained in either German philosophy of the Hegelian variety or Darwinian theories of evolution in either European or leading American universities, such as Harvard. At Harvard, the theory of evolution had taken hold even in the 1860's under the sponsorship of Asa Gray. Thus, scholarship—scientific, philosophical, and theological—was increasingly oriented toward the theory of evolution and sought to apply it not only in their disciplines, but to the whole of the intellectual, religious, and social life of the West, including Russia. Their efforts were aided by the optimism with which the Western world greeted the opening of the twentieth century. It was widely believed that the present century would see the fruition of all the hopes and dreams of previous eras; that war, disease, and poverty would be banished, and that mankind would enter upon a secular millennial age such as the world had never before experienced. This optimism permeated much of the thinking of the first decade of the twentieth century, and one editor confidently wrote that even though there might be occasional setbacks, there lurked in every day a better tomorrow, and that these setbacks would only be temporary detours on the road to progress. He was equally confident that war would become a thing of the past because humanity had learned its lesson and would use peaceful methods for settling international disputes. Pacifism was, in fact, a prominent aspect of the unlimited optimism which pervaded Western thought. Woodrow Wilson and Theodore Roosevelt, each in his own way, made glowing predictions for the future during the political campaign of 1912. The campaign revolved around which party was most capable of bringing these rosy predictions to pass. Not even the outbreak of war in Europe in 1914, or the American involvement in 1917, extinguished the bright hopes for the twentieth century. They were dampened a bit, however, but Wilson's impassioned pleas and promises for the effectiveness of the League of Nations rekindled the hopes for a utopia. The Great War was the last war to be fought, and it would be waged for the purpose of making the world "safe for democracy." Not until the late 1920's did the optimism of the first decade of the century yield ground to the demands of an unrelenting realism and finally bring forth its harvest of despair in the 1930's.

---

see C. Gregg Singer, *A Theological Interpretation of American History* (Nutley, N. J.: Craig Press, 1964); Paul E. Boller, *American Thought in Transition: The Impact of Evolutionary Naturalism, 1865–1900* (Chicago, 1969); George Daniels, ed., *Darwinism Comes to America* (Waltham, Mass., 1968); R. J. Wilson, *Darwinism and the Intellectual* (Homewood, Ill., 1967); and Charles Hodge, *What Is Darwinism?* (New York, 1874).

The seeds for the transition had been sown in the thought of the nineteenth century, but only gradually did it bring the change which was inherent in its basic presuppositions. The optimism brought on the widespread belief in the evolutionary hypothesis which was too firmly entrenched to easily yield to its own offspring. Several transitional figures, however, played a prominent role in preparing the ground for the conquest.

Henri Bergson (1859–1941) was one of the first to be a philosophical link between these two eras. His interests were more strictly philosophical in character than those who followed him, but he also plowed the ground and fertilized the intellectual soil of Europe for the growth of irrationalism. Even more than John Dewey, he centered his attention on questions that were essentially philosophical in nature rather than practical. His philosophy is very difficult to grasp or discuss, since he based his whole system on an attack on the possibility of conceptual knowledge in a manner which is reminiscent of that of Schopenhauer. His approach arose out of the continuing controversy in philosophical circles over vitalism versus materialism. He denied the capacity of human reason to know "inner" reality and held that such a reality could be known by intuition alone.

In his early years as a thinker, Bergson had been devoted to science as the only valid approach to the meaning of reality, and to positivism as the only correct philosophical system based upon the scientific methodology. But he came to a realization of a basic question which neither Comte nor Marx had ever faced or answered. This was the question of the origin of human consciousness. He rightly came to see that to place its source in matter was totally unsatisfactory as an answer to the very basic philosophical issue. He further came to the conclusion that this scientific methodology could yield no knowledge of the inner spiritual world which was peculiar to man and which differentiated him from the outside world of nature. Only intuition can give to man this true knowledge of his inner self. This conclusion led him to make a further break with the evolutionary philosophy as it was then widely held among sociologists and psychologists as well as biological scientists.

Although in his first major work, *Time and Free Will* (1889), he launched an attack on the Kantian concept of reality, he soon turned his attention to the major area of his developing philosophical system, the problem of consciousness in man. This theme began to take form in his *Matter and Memory* (1896), and was even more fully developed in his *Introduction to Metaphysics* (1903).

Basic to Bergson's whole position was his concept of consciousness or the intuition of self.

> I find, first of all, that I pass from state to state, I am warm or cold, I am merry or sad, I work or I do nothing. . . . I change then without ceasing. . . . Duration is the continuous progress of the past which gnaws into the future and which swells as it advances. And as the past grows without ceasing, so also is there no limit to its preservation. . . .[2]

It would thus seem that for Bergson, consciousness itself was the only reality, and its function was to use the knowledge brought by science to translate these impulses into material forms. The function of science is limited to bringing to man the raw data concerning the outer world, which must then be interpreted by the inner world of consciousness. The human body is thus the agency through which spirit comes to know and to act upon the world as brought to it through the senses. But this knowledge which comes to man through his senses is not absolute, but relative. Absolute knowledge is intuitive in nature, but, Bergson also admitted, or perhaps insisted, intuitive insights are the province of only a relatively few people. This important problem arose out of his position, and his critics were not slow to press this point to their advantage and his discomfiture.

He compounded the difficulty by insisting that the intellect, by its very nature, cannot comprehend reality. From this seemingly hopeless impasse it is redeemed by its instincts. Instinct, in turn, is the key to the vital operations of life.

Once again Bergson created a new difficulty in his definition of life. Holding that it was unique reality and the source of both spirit and matter, space and time, instinct and consciousness, science and intuition, he went on to declare that the cosmos is a field of vital force or *élan vitale.* This definition, however, is not actually a definition which is easily understood, since Bergson did not identify its components.

Since the cosmos had as its purpose the proliferation of the various forms of life, Bergson also held that man is not, and cannot be, the sole end of the evolutionary process. He must have achieved this conclusion through intuition, since it cannot be known through the scientific methodology. Bergson did not deny, however, that man occupies a unique place in the evolutionary scheme of life, even if he is not its chief end. Man, for him, was the agency or instinct through which spirit is able to liberate itself from the confines of material reality.

How does Bergson know that man is not the chief goal of the evolutionary process? How could he affirm that man is the agency liberated from matter? What is matter? There is in Bergson no satisfactory answer

---

2. Henri Bergson, *Creative Evolution,* trans. A. Mitchell Holt (New York, 1911), p. 22.

to these very important questions. His metaphysics is underscored by a series of assumptions which lack both metaphysical and scientific evidence. Granting that Bergson was at war with science and the scientific methodology and that, therefore, he could not use scientific evidence as answers to these important questions, we must still insist that his metaphysical assumptions are not answers and fail completely to offer a satisfactory solution to the great questions of human life.

The difficulties of his position are even more clearly etched when we examine his moral and religious position, which is the theme of his last major work, *Two Sources of Morality and Religion* (1932). In this last effort to set forth a meaningful philosophy, Bergson held that morality and religion have two different sources. One is the eternality of the creative force. The eternal creative force results in a dynamic religion and "open morality, while the external force produces a static religion and closed or formalized morality. The eternal creative force thus produces a religion and morality in which a morality of love and freedom predominates, while the external force produces a religion in which the morality of obligation and law are the chief characteristics."[3]

The open morality is the result of an awareness that the world is changing and that it is moving toward what he called a radical spirituality. History, for Bergson, is a dialectical conflict between an open society on the one hand, and a closed one on the other. At this point the influence of Hegel on his thinking is quite apparent. Furthermore, this dialectical interaction is evolutionary in its character, and its goal is the attainment of an open society in which humanity will enjoy a state of perfect freedom because it will be in perfect union with a consciousness which has been released from every material limitation. Unlike Hegel, Bergson did not foresee an unending dialectical process and bequeathed to the dialectical process in history a definite goal, even though this goal is certainly mystical in its form and means of attainment. On the other hand, it is a far cry from St. Augustine's *City of God* and the biblical teaching in regard to the second coming of Christ and the establishment of His kingdom of the New Jerusalem.

Coates and White have perhaps given the best summary of Bergson in their conclusion that "in deifying life, he justified everything that happened in life."[4]

3. Wilson H. Coates and Hayden V. White, *The Ordeal of Liberal Humanism* (New York, 1970). See Henri Bergson, *Deux Sources de la morale et de la religion,* 10th ed. (Paris, 1932), p, 271.

4. Ibid., p. 277.

The result of this was a negation of man's moral responsibility and an admission that what has happened in history is right simply because it has taken place.

Bergson was correct in seeing that the uncritical adoration which the nineteenth century was lavishing upon the scientific method and the discoveries of scientists was unwarranted and even dangerous, since it led to the materialistic philosophy and religion. But he had no satisfactory substitute to take the place of the religion and philosophy which he sought to destroy. His whole approach to reality was based upon a series of assumptions which had no foundation in either science or philosophy, and his mystical approach to the problem would logically have led him into a position where he could not even use language to discuss the issues he was treating. In this respect he was a forerunner of the modern existentialists, whose logic leads them into almost the same impasse.

Bergson's failure stemmed from his complete departure from biblical truth. He did not use any biblical presuppositions in the construction of his system. As a result, he had a faulty concept of reality in general and of man in particular. He had no theistic foundation for his epistemology, making his concept of intuition and instinct woefully inadequate for the task he imposed upon these sources of human knowledge.

Inevitably his attempt to provide a moral and ethical theory led to dismal failure. His inability to find a satisfactory meaning of reality doomed him to an inability to provide a satisfactory ethical and moral philosophy, even as he had failed to find a true picture of reality in general. It might be observed that Bergson may well have been aware of his own failures, since he had been a Jew and ultimately turned to find peace in the Roman Catholic theology and church.

Max Weber (1864–1920)

Max Weber was a scholar of very broad interests and scholarly activity. Although economic theory and organization claimed much of his intellectual activity, he was, nevertheless, by the very nature of his studies, drawn into sociology and religion. He became one of the leaders of the twentieth-century mind of the West. Perhaps the best evaluation of the role of Weber in this development is that given by Coates and White, who describe him as "a scholar who turned to the problem of the place of the irrational in the life of civilization."[5]

In his basic assumption that irrationalism is the essential ingredient of

5. Ibid., p. 262.

human life, he created his own dilemma which he never solved, for he also believed that reason is the tool through which man should and could attain his irrational drives. For Weber, man's reason is the means for the realization of the irrational.

All of Weber's writings reflect his deep distrust of metaphysics and theology as a key to the understanding of human life and an equally great repugnance that human life, either individually or collectively, can be regarded as having a purpose or goal.

In spite of his extensive work in the field of economics, his greatest influence has been in the realm of sociology. Sociology both as an academic discipline and as a field of social action bears the mask, or stigma, of his pervading influence on it. It most certainly can be said that he gave a tremendous impetus to the growing belief that human life in all of its social, economic, and political activities is essentially irrational. In fact, Weber gave a tremendous impetus to the growing assumption that since all cultural activity is essentially irrational and that culture itself is both irrational and blind in its working, its products are nothing but a means or agency through which it achieves its irrationally chosen goals. In all of this Weber held that the function of reason is to tell man what the world is, but it cannot by its very nature tell him what his world ought to be. Reason is incapable of providing man with the knowledge of what the world ought to be because the decisions as to what it ought to be are irrational in their origins. Reason determines the facts for man, but the ideals of any given society must be irrational. Thus, Weber saw all societies as the scene of a continuing tension between reality and their ideals, between facts and their aspirations for the future. The importance of the role which Weber has played in the breakdown of Western culture is so obvious that it is beyond dispute. He extended the realm of the irrational in two directions: first, so as to include within its scope the whole of what is now considered to be the realm of the social sciences and, also, into the future.

Weber also included the field of religion within the scope of his approach and brought this aspect of culture into the area of sociology.[6] This evolutionary interpretation of all religions, including Christianity, was not entirely unknown before Weber, but his work was revolutionary in its extension of the evolutionary concepts of both the origins of religions and their rites and practices to a degree not generally accepted. Marx and

---

6. Weber treated this theme extensively in his *The Sociology of Religion,* first published in 1922, and his very controversial *The Protestant Ethic and the Spirit of Capitalism,* first published in Germany in the *Archiv fur Sozialwissenschaft* in 1904 and 1905, vols. XX and XXI.

Feuerbach had made this thesis part of their communistic philosophy, but not with the allegedly careful scholarship which Weber displayed in his works.

As a result of Weber's influence the whole study of religions became comparative in nature and evolutionary in basic assumptions. Religion was now to be considered as a part of sociology and therefore irrational in all of its aspects.

Although Weber held that religious or magical behavior or thinking should not be divorced from normal daily conduct on the ground that "even the need of religious and magical action are predominantly economic," he did not insist that all religious activity had to become economic in its origin. He did hold that the Reformation brought with it a new relationship between the economic and political life of man in that these institutions were freed from the idealism which had united them to the church during the Middle Ages. Thus, both the Protestant ethic and the spirit of capitalism were instrumental in bringing to Western culture a new spirit which had the effect, according to Weber, of "dispiritualizing" the Western mind. That Weber displayed a gross misunderstanding of the real meaning of both Lutheranism and Calvinism cannot be denied. A casual reading of his *The Protestant Ethic and the Spirit of Capitalism* makes this quite clear. He utterly failed to appreciate the real meaning of the doctrine of the sovereignty of God in human affairs and presented a caricature of the doctrine of election which is simply not true; it is a gross misrepresentation of both the Scriptures and Calvin's exegesis of those passages which present this important doctrine. It must also be observed that in his effort to draw a sharp contrast between the Middle Ages and the Reformation, Weber is also guilty of failing to give an adequate account of the views of St. Thomas on these doctrines.[7]

Weber's hostility to historic Christianity and his evolutionary views of all religions lay at the very heart of his writings and were thus allies of the very irrationalism which he was indicting in his works. His attitude in regard to religions also led him to some very dangerous conclusions which were, consciously or unconsciously on his part, in an effort to offer a corrective, a new norm for the norms he had torn down. In these efforts he was far from successful. His reliance on science and the scientific methodology, and the evolutionary approach to life brought him to an

---

7. The author is not attempting to gloss over important differences between the position of St. Thomas on the one hand, and that of Calvin on the other, but he would insist that St. Thomas did teach this doctrine in a modified form.

impasse. On the one hand his works reflect his conviction that the triumph of modern science (the theory of evolution) was the triumph of truth, but, on the other hand, it was also the cause of the widespread feeling that life is without meaning. It was an impasse for which he had no answer for his diagnosis of the cause of this illness which had, and has, the Western mind in its grip. The science which Weber and his contemporaries worshiped betrayed them and robbed them of their dearest possession, a conviction that life was worth living, possessing goals and purpose. Asserting the autonomy of man in his possession of his new key to thought, these men had unknowingly dethroned the God who is the source of all truth and had plunged themselves and their disciples into a world of chaotic meaninglessness. This has become for the reader a frequently repeated part of the account of the descent of the Western mind, and will become an increasingly familiar story as we continue our journey through the first three quarters of the twentieth century.

The impasse was of peculiar significance as it emanated from the mind of Weber. It is significant not only because he was a transitional figure in the history of Western thought, bridging the last few years of the previous era with the new age that was dawning, but his impasse is also important because of the remedy which he suggested. To be sure, the remedy was not entirely new, but because of his sociological studies, Weber gave it a new role to play in sociological theory. As a result, it has become part and parcel of the sociological prescription for the ills of modern society. Weber himself suggested that social scientists, by which he meant sociologists, themselves should supply the remedy for this disease. The social scientist should claim for himself the role which he would usurp from the political scientists and statesmen. It should become the task of the sociologist to work for the creation of a kind of political structure which would be a mediating institution between the irrational impulses of the masses and the realities of the power of the state and its role to bring a rationality to the political life of a nation. He recognized that political parties attracting the support of the masses would continue to be a part of the political life of a nation, but these must be offset by a bureaucracy, staffed with a group of specialists who would be trained for the various functions of government within a state.

Although Weber did not spell out the implications of his political proposals, it is obvious that he regarded the masses with a degree of philosophic contempt as the source of irrational actions within the area of political activity. He felt the sure corrective for such irrational action would be a bureaucracy which would modify the irrational demands of the masses and attempt to supply rational solutions to political, economic, and social problems.

On the surface this plea for trained specialists has merit and appeal for thinking people. But there was a basic flaw in Weber's solution which could only intensify the problem rather than solve it. His trained elite, the bureaucracy, was to be trained in a philosophy just as irrational as that which characterized the thinking of Weber's masses. Weber himself was caught in his own trap of irrationality, and he gave to sociology an almost indelible stamp of irrationalism which has characterized it from his day on until our own.

It is thus no accident that the modern welfare states such as Sweden, Great Britain, France, Italy, and the United States are plagued with bureacracies which are the fruits of Weber's thinking. These welfare states have urged on their respective governments and peoples, political, economic and social policies which bear the stamp of an irrationality which is the inescapable corollary of any system of thought which rejects the presuppositions of biblical theism. Weber either forgot, or never realized, that there lurked in the system which he proposed a very real danger that the irrational masses would gain the upper hand and demand bureaucracies which would be untrained and share their own peculiar brand of irrationality. The modern democratic state, wherever it is found, is both an illustration and a warning of the dangers inherent in Weber's solution to the problems which he foresaw and which he helped to bring to reality.

The very breadth of Weber's interests enhanced the dilemma confronting modern liberalism in that it spread the virus of its irrationalism over the entire realm of the social sciences area and impregnated religion to an alarming degree. Weber succeeded in removing social, political, and economic thought from their remaining connections with the Christian ethic and plunged them into the abyss of his own version of irrationalism as he sought to give an evolutionary interpretation of the human culture in all of its ramifications. Coates and White have summarized his contributions to our era with a diagnosis which can only spell death to the patient:

> There were no absolutes in the world, and so each man constantly had to measure his responsibilities to his own personal ethic of ends against the more general ethic of responsibility to his calling. In the interplay of irrational drives and rational apprehension of the real, human life staggered to a final fate of which only the gods were certain.[8]

Sigmund Freud (1856–1939)

Psychology as a discipline was rather late in becoming a major factor in

8. Coates and White, *The Ordeal of Liberal Humanism,* pp. 269-270.

the life of the Western mind. Wilhelm Wundt (1832–1900), a German scholar, was the pioneer in experimenting with animals and established the first psychological laboratory for this specific purpose. His work was continued by Ivan Pavlov (1849–1936), who used dogs to prove that animals, and presumably human beings, can be conditioned to respond to stimuli. The implication of these early experiments was that men do not have freedom of the will, but are subject to external environmental conditions. The work of these men, however, was overshadowed by investigations in the area of psychotherapy by Sigmund Freud, whose conclusions proved to be an even greater challenge to the long-held assumptions concerning the rational nature of man and his ability to make intelligent decisions on that basis.

There is scarcely a student of the intellectual history of the West who does not recognize the enormous influence which Freud has exercised over the Western mind during the twentieth century.

> Many facets of modern thought have been traced in Sigmund Freud . . . : rationalism, scientism, romanticism, primitivism and Darwinism, among many others. Behind all of these movements, and basic to them all, as to Freud, is the Enlightenment, and we are told Freud belongs to the Age of the Enlightenment.[9]

It is true that the well-springs of Freud's philosophy are to be found in that of the Age of the Enlightenment; yet it would be a serious mistake to assume that he reflected its basic assumptions in regard to nature and man. As we have seen, the Enlightenment had replaced historic Christianity with a faith in, and worship of, nature. But Freud carried to a logical extreme the implications of this negation of Christian orthodoxy and assaulted the Enlightenment trust in man and natural law. Rushdoony is entirely correct in insisting that Darwin, Marx, and Freud are the culmination of the philosophy of the Enlightenment. It is important to note that Freud, although a child of the Enlightenment, turned against his intellectual ancestor with a devastating zeal.[10]

Freud began his career with a passionate devotion to science and believed that in science he would find the solution for human problems, not in the sense that this knowledge would bring about a millennial experience of some kind on earth, so much as that such an understanding of scientific principles would help man to accept his destiny. From the beginning of

9. Abraham Kaplan, "Freud and Modern Philosophy," in Benjamin Nelson, ed., *Freud and the Twentieth Century* (New York: Meridian Books, 1957), p 226. Quoted in R. J. Rushdoony, *Freud* (Nutley, N. J.: Presbyterian and Reformed, 1965).

10. Rushdoony, *Freud,* p. 9.

his career in medicine and psychotherapy, Freud was thus a determinist.

Freud was also a thoroughgoing materialist. Thus, science was the highest form of knowledge possible for man to achieve, even though he freely acknowledged its limitations in dealing with the human mind.

In spite of his materialistic view of man, Freud dealt with issues that were closely related to theology. For this reason he has had a great influence not only on theology proper, but on philosophy, sociology, and social practices. There is scarcely an area of human intellectual activity which has not felt the impact of his psychology and philosophy. His insistence that man is naturally "brutish" at first glance would seem to place him in the ranks of those who held, in some form, the doctrines of original sin and total depravity. His tremendous emphasis upon the sense of guilt served to reinforce this apparent kinship between Freud and religion. However, such a conclusion is entirely unjustified. In his outlook for the life of man he was a Stoic and nothing more. He did not even think his psychotherapy could bring about a utopia on earth, or even bring true happiness to man. The most that it could do would be to make his life on this earth more endurable. That was the most to be expected from his psychological system. And why was this the case? Why was man brutish and why is this brutishness an incurable burden or disease? A brief answer to these questions is simply this: Freud held to a low view of man. Unlike many of his predecessors and some of his contemporaries, Freud proceeded on the assumption that there is no real distinction between man and the animals. Even Bergson had assumed that there was a kind of spiritual nature present in man which distinguished him from the animals. Freud, on the other hand, agreeing with Weber, regarded these so-called higher faculties as instrumentalities of human nature (whatever that might be) and not as an essential possession of that nature. These so-called higher faculties must be regarded as an evolutionary development, the result of the efforts of the human organism to adjust to those limitations placed upon it by its environment.

So far, this analysis of Freud may seem to be rather prosaic, yielding nothing very novel. It would seem that Freud was merely applying the Darwinian evolutionary hypothesis to the mental and "spiritual" life of man. If this were the sum total of Freud's view of man, it would not be novel nor explain the tremendous influence which he has gained in this country. What has been said thus far is simply a prelude to further views on the nature of man and his cultural development.

Freud's importance lies in the further application of the Darwinian view to the human condition stated in terms which are completely materialistic and which, at the same time, are portrayed with a sufficient tincture of religious language to act as a kind of satire on the entire biblical account of creation and man's appearance on earth. Freud's influence was the result of his liberal attack against God and his criticism of the long-cherished conviction that man bears the image of the God who created him.

The destruction of the Christian view of God at the hands of Weber and others logically led to the destruction of the biblical view of man. Freud, in sheer hatred of his own Jewish background, set himself to this task with a devotion and ferocity that has seldom been equalled, even by Marx and Engels, or the extremists of the French Revolution. For this reason, it has often been supposed that human sexual drives and activities form the pivotal theme in Freudian thought. While sex does play an important part in his writings, it is not the key to his psychology. The central theme is guilt, a guilt from which man can never be freed.

Freud correctly diagnosed man's problem as guilt, but a guilt totally divorced from sin. This sharp distinction between guilt and the biblical doctrine of sin is an essential element in the approach to Freud's psychology. Rushdoony has correctly interpreted Freud at this point. He points out that Freud was facing a basically religious issue as a scientist, and for this reason he turned to anthropology to seek an explanation for this phenomenon, for how can there be the sense of guilt if there is no God against whom man can sin?

Freud sought for his solution to the problem in anthropology and not in theology. His solution is fanciful and is not accepted by the most respected anthropologists. In his *Totem and Taboo* he elaborated on his sociological and anthropological conception of the origin of the feeling of guilt. In brief, he held that in every culture the holy, or the sacred, has a double meaning. In one sense it means the sacred, while in another it refers to the forbidden and the unclean.

It is at this point that conscience comes into the picture and creates a feeling of guilt when it is violated; but conscience is violated by wrong feelings also. Freud found the source of the problem in those "sins" which are found in man's past: incest, cannibalism, and other such beastly acts. At this point he relied on what he preferred to call the Oedipus Complex. By this he taught that the violent primitive father drove out from the family the sons because they threatened his exclusive claim to his sexual possession of the mother and his daughters. The sons then killed the father, but this deed did not settle the conflict. Freud argued that the stronger sons then claimed the place formerly held by the father, which in turn caused another rebellion, and so on, one such rebellion following another. The killing of the father brought with it a sense of guilt, but did nothing to settle the issues.

> The brothers did their deed by declaring that the killing of the father substitute, the totem, was not allowed and renounced the fruits of their deed by denying themselves the liberated women. Thus they created two fundamental taboos of totemism out of the sense of guilt of the son . . . whosoever disobeyed became guilty of the only two crimes which troubled primitive society.[11]

Freud carried out his explanation of the sense of guilt even further. He argued that the two taboos of totemism were not of equal strength, and the prohibition against incest had a stronger practical value or force.

> Sexual need does not unite men: it separates them. Though the brothers had joined forces in order to overcome the father, each was the other's rival among women.[12]

But there was no one to take the place of the father and thus the brothers were forced to erect the prohibition against incest. It is only necessary to point out that Freud was offering nothing more than an understanding of the origin of the feeling of guilt. By no means was he offering a solution, for in the light of his basic assumption that there is no God he was under no logical compulsion to offer any solution. Indeed, his explanation in no way suggests that either murder, incest, or any other form of sexual aberration is wrong, per se. But if these acts are not wrong, per se, how then can there be the sense of guilt? It would seem that at this point Freud borrowed a theological concept, and then secularized it to offer an explanation of what he could not otherwise account for.

With this analysis of Freud's reliance upon anthropology as he understood it, we are now ready to enter upon an examination of his psychology. As Freud relied upon an evolutionary interpretation of anthropology, so did he rely on his psychology for an evolutionary explanation for man. Particularly did he look to Lamarck. Although Lamarck had been largely discredited in scientific circles by the contributions of Darwin and others to the growth of the evolutionary hypothesis, Freud professed to see a value in his approach that was lacking in Darwin.

However, Freud rejected the conclusions of previous schools of psychology as to the component aspect of human personality and substituted his own concept—the *Id*, the *Ego*, and the *Super Ego*. He developed this theme very clearly in his *An Outline of Psychoanalysis* and *The Ego and*

---

11. Freud, *Totem and Taboo. Basic Writings of Sigmund Freud,* Modern Library ed. (New York, 1938), pp. 916 et sq.

12. Ibid., p. 945.

the Id. He brought his theory into an even clearer focus in his *New Introductory Lectures on Psychoanalysis.*[13]

This division of man's personality was really little less than Freud's attempt to formulate a materialistic and secularized doctrine of a trinity within man with the Id replacing the God revealed in the Scriptures, the Ego replacing Christ as the Second Person of the Godhead, and the Super Ego taking the place and assuming the role of the Holy Spirit in the inner life of man. This secularization of the doctrine of the Trinity was not accidental, for it revealed what Freud had publicly declared—that he hated Christianity.[14]

Freud defined the Id as that component aspect of human personality which is the oldest and represents all that man is in his nature at birth. It is essentially instinctual and is thus basically illogical and irrational. Hence it has no knowledge of any values such as good and evil, or of purpose in life for man. Freud argued that man has no purpose in life. We are born, we suffer, and we die, and there is nothing beyond death.

And yet, the Id is the foundation of all personality, seeking pleasure and self-gratification. Freud defined it further as being unconscious and the unorganized libido. This definition raises some serious questions. If the Id is what Freud claimed it to be, on what grounds could he properly speak of personality? How can an impersonal Id give birth to a personality?

Freud defined the Ego as the center of human personality, the "I."[15] It is the organized Id. It is a mediating psychical entity which mediates between the senses of man and his needs. Governed by the reality principle, it is the center of consciousness. As the center of consciousness, it receives information from the outside world through the senses. It brings the information into a kind of harmony with the instinctual impulses and demands of the Id since it is aware of reality, while the Id demands only pleasure and gratification.

The basic role of the Ego is to bring about a synthesis, or harmony, between the person and the world, and to direct the human organism in such a way as to allow a maximum of self-gratification on the one hand, within the limitations imposed on the person by its environment.

Freud's thinking in regard to the nature of both the Id and the Ego is not at all clear, for he insited that both the Id and the Ego could be said

---

13. Sigmund Freud, *An Outline of Psychoanalysis, The Ego and the Id,* trans. Joan Riviere (New York, 1960).

14. Freud even attempted to psychoanalyze Moses, because of his great hatred for his own Jewish past and everything Jewish.

15. Rushdoony (in *Freud*) speaks of the Id as representing "I" to some degree.

to exist in lower forms of life. However, his position does not allow for lower forms of life in one sense, since man is, in his thinking, nothing but an animal. This is seen in his view of human personality, which he held was a result from the conflict between these two principles in the life of every individual. He admitted that consciousness was no indication of a higher form of life, per se, since it is only the result of a conflict between desire and gratification.

On the other hand, Freud also insisted that the Id and the Ego are not necessarily at war:

> Just as the pleasure-ego can do nothing but *wish,* work towards gaining pleasure and avoiding "pain" so the reality-ego need do nothing but strive for what is useful and guard itself against damage. A momentary pleasure, uncertain in its results, is given up, but only to gain in the new way an assured pleasure coming later. But the end psychic impression made by this substitution has been so powerful that it is mirrored in a special religious myth. The doctrine of rewarding future life for—voluntary or enforced—renunciation of earthly lusts is nothing but a mystical projection of this revolution of the mind.[16]

By this chain of reasoning, Freud arrived at what came to be, in the minds of many, his most famous conclusion, namely, the neurosis. This he defined as the result of a conflict between the Ego and its Id. On the other hand, the psychosis is the similar disturbance arising between the Ego and its environment, by which he meant the outer world.[17]

When the Ego is compelled to oppose the other faculties by aberration, criticism, and prohibition, a new process emerges, which Freud called the Super Ego. Its function, which usurps the place of the parents, is to keep the Ego in continuous dependence on it and exercise continuous pressure upon it. Thus, the Ego must consider the objections of the Super Ego before it can satisfy the demands of the Id. If the Super Ego unites with the Ego, it becomes a repressive force in human personality.

There is one other aspect of human personality which needs a brief discussion if we are to fully understand the almost unrestrained irrationalism which dominated both Freud's philosophy and his psychology. This is his theory of the libido. It is here that his connection with sex comes into full view. Freud defined the libido in such a way as to insist that man's instinctual energy (that found in the Ego) is sexual in nature. The Ego is

---

16. Sigmund Freud, "Formulations Regarding the Two Principles in Mental Functioning," *Collected Papers,* IV, p. 18.

17. For a discussion of this aspect of Freudian thought see Sigmund Freud, "Neurosis and Psychosis," in *Collected Papers,* II, p. 250, et sq.

the original dwelling place for libido in the human personality. It is this concept of libido which allowed Freud to conclude the causes of neurosis are to be found in the sexual life of man. Sexual life is burdened with guilt which arises from both the Super Ego on the one hand, the early training of children which is repressive in character, and from the Id, where the taboos are very strong. According to Freud, men are torn between the desire to violate the taboos on sex, on the one hand, and to obey the desire, on the other. The result is conflict arising over the continual effort to repress libido, and this repression, in turn, produces anxiety.

Freud and Christianity

We have noted on our journey through the nineteenth century that many thinkers either rejected orthodox Christianity or attempted to create some kind of a synthesis between their respective philosophies and historic Christian doctrine for the sake of attempting to maintain peace between themselves and the Christian church. Even though their systems were virtually at war with Christian thought, they sought to minimize the intensity of the conflict by the usè of religious terminology or the semblance of an acceptance of its doctrinal position. We have seen that near the end of the century, in Nietzsche and Weber, this veneer of peaceful coexistence broke down and philosophers and social scientists were less careful to conceal the basic conflicts between their respective philosophies and Christianity. In Nietzsche and Weber the conflict broke out into the open when Freud's secularism and the social sciences declared war on the Christian church with a vitriolic hatred which appeared with full force.

Freud hated Christianity as well as Judaism. He regarded himself as one of the most dangerous enemies religion had. Coercing God, Freud wrote:

> I stand in no awe of the Almighty. If we were ever to meet, I should have more reproaches to make to Him than He could make to me. I would ask him why he had not endowed me with a better intellectual equipment, and He could not complain that I have failed to make the best use of my so-called freedom.
>
> . . . .
>
> Religion is the universal obsessional neurosis of humanity. . . . Your religious doctrines will have to be discarded no matter whether the first attempts fail or whether the first substitute informations prove to be unstable.
>
> . . . .
>
> Religion is an attempt to get control over the sensory world in which we are placed by means of the wish world which we have developed inside us. . . . It will not achieve its ends, its doctrines bear . . . the stamp of

the times in which they originated, the ignorant childlike days of the human race.[18]

Freud hated Judaism even more than he hated Christianity, and he vented his wrath in *Moses and Monotheism* by putting forth the thesis that Moses was an Egyptian. The purpose of this was to destroy the law of the Old Testament and thus banish the sense of guilt.

Freud: Political Thought

Freudian psychology has come to have an influence far beyond the halls of learning, and his psychiatry has invaded nearly every segment of American intellectual activity. It has furthermore achieved a dominant influence in the administration of justice in this country, including the Supreme Court, in sociological theory and practice, in educational circles, and in many pulpits of the land.

Richard La Pierre describes this growth in popularity of Freudian thought as a change of permanent significance for the United States because it provides a unique idea of the nature of man and of his relationship to society. He further wrote that the introduction of this Freudian ethic into American life meant the adoption of a new set of values, and "the result is a number of changes which seem likely to stultify individual enterprise and which may well bring American society into an era of stagnation."[19]

At first glance, this seems to be a very strong charge, but La Pierre is by no means the only scholar in the field of psychology to raise doubts. Hobart Mowrer can only regard this penetration by Freudian thought into American life as a crisis in psychology. He charged that American psychology has been "biologized," and that Freud, following Darwin, held that neuroses are the result of moral and religious interference with normal psychological (by which he meant physiological), instinctive processes. Not content with making this charge, Mowrer then raised a more pertinent question: "What would happen if modern man were forced to confront his guilt and insecurity for just one week without these masks and crutches? Would it destroy us completely or perhaps point the way to a better saner life?"[20]

This is an important question, and many psychologists today are re-

18. Ernst L. Freud, ed., *Letters of Sigmund Freud* (New York: Basic Books, 1960), p. 307; Freud, *The Future of an Illusion* (New York: Doubleday Anchor Books); Freud (in an earlier work), *New Introductory Lectures on Psychoanalysis* (New York: W. W. Norton).

19. Richard La Pierre, *The Freudian Ethic* (New York, 1959).

20. Hobart Mowrer, *The Crisis in Psychology and Religion* (New York: Van Nostrand Reinhold, 1961), p. 57.

visiting Freud, searching in his works for the answers to many questions which he raised and for which he provided no answers. In some respects the widespread popularity of Freud is difficult to understand and explain. In spite of his reverence for science as the ultimate key to the mystery of human personality, Freud, like Marx, did not adhere to the scientific methodology in the formulation of his theories. In fact, he has been widely criticized for erecting a system of thought that lacked scientific evidence.[21] It was not intended to justify sexual laxity, but because it was essentially negative in character it did, however, lend itself to such an interpretation. It is most likely that its current popularity can be traced to this aspect of Freud's thought, but it was not designed to be a code for licentiousness. Hobart Mowrer has probably given the best explanation for the popularity of a theory of man which is most degrading and denies to human life any plan or goal. "But the plain fact is that professional psychotherapy is a business and if it turns out that what the patient secretly hoped to buy (and the therapist implicitly promises to sell) it is a cheap form of forgiveness and expiation."[22]

Mowrer further suggests that the psychoanalytic physician sets out to cure neurotic individuals "by championing the rights of the body in opposition to a society and moral order which was presumed to be unduly harsh and arbitrary."[23]

Mowrer in his analysis of Feudian psychology is not arguing for a divinely instituted moral order, for Christianity, or the biblical view of sin. His own position is not that of Christian theism, but he is simply arguing that Freud has created a sense of guilt arising from the desires of an individual who feels the restraining influence of society on a generally accepted moral code. Mowrer makes this very clear in a most enlightening comment which is worthy of serious consideration. He admitted his own lack of understanding as to why Protestant leaders could so easily accept Freud.

> For a long time it was a mystery to me why Protestantism and Freudian psychoanalysis have hit it off so well. In many ways they are very strange bedfellows indeed. The New Testament, to say nothing of the Old Testament, seems fairly to cry out in opposition to everything psychoanalysis stands for and Freud in his book, *The Failure of an Illusion* makes his opposition and contempt for religion, crystal clear.[24]

We may well agree with his analysis of the incompatibility of Freudian-

21. For an interesting discussion of the unscientific character of Freud's work, see La Pierre, *The Freudian Ethic,* chap. 3, p. viii
22. Mowrer, *Psychology and Religion,* p. 77.
23. Ibid., p. 84.
24. Ibid., p. 159

ism with Christianity, both Protestant and Roman Catholic, but Mowrer was in error when he blamed Freud's hatred of Christianity on Calvinism, particularly his emphasis on the helplessness of man in achieving redemption and the doctrine of election. Freud replaced the doctrine of divine sovereignty and election with his own fatalism and the ensuing hopelessness of man to face his guilt, which he could never overcome. For Freud had insisted that "we do not live but are lived by unknown and uncontrollable forces."

In 1908 the International Congress of Psychoanalysis was formed to systematically promote Freudian views in both Europe and the United States, but it was in this country that Freud met with his greatest success. His system replaced the earlier Behaviorism of John B. Watson and his group and other schools of psychology as to the basic therapeutic approach to the problems of the patients in mental institutions of various kinds in this country. It also gained great currency in American educational circles and schools for the training of social service workers, who became the apostles of Freud in applying his theories in the various social services provided by the federal and state governments and by various private agencies.

It has also inundated many courts of the land. The Supreme Court of the United States on many occasions has given evidence that in its decisions it is much more interested in what Freud, psychologists, and sociologists have to say than they are in what the law is. The influence of Freud has been most obvious in capital cases in which the courts have, to all intents and purposes, freed those charged with murder from the death penalty on the ground that society, rather than the accused, is really guilty because it has not provided a satisfactory environment. Thus the accused should be excused on the ground that they were driven to their crimes. Thus they are not responsible for their crimes and should not be punished.

Freudianism has thus become an important factor in the breakdown of justice in the American judicial system. The main concern has centered around the unfortunate criminal who is the victim of his environment, rather than on the victims of these criminals. Even less attention has been given to the fact that primarily all such crimes, while obviously against both the victim and society, are still basically crimes against the law of God and should be dealt with on this basis. To deal with criminal acts and criminals on the basis of the biblical ethic requires first of all a belief in the majesty of that ethic and the sovereignty of the God whose law has been broken. Self-conscious Freudians in the various areas of modern life must first have repudiated their allegiance to Christianity and the biblical ethic before they could embrace the Freudian approach to sociological and criminal issues.

It was to be expected, perhaps, that sociology and social welfare should be among the first areas to surrender to the allurements of Freud. Their entire development and philosophy in this country can be traced back to those European and American thinkers who prepared the way for the advent of Freudian psychology. The strange attraction which Freud has had for modern liberal Protestant thinkers is not, at first glance, easy to explain. By 1930 he had gained the ear of many liberals within Protestant circles, and more recently liberals within the Roman Catholic structure have been giving him an increasingly favorable hearing.

Between Roman Catholic doctrine formulated by the Council of Trent and Protestant doctrine as it was formulated by the Reformers and their successors, there is a great gulf which cannot be bridged. We must also remember that theological liberalism, which entered into continental theology during the second half of the nineteenth century and which came to the American denominations of the North somewhat later, also had its roots in the same philosophies which had made both Weber and Freud possible. The simple statement that these philosophies made Freud possible does not, in itself, answer the question. The full answer lies in the fact that Freud divorced the sense of guilt from the fact of sin as being basically an offense against an almighty God who is judge of both the quick and the dead. In the same way it has ultimately found its way into Roman Catholic circles for the same reason. In each case it apparently removes the sinner from confession to God and places him under the care of a psychiatrist who tells him what he wants to hear rather than declares to him a message from the Scriptures which he does not wish to hear.

Theological liberalism is blind to the fact that the Freudian therapy cannot work and has not worked. Hobart Mowrer severely criticized Paul Tillich for his continuing emphasis that this Freudian approach was successful and should be used by Protestant ministers.[25] Liberal and radical theologians persist, however, in regarding Freudianism as an excellent and more authoritative approach for dealing with the problem of sin and guilt than that provided either by the Council of Trent or by Calvin, Luther, and their colleagues.

It must be concluded on the basis of all the available evidence that Freud must be held accountable for the breakdown of justice in this coun-

---

25. For an excellent criticism of this Freudian approach by ministers, see Jay Adams, *Competent to Counsel* (Nutley, N. J.: Presbyterian and Reformed, 1975).

try, for the failure of the modern techniques sponsored by him and his followers to provide adequate treatment for mental illness by its inability to treat its cause, namely, the consciousness of sin and guilt and for the breakdown of public education in the twentieth century.

Above all, Freud must be regarded as a transitional thinker bridging the gap between the two centuries and contributing to the ultimate collapse of Western thought by bringing under the mantle of psychology much of the philosophy and the educational psychology of our day. His outspoken rejection and hatred of Christianity was the shaky foundation on which he reared a concept of man and the human mind which strengthened those forces working for the destruction of Western thought by destroying the historic doctrine of man as a responsible moral agent and replacing it with a view which, at best, regarded him as an animal, higher to be sure, but failing to give any meaningful explanation as to why he should be regarded as superior to any other animal. Freud gave a new support to the growing darkness which was overtaking the Western mind. The mantle of irrationality was being wrapped around the slender beams of light which were still shining within the Christian church.

Van Til's summary of Freud may well be taken as a final evaluation of this important, but tragic, figure in the history of Western thought:

> Looking at this general argument of Freud, it is difficult to understand how he could be unaware of the fact that he is, in effect, making a universal *a priori* assertion about all possible existence while yet pretending to base his entire explanation of the origin of religion on scientifically ascertainable knowledge
>
> From the historic Protestant or Christian point of view, Freud's position may itself be taken to be the expression of a wish-world that he seeks to impose on reality. He is anxious to suppress the claims of God and of Christ that press upon him from within and from without. It is true that the Christian is bound to give his own psycho-analysis of the process employed by Freud. By this method of psycho-analysis modern man, sinful as are all other men in themselves, seeks to suppress the truth of his responsibility to God and to ignore the call to repentance that comes to him in the name of Christ. Such opposition to God and to His Christ would be meaningless except for the fact that through it God is showing to man that his wisdom is foolishness and that only in turning to Christ is life and meaning to be found.[26]

Erich Fromm, one of Freud's disciples, endeavored to furnish Freudian thought with a religious outlook. But in no way did he surrender to the

26. Cornelius Van Til, *The Search for Meaning in Modern Thought,* unpublished lectures for classes at Westminster Theological Seminary (October, 1961), p. 38.

claims of a biblical theism. He held that basically there are two kinds of religious systems—the authoritarian and the humanistic. Fromm placed himself within the camp of the humanistic. He further held that Christianity was an authoritarian religion, and he suggested that it was man's effort to escape from the control of a tyrant. According to Fromm, Calvin put forward this concept in its most objectionable form.

Fromm defined humanistic religion as one which is centered around man and his strength. In treating this theme Fromm endeavored to place Jesus Christ within the orbit of this humanistic approach, contending that Christ's teaching that the kingdom of heaven is within you is the clear expression of a non-authoritarian idea of religion, that virtue is self-realization. In other words, this non-authoritarian religion is democratic in its nature. Fromm further held that in authoritarian religions, such as the Augustinian-Calvinistic interpretation of Christianity, the psychological mechanism of projection enriches God at the expense of man. In projecting the best that he knows and possesses, he enriches God at his own expense. Fromm held that authoritarians do not realize that, although men are dependent on forces beyond their control, it is nothing less than self-destructive to worship such forces. He was convinced that although authoritarians do not realize that man longs to relate himself to something beyond himself, this longing is not proof that such a God actually exists.

The biblical answer to Fromm's endeavor to give to Freud a cloak of religious acceptance, if not respectability, lies in the fact that "if we with him reject the idea of man's dependence upon God through Christ, we then place man in a vacuum for it is only on the presupposition of the truth of the Christian position that human personality stands in an intelligible relation to his environment. . . . Christianity finds no intelligibility in the idea of man except in terms of his creation and direction by God in Christ."[27]

Fromm's efforts to refurbish Freud and remove some of the sharp sting of his scientific naturalism foundered on the same destructive assumption on which Freud built his whole philosophy and psychology—the doctrine of human autonomy.

John Dewey (1859–1952)

Although John Dewey made his major contributions to American thought during the twentieth century, in many respects he was the offspring of the previous era and was deeply indebted to nineteenth-century thinkers. In fact, it can well be argued that he merely redirected and popularized

27. Ibid., pp. 39-40.

what he had learned from his predecessors and contributed very little that was original. Instrumentalism might be considered as the one contribution to the heritage he had received. It is for this reason that he can be considered as a transitional thinker. Because of his interest in the field of education and his insistence that true education must have a social value, he had an enormous influence not only in molding the modern American public school system, but in creating a public opinion on many social issues as a result of his commanding influence in educational thought and practice. It can well be said that perhaps more than any other educator he brought about the downfall of the public schools of the nation and turned them from their traditional function of serving as educational institutions. Dewey and his philosophy directed the schools into becoming institutions whose chief purpose has been the manipulation of young people into being willing tools and supporters of a democratic totalitarianism of a communistic type. All of his educational efforts were directed toward the realization of this goal, even though it may not have been too apparent in some of his writings. Try as they will, his admirers and successors in this continuing project cannot successfully deny that his total influence was in this, and no other, direction.

Although there are many facets to his philosophy, behind them are two basic themes which control all of his thinking. In the first place, he began his professional career as a teacher with a disdain for Christian theism and with the profound conviction that through the proper use and application of the scientific methodology he could fashion a philosophy which would solve all the intellectual, political, educational, and social problems of the day. In fact there was, in his opinion, scarcely any aspect of the human scene which would not benefit from the application of such a philosophy. His lasting admiration for the achievements of science and its methodology implied a corresponding rejection of historic Christianity. The scientific methodology was for him the new epistemology which would lead to a kind of ultimate knowledge, if not to ultimate truth; at best only a warranted assertibility. Thus his philosophical system has become known as Instrumentalism.

He revealed his antipathy to Christian theism in particular, and Christianity in general, in the opening pages of his *Common Faith,* in which he announced that it would be his purpose in this work to develop another conception of the nature of the religious phase of experience which would separate it from the supernatural and the things that have grown up about it. "I shall try to show that these deviations are encumbrances and what is genuinely religious will undergo an emancipation when it is relieved from them; that then the religious aspect of experience will be free to develop freely on its own account."[28]

Dewey claimed that in this project he was endeavoring to save religion from the attacks of those who were insisting that because of recent psychological and scientific discoveries, everything religious must go.

Gladly admitting that historic religions have been relative to the conditions of social culture, Dewey felt compelled to inquire how much in religions now accepted are survivals from outgrown cultures. He also claimed that the logic involved in this argument compelled him to ask what conception of unseen powers and our relation to them would be consistent with the best achievements and aspirations of the present.[29] In short, said Dewey, this logic demands that we wipe the slate clean and make a fresh start by asking "what would be the idea of the unseen in the manner of its control over us, and the ways in which reverence and obedience would be manifested, if whatever is basically religious in experience had the opportunity to express itself free from all historic encumbrances."[30]

Dewey, in his introduction to his argument in this work, makes it supremely clear that he is no theist and has little or no use for historic Christianity. He would emancipate Christianity, and Judaism also, for that matter, from accretions from the past which sap their strength and prevent their followers from being truly religious. He would willingly take one other step. He would argue that to free Christianity from these accretions picked up during its two thousand years of history would actually be beneficial in that it would help to promote this process of purification because of the historic increase of the ethical and ideal content of religions. Thus he is suggesting that Christianity itself is part of an evolutionary process in the development of religious experience.

Dewey paid scant heed to the usual proofs of the existence of God or to the uniqueness of the Christian experience of conversion.

> In reality the only thing that can be said to be "proved" is the existence of some complex conditions that have operated to effect an adjustment in life, an orientation that brings with it a sense of security and peace.[31]

The particular interpretation which a person may give to his experience is not inherent in the nature of the experience itself, but is derived from that person's particular cultural exposure. Dewey hastened to add that it was not his purpose to deny the genuine importance or result of such an experience, but to point out the possibility of a purely naturalistic explanation

---

28. John Dewey, *A Common Faith* (New Haven: Yale University Press, 1934), p. 2.
29. Ibid., p. 6.
30. Ibid.
31. Ibid, p. 13.

of the event.[32] He then goes on to deny the generally accepted order of events in a "religious experience."

> It is the claim of religions that they effect this generic and enduring change in attitude. I should like to turn the statement around and say that whenever this change takes place, there is a definitely religious attitude. It is not a religion which brings it about, but whenever it occurs, from whatever cause and by whatever means, there is a religious outlook and function.[33]

Thus Dewey's common faith becomes no faith at all in the supernatural. A man becomes religious by "doing" and not by believing. In this work not only does he set aside Christianity as such, but all idealism of whatever nature it may be.

Dewey insisted that desire has a powerful influence upon intellectual beliefs. From this basic premise he then drew the conclusion that the "inherent vice of all intellectual schemes of idealism is that they convert the idealism of action into a system of beliefs about antecedent reality. The character assigned this reality is so different from that which observation and reflection lead to and support that these schemes inevitably glide into alliance with the supernatural."[34]

Enough has already been said to clearly demonstrate Dewey's avowed hostility to the supernatural in general, and to Christian theism in particular. He rejoiced in the fact that the discoveries of science have made the acceptance of the long-established religious beliefs increasingly difficult. He also rejoiced that the Christian church persisted in maintaining the validity of the historic creeds, with the result that the majority of the intelligent people are driven away from the church. The discoveries of astronomy, geology, biology, and anthropology have had a tremendous impact and have largely dispelled the "myths" upon which Christianity was founded, according to Dewey.

> Psychology is already opening to us natural explanations of phenomena so extraordinary that once their supernatural origin was, so to say, the natural explanation.[35]

For Dewey, these discoveries and intellectual advances could have but one meaning and one result—a new final authority in a world of flux from which absolute truth had been banished as an obsolete conception.

> The significant bearing for my purpose of all this is that new methods of inquiry and reflection have become for the educated man today the final arbiter of all questions of fact, existence and intellectual assent.

32. Ibid., p. 15. 33. Ibid., p. 17. 34. Ibid., pp. 23-24. 35. Ibid., p. 31.

> Nothing less than a revolution in the "seat of intellectual authority" has taken place. . . . In this revolution every defeat is a stimulus to renewed inquiry; every victory won is the open door to more discoveries, and every discovery is a new seed planted in the soil of intelligence from which grow fresh plants with new fruits. . . . There is but one sure road of access to truth—the road of patient, co-operating inquiry by means of observation, experiment, record and controlled reflection.[36]

What then is left of religion, of Christian theism? Here Dewey showed a spark of honesty which is refreshing. He condemned religious liberals for their willingness to surrender what they at one time held to be basic religious truths on the ground that a doctrine, now no longer tenable, never was an intrinsic part of religious belief. On the other hand, he commended the fundamentalists of his day for their insight that the basic issues did not concern various items of religious belief but "centers in the question of the method by which any and every item of intellectual belief is to be arrived at and justified."[37]

Dewey's comments upon these two attitudes are most revealing as to his own religious position:

> The positive lesson is that religious qualities and values if they are real at all are not bound up with any single item of intellectual assent, not even that of the existence of the God of theism; and that, under existing conditions, the religious function in experience can be emancipated only through surrender of the whole notion of special truths that are religious by their own nature, together with the idea of peculiar avenues of access to such truths.[38]

In this manner Dewey thus banished the uniqueness of Christianity and special revelation through the Scriptures and insisted that religious values do not even depend for their reality on the God revealed in the Scriptures. The result is a completely humanistic philosophy bolstered by a reliance upon the recent discoveries in the area of science and psychology. Biblical truth delivered once and for all by God to His people has been banished by scientists from the scene of human intellectual endeavor. This truth is to be replaced by a concept of human knowledge about the world and the universe as psychologists unravel the mysteries of human nature and as both groups of scholars pursue their inquiries without any regard for the sovereign God who created the universe and man—the God who gave to both their meaning and role in His plan.

It is now obvious that Dewey's religious views, as he embraced them in his "common faith," are extremely important for an understanding of his

36. Ibid., p. 32. 37. Ibid. 38. Ibid., p. 37.

general philosophy and his educational thought, which swept the nation and have had an enduring impact upon educational thought and practice. In this manner he has greatly contributed to the crisis and chaos which have contemporary education in their grip.

It was not merely the fact that he rejected theism as an explanation for all reality, but he further condemned all religious doctrines on the ground that they have consumed entirely too much intellectual energy, which would have been better employed if it had been put to a better use. This continuous effort has, claimed Dewey, given assent to the general mind which has been even more harmful than the consequences of any one particular item of belief.[39]

It would be very misleading to assume that Dewey's philosophy consisted largely in his attack upon Christianity and was essentially negative in character. This is far from the case. Actually his philosophy was quite similar to that of William James. Relying largely on Darwinism, he tried to erect a philosophy which would adopt the method of the natural sciences for the interpretation of reality and man's place in nature. Discarding the doctrine of absolute truth, he replaced it with a concept which he called a "warranted assertibility," by which he meant that truth is what people think it to be. Thus the search for a non-existent truth was by its very nature more important than its discovery. Repeatedly Dewey reiterated his conviction that thinking as an activity is more important than thought as a body of content of rational meaning. Necessarily he was compelled by his own basic assumptions to abandon any quest for first causes or ultimate purposes in human life. "Philosophy forswears inquiry after absolute origins and absolute finalities in order to explore specific values and specific conditions that generate them."[40]

Paradoxically for Dewey, thought was a product of the process of evolution or absolute change, and absolute change of an evolutionary character, and thus became his ultimate absolute. Although he started from very different assumptions, his logic led him to a conclusion startlingly similar to that of Hegel. If the process of evolution is the only lasting truth, why explore for specific values and conditions? If there is no absolute truth, how can one define the concept of "value" except in terms of the concept of evolutionary change. Why search for values which do not and cannot exist? Like his predecessors who were quarrying in the worn out mines of relativism, Dewey had no satisfactory answer to these vital questions. This

39. Ibid., p. 33.

40. John Hallowell, *Main Currents in Modern Political Thought,* p. 548, quoted from John Dewey, *The Influence of Darwin on Philosophy* (New York, 1913), p. 10.

is not to say that he did not attempt to provide an acceptable answer. Having made such declarations, Dewey then proceeds to build a philosophy on assumptions which are, on the surface at least, quite contrary to his basic beliefs. He speaks of values, goals, and similar concepts in terms which can mislead the unwary into a misconception of the true nature of his philosophical position, and they can easily be tempted to conclude that his philosophy is not as bad as it has been described. This results from the fact that if he were true to his own presuppositions he would find it very difficult to state his case in meaningful language.

Dewey's philosophy, although much like that of William James, and although essentially pragmatic in its essence, should be called Instrumentalism, since he insisted that all knowledge, empirically or pragmatically obtained, must ultimately be tested by its usefulness, not for the individual, as in James, but for the community. All knowledge for him had to be practical, socially practical. For this reason he rejected intuition as a source of knowledge and depended upon the "collective experience of society to achieve or discover its warranted assertibilities."

Thus for Dewey the purpose of human life was power—power over its environment. This power must be achieved through the proper kind of education. Through the use and control of the scientific method man can be the master of his own destiny, but for such a mastery intelligent planning is a primary prerequisite. Once again, at this point, Dewey departed from his previous conception of the purposelessness of human life and falls into a serious contradiction. For if man is to be the master of his destiny, the very concept of destiny presupposes some kind of purposive aspect to human nature and the natural environment to which the scientific method is to be applied.

This is not the only contradiction which appears at this point in Dewey's philosophy. If the word destiny implies some kind of ultimate goal, however vaguely he defined it, it must also imply something more than a warranted assertibility. Dewey, even in his hatred of Christianity and the older metaphysics, could not escape from borrowing some of their basic assumptions to make his own position acceptable. He had to confer upon his irrationalism a veneer of rationality borrowed from Christian theism.

With this background now before us, it is possible to examine Dewey's philosophy in greater depth and to understand its wider implications for the political, social, economic, and educational life of the American people.[41]

41. It is difficult to describe or discuss Dewey's metaphysical views. He held this branch of philosophy in great disdain and, as a result, pays it little attention in all of his writings.

Of equal importance for the understanding of his total system is the comprehension of his doctrine of man, if indeed it may be called a doctrine. He regarded man as an animal and nothing more, even though he also insisted that man represented the most complex form of animal life; but this complexity was only a matter of degree and did not represent a higher form of life inherently different from that of the animal kingdom. He held that man is both a natural and social animal, that his personality (if the term may be used to describe Dewey's view of man) is based upon habit and impulses. He taught that habits involve a functional relation between the organism and its environment, and, as such, it is a relationship which maintains life in the organism. Habits are acquired or learned by the individual in his process of adjusting to his environment. On the other hand, impulses are quite indefinite and flexible. But what about intelligence in his view of man? Does man possess that precious commodity and, if so, where is it located and what is its function. He defined intelligence as an unusually flexible and finely adjusted habit, and its function is to improve the relationship between the organism and its environment. It is quite apparent that at this point Dewey has abandoned the biblical view of intelligence and discarded the views of earlier philosophers. In fact, in his concept of the learning process there is little or no room left for the role of conceptual thinking. In Dewey's philosophy man cannot think God's thoughts after Him, for it is very doubtful that there is a God and equally uncertain as to whether man could possibly think His thoughts after Him, even if He did exist. Man, according to Dewey, most certainly was not created in the image of God, whose existence is open to serious question.

In spite of this fatal weakness in his system, Dewey plunged boldly ahead to formulate an epistemology and theory of learning which negated and even denied his previous negations. Perhaps the key to Dewey at this point is his oft repeated assertion that all living is learning. In his discussion of the nature of intelligence and inquiry Dewey introduced his topic with the affirmation that

> whatever else organic life is, or is not, it is a process of activity that involves an environment. It is a transaction extending beyond the special limits of the organism. An organism does not live in an environment; it lives by means of an environment. . . . The processes of living are enacted by the environment as truly as by the organism, for they are an integration.[42]

Dewey sought to escape from the obvious determinism involved in such

42. Irving Edman, ed., *John Dewey: His Contribution to the American Tradition* (New York, 1968), p. 225.

a definition by insisting that "nature is an environment only as it is involved in interaction with an organism, or self, or whatever name be used."[43]

He further maintained that every such interaction is a temporal process and the situation in which it occurs is indeterminate. But his efforts to escape determinism were in vain. Even more so were his efforts to frame an adequate concept of intelligence on the basis of a set of epistemological assumptions which offered no possible basis for a satisfactory answer as to what either intelligence or inquiry is. Having rested his case upon the significance of the natural sciences and the scientific epistemology to provide an answer, his conclusions are fallacious and leave his readers in the dark. The rationalism which he sought in the scientific method of inquiry turned into irrationalism as he plodded his way through his tedious mode of thought.

Gordon Clark has pronounced an excellent epitaph not only on Dewey's reliance on the scientific methodology, but on those who, like him, have worshiped at this altar of the god of the twentieth century.

> At any rate, the rapidity with which in the recent past scientific theories have been invented, accepted and discarded, warns us that science is not a fixed and absolute truth. Newtonian science lasted two centuries. Today's science hardly lasts two decades.[44]

The Ethical System of Dewey

Dewey's interest in the scientific method was not the result of any scientific mindedness on his part, but rather was it the result of his conviction that it offered the most probable or certain ground for the system of ethics which was his major interest, if not consuming passion. He had a wide range of interests in regard to political, social, and economic issues, and his educational philosophy was devoted to the solution of the ethical problems which he found in these basic areas of human interest and activity.

For him, the scientific method was the key to the solution of problems in the realm of ethics and morality. He admitted that the consistent use of the naturalistic method would destroy many long-cherished assumptions and ethical convictions, but at the same time, experience discovers new values in nature, values which are practical and not metaphysical in nature. This was quite in harmony with Dewey's insistence that in its ethical en-

43. Ibid., pp. 230-231.
44. Gordon H. Clark, *Dewey* (Phillipsburg, N. J.: Presbyterian and Reformed, 1960), p. 13.

deavors, philosophy is the only search for the proper method of making intelligent choices.

But what are these intelligent choices which Dewey would have men make? They were neither theological nor metaphysical in their origin and nature. Whatever standards may result from what Dewey delighted to call intelligent choices, they could not be ultimate standards or final norms. In his work on logic he used an interesting but faulty comparison between standards of justice and truth on the one hand, and the platinum bar which is used as the standard for the measurement of length on the other hand.[45]

Dewey based his entire ethical systm on evolutionary principles. This reliance upon Darwinian principles is unmistakable in his discussion of the origin of moral standards. Any system of absolute moral standards, he argued, is, like human language, simply the product of custom. He maintained that even as there were no original principles of human grammar and that language evolved from unintelligible and even irrational babblings of primeval man, so rules of grammar appeared at a later date. But language continued to change to meet the emerging needs of mankind. Even though grammar and literary procedures were subject to change, they somehow obtained a mastery or tyranny over human ethics. Dewey insisted that for morality to be consistent with the needs of human nature it must be based upon the realities of that human nature and not forced upon it by parents, priests, or social monitors. He felt that a system of morality arising from such a perspective would be much better than an alien code of ethics not arising from actual human needs.

> The intelligent acknowledgement of the continuity of nature, man and society will at once secure a growth of morals which will be serious without being fanatical, aspiring without sentimentality, adapted to reality without conventionality, sensible without taking the form of calculation of profits, idealistic without being romantic.[46]

Dewey's sublime faith in nature is given its supreme exhibition in this passage. The intelligent acknowledgement that man and his society and nature are somehow virtually one will solve all of man's ethical and moral problems. In one sense this would be true. If we could reduce man to the state of animal existence for which Dewey is really calling, then without any moral consciousness men could, in one way, solve their moral dilemma by returning to the Darwinian concept of the survival of the fittest. No doubt Dewey would seriously object to having such a conclusion drawn

---

45. John Dewey, *Logic: Theory of Inquiry* (New York: Harper and Row, 1938), p. 216.

46. John Dewey, *Human Nature and Conduct,* p. 13.

from his thinking, but he could hardly deny the implications of his own logic.

This objection does not answer his optimistic conclusion that such an assumption would bring a serious concept of morality which would not be fanatical (a thrust at the Puritans), aspiring without being sentimental, and somehow adapted to reality without any trace of conventionality. His entire ethical theory was obviously irrational and void of any goals for human society. It would plunge humanity into the maelstrom of meaninglessness if it were to be adopted.

Perhaps we should drop the conditional clause in the foregoing paragraph. Much of Dewey's thought has already been accepted by contemporary leaders in the field of education, and it is actually being taught in the public schools of this nation. This is so because it has become the accepted point of view of most schools of education and in many educational textbooks used in these centers for the preparation of the teachers of American youth. Dewey cannot be dismissed as a philosopher who dwelt in ivy-covered halls and relegated to a mere handful of philosophers who were in essential agreement with him. He talked to the teachers and the school administrators of this nation, and his voice is still heard in these circles two decades after his death.

Dewey continued in his theory of ethics to insist that ethical values must, in some way be related to preferences or desires and thus they are not the result of any random preference. Not at all. They can only be related to those preferences which have been rationally approved and are pragmatically acceptable.

Although Dewey had criticized other systems of thought for their efforts to find certainty, he himself could not avoid paying some attention to this problem. The very fact that he attached value to certain preferences which have been pragmatically approved implied the need for some kind of certainty that the values adopted would provide future satisfaction. Gordon Clark rightly criticizes Dewey and points out that his three basic assumptions are not valid. Clark pinpoints the basic fallacy involved in Dewey's position. Granted that the scientific method and its results, such as improved speed in travel, improved methods of communication, do not, in themselves, guarantee a greater degree of satisfaction and enjoyment to those nations which possess them. These very technological advances have also made modern warfare more horrible and destructive. His concluding question is devastating to Dewey's entire ethical outlook.

> In other words, must there not be a value, a good, an end whose intrinsic goodness can motivate our choice before our knowledge of

> means, conditions and circumstances will lead us to secure it? Can science possibly justify such ideals?[47]

This question must be answered in the negative. But is there not yet another question which must be asked at this point? Can the scientific methodology produce such values and then is it not true that these values must exist without any reference to scientific or technological developments? Dewey's pragmatic approach on ethical issues underscores both his political and educational thought. We must now turn our attention to these aspects of his total philosophy.

Political Thought

That Dewey's basic philosophy and ethical outlook should lead directly to the conclusion that socialism is the most desirable, and even the necessary, form of government was almost inevitable. His rejection of any divine norm for individual human conduct left him with either the alternative of anarchy, which he also repudiated, or the necessity of creating a strong socialized state equal to the needs of a modern technological society. It is true, of course, that this trend has been an ingredient of all political philosophies which have looked to the eighteenth-century doctrine of natural rights for their sanction. All philosophies which are naturalistic in origin regard man as part of nature and determined by it. Dewey did not introduce this concept to American political thought, but he gave it a new impetus at a time when many were questioning the ability of the American constitutional system to deal with twentieth-century problems and were searching elsewhere for a meaningful political theory and practice which they felt would be adequate for the solution of the problems which were confronting the American people.

Although Dewey was guarded in many of his statements in regard to his political thinking, his writings contain some basic insights which indicate its direction. Having rejected subjectivism and individualism as ethical concepts, and having denied any divinely given sanctions for the nature and conduct of human political activity, Dewey, by the very nature of the case, was forced to seek elsewhere for a means of social control. He found it in his concept of a social sanction as over against a divine sanction for the proper power and limits of human government. This social sanction had its roots in the scientific method and technological advances and highly indicated he favored a socialistic form of government.[48]

---

47. Clark, *Dewey,* p. 27.
48. He was also addicted to either joining or supporting many organizations which favored socialism for this country.

But how was such a regime to be introduced into this country? Dewey believed that because human nature is malleable, it could be manipulated in such a way as to bring about socialism, and the public schools of the nation would be the agency through which the desired manipulation could be achieved.

It is thus obvious that socialism, in its own right a despotism, would be achieved by an authoritarian approach—the use of public education. But how could Dewey select such a goal for the governing of the American people when his own philosophy precluded any knowledge of absolutes such as right and wrong and any certain goals for the future of the people? In brief, how can a socialist regime be right? Although Dewey would probably have shunned the logical answer to this question, it nevertheless remains true that it would be right only because it would have the absolute power to proclaim what is either right or wrong. Dewey's social sanction in the end turns out to be nothing more than the sanctions of a democratic majority which have the force of law only because they are enforceable by a majority group or party within the state.

In such a political situation human rights, as they have been traditionally revered, become extremely tenuous in nature. It must be granted that Dewey had no intention of endangering these long-cherished rights. But his belief in the inherent goodness of man and in the potential perfectibility of human nature blinded him to the almost inevitable consequences of his own political outlook. Improved public education, in alliance with scientific techniques and discovery, would bring about a socialistic millennialism beyond the wildest dreams and highest hopes of previous philosophers, who had only dimly seen the possibilities of what the twentieth-century man could achieve.

Dewey's political thought vividly outlines the basic weaknesses of his philosophic system. His renunciation of the Christian view of God and of knowledge and his negation of the biblical ethic could only produce a political thought which would be thoroughly irrational. This very irrationality would, in turn, bring him into a theoretical, and at times practical, alliance with the totalitarian regimes of the day. His denial of the sovereignty of God in the political affairs of men could only lead him to an acceptance of the sovereignty of the state, a state possessed of all the necessary power needed to manipulate its citizenry into an acceptance of its dictates as to what the people must believe and do in every area of life. Socialism is a dictatorship, and it cannot for long allow any serious deviation of thought or action from the party line. Such deviations are a form of heresy, since they are denials of truth as it has been set forth by the ruling powers within that society.

Dewey's Philosophy of Education

Dewey's thinking on education is probably the most important aspect of his whole system, for it was through his influence on Teacher's College of Columbia University that his philosophical system as a whole gained credence over the nation at large. Because of its virtual monopoly over the training of teachers, which it gained after 1920, this institution was able to disseminate Dewey's philosophy in every state of the nation and in virtually every school district.[49] It can be safely said that very few students escaped the influence of Deweyism. Not only were the great majority of teachers who were trained in this era from 1920 to 1950 thoroughly impregnated with Dewey's philosophy, but the textbooks which were used in the schools of education and the textbooks which were used in the classrooms of the nation based upon Dewey's approach to the goals and methods of public education.

The key to his views of education and its close relationship with the reforming of human personality according to his preconceived pattern of what it should be, is found in his *Democracy and Education*.[50] In a brief preface Dewey stated his aim in writing the book and the philosophy which underlay his efforts. In brief, it was to relate the ideas implied in a democratic society to the problems of education. He freely admitted that his philosophy of education connected the growth of democracy with the development of the experimental methods in the physical and biological sciences, particularly with the theory of evolution as it was found in the area of biology.[51] He did not stop at this point. It was also his aim to relate this development of the experimental method of the natural sciences to the problem of industrial organization. Here, in guarded language, we see a purpose dear to the heart of John Dewey—the use of the scientific method in the schools to produce a socialist society.

In his discussion of education as a necessity of life Dewey brought in the idea of the necessity of control, through the back door, in his definition

---

49. To an amazing degree, Teacher's College was able to gain entry into nearly every school of education in the large universities and in most of the smaller schools which trained teachers. Through this "alliance" Columbia graduates placed later Columbia graduates in places of great influence in nearly every school district of the nation, and they worked in harmony through professional associations to realize Dewey's basic aims for education and for the nation.

50. John Dewey, *Democracy and Education* (New York, 1916).

51. Ibid., p. v.

of education. Defining it as the means for maintaining the social continuity of life, he suggests that by its very nature this kind of education involves, as its collateral, the necessity of control; the control of the more mature exercised over the less mature. As civilization advances, the gap between the capacities of the young, or immature, and the concerns of the mature adults widens, hence the need for control becomes great if the civilization is to endure. This analysis led him to the conclusion that education must, therefore, be a socialist function. To "socialize" the young members of any society is thus both its goal and its purpose.

> Our net result thus far is that social environment forms the mental and emotional disposition of behavior in individuals by engaging them in activities that arouse and strengthen certain impulses, that have certain purposes and entail certain consequences.[52]

This definition in turn led Dewey to admit that in the educational process there must be direction, control, or guidance. Dewey quickly denied that his definition of control contained any implication of coercion. Rather did he view control as "an emphatic form of direction of powers, and covers the regulation gained by an individual through his own efforts quite as much as that brought about when others take the lead."[53]

Dewey furthermore denied that purely external direction or control is impossible. Nothing can be forced upon students. He contended that to overlook this fact is to distort and pervert human nature. Thus, all direction is only redirection. But how is this redirection to be accomplished? Dewey was ready with an answer. It is the function of the teacher to inform the students of the outcome of undesirable actions so that they will act more intelligently. Dewey concluded that the very existence of the social medium in which the students live and move will be an effective agency for directing their activity. This approach is Dewey's instrumentalism in action.

However appealing it may seem to be at first glance, it rests upon assumptions which are a serious distortion, if not absolute negation, of the nature of man in the light of the Scripture. Furthermore, they assume an inherent goodness in man and deny the doctrines of original sin and total depravity.

The breakdown of Progressive Education and the chaos which has most of the public schools of the nation in its grip today are the result of the application of this philosophy to the educational process. Generations of

52. Ibid., p. 19.
53. Ibid., p. 29.

teachers and school administrators have been thoroughly imbued with the idea that discipline is an outmoded concept and that the role of the teachers in maintaining discipline in the classroom should be restricted to reasoning with the student as to what the outcome of his "anti social" behavior might mean.

At first glance it might well seem that Dewey's antagonism to the historic or traditional means of maintaining discipline in the schools was at variance with his insistence that the schools should prepare the students for a socialistic society. On the surface this does not seem to be the case. But actually what Dewey had in mind in his opposition to the traditional approach was a preparation for a new type of discipline which would be induced and encouraged by teachers, who would then be preparing their students for the manipulative process which Dewey had clearly in mind. He had no thought of undermining his own program. His attack on tradition was only a subtle method of preparing the way for a manipulative process.

Dewey's concept of the purposes of education not only dictated the general approach to be used in the schools, but also had specific implications for the method of instruction to be used and the curriculum to be presented. The idea that the students and the teachers were to be in a cooperative enterprise in which they would share learning experiences and thus pursue "truth" together in a common experience was an inherent aspect of his approach. Through this common sharing of the learning experience, Dewey's theory of direction or control was to be realized indirectly. Discipline in the classroom was to be a cooperative affair democratically conceived and applied. The authoritarian role traditionally exercised by the teacher was to be replaced by an entirely new principle of democratic self-government for the schools. Here the students would have a role equal to that of the administrators and teachers. Student "self government" would replace the traditional strict discipline approach of subjects being taught to the tune of the hickory stick. The virtual anarchy which reigns in the public schools today can be traced directly to this insistence that all learning is a democratic process, and the teacher and the students form a kind of team which sets out in search of the non-existent body of truth.

Obviously this approach to education demanded a radical change in the curriculum. Dewey was ready with his suggestions for revamping the entire curriculum offerings throughout the schools of the nation. Traditional subject matter must be banished along with the traditional methodology, for they formed one parcel and they must suffer a common banishment.

As the older methods of teaching reading and spelling were dethroned, so was the material that was offered in the reading courses.[54]

The deterioration, however, was not confined to the lower grades, but gradually made its way into the high schools and is now evident in the colleges and the universities.

The curriculum offered in the first two years of college today is quite frequently what was offered in the high schools in the period from 1900 to 1920. History has been replaced with a nebulous array of courses known as the "social sciences," in which there is little real history content and a great deal of misinformation in what is often regarded as sociology, economics, and government. Very few high schools give any real introduction to the great literature of the past and perhaps even a lesser number give a meaningful course in history. The very term "social sciences" precludes the possibility of solid scholarship in these areas.[55] This decline is is not accidental. It was inherent in an essential part of the Dewey program for the schools. True enough, some have complained that Dewey's followers have complained that educators have taken him much further than Dewey had contemplated or desired. Whatever truth there may be in such a complaint, the fact remains that these educators have only followed the logic of Dewey's position.

This reduction of the curriculum to an almost meaningless and empty form was necessary as a part of the manipulative program inherent in Dewey's program for remaking the American political system into a vehicle suitable for the introduction of socialism in this country. In his thinking, a meaningful contact with the rich truth of the American heritage could only be a hindrance to his purposes; and, a meaningful acquaintance with great literature, both English and American, would only defeat the realization of his goal. The curriculum was to be revamped so it would be a useful vehicle for the coming of democratic socialism and not a hindrance. Any knowledge which would impede the process of manipulation must be banished from the school systems of the nation. By 1936 this had been ac-

---

54. A few years ago the author was a participant in an accrediting program for a certain high school. He was given a textbook of a radical nature. The Foreword contained the statement that this textbook was not intended to present many facts of history but was designed to have the students raise questions. Needless to say, it more than lived up to its promise in the paucity of facts it presented and could hardly help the students to raise questions as a result.

55. It is worthwhile to make a comparison between present textbooks in the area of reading with those used before 1920. The difference is striking and such a comparison will answer the questions as to "why Johnnie can't read." A similar comparison of mathematics will answer the question as to why Johnnie cannot understand or use mathematics either.

complished to a far greater extent than the public had realized. Today in many quarters, Dewey's followers are firmly in the saddle in most schools of education, boards of education, and in the ranks of school administrators. Although the Progressive Education Association has been disbanded, it did not bring its program to an end until it had gained the victory. The ultimate result of Dewey's philosophy of education is the mournful conclusion that there is no truth to teach, no teacher to teach it, and no students to learn, simply because man is an animal—a high grade animal to be sure, but only an animal. These younger animals are to be manipulated by older animals who guide and direct them to goals selected for them by the educational hierarchy.

In Retrospect

In its essence Dewey's philosophy was probably no more irrational than that of William James, Max Weber, and other members of what we have called the Transitional School of Western Thought. Like them, Dewey denied biblical theism as the basis of all intellectual activity. Like them, he attempted to find a new source of authority in the mind of the democratic majority, and he believed that proper educational techniques could so manipulate the human mind that this democratic majority would seize upon Instrumentalism (truths that have a certain warranted assertibility) so that they would be used in the right way. By the right way, Dewey meant that the schools should be used as the instruments for the introduction of a socialist "democracy."

The importance of Dewey lies in the fact that to a far greater degree than others he was able to influence educational theory and practice in this country and bend the American school system to become the agency for realizing his goals for American society.

Under the impact of his philosophy many, if not most, of the public schools of this nation have become the agencies for sowing the seeds of irrationalism and the destruction of the American cultural tradition, with its Christian foundation, in favor of a thoroughly humanistic and naturalistic philosophy which in its political implication can only transform this constitutional republic into a democratic despotism of some sort. It is for this reason that our educational system has become one of the greatest dangers which this republic faces today. It is not producing good citizens in the traditional meaning of the term, but a new generation which has been thoroughly tutored and brainwashed into accepting the glories of a political, social, and economic philosophy which denies the existence of absolute truth and yet which, at the same time, sets itself up as the absolute before which all must bow in abject submission.

This new god, the creation of Dewey's Instrumentalism, cannot tolerate any other god before it. It is for this reason that we, as a nation, cannot have the reading of the Scriptures or prayer in the public schools of the nation. To admit the worship of another deity is a heresy worthy of exclusion for students who insist on their right of free worship. This also applies to the teacher, who may well lose his position if he continues to hold and practice such outworn and untenable, even though long-cherished, convictions. To worship the God of heaven in place of the god of the evolutionary process is gross idolatry in the eyes of the Deweyites and therefore cannot be tolerated.

Chapter 10
Transitional Thinkers — Part Two

Although any division between the more important and less important thinkers of any era may be a highly subjective process and open to serious question, some such selection must be made. It would seem that there is a group of thinkers and scholars in various disciplines, particularly in the emerging field of sociology, who are important, and yet cannot be regarded as equals of those who were discussed in the previous chapters. Granted that these writers opened the door for later development of sociology and the social sciences, and granted that these studies have become increasingly important in our day as man has turned to himself and to his society to find the answers for the perplexing questions which confront him on every hand, it is nevertheless the conviction of this writer that they are of lesser importance in the light of their own contributions to contemporary thought. The seed of later developments may appear in their works to varying degrees of clarity, and because of this they are worthy of study. The total picture of contemporary thought would not be complete without some understanding of what these writers have contributed to the modern spectrum of the field of the social sciences as we have them today.

It may also be debated whether they are transitional figures at all, but actually belong to the twentieth century. It could be argued that Durkheim is actually a twentieth-century figure. In one sense this is quite true, in that his works have achieved a hearing after 1900 which they did not receive when they first appeared. The same could probably be said of Pareto. But in their own roots they looked backward to Comte, Herbert Spencer, Darwin, and other writers who are clearly within the fold of the nineteenth century, and for this reason it has seemed wise to include them as part of the great transition. For these writers the theory of evolution provided the only answer to the ultimate questions concerning the origin of man and his institutions. Although their interpretations of Darwin were somewhat different, they were in agreement as to the authority of his evolutionary thought in its application to social and economic issues.

Emil Durkheim (1858–1917)

Emil Durkheim, the prominent French sociologist, played an important role in the development of sociology as a separate discipline and gained for it a new respect on the part of scholars in other areas of intellectual activity. He also placed this discipline firmly within the Darwinian camp, even though he differed at some points with those who also looked to Darwin as their master teacher. Durkheim was equally interested in developing a sound methodology for his emerging branch of the knowledge of society, and he logically looked up to science as the source for such an approach to sociological inquiry.

For the purposes of this study of the descent of the Western mind into the abyss of irrationalism, the proper approach to the understanding of Durkheim is his concept of the role of religion in human history. Granted that this is not the usual beginning of any inquiry into his sociological thought, for Durkheim himself did not begin here, but it is nevertheless true that his assumptions in regard to the origins and rise of religion lie at the very base of his sociological outlook. In his discussions on religion we see how he firmly anchored his philosophy to the evolutionary hypothesis.

It is perhaps unnecessary to make the point that Durkheim completely rejected the notion that religion in general, and Christianity in particular, is of divine origin. To say this is not to place other religions on the same plane with historic Christianity. Rather does this statement mean that Durkheim did not subscribe to any theistic concept that man is innately religious and feels the necessity of worship even though his worship may take the form of gross idolatry.

In short, his religious philosophy, if indeed he may have had one, was based upon humanistic presuppositions interwoven with a naturalistic outlook. Durkheim was under a strong necessity to divorce his approach from any possible contamination with theism at any point, and he thus attempted to find the sources of religion in the area of evolutionary thought.

He found the origin of religion in two sources which he called the need to understand and sociability, but he felt that sociability was the determining factor in the rise of religious sentiments.[1] Particularly did he locate the origin of religion in those social sentiments which bind individuals to the social entity as a whole. In this kind of a relationship Durkheim found the concept of obligation which he felt was an important aspect of religious thought and activity.

---

1. Emil Durkheim, *Selected Writings,* ed. and tr. Anthony Giddens (Cambridge University Press, 1972), p. 219.

> Religious society is only human society stretched ideally to beyond the stars; the gods were not conceived of as members of the tribe, but formed one, or rather several societies located in specific separate regions, some of which were friendly, others hostile and with which men have entered into relations of an international character.[2]

Durkheim felt that theory would explain why the superstitious natural philosophy of religion is obligatory, while the scholar's is not. Thus, the origin of religion is to be found in what Durkheim called the group consciousness, and he denied that it was to be found in mythology. Man created his gods for socially necessary purposes. His negation of mythology as an explanation in no way conceals his basic humanism and his antitheistic position. For Durkheim all religions were inherently human phenomena, and the resulting deities were cast in the image of their creators. "It is because of the fact that the existence of gods depends upon human thought that men are able to believe in the effectiveness of divine assistance."[3]

Thus, prayer and religious worship are simply psychological experiences. Man worships a god whom he has created, but in so doing seemingly obtains some mental or moral strength for daily living. The effectiveness of such a worship, however, depends upon its collective character. When religious faith lags, according to Durkheim, it can be rekindled only by groups assembled for religious worship.

> Common faith becomes quite naturally revived in the heart of this reconstituted group; it is reborn because it again meets the very conditions in which it was created in the first place. After having been restored it easily triumphs over all the private doubts which may have arisen in the individual.[4]

This is obviously a statement of the pragmatic need for religion. Durkheim is here upholding a kind of civil religion of a purely human character as necessary for the well-being of the social structure. It makes very little difference what form this worship may take, just so long as it has a cohesive power within the society which practices this particular form of religious exercise. For Durkheim, religion, then, constituted the primary form of the collective conscience, and around this concept he built his whole concept of sociology as an independent discipline. Religion as the collective science originally absorbed all the intellectual and practical functions, constituting a humanistic rival to Christian theism at this point. He ventured the prophecy that in the future religion would play a much smaller part in the life of man than it played in early times, or in the Middle Ages. Social evolution would bring about such an era.

---

2. Ibid., p. 220. 3. Ibid., p. 221. 4. Ibid., p. 225.

> If there is one truth history teaches us beyond doubt it is that religion tends to embrace a smaller and smaller sector of social life. Originally, it pervaded everything; every big society is religious. . . . Then political, economic, scientific functions free themselves from religious control, establish themselves separately and take on more and more openly temporal character. . . . This regression did not begin at some certain moment in history; we can follow its development from the early phases of social evolution. It is thus linked to the fundamental conditions of the development of societies and this shows that there is an increasing number of collective beliefs and sentiments which are both collective and strong enough to assume a religious character.[5]

Having thoroughly anchored his approach to knowledge in the theory of evolution, Durkheim felt free to proceed with the development of his goal to provide not only a sociology, but all the social sciences, with a distinctive methodology which he regarded as scientific in nature and yet distinct from that methodology used by the natural and biological sciences. The irrationalism inherent in these primary assumptions stalk his efforts to achieve his goal at every point. This acidity of irrationalism dissolves the possibility of an effective use of the scientific method at the very outset, since he was forced to redefine truth in terms of constant change. As a result, his sociological formulations and theory were subject to this ruinous defect.

For his sociological millennium Durkheim looked to the past rather than to the future. Along with Max Weber, he may well be considered the founder of modern sociology.[6]

Durkheim was no slavish follower of either Weber or Comte. He insisted that the social order is governed by its own laws, and thus sociological insights could not be deduced from, or reduced to, either material power or the modes of production alone. In fact, he was quite anti-Marxist, even though he shared many of the basic presuppositions which had entered into the formulation of the communist theory and practice.

Curiously enough, Durkheim based his methodology on an assumption which, by its very nature, must exclude any kind of scientific proof. He assumed the existence of a collective consciousness or social mind. But he had rejected the idea of the soul in man, so he could not speak of a social soul. If we keep in mind the fact that Durkheim was searching for an answer to the question as to how it is possible to maintain order in a society composed of individuals with sharply conflicting interests, we will

5. Ibid., p. 245.

6. His main writings are: *The Division of Labor in Modern Society* (1893), *Rules of Sociological Method* (1895), *Suicide* (1897), and *Elementary Forms of Religious Life*.

have some inkling as to why he accepted and used a presupposition which was so foreign to the scientific methodology which he professed to follow. His solution is strangely similar to that of Rousseau, with a bit of Hobbes added as an extra and somewhat incongruous ingredient, to the sociological pie. The basic purpose which Durkheim had in view was a method by which he could unite the interests of the individual members of society (or at least a majority of them), in such a way that these individuals would become unconscious representatives of the communal ideals as against their own individual interests. He further believed that these collective ideals would serve as the collective consciousness of a society. This aspect of his thought strongly resembles Rousseau's theory of the corporate will. Using the mixture of chemical elements to produce substance which becomes quite different from its original constituents in its properties, Durkheim then applied this principle to sociology.

> Let us apply those principles to sociology. If . . . this synthesis constituting every society yields new phenomena, differing from those which take place in the individual consciousnesses, we must, indeed, admit that these facts reside exclusively in the very society itself which produced them, and not in its parts, i.e., its members. They are, then, in this sense external to individual consciousness . . . just as the existing characteristics of life are external to mineral substances composing the living being. . . . Thus, we have a new justification for the separation which we have established between psychology, which is properly the science of the mind of the individual and sociology.[7]

At first glance, it would seem that Durkheim was not only divorcing sociology from psychology and placing it in the realm of the sub- or unconscious state of society as a whole, but that he was also abandoning once more the scientific methodology on which he was seeking to build his system. Apparently he was aware of such a charge against his position being a possibility and he hastened to deny that this was his intent. He seemed to realize that in making this distinction he opened himself to the charge that he was drawing too great a distinction between social and psychological facts. Having advanced from the shallow waters of irrationalism, he was now in the position of nearly being over his head. He saw that some kind of a retreat or restatement of his position was necessary.

> Social facts do not differ from psychological facts in quality only; *they have a different substratum;* they evolve in different milieu; and they depend on different conditions. This does not mean that they are not also mental after a fashion, since they all consist of ways of *thinking* or behaving. But the states of collective consciousness are different in

7. Durkheim, *Rules of Sociological Method,* pp. xlviii-xlix.

> nature from the states of individual consciousness. . . . The mentality of groups is not the same as that of individuals; it has its own laws. The two sciences are thus as clearly distinct as two sciences whatever relationship there may be otherwise between them.[8]

This explanation is far from convincing and should even be acceptable to convinced evolutionists. Durkheim, in his efforts to extricate himself from the embarrassment of his own position, was really insisting that both psychology and sociology are subject to the evolutionary process, but the laws of evolution do not apply to both of these sciences in the same way. Unfortunately for Durkheim, he did not, or was not able to, muster any scientific evidence in behalf of this unsupported supposition.

For the Christian, his defense is even less impressive. His doctrine of social restraint (his theory of collective consciousness) is, by his own confession, based upon the presupposition that the key aspect of his whole social theory rests upon its irrational operation within a given society, for,

> . . . it is the very essence of the idea of social constraint; for it merely implies that collective ways of acting or thinking have a reality outside the individuals, who, at every moment of time, conform to it. These ways of thinking or acting exist in their own right. The individual finds them completely formed and he cannot evade or change them. He is therefore obliged to reckon with them.[9]

Durkheim admitted that it was possible, although difficult, for an individual to modify these collective ways of thinking and acting. He also admitted that the individual played a role in their origins. But for there to be social facts, several individuals must have contributed to their action, and such a joint activity contributes the origin of a new fact. Since this joint action takes place outside of the individuals who initiated it, "it thus becomes necessary to institute certain external ways of acting and certain judgments which do not depend on each particular will taken separately."[10] Durkheim concluded this portion of the argument by insisting that "institution" best defines this portion of reality, and he defined "institution" to mean that special mode of reality. Thus society as a science, for Durkheim, was the science of institutions, of their origins and their functions.

When we look beneath this sociological jargon, a startling meaning appears. As harmless as it may appear to be on the surface, a closer inspection reveals the frightening character of his definitions. In the first place, this collective consciousness, which lies at the very heart of his system, should be called a "collective unconsciousness" with much greater accu-

8. Ibid., xlix. 9. Ibid., lvi. 10. Ibid.

racy. Since Durkheim denied that individauls possess souls, he was, at the same time, denying logically that they would be truly conscious. If men are not conscious of the image of God within them, how can they be conscious either of themselves or of created reality of which they are a part? If this be the case, how can a collective consciousness somehow emerge from many unconscious individuals? Durkheim had no answer for this all-important question.

The denial of an individual consciousness must, by its very logic, be a denial of the doctrine of moral consciousness and responsibility. Logically, moral anarchy could only be the result of such a definition of man. Durkheim, however, attempted to avoid this logical implication by creating a fictitious doctrine of moral compulsion resident in this collective will. Even as a collective consciousness was somehow supposed to grow out of a state of individual unconsciousness on the part of those who initiated this new social fact, so does a power of moral compulsion rise out of this anarchistic concept of man.

We must go even further with this analysis of Durkheim's contributions to modern sociology, if they can be so called. His doctrine of collective compulsion is not only irrational, but politically dangerous. If he, along with Max Weber, committed the study of social relationships in their institutional form to the embrace of an unmitigated irrationalism, and they did, in the same way they committed this discipline to the cause of political tyranny and the destruction of human political, social, and economic freedom. They achieved their goal through the thinly veiled use of Rousseau's doctrine of the collective will and the introduction of some Hobbesian principles through the back door of the social sciences. It is no accident that most contemporary sociologists can be counted as members of that group in this country who are insistent in their demands for a greater and greater governmental control over the American people, their homes, their family life, their political institutions, the schools, the church, and other social institutions. Although they speak loudly and fondly of human rights, they speak as tinkling cymbals, for they prefer to destroy freedom—the freedoms still remaining to us—in the name of some tenuous conception known as human rights, which they frequently interpret as the right to abort, to cut off life, to sex without marriage, to engage in rioting, and to engage in revolution.

Some will immediately object that such a result was quite contrary to Durkheim's purpose, and they will insist that he was against such an order and desired by his approach to the study of human institutions to lay down a chart for achieving and maintaining civil order. With this we must agree. The answer lies in the fact that he chose certain basic presuppositions and a methodology which were destructive of these basic and desirable goals. Using a faulty view of man, he could only build on a faulty view of human freedom and erect a view of society which would be dangerous for the maintenance of the very values which he professed to cherish.

The dangers inherent in the application of his theories to the state become very obvious in his writings on political topics. His definition of the state is positivistic. For him it consisted of the union of a fairly large number of secondary social groups which are subject to the same authority and which, in turn, is not itself subject to any other permanently constituted superior political authority.[11]

The development of states has, through history, followed an evolutionary pattern and at the same time, Durkheim argued, "while the cult of the individual is a superstition of which we ought to rid ourselves, to do so would be to go against all the lessons of history, for the more we investigate history the more we find the human person tending to gain in dignity."[12] It is doubtful that Durkheim could hold such a presupposition if he had lived through the first fifty years of the twentieth century. The historical trends of our era would have almost certainly destroyed his buoyant hope in the beneficent outcome of the evolutionary process. His insistence that no law is more firmly established than that which promises the continued development of human dignity has a hollow ring today. But why and how could Durkheim be so confident of the enduring quality of this law of history? We cannot force things to be other than they are. We cannot stop the individual from having become what he is—an autonomous center of activity, an imposing system of personal forces whose energy can no more be destroyed than that of cosmic forces. It would be just as impossible to transform the physical atmosphere in the midst of which we breathe.[13]

Once again we are brought face to face with an insurmountable contradiction in Durkheim's thought. How can an impersonal individual without a soul become an autonomous center of activity in the midst of a set of natural forces and laws over which he has no control? Is it not true, even for Durkheim, that death, a natural force, places a fatal limitation on this imposing system of personal forces whose energy cannot be destroyed? Durkheim, at this point, then admits another insoluble contradiction to his system:

> On the other hand we establish that the state goes on developing more and more; on the other, that the rights of the individual, which appear

---

11. Durkheim, *Selected Writings*. 12. Ibid., p. 195. 13. Ibid., p. 196.

to be antagonistic to those of the state, have a parallel development. The government organ takes on an even greater scale, because its function goes on growing in importance and because the aims that demand its intervention increase in number, and yet we deny that it can pursue aims other than those that concern the individual. But these aims seem to belong to the individuals alone. If . . . the rights of the individual are given in the individual, the state does not have to intervene to establish them, they depend only upon the individual. But if this is so, and these rights are outside its sphere of action, how can this sphere of action go on expanding, if on the other hand it must avoid those things which compromise the interests of the individual?[14]

It will be observed that at this point Durkheim, looking ahead, saw the issue which confronts all democracies: How to maintain either the historic seventeenth-century concept of the origin and nature of natural rights on the one hand, or the biblical view on the other, in face of the democratic principle involved in the paradoxical situation which occurs when people who possess these rights also demand that the powers of government be expanded in such a way that their historic rights are threatened, even to the point of virtual destruction, as happened in Nazi Germany, Soviet Russia, and other such totalitarian states. Durkheim offered an answer for this apparently insoluble dilemma which has become very popular in the Western world and is most certainly not absent from contemporary American political thought and practice. His answer:

The only way of disposing of this difficulty is to reject the postulate that the rights of individuals are given in the individual and to admit that the institution of these rights is in fact precisely the task of the state. Then, in fact, everything becomes clear. We can understand that the functions of the state may expand without any diminishing of the individual. We can see too that the individual may develop without causing any decline of the state since he would be in some respects himself the product of the state, and since the activity of the state would be essentially one of individual liberation.[15]

If we translate this sociological jargon into a more suitable form, we will then see that Durkheim is insisting that the only solution to the problem is for the individual to recognize that he has no inherent rights, inalienable because they are divinely bestowed upon him, and to accept the fact that they are the gift of the state, and in some mysterious way this recognition will advance both individual liberty on the one hand, and the role of the state as the champion of collective liberty on the other.

---

14. Ibid.
15. Ibid., p. 196. It should be noted that this is essentially the Hegelian view of freedom. For Hegel, the state conferred personality and rights upon its citizens.

Durkheim offered a further defense of his position by stating that democracy existed only in the early history of a society: "If everyone governs, it means in fact there is no government." But as he redefined democracy according to his basic postulates—a definition which really spells out a "democratically controlled totalitarianism"—Durkheim could offer this cheering note on what such a state could expect: "Seen from this [his] standpoint, a democracy thus appears as the political system by which the society can achieve a consciousness of itself in its purest form."[16]

This view of the state and democracy has become very popular during the twentieth century. This is the reason why Stalin could refer to the Soviet system as the most highly developed form of democracy. It also explains how Hitler could achieve power in Germany by a similar argument, using the legitimate political means placed at his disposal through the Weimar Constitution.[17] Durkheim offers a blueprint for the erection of a totalitarian regime using his sociological theory as the basic guide for its realization.

It might also be well to remember that this kind of thinking was part of Roosevelt's strategy in the 1932 presidential campaign, when he was able to defeat Herbert Hoover by a very large majority in the popular vote. Roosevelt was very careful in relating his campaign addresses to the particular audiences, whether they would consist largely of farmers, the laboring classes, Southerners, or professional people of various kinds, as well as the professional radicals who were eager to climb aboard his bandwagon. Very seldom did he reveal his basic political thought. On one occasion, however, he spoke with great clarity and to some length on his basic political thought, but this speech did not receive nearly as much attention from the press as his other addresses, and was not broadcast over the networks. At the Commonwealth Club in September, 1932, he was very forthright and related his New Deal to Jefferson's political philosophy with political embellishments which Jefferson would have repudiated, at least in 1776. In this "Commonwealth Club" address Roosevelt made it very clear that he wanted the kind of a political democracy which Durkheim favored.

> The Declaration of Independence discusses the problems of government in terms of a contract, perforce, if we should follow the thinking out of which it grew. Under such a contract rulers were accorded power

16. Ibid., p. 199.
17. This is not to say that other factors, political, social, and economic, did not aid the rise of these dictatorships. But underlying these factors was the motivating power of irrational political philosophy, which was ideally suited for their use.

> and the people consented to that power on the consideration that they were accorded certain rights. The task of statesmanship has always been the redefining of those rights in terms of a changing and growing social order. New conditions impose new requirements upon government and those who conduct government.[18]

That this is a gross misrepresentation of the thinking of Jefferson and the other members of the committee who aided him in drafting the Declaration of Independence is hardly worth debating. Roosevelt was guilty of a flagrant misrepresentation of that document, and it is very difficult to believe that he was unaware of this. Whatever else these men had in mind, it is clear that the social contract they had in mind did not involve the idea that rulers were accorded power on the consideration that they accorded certain rights to those whom they ruled. The opening paragraphs of the Declaration make such an interpretation absolutely impossible.

Nevertheless, it is equally clear that Roosevelt had in mind a totalitarian pattern for the future shape and conduct of the government of the United States as a result of which a false interpretation of the Declaration of Independence would repeal the Bill of Rights and other parts of the Constitution of 1787. Under Roosevelt a radical and irrational sociology would triumph over the theistic English and colonial political tradition as that tradition had been enshrined in the work of the Philadelphia Constitutional Convention.

It has never been the task of responsible statesmanship in either the United States or western European countries to define human rights according to the changed conditions of the times. This is sheer relativism. Granted that changes are ever taking place in human society. But it has never been maintained by those who hold to the historic political traditions that such changes ever impose upon government the requirement that it redefine the very rights that it was, according to Locke and the Social Contract, designed to protect. With even less force can it be maintained that at any time has it ever been the task of statesmanship to redefine those rights granted to mankind by a sovereign God. But Durkheim, Stalin, and their followers had solved this problem by dethroning, in their own thinking, that sovereign God who instituted human government for the proper regulation of human affairs.[19]

The invasion of political affairs by sociologists has given a new strength to the irrationalism inherent in modern political thought and a new impetus to run government according to these sociological dictums, which are

---

18. Franklin Delano Roosevelt, *Public Papers* (1928–1932), pp. 742-756.
19. See Romans 13:1-8.

extremely dangerous.[20] Because of the tendency of governmental officials to be more attentive to the pontifical pronouncements of sociologists and psychologists and less attentive to the demands of the Constitution and common law requirements, the irrationalism which has inundated the areas commonly known as the social sciences has spread like an uncontrolled cancer over the whole of the body politic, not only in this country but in most of the countries of Europe as well. Thus, the basic philosophy of the federal government today has become tuned to the demands of cancerous irrationalism, which can only destroy the American legal and constitutional heritage and our political system as well.

Vilfredo Pareto (1849–1923)

Many historians of social and political thought regard Vilfredo Pareto as one of the most important sociologists. Although he was born in Paris, his parents had fled to Italy, apparently because of his monarchistic opinions of his allegiance to the cause of Mazzini. His early training was in the field of civil engineering, and this fact undoubtedly gave him a background and approach to social and economic problems not usually associated with social theorists. Something of the elements of his later social thought can be traced back to his graduation thesis written for the Turin Polytechnic Institute, *The Fundamental Principle of Equilibrium in Solid Bodies*.

After a career in business he became tremendously interested in economic problems and wrote a host of pamphlets on economic topics. In 1893 he was named to the chair of political economy at the University of Lausanne. He was still ardently democratic in his outlook, and this philosophy was clearly reflected in his first major work, *La Liberté economique etles evenments d'Italie*.

By 1900 his political philosophy had undergone a dramatic change, and he became passionately anti-democratic in his outlook. The cause for this change seems to lie in his disappointment at the way the Dreyfus Affair was handled in France and the tremendous growth of communist thought in Italy. According to S. E. Finer, this intellectual revolution took place suddenly in 1897, when he turned his back on his previously held libertarian outlook and came to the conclusion that most human activity was not the product of rational thinking, but of sentiment. In brief, human history is the story of the irrational acts of men who try to find a rational

20. Modern sociology vies with contemporary psychology and philosophy for being the most irrational of the academic disciplines. An impartial judge would have great difficulty in deciding which would be awarded first place in this dubious contest.

justification for what they have already done. Pareto decided to write a sociology devoted to this principle of irrationalism. Basic to his system was his insistence that there must be a sharp distinction between human thought and human action. He thus sharply restricted the role of reason, admitting that it can tell people how to do what they have already decided to do, but it cannot help men to come to any judgment as to the desirability or merit of human wants. It was by such a sharp distinction that he could assert the irrationality of human actions. He admitted that in scientific research logic reigns unchallenged, but although science is important in the quest for knowledge of certain kinds, it is of practically no value as a guide to conduct.

After indicting political and social theorists for laying down useless prescriptions of a metaphysical nature, which are not useful because they actually represent the intrusion of metaphysics into the area of human conduct, Pareto then outlined in principle the role of science and the scientific method in obtaining knowledge.

> For the purpose of knowing, logico-experimental science is the only thing of any value; for the purpose of doing, it is of much greater importance to follow the lead of sentiments. And here again, another important fact comes to the fore: the advantage as regards eliminating that conflict, of having a community divided into parts, the one in which knowledge prevails ruling and directing and the other in which sentiments prevail, so that in the end action is vigorous and wisely directed.[21]

Pareto's system did not achieve its maturity until the appearance of *The Mind and Society* (1915–1916), although some of its basic insights are found in his earlier works such as his *Cours d'Economie Politique* (1896).

The key to the understanding of Pareto was his concern for social order in a world of irrationality. This is the main theme of his writings after 1900, and he devoted his *Mind and Society* to the achievement of such a goal. In his search for such an order he devoted considerable attention to the description and classification of what he considered to be the non-logical or irrational drives that motivate human conduct. He came to the conclusion that in all periods of human history there was a fairly small number of such motivating factors which have been possessed by every society in every period of history. Denying that these drives are instincts, he preferred to call them residues, and he defined them in more or less satisfactory terminology:

---

21. Vilfredo Pareto, *The Mind and Society*, 4 vols. (New York, 1935), II, 1241.

> The residues must not be confused with the sentiments or instincts to which they correspond. The residues are the manifestations of sentiments and instincts just as the rising of the mercury in a thermometer is a manifestation of the rising of the temperature. Only elliptically and for the sake of brevity do we say that the residues, along with appetites, interests, etc., are the main factors in determining the social equilibrium, just as we say that water boils at 100 degrees Centigrade.[22]

Pareto then proceeded to delineate six different types of residues.[23] The first, residues of combination, he defined as those characteristics of human beings which cause men to strive to enter into cultural activity of various kinds. The second class of residues he defined as those which cause men to enter into various kinds of social relationships and then defend the resulting institutions. In this category he placed the family and various social classes. Class three he looked upon as comprising those social combinations which were the result of the need of doing something and included within this category what he called religious ecstasies, by which he meant what is commonly called religious worship and accompanying activities. This third group also explained, in his thinking, human political activities. His fourth group consisted of those human characteristics which he connected with sociability, by which he meant the human tendency to conform to group standards of various kinds and to enforce conformity upon others. The fifth category of residues centered around those tendencies which cause men to safeguard their own integrity and strive for certain kinds of equality. The sixth category he called the sex residue, to which he devoted considerable attention. While he was not a Freudian and did not find in sexual activity the dominant drive in human life, he nevertheless held in contempt the Christian view of sex. His attitude became very evident in his discussion of prostitution:

> It is one of the dogmas of present day religion of sex that prostitution is an absolute "evil" and like every other dogma, it is not debatable. But from the experiential standpoint it is still a question whether prostitution may, or may not, be the occupation best suited to temperament of certain women, as being more congenial to them than any other that they might follow; and whether prostitution is, or is not, within certain limits beneficial to society as a whole. Followers of the modern religion of sex offer no proof whatever in support of their answers to these questions.[24]

Pareto adopted his theory of moral relativity as answer to the question

---

22. Ibid., p. 511.
23. For his definitions and explanations of these six types, see ibid., pp. 517-884.
24. Ibid., pp. 863-864.

and pointed out that prostitution had existed at all times in human history and in all societies, and that it differed in no way from other commonly accepted religious rites. His conclusion was that legislation against this practice was futile and that it would continue throughout human history. It was therefore, in his thinking, "right" simply because it was socially acceptable and an even necessary residue.

Pareto's Political Theory

After his conversion from liberalism to his new outlook, it is quite evident that Pareto assumed a low view of human nature and actually held men in disdain and even contempt. This low estimate of the human race dominated his sociology, and it should be no surprise to learn that it also dominated his political thought as well. In fact, his whole outlook on man as an individual and his society was a logical and necessary consequence of his acceptance of the Darwinian thought. In his efforts to exalt man and to emphasize human autonomy, Darwin had actually dehumanized and debased man by robbing him of stature as a creature bearing the image of the personal God revealed in the Scriptures.

Pareto's reliance upon the Darwinian hypothesis has the same irrational character as that possessed by his sociology. Because the theory of evolution was so deeply imbedded in his political philosophy, it made his outlook on the powers and function of the government extremely dangerous. It was no mere coincidence that his *Mind and Society* appeared a few short years before the emergence of Mussolini and the fascist state in Italy and the rise of the Nazi system in Germany. After his dramatic conversion from his earlier liberalism to his later outlook on government, his views were accompanied by a cynical attitude toward government as an institution. It could well be argued that his position was no more irrational than his previous liberal outlook, but his later position was that which carried a far greater weight in European thought and was, therefore, more dangerous to the cause of human liberty.

One can appreciate his cynicism as he unfolded his insight into the rise of the democratic movement in the various countries of Europe and can share with him his deep apprehension of the pious pretensions which the various absolutist and despotic regimes put forth as a justification for their rise to power.[25] We can also appreciate his sharp criticism of the defenses usually put forth by these various kinds of absolutist governments as a justification for their seizure of power.

---

25. See ibid., vol. IV, pp. 1503-1540, for an interesting treatment of this aspect of Pareto's philosophy of government.

> All governments use force, and all assert they are founded on reason. In fact, whether universal suffrage prevails or not, it is always an oligarchy that governs, finding ways to give to the "will of the people" that expression which the few desire, from the "royal law" that bestowed the *imperium* on the Roman emperors down to the votes of a legislative majority elected in one way or another, from the plebiscite that the empire gave to Napoleon III down to the universal suffrage that is shrewdly bought, steered and manipulated by our "speculators." Who is this new god called Universal Suffrage? He is no more exactly definable, no less shrouded in mystery, no less beyond the pale of reality than the hosts of other divinities; nor are there fewer and less patent contradictions in his theology than in theirs. Worshippers of Universal Suffrage are not led by their god. It is they who lead him—and not by the nose, determining the forms in which he must manifest himself. Oftentimes, proclaming the sanctity of "majority rule," they resist "majority rule" by obstructionist tactics, even though they form but small minorities, and burning incense to the goddess Reason, they in no wise disdain, in certain cases, alliances with chicanery, fraud and corruption.[26]

Along with this disdain of popular government, Pareto also held to a view of the composition of society which was by no means original with him and which was not an essential ingredient of his evolutionary outlook. However, Pareto gave to this view an interpretation which was different from that of John C. Calhoun or even of Arnold Toynbee. Pareto was convinced that every society known to history had been divided into two groups—the elite and the non-elite. But he also gave this view a peculiar twist. Within each of these societies there is an almost constant circulation of the members of the elite, by which he meant a constant shifting from this upper and privileged class within a society to the lower classes. From this assumption he drew the conclusion that every such elite group is doomed to disappear.

> Aristocracies do not last. Whatever the cause, it is an incontestable fact that after a certain length of time, they pass away. History is the graveyard of aristocracies . . . they decay not in numbers only. They decay also in equality, in the sense that they lose their vigor.[27]

Stability is achieved in any government only when the elite is willing to assimilate or destroy those who seek entrance into its ranks. If, however, the elite group refuses to accept new members and becomes so weakened by what Pareto called the poison of humanitarianism and is thereby unwilling to destroy those who seek entrance, then revolution becomes a

---

26. Ibid., pp. 1526-1527.
27. Ibid., vol. III, p. 1430.

real threat. What then is the conclusion which he drew from this picture of humanity? In him we hear the echo of Machiavelli and other political philosophers whose rationalistic approach to the problem of government was essentially irrational.

> That being so [that humanitarianism begets revolution] the art of government lies in finding ways to take advantage of such sentiments, not in wasting one's energies in futile efforts to destroy them, the sole effect of the latter course very frequently being only to strengthen them. The person who is able to free himself from the blind dominion of his own sentiments is capable of utilizing the sentiments of other people for his own ends.[28]

If any doubt remains as to exactly what Pareto had in mind, the following quotation should end any uncertainty as to what this leading modern sociologist had to say:

> To ask whether or not force ought to be used in a society, whether use of force is or is not beneficial, is to ask a question that has no meaning.[29]

To raise moral issues involving the use of force is a meaningless question and also dangerous. The echo of Machiavelli is gaining strength as we continue our study of Pareto.

> The use of force is indispensable to society; and when the higher classes are averse to the use of force, which ordinarily happens because the majority of those classes come to rely wholly on their skill at chicanery, and the minority shrink from energetic acts now through stupidity, now through cowardice, it becomes necessary, if society is to subsist and prosper, that the governing class be replaced by another which is willing and able to use force. Roman society was saved from ruin by the legions of Caesar and Octavius. So it may happen that our society will one day be saved from decadence by the heirs of the Syndicalists and anarchists of our day.[30]

We can and must sympathize with Pareto as a thoroughly disillusioned liberal. He saw clearly that liberalism as a philosophy had been betraying and was continuing to betray its followers, even to the point of duping them. But what he apparently did not realize was that it was not possible (and is not possible today) to fight one form of irrationalism with another form drawn from the same original sources. The Renaissance cannot be used to overcome the decadent forces inherent in its irrationalism. Pareto's own efforts were an exercise in futility. John Hallowell has given to us a mag-

28. Ibid., p. 1281.
29. Ibid., vol. IV, p. 1512.
30. Ibid., vol. III, p. 1293.

nificent insight and criticism of Pareto's whole system of thought:

> A disillusioned liberal, Pareto's work is premised upon cynicism and a frank contempt for human personality. It is a curious twentieth century phenomenon that so many intellectuals should be so actively engaged in the task of persuading other intellectuals by *reason* that men are essentially irrational. That rational justification for such a view of man should be thought either necessary or possible is itself a refutation of the conclusion that intellectuals seek by rational arguments to persuade others to accept.[31]

The answer to the dilemma which Professor Hallowell so ably posed lies in the fact that even though they endeavor to disavow their divine origin and the God-given meaning and purpose of life, they cannot even persuade men to accept irrationalism unless it is presented within the framework which is premised upon the assumption that man possesses a spark of rationality by which he understands the irrational as it is conveyed to him by those whose frame of reference is irrational.[32]

However contradictory and hopelessly irrational Pareto's view of society and government were, and are, the unhappy fact is that they appealed to many illusioned liberals who were equally devoted to the cult which Pareto sponsored, and this group, its numbers greatly enlarged by the turmoil brought on by World War I both in Germany and in Italy; this group was ready to welcome an "elite" leadership which was eager to use the very force which Pareto suggested as the means of resorting to that political, social, and economic equilibrium which he and other intellectuals regarded as the only possible solution for the serious problems which the nations faced. The irrationalism of Western philosophy produced the irrationalism inherent in the modern totalitarian state.

Alfred North Whitehead (1866–1952)

Assuming a somewhat different approach and pursuing a goal of interpreting philosophy in the light of recent scientific developments, Alfred North Whitehead is nevertheless to be classified as a member of the Transitional School of thinkers who were trained in the nineteenth-century brand of philosophic liberalism, yet who at the same time were greatly influenced by the more recent scientific developments of the first half of the present century. Although the members of this group responded in different ways to their own heritage and to these contemporary influences, they were

---

31. John Hallowell, *Main Currents in Modern Political Thought* (New York, 1950), p. 542.
32. For the theistic solution to this dilemma, see chapter 14.

transitional in the sense that they brought elements of nineteenth-century thought to bear upon the sociological, economic, political, and philosophical issues which were derived from the integration of the thought of these two centuries in an effort to forge a new pattern and harmony of the old and the new. Whitehead's long life span gave to him an unusual opportunity to be a philosophic bridge between these two eras. To this goal he devoted his entire academic and intellectual career.

Whitehead's philosophy has frequently been called a process philosophy on the ground that he rejected the older or static view of science. He did this in the interest of human freedom. Beginning with the insistence that "we must start with the event as the ultimate unit of natural occurrence,"[33] he defined "event" as the most concrete finite entity and then went on to conclude that "this idea of 'event' is a process whose outcome is a unit of experience."[34] In the light of this definition, Whitehead then proceeded to enthrone freedom above all forms of necessity that may be found in reality. Cornelius Van Til interpreted Whitehead to the effect that his idea of events sets man above the older static notions of science. It is also true that this idea of event enabled Whitehead to avoid "paying metaphysical compliments" to God.

Paradoxically, many thinkers of the twentieth century, in their desire to establish what they call the religious significance of the concept of God, regard Whitehead as their ally, "as the foundation of the metaphysical situation with its ultimate activity."[35] Whitehead was, and is indeed, a weak reed upon which to lean for the introduction of any theistic concepts in a philosophical system. In fact, his system was carefully designed to prevent any such "disaster" from taking place. Although he had been reared within the folds of the evangelical wing of the Church of England, he broke out of these restricting fetters as a young man and sought a substitute for evangelical Christianity, first in science and then in philosophy. It was not his intention to provide a platform for the entry of historic orthodoxy into process philosophy. To read Whitehead in any other way is to misread him completely.

Whitehead first broached his view of God in his *Science and the Modern World.* (1925). This presentation does not present his more mature insight and reflects his earliest scientific interests rather than his metaphysical.

---

33. A. N. Whitehead, *Science and the Modern World* (New York, 1925), p. 105.
34. Ibid., p. 179. See also Van Til's unpublished lecture on "Kant and Protestantism," pp. 5-6. This most valuable collection of his lectures is found in a complete set in the library of the Westminster Theological Seminary, Philadelphia, Pa.
35. Whitehead, *Science and the Modern World,* p. 179.

This incomplete view of God is developed in his later works and most importantly in his *Religion in the Making* (1926), *Process and Reality* (1929), *Adventures in Ideas* (1933), and finally in his *Modes of Thought* (1938).

His stating that his views of God and religion underwent important changes as Whitehead himself shifted from his interest in science and mathematics does not imply that he came closer to the biblical doctrine of God or any form of theism in general. Such is not the case. The changes do not imply a spiritual development in Whitehead's outlook. This is not the case if we are thinking in terms of the biblical concept of spirituality. His reliance upon process philosophy would prevent any such development, for Whitehead looked upon theology of any kind with deep suspicion. An unchanging orthodoxy, whether it be that of the Roman Catholic Church or that of historic Protestantism, was little less than anathema to him. For him, theology must always be a continuing activity. The roots of true religion do not lie in theological formulations, but in religious experience and history. Theological dogmas, like metaphysical systems, are, at best, only bits of truth. He maintained that "religions commit suicide when they find their inspiration in dogmas."[36] Theology must always be in the process of developing, even as is the study of metaphysics. His entire position implies that without metaphysics there cannot be a real theology.

Whitehead offered several definitions of religion which, because of their contradictions, are confusing and do very little to shed light on what he really thought. From the Christian perspective it is perhaps better to explain what he felt religion was *not,* rather than what it actually is. One or two examples will illustrate the perplexity of his thinking and the difficulty of finding a focal point for understanding his position.

> Religion is an ultimate craving to infuse into the insistent peculiarity of emotion that non-temporal generality which primarily belongs to conceptual thought alone.[37]

In another place he defined religion: "Religion is centered upon the harmony of rational thought with the sensitive reaction to the percepts from which experience originates."

The tragic nature of his thinking in regard to religion appears most strongly in his concluding chapter of *Process and Reality,* in which he wrote:

> Throughout the perishing occasions in the life of each temporal creature, the inward source of distaste or of refreshment, the judge arising

36. Alfred North Whitehead, *Religion in the Making* (New York, 1926), p. 144.
37. Alfred North Whitehead, *Process and Reality* (New York, 1929), vol. I, p. vi.

> out of the very nature of things, redeemer or goddess of mischief, is the transformation of itself into everlasting in the being of God. In this way, the insistent craving is justified—the insistent craving, that zest for existence be refreshed by the ever-present, unfading importance of our immediate actions, which perish and yet live forevermore.[38]

This tragic affirmation of a kind of immortality which is man-made and which arises only out of his desire for some kind of immortal existence was the logical conclusion to his view of God which precedes this definition of religion and immortality.

> Thus the consequent nature of God is composed of a multiplicity of elements with individual self-realization. It is just as much a multiplicity as it is a unity. . . . Thus the actuality of God must also be understood as a multiplicity of actual components in process of creation. This is God in his function of the Kingdom of Heaven. Each actuality in the temporal world has its reception into God's nature. The corresponding element in God's nature is not temporal actuality, but is the transmutation of that temporal actuality into a living, ever-present fact.[39]

It is evident from the foregoing that Whitehead's god, whatever else he may be, is not the living God of the Scriptures, nor is he the Creator and Sustainer of the universe. If there is any doubt as to his finite nature, it should be removed by the following:

> An enduring personality in the temporal world is a routine of occasions in which the successors with some peculiar completeness sum up their predecessors. The correlated fact in God's nature is an even more complete unity of life in a chain of elements for which succession does not mean loss of immediate unison. The elements in God's nature inherit from the temporal counterpart according to the same principle as in the temporal world the future inherits from the past. Thus, in the sense in which the present occasion is the person now, and yet within his own past, is the counterpart in God is that person in God.[40]

Whitehead's theology, or process philosophy and its correlative of the Great Chain of Being, is a form of pantheism, albeit a confusing form, and a futile effort to prevent atheism from creeping into his system.

Van Til rightly sees that if Whitehead consistently adhered to this view of God, there could be no alternative except to discern in this being the origin of all evil as well as of all good. This must be the case of every actuality in the temporal world which has its reception into God's nature.[41]

---

38. Ibid., p. 413.
39. Ibid., p. 412.
40. Ibid., p. 413.
41. Van Til, "Kant and Protestantism," p. 6.

For Whitehead, God is the ultimate limitation, and it had to be this in order for him to limit science so as to make way for faith. But this limitation posed a difficulty for his system which was not easily overcome. To accomplish this limitation, Whitehead found that the notion of matter must be replaced by the organism, its notion of static substance by that of function.[42] "Every actual occasion exhibits itself as a process; it is a becomingness."[43]

It was by such a maneuver that Whitehead felt that he had made room for religious faith in a system which did not logically make any provision for such an aberration. He virtually confessed his failure in the definition of religion which he gave at this point:

> Religion is the vision of something which stands beyond, behind and within, the passing flux of immediate things; something which is real and yet waiting to be realized; something which is a remote possibility, and yet the greatest of present facts; something that gives meaning to all that passes, and yet eludes apprehension; something whose possession is a final good, and yet is beyond all reach; something which is the ultimate ideal, and the hopeless quest.[44]

Whitehead's god is enmeshed in a quagmire of sheer relativity and the search to find him could only be a hopeless quest, but certainly not the final good. The irrationality which permeates this definition lurks beneath, and sometimes rests on the surface of his total thought. His denial of creation and divine providence, and his reliance on a theory of evolutionary thought, could hardly produce anything else but the irrationalism which grips his system and presses it into meaningless confusion. With him, process philosophy reached the nadir of despair. With it the freedom of man disappears into a sheer determinism resulting from the impersonality of his deity and the relentless forces of nature before which Whitehead bowed in abject submission.

We can only conclude that, like his contemporaries, he was a victim of the very irrationalism which he condemned. As a result, he condemned philosophy to it and pushed it towards its ultimate dissolution in clouds of agnostic pessimism. Denying the God of Scripture, he was forced to deny the reality and dignity of man and the achievement of any absolute truth for man. Only the process of change was truly real in Whitehead. Although his influence is strictly limited today, and some thinkers dismiss him as relatively unimportant, no study of the decline of the Western mind can be

---

42. Whitehead, *Science and the Modern World,* p. 180.
43. Ibid., p. 176.
44. Ibid., p. 191.

complete without paying due attention to Whitehead as one of the architects of its fate.

Bertrand Russell (1872–1970)

Bertrand Russell began his career as an idealist and held much in common with Alfred North Whitehead. By 1903, however, Russell turned from idealism and became a dualist, believing that mind and matter were the only realities, and this conviction became a veritable passion with him, since he felt that if he could find a relationship between them it would bring order into what he insisted was the muddled world of philosophy.

Although differing markedly at various points with his contemporary, Alfred North Whitehead, Russell offered no relief from the determinism and irrationality which characterized Whitehead's thinking. In fact, he cast aside the attempts of Whitehead to make a religious dimension in life as futile and not worthy of serious intellectual effort and accepted the dreary pessimism which Whitehead apparently refused to face as the logical consequence of his system.

After World War I, Russell emerged as a materialist in philosophy and a socialist in political interests. Morris Weitz is probably correct when he concludes that there is in Russell's career as a philosopher a unity which lurks beneath these changes, and that unity was "the justification of science, considered as a body of knowledge, and not as a set of techniques or principles."[45]

In his early years Russell was primarily concerned with the problem of reducing mathematics to a finite set of logical relationships and to show that, viewed in this light, this discipline was the only correct method of representing reality. To accomplish this aim he set out to construct an ideal language which would make it possible to translate any proposition into a logically correct form. In collaboration with Whitehead, his own professor at Cambridge University, he offered a solution to the problem in *Principia Mathematica* (1913). In this work he set forth what he called a syntax in the light of which he felt that any linguistic usage could be analyzed and its truthfulness or accuracy as a function of our expressions determined. Russell's philosophic system came to be based upon the assumption or conviction that the structure of language is the key by which we can be led to understand the structure of the world.[46]

Russell's further development of this theme led him to considerable

45. Morris Weitz, "Analysis of the Unity of Russell's Philosophy," in Paul A. Schlipp, ed., *The Philosophy of Bertrand Russell* (New York, 1963), vol. II, p. 103.
46. Bertrand Russell, *Inquiry Into Meaning and Truth* (Edinburgh, 1940), p. 341.

difficulties and brought him to a position which was close to that of logical positivism. It is obvious that this philosophy (if indeed it is a philosophy) made any kind of metaphysical concept impossible; and, driven to its logical conclusion, it actually made any reliable knowledge equally impossible. Its basic presupposition is that the correspondence existing between words and the things those words represented must be verified in terms of itself.

Russell rejected three modern theories concerning truth: the warranted assertibility concept as it had been set forth by John Dewey; the theory of probability; and, the theory which defined truth as coherence, advocated by the Hegelians and some logical positivists. Having rejected these three widely held contemporary epistemological theories, Russell boldly declared himself in favor of the fourth view, known as the correspondence theory of truth, "according to which the truth of basic propositions depends upon their relationship to some occurrence and the truth of other propositions depends upon their syntactical relationship to basic propositions."[47]

Russell gave a weak defense of his reliance upon this fourth view, which is important only to the extent to which it revealed the anti-intellectualism of his own position and an apparent fear that somehow he would find truth.

> For my part I adhere firmly to this last theory. It has, however, two forms, between which the decision is not easy. In one form, the basic propositions must be derived from experience, and therefore propositions which cannot be suitably related to experience are neither true nor false. . . . In the other form, the basic propositions need not be related to experience, but only to "fact," though if they are not related to experience they cannot be known. Thus the two forms of the correspondence theory differ as to the relation of "truth" to "knowledge."[48]

The real difficulty which Russell faced at this point is revealed in his use of quotation marks around the words *truth* and *knowledge.* Neither his logic nor his epistemology allows him to believe in truth as an unchangeable absolute. Not even Dewey's vacillating "warranted assertibility" could satisfy Russell. Although he placed a seeming importance on the relation of "truth" and "knowledge" in the discussion of the four theories in regard to the nature of truth, this importance was more superficial than real. The relationship can be of real importance only if both exist as absolutes and not as constructs of logical posivitism.[49]

Russell was not unaware that his position could easily lead to a complete

47. Ibid., p. 289.
48. Ibid.
49. For a more complete discussion of his position, see ibid., pp. 289-347.

agnosticism as far as the achievement of any certain knowledge or possible truth was concerned. Therefore, he fought off the attacks which would certainly be leveled against his position.

> We have arrived . . . at a result which has been, in a sense, the goal of all our discussions. The result I have in mind is this: that complete metaphysical agnosticism is not compatible with the maintenance of linguistic propositions. Some modern philosophers hold that we know much about language, but nothing about anything else. This view forgets that language is an empirical phenomenon like another, and that a man who is metaphysically agnostic must deny that he knows when he uses a word. For my part, I believe that, partly, by means of the study of syntax, we can arrive at considerable knowledge concerning the structure of the world.[50]

It is difficult to understand how Russell can conclude that he has escaped the impasse of the metaphysical agnosticism which he sees in some of the logical positivists. His religious agnosticism stares him in the face and stalks his every effort to escape the pitfall which he seeks to avoid. His view of the origin and function of language is embedded in the anti-intellectualism and irrationalism which haunted the efforts of Wittgenstein and his group to attempt the formulation of an epistemology on the basis of linguistic analysis.

The weakness of this position and its ultimate futility is rooted and grounded in the denial of the biblical view of man as a being created in the image of God. Only in the light of such a theistic conception of man and his intellectual faculties does the study of language come into its own. All other approaches to this question bog down under the weight of their repudiation of this biblical insistence that man was created with the power of conceptual thought to think God's thoughts after Him and to place his thinking in meaningful linguistic patterns. Language is not a product of the evolutionary pattern and development through which man has allegedly passed, but was native to him from the very moment he emerged from the hand of his Creator, possessing that image which alone made him man in the fullest sense of the word in an instant of time, fully endowed to assume his role as a steward over the whole of the created realm and endowed with the linguistic ability to give all of creation appropriate names as an expression of the meaning of every single aspect of that created reality.

Bertrand Russell was quite outspoken in his rejection of Christianity. He admitted, however, that the decay of religious beliefs and the denial of

---

50. Ibid., p. 347.

dogmas did not settle the issues involved: ". . . the question of the place of religion in life is by no means decided."[51] In a lecture given in London on March 6, 1927, on "Why I am not a Christian," Russell was very emphatic in his opposition to the historic Christian faith.[52]

In this lecture, in a rather cavalier manner, he dismissed the traditional Thomistic arguments for the existence of God and concluded that there is no reason to suppose that the world had a beginning at all and insisted that the idea that it must have had a beginning is due to the poverty of the human imagination. He did not end the argument with the dismissal of these traditional arguments, but went on to add one which was hardly original with him, namely, the defect of sin in the teachings of Christ.[53]

Having thus dismissed the concept of God as a reasonable prospect for the human race, he then tried to face the question as to what man must do to replace the vacuum which he had created.

> We must stand upon our own feet and look fair and square at the world —its good facts, its bad facts, its beauties, and its ugliness; see the world as it is, and not be afraid of it. Conquer the world by intelligence and not merely by being slavishly subdued by the terror that comes from it. The whole conception of God is a conception derived from the ancient Oriental despotisms. It is a conception quite unworthy of free men. When you hear people in church debasing themselves and saying that they are miserable sinners, . . . it seems contemptible and not worthy of self-respecting human beings. We ought to stand up and look the world frankly in the face. We ought to make the best we can of the world, and if it is not so good as we wish, after all it will still be better than what these others have made of it in all these ages. A good world needs knowledge, kindliness and courage; it does not need a regretful hankering after the past, nor a fettering of the free intelligence by the words uttered long ago by ignorant men. It needs a fearless outlook and a free intelligence. It needs hope for the future, not looking back all the time towards a past that is dead, which we trust will be far surpassed by the future that our intelligence can create.[54]

In such a manner did Bertrand Russell endeavor to free contemporary man from the shackles imposed upon him by the ignorant voices of the past, by which he meant the writers of the Scriptures, and those who followed them in the creation of a theistic world and life view. In these proud and boastful statements we hear echoes of Nietzsche and others

51. "The Essence of Religion," in *The Basic Writings of Bertrand Russell,* ed. Robert E. Egner and Lester E. Denonn (New York: Simon and Schuster, 1961), p. 565.

52. Ibid., pp. 584-597.

53. Ibid., pp. 532-593.

54. Ibid., p. 597.

who offered a similar slavery in the name of freedom.

Russell seemed blissfully unaware of the inconsistencies in his position. In his references to freedom, kindliness, and courage in his hope for a better world to be born, he did not seem to realize that he was calling for a system of absolutes in the ethical realm which depended upon the God of the Bible for their existence and for the fact that man can know of their existence. Repudiating the source of his hope, he clung to the shell of a hope which he had deprived of its sense and meaning.

With his devotion to mathematics as the explantaion of life and natural law, his devotion to the cause of freedom was but a superficial commitment. His renunciation of God had as its necessary corollary the revocation of true freedom and, with this, the negation of its political, social, and economic corollaries. Beneath the slavish service of the free man and his kindly qualities and his hope for a greater freedom for the human race, Russell was a hopeless pessimist. We need only to look at the following passage to see where his irrationalism led him.

> Brief and powerless is Man's life; on him and all his race the slow, sure doom falls pitiless and dark. Blind to good and evil, reckless of destruction, omnipotent matter rolls on its relentless way; for Man, condemned today to lose his dearest, tomorrow himself to pass through the gates of darkness, it remains only to cherish, ere yet the blow fall, the lofty thoughts that ennoble his little day; disdaining the coward terrors of the slaves of fate, to worship at the shrine that his own hands have built; undismayed by the empire of chance, to preserve a mind free from the wanton tyranny that rules his outward life; proudly defiant of the irresistible forces that tolerate, for a moment, his knowledge and his condemnation, to sustain alone, a wearying but unyielding Atlas, the world that his own ideals have fashioned despite the trampling march of unconscious power.[55]

In a very real and frightening sense Russell here at an early age was declaring that the quest for certainty, for hope, for meaning and purpose in life was hopeless, for man is doomed by the tramping march of an unconscious power.

One can only wonder what inner force drove Russell on to seek a philosophy of life in the midst of such a confession of absolute hopelessness. If all is irrational, how can any search for meaning achieve meaningful results? The question becomes even more depressing when, in his later

55. Ibid., p. 72. This was first printed in *The Independent Review*, December, 1903. Later it was reprinted in *Mysticism and Logic* (London, 1917, New York, 1929). It might also be noted that this was written after his conversion from his idealism to his devotion to the scientific frame of reference for his world and life view.

writings, he insisted that man himself is irrational. In 1955 he penned a confession of failure as penetrating as that which he gave in 1903:

> Man is a rational animal—so at least I have been told. Throughout a long life, I have looked diligently for evidence in favor of this statement, but so far I have not had the good fortune to come across it. . . . On the contrary I have seen the world plunging continually into further madness.[56]

Russell concluded this eulogy on mankind by agreeing with Erasmus that folly is perennial and that the follies of our own day are easier to bear when they are compared to the follies of the past. For Russell, the one word that could be written in large letters over the human scene would be FOLLY. Inescapably Russell had followed his own basic premises to their conclusions that even as life has no purpose or goal for men individually, so does history offer no hope for the race. The most that we can expect is the perennial repetition of past follies. Well has he named this essay "Intellectual Rubbish"!

In the writings of Russell, once again we see the liberalism of the Renaissance in all of its stark nakedness, naked of any awareness of the meaning and purpose in human life through divine creation and equally barren of any meaning in its collective history because of its denial of divine sovereignty. In Russell the tendencies of the nineteenth century have become the sickening and degrading intellectual realities of our own day boldly etched in what passes for philosophy.

Benedetto Croce (1866–1952)

It should not be assumed that all members of this traditional group of thinkers took refuge in a cynical pessimism and were content to pronounce a secular benediction on what they regarded as the futile struggles of the human race to thwart the inevitable consequences of their imprisonment on this earth. Benedetto Croce was one of those observers who were thoroughly aware of the plight of Western culture at the beginning of the twentieth century, and who sought a remedy for this cultural impasse. In his concern for the future of Western man Croce did not stand alone, but he did not follow the path of renewal which had been laid down by many of his contemporary philosophers, psychologists, and sociologists. In fact, he was not at all interested in developing rational explanation of the irrational. Rather was he interested in finding a basis for rational thought which would exclude the worship of the irrational as the foundation for Western culture.

56. Ibid., p. 73.

This quest led Croce back to the humanism of the Renaissance, for he believed the real genius of modern civilization had its origin in that era of European history. Unlike his contemporaries, who were products of the universities, Croce was not a university graduate and harbored a certain disdain for the academic outlook on life, believing university training was quite irrelevant to the problems of the day, and that these institutions were not addressing themselves to the basic problems confronting Western man. In fact, he felt they were contributing to the growth of these problems. He was convinced that it was the task of scholarship to review the humanistic tradition in an effort to evaluate its contributions to modernity and to appropriate the most valuable of these for the promotion and development of Western culture. He was convinced that the Renaissance had much to say to his day, and he undertook the task of listening to its message and injecting this message into the cultural efforts of his day. For this purpose he founded a journal, *La Critica,* for the purpose of applying what he felt were the enduring principles of Renaissance humanism to the intellectual, moral, social, and political issues confronting the Western mind. This interest in the Renaissance and its message soon turned him to a study of history and its meaning; as a result he wrote *History Subsumed Under a General Concept of Art.* In this essay he argued that history was more an art than a science, since it was mainly concerned with specific events rather than with general laws. He further argued that it was a special kind of art in that its purpose was to set forth a picture of the real world of real events rather than an imaginary presentation of events as the product of the human imagination. This new interest eventually led Croce into the field of philosophy, but with a basic concern for the meaning of history.

For the next two decades, Croce centered his attention and literary efforts toward presenting an interpretation of history which has been called a fully developed "philosophy of the spirit," which was intended to comprehend all aspects of human achievement—art, history, science, and philosophy—into a world and life view which he later came to call historicism. At first he preferred the term "critical, or realistic idealism."[57]

57. His early distaste for historicism as a descriptive term for his system was well founded, for sharing the nineteenth century had been Troeltsch, Dilthey, and other scholars to denote historical relativism, by which they sought to deny the existence of all absolutes and to explain what had been regarded as absolute as purely human responses to specific crises or challenges at any given time. Although this concept had been used at first by nineteenth-century theologians to destroy the belief in the Scriptures as the infallible revelation of God to man, it could easily be, and was, used to deny any absoluteness to history and secular historians were soon engaged in furious debate in an effort to save their profession from its destructive attacks.

However, Croce's attempt to find enduring elements in history was made quite difficult for him by his own negations of biblical truth and his devotion to humanism. He did not seem to realize that the very philosophies which he was criticizing and attacking were the ultimate product of the humanism to which he had given his allegiance. His efforts to find a basis for optimism in viewing the historical process were confronted with a very serious difficulty—his insistence that man is free only if there are no absolutes. This was a basic conviction of Renaissance humanism, and it inevitably thwarted his every attempt to find a foundation for an enduring optimistic interpretation of the history of Western man.

An equally formidable opponent of his efforts was his insistence that if man was to be truly free there could be no transcendental realm of ideal values. If this was the case, how could Croce speak of freedom, for if freedom means anything, it must mean the existence of transcendental value which all men seek.

Once again Croce found an answer for this question, but he found it in Renaissance humanism. For man to work out his own destiny there must be no transcendental realm of absolute values (spirits) but only the human spirit. This human spirit must be regarded as the supreme spirit for man. In brief, man is sovereign, for his own spirit is the ultimate reality. Croce was calling on the Renaissance to wage warfare against its own offspring. But if this be the case, why did Croce call on the products of art, religion, science, philosophy, and other branches of human intellectual achievements in such a warfare? If historicism is correct and there are no absolutes in history, why and how do these cultural achievements have anything to say to modern man? If they are the products of one era, how can they have any authority for a later period of time? Croce again had his answer, insufficient as it is. This cultural inheritance was not without any value; its value lay in the fact that it represented previous achievements in man's unending quest for self-comprehension. This cultural heritage is valuable evidence as to the ways or means which the human spirit has used to establish its kingdom over the world. The solution of Croce lay in his belief in the necessity of union between man's historical consciousness with his power of philosophic reflection for a proper understanding of the role of the human spirit in the historical process.

Croce also insisted that man's cultural heritage from the past could not be properly used as evidence in a meaningful philosophic inquiry until it had been put into a meaningful form by the historical imagination. It was the function of the historical imagination to present this heritage in such a form that philosophy could extract from the products of art, science, religion and philosophy the basic principles which govern the operation of spirit in general.

The basic weakness in Croce's approach to history through philosophy lay in his concept of "spirit." He never defined its content and only presupposed its existence. Some commentators have likened his use of "spirit" to Freud's use of the unconscious, or Bergson's assumption of the *élan vital* as the moving force in history. Even more than Bergson's *élan vital,* Croce's "spirit" has no goal or purpose and is as impersonal as Freud's concept of the unconscious as a force in human life.

Croce endeavored to soften this dilemma by insisting that this spirit can be experienced directly by the individual, but he immediately weakened the strength of this position by his insistence that it could be understood only through its results. The result of such a comprehension Croce set forth in what he called his four moments of expression: the good, the true, the beautiful, and the useful. It must be noted that the four moments in the life of humanity, which Croce delighted to call the "circle of the spirit," were impersonal entities resembling the ideas of Plato.

Croce's humanism thus broke down into an ultimate impersonalism which, to a degree, echoed Hegel and perhaps even Kant. Whatever strains of previous philosophy it may have reflected, it cannot be regarded as theistic. Croce did not look to God or to the Scriptures for the basic presuppositions of his philosophical system, and his introduction of the rationalism inherent in the thought of the Renaissance failed to provide him with any effective weapon against what he regarded as the destructive forces which he felt were destroying Western culture.

Although Croce was not one of the most important figures in this era of transition, he is of interest, largely because he was aware of the decline of the Western mind and because his efforts reveal the futility of relying upon the rationalism of a previous era as a weapon against the corroding influence of rationalism of a more advanced stage of development. Croce gave a fairly good diagnosis of the illness from which Western culture was suffering, but he was unable to prescribe the proper remedy, for he was a victim of the same illness in an earlier stage of its development in his own thinking.

José Ortega y Gasset (1883–1955)

Like Croce, although in a somewhat different manner, José Ortega y Gasset combined his approach to the history of culture in union with a study of philosophy. It may even be questionable as to whether he should be included among the transitional thinkers. However, as a young man he studied in Germany in a neo-Kantian atmosphere, and those contacts were quite influential in his formulations of the relationship between the history of culture on the one hand, and its relationship to the world of thought on the other. There can be no doubt that this early association with the German neo-Kantians led him to the conclusion that all forms of cultural expression must, by their very nature, be provisional. It also conveyed to him the conviction that all cultural activity is, at best, irrational.

We see very clearly the direction in which his thought was headed when we look at his definition of truth.[58] He spoke of the frailty of truth and of its non-durable character. This frailty becomes quite evident when truths enter into history and are acquired by real persons. It was the realization of this frailty which compelled Plato to place Ideas (or truths) outside of the temporal world.[59] However, these transmundane truths filter into our world, and this filtering process takes place through the mind of man. The result of this filtering process is what Ortega called the articulation of history with philosophy. It would seem that he, at this point, was a modern Plato, but he hastened to deny any such affinity:

> Here, for the first time we stumble on a basic distinction which differentiates our philosophy which held the stage for centuries. This distinction consists in taking into account of something that is very elemental, namely that there is no direct resemblance between the person who thinks, sees, or imagines something and things seen or imagined by him; on the contrary there is a generic difference between them.[60]

This fact, for Oretga, constitutes the basis for the necessity of the articulation of history with philosophy. Arguing that the fundamental task of history must be to show how this philosophy or that political system "could only have been discovered, developed, and, in short, lived" by a particular type of man at a particular date, he concluded that if truth has value for anybody, it is history which must bring the truths of an era into harmony with the idea that somehow these truths come to be known by a few people of that era. By such an ingenious solution did Ortega seek to avoid the trap of relativism by showing that these truths did filter into the minds of at least a few people at a given time.

He also sought an additional defense against such a charge of relativism in his insistence that although truths do not change, man's understanding of them undergoes a change.

---

58. Ortega y Gasset was a disciple of the Spanish thinker Miguel de Unamuno y Jugo (1864–1936), who was regarded as a forerunner of existentialism.
59. José Ortega y Gasset, *What Is Philosophy* (New York, 1960), p. 23.
60. Ibid., p. 24.

> We must recognize variations in thinking not as changes in yesterday's truth which convert it into today's error, but changes in man's orientation which lead him to see other truths that are different from those of yesterday. It is not truths that change, but man who changes and who, because he changes, goes on scanning the series of truths, goes on choosing from that transmundane sphere to which we earlier alluded the ones that are right for him and blinding himself to all the rest. Note that this is history's basic and fundamental *a priori.* Is it not the history of man?[61]

The minimum task we can assign history, then, is that it must assume that the subject of which it speaks can be understood, and a thing to be understood must possess some degree of truth. History cannot fulfill its mission unless it achieves an understanding of man in his period, but it cannot accomplish this task if man himself, in that period, leads a life that has no meaning and if what he thinks and does has no rational structure. In the final analysis, Ortega argues that it eases the task of philosophy to bring both the temporal and the eternal together through its proper use of history.

This thesis gives rise to several important questions. In the light of Ortega's own presuppositions, is it possible to maintain that truth does not change? If the thinking of men changes, and we must admit that it does, why is it that he holds something to be true in one era and then decides at a later time that it is false, that he can insist that there is no change in truth, as such? Were all scientific theories before Newton true simply because men affirmed that they were. If Newton was correct, then were not the previous interpretations of the nature of the universe in error? Then, if Newton's interpretations are true, why are later theories of the universe equally true though they may set aside some Newtonian laws?

Ortega answers this question with the affirmation that as man continues to scan the series of truths which he obtains from his penetration of the transmundane sphere, he is free to choose those truths which are right for him. This only raises a further question. How can men obtain conflicting truths from that transmundane area, or sphere, of unchanging truths? Does not this solution leave man in a serious predicament? If various groups of men, in scanning this sphere of transmundane truth, come upon truths which seem right to them but which contradict each other, which set of truths is actually true, and how is their validity to be determined? To be more specific, if, according to this theory, the Nazis of Germany scanned this transmundane sphere and found those truths which seemed to be

61. Ibid., p. 26.

right to them, but which we in this country could not possibly accept, then which set of truths would be right, and how would the question of the suitability of Nazi truths be determined? For Ortega to say that it is the function of philosophy to unite the temporal and the transmundane with the aid of history is no answer at all. Such an answer but confuses to a greater degree an already confused, and confusing, view of both history and philosophy. Thus we must conclude that he, like the other thinkers included in this transitional period, also failed to deal in a satisfactory manner with the great issues of life. This is true whether they are in the area of philosophy and history, or with political, social, economic, and educational thought and activity. They failed because they did not reach the crucial point of dealing with the questions which underlie the issues with which they dealt.

All fail because they refuse to accept the biblical view of God and man. They reject the doctrine that man was created in the image of God to think His thoughts after Him and that man is, therefore, a steward, responsible to God for his intellectual activity.

Furthermore, as a result of these denials they refuse to acknowledge that truth is personal in its nature and that it is resident in the personal God of the Scriptures; that only through His revelation of Himself to men can they know and appropriate the truth. However much Dewey, Weber, Freud, and others differ among themselves in their metaphysical and epistemological positions, they are at one in their common rejection of the biblical revelation as the norm for all truth. Thus, although it may take different forms for them, truth is not absolute and unchanging in its nature and content, but changes as men select these truths which seem appropriate and relevant to them in the age in which they live. This is the inescapable conclusion of Ortega Gasset's position at this point. He may speak of eternal truth, but his contention that men select what seems best to them must sweep away his contention that he avoided the charge of relativism. History does not save him from this conclusion, although he insisted that it did. He held that history does not properly fulfill its mission unless it achieves an understanding of man in his period, and although he also argued that history is bound to justify all periods, he did so in a way as to also include the idea that history has to give full meaning to each relative position that man takes, and must reveal to man the eternal truth which each generation in every period has lived.

By this line of reasoning, Ortega hoped to educate Europe and the West in general to a proper recognition of the relationship between life and culture. But he constructed a weak reed upon which to build this educational venture. His conviction that the ultimate reality which he called life, or life force, was unknowable, and thus culture and civilization could be built only upon this speculative conception of the nature of true reality. Inevitably his efforts to relate his philosophy to history in such a way as to serve as the interpretation for the decline of Western culture was, in itself, part of the problem.

Defining life as a process, a kind of flux, he concluded that civilizations, in the true sense of the word, were possible only when civilization was lived in harmony with the demands of the life force as it had appeared at a given time and a given place. For this to take place, the cultural leader had to recognize the fact that since life is flux, it is also dissolution, and by this he meant that it involved the dissolution of the antiquated methods by which it had been expressed in a previous era. His diagnosis of the difficulty facing modern European culture lay in the fact that its ills, war, social upheavals, revolutions, the continuing revolt of the masses, and what he called the dehumanization of the arts were the result of the unwillingness of the elite to allow this dissolution to occur in their desire to retain the status quo. Instead, this group was in opposition to the demands of the life force and would destroy Western culture.

As early as 1923 Ortega painted a gloomy picture of Europe: "Our institutions, like our theatres, are anachronisms. We have neither the courage to break resolutely with such devitalized accretions of the past nor can we in any way adjust ourselves to them."[62]

It is precisely at this point that his philosophy became intertwined with his view of history, so that the study and knowledge of history became for him the vehicle which he could give expression to his philosophy. For him, the elite are the key to the survival of culture. It is the function of this group to create and then transmit to the masses the necessary myths concerning the nature of reality. By this process a sense of purpose is given to the incoherent masses, who serve as the raw material for the advancement of culture. They cannot do this on their own without the stimulation of the culturally elite minority.

At this point, Ortega approaches the position of Arnold Toynbee in his concept of the creative minority. However, he used the concept with a somewhat different meaning. In somewhat the same manner he gives a different role for the masses than that assigned by Toynbee. He hastened to point out that the division of society into the masses and select minori-

---

62. José Ortega y Gasset, *The Modern Theme,* tr. James Celugh (New York, 1961), pp. 20-21.

ties is not the equivalent of a division into social classes. He held that both the "upper" and the "lower" classes contained some of the elite.[63]

Ortega did not regard this division as a necessary characteristic of all previous civilizations, as Toynbee insisted. The advance of the masses into a position of social and political importance is a new development. He traced the advance of the masses in our day as a result of the recent intellectual and social changes.

> I believe that the political innovations of recent times signify nothing less than the political domination of the masses. The old democracy was tempered by a generous dose of liberalism and of enthusiasm for law. By serving these principles the individual bound himself to maintain severe discipline over himself. Under the shelter of liberal principles and the rule of law, minorities could live and act. Democracy and law, life in common under the law, were synonymous. Today we are witnessing the triumph of a hyperdemocracy in which the masses act directly, outside the law, imposing its aspirations and its desires by means of material pressure.[64]

Ortega was fearful of this rise of the masses to a position in which they could and would use pressure. He wrote quite candidly of this danger.

> They [the facts] all indicate that the masses have decided to advance to the foreground of social life, to occupy the places, to use the instruments and enjoy the leisures hitherto reserved for the few. It is evident . . . that the places were never intended for the multitude, for their dimensions are too limited, and the crowd is continuously overflowing: thus manifesting to our eyes and in the clearest manner the new phenomenon: the mass, without ceasing to be the mass, is supplanting the minorities.[65]

In fact, Ortega went further than to merely voice his fears about this new phenomenon. In his view it threatened the very existence of human society in its civilizational and cultural form. On this point he was crystal clear.

> I have never said that human society *ought* to be aristocratic, but a great deal more than that. What I have said, and still believe with ever-increasing conviction is that human society is and always will be . . . aristocratic by its very essence, to the extreme that it is a society in the measure that it is aristocratic, and ceases to be such when it ceases to be aristocratic.[66]

All of these observations brought Ortega face to face with certain com-

---

63. He defined the masses as the average man.
64. José Oretega y Gasset, *Revolt of the Masses* (New York, 1932), pp. 18-19.
65. Ibid., p. 17.
66. Ibid., p. 22.

plexities for which his system had no answers. His philosophy and his predilections were obviously in sharp conflict. He supported the republican cause during the Spanish Revolution in the 1930s. At the same time he taunted the liberals of recent decades for the fruits of their own democratic convictions, and it is quite obvious that he was not very happy with what he was witnessing.

The problem for him and his fellow liberals lay in the fact that his taunts were based upon what had been regarded as undebatable scientific facts and positions furnished by the scientific discoveries of the seventeenth century. Ortega pointed out that the doctrine of human rights as set forth by the thinkers of the late seventeenth century had become an ideal during the eighteenth century, but it remained an ideal and was not put into practice. On the other hand, the history of the nineteenth century must be construed as the story of that era in which the people, while becoming enthusiastic for that ideal, did not exercise rights or even attempt to make them prevail, "but in fact under democratic legislation continued to feel itself just under the old regime."[67]

Ortega explained this dichotomy in the light of his observation that the people had learned they were sovereign, but did not really believe it to be true. Today all of this has changed, and in this change he professed to find the key to what was happening in the Western thinking of the twentieth century.

> The sovereignty of the unqualified individual, of the human being as such, generically, has now passed from being a judicial idea or ideal to being a psychological state inherent in the average man. . . . The levelling demands of a generous democratic inspiration have been changed from aspirations and ideals into appetites and unconscious assumptions.[68]

Ortega dismissed the logical implications of this position in his idea in that this leveling process was, in the long run, a sign of hope for the future. "Consequently the uprising of the masses implies a fabulous increase of vital possibilities, quite the contrary of what we hear so much about the decadence of Europe."[69]

However, this question arises: How could Ortega hold to such an optimistic view in regard to the future in the light of his own basic concepts concerning culture. It must be remembered that in essence these aspirations were, and are, unconsciously formulated, and history has sense of direction, or purpose, for this reason. Under the guise of such optimism

67. Ibid., p. 25. 68. Ibid. 69. Ibid., p. 28.

Ortega smuggled into his evaluation of history a philosophy which rests upon an irrationalism. He admitted and even insisted that he was not a Christian, and the whole tone of his system is one of antagonism as far as Christianity is concerned. The sovereignty of the triune God, the doctrine of creation and divine providence in human affairs as well as in the government of nature are quietly pushed to the sidelines as unworthy of consideration in the light of the intellectual developments which have taken place since the close of the Middle Ages. For him all world and life views, by their very nature and origin, must be fictitious. Such a vacuum provided him with no real view of man and no possibility of purpose in human life and history.

Conclusion

As the curtain is closed on the intellectual activity of the nineteenth century, it concludes on a dreary note. With some few exceptions in orthodox theological circles, the vast majority of philosophers and scholars in other disciplines had accepted the theory of evolution and with it the fruit of social, political, and economic unrest, of political totalitarianism, theological decline, and the ultimate collapse of the Western mind as it yielded to the increasing pressures of irrationalism bequeathed to it by the preceding era. Existentialism in philosophy, irrationalism in political, social, and economic thought, and totalitarianism in several forms were to be the ultimate outgrowth of this resort to an irrational interpretation of life. Man's futile quest to overthrow the demands of a sovereign God in whose image he had been created would ultimately bring man to deny himself and his purposes on earth as he vainly attempted to create a new political sovereignty on earth to take the place of the sovereign God in heaven whom he had eagerly deposed in his own thinking.

The deluge which had been gathering force in the nineteenth century broke with unabated fury upon the era which had been looked upon as the beginning of a humanly created and sustained millennial existence on earth.

Chapter 11
Earlier Twentieth-Century Thought

The transitional thinkers discussed in the preceding chapter did not do their work in isolation, but produced a crop of followers who not only developed their irrationalism to greater lengths, but who, like John Dewey, were able to permeate the thinking of large and important segments of American society. These scholars in the Age of Transition further advanced the decline of thought inherent in their predecessors and, at the same time, provided the soil as well as the seed for the more devastating decline which would dominate the philosophical activity of the twentieth century. Protest as they would, and some of them did, against the intellectual developments which were already in progress in their own lifetimes, they had no valid argument against them. Once the open break with theism had been completed, there could be no logical stopping place short of an existentialist chaos. Every way-station on this main line of intellectual dissolution was an illogical halting against which there is no defense.

Thus, the history of twentieth-century thought in both Europe and the United States is the unhappy unfolding of the logical consquences of the departure from the biblical foundation of human knowledge and of the acceptance of naturalism as the new *Weltanschauung,* if such a term may be used to describe the present state of intellectual affairs. Strictly speaking, existentialism and its cohorts cannot properly be called a *Weltanschauung,* since these philosophies deny that there is any meaning to either life or the world. Yet, in this negative sense, it may be used to describe those negations which are an inescapable and essential aspect of what is left of the modern mind. These remnants of biblical theism are fast crumbling under the attack of modern theologians and philosophers. As a result, the magnificent citadel of religious and intellectual certainty bequeathed to us by the Reformers is fast becoming a kind of museum piece cherished by orthodox Christians, lamented by some liberals who are aware of what is happening and who lack any solution to the issues of the day; and, hated by the devout humanists who have long sought its destruction. It is not too much to say that many humanists would gladly see it banished and remove Christianity from the modern scene. The disdain and neglect of the liberals of a previous age have been transformed into active hatred, hatred in our day as various schools of modern theology and philosophy seek to remove the very concept of the God presented in the Scriptures from academic and theological circles. Their religion is a humanistic naturalism based upon the theory of evolution. It has been well stated that the modern mind has become saturated with this theory to the extent that it has become poisoned to its very depths. The study and writing of history, sociology, economics, political science; the study of literature; and the development of the various languages and arts have literally been inundated by the proponents of evolution. It is almost impossible to find books in these various areas which do not clearly reflect the bias of the writers toward the unproved theory.[1]

The theme which was to be that of the present century was stated clearly in the following declaration of human independence:

> We are now able to erect for ourselves a philosophy that can find a natural and intelligible place for all human interests and aims, and can embrace in one natural world, amenable to a single intellectual method, all the realities to which human experience points. Symphonies as well as atoms, personality as well as reflex action, religious consecration as well as the law of motion or the equation of the field theory.[2]

To the extent to which this era has followed this assertion of freedom from the past, and particularly the Christian past, it can be called the epitaph of Western culture, written for it by the humanists and the naturalists who were standing by as it breathed its last. As these irrational irrationalists gaze upon the coffin, they must indict themselves for their participation in bringing about the death of the culture of which they expected so much and from which they have garnered so little.

The almost frenzied desire to assert man's independence of God, the equally intense determination to demonstrate this independence by inverting the traditional order of human life, the insistence that the rational must

1. Indeed, today those scholars in these various areas who do not accept this theory are treated with disdain and regarded as unscholarly; their books and pictures are laughed out of court all too often. It also should be noted that a large number of scholars reject this theory, some for logical reasons and others because they regard it to be unproved and unprovable.

2. Yervent Krikorian, *Naturalism and the Human Spirit* (New York: Columbia University Press, 1944), p. 369.

be irrational, was to become the dominant feature of the cultural deterioration of the twentieth century. Having its roots in theology and philosophy, it found expression in every area of human activity and brought with it the rise of a rebellious attitude toward a sovereign God.

This bitter attitude toward Christianity and the traditional social order which it had nurtured was, of course, not new with the dawning of the new century. It was explicit in some writers like Marx, Freud, and Nietzsche, but was implicit in many more, and by 1900 the stream of revolt was at full tide.

This bitterness, or contempt, was also accompanied by an optimism that this independence from God which man was now proclaiming was for his own good. The shackles of Christianity had now been broken, and mankind was about to enter upon a millennial existence of his own making. This strident naturalistic religion was not lacking an eschatology. Vastly different from that of the Scriptures, to be sure, it was confident that it could offer to the human race a heaven on earth, a heaven of man's own choosing and making. These secularists would offer a heaven in which man would be sovereign and in which his wishes, or at least the wishes of a sovereign majority, would be realized. It would take the advent of World War I, and the ensuing depression, to turn this optimism into the channels of despair; to break the bubble and crush the idea of inevitable progress as the proper destiny of a race inherently good and needing only the proper techniques to bring this inherent capacity for the good life into fruition as had never before been achieved in the annals of history.

In both this country and Europe the closing decades of the nineteenth century and the opening decade of the present century were regarded as the fulfillment of the dreams of the evolutionary age, an age in which the theory of evolution became the new deity worthy of human worship. It is perhaps impossible for the people of our day to recapture in their own thinking the optimism which flooded the literature of that era and the mood resulting from an almost utter abandonment to the promises which this scientific theory held out to its millions of devotees. The editors of *The Outlook* virtually promised their readers that never again would war scourge this earth, for there were better ways of solving international problems. The medical and technological advances were ushering in a new day in which sickness, poverty, and other social ills would be banished if men would but listen to the dictates of scientists and follow their prescription. Statesmen, politicians, teachers, and ministers all fell victim to this cancer of the human spirit, this false ideology which promised much and failed miserably in the fulfillment of what it held out to those who looked to science as the new messiah of the twentieth century.

This optimistic spirit proved to be peculiarly fascinating to the liberal political leadership of the United States in the period from 1892 to 1912; also to the professional socialists who camp on the outskirts of both political parties and, at times, unsuccessfully experimented with the formation of third parties.[3]

The devotion to the evolutionary spirit brought about the formation of new intellectual and political movements and also gave birth to the extremely liberal *New Republic,* which soon rivalled *The Nation* as the voice of this new liberalism in American political life.

Many, if not most, Americans look on this period from 1900 to 1912 as the great Era of Normalcy, and in the decades which followed World War I many people looked back with yearning hearts to this era.

The outbreak of war in Europe proved to be a rude shock to this nation, for its people were not ready to believe that such a war could be possible. Preparing them for our involvement required a tremendous amount of well-planned propaganda, which was admirably provided by the British and their American collaborators. Even though President Wilson retained enough of the earlier optimism to develop his League of Nations and drew fervent support from those who believed that such a device would bring perpetual peace, this post-war liberal optimism lacked the popular support necessary for bringing its program to reality. As a result, American liberals became pessimistic, and many of them withdrew from the battlefield to sulk in silence in their philosophic tents, bemoaning the fate of their movement and of the country which apparently had repudiated them.

This mood, which gripped many professional political, social, and economic liberals, reflected the more basic intellectual currents which were evident in this country after 1914. Both European and American thought were now captive to the sterility which was the necessary and even logical result of the heritage of the nineteenth century. The twentieth century has been notably lacking in its production of important leaders in the world of thought who were not part of the great transition examined in chapter 10. The anti-intellectualism inherent in this former era was soon translated into an intellectual poverty by 1920. Nineteenth-century liberal thought proved to be incapable of maintaining even its own level of scholarly insights into philosophical and theological problems. Thus, the theological

3. *The Outlook* under the editorial leadership of Lyman Abbot and Theodore Roosevelt during the presidential campaign of 1912 used this evolutionary appeal in the fervent support of Roosevelt's Progressive, or Bull Moose, Republican Party.

and philosophical leadership has been but a feeble echo of its nineteenth-century antecedents.[4]

Granted that some philosophical figures even in the twentieth century have risen to places of some importance, nevertheless it remains true that philosophy per se has come upon evil days. Much of the intellectual history of the twentieth century cannot be found in the works of important philosophers, but all too often in the influence of scholars in other disciplines. Thus, the intellectual history of the West must be sought in political thinkers and leaders, economists, educators, social scientists, literature, and the fine arts.

Apart from the transitional figures already discussed, whose roots were firmly imbedded in the philosophical soil of the nineteenth century, it must be admitted that a sterility of thought has characterized the philosophic endeavors of the present era. Those philosophers, who have appeared in both Europe and this country, are the offspring of the main currents of the previous era and simply carried Western thought nearer to the abyss of nothingness into which it has fallen. It could be said that philosophy as a humanistic study has already taken the fatal plunge and, in so doing, has brought the social studies, the arts, and theology to the brink of irrationalism. They too have yielded to the embrace of an enveloping existential attitude of mind. For this reason it seems appropriate to begin the study of twentieth-century thought with an examination of existentialism as a philosophic movement which is perhaps the most significant development of our day. In making such a statement we are not implying that it is an original or valuable contribution to Western thought. It is a movement which must be reckoned with, but it is, at the same time, a movement whose roots are deeply buried in the intellectual soil of the previous era. Some students of this movement profess to find its roots in Kierkegaard, while others look back to either Kant or Hegel for its inspiration. Some writers insist that it is the fruit of Kierkegaard's rebellion against Hegelianism. A good case can be made for this position, but it must also be remembered that Kierkegaard did nothing to relieve Western thought from the burden of the irrationalism which was, as we have seen, inherent in both Kantian and Hegelian philosophies. Kierkegaard's re-

4. No doubt some will rise to take issue with this statement and will point to Karl Barth as a great leader of thought during the first half of the present century. There is much truth in the contention that he was very influential, but he was an echo of Immanuel Kant, even in his efforts to formulate a theology which would break loose from nineteenth-century liberalism and recover some of the truths of historic Christian orthodoxy under the shield of an existentialist approach. Barth will be dealt with at some length in a succeeding chapter.

bellion is irrationalism in another, and probably more attractive, form than the Kantian and Hegelian versions.[5]

Very few scholars would deny the contention that modern existentialism has its roots in Kierkegaardian principles, even though some would deny that he was an existentialist. There is no doubt that we can safely assume that he was the father of both the philosophical existentialism of the twentieth century on the one hand, and of dialectical (neo-orthodox) theology on the other. Thus, he carried the irrationalism of Kant and Hegel to a new height and set the stage for the ultimate debasement of philosophical activity in our day; and, he also inspired the irrationalism inherent in the neo-orthodoxy of Barth and his many followers.

Van Til rightly concludes that Kierkegaard gave the first major expression to the most salient features of modern existentialism in his *Philosophical Fragments* and *Concluding Unscientific Postscript.*[6]

In the introduction of the first of these two works, Kierkegaard sets the problems sharply before us and in so doing drives a wedge between the noumenal world of Kant, or the supernatural world of Christianity, and the world in which factual history takes place.

> Is an historical point of departure possible for an eternal consciousness: how can such a point of departure have any other than a mere historical interest: is it possible to base an eternal happiness upon historical knowledge.[7]

The thrust of the questions gives to the reader the very distinct impression that the author is implying that these questions must be answered in the negative. In the discussion of these questions it is obvious that Kierkegaard has both philosophy and Christanity in mind.[8] Although he is raising the question as to whether Jesus Christ can be found in history, a religious issue, he is, at the same time, raising philosophical issues of very great importance. In both of these works he assumed a vigorous, if not hostile, opposition to the idea of truth as an intellectual system. In his

5. It is, of course, true that existentialism, as a philosophy, must be given due weight and consideration as an important aspect of the intellectual life of both Europe and America, but this philosophy is itself the dying gasp of the liberal bent toward the irrational. For a brief discussion of this issue, see William Barrett, *What Is Existentialism* (New York: Grove Press, 1964), pp. 8-12. For a somewhat different interpretation, see Calvin Schrag, *Existence and Freedom* (Evanston, Ill.: Northwestern University Press, 1962), pp. 142-145.

6. Søren Kierkegaard, *Philosophical Fragments,* 5th printing (Princeton, N. J.: Princeton University Press, 1952). See also ibid., 2nd printing, 1944.

7. Ibid., title page.

8. We shall discuss the theological and religious implications to this question in our treatment of Barth and neo-orthodoxy.

reference to "system" he had Hegel in mind and took issue with the Hegelian effort to explain the course of history by means of a comprehensive system of logical relations. Kierkegaard asked:

> How can finite man, whose very essence is that of becoming and change presume to discover a system of truth? How can he ever attain to the identity of being and thought?[9]

In pursuing this line of argument, Kierkegaard was admitting that God is far above man. From this admission he then drew the question as to how human reason can know that which is absolutely other than itself. But in Christ the eternal becomes temporal. However, he insisted that such an event is logically impossible. Thus, we must therefore believe that which cannot happen.

Van Til admits that while we are now entering doubtful territory it is true that

> Man cannot and must not seek to attain a system of knowledge in the way Hegel did, for any non-Christian system of philosophy is immanentistic. . . . they are all controlled by the idea of abstract form and equally abstract matter. And the modern freedom-nature scheme is but an expression in modern form of the general form-matter scheme. The modern dialecticism of Kant and of Hegel is no less destructive of the true revelation of God and man than was the ancient dialecticism.[10]

Van Til is unquestionably correct in his contention that Kierkegaard was merely carrying on in the spirit of Kant. Van Til correctly asserts that Kierkegaard's final reason for rejecting the system arose from his conviction that there is no God who can give a final revelation of Himself to man in history. It must follow, then, that his position is actually no less speculative than that of Hegel. Both thinkers were irrational in that they allowed for the idea of mere contingency. At the same time, they were both rationalists in that they used the laws of human logic for the purpose of excluding the truth of historic Christianity. According to Van Til, the difference between them was merely one of degree, and with this conclusion we must agree. Kierkegaard's purpose of excluding any philosophical system had as its necessary correlative the negation of historical truth.[11]

The philosophy of Kierkegaard is a form of Kant's ethical dualism and ethical monism. At the same time, his theology is adapted to that philosophy, and it is for this reason that the essentially irrational character of his thought has carried over into secular and "religious existentialism on the

---

9. Kierkegaard, *Fragments,* p. 97.
10. Van Til, *Christianity and Barthianism,* p. 289.
11. Ibid., p. 291.

one hand, and into neo-orthodoxy in Christian thought on the other. There cannot be, therefore, for Kierkegaard objective truth. It is well known that over against every form of 'objective' truth Kierkegaard maintained the qualitative difference between God and man."[12]

Van Til hastens to point out, however, that in insisting upon such a difference Kierkegaard did not mean the difference in the biblical sense, the difference which must exist between God as the Creator and man as a created being. Kierkegaard did not begin with the doctrine, or idea, of creation, but with the notion that man is free over against all objective revelation. With Kant, he argued that man is ethically free, but the realm of nature is the realm of necessity. It is this stress on human freedom that forms the nexus and starting point for Kierkegaard's thinking. Rejecting the biblical teaching that man is ethically alienated from God because of the fall of Adam and the resulting total depravity of the human race, following Kant he maintained that man is free because he is autonomous.

Van Til argues that Kant's ethical dialectic was perfected by Kierkegaard. God was first excluded from the realm of nature and therefore from the consciousness of man as revelatory of God's presence and claims. Van Til then points out that human knowledge is first interpreted as something which takes place when it imposes man's own organizing principles of thought upon material which is purely contingent material in character.[13] But since man thinks in terms of concepts and general principles, it is assumed that nature operates according to these concepts. At the same time, it is recognized that these human concepts cannot exhaustively order contingent reality. "So that which is not ordered is thought of as irrational or non-rationalizable and ultimately mysterious something. This realm of the irrational or unknown is then made the object of faith. It is in this field that man is said to be free."[14]

Van Til points out that Kierkegaard according to this view set human reason over against the natural because it is regarded as operating in a realm that lies beyond the natural.

Also in this Kierkegaardian approach the intellect of man as the source of nature is set over against the will of man as operating in the realm of the irrational. This irrational realm is regarded as the realm of possibility, in which the free man must seek to realize himself.

At this point a very real difficulty confronts the entire Kierkegaardian scheme. To the extent that man must realize his possibilities in this realm

12. Ibid., p. 292.
13. The theological implications of this position will be discussed later.
14. Van Til, *Christianity and Barthianism*, p. 296.

of freedom through the medium of nature, he thus cannot escape the mediation of nature, and consequently his freedom is compromised. For the same reason, when this free man desires to communicate his ideas to his fellow free men, this communication is stifled by nature. Logically neither Kierkegaard nor his followers are free to communicate their ideas. Van Til has given an excellent and penetrating analysis of this dilemma. "The ethical freedom which forms the starting point of Kierkegaard's philosophy is a freedom that requires pure possibility for its environment. It requires this pure possibility in order to develop itself according to its own purpose."[15] To say this is to say that man's freedom requires pure contingency and pure chance as the environment in which it can express itself, which is to say that this freedom requires irrationality in which to express itself, and this freedom is irrational in its nature. Obviously, these aspects of Kierkegaard's thought have tremendously important religious and theological implications. These will be discussed in much greater detail as we come to examine irrationality in modern Christianity and particularly in neo-orthodoxy.

In this chapter we shall pursue the philosophical aspects of his thought to the extent to which it is possible to extricate the philosophical from the whole and treat it separately. Kierkegaard's insistence that faith is not knowledge has very dangerous implications for historic Christianity, and these dangers cannot be minimized. However, it is also true that they have just as dangerous consequences for knowledge in Kierkegaard's concept of knowledge and its nature in every area of human intellectual activity. Irrationality cannot be confined to either philosophy or theology. By its very nature it must overrun these bounds and enter into the general stream of intellectual inquiry, in the natural and the social sciences, and in the arts as well.

These basic presuppositions (if we may be allowed to call them that) bear directly upon his view of man, as Kierkegaard believed that man is spirit. But what is the spirit which is the essence of man? Kierkegaard supplied an answer. Spirit is the self. Then the question must arise: What is the self? To which question he offered this answer: "The self is a relation which relates itself to its own self, or it is that in the relation (which accounts for it) that the relation relates itself to its own self; the self is not the relation but (consists in the fact) that the relation relates itself to its own self."[16]

15. Ibid.

16. Søren Kierkegaard, *The Sickness Unto Death* (Princeton, N. J.: Princeton University Press, 1941), p. 17, quoted by Van Til in ibid., p. 300.

In this rather unclear and even more unsatisfactory explanation of the meaning of the self, Kierkegaard was asserting that man is a synthesis of the finite and the infinite, of the temporal and the eternal, of freedom and necessity. Regarded as a synthesis, a relation between two facts, man is not yet a self.[17]

The problem in Kierkegaard becomes more acute when we remember that he insisted that the free man must express his freedom, his self, through nature. Thus, the free man stands in a dialectical relationship with nature: "The self is freedom. But freedom is the dialectical element in the terms of possibility and necessity or contingency and necessity."[18]

At this point he would lose the reader in a maze of contradicting elements. Van Til summarizes Kierkegaard by pointing out that as a synthesis between time and eternity, the self does not actually exist at any specific time. Yet the task of this identity is to become self. But how can this be achieved? Once more we turn to Kierkegaard, at the point of sharing his despair:

> The self is the conscious synthesis of infinitude and finitude, which relates itself to itself, whose task is to become itself, a task which can be performed only by means of a relationship to God. But to become oneself is to become concrete. But to become concrete means neither to become finite nor infinite, for that which is to become concrete is a synthesis. Accordingly, the development consists in moving away from oneself infinitely by the process of finitizing.[19]

Since this process of gaining self-realization is an infinite one, and man can never achieve true selfhood, he is condemned to despair. Not to be one's own self is despair.

It is obvious that although he proclaimed himself in rebellion against Hegel, Kierkegaard could not escape him, and this becomes evident in his insistence that the becoming self is an infinite process of actualization.

Van Til's evaluation of Kierkegaard's efforts are to the point. In taking his point of departure in the consciousness of man independently of the revelation of God through Christ directly revealed in the Scriptures, Kierkegaard has found his result in a complete secularization of Christianity.[20] Kierkegaard virtually admitted that this charge launched against him is correct. He admitted that the philosophy which he set forth in his *Fragments* and *Postscript* takes its point of departure in the pagan conscious-

17. Kierkegaard, *Sickness Unto Death,* p. 17.
18. Ibid., p. 43.
19. Ibid., p. 44, quoted in Van Til, *Christianity and Barthianism,* p. 300.
20. Van Til, *Christianity and Barthianism*, p. 306.

ness in order to seek out experimentally an interpretation of existence which might truly be said to go further than paganism.[21]

His modern man is in a serious predicament from which he cannot be rescued. Condemned to live in a constant tension between freedom and necessity, between infinitude and finitude, he must live in despair and dread. Caught in a never-ending process of self-actualization, he cannot find any meaning to life nor truth to live by. He can never become himself. His philosophy condemns its followers to an endless pursuit of the unobtainable and the impossible. Kierkegaard began by loving despair and ended by rationalizing it as the belief in the impossible.[22]

For him there cannot be absolute truth in the historic meaning of that phrase. For, for him, faith became belief in the logically impossible. He wanted to believe. He wanted to believe in the absurd, but found that he could not. Yet, for him a specious form of Christianity denuded of objective truth and of its setting in historical factuality, he set the stage for the advent of twentieth-century existentialism with its more sweeping denial of the very possibility of any objective truth which could be communicated to any other person, even though they made such an effort in their own writings. Kierkegaard sanctified a kind of irrationality which would seek dominion over the mind of the twentieth century, and by the end of World War II it was well on its way to gaining the victory which it was seeking.

Existentialism in the Twentieth Century

Although Kierkegaard undoubtedly set the stage for the advent of existentialism, it is misleading to suppose that he was its only nineteenth-century source. Some members of this school show the influence of Nietzsche and even Kant. Some scholars would argue that its roots are to be found in the dualism of Descartes, and this is a plausible argument. But the more immediate source is to be found in the whole drift of Western thought to which most of its philosophers contributed in one way or another. This was the drift away from the certainty afforded by the great verities of historic Christianity to the uncertainties found in all forms of nineteenth-century substitutes. Evolutionary theories, pragmatism, and positivism all helped to prepare the European mind for the growth of existential thought. All of these philosophies aided in the destruction of

---

21. Søren Kierkegaard, *Concluding Unscientific Postscript,* tr. Walter Lowrie (Princeton, N. J.: Princeton University Press, 1941), p. 323.

22. Arland Ussher, *Journey Through Dread: A Study of Kierkegaard, Heidegger and Sartre* (New York, 1968).

the intellectual certainty which, to varying degrees, remained within the rationalist and empirical traditions. The intellectual efforts of the nineteenth century not only rather effectively completed the divorce between philosophy and theology begun by Descartes, but continued the progress of separating the philosophy from Cartesian rationalism and Lockean empiricism.

The confluence of the streams of the nineteenth-century irrationalism during the early decades of the present century provided the fertility in which the seeds of intellectual dissolution would take place. True enough, the collapse of democracy and the rise of totalitarianism in Germany, Russia, and Italy, and the threat of such a development in France in the years just before World War II, furnished further intellectual climatic conditions for the seeds of disillusionment and despair to come to fruition.

Some scholars would add one more ingredient to this miscellany of facts which lie behind the rise of existentialist thought—the loss of the feeling of individuality and of the worth of the individual in the face of the emergence of a technological civilization which seemingly threatens to overwhelm the individual in one vast holocaust of an impersonalism inherent in modern society run by machines of various kinds. In such surroundings and in the light of the philosophical heritage of the previous century there came forth a philosophy which accentuated the absurdity and the meaninglessness of human life in a world devoid of both meaning and purpose.

France was on the verge of political collapse even before the war machine of Hitler threatened its very existence as a nation. It was here that existentialism, as a philosophical movement, first gained prominence, largely through the personal prominence of Jean Paul Sartre as its champion.

Although all of these factors undoubtedly played a role in the emergence of this philosophy to its place of dominance in the West after World War II, it must be emphasized that this could not have taken place without the prior decline of religious thought in general and the loss of influence of Christian theology and biblical theism. This decline of Christianity as a central factor in the life of the West left a vacuum at the very center of its intellectual and cultural activity. The human mind can no more tolerate such a vacuum, such an absence of a controlling world and life view, than nature can tolerate a vacuum. Man was created in the image of God to think His thoughts after Him, and if he will not think as God ordained him to think, he then creates his own idols of the mind, his own world and life view, which he finds either in himself (rationalistic humanism), or in the world of nature (rationalistic naturalism).

However, there is a third possibility. When the modern mind has found both of these approaches unfruitful and unable to provide the necessary answers to the basic questions of human existence, it attempts to find a solution in this third approach with its radical re-definition of man, his nature, and the nature of the world in which he lives; also, of the nature, and even the possibility, of knowledge. Despair and dread replaced the optimism which had permeated the humanist approach to the great questions of life and the recourse to scientific naturalism. Both of these had been tried and found wanting and were unable to furnish any satisfaction to those who had looked to man himself for his conquest over nature for a solution to the besetting problems of contemporary life. Thus, they resorted to vacuous philosophy to fill the vacuum created by the retreat from Christian thought. Existentialism may well be called the nadir of despair for the Western mind even more than communism. Communism at least echoed, in its dialectical materialism, some kind of hope for continued progress and the realization of a secularized millennial period in human history. But existentialism can offer no such hope.[23]

Existentialism can offer no hope or solution for the besetting problems confronting the modern mind, for it binds together all of the irrational and pagan elements of nineteenth-century thought into one bundle and gives an added impetus to the anti-Christian momentum inherent in the philosophy of the preceding centuries. Existentialism is the final expression of the aimlessness of modern thought as it began its course with Descartes and his immediate successors. It is noteworthy that nearly all of the existentialist writers refer to Descartes as the grandfather of their movement in the sense that he inaugurated currents of thought which brought modern philosophy to its critical juncture which their movement is designed to correct. Many scholars must disagree with their remedy while admitting the truth of their contention that the trend (or trouble) did begin with Descartes.

All existentialist thinkers betray a haunting dissatisfaction with modern

23. Many writers in their discussion of existentialism attempt to draw a distinction between those members of the existentialist school whom they classify as self-conscious atheists and those whom they call Christian existentialists. This author regards this effort as a rather arbitrary distinction which lacks any real substance. He would admit that some within this group have made serious, and perhaps desperate, attempts to maintain a place for some kind of faith in their philosophy, while others have made no pretense of providing a place of refuge for their dethroned mythological sovereign. The author would insist that all existentialism in its basic presuppositions must, by its very nature, be atheistic in its intent. The god of the existentialists is a god of their own creation to whom they grudgingly allow a limited existence, but he must conform to the dictates of their nihilistic philosophy to retain even this precarious footing.

philosophy and an emptiness of spirit which they seek to overcome. Most of them describe this as a feeling of alienation. It can be said that this feeling of alienation and dread is the one feature which is common to all members of this school. In fact, the common bond which more or less binds the existentialist thinkers into a school of thought is to be found in the negations which underlie their thinking. But even in their negations they differ widely in their interpretation. Many observers find it difficult to define and characterize the thinking of those who are popularly called existentialists. Heidegger vigorously denied that he was an existentialist.[24] However, his denial is offset by the fact that he shares many, if not most, of the basic assumptions of the various members of this school, and it is almost impossible for him to extricate himself from those who are avowedly existential in their thinking.[25] In spite of some major and some minor variations in the thinking of the leading exponents of this philosophy, those assumptions which they hold in common outweigh in their importance those which separate them. For this reason the claim of some that they are Christian existentialists is suspect and open to serious question. The theism to which they claim allegiance is not that of historic Christianity and the teaching of the Scriptures. This common rejection of Christianity becomes very evident as we examine the position of the leading existentialist thinkers in regard to the doctrines of God, creation, man, truth, sin, evil and redemption, time and human history.

The biblical doctrine of God, so basic to Christian theism, plays a minimal role in existentialist thought. Heidegger and Jaspers, following Kierkegaard, pay Him some attention and a limited recognition in their systems, but Sartre is truculent in his dogmatic denial of this vital Christian doctrine. Even the so-called Christian existentialists failed to make the triune God of the Scriptures the focal point in all of their thinking.

Commentators on Heidegger's existentialism differ on his view of God. Some believe that he had a high regard for Christian theology, but they also admit that he strongly insisted that it should not be allowed to speak on metaphysical or other questions. His writings scarcely mention God for this reason. Heidegger disavowed any great interest in the problem of the existence of God because he was more interested in "Being" than with

24. Some draw a sharp distinction between the theistic and the atheistic members of this school. The theistic members are regarded as the successors of Kierkegaard, while the atheistic members are regarded as the colleagues of Sartre.

25. In one sense this distinction between the atheistic and the theistic varieties of existentialism is legitimate. Jaspers and Marcel certainly speak of God and try to make room for Him in their systems. Heidegger and Sartre openly announced their allegiance to atheism.

existence, and to the accomplishment of the purpose of building a metaphysic of "Being" he devoted his *Sein und Zeit* (1927). He agreed that the concept of "Being" is the most universal one in philosophy, but at the same time he rejected the previous definitions of Aristotle, St. Thomas, and Hegel. He insisted that it is both universal and indefinable. It cannot be regarded as anything that is, neither can it be deduced from higher concepts. In something of a Hegelian sense, he attempts to define it in terms which are reminiscent of Hegel's dialectical system. He referred to it as the reality which is encountered in everything and which, at the same time, makes possible everything that exists. For Heidegger, "Being" is the evolution of this all-pervading reality toward its actual existence. Nevertheless, he is very careful to prevent the identification of this "Being" with God.

It is evident at this point that Heidegger's position leaves a great deal to be desired and many fundamental questions unanswered. Not the least of these is that which pertains to the relationship of Being and Nothingness, and which of these two concepts is the ultimate ground of those things which exist. The difficulty involved in this question is that Heidegger leaves a great void in his discussion of it. When there is no God, then the great issues of philosophy can be neither discussed in a meaningful way nor answered. This serious inadequacy in his system brings in its wake a series of failures as he sets out to provide answers to the other great issues which haunt the minds of men in every age in spite of the continual efforts to banish them from the sight of human intellectual endeavor.

Heidegger's casual dismissal of the God of Christianity as a possible being unworthy of serious philosophical attention necessarily influenced his entire outlook and his total system. Inescapably the low view of God shared by all existentialists brought in its wake a low view of man and the world. Strive as they might to fashion a philosophy of being, their lack of a meaningful account for the original of all temporal reality rendered their efforts futile. In his *Sein und Zeit,* Heidegger attempted to develop a universal ontology, but this approach necessitated an existential analysis of the *Dasein,* which he defined as the "human being there."[26] But *Dasein* does not represent the ontology of man. Although it is not translatable into English, it is generally accepted as meaning the mode of existence of the human being. This *Dasein,* or existence, does not comprise all of the

---

26. This work was never completed, and some students of Heidegger contend that if he had been able to complete this project, we would have a satisfactory presentation of his ontology. Christian theists, on the other hand, reply by pointing out that the basic approach in the volume could lead only to a more unsatisfactory analysis in a second volume.

temporal aspects of man. It is only an abstraction of his existence, and the natural aspects of human existence such as number or space, motion, or even life itself are part of this *Dasein.*

According to this view, the essence of *Dasein* is its existence. Heidegger, at this point, is asserting that human reality cannot be defined because it is not "given." A man is to be regarded in terms of possibility, and his existence consists in his ability to make choices of the possibilities which confront him. But his choices are not final. He is constantly confronted with a series of choices. As Heidegger further explains his system and seemingly has real solutions to the contradictions involved in it, he faces more complex involvements which do not admit of any solution. The discussion of his view of man, thus far, indicates that man is the product of chance and that his existence is largely subject to chance. Heidegger retreats from such a conclusion, in theory at least, by insisting that the mode of human existence has a structure. This being in the world—of which we have been speaking thus far—is the being of a self in relationship to what he calls a not self, by which he means a world of external relationships, both personal and impersonal. He further insists that the manner of existence is not accidental but is a necessity of thought, by which he means that the world as man finds it is constitutive of his existence. This is the basic meaning of *Dasein* in Heidegger's works. *Dasein* is the source of possibilities confronting man and, as it is constituted by its relations with objects which are enabling possibilities, confers intelligibility upon the world.

This intricate view of man in the world is based upon pure conjecture and raises many important questions, the answers to which leave his system in shambles. In one moment Heidegger rests his case purely upon chance, the contingency involved in the many possibilities which an individual confronts. Yet, at the same time, the *Dasein* is also constituted by its relations with external objects.

Why is man capable of choosing among the possibilities which confront him? What is there in man which makes such a choice possible? Obviously, Heidegger's man is not the normative man we find in the Scriptures. He gives no credence or place to the human soul and its faculties as he meanders through this strange exploration of the meaning of Being.

Secondly, we see no reason for man making such choices. There is in Heidegger no hint of purpose in creation or life. In fact, he assumes the world and man as given and makes no effort to explain their origin. Even his use of Hegel's dialectical process lacks the impressive meaning which Hegel sought to give to his system. Heidegger is also strangely, and yet logically, silent on the nature of the possibilities open to man. There is a good reason for this. His reliance upon contingency deprives him of any meaningful answers to such a question. Caught on the horns of a dilemma, a meaningless contingency on the one hand as an explanation of human behavior, and an equally meaningless determinism on the other, Heidegger fled from the question into the quagmire of greater complexities which are even more baffling both to his disciples and to those who are seeking to unravel the threads of his system to better understand his existentialism merely for the sake of obtaining an insight into the contemporary streams of thought.

As his system unfolds, the plunge into irrationalism becomes more obvious. It is at this point that we venture into deep and murky waters. The point has already been made that the *Dasein* cannot be defined. How, then, can we know that which cannot be defined? Heidegger insists that man cannot know the *Dasein* by objective thought. On this he is very clear. It cannot be known through rational thought. In this sense it is unknowable, but it can be known from revelation from the *Dasein* to *itself*.

In spite of its inaccessibility to any objective rational thought and in spite of the fact that it cannot be defined, Heidegger bravely sets forth to make propositional statements about its nature. He made a sharp distinction between what he called authentic existence and unauthentic existence, by which distinction he meant the fundamental existence which truly exists and one which is concerned with the externals of humanity.

Unauthentic existence is the characteristic of the mass man, *Das Man*. At the same time, Heidegger held that both forms are *Dasein* and these two forms cannot be separated from one another. For him, unauthentic existence is the material environment in which man finds himself—a totality of all objects. The masses exist on this plane. On the other hand, authentic existence is much broader than this living in the environment. It is the transcendence, or the projection, by which the *Dasein* constitutes or realizes itself. The person who achieves authentic existence must transcend the pragmatic existence of his life in the world.

But how does man pass from unauthentic to this authentic existence? He provides the answer to this question in his concept of *Angst*. This *Angst* is not fear. Fear arises by contact with something which causes it. *Angst,* on the other hand, arises suddenly out of the depth of human existence. This concept was not original with Heidegger, for he borrowed it from Kierkegaard, who defined it as the reality of freedom as potentiality.

For Heidegger anger, or dread, has a revelational function. It discloses *Dasein* to itself, and in so doing it brings about a great change in human existence. This results in authentic experience or authentic *Dasein*. It reveals to men our freedom to choose and produce our possibilities. It also reveals to men that existence is "Being toward death." Existence is determined by death, from which there is no escape.

But, curiously enough, our conscience is somehow awakened by the *Angst*. However, Heidegger's view of the awakened conscience is not that of the Scriptures. There is no operation of the Holy Spirit working on the conscience of man to bring him to an awareness of his state of sin and guilt. For Heidegger the function of the conscience is to call men out of the state of unauthentic existence into that of authentic existence by making men choose and then actualize their possibilities. When conscience is thus awakened, there also arises a sense of guilt. It is strictly a humanistic conception by which men are led to the realization that human existence is an actual fact and that they have been forced to accept the burden of having been thrust into existence.

Heidegger's view of freedom is a curious fabric, a compound of pure chance and determinism. His freedom is conditioned by the *Angst* which suddenly arises from the depths of human existence, and its final lesson for mankind is that existence is toward death. The *Angst* also teaches men that in authentic existence he can no longer feel at home in the world. The freedom in existentialism as it is found in Heidegger is the freedom to accept one's fate.

In brief, his view of freedom is humanistic to the core, thoroughly irrational in its character. It is heavily tinctured by a pessimism resulting from its underlying nihilism. It is humanism run amuck, a humanism stripped of the glow which at an earlier time in its arduous history surrounded its earlier disciples.

Heidegger leaves no room for a doctrine of creation or purpose and goal in nature and human history. Thus, there is no possibility of a doctrine of truth. This negation of truth is common to all existentialists, but it is especially prominent in the thinking of Heidegger. What truth or "purpose" there may be for man in his thought, man confers upon himself when he achieves his authentic existence.

For Heidegger, man is a pathetic creature, devoid of meaning and purpose, an irrational being cast adrift in an irrational universe, doomed to a death which ultimately denies even the tenuous existence which he does not enjoy so much as endures. He is a prisoner of fate, for he cannot escape, and is the product of chance, over which he has no control.

This introduction to existentialism through the eyes of Heidegger may well raise the question as to why and how this intellectually, morally, and spiritually devastating mode of thought has been able to gain such a hold on the modern mind. It is doubtful that the study of the other existentialists will shed more light on this important question, for although there are differences between Heidegger and those who followed him in this tradition, these differences do not in any way begin to provide the answer.

Karl Jaspers (1889–)

It is sometimes asserted that Karl Jaspers represents a kind of Christian strain in existentialist thought, and that for this reason his system, if we may use the term, is something different from the existentialism we have found in Heidegger. There are differences, but these differences are insignificant in view of the much more basic similarities found in these thinkers. The Christian thought allegedly contained in Jaspers' thought and philosophy is assuredly not that of historic Christianity.

Along with other existentialists, Jaspers' primary concern was with the nature of being, but he insisted that being in general cannot be defined. In his life upon earth man is confronted with three specific forms of being. The first form Jaspers called "in-itself," a degree of being which comprised things, the existence of which is known to man apart from himself through science. Science is the necessary tool for acquiring the knowledge of this first stage of being. In this first stage man is forced to come to terms with an objective world through the empirical process. But the scientist or philosopher soon realizes that he is strictly limited in this approach to a knowledge of being. The philosopher realizes that he can neither think absolute being and yet at the same time deny the necessity which he feels to think it, even though it is unthinkable.

The second degree step in the knowledge of being is the knowledge which he called "being-object" of those things which can relate to the person as a subject. In this second stage things relate to man as the subject. The third, and most important, form of being for Jaspers is that form which is found only in man, which he describes as Being I, which includes being and being known.

All of these three forms are not of equal importance for Jaspers, but they are all simultaneously present in man. For man his *Dasein,* his being, is actually his self-consciousness. In this state man is conscious of his own consciousness in which he becomes thoroughly conscious of his solitude on the one hand, and liberty on the other. Man is conscious of objects external to him and of himself. They can never be separated from each other as two coterminous ingredients of self-consciousness. This kind of consciousness cannot be achieved through science, psychology, or logic, but only through philosophy. Philosophy brings this to man and makes him able to penetrate to the depths of his existence through its power of enlightenment, or the illumination of his experience. It brings to man a consciousness or revelation of his existence. At this point there is revealed to him his liberty, which Jaspers described as the source of human possibilities. Man can never say that he is, for he is in a state of permanent unfolding and self-realization or actualization. It is for this reason that a man can never say "I am," because he is constantly changing and is never the same. It thus follows that man cannot have an essence. It also follows, according to Jaspers, that man must realize his liberty in the world and then lose it in the transcendence on which it is grounded and by which it is also limited. However, this transcendence also provides the goal of human existence. As an existential being, man must transcend himself, even as he is also his own origin and creator. J. M. Spier summarized this difficult portion of Jaspers' thought:

> As an existential person I am the origin of myself, the creator of the actualization of my potentialities. In my existential being I transcend myself, I go beyond my factual being, my being in the present, but I project myself into the future.[27]

The choice of possibilities involved in the process has its source in man and returns to him in making him what he is at any particular moment. At this point, Jaspers proceeded to erect a theory of ethics which clearly shows his break with historic Christianity. Like his fellow existentialists, Jaspers has always been concerned with maintaining a doctrine of human freedom within the determinism which underlies existentialist thought. He insisted that the choices which men make are not uncertain decisions in the presence of alternatives; rather they are elicited from man, and at the same time they are disciplined choices. His thought is that in this process duty plays a role, but he denies that man is under an ethical law; he simply adopts it as his own. But what is the origin of this sense of duty? To whom is this duty owed? The answers are obvious. Man is the source of the sense of duty which he feels and of the ethical law which he adopts as his own. Man thus accepts determination by law, and this is the essence of human liberty. Jaspers teeters on the brink of the abyss between determinism and liberty—a common dilemma faced by all existentialists and solved by none.

Jaspers clings desperately to human autonomy, even to the point of giving the very distinct impression that man creates himself and becomes the arbiter of his own ethical outlook and destiny. It is humanism run riot.

27. J. M. Spier, *Christianity and Existentialism* (Philadelphia, 1953), p. 20.

The irrational character of his system becomes so transparent that it finally makes it almost impossible for those who are searching for its meaning to trace the development of his thought.

He admits that all of life is dominated by a sense of insecurity and futility, for man cannot transcend the limits of his finite environment, and the greatest of these limitations is death itself. It does not bring him into contact with God, for in his thought there is no personal God, no immortality in heaven, and no eternal punishment in hell. Death, in spite of his efforts to evade its meaning is, for Jaspers, the end. His philosophy is pessimistic in the extreme. His one conclusion which he offers to mankind is that the philosophy which brings him to the realization of his condition and tempts him to despair, also brings to him a kind of faith which enables him to continue living in spite of the ultimate hopelessness of his situation.

What kind of a faith is this, and what is its focal point? It is obviously not the faith of the Scriptures. It is not a faith placed in a personal God as He is revealed in Jesus Christ. It is not faith such as that set forth in the eighth chapter of the letter to the Romans, in which the Apostle Paul declares that a sovereign, holy, and personal God is working all things together for the good of those who have placed their faith in Him. One searches in vain for that kind of faith in Jaspers.

Jaspers also does not reveal any purpose in living, for there is no real meaning to be found in human history, or in the lives of any who have lived on this earth. The faith of which he speaks is an empty and hopeless faith in human transcendence, which man manufactures for himself.

In short, this faith is no faith at all. It is an irrational, anti-intellectual, blind hope, devoid of any sure foundation. Lacking such a foundation, Jaspers' claim that he has built on a Christian foundation is, in itself, without foundation. It is a humanistic philosophy which uses science in the first step toward a knowledge of the outer world, and then abandons it as a useless instrument in the quest of self-realization. It is an irrational system which employs rational language for the statement of its position. Jaspers disclaimed the value of language as a means of communication. For him, there is no truth to proclaim and no real reason for proclaiming it if it should exist. Finally, there is no one to proclaim it and no one to receive a proclamation if it should be made.

According to Jaspers, existence as such can never be perceived, and for this reason we cannot perceive, or observe, the existence of another person. Since men can experience existence only in themselves as their own personal property, it follows that men can experience their own existence only as they are in contact with other people. In other words, personal contacts between men call forth the experience of existence in each of them having such a contact. Such a contact is never permanent, however, and is only for the moment. Thus it follows that each individual is not continually aware of his own existence, but only to the extent that such an awareness is called forth by personal contacts with other individuals. Jaspers insists that these contacts constitute the highest form of personal contacts because they allow individuals to make it possible for other people to discover their true selves in the discovery of other individuals.

For Jaspers this is actually a kind of secret contact or discovery. It cannot be stated in meaningful language because it is so highly personal and temporary. These glimpses of the true self are but fleeting insights into the human self. For him the world outside of persons, other individuals, is a secret text which can be experienced only in a secret manner. The content of such contacts cannot be put into meaningful language, for to do so is to destroy their inherent nature and value. They must be "existential" and not "essential." He further insisted that not until an individual thoroughly grasps the individuality of his own existence does he seem to see the need for other persons and thus the need for society. Yet, at the same time, he insists that there is a deep-seated tendency in existence to hide itself from other people. The cause of this is the "dread" which arises out of the realization, or feeling, that a personal confrontation between individuals produces a kind of nakedness in the disclosure of one to another.

Jaspers, along with the other members of the existentialist school, is confusing because of the basic irrationalism which underlies his entire approach. If they were consistent in the pursuit and teaching of their philosophy, they would avoid the use of rational language entirely in their writings. They face the dilemma of having to use rational language (even though it is highly ambiguous) to express their irrationality. They must use terms which are not only foreign, but even hostile, to their basic presuppositions. Actually the presuppositions themselves are hostile to the existentialist philosophy. To be sure, they employ such terms as thought, science, reality, experience, being, and essence, but their logic should preclude such an indulgence.

Lying behind these obviously critical difficulties and weaknesses in the position of Jaspers and his fellow-existentialists, there are even more critical weaknesses, which make a mockery of their claims that existentialism is compatible with Christianity, or even that it is a meaningful philosophy and a useful tool for the solution of the problems confronting twentieth-century man. The logical contradictions and irrational presuppositions which are so apparent in the work of Jaspers have their roots in his basic negations and affirmations. It has already been noted that in a very real sense man is the creator of his own personality. This is, of course, truly absurd, and at one time in the history of liberal thought would hardly have been regarded as worthy of any serious attention. But today it passes almost without question in some philosophical and even theological circles.

Nevertheless, nagging questions persist. If there is no God and man is not created in His image, what then is the origin of consciousness of the soul, and how is it possible for two or more individuals through these existential confrontations which result in fleeting glimpses of the true self, to create this consciousness and the realization of what man truly is? How can one man who does not have such an awareness communicate to others such an awareness which he does not possess in regard to himself? The existentialists have no real answer to these questions. It is an act of faith on their part to make such an assertion; it is a veritable leap in the dark. Logically they should avoid using rational language to express their irrational philosophy, as they decry the use of language as a legitimate mode of expression. Existentialist thought and practice is studded with inconsistencies, both in its reliance on "unauthentic" presuppositions and in its application of these presuppositions.

Even more glaring are its negations of Christian theology. The virtual rejection of the biblical view of God brings in its train a host of problems which Jaspers either ignored or sought to answer in a manner which, in itself, contradicted his own frame of reference. In him, as in Heidegger, the problem of the origin and nature of human consciousness is a major issue as well as a major weakness in his system. The ethical implication of Jaspers' denial of both the biblical teaching in regard to the human soul and its correlatives of the nature of consciousness and the conscience are staggering. His solution is frightening. His casual proclamation that the individual is free from ethical law except as he creates his own is dangerous in the extreme. This gives rise to untrammeled relativism in ethical theory which can only create the grounds and motivation for the creation of political dictatorships in those societies or nations which accept his theory.

The one redeeming feature in existentialism is its negation of propositional or absolute truth. If there is no absolute truth, then it must follow that existentialism cannot be true. This redeeming feature is somewhat offset in its value, as many people prefer falsehood if that falsehood proclaims the autonomy of the human reason and will. It is this assertion, common to all existentialists, which accounts for the popularity of a philosophy which is utterly irrational and meaningless, and which degrades man to the level of animal life. In seeking to enthrone his own autonomy, modern man has committed himself to a philosophy which denies to him the ground for believing in that autonomy and dignity.

Jean Paul Sartre (1905–)

A brief treatment of the even more radical existentialist, Jean Paul Sartre, seems to be in order. Implicit in Heidegger, inherent in Jaspers and in Sartre, atheism became the overriding passion which permeates their various writings. In Sartre the accumulated antagonism to historic Christianity, both Roman Catholic and Protestant, comes to its own with a vitriolic intensity almost unmatched in other existentialist literature. All of the latent hostility inherent in the existentialist position finds open expression in Sartre, which makes him somewhat different from his contemporaries. It is for this reason that some scholars have argued that he is not the most typical existentialist philosopher, and their case has some cogency and merit. It is true that in the vehemence of his antagonism and the manner in which he has flaunted it before the public, he is probably not the most typical representative of this school. However, there is another side of the picture which, to a degree, mitigates against the idea that he is not typical. At least one modern commentator insists that Sartre is a typical French intellectual.[28] He even insists that France can, and should, feel national pride in this exhibition of French intelligence.[29]

Sartre's main work is *Being and Nothingness,* written in 1943. He has also given a briefer statement of his position in his *Existentialism Is Humanism.* It must be admitted that he was quite familiar with nineteenth-century thought and drew freely upon Husserl, the philosopher of phenomenology, Heidegger, and some of his writings reveal that he was somewhat influenced by Descartes, Hegel, and Freud. The very fact that some of the Cartesian lines of thought can be discerned in his writings is also evidence that the descent of rationalism into irrationalism began with Descartes. Although Sartre became famous in France and elsewhere with his *Being and Nothingness,* this publication was not the first announcement of his philosophy, for he had previously written a novel, *Nausea,* in 1938, in which being and existence constituted the main theme.

---

28. H. J. Blackham, *Six Existentialist Thinkers* (London, 1961), p. 110.

29. For a different point of view see Kurt Reinhardt's *The Existentialist Revolt,* 2nd ed. (New York, 1960), pp. 157-158. This author argues that three intellectual forces are struggling today for the control of France: Christianity, Marxism, and atheistic existentialism. He says that Sartre is the chief representative of the latter movement.

Sartre defines existence as pure contingency. In his thinking it means "to be there." He was convinced that such an explanation relieved him from any added necessity of formulating a theory of necessary being. Spier is correct when he says that the key to Sartre's entire theory is found in his insistence that it is built upon the experience of finiteness and on the antithesis between what Sartre calls the *en-soi,* the being in itself of the material being of the world, and the *pour-soi,* the being for itself of human consciousness.[30] However, there is a danger in this simple approach to Sartre. It can lead to a misleading simplification of his thought for the unwary reader.

Many interpreters of Sartre insist that the key to Sartre is an understanding of what he means by the term "consciousness." This approach is not in contradiction to Spier's interpretation, but it would seem to be more inclusive and, therefore, more helpful. For Sartre, to be conscious is to be conscious of something. Furthermore, to be conscious is to be aware of being conscious. He argues that if this is not the case, then we would not be aware of being conscious of something. For Sartre, human consciousness in its essence is contradictory. On the one hand, it is finite and contingent, but on the other its activity is also directed toward the pursuit of an unapproachable Absolute. He confessed this in his insistence that the Absolute is a contradiction, for Absolute Being by its very nature would mean that it is the conscious source of everything that is. The contradiction lies in the insistence that while this Absolute is a unity, consciousness is a duality, since this consciousness is always a consciousness of something. Thus Sartre insisted that man is built upon contradictions, for he exhausts himself in the vain search for another contradiction. This thinking logically led him to the famous conclusion that man is a useless passion.

We cannot fully comprehend Sartre's definition of consciousness until we carefully examine his understanding of the Absolute. This notion contains both being-in-itself, *en soi,* a self-sufficiency, and also consciousness, *pour soi.* It is at this point that a kind of irrationality takes over in his thinking. The *en soi* and the *pour soi* are also two modes of consciousness. However, the Absolute Being cannot possibly exist. This material being of the world possesses *en soi,* being-in-itself, and is therefore contingent and absurd. Consciousness cannot be deduced from this world, which is independent and self-sufficient, but the world can be deduced from consciousness. In short, consciousness is related to the objective world and

30. Spier, *Christianity and Existentialism,* p. 60.

dependent upon it. We must conclude that this is true because that of which Sartre speaks is *pour soi,* independent of this world. This is not the case.

Neither can we conclude that Sartre holds that consciousness is something other than the world. He insists that this consciousness constantly reconstitutes itself, by which he means that the consciousness of man is constantly seeking a self-sufficiency or self-realization which it can never achieve. He seeks to realize or achieve the idea of God, but this human consciousness can never achieve this goal. The idea of God is a self-contradiction. Man as *pour-soi* seeks some kind of a unity of the *pour-soi* with the *en-soi.* This is true because man's consciousness of himself implies a projection of himself toward his possibility. This unity between the two is impossible because man as *pour-soi,* as existential self-consciousness, for this reason can never be himself but is always in a process of becoming himself. Thus, for Sartre, human existence is a continual pursuit of an illusion which can never be obtained. By its very nature it would crumble to pieces if he were ever able to lay his hands upon it. Man is driven by a useless passion for the unobtainable.

It is obvious that Sartre has plummeted to the depths of irrationality. If a brief review of his thought leaves the reader in confusion and perhaps in a state of despair as to his ability to comprehend Sartre's version of existentialism, it is very doubtful that a more complete presentation would do much to displace the darkness with light, or the despair with hope. Light and hope can hardly emerge from the muddy waters or the muddled thinking of a philosophy which is saturated with the poisons of a determined atheism.

Sartre denies the possibility of true knowledge of the external world and the existence of Absolute Truth. He dangles before us the idea that knowledge is to know the thing as it is. But such knowledge is possible only if consciousness can somehow identify itself with the thing to be known. If this were the case, then there would be no consciousness and thus no possibility of knowledge. Our consciousness renders the world unreal. All consciousness, according to him, is an escape from reality. If we are conscious of something, or someone, this very consciousness renders the world unreal. Consciousness is a kind of relation with reality which destroys its reality as far as the man who is conscious of it is concerned.

From this it must follow that a human being cannot ever make a pronouncement about himself or others. To do so is an escape from reality. This consciousness is nothing more than an awareness on the part of human beings that they cannot identify themselves with the factuality of reality. It is for this reason that existentialism in general, and particularly that of Sartre, has been described as shadow-boxing with the world of nothingness. Reality is a shadow with unreal people clinging to some sort of contact with it in a manner which disproves any reality which may pertain to it.

Sartre's insistence that man is always becoming and never arriving or achieving has tremendous implications for his views on truth and ethics. For him there can be no absolute of any kind of a propositional nature. There is in his thought not even the possibility of the "truths" of an existential moment. If any factual reality is a being, then the consciousness which a man has of such a being is non-being and therefore non-propositional in nature. There is no objective truth to transmit, and even if there were, the act of communicating it would render it unreal and therefore beyond the power of man to communicate. Indeed, the one to whom it is being communicated must become unreal to the one who is attempting to communicate it. To become conscious of the other person is to render him unreal.

We may well wonder what attention Sartre has paid to the question of human freedom and ethics. We may even wonder if these human attributes can find a place in his system. Our doubts would be legitimate, for Sartre's logic hardly leaves any place for the traditional view of either ethics or freedom. To reach such a conclusion presumes that there is a certain logic in Sartre's version of existentialism, and there is certainly no logic in his position. But it would be quite misleading to conclude from this that Sartre paid no attention to these two important issues. It must always be kept in mind that the real purpose of Sartre was to erect a system of thought which would make man a kind of god and would ascribe to him, as god, the sovereignty and authority which the Scriptures ascribe to the God revealed in them. His existentialism is a determined effort to dethrone God in order that man may assume His place and be enthroned as king of both heaven and earth.

But how can Sartre provide for a system of ethics possessing meaning and authority in a world devoid of both? At first glance this would seem to be a contradiction too gross and too absurd to be considered. Those who have arrived at such a conclusion have overlooked both the grossness and the absurdity of his position. As absurd as it may seem for Sartre to assert ethical considerations with meaning in a world which lacks meaning, this is exactly what he has done. This does not mean that he has accepted any traditional ideas concerning ethics or freedom, or that he has presented a meaningful theory or view of liberty. To have done so would be contrary to the logic, or perhaps better, the thrust of thought and purpose which he had in mind in constructing his philosophy. For him, there cannot be any right in the propositional sense of the term, and thus there cannot be any wrong or evil. If there is no objective truth, it must follow that there cannot be any objective standards of right and wrong. To become conscious of them is to destroy their reality. Even if there were such objective standards in his thinking, there is no possibility of communicating them to other individuals, for language is meaningless. To communicate truth is to destroy it.

Truth, then, is relative in its character; it pertains to the individual only at any given moment in his life experiences, for the individual is constantly becoming. Thus, his ethical insights are not only constantly changing, but cannot be communicated to other individuals, who are also captive to this state of constant flux. It must therefore follow that man sees ethical truths as that which is right in his own eyes at any given moment. What is right for him today was wrong yesterday, and what is right today can very well be wrong tomorrow. This relativism is for Sartre the ethical norm for all people. Logically, in a society controlled by existentialist thought it would be not only undesirable, but utterly impossible, to establish and maintain norms of public behavior. Social anarchy must ultimately result from the dictum that "everyone should do his own thing." No society can long survive the social, economic, and moral anarchism inherent in such an ethical outlook. It soon takes steps to preserve itself against the inroads of the moral relativism which grows out of a widespread acceptance of this ethical philosophy by a large segment of its own members. The political result of this effort produces within the body politic a totalitarian despotism of some kind which embraces the total life of all the people. Translated into more specific terms, the result is the Nazi state in Germany, the Fascist state in Italy, or the emerging absolutism which threatens the traditional constitutionalism of Great Britain with a communist regime of some kind.[31] In a somewhat broader pattern of application, moral relativism forms the foundation for the trend inherent in all modern democracies to become the womb of dictatorships.

Closely related to Sartre's view of ethics is his concept of human freedom. Here again we must keep in view that Sartre does not have in mind a tradi-

31. At the time of writing (October, 1976), Harold Wilson, former Labor-Socialist Prime Minister of Great Britain, issued a solemn warning to the English people that the welfare state and its moral accompaniments must be changed toward a conservative pattern, or the country would face the very real possibility of a communist take-over.

tional view of freedom based on a biblical foundation. The relativism inherent in his philosophy strikes the reader with renewed force. He demands for man absolute freedom in a world in which there can be no absolutes. Man is absolutely free. In fact, he is so free in his deeds that he creates his own world and confers upon it its meaning, or lack thereof. Sartre insists upon the necessity of atheism because if there is a God, and if man believes in Him as the sovereign Creator of all things, then that man evades his own responsibility and flees from his freedom. What, then, is freedom? In essence it rests in the absolute autonomy of man, but it also has been defined as the absolute arbitrariness of man. To understand this we must retrace our steps for a moment and return to his ethical outlook, particularly to his view of law. Man is outside the law in the sense that in his actions he is responsible only to himself. There is no ethical code to which he is subject, not even that categorical imperative described by Kant to which he is bound, no higher authority to which, or to whom, he must yield obedience. The truly responsible man is truly responsible to himself and to no one else. Sartre's doctrine of freedom reenforces the anarchistic tendency in his ethical outlook and hastens the creation of a social anarchy which, in turn, yields the fruit of a totalitarian political regime as its antidote.

In this fashion the irrationality of the existentialist philosophy is communicated to the totalitarian regime which emerges to check the anarchy inherent in its view of freedom and ethics. The irrational behavior of modern totalitarian regimes is the necessary fruit of its philosophical background. It is ironic, in one sense, that Marxist thinkers have denounced Sartre for his highly idealistic view of freedom, for they rightly see that this unbridled individualism is directly contrary to their own version of the solidarity of the proletariat and the absolute truth which they profess to find in the dialectical logic of Marx. The irony all too often has escaped both the followers of Sartre and those of Marx.

Christian Existentialism

In spite of the contradictory nature of such a terminology as "Christian existentialism," there have been, and still are, those philosophers and theologians who have sought to find a synthesis between the basic principles of existentialism on the one hand, and Christian theology on the other. They find their inspiration in Kierkegaard, but have advanced beyond him in that they have tried to come to terms with the intellectual descendants of this nineteenth-century Danish thinker. Some of these have attacked the problem from the philosophical view, while others have sought to achieve a harmony between Christian theology and existentialism.

The leading member of the first school is Gabriel Marcel (1889–). His efforts to erect theistic existentialism are not very impressive, for he had chosen for himself an impossible task. It is important to note that not until 1929 did he join the Roman Catholic Church, and this came about after a long struggle within himself. Thus, his first ventures as a thinker took place before he had entered into a Christian belief. For this reason he denied that he was an existentialist, and many scholars do not regard him as a member of this school of thought. However, his methodology and attitude reflect much existential influence on his approach to philosophical problems, and it is very doubtful that he ever approached a truly theistic answer to the problems which he discussed. He began with the assumption that it is impossible to construct a satisfactory philosophical system in the manner of a St. Thomas Aquinas or a Descartes. He distrusted all metaphysical systems, regarding them as a kind of prison which would imprison him.

> No step seems to me metaphysically more important than that by which I recognize that I cannot without contradiction think of the absolute as a central observatory from which the universe would be contemplated in its totality, instead of being apprehended in a partial and lateral way, as it is by each of us.[32]

Christian theists can well appreciate his efforts to escape the snares of philosophical systems which seek to interpret the universe from the vantage point of an impersonal absolute. They would quickly insist that the determination to escape from this trap does not mean that we must also avoid looking unto the personal God of the Scriptures as the great observatory in the light of which we must interpret all reality.

Even though Marcel entered the portals of the Roman Church, with its vast cathedral of Thomistic philosophy, he never brought his thinking into captivity to Thomism, and at heart remained an existentialist in his philosophical methodology. Like Jaspers, he centered his attention on the problem of "Being." In the light of this approach he then turned his attention to man. He did not regard being as a problem, but as a mystery.

It is not necessary to deal with the intricacies of a system which denies that it is a system. It is necessary, however, to refute the idea that Marcel is a Christian existentialist and that Christian existentialism is a possible option in his philosophy. For this reason his discussion of man is important,

---

32. Quoted in Ronald Grimsley, *Existentialist Thought* (Cardiff, Wales, 1967), p. 189.

not only because of the light it sheds on his view of man, but also because of the light it sheds on his view of God. Marcel declared that the essence of man lies in the fact that he is in a situation and that he is unconscious of the situation. He insisted that his awareness of his existence cannot be first of all the awareness of himself as a knowing subject from his body as known object, because it is the existence of the body of a human being in the world that constitutes him a subject before it is given to him as an object to a subject. In brief, man has a kind of primordial participation of his bodily existence in the life of the world in which state he has a confused consciousness of universal existence before he goes to a separate awareness of his own existence.

This concept of man and his conscious state is a far cry from the biblical view. There is no recognition of the biblical doctrine of creation or the fact that man is created in the image of God and that the possession of a soul is the seat of conscious existence. The basic note of Christian or biblical theism is lacking in Marcel. This is not to say that Marcel lacks any idea of some sort of creation, rather does he refuse to accept the biblical view.

> My most intimate and unshakable conviction—and if it is heretical so much the worse for orthodoxy—is, whatever so many of the pious and learned people may have said about it, that God does not at all want to be loved by us over *against* the created, but to be glorified through the created and starting from it. That is why so many pious books are intolerable to me. This God standing against the created and in some way jealous of His own works is in my eyes nothing but an idol. It is an escape for me to have written this. And I do declare till a new dispensation that I shall be insincere each time that I shall seem to affirm anything contrary to what I have just written.[33]

Marcel's philosophy has been called Christian humanism, but this term is, in itself, a contradiction in the light of Christian theism. His philosophy is devoted to a study as to how men participate in being. This approach is quite the reverse of that which is dictated by Christian theism.

This negation of biblical theism runs throughout his thought and supports the description given to Marcel that he was always an obedient churchman, but never the orthodox theologian. This evaluation of Marcel's thought involves the recognition that he did not accept the historic Christian view of such doctrines as the Person and nature of the triune God, creation, man, sin, the nature of redemption, the meaning of the Christian

---

33. Quoted in Blackham, *Six Existentialist Thinkers,* p. 72.

life, the role of the church, or the doctrine of the resurrection in its relationship to the meaning of death. Because Marcel never came to an appreciation or acceptance of these basic Christian truths, he never achieved a meaningful insight into their implications for philosophy. Particularly did he fail to understand their implications for such philosophical issues as the meaning of truth and human liberty.

Marcel's view of freedom illustrates very clearly that existentialism dominates his thinking on this vital issue. Freedom for him consists in a man's horizontal relationship which he is able to establish with other human beings. Freedom is experienced or encountered when man stands in what Marcel calls ontological mystery, but he also held that man achieves it in the sense that his relationship with other human beings was a necessary means for achieving and experiencing it. This concept is the logical result of his emphasis upon the I and Thou encounter which brings about the realization of freedom. Thus, his view of freedom is essentially humanistic in its nature and cannot in any way be related to the biblical view. Man by a human encounter with other human beings experiences a freedom, but the question remains: a freedom from what? Marcel further argued that the absolute Thou, God, emerges out of this experience of freedom. This is far different from both Roman Catholic and Reformed views of freedom. The experience of God in a personal encounter results from an action initiated by man with other men. Marcel, at this point, is affirming the autonomy of both the will and mind of man as over against divine sovereignty, and try as he would, there is no way of reconciling the biblical view of God with his existentialist presuppositions. There is no sense of the slavery of man to sin and no affirmation of the new freedom which believers have in Christ. Marcel gives no indication of any appreciation of the biblical teachings of the meaning of freedom or how man can achieve such a liberty such as that of which Christ spoke when He declared that man shall know the truth and the knowledge of the truth would make him free.[34]

Marcel not only rejected the traditional Roman Catholic arguments for the existence of God as they were set forth in the works of St. Thomas Aquinas, but he also refused all creedal statements concerning the nature of God on the ground that such creedal affirmations only objectify God and prevent the personal encounter out of which the knowledge of God and the experience of freedom must emerge if they are to be known at all.

This rejection of creeds and systematic statements of the Christian faith

---

34. John 8:32.

necessarily arises out of Marcel's distinction between non-existential and existential knowledge. Non-existential knowledge uses propositions to set forth objective truth. But this non-existential thinking not only fails to bring valid knowledge, but is also quite dangerous when it is accepted as the only valid truth, since it deprives men of all that is really important. On the other hand, existential knowledge is a knowledge born of personal encounter, arising out of the struggles of a free person.

The question must necessarily arise: How does man achieve truth, and is there any truth to achieve? Is not such knowledge a purely subjective experience, since it is not based upon propositional truth? The answer to this question must logically be in the affirmative. However, Marcel sought to guard against such an interpretation of his position by his insistence that this search for knowledge is not an aimless procedure in which man gropes in the darkness. Somehow or other, man is met half-way by God, who actively reveals Himself to the seeking person. This search for God arises out of man's desire for such an experience with the Absolute I, and God graciously responds to this search. In this process God and man are no longer rigidly separated, but become participants in the same reality. Thus, for Marcel, truth is achieved as a result of this personal involvement between the subject and the object. Truth, if it can be found at all, is found only as men participate in their own personal search for God, and thus the truth revealed in such an encounter is not a unity in any sense of the word, but is the personal experiences of those who participate in the search for it. For Marcel there can be no real communication of objective truth, for to objectify truth is to destroy it. His version of existentialism is contrary to both the Roman Catholic insistence on an infallible papacy and its objective pronouncements and to the creedal statements of the Reformed and Lutheran churches. Truth thus becomes vaporized in the subjectivism of existentialism, and while there might seem to be crucial differences between the atheistic versions of this philosophy and those espoused by "Christian existentialists," they are basically the same. For this reason they must be regarded as equally irrational and destructive of the culture of the West.

The Theistic Evaluation of Existentialism

There can be no doubt that existentialism has added momentum to the process of intellectual deterioration now taking place in the West. It has now joined communism and the Freudian psychology as one of the three great enemies of historic Christianity in the modern world. In assuming such a role it has also joined the ranks of those philosophies which have contributed so much to the growth of irrationalism and anti-intellectualism in the name of rationalism.

This insistence on the meaninglessness and lack of purpose in history and the life of man is deeply ingrained in the entire existentialist movement. Because these philosophers insist that man is history and is therefore in a state of becoming, it must follow that man becomes what he is at any given moment and that he is also what he becomes for the same reason. In such a state of flux there is no place for any absolutes, yet, in spite of this, existentialism insists that man is autonomous. How can he be truly autonomous in a state of constant flux? Is not the flux in which he is a prisoner a distinct limitation on his autonomy?

Existentialism also rules out the divine creation of the world and of man. Therefore it has no satisfactory explanation for the existence of the material world or man. Some members of this school of thought have gone to the absurd extreme of giving support to the theory that man somehow creates himself. The absurdities in such a position are too severe a strain upon common sense to demand a serious response.

Existentialism also rests upon the foundations of an unabashed humanism which represents man as essentially good without taint of sin in the biblical sense, without any need of repentance or a change of ethical life. What changes are needed are thoroughly within the province and ability of man to achieve, and there is no need of divine grace to achieve an authentic existence. Existentialism deifies man and with great consistency proceeds to confer upon this deified human personality a creative power and absolute freedom consonant with the biblical idea of deity. It is ironic that the existentialists confer upon man those characteristics of a deity whom they deny and whom even the so-called Christian existentialists restructure to their own purposes and liking.

Existentialism either openly, or somewhat more cleverly, denies the historic Christian faith at every essential point. It has been described as a philosophy in which "all things proceed from man and exist for him."[35] Spier makes the further observation that "Existentialism is not only foreign to the revelation of God in His Word, but it is also alien to the God of revelation."[36] Although Sartre attempts to place Jaspers and Marcel within the Christian camp, specifically within the Roman Catholic world, he also insists that existentialism is not only atheism in the strict sense of the word, meaning that God does not exist, but adds the further negation

35. Spier, *Christianity and Existentialism,* p. 136.
36. Ibid., p. 137.

that it would not make any difference to His particular brand of existentialism if He should somehow exist.[37]

Existentialism is an apostate philosophy, and because of this apostasy it has brought Western thought to the brink of nihilism, denying purpose and meaning to all of reality. Because it is theologically apostate, it is also religiously apostate. It is the ultimate admission of the futility of the humanism by which it was inspired and through which it has been nurtured. It is the ultimate affirmation of the cultural and intellectual decadence of the Western world which was its womb and of the theology which sought an alliance with it.

The Impact of Existentialism on Western Culture

It might be supposed that because of the rather narrow vision of the existentialist philosophers and their apparent lack of interest in the broader aspects of the outreach of the more traditional philosophers, that existentialism would not have obtained a wide hearing in Western culture, and that it would have had a rather limited influence in contemporary intellectual affairs. This has not proved to be the case. It has gained an influence far beyond the bounds of philosophy proper. The question may well arise: How could such an anti-intellectual philosophy find a welcome in the ranks of academic disciplines and cultural interests such as political philosophy, sociology, psychology, literature, linguistics, and even theology? That it has had such an impact is of great importance and is the justification for devoting an entire chapter to this philosophy which, at first glance, might seem to be an aberration too small to merit anything more than a cursory footnote or a few paragraphs. This is not the case. The next chapter will be devoted to an examination of its expanding influence in nearly every aspect of Western culture and its attendant growth of irrationalism in the areas of human activity: intellectual, political, economic, social, educational, and religious.

The Wider Impact of Existentialism and the Development of Other Forms of Irrationalism

Why has an irrational philosophy of the dimensions of existentialism been able to permeate so much of Western thought, and to such an extent as to virtually paralyze much of current intellectual endeavor and to sentence it to futility and frustration? That this is the case can scarcely

---

37. Jean Paul Sartre, *Existentialism Is Humanism,* p. 16.

be denied, and the very importance of the question demands an honest investigation and a satisfactory answer. One answer to the question lies in the proposition that the Western mind was prepared and awaited the arrival of such an explanation of life. Already imbedded in a morass of irrationalism, the Western mind was a field already furrowed, fertilized, and ready for this nihilistic philosophy. Freud, Weber, and Dewey, and their colleagues in the various disciplines, had done their work well.

However, the truth of these propositions, in itself, raises further questions which need to be answered. Why were Dewey, Freud, Weber, and their predecessors able to have such an impact on the West? How had they been able to prepare the soil until it had reached its zenith of fertility for the successful planting of the seeds of a nihilistic irrationalism? The answer lies in the theological decline which had taken place in the latter half of the nineteenth century as a result of the invasion of Darwinism and Marxian thought into the West.[38] Theological liberalism by the fourth decade of the twentieth century had already gained a firm footing in the "mainline" Protestant denominations in this country and was beginning to influence Roman Catholic theologians, although this influence was not to become visible to the American public until Vatican II and after. Theological liberalism, to greater or lesser extents, was an ally of irrationalism and often quite openly in alliance with Marxian thought and practice.[39] These major denominations had already capitulated to the irrationalism inherent in the attempt of nineteenth-century thought to offer interpretations of man and the world which were divorced from Christian theology and yet which represented the most advanced rationalistic insights of the era. This growing commitment to the scientific theories of the latter nineteenth and early twentieth centuries prepared the church for the later onslaughts of existentialism, but the concepts of man and his world, which had once seemed so certain and so alluring, soon turned to ashes in the hands of the twentieth-century heirs of this legacy, and they quickly lost their luster. The faith, so popular in many quarters, that science could answer with certainty the questions with which Christianity was seemingly unable to cope, now seemed sadly misplaced, and disillusionment set in, not only with science as such, but even with the ability of man to solve his problems and come to friendly terms with the unfriendly fates which he be-

38. The further impact of existentialism on Christian thought will be explored in the latter sections of this chapter. We are concerned at this point with the theological preparation for existentialism.

39. For a detailed study of this aspect of American ecclesiastical history, see C. Gregg Singer, *The Unholy Alliance* (Arlington House, 1976).

lieved were in control of human destiny.

Those individuals who still clung to the fabric of organized Christianity found in the neo-orthodox appropriation of existentialism a haven, or refuge, while, for the secular-minded, existentialism proved to be the voice of organized doubt and despair for which they had been seeking. Existentialism offered philosophic justification for their disillusionment, and they joyfully claimed it as their own. The intellectual climate of the day provided a fallow ground in which existentialism could and did easily take root. This climate included every avenue of contemporary thought. The anxiety and dread concepts which underlay so much of existentialist thought found a ready response in a world which had faced the agony of a widespread totalitarianism and devastating World War which was quickly followed by wars in almost every quarter of this terrestrial globe. The resort to this philosophy went hand in hand with the widespread efforts to find escape from life in the use of drugs, the glorification of sex, and the activism of the last two decades.

In literature, art, music, and historical thought existentialism left its mark. At the same time, in some writers of the twentieth century evidences of an existential mode of thought appeared before existentialism had gained formal recognition as a philosophy. These writers shared a common background of the legacy of the nineteenth century with Heidegger, Jaspers, Sartre, and their colleagues, but sought to give expression to this legacy in a different form of literature, while others turned to art and music as the vehicles which they used to give expression to this new *Weltanschauung.*

The writers to be discussed in this part of the chapter are not to be regarded as formally existentialist in their philosophy, but rather are they representative of it in various ways, in varying degrees, in their respective fields of cultural activity.

Andre Malraux used the novel as the primary vehicle for the expression of his philosophy, which bears the stamp of his activities in Cuba during the revolutionary upheavals which took place in that country during the 1920's. At a rather early age he repudiated the Roman Catholic Church and its theology, and adopted communism as his ideology, for the time being at least. In two of his earliest works, *Temptations of the Occident* (1926) and *The Conquerors* (1928), his attraction to communism is quite evident. In the first of these novels he repudiated the traditional values of the West in which he had been reared. In the latter novel he argued that a new conception of man and the meaning of human life could be achieved if Marxism were successful in Russia and China. But in his *Man's Fate* (1934), his mood shifted away from his earlier optimism, and he no longer believed that the success of the revolution in these nations would guarantee the emergence of a new man.[40] The basic theme of this novel is the death of the old order known as Western civilization and the emergence of a new one to replace it. Underlying this struggle is the specter of despair and futility. Here he painted a picture of men involved in the revolution in China who fight bravely for the goals they have in view, but they wage a futile conflict. Fighting bravely, they die in vain. In essence, the novel is a defense of the revolutionary spirit, while at the same time it presents a profound contradiction. It calls on men to change the conditions of life and control the blind forces that shape human destiny and give it meaning. Somehow man is to control the blind and irrational forces of Fate and put meaning into these forces, so that they may, in turn, confer meaning and dignity upon human life.

Malraux's entire philosophy is summed up in the words spoken by a leading character in *Man's Fate:*

> You know the phrase "It takes nine months to make a man, and a single day to kill him." We both know this as well as one can know it. . . . May, listen: it does not take nine months, it takes fifty years to make a man, fifty years of sacrifice, of will . . . of so many things. And when this man is complete, when there is nothing left of him of childhood, nor of adolescence, when he is really a man—he is good for nothing but to die.[41]

Malraux's thought was, man was, and is, engaged in a continuous struggle against nature. In his earlier novels he thus turned to his conception of the hero as a means of finding something real in life, but Malraux found that his heroes would fail him in the moment of crisis, and thus the deaths of men, as well as of heroes, are seldom important. Men and their heroes align themselves with lost causes. Their acts are basically meaningless because life itself has no meaning. The only slight strand of meaning there might be is to be found in the contemplation of the death of an individual human being. Malraux thus came to the conclusion in his *Art As Ideology* that human life is absurd and can achieve nothing more than moments of existential meaning at times of intense personal danger. Fate has man in its grip, and yet, in his last work, *The Psychology of Art* (1940), he attempted to refute Spengler's deterministic view of history by insisting that art is a repudiation of fate rather than a fulfillment of it, as Spengler held. As a revolutionary, Malraux was caught in a serious di-

---

40. Trans. from the French by Haakon Chevalier as *Man's Fate* (New York, 1934).

41. Ibid., pp. 359-360.

lemma. Assuming the essential irrationality of life and the absurdity of human existence, he struggled to find a rationale for engaging in revolution. But why should man engage in revolution to struggle against fate? For this question, Malraux had no answer. There is, and was, for him no power sufficiently strong to ward off the inevitable results of fate in human life.

Albert Camus (1913–1960).

Like Malraux, Camus reflects the strains of existential thought and the accompanying fatalistic outlook on life. Both men personify the decadence which has overtaken French thought to an alarming degree in the twentieth century.[42] The same basic themes appear in Camus which mark the writings of Malraux, but in somewhat different form and a minor difference in emphasis. However, the similarities far overshadow the differences, and both writers have placed themselves in the same general school of thought.

Much of Camus' novels are couched in a stream-of-consciousness style which makes it possible for him to have his characters give forth in a rambling and disconnected manner their basic attitudes toward the important issues of life. In so doing they speak for Camus himself in a way which leaves no doubt concerning his own attitudes. He not only represents the irrationalism and degeneracy of the contemporary French mind, but gives additional impetus to the degenerative influences in a powerful manner, since he was the darling of the New Left, not only in France but in this and other countries. In this sense he is perhaps a more important figure in modern thought than Malraux, not because of the superior quality of his writings so much as because of their wider appeal beyond the confines of professional philosophy and literature. As a novelist and playwright, he was able to gain an influence that many professional philosophers have had difficulty in achieving.

Basic to the thought of Camus is his rejection of Christianity. His rejection, however, was not generally couched in the vitriolic hatred voiced by a Marx or a Sartre. His position was expressed in a different terminology, but the total effect was the same and the results not vastly different. He expressed his religious sentiments in various ways, sometimes giving the appearance of harboring little more than an indifference to to all re-

42. The decline of French thought and its fall into the embrace of irrationalism is all the more startling since France was the intellectual capital of Europe during the Middle Ages, and its position of leadership continued to the modern period. The beginning of the visible decline was at the outbreak of the Revolution of 1789; the invisible had already set in with the appearance of Descartes.

ligions and their doctrines. At other times he came closer to a more determined opposition to them and to Christian doctrine in particular.

At other times, Camus dismissed religions in general as being unnecessary. In speaking of human guilt he wrote:

> Believe me, religions are on the wrong track the moment they moralize and fulminate commandments. God is not needed to create guilt or to punish. Our fellow men suffice, aided by ourselves. You were speaking of the Last Judgment. Allow me to laugh respectfully. I shall wait for it resolutely, for I have known what is worse, the judgment of men.[43]

Behind this attitude toward God lies the assumption of human autonomy and the collective conscience of mankind which, for Camus, was a much worse kind of judgment—the judgment of his peers.

Again, in *The Stranger,* Camus expressed his disdain for Christianity in a different, yet essentially similar, manner. In this novel Camus, speaking through Meursault, a man condemned for murder and awaiting execution, in answering the questions as to why he would not allow the chaplain to visit in his cell, replied that he did not believe in God and saw no point in troubling his head about the matter.[44]

Camus' writings abound in such passages, which are not isolated, but form the very nexus of his outlook on life. At times he was quite specific in regard to his attitude toward Christianity and its doctrines of God, evil, and judgment. Some of his commentators attempt to make a distinction between his attitude toward communism and Christianity, insisting that he was anti-communist but not anti-Christian, merely non-Christian. Such description is contrary to the statements of Christ Himself that he who is not for Him is against Him, and also ignores the attitude displayed by Camus himself. The fact that the writings of Camus contain frequent references to Christianity can hardly be used as an argument that he was simply non-Christian. His basic conception of human life (if, indeed, he had one) does not allow this assumption.

Granted that for Camus the problems of evil and death are of overwhelming importance to which the problem of God must take second place, for he insisted that man does not know himself by the same act by which he knows God, nor does he know God by the same act by which he knows himself. How, then, does Camus know that man exists? He answers this problem by stating that suffering and death are the primary evidence for

43. Albert Camus, *The Fall* (New York, 1964), p. 111.
44. Albert Camus, *The Stranger* (New York, 1973), p. 145.

human existence. Evil and death are, for him, the abiding condition of man. Only after man knows the reality of evil does the question of the existence of God have any importance to him.[45] But the fact that the question arises does not mean that he will give an affirmative answer to it.

The question must arise: How does man know that the abiding condition of his own existence is evil and that death is a part of the absurdity of human existence? Camus reverses the biblical order of apprehension at this point. The Scriptures insist that man must first know good before he can know evil, because the God in whose image he was created is the author of all good. Evil and death have an existence prior to the God whom man comes to know through them. It would seem that for all practical intents and purposes, Camus must be regarded as an atheist in the sense in which the Scriptures describe an atheist as the fool who says in his heart there is no God.

For Camus, Christianity can do little more than bring an acceptance of the reality of evil and death. This is true even though Camus admits that, at its best, Christianity can help to cultivate both beauty and goodness, but these two qualities are independent reals (if we may use that term as applicable to his thought) and not dependent on the sovereign God who has revealed Himself in His perfection of these and other qualities, which are comprehended in the Trinity.

In the light of his view of God, evil, and goodness, it is to be expected that he lacked a meaningful doctrine of creation and purpose in life. There is no recognition of the divine role assigned to man, intellectually, volitionally, and morally. There is nothing to be known and no way for man to really know it if it were knowable. Man leads a dreary existence in an absurd world, and his only escape is in death. There is no doctrine of a Redeemer or of a redemption and no hope for the future. It is a dreary picture which he paints of the human predicament. In him, as with the other existentialist thinkers, relativism has become the absolute, the only absolute which can be known, and it, at best, can offer only fleeting glimpses of an almost unreal reality.

Thus, there can be no absolute values to claim the loyalty of these thinkers. Even though Camus vigorously denounced communism and communist tactics, he did not, and could not, do so on the basis of his philosophical outlook, but was forced to borrow the terminology of Christian theism in his denunciation. This terminology, in itself, lacked vigor because he gave to it an existential meaning which robbed it of its strength.

Thus, we must conclude that Camus reflected the irrationalism of ex-

45. This is the basic theme of *The Rebel.*

istentialism in his main works, novels, dramatic productions, and short stories. All his writings bear the stigma of presenting a meaningless and purposeless view of human existence.

Existentialism thus became one of the two "big umbrellas" which have sheltered irrationalism in its various forms during much of the twentieth century. These two forms of irrationalism have combined in their efforts to virtually destroy the fabric of the Western intellectual tradition and bring it to the depths of the chaotic confusion in which it now finds itself.

Chapter 12
Existentialism and Theology

Existentialism has had its most disastrous impact on Christian thought. Along with naturalism, it has reduced much of theological activity to a degree of sterility virtually unknown in the West, even in the post-Thomistic era of the medieval Catholic Church. It has become a common meeting ground on which many evangelicals felt they could come to terms with the older liberalism. Many liberals, in turn, looked upon this philosophy as a means by which they could re-open communication with the world of evangelical scholarship and thus recover much of the earlier fervor which had characterized the early years of the Protestant movement and which had been largely lost by the liberalism of the eighteenth and nineteenth centuries. These liberals were furthermore convinced that they could recover much of the historic doctrine of Protestantism without surrendering what they felt were the beneficial results of nineteenth-century biblical criticism and scientific achievements. In much the same manner, many conservative scholars looked upon existentialism as a means by which they too could re-open communication with their liberal antagonists and thus find a common ground on which both could agree as they faced a common foe in the secularism and naturalism of the twentieth century. As erroneous as they must be, and however naive scholars in both camps now appear to have been, there can be little doubt that such convictions underlay much of their theological speculation in the earlier years of the century. The result was the appearance of a movement known as neo-orthodoxy. Like its parentage, this movement too proved to be a very broad theological umbrella under which many theologians took refuge, often without an understanding of the meaning of existentialist thought from which it was derived, and with perhaps even less comprehension of the ultimate impact of such an alliance on the very values they were seeking to preserve. For the evangelicals who sought such a place of refuge, it meant the ultimate surrender of the basic concept that the Scriptures are based upon and teach propositional truth. For the liberals it meant that the minimal biblical doctrines to which they still clung would be utterly dissolved in the unbelievable phenomenon of the "God-is-dead" movement. For both camps this reliance upon existentialism meant the ultimate dissolution of the theories, or philosophies, to which they had been clinging and the descent into an irrationalism closely akin to that into which philosophy, literature, the humanities, and the social sciences had fallen.

In neo-orthodoxy there was very little that was orthodox and even less that was new. As Cornelius Van Til has so aptly written, it was nothing more than the old modernism in a new form and should be called the New Modernism. The only real difference between it and the older liberalism was that it was a theological wolf appearing in the dress of scriptural phraseology, and was thus able to conceal its real meaning of anti-intellectualism. For this reason it constituted a peculiarly pernicious danger to the church, both Roman Catholic and Protestant.

Its Origins

Many commentators and students of existentialism profess to find its religious as well as its theological roots in the religious philosophy of Søren Kierkegaard. There can be no doubt that he was a powerful inspiration for the later budding of neo-orthodoxy. Van Til is much closer to the truth in his insistence that as a theology it has its origins in Kant and in his distinction between the noumenal and phenomenal worlds as constituting reality.

Although Kierkegaard was vigorous in his reaction against Hegelian philosophy, he was never able to free himself from Kantian metaphysics and its anti-supernaturalistic implications.

In fact, it is not too much to claim that all liberal theological activity during the nineteenth century was, to varying degrees, influenced by this Kantian dualism, and even those theologians who reacted against certain aspects of Kantian philosophy were never able to emerge from its shackles unharmed. Twentieth-century neo-orthodoxy falls neatly into this pervading pattern.

Not only must Kant be regarded as the "villain" in fomenting and developing irrationalism in modern philosophy, but he must also assume the same role in the theological movement of the nineteenth and twentieth centuries. The admission that Kierkegaard struggled to free himself and Christian thought from any entanglement with Kantian thought by no means implies that he was successful in his effort. The Kantian imprint was too firmly etched on the European mind to be so easily erased. Richard Kroner rightly insists that there is nothing essentially new in recent dialectical ontology and that it is actually the fruition of Kant's concept of the primacy of practical reason.[1] Kroner goes a step further and insists that there is in contemporary dialectical theology an even greater stress on the contrast between the noumenal and phenomenal worlds than can be found in Kant. Kroner maintains that the chasm between the divine and human minds is far deeper than Kant and Hegel realized. This great difference, or bridge, between the two came into theological prominence in the works of Kierkegaard, particularly in his *Philosophical Fragments* and *Concluding Unscientific Postscripts*. It is in these two works that the major features of contemporary existentialism received their first major expression. In his approach to the religious problems which he was personally facing, he set the stage for the appearance of the existentialist philosophy of our day and thus for neo-orthodoxy. Van Til states that Kierkegaard set this stage by the priority which he gave to his questions. He did not begin his religious quest by seeking what Christianity is, but rather by "How may I become a Christian?"[2] For Kierkegaard, Christianity was primarily a matter of personal religious involvement rather than a matter of objective truth. Van Til's analysis of Kierkegaard bears further study for use at this point.

Kierkegaard saw that it was so easy to be a Christian when Christianity is the commonly accepted pattern of life, but he insisted that one must become Christian inwardly, and that for an individual it is a matter of life and death. "It is so easy to become a Christian if the Christ I believe in fits into the pattern of general human knowledge. But the true Christ does not fit into any pattern of human knowledge; He transcends all human knowledge."[3] This very fact makes Him a scandal. Kierkegaard was correct in his insistence that men are not Christians simply because they assent to the articles of the creeds of the church, but that they must possess a personal experience and have a deep trust in the Christ set forth in those creeds.

Van Til further points out that Kierkegaard's championship of a personal identity with Christ does not end at this point. He vigorously objected to the whole idea of truth as an intellectual system and insisted that Christianity is not, and cannot be, an intellectual system. It is true that in his attack on philosophy and systematic theology Kierkegaard had Hegel and the entire Hegelian philosophical movement in mind, but once again he carried this philosophical concept too far and applied it to Christian theology, even though we grant the truth of his contention that Kierkegaard was correct in contending that God is far above man. That is the message of the Scriptures. But Kierkegaard then posed the question: How can hu-

1. Richard Kroner, *Culture and Faith* (Chicago, 1937), p. ix.
2. Van Til, *Christianity and Barthianism*, p. 288.
3. Ibid., p. 283.

man reason attain a knowledge of that which is absolutely other than itself (the wholly other God of Barth)?[4] The dialectical aspect of Kierkegaard appears at this point. He argued that in Christ the eternal became temporal, but such an event is also logically impossible. Yet he would have the Christian believe that which is logically impossible.

Van Til appreciates the fact that at this point Christians come into "doubtful territory." Kierkegaard's rejection of system did not stop with the non-Christian schemes of Kant and Hegel, for he extended it to the theological schemes of Calvin and Luther. He concluded that any directly revealed knowledge of God in history is an impossibility. He intended to defend the uniqueness of the event of the incarnation, and thus he refused to allow the birth of Christ to be reduced to the "instance of a law." It was his intention to establish this uniqueness of Christ and the Christian faith against the inroads of any kind of philosophical speculation, but in order to achieve his goal he concluded that he must deny the role of history as the medium of direct revelation. He felt that if the incarnation were to be regarded as identical with historical fact, then "the purveyors of the system would be in control of it."[5]

Kierkegaard held that man cannot have a true existential relationship with any fact of history and thus cannot base his hope for eternity on any fact of history, as such. In history there can be, at best, only an approximation of truth. He made this point very clear. "If all the angels in heaven were to put their heads together, they could still bring to pass only an approximation, because an approximation is the only certainty obtainable for historical knowledge—but also an inadequate basis for eternal happiness."[6]

What, then, was his solution to the problem he posed for Christians of the nineteenth and twentieth centuries? If history is such a frail vessel for the communication of redemptive truth, how, then, can men of our day find this Christ? Kierkegaard had his answer for these questions. "If the thing of being or becoming a Christian is to have its decisive qualitative reality, it is necessary above all to get rid of the whole delusion of after-history, so that he who in the year 1846 becomes a Christian, becomes that by being contemporaneous with the coming of Christianity into the world, in the same sense as those who were contemporaneous before the eighteen hundred years."[7]

---

4. Kierkegaard, *Philosophical Fragments,* p. 37.
5. Van Til, *Christianity and Barthianism,* p. 289.
6. Kierkegaard, *Concluding Unscientific Postscripts,* p. 31.
7. Kierkegaard, *On Authority and Revelation* (Princeton, N. J.: Princeton University Press), p. 58.

At this point Van Til points out a fatal weakness in his argument. To brush aside the centuries intervening between us and the first century does not in any way mean that we draw closer to Christ. Men of the first century were close to Him historically but far away in their hearts. Kierkegaard was not unaware of this difficulty and attempted to draw a distinction in an effort to solve the dilemma. He insisted that a distinction be drawn between the historical element in Christianity and history in the ordinary sense of the term.

> But though a contemporary learner readily becomes an historical eye-witness, the difficulty is that the knowledge of some historical circumstances, or indeed a knowledge of all the circumstances with the reliability of an eye-witness does not make such an eye-witness a disciple, which is apparent from the fact that this knowledge has merely great historical significance for him.[8]

There is a sense in which Kierkegaard is correct. It is true, as the Scriptures not only declare but insist, that many who heard and saw Christ in the flesh did not believe on Him. But a close examination of Kierkegaard at this point reveals that this is not what he had in mind. Rather was he insisting that no one has ever been directly confronted by Christ in history; that although revelation is historical in its nature, it is not true that history is revelational.

Barth and the other neo-orthodox writers find their roots not only in Kant but also in Kierkegaard, for Kierkegaard was carrying on the spirit of Kantian philosophy. Van Til, therefore, has argued with cogency that Kierkegaard's final reason for rejecting any philosophical or theological system arose from "his conviction that there is no God who can give a final revelation of Himself to man in history."[9] Thus Kierkegaard sought to attain a uniqueness for Christ in terms of the idea of pure contingency: "And this idea of pure contingency of necessity has for its correlative the formal ideal of pure rationality."[10]

Van Til further draws the conclusion that Kierkegaard, as well as Hegel, is speculative, and therefore both are irrational, and yet they are rationalists in that they allow for the laws of human logic in order to allow for the exclusion of the truth of historic Christianity. At this point the difference between Hegel and Kierkegaard is merely one of degree. True enough, Kierkegaard's philosophy is open to Christianity, but only to that kind of Christianity which features an indeterminate God and an unknowable

---

8. Kierkegaard, *Philosophical Fragments,* pp. 47-48.
9. Van Til, *Christianity and Barthianism,* p. 291.
10. Ibid.

Christ. Thus, the irrationalism appearing as the correlative of Kierkegaard's rationalism was taken over by Barth and his numerous followers, into the very essence of neo-orthodoxy.

The Existentialist Theology of Karl Barth (1886–1968)

The question must arise: Why did Karl Barth look to Søren Kierkegaard for the answers to the problems which he felt were confronting Protestant theology during his lifetime? Why was he captivated by Kierkegaard's idea of the absolute qualitative difference between God and man? The answers to these questions lie partly in Barth's own internal spiritual development and partly in his growing awareness of the perils which confronted Christianity in the sterile liberalism involved in the German high criticism of the latter part of the nineteenth and early twentieth centuries. He realized the dead end to which the whole thrust of nineteenth-century thought was leading the Protestant movement, not only in Germany but throughout the Western world.

On the other hand, Barth was deeply steeped in the nineteenth-century tradition of biblical higher criticism as it had been developed first by the immediate successors of Hegel and the Graf-Wellhausen school. This radical approach to the Scriptures had virtually destroyed the belief in the infallibility of the Scriptures as the Word of God in Protestant churches on the continent of Europe and in this country as well. But Barth was too much a child of this intellectual climate to free himself from this approach. Nevertheless, he realized that liberalism in conjunction with higher criticism had robbed the church of its vitality and message and that a remedy for this distressing condition must be found. In Kierkegaard's adaptation of Kant to Christian thought, Barth felt that he had found the answer to the dilemma. Kierkegaard's theology seemed to offer an escape from the dilemma which confronted Barth. In it he felt he had a solution: He could accept the findings of higher criticism as to the discrepancies and errors in the Scriptures on the one hand, and yet, at the same time, recover the evangelical teachings of the Reformers on the other. In short, Barthian theology may be looked upon as a desperate effort to accept the destructive force of modern biblical scholarship while rejecting its efforts to discredit the religious, or theological, treasures of a book which could no longer be regarded as infallible, as the whole counsel of God according to the Westminster Confession of Faith and the historic credal statements of the Christian church throughout the ages.

The basic theme of Barth's theology is "the freedom, sovereignty and actuality of God" in His revelation. But Barth does not mean by these terms what traditional theology has always meant. Neither should we be misled by the similarity of the terminology of neo-orthodox theologians with the traditional usage. Acting in accordance with the basic principle derived from Kierkegaard, Barth began his system by rejecting the idea of the verbal inspiration of the Scriptures and therefore of their infallibility and authority. He held that to believe in the verbal inspiration is actually to take away the revelational character of Scripture. The idea of verbal inspiration implies the correlative idea of direct control. Thus, to speak of direct revelation is to imply that man possesses and controls revelation and that man loses God. All of this is comprised in Barth's *Urgeschichte.* In this concept Barth felt that he had accomplished the contemporaneousness of the believers with Christ. For Barth there is no *historia revelationis* in the traditional sense of the word. He rejected the very possibility of a general revelation in history. In formulating this view of revelation it was his purpose to escape from the clutches of consciousness theology, and thus in his *Commentary on Romans* and in his *Christian Dogmatics* (1927) he sought for a transcendent God. In seeking for such a God who would be immune to the attack of Feuerbach, he suggested that the Christian church should frankly admit that all theology, as human speech, is nothing but anthropology, that it is a matter of knowledge, and that the field of knowledge is the field of historical relativism and psychological subjectivism: "He who dares to speak of God, must in the last analysis, dare to do so with God alone. . . ."[11]

> Every way to the knowledge or conceivability of God is in any case so dark, known to so few, that he who speaks of God thereby maintains a position which, regarded from the point of view of the world, is nothing more than a fantastic if beautiful dream.[12]

This led Barth to call upon Christians to calmly accept the idea that the words of the Bible are tinctured with a human fallibility. At the same time, he also insisted that God's revelation does not take place behind, but in the words of Scripture. However, this identification of revelation with the Scriptures can never be direct and must always be indirect. No document of history can ever be anything more than a witness to primal history.

Thus, for Barth, the true approach to theology must be existential. But this approach is not possible on any idea of direct revelation. Man must meet God not through any direct revelation, but by becoming contempo-

11. Van Til, *Christianity and Barthianism,* p. 308.
12. Karl Barth, *Die Lehre vom Worte Gottes,* vol. I of *Die Christliche Dogmatik im Entwurf* (München, 1927), cited in Cornelius Van Til, *Christianity and Barthianism* (Philadelphia: Presbyterian and Reformed Publishing Co., 1962), p. 308.

raneous with God in *Urgeschichte*. According to this principle, the incarnation and the resurrection of Jesus Christ are not history in the ordinary sense of the term. Revelation *Urgeschichte* and ordinary history simply point to *Urgeschichte,* and primal history is the meaning of ordinary history.[13]

He maintained that the realm of *Urgeschichte* is free from ordinary historical continuity, for its unity is found in his concept of contemporaneity. At this point Barth's dialecticism comes to the forefront. How, then, does man know God? He answers this important question in terms of his concept of *Urgeschichte*. God, the whole God, becomes man, and man—in response to this—becomes a new subject. Because revelation on God's part is "no revelation" to ordinary history, so man as the "old subject" cannot receive true revelation.[14] Barth therefore felt that man must know himself as non-existing before he can hear the Word of God. However, to know himself as non-existent, he must already exist as the new man. He argued that as God had to become wholly man to reveal Himself to man, so to receive this revelation man must participate in the divine Subject. Thus, in this act of revelation and in the act of faith as a response to God, the dialectical, or existential, relation between God and man takes place.[15]

Some students and defenders of Barth's version of neo-orthodoxy have argued that in his later works, namely, in his *Kirchliche Dogmatik,* he rather dramatically shifted from this existentialism to a more biblical view. This assumption is difficult to sustain in view of the fact that in this monumental theological work his entire outlook centers around the Christ-Event, and in this Christ-Event God is at once wholly revealed and wholly hidden. It can be safely maintained that Barth never forsook his basic principle that revelation is historical but history is never revelational. In his discussion of biblical events such as the resurrection, Barth insisted that when the apostles witnessed the resurrection of Christ they were giving witness to an incontrovertible fact, an event in time and space. This sounds quite orthodox. But Barth never identified such events as the incarnation or the resurrection with ordinary history, which he called *historie*. For Barth it was *geschichte,* by which he meant that this is an event to which we cannot ascribe a historical character. Van Til even insists that in his later works Barth laid a greater stress on the hidden nature of revelation than he did in his earlier works, and makes the point that only by such an increased emphasis could he escape the charges of Feuerbach.[16]

13. Ibid., p. 223.
14. Ibid., p. 287.
15. Van Til, *Christianity and Barthianism,* p. 310.
16. Barth, op. cit., p. 312.

It must therefore be concluded that in his efforts to rescue theology from the clutches of its nineteenth-century foe, Barth simply accelerated its descent into the embrace of irrationalism. The correlative of his rationalism was the inescapable irrationalism inherent in his use of existentialism as the means of escape. Of special importance is the observation of Van Til at this point:

> Our general conclusion then must be that in all stages of the development of his thinking, Barth has followed without basic alteration the type of dialecticism that we found in Existentialism and, back of it, in Kant. . . . And his attempt to go beyond modern existentialist dialecticism by means of his Christ-Event cannot be accounted as successful either. With Berkouwer, we would hold that he who sets his feet on the way of subjectivism cannot suddenly stop himself from sliding into illusionism.[17]

Even as modern existentialism has denied the possibility of propositional truth in all of man's intellectual endeavors, so Barth has denied its possibility in God's revelation of Himself to man. He thus erected his entire theological system on this basic presupposition. The God we find in Barth's theology is the projection of the would-be-autonomous man. He rejected all positive revelation. "In his theology the whole of positive revelation has been absorbed by the actualistic unapproachable reality of God."[18] For this reason every theological truth long held by the Christian church has been thrown into the maelstrom of uncertainty. No doctrine has escaped the devastating impact of Barth's view of revelation and its relationship to the Christ-Event. The almost lethal form of irrationalism has been let loose within the church.

In Barthian thought there is no room for the biblical doctrine of the creation and no place for man in the scheme of creation. Man becomes "Man" only when he enters into the meaning of the "Christ-Event." There is no place in the Barthian or neo-orthodox scheme for the biblical existence of creation as an act of God in time and for the creation of man as the crowning completion of the divine plan for this world. There was no actual Adam and no real purpose for creation or for the role of Adam within it. For Barth, there are no men except as they are men by participation in Christ. But we must remember that in his theology the "Christ-Event" stands for the idea of Reality as a whole.

Because of his existentialist view of anthropology, Barth did not allow

---

17. Van Til, *Christianity and Barthianism,* p. 315.
18. G. C. Berkouwer, *Karl Barth* (Kampen: J. H. Kok, 1936), quoted by Van Til, *Christianity and Barthianism,* p. 430.

for the fall of Adam as a fact in history. It is a primordial supra-historical fact which did not, and could not, take place within human history as a propositional fact. Thus if there is no actual fall, sin is not truly real, and sinners are not truly sinners in the biblical sense of the word. Accordingly, as we have seen, the incarnation, including the virgin birth of Jesus Christ, His resurrection and ascension, are also supra-historical in character. Redemption comes to man when he achieves his contemporaneity with Christ through the "Christ-Event."

Because of his existentialist concept of the nature and the historicity of the scriptural narrtion of the events used to describe God's dealings with His creation and with His plan of redemption as it has been carried out through the ages, Barth's whole theology suffers from the incurable disease of irrationalism. Furthermore, his treatment of the great topics of theology such as the doctrine of the covenant, election, effectual calling, justification, conversion, and sanctification is seriously misleading. In brief, his theology is by no means a return to that of Calvin and the other Reformers in opposition to modern liberalism, and in spite of the fact that he shared with Rome certain assumptions, his entire outlook is quite different from that of Roman Catholic theology as it was voiced by St. Thomas Aquinas and the Council of Trent. It has in actuality been a kind of Pandora's box, from which have sprung the even more radical theologies of Rudolf Bultmann, Paul Tillich, and their successors. It had its final outburst in the "death-of-God" theology, which enjoyed a phenomenal but brief popularity in the 1960s.

Van Til has summarized with great insight Barth's position, and we can do no better than pay close attention to his analysis of the Barthian theology in its relationship to the Christian theology and, therefore, to the declining health of Western thought.

> It is the Christian view of things as a whole that must be placed over against the Barthian view as a whole. Only then will men be saved from the tyranny of words. Men will then use such words as causation, reason, faith and give them their true biblical meanings. The simple believer knows that the Heavenly Father controls his birth, the circumstances of his life, even to the last microbe that might affect him. He belongs with his body as well as with his soul to the Savior. Barth in effect demythologizes all of this.[19]

Van Til then concluded with the observation that the humble believer

19. Van Til, "The Triumph of Grace," lecture series at Westminster Theological Seminary (Philadelphia, 1962), p. 152.

can no more remain in a church where the Barthian theology is taught than he can remain in a church where the theology of either Schleiermacher or Ritschl holds sway. He gives the reasons for this strong stand. In the first place, Van Til rightly insists that "Barth's theology is no more based on Scripture as the "Word of God" than is the theology of these other nineteenth-century theologians:

> All three are basically speculative. Granted that the Bible has a greater influence on Barth than on them, it remains true that Barth is no nearer to the thinking of the Bible as the Word of God than are these three men. When Barth says that the Bible *is* the Word of God, he says something that is more orthodox in words than what these men say, but it is not more orthodox in content.[20]

In the second place, Van Til insisted that Barth's Christ is no more the Christ of Scripture than is the Christ of these other scholars.

> Schleiermacher and Ritschl also wanted to interpret all things Christologically. And Ritschl was anxious to escape the speculation and mysticism which he found in Schleiermacher. Barth is far more Christological than either. But his Christ is no more the Christ of Scripture and of the historic Christian confessions than is the Christ of these men. The real transaction between God and man, according to Barth, takes place in *Geschichte* rather than in history. To be sure, history is involved. But there is never in history any direct and clear revelation and therefore any act of salvation by God for man.[21]

Van Til interprets this second reason in a very clear manner. He points out that to follow Barth means that we must re-interpret the Apostles' Creed (and all other historic creeds as well), according to Barth's dialecticism. We must then interpret all the great historical affirmations of this creed in such a way that they are not history as such, but only supra-history. God's creation of the world can be only saga or myth and not an actual fact of history. We can never again say with Chalcedon that Christ is truly God and truly man. Now, with Barth, we must say that in the "second mode of his being God turns into the wholly opposite of Himself," and that when we affirm our belief in Christ as the Son of God, we are giving voice to the idea that we are giving expression to the idea that what the Son expresses is only the principle of world-immanence and "the secondary absoluteness of God."[22] In turn, we must surrender the great affirmation of Chalcedon and realize that it cannot furnish any solid foundation for the atonement.

Likewise, when we affirm that Christ was born of a virgin, we must re-

20. Ibid. 21. Ibid. 22. Ibid., p. 153.

member that this was not really the case, since revelation is never a predicate of history. Thus, we can never regard the virgin birth as a biological event in history. What, then, is the virgin birth? It is only a sign of the hiddenness of God, according to Barth. In the same manner, Barth banished Christ's miracles on earth as being in any sense a direct revelation of the will of God.

But this is not the end of the story. When we affirm our belief that "He suffered under Pontius Pilate; was crucified, dead and buried; He descended into Hell,"[23] we only say that even here what actually took place at Calvary and in the atoning death of Christ took place as *Geschichte* and only secondarily as history.

But the destructive force of the Barthian position does not end here. Barth did not place the resurrection in history, and he insisted that the real presence of God in Christ was in *Geschichte* and not in human history, for history is only the border of *Geschichte*.

In the same fashion Barth dismissed the ascension and the final judgment as events taking place only in *Geschichte*. Thus, neither the resurrection nor the second coming of Christ is to be regarded as an event which will bring history to a close because neither takes place there, but in *Geschichte* alone.

Van Til's final statement in his evaluation of the Barthian theology is a well-founded indictment: To follow the Christ of Barth is to deny the Christ of the Scriptures.[24] But in denying the Christ of the Scriptures we deny all that to which the Christian faith commits us and cast ourselves adrift upon the stormy seas of theological, moral, intellectual, and political uncertainty, without a compass for the mind or an anchor for the soul.

We must, therefore, conclude that Barth's valiant efforts to free theology from the shackles of German higher criticism and romanticism, and the ensuing religious liberalism, brought disaster to the Christian church in both Europe and America and gave added impetus to the decline of Western thought. Neo-orthodoxy as the result of the invasion of philosophical liberalism into the thinking of the church in turn inspired a further decline in its theology; and it also inspired an even greater disintegration of the fabric of the philosophy and the social, political, and economic thought of the West. The popularity of neo-orthodoxy popularized the irrationalism on which it was founded and weakened the theological strength of the church, both Protestant and Roman Catholic.

Because of its very nature and also as a result of its deceptive charm

23. Ibid., p. 156.

24. Ibid.

for many evangelicals, its true nature was not easily perceived by those uninitiated into the meaning of the dialectical system on which it was founded. The use of evangelical language to convey non-evangelical truth made it a dangerous weapon in the hands of those who sought to use it as a means of denying the historic faith. At the same time, it contained many implications which invited the emergence of a flood of theological and philosophical derivatives which led both Christian theology and Western thought further down the road of irrationalism and unbelief. Barth's insistence on the unhistorical character of the factual contents of the Scriptures invited further distortion of the biblical message in the hands of such thinkers as Rudolf Bultmann, Paul Tillich, Reinhold Niebuhr, and many others within Protestantism and in the thinking of Hans Kung in the Roman Catholic Church.[25]

Heinrich Emil Brunner (1889–1966)

The full burden of blame should not be placed on the shoulders of Karl Barth alone. Nearly as influential in the popularization of neo-orthodoxy were the voice and the writings of Emil Brunner. Even though important differences emerged between Brunner and Barth as they developed their common heritage, their similarities outweighed any points of divergence between their respective positions. As a result, Brunner became an important instrument in helping to popularize neo-orthodoxy within the church in this country.

Some scholars would argue that Brunner's development was quite independent of Barth's, and to an extent this is certainly true, in that they parted company over the question of natural theology in the 1930s. Barth sharply rejected this aspect of theology, while Brunner warmly championed it. Like Barth, he was intensely critical of Schleiermacher, and in 1924 he published his *Die Mystik und Das Wort.*

Brunner's theological development was deeply influenced by Kierkegaard's philosophy, and this influence, which he shared in common with Barth, is very evident in his *The Mediator,* which appeared in 1927.[26]

For Brunner, revelation was regarded as taking place within a personal encounter between a God who communicates Himself and man. He came to this because of his insistence that God Himself is a personal subject who can be reduced to an object. Thus for Brunner, as for Barth, revelation

25. There is no satisfactory order in which these neo-orthodox scholars can be treated, and so the author has followed a chronological approach.

26. Brunner also combined with Kierkegaard the I-Thou relationship which is so much a part of Martin Buber's existentialism.

is always indirect, and it can never be direct.

Brunner's doctrine of Scripture, like his view of natural theology, was somewhat indefinite. For him, the Scriptures are a norm for belief, but not an infallible norm and, therefore, not above criticism. He rejected the traditional orthodox view that the Scriptures are infallible and therefore authoritative. He even went so far as to admit that revelation can be mythical in form, but this admission was not a concession to unbelief. Brunner regarded the presence of myth[27] in the Scriptures as a necessity because of the great gulf which exists between God as the Creator and man as His creature. He maintained that because of this yawning gulf there could not be any direct revelation between the two. Like Barth, Brunner was using this philosophical position as the means by which he would accommodate his version of the Christian gospel to the findings of higher criticism. Some have regarded this as a noble effort, while others have viewed it with horror and disgust as a dishonest approach to the problem.

However, there can be no doubt that Brunner's dependence upon Kierkegaard, Buber, and myth removes his theology from the orthodox position and places him within the ranks of those who substituted an irrational philosophical theology for the historic faith. Brunner's surrender to irrationalism appears at exactly the same point which characterizes nearly all of modern thought, namely, in his approach to the knowledge of God and therefore of man's knowledge of himself. Whatever deviations he may have entered upon from the position of Barth, Kierkegaard, and other existentialist thinkers, his basic assumptions were from the same root. Therefore, branches of his system bore a marked similarity in their basic essentials to that of his colleagues.

Yet there is in Brunner's approach to the gospel a sincerity which can easily captivate his readers. In his Preface to *The Mediator,* he makes this very evident. He maintained that it is the duty of the church to make the name of Christ known: "Without this name, inevitably the world will rot, and no social reform, no Church activity, however well intentioned, can arrest the process of disintegration."[28]

But almost at once Brunner beclouded the issue by insisting that he was only trying to restate old truths and that he would add nothing to the gospel.

> I would have no right to venture upon this task, were it not a restate-

---

27. Although it must be admitted that he did not use "myth" in the Greek or popular meaning of the term, there is no doubt that his use precluded any adherence to a belief of propositional truth in the Scriptures.

28. Emil Brunner, *The Mediator* (New York, 1934), p. 14.

ment of old and well-known truth. I have nothing new to say; on the contrary, my main concern is to make clear that what is said here has been the faith of the Christian Church from the very earliest days.[29]

It was his task to make clear to the church its heritage and the function of this heritage during the first half of the present century.

The present work is predominantly intellectual; it is not intended to produce faith, but to make faith conscious; and to help it steer clear of error.[30]

It is at this very point, however, that Brunner enters into murky and troubled waters. After admitting that it is his hope that the book will be superfluous because the church would proclaim the name of Christ with such a mighty fervor that the whole world would be convinced of the truth of the gospel, this hope becomes fuzzy in the ensuing declaration.

This clear reverberating sound, as of a trumpet call, does not echo through this book, for this should not be expected in a work of this character. For it is not itself a proclamation of the truth; it simply deals intellectually with the contents of the true message.[31]

Here we see the appearance of the dialectical nature of Brunner's approach to scriptural truth and the resulting epistemological problems which will confront him throughout the rest of his theological pilgrimage. If the clear sound of the call of the trumpet is not to be resounded through this work, and if it is not the proclamation of the truth of the gospel, how can this book possibly stir the church to proclaim the name of Christ with an overpowering conviction? But this is not the end of the mystery. What did he mean when he limited the scope of this book so that it would deal only "intellectually with the content of the truth"? How can it deal intellectually with the content of the true message and yet not be a proclamation of the truth thus dealt with? For those who are not initiated into the subtle meaning of dialectical theology, there appears to be no satisfactory answer to this epistemological and theological riddle. In the succeeding chapters Brunner unfolds the neo-orthodox answer to this perplexing question and in doing so reveals the existential, and therefore the irrational, character of his theological position. The dialectical approach to the knowledge of God through revelation is clearly stated by Brunner in his treatment of general and special revelation.

In the Christian religion "salvation" is always indissolubly connected with an historical fact: with the fact of the Incarnation of the Divine Word, with the fact of the Atonement of Jesus Christ. Although the

29. Ibid. 30. Ibid. 31. Ibid., p. 15.

> time and space element, that is, the element of historical contingency, does not in itself constitute a revelation, yet the revelation upon which the Christian faith is based is founded upon this fact alone and apart from it Christianity could not exist.[32]

At first glance this sounds exactly like the historic testimony of the Christian church throughout the ages: that Christianity is a historical religion and that the incarnation and atonement are facts of history. True enough, it does have the ring of orthodoxy, and Brunner will even insist upon a distinction between general and special revelation, a distinction so dear to the hearts of Reformed theologians. But is this a valid distinction, and did he mean what Reformed and other theologians have meant by this distinction? When we look at his passage as a whole, we see that he had something else very clearly in mind, and the difference appears in his view of time and space as the element of historical contingency and his denial that they constitute a revelation. The contingent character immediately reveals the nakedness of his doctrine of natural revelation. Events in time and space in their contingent character can be the vehicle of natural revelation, even though they do not constitute a revelation. At the same time, the revelation on which this Christian fact is based is founded upon the fact of the time and space element as historical contingency. Apart from it, according to Brunner, Christianity could not exist.

Thus natural revelation for Brunner could be founded only upon facts which are contingent in nature, and accordingly the incarnation and the atonement are factual but also contingent. Thus, Brunner's insistence upon general revelation, at first glance, may seem startlingly different from Barth's original violent reaction to Brunner's position as he uttered it in 1929, but the two theologians were not as far apart as it might have seemed. Later, in his *Church Dogmatics,* Barth drew much closer to Brunner's position.

Brunner, in asserting that facts of history are in the realm of the contingent, and in placing the incarnation and the atonement in this area, went beyond the subjects generally reserved for general revelation and placed two very essential facts of redemptive history in the realm of the contingent. Is this not a contradiction, a dilemma beyond solution? In terms of the historic position of the church, this question must be answered in the affirmative. But Brunner was not to be caught in such a trap and supplied an answer through his resort to the dialectical method inherited from Kierkegaard, and his work, *The Divine Mediator,* is dedicated to this task.

---

32. Ibid.

Brunner insisted that the dilemma would not have arisen if the church had not committed a serious error and equated the Scriptures with revelation. He lamented the fact that the Christian faith in the sense that it is faith in a Mediator has almost disappeared from the consciousness of twentieth-century Christianity as he knew it. Why was this the case? According to Brunner, the church itself must bear the guilt for this unhappy situation.

> The Christian Church must bear some of the blame for this situation, not only on account of the weakening of its idea of revelation in the Catholic system . . . but scarcely through its false interpretation in the orthodox emphasis on the Bible among Protestant Christians. Orthodoxy has placed the Bible itself, as a book, in the place which should have been reserved for the fact of revelation. It confused the fact of revelation with the witness of the fact.[33]

Brunner throughout his writings is quite insistent on this distinction between revelation as such as being found in an act, an act of God, and the Scriptures as being a witness to that fact, the act of God. He becomes somewhat passionate in his denunciation of the orthodox view of the Scriptures as the revelation of God to man and accuses the church of distorting the biblical message.

> All the passionate interest which belonged to the unique event, to the Mediator and his act, was thus diverted from its true object and directed toward the Scriptural testimony to it. Hence the destruction of the dogma of Verbal Inspiration, with its emphasis upon an Infallible Book, by the modern process of research in natural and historical science inevitably carried away with it the whole Christian faith in revelation, the faith in the Mediator.[34]

Brunner was thus accepting the findings of scientists in the areas of biology, physics, and geology, and the results of nineteenth- and twentieth-century higher criticism as legitimate weapons for the destruction of the historic belief of the church in the divine inspiration of the Scriptures. In fact, he was willing to go even further and make the claim that such a belief was, in itself, the cause for the growing lack of belief in Christ as the Mediator, the fact and act of revelation.

An important question naturally occurs at this juncture. Since Brunner is willing to grant the Scriptures are a witness, even the most important witness to Christ, we may well ask him this question: If the Scriptures are in error at important points, how can the church be sure their witness to Christ as the Mediator is itself worthy of our acceptance? Cannot the

33. Ibid., p. 34.

34. Ibid.

Scriptures as witness to revelation in itself also be in error at this point? At no place in his writings did Brunner ever give a satisfactory answer to this transcendentally important question. Rather did he build his entire case in *The Mediator,* and other works, upon the very issue in question.

Brunner insisted that in Christianity faith in the Mediator is not something optional, not something, in the last resort, on which it is possible to hold different opinions, if we are only united on the main points. Brunner was adamant about this.

> For faith in the Mediator—in the event which took place once and for all, a revealed atonement—is the Christian religion itself; it is the "main point"; it is not something along side of the center, but it is the substance and kernel, not the husk; this is so true that we may even say: in distinction from all other forms of religion the Christian religion is faith in the Mediator. There is no other form of belief which is, in this sense, faith in the Mediator because no other form of faith knows and takes seriously the category of uniqueness (once-for-allness).[35]

There is no doubt that Brunner believed in Christ as the Mediator, and he further asserted that those who refuse to believe in Christ as the Mediator cannot be regarded as Christians even though they may be very pious folk, and he would be willing to speak all the good he could of them.

It must be admitted that on the surface this sounds like evangelical language which places Brunner within the realm of historic orthodoxy. But we must keep in mind the preceding quotations in which he very clearly stated his view of the Scriptures, and the questions raised then must be raised again at this point. Is this Mediator truly knowable, is He truly unique if the fallible Scriptures are the best and probably the most accurate for our knowledge of Him? If the best witness is necessarily unreliable, and, according to Brunner, has been the cause of unbelief, how then can he insist that a fallible Scripture can gain strength in arousing belief in Jesus Christ as the Mediator? The necessary conclusion to his logic, that a fallible Scripture can present a stronger argument for belief in Christ as Mediator than an infallible testimony of the authoritative Scriptures of orthodox Christianity, is totally untenable.

Beneath the seemingly placid and even orthodox seas on which Brunner's version of neo-orthodoxy sails there lurks the dangerous rock of this irrationalism which threatens his system at every point, and which will ultimately sink the entire venture beneath the waves of this attempt to redress evangelical thought in a linguistic form which denies its essence.

35. Ibid., p. 40.

The rocks become very apparent in his treatment of the Christian faith and its relationship to historical research where Brunner as the skillful pilot attempts to steer his ship on a perilous voyage toward the achievement of his goal. It was his purpose to so chart his course that he would not surrender the achievements of higher criticism on the one hand, or faith in Christ as the Mediator on the other.

He set his course on the assumption that it is of the very essence of the Christian faith that its relation to history should be entirely different from that of any other religion or philosophy. In fact, in the ordinary sense of the word, it is not concerned with history at all. Dialectically speaking, however, Brunner also insisted that "it is what it is through its relation to that unique event, which, although it is fact of history, does not gain its unique character from its historical connection."[36]

Brunner, however, could not easily free himself from this historical connection, for he also held that it is this historical connection which determines the peculiar relationship of the Christian faith to history in general. His dialectical theology rushed to his aid at this juncture.

> To the Christian faith revelation does not mean a reverent process of tracing the ways of God in history. Indeed, history as such is not a divine revelation; it merely represents humanity as a whole in its need of redemption. But precisely because something super-historical, unique, absolutely decisive has entered into human history, to faith history means something entirely different from its meaning for all other forms of thought.[37]

For him, then, Christianity is not rooted and grounded in history, even though it is concerned with an external historical fact. But "it is not the external fact itself with which it is concerned so deeply but with the fact of the reality of that upon which it depends . . . all depends upon the fact that the Word did become flesh."[38]

However, this leads back to the main contention voiced in the previous question. If, according to Brunner, the Christian faith does not involve "a reverent process of tracing the ways of God in history," how, then, can we be sure that this breakthrough of God into history in the person and fact of the Mediator is historically true? If Christianity is not a historical religion, why, then, should this one historical fact assume such an importance for Brunner or for any other believer? In short, how can this one fact make a believer out of an unbeliever? If the other great facts of history around which the Apostles' Creed and other great creeds of the church revolve are not necessarily accurate, but are subject to error,

36. Ibid., p. 153. 37. Ibid. 38. Ibid.

how, then, does this one fact take on that significance which Brunner attributes to it? He found his answer to the problem in the I-Thou concept which he borrowed from Martin Buber, the Jewish existentialist.

Thus the validity of a belief in Christ as Mediator is established in this personal existential encounter between God and man. But since this encounter by definition is extremely personal, how can it be communicated to others? Brunner objected to the orthodox view of revelation and revealed truth because God as a personal subject cannot, and must not, be reduced to an object. If this be the case, does it not necessarily follow that there can be no meaningful communication of normative biblical truth to other people by the one who has had such an encounter?

Although different from Barth's position in some respects, we must conclude that these differences are ultimately minimal in their total effect and that, therefore, Brunner's solution to the theological issue of man's knowledge of God is faulty and even dangerous to historical Christianity, as was that of Barth. The danger inherent in the theology of both the theologians is not limited in any way to the problem involved in man's knowledge of truth, but immediately involves the range of their respective theologies. The fact, or the supposition that Brunner was less extreme than Barth is true in some respects, but the difference between them was not, and is not, sufficiently great to redeem them from the charge that they, along with their neo-orthodox colleagues, have undermined the validity of the Scriptures as a whole and rendered attempts to communicate the gospel in any objective manner sheer futility. They become a part of *Urgeschichte,* or "holy history." Brunner, like Barth, cast aside the historicity of the Genesis account of creation, the creation of Adam and Eve, and all the other great doctrines of the Bible, assigning to them a rather hazy place in which they become unhistorical vehicles for the communication of divine truth; thus they become suprahistorical in character even though, in some way, they took place in the arena of history as such.

In the light of what has been discussed so far, several great issues emerge which are of tremendous importance to the history of Western thought. One of these is embodied in this question: "How does man know himself?" If man can know God only through the Mediator in an existential encounter of the I-Thou variety, how can he encounter himself? If we follow the prescription of Augustine and Calvin—that man can know God only by the means by which he knows himself, and that he can know himself only as he knows God—then how can he know himself according to either Barth or Brunner? Is such knowledge possible and, if possible, to what extent is it reliable? For the problem of Western thought and its apparent dissolution in the twentieth century, these are questions of overwhelming importance. Has neo-orthodoxy helped to stem the tide of a rising irrationalism and despair, or has it aided the growth of these characteristics of much of Western intellectual activity in the last 75 years?

Brunner dealt with these issues in his *The Mediator* and fashioned an epistemology based on his concept of Christ as the Mediator through whom man knows God. At every point in *The Mediator* we are confronted with the I-Thou relationship as the key which unlocks the answers to the problems. As a Mediator, Christ reveals God to man, and as Mediator He is also the one who reconciles God to man, and the whole plan of redemption rests on this concept. Outside of Christ man does not really know himself, even though he is a sinner. Only in Christ can we know ourselves as we really are. This, at first glance, sounds as if it were strict orthodoxy come to birth in the midst of a neo-orthodox frame of reference. But such is not the case. If we know God only through an existential encounter, or series of such encounters, none of which can be verified by an appeal to an objective revelation of God in the Scriptures, how can we be sure that we really know God, and thus how can we be sure that we really know ourselves; how can we be sure of the world in which we live, or of our roles in that world? If all our knowledge is subject to contingency, how can we be sure of the answers to any of these great questions? The answer is that there cannot be any certainty for man in dialectical theology any more than there can be in existentialist philosophy. Uncertainty is the order of the day in the life of the church when it adopts such a philosophy or theology.

Furthermore, by his own admission, the Christian can have no vital or real concern for history as a whole because history has no concern for him. In reverse, the professional historian and student of history cannot know the real meaning of the incarnation. There is a sense, of course, in which this statement is true. The unregenerate, unbelieving historian cannot think God's thoughts after Him in relation to the meaning of history. He cannot see events as they relate to the sovereign will of God in the history of mankind and the meaning and purpose which God assigns to these events. To the extent to which Brunner has this in mind, he is in accord with the biblical view of history. But it is very doubtful that he had this in mind or could have intended this. For Brunner, history lies in the realm of contingency and is thus subject to chance for its unfolding and development. This concept vitally affects the concept of the purpose of historical studies.

> The aim of history, of historical science, is primarily to fill in the spatio-temporal continuum of the imagination with representations which

> correspond to reality, and, secondly, to relate this spatio-temporal continuum to the "analogous continuum," that is, to that which we call the sum-total of all the possibilities of nature and of history. Its aim, therefore, is to create, as far as possible, a complete "film picture of the past," and to interpret the pictures of reality which have thus been completely recaptured in the light of previous happenings, and of that which is intelligible to humanity as a whole.[39]

Brunner then admits that the first task is impracticable and the second is impossible, "because of the great variety of aspects of all events within time and space. The result then can be only an approximation of the meaning of these events, which in turn yields only a relative certainty—the certainty of probability."

Once again we must admit that to an extent Brunner is correct. It is certainly true that the most able Christian historians can never learn all there is to know about an event in history, and therefore their interpretation bears the mark of the incompleteness of their data. All historians, Christian and non-Christian, share this problem. But Brunner's assumption that part of the problem lies with what he calls "relative certainty" or the "certainty of probability" does not confront the Christian historian because he does not have to deal with contingency. He does not look upon any fact (no matter how incomplete his knowledge of it may be) as the product of chance.

Brunner admits that the fact of sin has made it impossible for the human eye to comprehend reality as a whole and therefore can achieve only a certain superficial aspect of reality: "Its depths, the secrets of God are inaccessible to us as human beings; they can only be revealed to us through revelation."[40]

Brunner was willing to go so far as to say that history comes alive only to those who have been illuminated by the Holy Spirit. Once again he appears to be on the very doorstep of accepting Christian theism. But we soon realize that this is not the case. He abruptly introduces into his discussion a new category of historical interpretation which he insists is necessary for the interpretation of the history of revelation.

> For the meaning of that history in which Christ manifested Himself is only revealed to faith. . . . What history can be interpreted by the Christian—only that history in which Christ manifested Himself to faith.[41]

At this point Brunner sharply limited the whole area of history which can

39. Ibid., pp. 160-161. 40. Ibid., p. 161. 41. Ibid., p. 162.

be interpreted by the Christian. It is not the historical process as a whole, since Brunner previously insisted that history is not revelational, and if it is not revelational, it cannot be interpreted by the eye of faith.

In essence, Brunner plunged the study of history squarely into the arena of contingency and the necessary consequence, of uncertainty. In the first place, he sharply limited that part of history which the Christian may interpret, as that interpretation is given to him by faith, to the events which deal with holy history, the events which deal with the incarnation of Jesus Christ. The meaning of other events is not given by revelation. Thus, other great movements and forces within the historical process cannot be understood. This is only one aspect of the problem. Since the revealed meaning of the incarnation is highly existential in character and not found exclusively in the Scriptures, since they are not infallible, every Christian who has this existential and highly personal encounter with Christ the Mediator will most likely have a very personal interpretation revealed to him concerning the meaning of the incarnation itself and of Christ the Mediator.

Thus, in Brunner's dialectical scheme, there is no room for propositional, objective truth in the study of history. Consequently, man is cast adrift upon the sea of chance and uncertainty as he seeks in vain to find the meaning of the collective history of the human race. Since history in its wide embrace contains all of the human past, not only political and constitutional events, but economic, social, cultural, and educational as well, man's cultural development becomes completely unintelligible. Hence, Brunner committed the church to the twins of his existentialist assumption—anti-intellectualism and irrationalism. If Professor Paul Jewett is correct in his writing that Brunner would probably say that his own contribution was the restoration of "theology to its proper task, namely to reflect upon the revelation of God in Christ in such a way as to challenge and renew the age in which we live with a genuine Christian approach to life," we must conclude that, as noble as this ideal was, Brunner was a failure. His basic assumptions contained the seeds of his own undoing, for he did not build his system on the belief in the Scriptures as the infallible Word of God and sought to implement their message with the findings of modern critical biblical scholarship on the one hand, and of modern scientific endeavor on the other.

Rudolf Bultmann (1884–1976)

Rudolf Bultmann, as a New Testament scholar and existentialist theologian, through his process of demythologization carried the Barthian epistemology and apologetics to an extreme which even caused Barth to shudder.[42] Although during his early years as a professor of New Testament at Marburg he pioneered in the advancement of the form-criticism of the Gospels, he later turned his attention to the broader question of the nature of the gospel material. He became convinced that the synoptic Gospels were not the actual historical records of the life and work of Jesus Christ but were simply an expression of the theology of the early church. He also assumed that the early church had borrowed mythical elements for its theology from its Greek environment and inserted these mythical concepts into the oral tradition which later became the basis for the written gospel as we have it today. In accordance with these presuppositions Bultmann concluded that the salvation history which Barth and Brunner had striven to defend was largely mythological in character, and under this umbrella of mythology he included the eternal deity of Christ, the fall, the incarnation, the death of Christ as the atonement for sin, the resurrection, the ascension, and the second coming. By mythology Bultmann meant that these doctrines were set forth in the New Testament, particularly in the four Gospels, in language which we derived from the mythology of the Jewish Apocalypse and the Gnostic redemption myth. In his commentary on the Gospel of John in 1941 he suggested that this book reflected Gnostic ideas. In his *Neues Testament und Mythologie,* published in the same year, he expanded this theme to the synoptic Gospels. It should be noted that he had already committed himself to an existentialist approach to theology in an earlier work, *Jesus,* published in 1926, in which he paid almost no attention to either the deeds or the teachings of Christ apart from his emphasis on a call to decision. It is clear that this existentialist approach was developed from Heidegger's analysis of the structure of being as a secularized philosophic version of the view of human existence which he professed to find in the New Testament.

It was but a short step from this inclusion of Heidegger's version of authentic and unauthentic existence to the process of demythologization. This approach to the study of the New Testament involved the assumption that it was no longer possible to discover the Jesus of actual history in the documents because they have been so infiltrated with the mythology previously noted. Bultmann had no difficulty in discarding the historical approach to the Jesus of the Gospels because for him, as for Barth and for Brunner, history had no real significance. History was actually dangerous to faith. Thus, this process of demythologization was conceived of by Bultmann as an actual aid to faith on the part of modern man. He argued

42. Karl Barth, in a personal conversation with a friend of the author of the book, remarked to him that if Bultmann were correct, then there was no gospel.

that this Jewish-Gnostic mythology of the New Testament has no appeal for the modern mind since twentieth-century man does not think in mythological terms. Modern man, on the other hand, accepts only the reality which he finds in the basic world and life view of our time, a world and life view based upon the findings of science and the concept of empirical causality. He felt that the New Testament should be so reinterpreted that its mythological character would be brought into harmony with the frame of reference used by modern man to interpret himself and the world in which he lives. Thus, myth must be interpreted as man's insight into the meaning of human existence, that is, in terms of existentialism.

By such an injection of the concept of myth, Bultmann felt he successfully presented the gospel in such a way that it would be attractive to the modern man. Its attractiveness would lie in the fact that it did not allow any place for miracles, for any other form of supernatural events, and would not allow for any discontinuity in the rational order of the universe as it is conceived by modern man.

In the light of this analysis the question naturally arises: How much, if any, of the gospel is left in Bultmann's demythologized edition? Here he resorted to the approach of Barth, but in an even more unbiblical and irrational manner. For Bultmann the divine activity in these historically known events is available only to the eye of faith. In other words, this divine activity can be known only through an encounter. At this point an important question emerges which is not easily answered in the light of Bultmann's basic assumptions. How can God's past acts be present in such an existential encounter as Bultmann demands for man's knowledge of divine events? Once again he turned to Barth for an answer.[43] He borrowed from both Barth and Brunner the distinction between *Historie* and *Geschichte*. *Historie,* for Bultmann, is that stream of events which historians discover and weave into a meaningful pattern. The fact of the cross is only a fact of *Historie* and does not have a redemptive impact. By *Geschichte,* Bultmann meant that certain events which take place within time and space have an additional quality. Such events have permanent significance for human existence. These events, which are *Geschichte* in character, are also eschatological in nature, by which term Bultmann meant that they are creative in character. In *Historie* the cross stands as a statement of fact, but as an eschatological occurrence it reveals the judgment of God as an eternal act of God. The significance of Jesus, therefore, is

43. It seems obvious at this point that even though Barth might be horrified by the trend of Bultmann's theology (if, indeed, it can be called that), he can hardly disown his theological offspring.

found in His role as a Revealer, by which Bultmann insisted that in the life of a man in *Historie* God encounters men existentially whenever the Scriptures are preached.

The inescapable conclusion of Bultmann's position is in the darkness of an inescapable irrationalism which must plunge modern man into the depths of despair. Van Til cogently summarized Bultmann when he wrote that the God of Bultmann's theology is the same unknowable wholly other of which modern philosophy also speaks.

> The Christ of modern theology is as unknowable as the God of modern theology. If theology differs at all from philosophy or from science, it is only in that it pretends to have a bigger flashlight and can therefore have a little deeper glance into the infinite impenetrable mists that surround modern man. When modern theology speaks of man's sin and of the saving grace of God in Christ, it merely uses religious language for ideas that philosophy has all the while expressed in concepts of its own.[44]

Van Til then drives this point with terrific force as he begins his study of the new quest for the historical Jesus. This quest deals with those men who followed Barth, Brunner, Bultmann, and Tillich. Concerning their notions he wrote:

> We must therefore meet Jesus in the I-Thou dimension. But if He is living in the I-Thou dimension, Jesus lives in the prison cell of His own isolation. How could He possibly give us any help? As one non-objectifiable self among millions of others, he could not know himself unless he, with all other men, were taken into and lost in an abstract principle of unity made after the pattern offered by Parmenides. In other words, the relation of Jesus to other men must, for existential theology, be explained by the principle of continuity and discontinuity that at once explains and explains away the difference between him and other men.[45]

This indictment of the existentialist approach to God and interpretation of His revelation to man through the Scriptures and Jesus Christ can hardly be questioned. Its irrationalism is too evident to be denied in that it is based upon and shares that of Kant, Kierkegaard, and other philosophers who prepared the way for its bursting into full bloom during the first half of the present century.

Inspired by nineteenth-century philosophy and bearing its burden of irrationalism, existentialist theology gave an impetus to the further development of irrationalism in modern thought. Before we enter upon such a

---

44. Van Til, *A Christian Theory of Knowledge,* p. 33.
45. Ibid., p. 341.

discussion, we must first take account of Paul Tillich's version of this theological phenomenon.

Paul Tillich (1886–1965)

A German-born and German-trained philosopher and theologian (Berlin, Tubingen, Halle, and Breslau), Tillich taught in four German universities until he was dismissed from his professorial post at the University of Frankfort by Hitler in 1933. He came to the United States and taught at Union Theological Seminary in New York and Columbia University from 1933 until 1955. From 1955 until 1962 he taught at Harvard University, and then went to the University of Chicago for three years (1962–1965). Of the European-born existentialist theologians he thus had greater contact with the American mind than his German contemporaries. It is doubtful that he ever obtained influence over theology in this country to the extent which Barth enjoyed. His break with historic Christianity was more openly announced than was that of Barth, and hence, for many, it was more unacceptable. It was much more difficult to bring Tillich within the framework of neo-orthodoxy than it was to make room for either Barth or Brunner.

Tillich was frankly and unashamedly existential in his thinking. His ideas reveal strong affinity with Platonism, medieval mysticism, the German idealism of Schelling, and the existentialist thought of Kierkegaard and Heidegger. He strenuously endeavored to bring Luther into the field of existentialism, and on occasion he even claimed the Apostle Paul. Not unexpectedly he is critical of Augustine, Calvin, and historic Christian orthodoxy at almost every point and sought to reinterpret it in terms of existentialism.

Tillich called his theological methodology the "Method of Correlation," in which he called for a complementary relationship between philosophy and theology, but the philosophy and theology he used were of the existential version. It was the role and duty of philosophy to pose the questions dealing with ontology or being, and the role of theology to answer them.

Basic to Tillich's whole system was his rejection of Christian theism. His doctrine of God and his ontological outlook demanded such a rejection. More specifically, his well-known concept of the "courage to be" made it absolutely necessary to reject the biblical view of God.

> The courage to take meaninglessness into itself presupposes a relation to the ground of being which we have called "absolute faith." It is without a special content, yet it is not without content. The content of absolute faith is the "God above God." Absolute faith and its

> consequences, the courage that takes the radical doubt, the doubt about God, into itself, transcends the theistic idea of God.[46]

At times Tillich became almost vehement in his negations of the possibility of Christian or biblical theism as a suitable religious vehicle.

> Theism can mean the unspecified affirmation of God. Theism in this sense does not say what it means if it uses the name of God. Because of the traditional and psychological connotations of the word God such an empty theism can produce a reverent mood if it speaks of God.[47]

Tillich then replaced this abrupt rejection of the traditional concept of theism with one of his own making. It is distinctly an existentialist definition and has almost no relation with any biblical view.

> Theism can have another meaning, quite contrary to the first one; it can be the name of what we have called the divine-human encounter. In this case it points to those elements in the Jewish-Christian tradition which emphasize the person-to-person relationship with God. Theism in this sense emphasizes the personalistic passages in the Bible, and the Protestant creeds, the personalistic image of God, the word as the tool of creation and revelation, the ethical and social character of the kingdom of God, the personal nature of human faith and divine forgiveness, the historical vision of the universe, the idea of a divine purpose, the infinite distance between creator and creature, the absolute separation between God and the world, the conflict between holy God and sinful man, the person-to-person character of prayer and practical devotion. Theism in this sense is the nonmystical side of biblical religion and historical Christianity.[48]

At first glance this would seem to be a statement of the case for Christian theism with which no Christian should disagree. The words are those of historic orthodoxy, but the meaning intended to be conveyed by that phraseology is that of existentialism. Tillich then proceeded to reject the first three versions of theism because they were either irrelevant, one-sided, or based on theology. His rejection of the third concept, the theological version, is of special importance because in his treatment of it he not only admits that from his point of view it is bad theology, but gives his reason for this evaluation.[49] In this form, according to Tillich, God appears as the invincible tyrant (simply because He is sovereign) :

> The being in contrast with whom all other beings are without freedom and subjectivity. . . . He becomes the model of everything against which Existentialism revolted. . . . This is the God Nietzsche said had

46. Paul Tillich, *The Courage To Be* (New Haven: Yale University Press, 1968), p. 182.

47. Ibid.

48. Ibid., p. 183.

49. Ibid.

> to be killed because nobody can tolerate being made into a mere object of absolute knowledge and absolute control.[50]

In these candid confessions, Tillich has made his position incontestably clear. Existentialism cannot tolerate any form of Christian theism which allows any room for the sovereign God of the Scriptures. For him, theism, in all of its forms, must be transcended in the experience which he called absolute faith. This form of theism is the "accepting of the acceptance without somebody or something that accepts. . . . it is the power of being-itself that accepts and gives the courage to be."[51]

But what does all of this mean? Tillich admits that this form of theism cannot be described in mystical terms, and it "transcends both mysticism and personal encounter, as it transcends both the courage to be as a part and the courage to be as oneself."[52]

The ultimate source of this courage to be is the "God above God," and this is the result of man's demand to transcend theism. To put it into other words, it is the result of man's insistence that he is not to be ruled by the sovereign God revealed in the Scriptures.

Tillich's further explanation is couched in somewhat different terminology:

> Only if the God of theism is transcended can the anxiety of doubt and meaninglessness be taken into the courage to be. The God above the God is the object of all mystical longing, but mysticism also must be transcended in order to reach him. Mysticism does not take seriously the concrete and the doubt concerning the concrete.[53]

It cannot solve the problem of meaninglessness. Tillich finally summarizes his presentation of the theism which he holds to be necessary:

> The God above the God of theism is not the devaluation of the meanings which doubt has thrown into the abyss of meaningless; he is their potential restitution. Nevertheless absolute faith agrees with the faith implied in mysticism in that both transcend the theistic objectivation of a god who is a being.[54]

Tillich was convinced that in this concept of the "God above God" he had removed the difficulties with the God revealed in the Scriptures and presented in traditional Protestant theology. This conception of God has given birth to a series of paradoxes which in turn drive the religious consciousness toward a God above the God of theism.

---

50. Ibid., p. 185.
51. Ibid.
52. Ibid., p. 186.
53. Ibid.
54. Ibid.

In this solution Tillich created his own god, not a sovereign but one whom men can control and this can resolve the so-called paradoxes which meet man in his efforts to worship the God of the Bible. The real sovereignty in Tillich's solution to the problem lies in man. He will create a god after his own image who will be obedient to the will of man. He frankly appeals to human effort, intellectual and moral, to create such a transcendent being in the belief that the result would produce "the courage to be."

> The courage to be which is rooted in the experience of the God above the God of theism unites and transcends the courage to be as a part of the courage to be as oneself. It avoids the loss of oneself by participation and the loss of one's world by individualization. The acceptance of the God above the God of theism makes us a part of that which is not also a part but is the ground of the whole.[55]

Tillich then issued a call for the church to stand for the power of being-itself or for the God who transcends the God of religions because it can then mediate a courage to be. A church which is based on the authority of God, according to Tillich, cannot make such a claim.

On the other hand:

> A church which raises itself in its message and in its devotion to the God above the God of theism without sacrificing its concrete symbols can mediate a courage which takes the doubt and meaninglessness unto itself. It is the Church under the Cross which alone can do this, the Church which preaches the Crucified who cried to God who remained his God after the God of confidence had left him in the darkness of doubt and meaninglessness.[56]

It is the duty of this church to interpret its symbols even when they have become nothing more than superstition and products of the imagination. "That which once was the power in these symbols can still be present and create the courage to be in spite of the experience of a chaotic world and a finite existence."[57]

There can be no doubt that Tillich has made use of evangelical or orthodox language to convey a meaning which is far removed from that embodied in historic Christianity. The god of whom he speaks is one of his own imagination, the concept of man derived from it is equally false, and the universe presented is not preserved from the concept of meaninglessness, dread, and anxiety. In short, Tillich is perilously close to pantheism, if he has not already crossed over the border into those regions of murkiness and despair.

In view of his definition of theism it was thus necessary, as Tillich recog-

55. Ibid., p. 187. 56. Ibid., p. 188. 57. Ibid., p. 189.

nized, to recast the whole body of traditional orthodoxy into a new form, to redefine man, the fall, sin, redemption, Christian ethics, and the Christian hope into an existentialist format. In fact, in view of his close affiliation with theism, Tillich could not, and did not, give any real explanation for the existence of man in the world. It would seem that he became dangerously close to the insistence that man somehow creates himself out of his courage to be.

In volume I of his *Systematic Theology* Tillich argued for the view that God is the ground of all being, but in a way which logically denies any possibility of a creation of the world or man *ex nihilo*. It is quite significant that Tillich makes little mention of such a doctrine in his three volumes on theology, and when he does it is strictly existential or even in pantheistic terms. In his discussion of revelation and the Word of God, Tillich admits that one of the uses of "Word" is in conncction with creation. He presents it as a medium of creation.

> The Word is the medium of creation, the dynamic spiritual which mediates between the silent mystery of the abyss of being and the fulness of concrete, individualized self related beings. Creation through the Word, in contrast to a process of emanation as elaborated in Neo-Platonism points symbolically both to freedom of creation and to the freedom of the created. The manifestation of the ground of being is spiritual, not mechanical.[58]

Tillich, thus far, has simply given us the Word as the medium of creation. This word is a dynamic spiritual entity, impersonal in nature and part of the ground of being. In his treatment of this aspect of Christian thought in the section on the reality of God, Tillich went into further discussion of the nature of creation which sheds little light on his positive solution to the problem, but which throws a great deal of light on his attitude toward the Scriptures.

He was very insistent that the Genesis account was not the story of an event which happened "once upon a time" and, as such, was a completed event within history. Rather is the term a basic description of the relation which exists between God and the world. It is the correlate to the analysis of man's finitude and discovers the meaning of finitude in man's loneliness. The doctrine of creation does not describe an event, but rather does it point to a situation of creatureliness and to its correlate, the divine creativity. Creatureliness in turn implies non-being, but it is more than that. It carries within itself the power of being, and this power of being is itself participa-

58. Paul Tillich, *Systematic Theology*, 3 vols. (Chicago: University of Chicago Press, 1951–1963), vol. I.

tion in being-itself, in the creative ground of being. Being a creature includes both the heritage of nonbeing (anxiety) and the heritage of becoming (courage).

Thus, according to Tillich, we are to believe that creation is a process of a transition from nonbeing to being and a transition from anxiety to courage. But this explains very little and creates innumerable difficulties. His reliance upon the Hegelian dialectic at this point as well as upon the evolutionary hypothesis sheds no real light on how the nonbeing came into existence with the potentiality of achieving being and how anxiety became attached to nonbeing and how the transition could possibly produce courage.

Tillich's answer to the question is less than satisfactory and a far cry from the biblical account. In his efforts to escape from what he considered to be the difficulties of the biblical version he has plunged his readers and followers into a labyrinth of meaningless language which contains a series of assumptions far harder to believe than the biblical account which he feels is so unrelated to the modern mind.

> There is no difference in the divine life between potentiality and actuality. . . . The creative process of the divine life precedes the differentiation between essences and existents. In the creative vision of God the individual is present as a whole in his essential being and inner *telos* and at the same time, in the infinity of the special moments of his life-process. Of course, this is said symbolically, since we are unable to have a perception or even an imagination of that which belongs to the divine life. The mystery of being beyond essence and existence is hidden in the mystery of the creativity of the divine life.[59]

Tillich insists that man exists, but beyond the foregoing quotation he has no explanation of how or why man exists. Inescapably this theology or philosophy is silent and must ever remain so as it confronts the problems of the fall, and human evil exists only in so far as it offers an existentialist answer to these issues and treats them in a symbolic manner. It is impossible to give a symbolic meaning to the doctrine of creation and then accept the biblical view of the fall and human sin. Consistency required Tillich to continue in his chosen point of view and vehicle of interpreting what he and his colleagues delighted to call the biblical drama of man and his redemption. He was quite clear that the fall was symbolic, but an important symbol—in fact, a decisive part of the Christian tradition—but its meaning transcended the myth of Adam's fall in the Garden of Eden. At the same time, he also held that "biblical literalism did a distinctive

59. Ibid., pp. 254-255.

disservice to Christianity in its identification of the Christian emphasis on the symbol of the Fall with the literalistic interpretation of the Genesis story."[60] Theology must clearly represent the fall as a symbol for the universal situation. Tillich preferred to describe this symbolic event as a "transition from essence to existence" in order to remove from the thinking of the church the idea that it was an event which actually took place within history. But the question remains: Since the effects of the fall are hardly symbolic but take place every day as events in history, can these daily evidences of a universal situation be explained in terms of a symbolic representation? Tillich professes to find in this symbolic expression of the fall the most profound and richest expression of man's awareness of his existential estrangement, and provides the scheme in which the transition from essence to existence can be treated.

In his further elaboration of this theme we come to the real purposc for this symbolic treatment. It is found in his desire to preserve the finite freedom of man.[61] He once again resorts to a dialectical approach to maintain this necessary aspect of human personality which he finds in the ontological polarity of freedom and destiny. In this third polarity he professed to find the fulfillment of the ontological structure and also its turning point. He defined freedom in the following:

> Freedom in polarity with destiny is the structural element which makes existence possible because it transcends the essential necessity of being without destroying it.[62]

To lay the foundation for his concept of freedom, Tillich wrote this paradox in terms of his meaning of polarity:

> Man is man because he has freedom, but he has freedom only in polar interdependence with destiny. The term destiny is unusual in this context. Ordinarily one speaks of freedom and necessity. However, necessity is a category and not an element. Its contrast is possibility, not freedom. Whenever freedom and necessity are set over against each other, necessity is understood in terms of mechanistic determinacy and freedom is thought of in terms of indeterministic contingency.[63]

Neither one of the explanations met with Tillich's full approval because neither, in his view, grasped the structure of being as it is experienced immediately in the one being who can experience it—man. Only man can experience freedom.

> Man experiences the structure of the individual as the bearer of freedom within the larger structures to which the individual structure belongs.

60. Ibid., vol. II, p. 29.
61. Ibid., pp. 31-32.
62. Ibid., vol. I, p. 182.
63. Ibid.

> Destiny points to this situation in which man finds himself, facing the world to which, at the same time, he belongs.[64]

The deficiencies in this definition of freedom must be obvious. They cannot be otherwise. Man's freedom is quite related to, and restricted by, his "polar destiny." Although Tillich attempted to avoid the inherent difficulty of the use of the word *destiny,* he was not able to do so, even though he also held that freedom is experienced as deliberation, decision, and responsibility, terms which he borrowed from Christian theism, but to which he assigned a very different role.

The tenuous nature of his position becomes even clearer in his discussion of destiny, which dissolves any meaningful concept of this aspect of man into a mirage of wishful thinking.

> Our destiny is not that out of which our decisions arise; it is the indefinitely broad basis of our centered selfhood; it is the concreteness of our being which makes all our decisions *our* decisions.[65]

Each man is responsible for what has happened through the center of his self, the seat and organ of his freedom. Thus man is the center and source of what freedom he possesses, but it is a freedom which is broadly, but nonetheless distinctly, limited by our destiny. To such lengths will men go to deny the sovereignty of God over human affairs—the only true source of human freedom. Tillich's doctrine of freedom turns out to be a doctrine of absolute slavery by which man is bound to the limits of his own destiny. Man is thus subject to a blind and meaningless force over which he can have no control. Tillich's efforts to escape these were futile and unconvincing.

> Since freedom and destiny constitute an ontological polarity, everything that participates in being must participate in this polarity. But man, who has a complete self and a world, is the only being who is free in the sense of deliberation, decision and responsibility.[66]

Tillich made a futile gesture toward a biblical frame of reference by a brief reference to the relationship between God and freedom. "Only he who has freedom has a destiny. Things have no freedom because they have no destiny. God has no destiny because he has no freedom."[67]

Tillich further insisted that the word *destiny* has an eschatological connotation, which is true in one sense and yet not in another. The created world has a destiny because God has so determined its ultimate destination or destiny. Tillich argued that this eschatological connotation made destiny

---

64. Ibid., pp. 182-183.
65. Ibid., p 184.
66. Ibid., p. 185.
67. Ibid.

qualified to stand in polarity with freedom, not as its opposite, but rather as a factor setting conditions and limits to it. This reference to God in no way sets aside the basic intent of Tillich's concept of man and his freedom and responsibility. These terms are not biblical in their use or intent, and man is not free because he is a new creature in Jesus Christ and is therefore undergoing a process of sanctification in which God's image in him is daily being restored. As it is being restored, man is recovering a freedom, because he has been regenerated and given a new power to do God's will. This whole biblical concept had no place in Tillich's system of thought.

If the question arises as to why little or no attention has been paid in this treatment of Tillich to the question of epistemology and our knowledge of God, its answer is to be found in the nature of Tillich's basic assumptions. His reliance upon a pantheistic idealism which virtually identifies God and man rendered any doctrine of revelation superfluous. To the extent to which we may say he had such a treatment we may say that he was one of the leading advocates of the concept that symbols or myths are signs that participate in the reality to which they point. Thus only through the use of myth and symbols can man achieve the real meaning and structure of reality—God who is the "Ground of Being." The existentialist position ruled out any meaningful doctrine of revelation, because if man and God are both participants in the same essential being, then revelation in the historic sense of the term is not necessary. Even Tillich's insistence that Jesus Christ is the New Being does nothing to alter the case. In His sacrifice on the cross Jesus became transparent to the "Ground of Being"—the New Being or the Christ. Tillich's Christ is not the Christ of the New Testament. Thus, the whole New Testament (as well as the Old Testament) was restructured to fit into this existentialist concept of reality with its pantheistic implications, to such an extent that its entire message became a grotesque philosophy rather than theology.

As a result, there is no theistic interpretation of man and human cultural activity possible in such an approach to the biblical message. Tillich must, therefore, be considered as another important figure who has contributed much to the decline of Western thought in general and Christian theology in particular. In his works theology first suffered because it was penetrated by existentialism. Then Western thought suffered because it, in turn, was penetrated by the poisons of an existentialism run riot. His ultimate impact was to further extend the doctrine of the sovereignty of man and to enhance the existential view that life is without meaning and is void of purpose. Without a meaningful doctrine of God, man, or creation, Tillich could not construct a theistic view of man or his knowledge which could adequately explain his role on earth and his cultural responsibilities as God's steward over the world which He had created and on which He had placed man.

At this point it seems not only fitting but even necessary to examine Van Til's analysis of Tillich in some depth, because he feels that Tillich has reached the depths of the abyss of meaninglessness in existential theology.

Van Til stresses the fact that Tillich shared the bitter hostility of modern existentialism against every form of orthodox thought:

> For him the idea of Jesus Christ as being directly identifiable with the man who walked in Galilee or the idea of Scripture as the direct and final revelation of God in Christ is intolerable. How could the depths of the mystery of being be exhaustively set forth in a form of words that finite man has produced and can understand?[68]

Van Til further maintains that Tillich believes that this was impossible because of his Kantian and Hegelian presuppositions. Thus Van Til concluded that Tillich, along with modern man in general, held that the God and the Christ of Scriptures, and therefore of the Reformation, cannot exist.[69]

Tillich's negations led him into further difficulties, which Van Til graphically portrays. In Tillich's position we have the post-Kantian view of reason. Thus Tillich was forced to seek for a principle of identity which "both in subjective and in objective reason, is both static and dynamic." But because Tillich stressed the dynamic, or irrational, side of being, his system of thought is not radically different from that of Hegel's idea of the self-realization of the Absolute Spirit. Inevitably this led Tillich to a denial of the Scriptures as the revelation of God to man.

> The idea of revelation as information would lack all the characteristics of revelation. . . . The sound of ultimacy would be lacking. . . . The "Word of God" contains neither revealed commandments nor revealed doctrines; it accompanies and interprets revelatory situations [Tillich maintained]. Knowledge of revelation does not increase our knowledge about the structure of nature, history and man. Whenever a claim to knowledge is made on this level, it must be subjected to the experimental tests through which truth is established. If such a claim is made in the name of revelation or of any other authority, it must be disregarded, and the ordinary methods of research and verification must be applied.[70]

Thus, in Tillich, there is no possibility of revealed knowledge in the

68. Van Til, *The Search for Meaning in Modern Thought,* p. 91.
69. Ibid.
70. Tillich, *Systematic Theology,* vol. I, p. 143.

historic sense of the term, and the church is plunged into the abyss of irrationalism, for Tillich's God cannot reveal Himself to man in any meaningful pattern.

Van Til's final summary of Tillich's philosophy, or theology, is most pertinent at this point:

> All of Tillich's predicates about Jesus the Christ hover like so many airplanes over an airport, unable to come down because of the fog. In fact, with the bevy of universals employed by Tillich (there is no good reason for thinking that there is such a thing as an air-strip at all. For them all is swamp.) If they pick on the particular spot of ordinary history occupied by the man Jesus, they do so for no good reason that they can give.[71]

Van Til is quite correct in pointing out that Tillich's theology (or philosophy) is only an expression of modern humanism. It makes man the center and supposedly intelligible foundation of all human predication. But it is a predication from which the God of the Scriptures has been carefully removed to the sidelines and a new god of man's own imagination has been created to take His place.

Reinhold Niebuhr (1893–1971)

Although Reinhold Niebuhr's major emphasis was in the field of Christian ethics, he became a major spokesman for the neo-orthodox school of theology in this country. This must be considered as an important influence in the history of American philosophy and theological development. Perhaps his most important role was in the application of the dialectical approach to social and economic issues and the interpretation of American history. Serving for thirty-two years on the faculty of Union Theological Seminary in New York, he was able to become the major voice in the role which he chose for himself.

As a young minister in Detroit he was quite radical in both his theology and his political and economic outlook. For a time he was a member of the Socialist Party and ran for Congress on its ticket in the 1930 congressional election. It has been alleged that the New Deal and the coming of World War II cured him of this radicalism and that he became a theological conservative. There is no real evidence that he underwent any radical change in either his theological or his political and economic outlook. It is true that he became opposed to communism and helped to found the Americans for Democratic Action to prevent the intrusion of communism into the political life of the nation. But his active participation in the founding of the

71. Van Til, *The Search for Meaning*, p. 112.

National Council of Churches in 1950 and in its development from that time on hardly supports the thesis that he became conservative in either his theology, or social and political outlook. Nor is any evidence for such a change to be gleaned from his writings.

It is true that Niebuhr's disillusionment with radicalism caused him to turn to neo-orthodoxy, and in this school of thought he found his permanent theological residence. But it is not the neo-orthodoxy of Karl Barth. In certain major respects it was his own. He took sharp issue with Barth and his followers who insisted that the church should remain aloof from political and social problems, and he made it his particular calling to find a mediating position in, and by which, the church would speak to the social, economic, and political ills of the day from the vantage point of neo-orthodoxy. In this sense there was something of a development in his thinking. Certainly the optimism which sparkled on many pages of his *Moral Man and Immoral Society* had vanished by the time he had produced his *Nature and Destiny of Man*. But his many writings all reflect certain basic neo-orthodox presuppositions which tended to saturate his political and social panaceas for the ills of American society and the world at large.

He became profoundly impressed with the reality of evil in both man and human society and a certain sense of the tragic in the human drama. This rather dominant feature of his work convinced many observers that he was orthodox and merely endeavoring to bring about some kind of a synthesis by which historic orthodoxy could speak to the ills of a modern technological society. This, however, was not the case.

Niebuhr was not orthodox, for he began his system with a thoroughly unorthodox concept of the nature of Scripture, which consequently led him to a false view of the nature of the fall and sin in man. The neo-orthodox concept of creation and the fall as myths underlie his whole theology. The statements of this position are neither isolated nor occasional, but form the very nexus of his entire approach. The defect in this view is, of course, the result of a more primary defect, namely, his doctrine of revelation. At no place in his works did he give any support to the biblical view of revelation, as that doctrine has no place in his thought. He offered instead a view of revelation which is Kierkegaardian in tone.

> The general revelation of human experience, the sense of being confronted with a "wholly other" at the edge of human consciousness, contains three elements, two of which are not too sharply defined, while the third is not defined at all. The first is a sense of reverence for a majesty and a dependence upon ultimate source of being. The second is the sense of moral oblightion laid upon one from beyond oneself and

> of moral unworthiness before a judge. The third, the most problematic of the elements in human experience, is the longing for forgiveness.[72]

He insisted that all three elements of revelation become more sharply defined as they gain the support of other forms of revelation. The cause of dependence gains its support from another form of what he called General Revelation, the content of which Niebuhr found expressed in the concept of the Creator and the creation. The second gains support from the prophetic-biblical concept of judgment in history. The third, the longing for conciliation, gains its support from the Old Testament interpretation of life.

In this view of revelation Niebuhr placed man, particularly the consciousness of man, at the very center of the process, man's consciousness of a "wholly other," man's consciousness of a sense of moral obligation, and man's longing for forgiveness. Thus, revelation depends upon man and his conscious need for God, rather than on God's conscious and infallible revelation of Himself to His creatures.

Niebuhr virtually admits the truth of this charge in his assertion concerning the nature of revelation.

> To speak of God as Creator of the world, is to regard the world in its totality as a revelation of His majesty and self-sufficient power. . . . The biblical doctrine of the Creator, and the world, is not itself a doctrine of revelation, but it is basic to the doctrine of revelation. It expresses perfectly the basic Biblical idea of both the transcendence of God and His intimate relation to the world. The doctrine is expressed in a "mythical" or supra-rational idea. Genetically the idea of creation is related to primitive concepts in which God is pictured as fashioning the world as the potter moulds his clay. The Bible retains this "primitive" concept because it preserves and protects the idea of the freedom of God and His transcendence.[73]

This is a very interesting and also misleading defense of this position. Several questions arise at this point. At what point is it a superior defense as over against the biblical view? What particular or peculiar virtues does it possess that the biblical position lacks? The answer lies in a basic observation. This is not a superior defense for the support of the biblical view of man and creation. The sovereign God of the Scriptures is hardly in need of the defense originating out of the murky fogs of neo-orthodoxy. The biblical view stands in safety from all its opponents. The truth is that Niebuhr needed to set forth such a view of revelation in order to escape from the biblical doctrine of creation and to stretch the limits of human

---

72. Reinhold Niebuhr, *The Nature and Destiny of Man,* 2 vols. (New York: Charles Scribner's, 1949), vol. I, p. 131.

73. Ibid., p. 137.

freedom. He wants a God that he can construct to fit the needs of his own neo-orthodox theology on the one hand, and his liberal, radical, social, political, and economic philosophy, on the other. He wanted and needed a theology which would allow man the prerogative of constructing a new social order which would reflect his own liberal outlook and which would be a long step on the road toward achieving a millennium on this earth. To achieve such a goal he found it necessary to construct a doctrine of creation and the fall which would allow him to redefine sin in such a way that it would not be an obstruction too great to be overcome. Standing in the way of all human dreams and efforts to usher in a human millennium stands the biblical doctrine of sin and its attendant doctrine of redemption in Christ alone.

Niebuhr was well aware of this fact. He rightly understood the impasse which continually confronts all humanistic schemes of reconstructing society. He had no intention of denying the reality of sin or of treating it lightly, as many of his contemporaries were, and are, prone to do. But neither could he afford to recognize the biblical concept without endangering his whole ethical and social philosophy. He committed himself to the fact that he was unwilling to accept the biblical doctrine of salvation because of the incredibile nature of the biblical account of creation and the fall.

> The whole Christian drama of salvation is rejected by modern man ostensibly because of the incredible character of the myths of Creation, the Fall, the Atonement, etc., in which it is expressed.[74]

It may be objected that Niebuhr is doing nothing more here than reiterating a commonly held point of view, and if this were the only occasion in which he presented such a description, the point could be sustained. But he himself held to the idea that the biblical truths, certainly those dealing with creation and the fall, are myths of a special kind and must be treated as such. The difficulty with his position is clearly seen. If the origin of sin is to be found in myth, why and how, then, is evil so horribly real in modern life? He admitted its reality but failed to answer this basic question. How can a symbolic fall produce such a horrifyingly real result? Niebuhr, perhaps more than any other neo-orthodox theologian, was convinced of the reality of sin in human affairs as a result of his early pastoral experience in Detroit, experience which did much to shape his future social philosophy.

His resort to a mythical explanation of creation and the fall launched his theological and ethical systems adrift on the stormy seas of irrationalism.

---

74. Ibid., p. 94.

Not only did he fail to have a view of creation which gives meaning and purpose to life, but he also failed to offer an explanation of evil which gave it significance in the light of the will of a sovereign God who both created man and ordains all that comes to pass in human affairs. Insisting that God and man are radically separate, his neo-orthodox outlook prevented him from accepting the biblical teachings in regard to the means by which God's sovereign control of man and history became a reality.

His reliance upon myth and symbolism also entered into his thinking in regard to the atonement and the resurrection of Christ. These events in the plan of salvation were for him supra-historical in character. Thus, the events in the life of Christ were, for him, symbolic of the plan of God for the redemption of man rather than the actual event by which this redemption was accomplished.

This ambivalence toward the origin and nature of evil ran throughout Niebuhr's numerous discussions of redemption, as well as his view of human history as a whole. He insisted that the whole character of human history "is thus definitely defined in the Christian symbolism of the 'first' and the 'second' Adam."[75] In accordance with this definition, Niebuhr stated:

> To define the norm of history provisionally in terms of prehistoric innocency is to recognize that a part of the norm of man's historic existence lies in the harmonious relation of life to life in nature. . . . The Christian faith appreciates what is valid in romantic primitivism as a part of the Christian affirmation of the goodness of creation. But the Christian interpretation of life and history has a too lively sense of the freedom which reaches into eternity to interpret life merely in terms of primitive innocency. To this innocency it relates the tragic perfection of the cross.[76]

Here Niebuhr is without question referring to Adam before the fall, in a state of prehistoric innocency in a symbolic terminology, and the Christian faith borrows this concept even though it goes beyond it to "the tragic perfection of the Cross." But even the cross is needed to perfect a symbolic fall from that of innocency.

In keeping with this approach to the factuality of biblical history, Niebuhr also spoke of the resurrection as a symbol. According to him, the idea of the resurrection of the body is a biblical symbol in which the modern mind makes the greatest offense and which

> has long since been displaced in most modern versions of the Christian faith by the idea of the immortality of the soul. . . . It is no more possible to conceive transcendent spirit, completely freed of the conditions

75. Ibid., vol. II, p. 80.

76. Ibid., pp. 80, 81.

> of nature, than to conceive the conditions of nature transmuted into an eternal consummation.[77]

Both positions, he thought, are beyond logical explanation, and he modestly admitted that only God can solve this problem, and we find this answer only in our Christian faith. Yet, he went on to cast his vote in favor of the resurrection of the body as a symbolic event in spite of his admission that even when we treat it symbolically, not all of the difficulties connected with a literalistic interpretation can be avoided. Nevertheless, Niebuhr preferred it as the most suitable explanation, which would at least remove some of the objections which the modern mind finds in such a primitive doctrine.

> In the symbol of the resurrection of the body, the "body" is indicative of the contribution which nature makes to human individuality and to all historical realizations. . . . The doctrine of the resurrection of the body implies that eternal significance belongs to the whole unity of an historical realization in so far as it has brought all particularities into the harmony of the whole. Consummation is thus conceived not as absorption into the divine but as loving fellowship with God.[78]

This explanation of this important aspect of God's plan of redemption for the race is a far cry from the biblical view. Niebuhr is here setting forth a concept of the resurrection which relates to human society rather than to the individual, the consummation of the historical process rather than to the ultimate salvation of the total man. It is a view of the resurrection suited to his view of society and its ultimate destiny rather than to the capstone of the salvation of the believer in Christ. Inevitably, this unbiblical, unorthodox view of the resurrection had very important implications for Niebuhr's view of history which was equally far removed from the biblical teachings on this important aspect of Christian theism.

With this examination of the thought of Reinhold Niebhur, our examination of modern theology must come to an end. In conclusion, as an evaluation of the neo-orthodox theologians as a whole, we can with approval quote the summary which Van Til gives of the situation:

> It may well be asked of Niebuhr and of modern theology as it follows the Kantian bifurcation between knowledge and faith how man can attain to any faith at all. Does faith in a vacuum have any meaning? How can human self-consciousness have any meaning unless its basic relation is that to God who through Christ had created and redeemed man? If with Niebuhr we begin our thinking about the meaning of life with the Kantian assumption of human autonomy it is a foregone

77. Ibid., p. 297.

78. Ibid., pp. 296-297.

> conclusion that we shall have to make artificial problems for ourselves and that therefore we shall never have any answers that satisfy them. The contrasts between a world of science of which there is impersonal conceptual knowledge and a world of faith to which man must stand in personal relation is a fatal one.[79]

And what is this fatal bifurcation Van Til presents in his answer? Logically the scientist who looks to an impersonal world of science either is bound to assert that this world is sufficient unto itself, or he must hold to his faith in a purely rational fashion. "Thus the nature of his faith is what it is because it is faith in man as autonomous and as able, in effect, to say that God *cannot* exist."[80]

For autonomous man in his modern world he must conclude that the God revealed in the Scriptures does not exist. To admit His existence is to admit that man is not autonomous. The consequences of this refusal is to live a life in the world devoid of meaning and purpose. The autonomous man can find only that meaning which he professes to seek and yet which he never finds. Thus, modern thought is characterized by a continuing and hopeless search for meaning and purpose, the ever-changing concepts which are afloat on the stormy seas of the philosophy of human autonomy.

Existentialism: A Flexible Edifice

In spite of the fact that existentialism, along with neo-orthodoxy as its correlative in theology, has failed to help modern man in his search for meaning within the universe and his own experience, this philosophy has spread its deadly tentacles into almost every segment of modern culture to an amazing degree. Many people are almost totally unaware of this. Its impact has been particularly important in the various areas of literature such as the novel, drama, and poetry and in the fine arts. Not even the social sciences have been able to escape from this deadly virus which asks man to insist on his own sovereignty to such an extent that he submits himself to the totalitarianism of meaninglessness as a substitute for that divine sovereignty which he has rejected.

Sartre paved the way for its invasion into literature, particularly the novel and drama. His associates were not slow to follow his example.

In this country, Tennessee Williams and Arthur Miller have probably been the pioneers and most influential purveyors of this philosophy in the field of drama, while the novelists have been almost too numerous to mention.

---

79. Van Til, *The Search for Meaning*, p. 10. He was speaking here of Richard and not Reinhold Niebuhr, but the analysis is equally applicable.
80. Ibid.

In such plays as *Street Car Named Desire, Baby Doll,* and Tennessee Williams' *Cat on a Hot Tin Roof,* the existentialist view of life is portrayed as a dreary existence, without meaning or purpose, in which men and women are helpless in the face of an unrelenting fate which governs their lives.

In similar manner, and yet perhaps with an even greater sense of despair and futility, Arthur Miller paints life in the light (or darkness) of the existentialist concept of man. In his *Death of a Salesman,* he has one of his characters say: "Figure it out. Work a lifetime to pay off a house. You finally own it, and there's nobody to live in it."[81] The reply of another character to this is: "Well, dear, life is a casting off. It's always that way."[82] Miller ends the play on this same plaintive note that life is futile and the goals we strive for vanish into thin air as we seem to be on the brink of achieving them. The same theme is presented in somewhat different manner in his *All My Sons.*

The fact that these and similar pieces of dramatic literature have enjoyed an amazing and continuing popularity in this country is a powerful witness to the widespread acceptance of existentialism by the people at large, even though many, if not most of them, are entirely unaware of their philosophical background and implications. The existentialist impact on the novel has been as great as it has been in the field of drama. But the novels reflecting this philosophy are too numerous to attempt to list, and furthermore it would be unnecessary or unprofitable.

In the realm of fine arts, particularly art and music, the impact has been equally devastating. The products in these fields have become so grotesque that the subject matter (if there be such) is hardly recognizable, and most of it is not worthy of notice except as it exhibits the degeneracy of the modern mind. Much of contemporary painting is dedicated to the proposition that there is neither meaning nor purpose in life and that "art" should feature this theme. The same decadence has overtaken much of the musical world and, as a result, much of contemporary music reflects the wild, savage beat of the jungle and clearly presents to the ear of man that same irrationality which much of modern art so grotesquely presents to his eyes. The attempt to evade the concept of order and rationality in the world has not left architecture unscathed. Churches and public buildings of various kinds reflect the retreat into the irrational as a kind of sanctuary for the modern mind burdened with the sense of meaninglessness and despair in

---

81. Arthur Miller, *Death of a Salesman* (New York: Viking Press, 1949), p. 15.
82. Ibid.

life. The effort to get away from Gothic or colonial architecture in newer church buildings and to use houses of worship as a means of denying a divinely instilled order in the created universe is a blatant form of the humanistic insistence that God has nothing to do with this world. There is also a desire to use the buildings in which God is worshiped as a manifestation of the desire of modern man to free himself from any remaining influences of the impact of Christian theism upon the world which he would like to reconstruct of what he considers to be the debris of a biblical world and life view has had its devastating impact.

Chapter 13
Science, the Scientific Outlook, and Irrationalism

Even as men have sought through the ages to use the processes of their own intellectual powers and the results of their own subjective experiences as the means of denying the sovereignty of God in human affairs, so have they also sought to harness the knowledge of science and its laws for this same purpose. The rebellious ego of man seeks every possible avenue for the expression of his rebellious spirit and the rejection of the divine sovereignty under which he lives. For the modern mind such a subjection is odious and intolerable. Thus, increasingly, since the Renaissance, secularists and humanists have used scientific discoveries as an important means for overthrowing the Christian heritage in favor of a new world and life view based upon naturalistic presuppositions.

This trend was in evidence in the rationalism of Descartes, Spinoza, and Leibniz, and then in the empiricism of Hobbes and Locke and their intellectual heirs. Even though in the development of Western thought a reaction set in with Kantian Idealism, Hegel and their philosophical derivatives, the march of scientific activity and discovery went on, steadily causing the nineteenth century to witness tremendous advances in scientific achievements. Even though the twentieth century has surpassed the nineteenth in its tremendous accumulation of scientific knowledge, we should not be blinded by the fact that many of the discoveries of the preceding era have made our advances possible. Neither should we forget that the proper scientific investigation of the realm of nature is part of man's mandate in his role of prophet, priest, and king over creation. The obvious abuses of this mandate by man through the ages should not allow Christians to turn against this aspect of their stewardship. Christians must never place a premium upon ignorance in any form and regard it as evidence of "sanctification."

However, the tremendous abuses of the scientific methodology and unfounded claims made in its behalf by unbelieving schools in the various scientific disciplines and their cohorts in other areas of intellectual activity have undoubtedly produced serious problems for orthodoxy throughout the ages. This issue has become peculiarly acute in our own day because of the seeming infallibility of the scientific method and the great popularity which scientists enjoy. Thus, they have not been slow to seize upon their widely respected authority to speak *ex cathedra* on many matters not related to their particular areas of study and give the appearance of infallibility. It is this widespread misuse of science and its methodology which has been the cause of much of the controversy between science and religion and which has been used to cast disrespect upon the authority of the Scriptures and upon those churches which refuse to grant to scientists a pontifical authority which demands a greater degree of obedience than was ever yielded to the papacy at Rome.

If this widespread willingness to accede to the demands of a scientific world and life view and its "priestly interpreters" is understandable to some degree, it is nevertheless reprehensible and dangerous for the intellectual, moral, social, and political stability of Western civilization. In fact, its very popularity is a cause for alarm, because its advocates tend to show a ruthless disregard for those who dare to disagree with their pronouncements and to declare them intellectual heretics. As a result, teaching and other academic and intellectual positions are closed to them because they refuse to bend the knee to this secular papacy, armed with great power and an even greater prestige, whose sphere of authority is far greater than any ever ruled by Rome.

How has this situation come into existence, and why has it gained such a foothold in Western thought? These are important questions and demand an answer if we are to understand how modern science, which accepts and rests upon concepts borrowed from the Scriptures, has somehow become the means for the advancement of irrationalism and the promotion of the idea that this world and universe are without any meaning.

The reliance upon nature and natural law as a source of ultimate authority and knowledge was a perennial characteristic of ancient thought and was by no means a stranger to the scholars of the Middle Ages. It is true, however, that St. Thomas and the scholastic philosophers and theologians gave to this concept a meaning quite different from that which it had received from the Greek and Roman philosophers. This difference was somewhat muted and modified by the nature-grace scheme which St. Thomas inherited from Aristotle, and which he wove into his philosophy and even into his theology.

We have seen, however, that with the coming of the Renaissance, and more particularly with the advent of the rationalism of the seventeenth century, natural law and the scientific methodology gained a new and much wider hearing and respect than had been the case during the Christian era. The increasing reliance upon science and its methodology as a kind of infallible oracle which would unlock all the secrets of nature had the effect of putting nature into the role of deity, whose authority could not be questioned.

As we have seen, political, social, and economic liberalism laid hold upon this new deity as one which could and hopefully would be of much greater service for the promotion of this philosophy than historic orthodox Christianity had been. Thus modern liberalism, in all its forms, gravitated toward nature for its support against the entrenched political, economic, and social orthodoxy which the liberals of the latter part of the eighteenth century and the nineteenth century associated with a reactionary world and life view, and opposed to the democratic aspirations of the masses and to their own dream of realizing a utopia upon this earth without any assistance from God, or even in spite of His revelation of the final destruction of this world order.

This secularistic concept of natural law and of the realm of nature in general gained an ascendancy in European thought as a result of the Newtonian revolution, which virtually made science the new deity. Science was now the infallible rule of faith and conduct to which the mind of man must conform and to which he must come for all valid knowledge. The scientific methodology became the new basis of the new scientific theology which a new priesthood would proclaim to the faithful; and this new priesthood would administer a new sacramental system as they would find it in the test tube and microscope. The oracles of nature would be the new revelation which would be preached to modern man, and from which he must draw his spiritual nourishment and intellectual inspiration.

Natural Law Theories and Modern Liberalism

The Newtonian discoveries became the source of a new theology for the mind of the eighteenth and later centuries. They also became a weapon which the emerging liberalism used against historic Christianity as a new theology. Liberals from Locke on, generally speaking, were intent upon maintaining the Christian view of human personality and a biblical morality, but they would achieve this task by erecting a new foundation for these desirable products of the historic Christian faith on the findings of Newton and his colleagues, as they ferreted out the secrets of God as they were being discovered in the temple of Nature, from which the Delphic oracles would now speak.

Hallowell is quite correct when he insists that "the essential postulate of integral liberalism is the absolute value and dignity of human personality."[1] However, this concept of human dignity and personality was not, and cannot be, found in natural law or in the scientific method. It was obviously derived from Christianity, with one important exception. In the biblical perspective these are not absolute values but result from the fact that man was created in the image of God and is therefore subject to His will.

This dichotomy raised for liberalism an insurmountable problem, with which it has wrestled from the late seventeenth century on until our own day, and which it has never been able to solve. Hallowell argues very persuasively that liberalism faced, and faces, the problem of solving the conflict that exists between its emphasis upon the absolute value of human personality on the one hand and that of maintaining social order on the other.[2] But there is an additional problem lying behind this one. It is the problem of the faulty and even dangerous foundation which liberalism has accepted for building its seemingly lofty edifice of its concept of man. In placing its concept of human dignity and worth upon the foundation of an impersonal natural law, it destroyed the basis of the concept of liberty which it had been endeavoring to maintain. In removing its doctrine of freedom from its basis within the biblical view of man, it necessarily destroyed the moral fabric upon which a meaningful doctrine of human rights could be erected. Hallowell is also correct when he points out that "integral liberalism bridged the gap between the natural liberty of the individual and the natural law of human kind, between subjective will and objective order by the sense of obligation."[3]

It is not enough to insist, as liberalism has maintained, that "it is the duty of the individual to carry out the dictates of objective reason, subordinating passion and desire, in order to realize the potential order embodied in reason."[4]

The sense of duty cannot be inspired in many by the concept of an impersonal natural law. Only the realization that man was created by a sovereign God and is responsible to Him for his actions can bridge the otherwise unbridgeable gap. Likewise, the insistence upon the supremacy of an impersonal natural law in human affairs brought with it the correlative of an irrational concept of human duty and human rights.

From this dilemma liberalism has erected two very different theories of law over the past two centuries, both of which are seriously lacking because they fail to recognize the sinfulness of man and his complete inability to

---

1. John H. Hallowell, *The Decline of Liberalism As an Ideology* (New York: Howard Fertig, 1971), p. 6.
2. Ibid.
3. Ibid., p. 7.
4. Ibid.

follow the dictates of right reason, even if the concepts of human duties and human rights should be subject to human discovery. As a result of a dilemma which the liberal theorists did not foresee, irrationalism has crept into the entire realm of contemporary liberal thought in regard to the nature of government and of law and has brought us to the impasse which we now face in these areas. The ultimate result has been the rise of determinism in its various forms, which in the twentieth century has made a mockery of the very freedom and human rights which liberalism professes to defend and protect against the inroads of their conservative opponents. It is liberalism which is destroying the human values which it professes to defend. The problem lies in the historic and congenital deficiencies of the liberal philosophy. It rests upon the autonomy of man, which breeds its own destruction. Liberalism, however, is not only a mode of thought, it is also a way of life and thus becomes a *Weltanschauung*. In its insistence on the autonomy of the human personality it constantly sets the stage for political, social, and economic anarchy, which in turn sets the stage for the creation of a government sufficiently strong to curb the autonomy of the individual. This can be achieved only by some form of a totalitarian regime. In other words, it brings about the creation of an autonomous government composed of autonomous individuals who seek to impose their stronger autonomy on the rest of the population or nation. Thus, what Hallowell calls integral liberalism becomes the invitation to the emergence of the modern totalitarian state simply because it refuses to recognize the sovereignty of God in human affairs and clings to an outmoded concept of human autonomy as the ultimate source of authority.

The nineteenth century witnessed the unfolding of the disintegration of liberalism as it shifted from its previous emphasis which it called democracy, but which should more accurately be called a democratic collectivism. In this process the absolute values which liberals professed to find in natural law have given way to a new set of values which the democratic majorities in the various nations have erected in place of those which were being rejected because they gave support to an unbridled expression of individualism, and freedom vanished from the scene.

In short, this is the history of the doctrine of natural law over the past 150 years. Because liberalism is a world and life view, then not only government, but every aspect of modern culture, has been invaded by this naturalistic, democratic liberalism.

Since we have dealt with the scientific point of view and its impact upon philosophy in a previous chapter, this chapter will be devoted to its influence on other aspects of modern culture, particularly to that area of human endeavor now known as the social sciences, psychology, education, and the writing and interpretation of history. In short, this scientific approach to the understanding of culture took the form of positivism, which became a substitute for metaphysics.

August Comte (1798–1857) *and Positivism*

By the nineteenth century the physical sciences had achieved an unprecedented prestige and had gained for science and scientists status which had long been held by Christianity. Science was widely believed to hold the key for the realization of the earthly utopia which had been expected by the eighteenth-century philosophers and struggled for by the leaders of the French Revolution.

> The method had been found; paradise on earth waited only upon the proper execution of the plans to be discovered in the truths and with the methods of the natural sciences. It was to Science that the nineteenth century turned for understanding and salvation as the men in the Middle Ages had turned to theology and the Church.[5]

It was this condition which led to the emergence of positivism as an inspiration which would guide social and political action of the nineteenth century into this long-expected utopia. Guido Riggerio has defined positivism as "a philosophical tendency oriented around natural science and striving for a unified view of the world of phenomena, both physical and human, through the application of the methods as the extension of the results whereby the natural sciences have attained their unrivaled position in the modern world."[6]

Comte was greatly influenced by the French philosophers, especially by Turgot and Condorcet. From them he was strengthened in his conclusion that science must be the new religion which would mold and give stability to the social order. If he was inspired by these men, it must not be concluded that he slavishly followed them in their philosophical outlook. He placed a much greater reliance upon the growth of human knowledge in the area of the physical sciences for an orderly and meaningful progress than did the philosophes. Society must be recognized in accordance with tested scientific principles. To the realization of this he devoted his life.[7]

In three important works Comte unfolded his basic concept: *Course of Positive Philosophy* (1830–1842), in six volumes; *System of Positive*

---

5. Hallowell, *Main Currents in Modern Political Thought,* p. 289.
6. Quoted in ibid., p. 290.
7. One of the first essays bore the title, "A Plan for the Scientific World Necessary to Reorganize Society."

Polity (1851–1854), in four volumes; and *The Catechism of Positivism* (1852).

Although Comte agreed with Locke and Hume that all knowledge begins with the senses, he could not and did not remain content with this simple epistemological formulation. It was his purpose to transform this epistemology into a new science by which he would develop a blueprint for the rebuilding of society. This new science was to be called sociology or sociocracy, terms which he apparently invented as a designation of the new society which he envisioned. Sociology would be the queen of the sciences. It is to be noted that he viewed it as a science, and it was to be for modern man what theology had been for the Middle Ages. Comte crowned sociology as the queen because he arranged the sciences into a hierarchy according to the order in which he believed that they had appeared in the history of human culture. In this historical development he also claimed to see a logical order. Thus the hierarchy began with mathematics (the simplest of the sciences) and moved on through astronomy, physics, chemistry, biology, and ultimately to sociology, which not only was the last to appear, but was also the most complex.[8] His view of the development of these sciences from the more elementary forms to the more complex was necessarily in character and this evolutionary influence became even more important in his law of the three stages. Comte also found it necessary to develop a philosophy or view of history in his concept of the new science of society, and, like Hegel, his philosophy heavily impinges on history and its interpretation.

The law of the three stages arose out of Comte's division between social statics on the one hand and social dynamics on the other. Under the heading of social statics he included the study of the mutual interaction of customs and ideas at any given time in history. Under social dynamics he placed his plan of the three stages. In essence, Comte was striving to formulate a social theory which would provide both order and progress. He recoiled from the turbulence of the French Revolution, feeling that here the desire for progress had destroyed the order necessary for the preservation of society.

In human history Comte thus found the stage of theology, the stage of metaphysics, and, finally, both of these were to be replaced by a third stage, the Age of Positivism, in which sociology would reign as queen. This division which he professed to see in human history is reminiscent of both

---

8. Comte devoted the first five divisions of his *The Positive Philosophy* to a careful delineation of the development of these first five sciences.

Vico and Hegel, although most students of Comte are reluctant to admit that he was influenced by the latter.

Comte defined the age of theology as one in which "the human mind seeking the essential nature of beings, the first and final causes (the origin and purpose) of all effects—in short, Absolute Knowledge—supposes all phenomena to be produced by the immediate action of supernatural beings."[9] He defined this first stage as the infancy of mankind and the era of warfare. Even though the polity which developed in this period was pernicious, he also saw great value in it.

> Pernicious as the theological polity may be in our day, no true philosopher will ever forget that it afforded the beneficent guardianship under which the formation and earliest development of modern societies took place.[10]

Nevertheless, its influence over the last three centuries, he argued, has been retrograde, and he further insisted that it was powerless to provide any future service for mankind. The law of social evolution clearly proved that it could no longer be of any service, and to restore it would be fruitless, even if somehow it could be restored. Because this stage represents the infancy of mankind, it must be replaced by the metaphysical, which represents the adolescent period in the life of man. He held that this period was represented in human history by the Middle Ages and the development of modern Europe down to the age of the French Revolution. The virtue of the polity of this age lay in the fact that, although it was critical and therefore revolutionary, it also had the virtue of being progressive. In fact, Comte credited it with most of the progress which Europe had achieved during the past three centuries. He also saw that the metaphysical stage was necessary as a "preparation for the advent of the positive school, for which the task is exclusively reserved of terminating the revolutionary period by the formation of a system uniting order with progress."[11] Nevertheless, the chief characteristic of a metaphysical stage is that of anarchism, and thus it must, in turn, be superseded by the positive stage, which represents the full manhood of the race. With a rare modesty Comte declared that this new age had begun with him and the annunciation of the positivistic philosophy.

> It is thus evident that the concept of progress belongs exclusively to the positive philosophy. This philosophy alone can indicate the final term which human nature will be forever approaching and never at-

9. August Comte, *The Positive Philosophy* (New York, 1974), p. 26.
10. Ibid., p. 403.
11. Ibid., p. 406.

taining; and it alone can prescribe the general course of the gradual development.[12]

At this point in Comte's development of his thesis a dangerous contradiction developed. If positivism represents the manhood of the race and if death is the ultimate end of each man, how could Comte conclude that the development of mankind in the age of positivism is never ending. The problem becomes all the more acute when we remember that Comte had borrowed his basic assumptions from the study of biology, and biology offers absolutely no assurance of a never-ending progression. Some will answer that he had also assumed the theory of evolution in formulating this science of society. This is true, but this only accents the difficulty inherent in Comte's position. His reliance upon the sensate epistemology should have precluded him from making any observation concerning the future, since the future must forever elude this epistemological approach until that future becomes the present.

Coates and White offer one solution to this dilemma in their observation that "Comte was never able to decide whether society should be envisaged on the analogy of a machine or on the analogy of a plant."[13] They further concluded that the two ideas of mechanism and organism vied for domination in his thinking, and only his involvement in a very emotional love affair brought him to the place where "the organistic concept began to predominate." But they only add to the problem with the added observation that with this triumph of the organistic view of society there came as a result "a concomitant irrationalism."[14] They even insist that as a result of this development Comte's positivism became "increasingly transformed into a melange of scientific jargon, ill digested idealistic motifs, religious rituals and mythopoeic constructs."[15]

There is, indeed, a certain truth in this last observation which cannot be denied. But the insistence that the irrationalism appeared only after the triumph of the organistic concept is unacceptable and apparently rests on the assumption that the mechanistic concept of life is thoroughly rational simply because it rests upon mathematical principles not found in the organistic approach.

Comte's positivism was inherently irrational from its early enunciation until the end of his life. The change from mechanism to organism may

12. Ibid., p. 440.
13. Coates and White, *The Ordeal of Liberal Humanism* (New York: McGraw-Hill, 1970), p. 136.
14. Ibid.
15. Ibid.

have caused him to offer this irrationalism in a new version and with a new veneer, but the basic presupposition which he claimed as his own throughout his writing career committed him to irrationalism.[16] This commitment to irrationalism was an inescapable derivative of his open hostility to Christianity in both its Roman Catholic and its Protestant forms.

Comte and the Biblical View of God: Positivism As a Religion

Comte held that modern man had outgrown the theological stage with the waning of the Middle Ages, and therefore he had outgrown any need for the revealed theology of the Scriptures. At every stage of his thinking his writings are saturated with an inherent hostility to Christianity and the organized church. He was convinced that the domination of theology precluded any real progress in human affairs, because opposition to progress was an essential ingredient of this theological state of mind. Human progress and historic Christianity were incompatible and contradictory elements in Western culture, and thus Christianity must give way to a new religion suitable for the age of positivism.[17] This restrictive influence was also present in Roman Catholicism, according to Comte, but he reserved his strongest indictment for Protestantism and Calvinism. He always admitted that the medieval church had served an unusual function, and he wanted to maintain the results of its elaborate structure and ensuing influence without the theology upon which it had rested. He was conscious of the fact that the religious or spiritual needs of man must also be met in the age of positivism. He pointedly remarked that everything pointed to the necessity of establishing a spiritual power as the sole means of directing this free yet systematic reform of opinion and of life with "the requisite consistency and largeness of view."[18] To bridge the gap and to fill the void caused by his arbitrary banishment of Christianity from the modern scene, Comte introduced his own religion, the Religion of Man, in which he would worship himself and proclaim himself to be God. The function of this new religion would be to encourage man to venerate the best in himself. To accomplish this purpose Comte was quite willing to use what he considered to be the best and most enduring values and practices of the medieval Catholic Church. In brief, he invented a religion with its features of worship because he recognized the human need for such a worship. He felt that he could improve the Catholic system by eliminating the Catholic faith and thus make the remnants a suitable vessel for fulfilling what he

16. Ibid., pp. 586-587.
17. Ibid., p. 670.
18. August Comte, *A General View of Positivism* (London, 1865), p. 91.

called the "spiritual needs of modern man." To promote the establishment of this millennial kingdom on earth, Comte proposed to translate theology into sociology, theocracy into sociocracy, and to transform the Catholic cathedrals of Europe into new temples in which men would worship this glorified version of humanity which Comte imagined would be the product of this new religion. There would even be a new priesthood, composed of those philosophers who were dedicated to positivism.[19]

In his rejection of biblical theism with its view of God, man and creation, and sin and redemption, Comte set the stage for the growth of this irrationalism in the field of the social sciences, particularly in the emerging area of sociology and in political thought and practice as well. It is of great significance that Comte is regarded as the father of sociology as a discipline and that he exercised a considerable influence on Spencer in England and William Graham Dumner, Lester Frank Ward, and their many successors in academic and political circles in this country. It is largely for this reason that modern sociological thought is such a strange mixture of irrational assumptions and conclusions which, in turn, have produced the confusion in the social thought and practice of our day in this country. Sociology as a study and practice has become an avowed enemy of historic Christianity on the one hand, and the stalwart champion of a totalitarian welfare state in political life on the other.

Because of his continuing impact on those areas of studies now popularly referred to as the social sciences, Comte has had a far wider influence on the thought of the West than many other philosophers whose positions were not so readily adaptable to the needs of these disciplines. As the "father of sociology" Comte has either directly or indirectly spawned many, if not most, of the dangerous social philosophies which have played such havoc in contemporary life.

The determinism and irrationalism of Comte's view of man and his society, based on scientific naturalism, made its way into nearly every area of human intellectual activity—in political thought, historical writing, psychology, economics, and literature. Thus, to varying degrees, modern culture has been permeated by this worship of nature and its scientific interpretation. Obviously, these disciplines have been forced to respond to the changing emphases and insights afforded scholars by the firmly entrenched priesthood of scientists who have no qualms about changing the

19. It is important to notice that Comte felt that the death of individuals was necessary for social progress and lamented the presence of too many old people, who would resist progress. In his ethical outlook there was a callous disregard of older people which makes a mockery of his pretension of a new spirituality based upon man.

tenets of their former infallible pronouncements to accommodate them to the latest scientific theories. Their disciples in these other areas have been equally willing to accept sudden changes in their religion and adapt themselves to the more recent pronouncements of these infallible oracles. In this continuing development the original theses propounded by Comte a century and a quarter ago, have been forgotten and discarded.

Comte's determinism and sociological thinking were largely determined by the scientific view of his own day. For this reason they were dated in this one respect, even though his basic identification of social phenomena with the laws of science was not. It was thus possible for his followers to adopt as their own the scientific developments which took place after Comte and adapt their own philosophy of the social sciences to the ever-changing pattern of scientific theories in both the physical and the biological areas.

In the areas of political, social, and economic thought, liberalism thus fell prey to determinism, and instead of viewing law as a limiting force on government action, it swallowed a large dose of determinism derived from its increasing dependence on the ever-changing scientific outlook and found itself in the peculiar position of championing the very doctrines which it originally had opposed. Finding no freedom for man in its scientific world and life view, it was logically led to a denial of its existence in human society. Thus by the early twentieth century liberalism came to espouse, in the name of freedom, government with unlimited powers over every aspect of the life of man and of being willing to support this view with the demand that government be centralized, even to the point of becoming an absolutism, to enforce the will of the people. Later liberal thinkers managed to forget Comte's famous dictum that there is no freedom in mathematics and engaged in a quest for freedom based upon a conception of the universe which afforded no support for this precious human commodity.

We have seen that in England the scientific outlook of Comte was woven into the stream of philosophical radicalism by John Stuart Mill in order to create a new liberalism based upon positivism. In the study of history, Henry Thomas Buckle performed a similar function. His most important work, *The History of Civilization in England* (1856), reflects this devotion to positivism. He viewed history as continuing conflict between man and nature, or, more specifically, between mind and matter. He, however, held to a materialistic view of mind, claiming that it was the product of geographical factors. Inevitably, according to this outlook, religion, literature, and particular forms of political organization are the products of a given civilization and not its causes. This determinism, in turn, gave birth to Buckle's theory of a relativism in regard to the values of any given civilization. Thus there cannot be any absolute moral or ethical standards which are universally true or binding. Every culture is to be judged in terms of the environment which produced it, rather than in the light of a universal moral standard as revealed in the Scriptures. How, then, do we seek to understand cultures? It would seem at first glance that if there are no universal moral and ethical standards, it would become impossible for historians, and other social scientists, to render any valid judgments in regard to past or present cultures.

Buckle evaded such a conclusion by insisting that cultures may be, and even must be, studied scientifically through the use of statistical analysis. He concluded that such scientific analysis reveals the fact that the basic moral concepts of mankind are the same everywhere.[20] Curiously enough, Buckle found much comfort in his general outlook and claimed that it offered a scientific hope for progress and support for liberalism. We must conclude that Buckle's use of Comte did much to bring irrationalism into the field of historical study and make it possible for this irrational concept of history in turn to become a tremendous influence in the fashioning of modern history. This disregard and even contempt for the biblical revelation, which had become a governing factor in modern social, political, and economic thought, has thus become a major influence in fashioning the total life of our age. Modern sociologists, political scientists, and economists not only analyze modern society, but they help to give it its shape and outlook. Their rejection of the biblical doctrine of man has spurred on the rise of the totalitarian state over most of the modern world. Modern liberalism has become the grave of the liberty once proudly defended.

In this development the study of history and historians played an important role even as Comte himself had featured his interpretation of history as the basic element of his positivism. In a somewhat different manner Leopold Von Ranke (1795–1886) used positivism in the interests of maintaining conservativism against the inroads of radicalism as it was gaining ground in the scholarship of Germany, France, and England. Von Ranke used the scientific approach for the purpose of opposing the Hegelian view of history. He did not deny that history had an inner meaning, a meaning given to it by God, but he held that this inner meaning must always remain obscure, at best, to the historian, whose chief function was to gather as many facts and as much data as possible in any given field of investigation

20. It should be observed that Buckle himself never made such a scientific analysis, nor has any other social scientist known to this author. Buckle thus failed to follow his own scientific methodology in arriving at such a conclusion, and that has been a pitfall for the social sciences down to our own day.

and then "let the facts speak for themselves." Vigorously opposed to the formulation of any philosophy of history, Ranke was not as neutral as he professed to be, and his positivistic approach was tempered by his basic dedication to Lutheranism and to his belief that God ruled this human drama. Hallowell makes the telling observation that Ranke's refusal to allow for the possibility of a philosophy of history was in actuality a philosophy of history, allowing his view to open the way for a scientific historicism which was little more than an affirmation that history was without purpose or meaning and should be studied in this light.[21]

The Second Scientific Revolution

By the end of the nineteenth century a new intellectual climate was developing which began to question the infallibility of science and the scientific methodology as it had unquestionably been accepted since the time of Newton. Hallowell sees the cause of this decline of confidence in science as a product of its progressive mathematization. It is doubtful, however, that this was the only cause of the growing unrest among philosophers and social scientists as to the validity and desirability of using science as the basis for their world and life views and the interpretation of ultimate reality. This is not to say that those who were losing confidence in the science of the nineteenth century as the basis for their conception of man and the universe in which he lived returned to scriptural norms. This was far from the case, but it is also true that this failure of science to convince the intellectual leadership of its infallibility, or even the possibility that it was worthy of their greatest confidence, served to deepen their pessimism and to cause them to doubt that life had either meaning or purpose. Not only the older Newtonian world and life view, but even the Darwinian view, came under suspicion. Unwilling to return, for the most part, to orthodox Christianity for their frame of reference, scholars in philosophy and the social sciences sought new bases for their intellectual activities. While not disowning science or the scientific methodology, they also sought to combine its findings with other intellectual assumptions which would provide a new basis for intellectual certainty.

Thus decline in confidence in science was aided by some scientiests themselves, who began to announce their own honest doubts about the sanctity and infallibility of their own discipline. These factors tended to combine to reproduce in the minds of many who worshiped at its shrines a feeling that somehow their religion had betrayed them. They were not sure

21. Coates and White, *The Ordeal of Liberal Humanism*, p. 160.

just how this betrayal had come about, but there was an uneasy feeling that all was not well within its holy temples. The scientific developments which helped to create this aura of doubt and uncertainty were the introduction of the new principles of the quantum and relativity theories. These theories necessitated a reorientation of theories previous to these two revolutions. Specifically, the Newtonian mechanics had to be given a new home within this new frame of reference.

Albert Einstein (1879–1955) made significant contributions along these lines with his announcement in 1905 of the theory of relativity with its formula, $E=Mc^2$. Max Planck (1858–1947) was responsible for the statement of the quantum theory. Both of these theories struck hard and possibly fatal blows at the Newtonian physics.

It must be pointed out that these announcements were not so disconcerting to scientists of the early decades of the present century. They had been prepared for such an apparent revolution in scientific thought by the previous achievements of their colleagues. Both Einstein and Planck, each with his own approach, had radically upset the Newtonian theory concerning matter existing as a continuum. The intellectual impact of these discoveries was largely contained in the widespread use of the resulting theory of relativity in the formation of a new world and life view. To be more accurate, perhaps, the theory was claimed by those who were intent upon using the latest scientific weapon in their continuing warfare against the Christian theistic conception of the nature of the created world as a means for a further attack against the biblical teachings in regard to the nature of God, man, sin, and ethics. Relativity, as a by-word and slogan in many areas of thought, became the order of the day. This attack was carried out in spite of the fact that Einstein openly denied that he was a "relativist," and he was convinced that his system did not destroy the basic Newtonian assumption of a universally valid science, if both his theory and the basis of the Newtonian system were properly understood. The difficulty lay in the fact that some who did understand the theory of relativity used it for purposes far beyond the confines of scientific studies and saw in it the vehicle for the construction of a new world and life view ostensibly based upon this second scientific revolution. For them the theory of relativity offered an opportunity which they quickly grasped and utilized. Relativity also had an impact on those who did not understand it, and they concluded that it had battered beyond repair the traditional concept of absolute moral and ethical standards which had been either found in the Scriptures or erected on the basis of the older Newtonian physics. The theory thus gained an influence far beyond the circles of scientific and mathematical studies and investigation.

This was true for many thinkers who, although they had to varying degrees lost faith in science and the scientific approach in their respective disciplines, were nevertheless inclined to adopt the new formulations largely because they had no other place to go or look. Having renounced biblical standards and insights into the nature of reality, they were unwilling to return to a theistic view of the world. Addicted as they were to following the sanctified pronouncements of scientists, they struggled to make their peace with the ever-shifting scenery brought into their view by these scientific upheavals. They apparently preferred the uncertainties of the voice of science to the discarded certainties of the voice of God. The possibility that all truth in all areas is relative was most appealing to them, and now they could claim that science itself supported such a position. For psychologists, sociologists, political scientists, historians, and even theologians it was a golden opportunity which they were not slow to claim as their own and to use for the advancement of their own particular, and even peculiar, points of view. The new science paved the way for the destruction of certainty in all other areas. The liberals took advantage of this opportunity to advance the cause of irrationalism through the scientific theory of relativity. This marriage of convenience between relativity and irrationalism created an intellectual, political, social, and economic vacuum. Thus for the next three quarters of a century liberalism found it necessary to be engaged in the fatuous task of creating an absolutism within the context of this relativism. No more than nature can the human mind tolerate a vacuum, and human society finds itself in the same position. Thus, relativism provided a frame of reference within a new and deadly absolutism which has grown and flourished during the twentieth century.

Twentieth-Century Political Thought

Although the nineteenth century laid the foundation for the political absolutism and the totalitarian regimes which have arisen to harass modern man, it remained for our own era to bring this incipient philosophy of absolutism to fruition. Out of the rubble of nineteenth-century liberal democratic thought there has arisen the specter of a tyranny which, in its intensity and widespread power, has probably never been equalled in human history. In this advanced despotism liberalism has found an antidote to its own anarchistic tendencies inherent in its insistence upon the doctrine of the sovereignty of the individual and the relativity of all truth. As a result, contemporary political thought, under the big umbrella of the democratic philosophy, has become a welter of conflicting political movements, having little or nothing in common except a reliance upon the irrationalism which they fondly call the autonomy and sovereignty of man. This doctrine is susceptible to many interpretations, but all are basically irrational in character.

The ultimate result of their philosophical presuppositions did not come easily to the liberals. In the early years of the present century they had rested in a somewhat naive belief in the inevitability of progress. Only gradually, with the advent of World War I, did disillusionment set in. The growth of absolutism in the form of the Fascist state in Italy, the Nazi regime in Germany, and the emergence of the communist dictatorship in Russia conspired to bring liberalism into disrepute and to cause many scholars in the area of government to reconsider many of their earlier assumptions. The advent of the knowledge of atomic energy and its destructive capabilities resulting from the monumental achievement of the splitting of the atom, brought with it a fresh wave of despair. The resulting dilemma confronting liberals has been very well expressed in the following by William Esslinger:

> The belief is gone that technical advance will by itself in due time lead to general progress. But modern man needs to believe in progress; his world is moving fast and he must feel that he is moving forward.[22]

Esslinger regards this loss of belief in the certainty of progress as one of the greatest dangers of our day. He further insists that the changes which have brought about the great transformation of the modern world are largely technical and scientific in nature. This fact confronts the modern liberal with his zeal for a belief in progress with a great impasse.

> Thus we are faced with the paradox that the progress during the nineteenth century and before was due to the advance of physical science and technology, and that their increasingly rapid continuation brought about the severe crisis of our day.[23]

What, then, is the answer to this paragraph? Esslinger supplies one which is hardly satisfactory. He claims that man in society must be willing to adopt the same evolutionary principle of adaptation which we find at work in evolutionary biology. Thus the answer to the predicament caused by scientific progress is a reliance upon those same scientific concepts. The irrationalism inherent in the cause is to be treated with another dose of the irrationalism inherent in the evolutionary hypothesis.

That this solution is not conjectural on the part of the author is clearly

---

22. William Esslinger, *Politics and Science* (New York, 1955), p. 4.
23. Ibid.

seen in Esslinger's insistence that the problem must be seen in the light of his corresponding belief that civilization as a concept must be separated from culture as a different concept. He furthermore defined civilization as consisting of machines and methods of government. Under culture he included religion, art, and poetry. Thus in the solution of our problems religion must be banished to the sidelines. He then maintained that our problems have nothing to do with the cultural sphere. It is the task of statesmen to adapt politics to technics, by which he meant scientific technology without any regard for religion.[24]

Esslinger is by no means alone in his attitude toward the problem confronting modern society in general and liberalism in particular. He quoted Alfred Russell Wallace, John Dewey, Harry Elmer Barnes, and other writers as they voiced their fears that the tremendous discoveries of the nineteenth and early twentieth centuries would lead to disaster unless they were accompanied by adequate moral values as safeguards against their flagrant abuse. These moral values will not come from religion, but they would come from education. He quotes with enthusiasm the dictum of H. G. Wells that "our solution is a race between education and disaster."[25]

Modern political movements reflect this general outlook. The biblical view of government has been either neglected or openly denied. Democracy has been enthroned as the great solvent for the problems of the century. If applied in well-measured and regulated doses in the hands of those qualified to administer them, it would bring a miraculous cure. This was the mood which prevailed in much of Europe and which also commanded a widespread loyalty in this country. It gained a new and wider hearing with the ascendancy of Theodore Roosevelt to the presidency and gained an even greater respectability with Woodrow Wilson's triumph in the election of 1912. It is not only difficult for conservatives today, but for the more chastened liberals as well, to understand the unfettered enthusiasm which abounded for this philosophy of government, let alone to accept the extravagant claims which were made for its therapeutic powers. It was popularly regarded as the great panacea for all of our national ills, so much so that Wilson was willing to go to war not only to preserve it, but to make the world a safe habitation for this wonder-working political philosophy. Thus a democratic program was erected upon a reliance on the combined effects of education, strengthened by sufficient doses of the evolutionary philosophy to make it more compatible with the needs of the day and fortressed by the theology of the social gospel.

---

24. Ibid., p. 7.

25. Ibid., p. 16.

In this country new periodicals were started to popularize this new religio-political-social philosophy on which the American political system must henceforth rely. Both education and religion must be updated, however, in order to fulfill their roles in bringing about this new political and social order. This updating must, in turn, come about through the accommodation of both education and theology in the new science. In his Introduction to his *Power: A New Social Analysis,* Bertrand Russell stated the case with great clarity:

> The fundamental concept in social science is Power in the same sense in which Energy is the fundamental concept in physics.[26]

Thus for many contemporary political scientists, there must be a close relationship between the study of the natural and physical sciences and the scientific methodology on the one hand, and the study of politics on the other. Democracy was to be closely allied to the determinism inherent in this approach to the study of man in his political activities. At the same time, the previous reliance on any biblical concept of the nature and powers of the state was to be studiously avoided. Theology was to be ruled out of the picture in favor of the view that man is the measure of all things as he measures himself in the light of his scientific knowledge and achievements. Furthermore, the scientific frame of reference in the light of which he would measure himself was evolutionary in character.

As a result of this invasion of this philosophic outlook throughout the West, political thought reacted accordingly and the result was a widespread surge of totalitarian regimes and systems. Although fascism, Nazism, and Russian communism were the most strident and menacing forms of this irrational political philosophy, it appeared in the democracies in more respectable, but no less dangerous, systems. Its virulence became very obvious in the regimes established in these three countries, striking a blow at human liberty whenever they appeared and assuming a militaristic posture under the guise of national defense and safety. It is true that the injustices perpetuated at Versailles in 1919 certainly aided the growth of totalitarianism, but it is not true that Versailles or the involvement of these nations in World War I furnished the philosophical ingredient for the philosophy lying behind these political developments. At most, the war and the treaty furnished either a reason or a pretext for putting them into

26. Quoted in Esslinger, *Politics and Science,* p. 22. Esslinger does not agree with Russell's emphasis upon power as the substance of political life, but he endorses the concept of order. His solution, however, is also open to serious question, since he would rely upon the use of the scientific method as applied to the social sciences to fund the substance of political life.

practice in those countries where the greatest instability prevailed.

This irrationalism in political thought had its most devastating impact in Russia and Germany. The writings of Lenin and Hitler furnish us with the most complete insight into the philosophic basis of both Russian communism and the Nazi movement in Germany. Although there were important differences between the Nazi tyranny in Germany and that of communism in Russia, it is important to observe that fundamentally they had a common origin, and were similar in the broad outlines of their nature. Both relied on brute force for the attainment of their purposes. Nazism relied on the force inherent in a comparatively small group rallying around a leader, whereas communism, as in Russia, relied upon a group known as the proletariat. However, in actual practice, the totalitarian Russian communist state has increasingly relied on a totalitarian regime whose methods are strikingly similar to those of Nazi Germany. The differences in technique have blinded many observers to their basic kinship and have led to the conclusion that there is a fundamental difference between the communist state in Russia and the Nazi state in Germany under Hitler.

Although we may agree with Hans Kohn that the Nazi philosophy did not meet the requirement that it present a coherent system, but was actually more a conglomeration of ideas, often inconsistent with each other, always vague and capable of contradictory interpretations, and hence adaptable to the exigencies of changing political conditions, we must also insist that it was a kind of political philosophy in the sense that it provided a framework for political action, however irrational and undesirable that action might be.[27] There can be no doubt that Hitler acted according to certain philosophic presuppositions. To call them ill digested and contradictory does not in any way deny that these presuppositions formed a political frame of reference according to which he acted. That it was a strange mixture of ideas derived from several sources only guaranteed that its practice would be equally strange, ill digested, and contradictory. Hitler was influenced by Machiavelli, Hegel, Darwin, Wagner, Nietzsche, and other thinkers whose philosophies bore the earmarks of an unmistakable atheism and irrationalism. If a brutality and violence unprecedented in modern history characterized German Nazism, Italian fascism, and Russian communism, as Hallowell suggests, this brutality was the logical consequence of the philosophical antecedents of these three expressions of the totalitarian philosophy.

Basically, Hitler's philosophy was one of determinism based upon the

---

27. Hans Kohn, *The Idea of Nationalism* (New York, 1944), p. 447.

Darwinian principles, as interpreted by Wagner in his music and Houston Stewart Chamberlain and other disciples of this nineteenth-century version of fatalism in human affairs.[28]

Coupled with this reliance on fate as a guiding principle was the reliance upon war as a clue to the struggle for survival.

> War is eternal, war is universal. There is no beginning and there is no peace. War is life. Let us go back to the primitive life of the savages. What is war but cunning, deception, delusion, attack and enterprise?[29]

War was highly regarded as a necessary experience of a nation, with therapeutic benefits. It had a necessary cleansing effect. In his writings, Hitler also cast aspersion and passed a savage condemnation on all forms of representative government.

Both Nazi and Fascist literature lavished the highest adoration on the leaders of these movements, claiming that they would redeem the nation, thus according to them a power which practically identified them as a kind of god. To be sure, a German or an Italian god, but a god, nevertheless. The Reich Minister for Church Affairs had no hesitation in claiming that Adolf Hitler was nothing less than a new authority as to what "Christ and Christianity really are."[30]

Thus, in the Third Reich Hitler was to be the new Christ, the leader to whom the German people owed their highest allegiance. Hermann Goering went one step further in his exaltation of Hitler as a national leader.

> Everyone who knows the close inner bond between Hitler and his men will understand that for us followers it is axiomatic that the Leader must possess any quality attributed to him in its highest perfection. Just as the Catholics consider the Pope infallible, in all matters concerning religion and morals, so do we National Socialists believe with the same inner conviction that for us the Leader in all political and other matters concerning the national and social interests of the people is simply infallible.[31]

In Hitler's Third Reich the irrationalism of nineteenth-century German thought came into its own. Dethroning God, the Scriptures, and the church

---

28. It is interesting to note that Hitler in *Mein Kampf* frequently refers to fate as the determining principle in the life of the German people. He refers to Wagner in high terms, and, according to Albrecht Speer in his *Inside the Third Reich,* Hitler habitually attended a performance of a Wagnerian opera nearly every Saturday afternoon.

29. Quoted in Hallowell, *Main Currents in Modern Political Thought,* p. 606, from Kohn, *The Idea of Nationalism,* p. 439.

30. Quoted in Hallowell, *Main Currents in Modern Political Thought,* p. 606, from Kohn, *The Idea of Nationalism,* p. 439.

31. Hallowell, *Main Currents in Modern Political Thought,* pp. 606-607.

—both Protestant and Roman Catholic—and enthroning a national leader who was accorded infallibility in his pronouncements on national affairs, the Nazi regime became the incarnation of evil and the absolutism which must follow in the wake of the repudiation of biblical theism and its philosophy of government.[32]

In the triumph of the Russian followers of Karl Marx in the Revolution of 1917–1918 we see in a slightly different form the emergence of a totalitarian regime thoroughly irrational in its outlook, but appearing in the guise of a rational criticism of the Romanov dynasty and the Russian nobility, along with the usual critique of capitalism.

It is generally contended, frequently believed, and seldom denied that the Russian revolution was not a truly communist movement because it underwent revision at the hands of Stalin and Lenin. There is no doubt that Stalin and Lenin refused to surrender the power which they had gained and place it in the hands of the proletariat, as Marx had expected. But it is a very dangerous fallacy to insist that this revolution was not truly communist. To refuse to see the hand of Marx in this revolt is to refuse to read the facts properly. What happened in Russia was, and remains, the logical unfolding of the Marxian philosophy, even though at first glance it seems to be a refutation of the dialectical logic employed by Marx in his explanation of human history. His system provided for a totalitarian regime just as surely as did that of the political philosophy which produced Hitler. Marx seriously violated his own epistemology when he made forecasts as to the future of the communist cause. His insistence that all we learn comes to us through the senses should have precluded any statements on his part concerning the future, since this epistemology prevents man from having any knowledge of future events. Liberals who try to defend Marx from any responsibility for what has happened in Russia are either blind to the meaning of the communist ideology, or they are engaged in a conspiracy to defend a movement which is not worthy of any defense and which, on logical grounds as well as moral, cannot claim any.

In a very informative and interesting passage, Lenin revealed why his totalitarian regime, composed of a few leaders, was necessary for the revolution in Russia to be successful:

> Since there can be no talk of an independent ideology formulated by

32. This statement should not be interpreted to mean that Hitler or his colleagues were irrational in the sense that they did not realize what they were doing. They were thoroughly aware of their course of action. In fact, Hitler's *Mein Kampf* is a very rational statement of his basic irrationalism, and it contains an interesting and terrifying mixture of historical fact and philosophic error.

> the working masses themselves in the process of their movement, the only choice is—either bourgeois or socialist ideology. . . . There is much talk of spontaneity. But the *spontaneous* development of the working class leads to its subordination to the bourgeois ideology. . . . Hence, our task, the task of Social Democracy *is to combat spontaneity,* to divert the working class movement from this spontaneous, trade unionist striving to come under the wing of revolutionary Social-Democracy.[33]

With this introductory explanation Lenin then went on to explain why the masses needed education as to the value of the Social-Democracy (the favorite phrase which he and his colleagues used to describe their communism).[34] In effect, he was admitting that the masses needed guidance to understand and embrace the benefits of the revolution. This need, in turn, gave rise to the need for a leadership in the hands of an elite group.

Lenin clearly admitted that this appeal to democracy as a rallying point for a revolution in Russia was a masquerade at best and that real democracy was dangerous to the safety of the movement.

> Reflect somehow over the meaning of the high-sounding phrases . . . and you will realize that "broad democracy" in Party organization . . . is nothing more than a useless and harmful toy. It is a useless toy because in point of fact no revolutionary organization has ever practiced, or could practice, broad democracy, however much it may desire to do so. It is a harmful toy because any attempt to practice the "broad democratic principles" . . . will divert the thoughts of the practical workers from the serious and pressing task of becoming professional revolutionaries.[35]

In view of these observations, Lenin openly called for the creation of a dictatorship, admitting that it was not in keeping with the Marxian program as outlined in *Das Kapital.* His justification for this dictatorship is interesting. Marx had confidently predicted that the most industrialized nations, like Germany, would be the first to become communist. However, in this as in other predictions, Marx proved to be seriously in error, and the triumph of the communist cause in Russia made a dictatorship necessary, even a dictatorship of the proletariat in the midst of the turmoil created by Russian involvement in World War I.[36]

---

33. James E. Conner, ed., *Lenin: Selected Writings on Politics and Revolution* (New York: Pegasus, 1968), pp. 45-46.

34. It is important to notice the meaning of this phrase which sought to relate communism with democracy and democracy with socialism. On many occasions, Stalin reminded the West that communism was the ultimate destiny of democracy and that Russian was the epitome of democratic striving.

35. Conner, ed., *Lenin: Selected Writings,* p. 76.

36. Ibid., p. 267.

> Every solution that offers a middle path is either a deception of the people by the bourgeois . . . or an expression of the dull-wittedness of the petty-bourgeois democrats . . . who chatter about the unity of democracy, the general democratic front, and similar nonsense. Those whom even the progress of the Russian Revolution of 1917–1918 has not taught that a middle course is impossible must be given up for lost.[37]

Lenin's solution for the difficulties confronting Russia in a revolutionary upheaval, caused partly by the war and partly by the revolution itself, was quite simple. Russia required rule by an iron hand, a dictatorship, not in the hands of democrats or even the proletariat, but in the hands of that small group which led the revolution to its triumph. They alone were worthy to hold this office and to perform its functions.[38] Thus, in Russia as in Nazi Germany and Fascist Italy, irrationalism was enthroned in the form of a totalitarian regime. All three of these regimes were essentially alike in philosophy, whatever differences there may have been among them in form and operation.

The American Political Scene: Democracy and Irrationalism

Many Americans have fondly imagined that this country, because it claims to be a democracy, can and will escape the ravages which have encompassed not only Europe, but China, India, and much of Africa. They proudly agreed with Sinclair Lewis that "it could not happen here." Actually, the history of American political development since 1900 offers no such guarantee and seems to suggest that, although our pace is slower, we too are heading for some kind of a totalitarian regime in the near future.

The demand for a strong central government, democratically controlled, emerged with the advent of the Populist Party in the election of 1892 and gained new strength in the campaign of 1912 with the formation of Theodore Roosevelt's Bull Moose Party. Building his campaign upon the need for governmental regulation of business, he coupled this demand with the insistence that such a government must be democratically controlled to a far greater extent than had ever been the case in our national history or was allowed by the Constitution.

The theological overtones and implications of this campaign are most interesting and clearly indicate that theological orthodoxy was in alliance with political conservatism, while social and economic radicalism was claiming the support of theological liberalism and radicalism.

The Outlook, the journalistic voice of the Progressive movement, gave

37. Ibid., p. 265.

38. Ibid.

to its readers a very interesting and important interpretation of the philosophical and theological differences existing among the three parties involved in the campaign of 1912. The sharp distinction which it drew between the platform of the Democratic Party and that of the Roosevelt "Bull Moose" Party is of special significance. Concerning the Democratic Party platform, it said:

> The Democratic Party appeals to those who are dissatisfied with present conditions and desire to return to the conditions of a previous age. They look to the past for their ideal; they wish to return to the simplicity of the fathers. They are men who in their theology go back for their beliefs to the creeds of the sixteenth century, or even to the fourth, and regard all new doctrines as heresies.
>
> In politics men of this temperament desire to make the principles and policies of the fathers of 1787 the standards for their children of 1912. They are Progressives in that they desire to get away from the present; but they desire to do so by going back to the past. He [the Wilsonian Progressive] wishes the understanding of the Constitution of 1787 to bind the nation in 1912. . . .[39]

The Progressive indictment of Wilson and the Democratic Party in 1912 was essentially theological in nature. They were guilty of wanting the theology of the Council of Nicea of A.D. 525 and that of the Reformation to determine not only the theology of the twentieth century, but its political program as well. But according to Theodore Roosevelt and Lyman Abbott, the editors of *The Outlook,* this revival of the orthodox theology and the political thinking of the founding fathers of 1787 was entirely inadequate to meet the needs of the twentieth century. A new theology and a new political philosophy were necessary. Concerning the Progressive Party, Abbott wrote:

> We look forward, not backward, to the Golden Age. We believe in a new theology, a new science, a new sociology, a new biology, a new politics. We believe that in every today waits a better tomorrow; the world is steadily growing better, though with lapses, failures and retrogressions . . . that the twentieth century is as competent to make its theological creed as was the sixteenth or the fourth, that the counsels of men of this decade are better able to decide the destiny than the voices from the graves of a century ago . . . that the Constitution is to be considered as an instrument to promote growth, not as impediment to prevent it. We believe that progress lies not in going back to the past, but in going forward to the future.[40]

This is a very frank and valid statement of the Progressive position.

39. *The Outlook,* September 21, 1912, pp. 101-102.
40. Ibid., p. 103.

They wanted to march forward into the future on the basis of a new theology (notice that this comes first), a new science, a new sociology, and a new politics. The dead hand of the past must not fetter the country today. Implied in this statement was the conviction that evangelical historic Christianity was no more adequate for the needs of man in the twentieth century than was the historic understanding of the Constitution. The Progressive was searching not only for a new view of man, but for a totally new foundation for the society which this twentieth century was seeking to erect in place of that bequeathed to him by the founding fathers. All of the orthodox theology of the past and the social, economic, and political philosophies which had developed from it must be set aside to meet the demands of a new and more democratic era.

It is most significant that the editors of *The Outlook* were cognizant of the need for changing the theological basis for the introduction of this new democratic era. We must commend them for their integrity in making such an admission, for this has not always been the case with liberalism.

What, then, was the nature of the change which must be made? Theology was to be made democratic and progressive. Professor Arthur McGiffert stated the case succinctly when he declared that democracy "demands a God with whom men may cooperate, not one to whom they must submit."[41]

The Progressives were not as sincere in their willingness to eliminate the dead hand of the past from their thinking as they professed to be. What they really had in mind was their desire to be freed from what they considered to be the dead hand of the orthodoxy of the past. They were quite willing to submit to the radical philosophies of the American and French Revolutions, to transcendental thought, and nineteenth-century Darwinian theories as a guide to their new order.

The Progressive Party of 1912 was an open acknowledgement of the alliance which was being forged between liberal theology and liberal social and political thought and practice. The party platform clearly revealed its affinity with the Methodist Social Creed of 1908 and the Social Creed of the Federal Council of Churches issued in this same year.[42] These social creeds and the platform of 1912 marked an interesting development—a growing willingness of the people, both in and out of the churches, to place

---

41. Arthur C. McGiffert, "Democracy and Religion, *Religious Education* XIV (1919), 161.

42. For a further discussion of this issue, see C. Gregg Singer, *A Theological Interpretation of American History*, and *The Unholy Alliance* by the same author (New Rochelle, N. Y., 1975).

a greater reliance upon the powers of government to achieve a utopian or socialist America than in the power of the gospel to revitalize American life. Liberalism had come to the conclusion that there must be a new theology to help them attain their goals. Orthodox Christianity was not a suitable vehicle for the realization of these radical aims for American society. All American thought must be brought into subjection to the evolutionary theory advanced by Darwin, and thus a new theology must be formulated which would be revolutionary in its outlook.

This union between political and social radicalism was largely the result of the influence of *The Christian Century,* founded in the early 1900s, and the writings of Washington Gladden (1836–1918) and Walter Rauschenbusch (1861–1918). Rauschenbusch became the theological father of the Social Gospel movement with his three major works: *Christianity and the Social Crisis* (1907), *Christianizing the Social Order* (1912), and *Theology for the Social Gospel* (1917). In the first of these he made a plea for the responsibility of the Christian church in coming to grips with the social crisis; in the second, he offered a blueprint for "Christian" social action; and in the third he offered a new theology as a support for the first two. He called for a Christian socialism as the remedy for the crisis and then offered a theology which would support this alliance between Christianity and a philosophy of government which invited the formulation of a democratic totalitarianism under the guise of Christian socialism.

The total impact of this Progressive movement in alliance with a liberal Christianity which denied the infallibility of the Scriptures and the biblical doctrine of creation, man, sin, and redemption was, for a radical concept of the nature and function of the state, based upon an evolutionary philosophy which could lead to an utterly irrational concept of human society and its purposes. Democracy was thus invited to become the agent for its own destruction. This evolutionary approach to the interpretation of history has been the basic characteristic of American liberalism from that day until our own, and liberals have sought to capture all institutions for the realization of this goal. At the same time, they have called upon all the other disciplines to aid them in their quest.

Perhaps the most striking display of the alliance between the evolutionary philosophy and American political thought and practice is seen in one of the least-quoted speeches of Franklin Roosevelt during the 1932 presidential campaign, delivered at San Francisco of that year and which has become known as the "Commonwealth Club Address."

> The Declaration of Independence discusses the problems of government in terms of a contract. . . . Under such a contract rulers were

> accorded power and the people consented to that power on the consideration that they were accorded certain rights. The task of statesmanship has always been the redefining of those rights in terms of a changing and growing social order. New conditions impose new requirements upon government and those who conduct government.[43]

This is an amazing confession and affirmation of the aims of the New Deal. Whatever else Jefferson or Locke had in mind, they would have been the first to arise in horrified denial that they ever believed that human rights can ever be redefined, or that it was the task of statesmanship to redefine these rights in terms of changing social, economic, or political conditions. This is precisely what both Locke and Jefferson intended to prevent.

Roosevelt's statement was a flat contradiction of plain historical fact, but it went virtually unnoticed at the time. Furthermore, it must also be noted that the philosophy which he enunciated is very similar to that announced by Hitler in his various addresses and by Lenin in his papers. Even as they were using democracy to transform their respective governments into totalitarian regimes, so was Roosevelt using the Declaration of Independence for the very same purpose.

Although the liberal *Christian Century* did not mention this address specifically, there can be little doubt that its editors were aware of it. Completely aware that the New Deal was pointing in the direction of a socialistic totalitarianism, its editors clung to the conviction that the church must cooperate in this venture.

> The churches will have to decide what kind of religion they will dispense. But there are sound reasons for believing that only when they are able to bring the intimate personal idea and the larger social relations of men into some kind of practical accord will they be able to satisfy the urge of men toward wholeness and compete successfully with the new totalitarian faiths.[44]

The wedding between theological liberalism and the radicalism of the New Deal was virtually complete by the end of 1933. It became an even closer relationship as the program unfolded and its purpose became more evident. In December, 1933, Oswald Garrison Villard was moved to comment:

> Certainly when the President declares he is for "prosperity socially controlled for the common good" and for "collective effort which is wholly in accord with the social teachings of Christianity," he states

43. Franklin D. Roosevelt, *Public Papers (1928–1932)*, pp. 742-756.
44. *Christian Century,* October 11, 1933, pp. 1262-1264. See also ibid., June 21, 1933, pp. 806-808, and August 30, 1933, p. 1079.

again the idea of liberals and Socialists, and even those further to the left.[45]

When the Congregational General Council at its meeting at Oberlin College in 1934 openly condemned capitalism as an economic system because "it depended for its existence upon the exploitation of one group by another" (a communist position), the *Christian Century* fairly gloated:

> Every true concept of religion now seems to be a social concept. . . . The conviction is growing among us that the individual can be saved only in organic relation to his world. Thus the world itself becomes the subject of redemption.[46]

The New Deal, an extension of the Progressive philosophy of 1912, was now in the saddle in American political life and was rapidly taking the American people far away from their Christian and constitutional political heritage. The evolutionary philosophy was leading the government and the people into the meaningless maze of evolutionary political thought from which they could only emerge with the conviction that our national existence could have only that meaning and purpose which an infallible New Deal could accord it.

With the triumph of the New Deal sociologists, economists, political scientists, and educators found a new inspiration to rewrite their respective areas of study and activity in the light of this thoroughly irrational and totalitarian philosophy. This effort is still underway although the New Deal, as such, has passed from the American scene. Nevertheless, its impact has been deeply etched in the American character, politically, socially, economically, and educationally. No area has escaped this deadly blight which, by its very nature, must destroy whatever it touches. Like the Nazi movement in Germany, the Fascist movement in Italy, and the Communist movement in Russia, the New Deal presents the decline of Western political thought and its ultimate embrace of irrationalism. That there has been a certain temporary respite or recession in the progress of this deadly disease in this country should not blind us to the fact that it is still present in the stream of American thought and it must soon break out again in all of its virulence.

This irrationalism has been the underlying factor in all the political, economic, and social programs inaugurated by succeeding administrations. Oftentimes the names applied to these programs are quite suggestive of their intellectual origins. Truman's Fair Deal, Kennedy's New Frontier,

45. *The Nation,* December 20, 1933, p. 697.
46. *Christian Century,* October 17, 1934, pp. 1304-1306.

and Johnson's Great Society not only suggest this irrational approach to political issues, but draw support from modern political thinkers whose own political thought was formerly anchored in a Progressive-Socialist ideology which looked to the sovereignty and inherent goodness of man as the key to their success. In fact, Lyndon Johnson openly borrowed his Great Society from a book written by Graham Wallas which was an unabashed plea for a socialistic collectivism.

If some would argue that Republican administrations escape this charge, they have failed to understand the ideology of those who have led that party in the last quarter of a century. The last Republican candidate to stand on an orthodox political philosophy or an orthodox platform was Herbert Hoover. Generally speaking, Republican candidates have not seen the basic issues involved in the campaigns in which they were taking part. Their conservatism has not been based on a solid conservative orthodoxy, but rather on a libertarian philosophy. Thus they could make some telling points against liberal policies, but they lacked the necessary theological and philosophical insights in the light of which they could offer alternatives to the liberal position. This has been a continuing weakness of most conservative political, social, and economic activity in this country for the past forty years.[47]

The decline in political thought throughout the Western world has likewise been accompanied by a similar movement in the philosophy of law and its application to human affairs. The denial of the sovereignty of the God of the Scriptures in human government could hardly have any other result than the negation of the biblical concept of law as the revelation and expression of His will. Gradually jurisprudence has come to accept a much lower view of the origin, function, and purpose of law and legal principles. Even as government has come to be regarded as of human origin, so has law come to be looked upon as the expression of the collective experience of men as they have sought to erect principles for the guidance of their relationships with each other. Not only has law been removed from its biblical foundations, but it is no longer even regarded as the collection of principles which are universally binding upon all men because they represent the dictates of right reason, as the men of the Enlightenment fondly believed.

To the extent to which we may speak of law as a binding influence on

47. For supporting data for this observation, see A. G. Heinsohn, *United States, 1932–1960: An Anthology of Conservative Writing in the United States, 1932–1960* (Chicago, 1962). See also M. Stanton Evans, *The Future of Conservatism* (New York, 1968).

human conduct, we may do so only in the light of the popular conviction that it represents the best majority opinion at any given moment on any given issue. This new concept of law was first voiced in an authoritative manner by Oliver Wendell Holmes, Jr., who served for over thirty years as an associate judge of the Supreme Court.

> The life of the law has not been logic; it has been experience. The felt necessities of the time, the prevalent moral and political theories, institutions of public policy avowed or unconscious, even the prejudices which the judges share with their fellow men, have a good deal more to do with the syllogism in determining the rules by which men should be governed.[48]

Holmes thus held to an evolutionary development of the law as it had emerged out of the murky past of human history. It is not the embodiment of eternal principles, but of an evolutionary development of the race. Thus, there can be no eternal principles on which statutory legislation must be based, but rather should this legislation be the product of the collective evolutionary experience of the race. It then can be adapted to ever-changing conditions.

> The law embodies the story of a nation's development through many centuries, and that in order to know what it is, we must know what it has been, and what it tends to become. Much that has been taken for granted has been laboriously fought for in past times; the substance of the law at any time corresponds fairly well with what was regarded as convenient by those making or intepreting it, but the form and the machinery and the degree to which it is able to work out desired results depends much upon its past.[49]

The insistence which Holmes placed upon the necessity of a historical knowledge of the growth of the law through the centuries is heartening, and it served to act as a restraint upon a thoroughly subjective interpretation of its content and meaning by those lawyers who accepted this evolutionary approach. But Holmes also afforded a place for expediency by his insistence that in past times the law also served as a guidepost for what a previous age regarded as convenient rather than what was right.

This open invitation to a reliance on the dictates of expediency opened the door to further departures from the historic conception not only of the role of the common law in society, but also of constitutional law as well. It awaited only the arrival of the sociological approach to the study and application of the law to bring a further and dangerous departure from the

---

48. Oliver Wendell Holmes, Jr., *The Common Law* (Boston, 1881), p. 1.
49. Ibid., p. 2.

belief that all law is based upon a body of fixed principles beyond the ability or right of man to change.

In recent years we have seen the havoc wrought by sociological interpretations of the law and the involvement of the courts in various issues in which they have listened to sociologists rather than to the law and to great jurists of the past as they have interpreted that law. As a result, courts in recent years have shown a much greater concern for the presumed rights of criminals than they havc in the rights of their victims, and a much greater concern for an erroneous conception of justice which has been hatched in the halls of learning.

Justice as a legal and biblical concept has virtually lost its meaning, and crime is thus lightly regarded. Inevitably this humanistic and irrational view of the law has led to a period of near social anarchy. Congress, the courts, and state legislatures have condoned abortion, pornography, and other immoral acts once condemned by the law and still condemned by the Scriptures.

Our concern with human rights has almost destroyed our concern for the duties which man owes to God primarily and then to the state and his fellowman. Modern legal and sociological theorists have so emphasized an unbiblical doctrine of human rights that they have practically removed from our thinking as a nation the concept of duty. In confusing rights and privileges they have all but destroyed those rights which man possesses because he is created in the image of God—life, liberty, property, and marriage—and replaced them with an equally dangerous concern for privileges, which must be earned.

Keen observers of the legal scene of that day were not unaware of the logic involved in such arguments. Writing specifically of the setting aside of the Constitution, and the rule of majority rather than of the law, Justice Stephen J. Field declared:

> If the provisions of the Constitution can be set aside by an act of Congress, where is the course of usurpation to end? The present assault upon capital is but the beginning. It will be but the stepping stones to others, larger and more sweeping, till our political contests will become a war against the rich, a war growing constantly in intensity and bitterness.[50]

Field was a far wiser prophet of the demise of constitutional government than he probably realized. His fears have become a gnawing reality which apparently knows no limits except possibly those imposed by the expedi-

50. *Pollock v Farmer's Loan and Trust Cp.*, 157 U.S., 607, 1895.

ency which he so greatly feared and which Holmes so greatly revered. Expediency knows no real limits, however, and the legislative and judicial history of the nation since the days of Field clearly proves that when expediency is used to defend one position against another, to defend one right or rights, against property, then those rights, in turn, become the victims of this same philosophy of law. The loss of the right of property is quickly followed by the loss of man's other rights. The privileges soon find themselves interred in the same grave in which totalitarian regimes have buried the God-given rights of man.

Irrationalism in Economic Thought and Practice

Although St. Augustine, St. Thomas Aquinas, Luther, Calvin, and other Reformation thinkers attempted to offer an outline of a biblical approach, or approaches, to the study and practice of economics, this discipline as an independent, or semi-independent, entity had its roots in seventeenth- and eighteenth-century philosophy. As such it suffered because of its identity with the empirical thinkers who attempted a formulation of economic theory and practice in the light of their philosophy. The efforts to find a basis for economic activity in natural law, even by professed Christians, was an obvious contradiction of their own religious convictions. It resulted in a concept of economic freedom which was undergirded by a philosophy which has alternately produced a chaotic form of freedom and then a stifling economic strangulation by attempts at socialistic collectivism. A free enterprise system which looks to eighteenth-century views of natural law and the deistic concepts of religion and ethics could hardly be acceptable to Christian thinkers, or even to a society which was forced to find a defense against this kind of economic freedom which could only bring forth a kind of anarchy as its natural fruit. Modern society is also the intellectual offspring of naturalism, and it has sought for a remedy in the very philosophy which caused the problem. As a result of the impact of the Renaissance, the Enlightenment, the French Revolution, and the rise of Marxism and Darwinian thought, modern economic thought has veered from one form of irrationalism to another and from the anarchy inspired by a false view of freedom under the law to an equally false remedy in a socialistic collectivism. Both of these patterns of economic thought are inherently anti-intellectual and irrational.

In Europe socialism developed during the French Revolution, but speedily turned to a communist economy during the radical period after the collapse of the French National Assembly. After the fall of Napoleon, collectivism again appeared in France and captured the radical mind in

England and other nations. It was inherent in the various radical movements which appeared in this country during the decades between 1820 and 1860.[51]

With the advent of Marx and Engels, communism arose as a major economic philosophy. Contrary to what many liberals claim, socialism and communism, however much they may differ in methodology, are of the same origin, both emerging out of the dust of the French revolutionary spirit and both rejecting the biblical view of God and man. Economic liberalism, as well as political and social liberalism, can thrive only in an anti-intellectual environment which has first rejected biblical theism as the proper foundation for man's intellectual, political, economic, and social activity. The history of modern economic thought and practice is the story of a series of fluctuations between the two poles of anti-supernaturalism, between a libertarian view on the one hand and that of collectivism on the other. Libertarians desiring freedom have sought to find it in natural law as interpreted by Darwin. Collectivists seeking freedom have sought it also in a differing interpretation of Darwin. In each case the appeal is to an impersonal authority which is quite contrary to that view of ultimate sovereignty found in the Scriptures. Thus modern economic thought, like its political counterpart, is in a constant state of fluctuation between libertarianism and authoritarianism. In Europe this pattern is reflected in the Nazi and Fascist economic programs of control as against the Russian, English, and French approach. Neither pattern can provide for men what it promises because neither pattern follows the biblical norm as the frame of reference for man's economic activities.

We need not confine our attention to the problems which have beset Europe in the twentieth century in its economic life. Mention has already been made of the many panaceas which have been attempted in this country, beginning with Franklin Roosevelt's New Deal, and apparently under different names in succeeding administrations. The names were changed, and some differences of emphasis have been discernible, but the basic philosophy remained the same: Man is sovereign and in his own autonomy he must find and apply the proper remedies for his economic and political ills. The basic approach has been that of the welfare state in never-ending doses, coupled with the fiscal theories of John Maynard Keynes.

The decline in economic thought in this country toward the abyss of irrationalism began theoretically with the acceptance of Darwinism by William Graham Sumner and Lester Frank Ward. It gained momentum,

51. See Alice Felt Tyler, *Freedom's Ferment* (Minneapolis, 1944).

however, as the study of economics as a separate discipline became customary in academic circles. It is important to note that these early economists, who were the early advocates of socialism for this country, were all liberal in their theologies even though they were reared in Christian homes. These three important members of the "new school" of American political science and economic thought, under the impact of Darwinian thought, all insisted that economic truth must be relative to time and place and that it evolved concurrently with economic development. If this be the case, then the question arises as to how economic development itself is measured. They took the position that the state must actively intervene in the economic life of the nation in order to help the laboring groups and to achieve what they called "a fairer distribution of the national wealth." Underlying their economic thought was a common denominator that economic laws are not immutable. They thus helped to cast this new and developing discipline afloat on the erratic seas of relativism.

In order to make the state a more important factor in the economic life of the nation, these young economists—Richard T. Ely, John Bates Clark, Simon N. Patten, and their colleagues founded the American Economics Association in 1885. Ely, perhaps the most influential member of this group, returned from his studies in Germany to urge a general reform of the economic life of the American people in the direction of a collectivist socialist state in which all natural resources and public utilities would pass under government ownership. The state would be the means of leading this nation into a secularized millennial era. In his later years, Ely turned from a rather crass materialism to a Christian brotherhood idea, or Christian socialism, and looked to the churches as the means for Christianizing the social order.

The history of John Bates Clark is much like that of Ely, except that in his early college days he had planned to enter the ministry. Weaned from this idea at Amherst and his advanced studies in Germany, Clark gave up this calling in favor of teaching and eventually joined the faculty of Columbia University. With this foothold in an important center of learning, coupled with the similar position assumed by Simon Patten in the Wharton School of the University of Pennsylvania, this school of economic thought gained an ascendancy in academic circles which was destined to have a profound and dangerous effect upon the economic life of the nation. Its ultimate devastating victory came with the triumph of the New Deal and its collectivist philosophy in the election of Franklin D. Roosevelt in 1932. Fortified by the crisis psychology engendered by the worst economic depression in the history of the country, Roosevelt was able to put this economic philosophy into actual practice without much opposition in the early years of his administration, even from fiscal and political conservatives, who either were unaware of the import of his planning, or were too bewildered by the turn of economic events to marshal their forces effectively against his program.

They were also somewhat baffled by Roosevelt's pronouncements, given at various times and various places, during the campaign; also by the relatively conservative stance of the Democratic platform of that year. Very soon, however, the radical nature of his program unfolded, and the trend became clear. Slowly the influence of John Maynard Keynes became apparent as it was put to use by a president who did not thoroughly understand the economic thought of any particular school—radical or conservative. The seriousness of the situation, coupled with Roosevelt's rather naive approach to economic problems, provided a splendid atmosphere for the triumph of Keynesian economic theory, an economic theory thoroughly irrational in character and a conscious departure from all previous traditional economic thought in favor of an economic system based upon government spending and taxation.

This Keynesian economic philosophy came to fruition with the publication of *The General Theory of Employment, Interest and Money,* in 1936.[52] To attempt to give any systematic presentation of his economic thought would be far outside the scope of this treatise. But to offer an indication of the direction of his thinking and the implications contained in this philosophy is in order, and is quite in accord with the basic thesis of this study. Keynes intended to offer a new economic philosophy, and to do so he openly attacked the basic theses of classic economic thought. In so doing he frequently misrepresented these theses. At other times he ascribed to the "classical" economists doctrines which they did not hold, at least not in the manner in which he attributed them to the said economists. The total effect of his economic theories has been to plunge economic thought and practice into a new era of illogical assumptions and even more illogical conclusions.[53] These illogical conclusions, when translated into practice, have brought the whole world to the brink of a disastrous inflation.

The astounding success and influence of Keynesian thought is difficult to

---

52. John Maynard Keynes, *The General Theory of Employment, Interest and Money* (New York, 1936).

53. This is not to say that the so-called "classical economists" were theistic in their outlook, but it is true that they often used theistic assumptions in relation to the study of economics and thus had a degree of biblical "traditionalism" in their philosophy, or philosophies, which is almost entirely lacking in modern economic thought.

understand. His works abound in contradictions, false assumptions, and equally false conclusions. These weaknesses have been noted not only by his numerous critics, but also by his even more numerous admirers. Even his style is forbidding and difficult to understand.[54]

In the light of these definite weaknesses in his writings, what then is the reason for his popularity and abiding influence? A careful reading will bring the conclusion that the answer to this question lies in the understanding of what he had in mind in what he set forth as the goal of his "New Economics."

The careful reader will be struck with the fact that one of his basic principles is his belief that saving money is a sin and squandering it is a virtue.[55] In essence then, Keynes was renouncing an economic dictum that was not only dear to the heart of classical economists but was an essential part of the biblical and Puritan ethic. While Keynes seldom treated religious themes directly, in his repeated insistence that saving is a sin and squandering a virtue, he was, in effect, turning his back upon the Scriptures as they speak to economic issues, and thus he was renouncing their authority. He was vehement in his attack upon thrift and left no doubt as to his attitude toward this Christian virtue.

> The more virtuous we are, the more determinedly thrifty, the more obstinately orthodox in our national and personal finance, the more our incomes will have to fall when interest rises relatively to the marginal efficiency of capital. Obstinacy can bring only a penalty and no reward. For the result is inevitable.[56]

Thus the reward for practicing thrift is a falling income. This obstinate loyalty to biblical principles does not bring a reward, but a penalty. The remedy is to squander income, both privately and nationally, and somehow this will bring an increase in personal and public wealth.

The reader may well ask the question: Just how and why do such statements account for the popularity which has greeted Keynes from 1936 until the present? The answer lies in the conclusions which he drew from these premises. His arguments are an invitation to statism and socialism and a repudiation of free enterprise and capitalism. This is the real explanation for his popularity. He is loved because of what he really had in mind rather than because of how he expressed his philosophy.

---

54. For an excellent chapter by chapter analysis of the contradiction involved in Keynes's *The General Theory of Employment, Interest and Money,* see Henry Hazlitt, *The Failure of the 'New Economics'* (Toronto, New York, and London, 1959).

55. Hazlitt, *Failure of the 'New Economics,'* p. 56.

56. Keynes, *The General Theory of Employment,* p. 131.

The key to this aspect of his thought is found in his admiration of what he called "a dynamicism" concept of economics rather than for the traditional "static" approach to this subject. Henry Hazlitt correctly points out much of his admiration of the "dynamic approach" can be traced to the philosophers Henri Bergson and John Dewey, and ultimately to Darwin.[57] We see in this affinity the real key to the understanding of Keynes. For him, economic activity is an evolutionary unfolding and must always be regarded in that light. The error of the classical economists lay in the fact that they did not appreciate the relation of Darwinian thought to man's economic thought and practice.

How, then, is this dynamic approach to economics to be translated into practice? Keynes had a ready answer. It is to be found in his concept of governmental activity in the economic life of the nation. This answer is closely related to his own philosophical presuppositions. His approach to the problem is both evolutionary and pragmatic, making it substantially anti-intellectual and irrational as the term is used in this book.

Nevertheless, Keynes was not the least afraid of becoming dogmatic in spite of his reliance upon Dewey's pragmatic approach to economic problems, and here his real bias becomes evident. Keynes insisted that the remedy for the economic problems of our day lies in increased government spending. He maintained this would promote economic growth. He interpreted government spending to mean that government should rely upon borrowed money, by which term he meant inflation.

In his *General Theory of Employment, Interest and Money,* Keynes vented his wrath against free enterprise and traditional economics in the following bit of fanciful reasoning:

> If the Treasury were to fill old bottles with bank notes, bury them at substantial depths in the disused coal mines which are then filled to the surface with town rubbish, and leave it to private enterprise on well tried principles of *laissez faire* to dig the notes up again . . . there need be no more unemployment and, with the help of repercussions the real income of the community, and its capital wealth would probably become a good deal greater than it actually is.[58]

Hazlitt is quite correct in his statement: "This sentence [of Keynes's] tells us much more about the prejudices and confusion of Keynes than it does either about gold, gold mining, the principles of private enterprise, or the purpose of employment."[59] Hazlitt was to the point in his analysis of

---

57. Hazlitt, *The Failure of the 'New Economics,'* p. 69.
58. Keynes, *The General Theory of Employment,* p. 129.
59. Hazlitt, *The Failure of the 'New Economics,'* p. 153.

the confused thinking when he criticized Keynes for his abysmal ignorance of the gold standard and insisted that gold is a far more satisfactory standard of value "than custard pies or overcoats as a medium of exchange."[60] This might seem to be a frivolous criticism, but it is a most accurate summary of modern economists who place their reliance on paper money issues totally divorced from gold and other solid backing to give stability as a medium of exchange.

The sum and substance of this Keynesian doctrine is that the government must drastically reduce the field of free enterprise in money management, capital investment, and related activities because government will not be tied down by the fetish of "liquidity," by which term Keynes meant nothing more than unsound finance and inflation.[61] More specifically, Keynes was saying that liquidity is wicked, a sin, and the freedom of the people to buy and sell their securities in accordance with their own evaluation of the state of the market is contrary to the public interest and should not be allowed. This function should be taken over by the bureaucrats, who, by some magic insight, according to Keynes, know what is best for the individual and for the nation as a whole.

Hazlitt states that the logical conclusion to Keynes's argument at this point is quite simple in one respect and deadly in another. It is a plea for the state to take over the function of the management of money, and when this happens, human freedom vanishes and totalitarianism enters into the picture with all the irrationalism and absolutism, nicely concealed in the robes of democracy.[62]

In modern economic thought and practice the irrationalism of modern philosophy has had a devastating effect upon the whole financial structure of the West. Inflation today is rampant in nearly every nation. This is true to such an extent that many statesmen and sound-minded economists doubt that it can be brought under control and that a rather imminent collapse of the entire monetary and financial structure of the United States and the nations of Europe cannot be avoided.[63]

Why has this situation developed? In brief, the answer lies in the fact that in our economic life, as well as in our political and social life, we have disregarded the biblical ethic and have adopted a relativist view of financial

60. Ibid., p. 155.

61. For this diatribe, see Keynes, *The General Theory of Employment*, p. 155.

62. For an analysis of the Keynesian doctrine at this point, see Hazlitt, *The Failure of the 'New Economics,'* pp. 179-185.

63. The entire federal debt of this nation, at the time of this writing, is about $700 billion, and the total future federal commitment reaches the staggering total of about $500 trillion.

and fiscal policy which denies any absolutes in the realm of economic thought. As a result, in the absence of such absolutes, modern man has felt the need of creating some for himself in the conduct of his economic and financial affairs. Hence he looks to government (man organized politically) to supply the absolute norms for the conduct of his economic life which he formerly found in the Scriptures. In the place of his prized economic freedom he has adopted an economic despotism, which he calls the new freedom because it came to him in the garb of democracy.

Contemporary Psychology and the Cult of Irrationalism

In the works of Sigmund Freud, modern psychology was well launched out into the stormy seas of irrationalism, and the currents of thought which he set in motion were continued by his disciples, and in other forms with some who even took issue with some of his basic presuppositions. As a result, the very term "psychology" in its historic and etymological sense as the study of the soul has become a mockery. Modern psychology denies the existence of the soul in both the traditional and the biblical acceptance of the use of the concept, and now it pours into it a purely material and mechanistic content which denies to psychology the role as a legitimate discipline in its own right, and which should result in its becoming an appendage of the biological sciences.[64]

Both Carl Jung and Eric Fromm were well aware of the impasse which Freud had created for this discipline, and they sought to save it from the consequences of his conclusions. As well intentioned as their efforts may have been, both of these successors were unable to provide a meaningful answer to the dilemma posed by Freud, for neither was willing to surrender many of the basic principles which he had used. They were under the spell of the same secular naturalism to which he had been captive and thus were unable to accept the biblical norm for the understanding of man and his behavior.

In our investigation of the irrationalism in contemporary psychology and psychiatry it is not necessary to investigate all of the writers in these disciplines. The investigation of Freud and B. F. Skinner will be sufficient to

64. There are, of course, exceptions to this generalization. There are Christian psychologists and psychiatrists who study their discipline in the light of the biblical view of God, creation, and man, and who earnestly seek biblical answers to the great questions with which their discipline attempts to deal and frequently with great success. Some traditionalists who disavow a biblical frame of reference nevertheless attempt to retain something of a traditional concept of mental processes and will not admit that psychology and psychiatry are simply dealing with materialistic and mechanistic concepts and realities.

show the trend and the resulting impasses of these disciplines in our own day.

It has often been asserted that Fromm made important corrections in the thinking of both Freud and Jung. Therefore, he may be said to have restored psychoanalysis to a place of some dignity, of which it had been deprived in the eyes of many thoughtful people by Freud's blatant misuse of the scientific techniques which he so often applauded and by the very erroneous conclusions which he drew from his methodology. Fromm insisted that when we turn to Jung, "we find at almost every point the opposite of Freud's views on religion."[65] However, Fromm admits that Jung's analysis of the concept of truth is not tenable. He attacks Jung's position that truth is fact and not a judgment. Therefore, the existence of an idea does not make it true in any sense.[66] Furthermore, he insists that although on the surface Jung's position might seem to be more friendly to religion than Freud's, it is "in its spirit fundamentally opposed to religions like Judaism, Christianity and Buddhism."[67] It is clear that Jung shares the basic irrationality of Freudian thought, although his approach is somewhat different.

We would agree that Fromm's criticisms of both Jung and Freud have much validity. But does such an admission mean that Fromm has crossed the boundary line from the irrational to the rational in the theistic sense of that term? Fromm is undoubtedly correct in his conclusion that Jung reduced religion "to a psycho-social phenomenon while elevating the unconscious to a religious phenomenon."[68]

Does such an insight mean that Fromm has escaped from the dilemma posed by Freud and Jung? Has he elevated religion in general, and Christianity in particular, to a more honorable position? In particular, can it be said that he has returned to a biblical theism in his view of religion, God, and man? The answer to this question must be a resounding negative.

Fromm is very hostile to any form of what he liked to call an authoritarian religion. This he defined as any recognition on the part of man of some higher and unseen power which controls his destiny.[69] He finds in Calvinism a vivid picture of this authoritarian theistic belief. In submission to such a powerful authority man seeks to escape from his feeling of loneliness and limitation, but on achieving this feeling he pays an awful price—his integrity and independence as an individual.[70] He had the audacity to

65. Eric Fromm, *Psychoanalysis and Religion* (New Haven: Yale University Press, 1972), p. 12.
66. Ibid., p. 15.
67. Ibid., p. 16.
68. Ibid., p. 20.
69. Ibid., p. 34.
70. Ibid., p. 35.

place Calvin as a theist in the class with such authoritarian secular religions as Nazism. It is clear that Fromm's correction of Freud and Jung is not more acceptable than their own positions. The best that Fromm can offer is a humanistic religion which centers around man's strength rather than around his weakness and misery. By this he meant that man must "develop his power of reason in order to understand himself, his relationship to his fellowmen and his position in the universe."[71] From Fromm the key to the problem is not the acceptance of authoritarian religion, whether it be Calvinism, Lutheranism, or the Roman Catholic theology. These theologies can only insure his continued bondage. Man must obtain full freedom for the unfolding and full emergence of reason. This man can achieve through psychoanalysis, for the psychoanalyst is the true physician of the soul. In what manner does the psychoanalyst fulfill this role which Fromm assigned to him? Fromm supplied the answer: "The psychoanalytic cure of the soul aims at helping the patient to achieve an attitude which can be called religious in the humanistic thought though not in the authoritarian sense of the word."[72]

Fromm further held that this pastoral role seeks to enable the patient to gain the ability to see the truth, to love, and to become a free man, responsible to the voice of his conscience.

It is evident that if Fromm did not plunge psychology and psychiatry to the depths of despair, he did nothing to retrieve it from the infamy into which it had fallen at the hands of Freud and Jung. At best, he had merely placed it in another setting with its dilemmas still unsolved and its basic irrationalism still unrelieved and uncorrected.

B. F. Skinner and Behaviorism

Although there are many schools of psychology and psychiatry offering their various cures to a bewildered and guilt-ridden modern society, there are relatively few which demand anything more than passing attention. They are all, for the most part, derivatives from Freud, Jung, or Fromm, and all share the basic weaknesses of their masters to varying degrees and in varying forms. Some have become very influential in modern psychiatry and in the social sciences at large and demand our attention.

Undoubtedly, at the present time, the most important of these is B. F. Skinner and his school of thought. His importance lies not only in his frank admission that man is an animal and little more, but that, as animal, he is to be manipulated for purposes provided for him by social engineers

---

71. Ibid., p. 37.

72. Ibid., p. 93.

who, although animals, have somehow managed to gain a superiority of intellectual powers over their fellow animals and thus are able to plan for them a future which they cannot either plan or achieve for themselves.

Skinner achieved major fame in the academic world with the appearance of his *Beyond Freedom and Dignity,* 1971.[73] The title reveals only too clearly his concept of man, which strips him of these two long-cherished ingredients which have been so basic to the traditional liberal view of human nature. It would be a serious error to conclude that this major work is the real clue to Skinner. This is not the case. The key to Skinner lies in his *Walden Two,* which was first published in 1948.[74] It is in this earlier work that we find the purpose of his psychology and thus the reason for his abysmally low view of man.

In his Introduction to this novel, Skinner depicts the condition of this country as he saw it at the end of World War II. Apparently he feels even more strongly about it today. In his *Behavior of Organisms,* published seven years earlier, Skinner gave the results of his laboratory experiments, but refused at that time to apply them beyond its walls. With the inspiration gained from a series of meetings with a small group of like-minded philosophers, and from the reading of the manuscript of Alice F. Tyler's *Freedom Ferment,* Skinner declared, "I decided to write an account of how I thought a group of, say, a thousand people might have solved the problems of their daily lives with the help of behavioral engineering."[75]

What was, for him, little more than science fiction became a very real possibility for solving the pressing problems facing the nation in the 1960s —the exhaustion of natural resources, overpopulation, pollution, and the possibility of a nuclear holocaust. Thus, *Walden Two* is dedicated to the presentation of a community in which behavioral engineering offers hope for the solving of these problems; it is presented as a kind of pilot project for the leaders of national affairs and the people at large to seriously consider as an alternative way of life. What we see in this utopian presentation is a blueprint for a society in which psychology of the behavioral type, in alliance with sociology, economics, and even political science, can bring about a millennial existence for mankind. The key to its success lies in behavioral engineering. This process presents a frightening picture of what is involved for those who are to undergo this "social engineering." It

73. B. F. Skinner, *Beyond Freedom and Dignity* (New York: Alfred A. Knopf, 1971).

74. B. F. Skinner, *Walden Two* (New York, 1948), reissued in 1976 as *Walden Two Revisited,* with a new commentary by the author.

75. Ibid., p. vi.

could well, and more accurately, be labelled "social manipulation," a process in which many institutions are to combine their respective talents and forces for the manipulation of people for the achievement of predetermined goals. Even more frightening is the fact that these goals are predetermined by psychologists and sociologists who are dedicated to the task of rebuilding society along the lines set forth a century ago by Lester Frank Ward, reinforced by the utopian ideas of Edward Bellamy in his *Looking Backward.*

The basic premise of this novel is that Christianity has nothing to say to the twentieth century. The biblical doctrines of God, man, and sin are meaningless and have no value for the solution of contemporary problems and are, therefore, discardable from our social thought.

Skinner has his apologist in the novel speak concerning the role of religion by dismissing it from the human scene as far as *Walden Two* is concerned.

> So much for our services. No ritual, no dalliance with the supernatural. Just an enjoyable experience, in part aesthetic, in part intellectual. Now, what else does organized religion provide? Aid to the sick and needy? . . . Comfort in time of loss? But why a professional comforter. Isn't that something we have outgrown like professional mourners? . . . Hope for a better world in the future? We like it well enough here on earth. We don't have to be consoled for a vale of tears by promises of heaven.[76]

Christian theism has no place in this utopian society as it is pictured by Skinner. There is no need for salvation, for there is no sin. There is no need for solace and comfort, or the teaching of the moral law and others services performed by the church. In fact, there is no need for the church; social planners have assumed those of its prerogatives which are deemed to have a social value and have banished those which are supernatural in their implications. "Original sin" is presented in terms of having interests which conflict with the interests of everyone else—a purely horizontal and societal definition. Such sins (the pursuit of individual interests at the expense of those of the group) are to be dealt with by the behaviorists. Punishment is to be avoided. It has failed. The apologist for *Walden Two* in the novel speaks to this point very graphically.

> What is emerging at this critical stage in the evolution of society is a behavioral and cultural technology based on positive reenforcement alone.[77]

---

76. Ibid., p. 186.
77. Ibid., p. 244.

Such a conclusion is the logical result of a social philosophy based on the theory of evolution and its resulting concept of the nature of man and society. If there is no God to whom man is responsible, he can be held to account only by society. But society must not punish these "sins," for it has now evolved out of such a state into a new era of social engineering, and the remedy is to be found in Skinner's therapeutic, which he calls "positive reenforcement."[78]

Skinner's moral philosophy (if indeed it deserves to be called this) is the logical consequence of his basic postulates. Although he apparently laments the disintegration of the family, this novel is primarily aimed toward its destruction. Declaring that parents lack the necessary training for the rearing of children, the parents in *Walden Two* commit their children to social experts; young people cohabit with, or without, the intention of marrying, entering into this agreement on an experimental basis. Allegedly, promiscuity is frowned upon strictly on a pragmatic basis—because of the possible unfavorable consequences for the parties involved.

The question may then be raised: What is the good life for the society that accepts his social engineering as a way of life?

Basic to the pursuit and eventual achievement of the good life for the whole community Skinner, through the mouth of his apologist, admits that there is a code to which all must subscribe when they become members of a community. But the function of the code is to act as an aid to the memory until good behavior becomes habitual on the part of all of the members of the community. The resulting good life is one in which all human needs would be met with a minimum of work, hopefully not over four hours a day, and the rest of the time would be spent in the pursuit of carefully chosen cultural activities.

This raises the question: What happens to human freedom in such a social context? Not surprisingly, it receives no serious attention. In fact, the traditional concepts of freedom are cheerfully disregarded. The underlying assumption of this novel is that freedom has been a costly human possession, and for the survival of modern man it must give way to a system of control by social engineering. Frequently this contempt for freedom is expressed in guarded language, for Skinner is well aware of the contemporary passion for this right and that many Americans would be on their guard against a panacea for modern ills such as that which he presents if they should become aware of the fact that it involves the loss of

78. This is dealt with at length in Skinner's *Beyond Freedom and Dignity,* a term which aptly describes his view of man. In his psychology, man is worthy of neither freedom nor dignity, but only of manipulation.

this precious possession. Again Skinner has his apologist ready with an answer which conveys this contempt for freedom:

> We want a government based upon a science of human behavior. Nothing short of that will produce a permanent social structure. For the first time in history we're ready for that . . . because we can now deal with human behavior in accordance with simple scientific principles.[79]

His meaning becomes somewhat more evident in another statement by this apologist:

> When a science of behavior has been achieved, there's no alternative to a planned society. We can't leave mankind to an accidental or biased control. But by using the principle of positive reinforcement—carefully avoiding force or the threat of force—we can preserve a personal sense of freedom.[80]

This is a most revealing statement. When society accepts the principle of social engineering presented by Skinner and his followers, it will have no choice but to accept the planned society it envisages. Its acceptance of its own slavery will not come through the use of force, or even the threat of force. Society will walk into the trap artfully set for it by the behaviorists, who will use the principles of positive reinforcement for the purpose of obtaining their goal. This goal will be a totalitarian society skillfully disguised by politicians in league with their sociological, psychological, and educational allies. This society delineated by Skinner is based upon a political and social theory which completely denies the biblical views of God, man, sin, and redemption. Its new priesthood is the Skinnerian psychologist, who draws up the code and executes the social engineering necessary to bring it into reality. Skinner has well called his book *Beyond Freedom and Dignity,* for the country which follows Skinner follows him beyond human freedom and human dignity into the morass of a totalitarian society which would be far more devastating than anything Hitler ever conceived, or attempted, and perhaps even more dangerous than the present communist totalitarianism, which has so much of the world within its grip. It is an irrationalism run amuck and signifies the end of Western man and his society, which even today somehow manages to confer upon our present culture some restraint and some meaning.

Irrationalism in Contemporary Education

If the influence of B. F. Skinner were confined to psychologists and

79. Skinner, *Walden Two,* p. 182.
80. Ibid., p 248.

psychiatrists, he would be dangerous for American society, but to a somewhat limited extent. However, this is not the case, for he has successfully invaded the ranks of education at all levels, particularly on the junior and senior high levels and the colleges and universities as well. His influence is not confined to the classroom, for he has successfully achieved a vantage point in state boards of education, departments of education, and in the Department of Health, Education and Welfare, where his formula for manipulation has had a peculiar appeal to those educators who, sitting in their ivory towers in Washington, state capitols, and departments of education in colleges over the country, loftily dream of remaking American society by revamping our educational process. The basic approach is Skinner's manipulation, but the word is seldom, if ever, used lest the taxpaying public become aware of how the public schools are being used for the destruction of their nation. Such a discovery would be nothing less than disastrous and must be avoided at all costs. To carry out this deception successfully, an elaborate vocabulary has been devised by which the unwary teachers, and even the less wary parents and the public at large, may be shielded from any real contact with the growing peril which they face and with the unpleasant realization that they are being taxed to support institutions which are engaged in the treasonable activity of destroying American culture and government from the inside.[81]

In the last few decades American education has become the avowed enemy of the American way of life and of the Christian religion as well. In these vital areas it has moved away from the basic purposes of education and from the preservation of our American heritage.

The schools have become agents of manipulation, the agents of social engineering by influencing generation after generation of American young people in the interests of the Skinnerian techniques.

In the first place, education has become anti-intellectual in the sense that the schools are no longer regarded as institutions dedicated to the teaching of truth in the various areas of study. In the second place, education has become either openly atheistic or nearly so in the sense that Christian theology is ignored where it is not more openly denied. Thus, morality,

81. This indictment of the system of education by no means implies that all teachers or professors, school board members or administrators are aware of the conspiracy in which they are involved. Very few of these groups are aware of what is taught in schools of education and to what extent this dangerous philosophy and lethal psychology have made inroads in American education. Some who are aware resist to the extent of their limited capacity. Many of them have found it impossible to buck the entrenched hierarchies in the state departments of education and their all-powerful ally in Washington, the Department of Health, Education and Welfare.

as such, is no longer given serious consideration as a proper aim of the educational process. In the third place, public education, at all levels, has to a much greater extent than is generally recognized by the public at large, become the vehicle for the teaching of radicalism to American young people.

A basic question emerges at this point: How have these developments taken place? How have these glaring failures taken such deep root in the public education system of this country as well as in many private institutions, most of which were founded for the purpose of training young people in the principles and implications of historic Christianity? It is obvious that these three developments have not taken place suddenly. By their very nature this could not be the case. The history of education in America reveals that their roots were planted in the schools even before 1850, and thus the fruits grew very slowly. In fact, they were not clearly observable before 1900. The period of greatest growth may be said to have begun with the arrival of John Dewey at Columbia Teacher's College.[82]

The developments which have taken place over the last half century are the logical fruition of the educational thought which Dewey taught so successfully from this vantage point to thousands of school administrators and teachers and which were adopted by practically every school of education in this country through his multitudinous writings and lectures. Dewey has come into his own in Skinner, who simply adopted his concept of the malleability of human nature to fit what he considered to be the educational needs in the latter decades of the twentieth century. The irrationality of Dewey's Instrumentalism has taken a new and probably even more dangerous direction in Skinner's Behaviorism.

The key to this dedication of the public schools (and universities) of the nation to the destruction of the Christian and traditional values which constituted their foundation in the colonial and early national era of our history is to be found in the rise and extension of the schools of professional education in which nearly all teachers are trained today. Because the states created boards of public instruction to oversee their school systems, it became an easy matter for these schools of education to enter into alliance with these agencies to gain control over teacher accreditation practices of the states and thus to insure that only those teachers who have been subjeced to "Deweyism" could be certified. It is doubtful that there is any state in which public education has not become a legalized monopoly

82. For an excellent and authoritative study of the educational philosophy held by the early leaders of the public school movement during the nineteenth century, see R. J. Rushdoony, *The Messianic Character of American Education* (Nutley, N. J.: Craig Press, 1963).

in the hands of this unholy alliance which exists between state boards of education and the schools of education within the states.[83]

The exaltation of irrationalism and anti-intellectualism thus begins with the professional training of teachers, and this trend is very evident in the textbooks used and the professional literature which pours forth in professional education journals in a veritable flood of words and confusing jargon which bewilder all those but the few who are familiar with the vocabulary used. Since the literature has reached the flood tide, it is impossible to present a wide survey of its contents in this study.

These textbooks are as important for what they do not mention as for what they do teach. An examination of their contents will reveal that such topics as Christianity, theology, religion, and morality are, with rare exceptions, not to be found in the indices of books used in the training of teachers. Where religion is discussed, it is solely in a historical context, generally in chapters concerned with education in the colonial period or in sections dealing with religious instruction or usages in the modern school. Religion is rarely included as a valid basis for education or as a guiding force in what is taught or how it is taught. Traditional Christian morality is also neglected and is replaced by such vague concepts as "acceptable social norms" or "desirable school objectives." These widespread omissions constitute in a very real way the problems besetting modern education.[84]

Modern educational philosophy and psychology, then, rest upon secular and even atheistic principles, fortressed by an unquestioning reliance upon the evolutionary hypothesis as the frame of reference for the understanding of man. Man is no longer seen as having been created in the image of God to think His thoughts after Him and to come to an understanding of culture and nature for the express purpose of fulfilling his cultural mandate. Indeed, the very idea of man having a cultural mandate is abhorrent to most modern educators, and it is never mentioned in textbooks dealing with education.

It is for this reason that it is doubtful that modern secular educators have a philosophy of their subject. Even this traditional aspect of teacher education has been dropped from usage. The courses in the history and philosophy of education which were part of the requirements for certification

83. With the advent of the Department of Health, Education and Welfare on the national level, these fifty different monopolies have now, for all intents and purposes, been congealed into a national monopoly of frightening proportions.

84. These glaring omissions have given rise to widespread protests all over the country, and a concentrated movement for a constitutional amendment to allow the schools to teach religious and moral values is in progress. Another fruit has been the amazing growth of the Christian school movement over the past quarter of a century.

in former days have now been replaced by courses which bear the title "Sociological Foundations of Education." Philosophies of education have been replaced by a reliance upon psychology, and the history of education has virtually been removed from the curriculum. As a result, teachers and administrators have very little real understanding or knowledge of the development and past history of their own discipline. Thus many of the innovations which they hold with such glee are little more than modern adaptations of methods and goals which their predecessors have tried and long since abandoned.

Today the entire process of education is viewed largely in terms of its setting in psychology and sociology. For this reason most literature on the training of teachers centers around the psychological factors involved in the learning process and their sociological impact. It is this reliance upon psychology which has led to the impasse in education today. Thc problem does not necessarily lie with psychology per se, but with the kind of psychology which has come to dominate the schools of education in twentieth-century America.

Contemporary educational psychology finds its premise in the assumption that psychology as a science is "the scientific study of human behavior," and by this the members of this school of thought mean the methodology of the biological sciences. For, in their thinking, man is an animal, complex to be sure, but nevertheless an animal, and is to be studied as such.[85] Granted that not all psychologists accept this environmental and mechanistic view of man, but the mentalist school does not differ materially in regard to the nature of man, nor docs it give any place to the biblical concept of man and the nature of the knowing or learning process. Perhaps the definition of educational psychology found in a rather widely used text offers the most satisfactory insight into what educators really believe about the nature of man and how he learns. "Educational psychology is the empirical foundation of education—that is, it represents those aspects of education which can be verified by experimentation, testing and observation."[86] From which definition the author draws the conclusion that in the final analysis the progress which has been made in educational psychology is bound to affect the philosophical basis of education.[87]

85. Leland H. Stott, *The Psychology of Human Development* (New York: Holt, Rineheart and Winston, 1974), pp. 11-13.

86. Henry Lindgren, *Educational Psychology in the Class Room,* 4th ed. (New York: John Wiley and Sons, 1972), p. 16.

87. Ibid.

This position represents a complete revision of the traditional approach, not only in the Christian approach to education, but also in the earlier forms of humanistic and secular thought as well. Until rather recently, educational philosophy furnished the frame of reference for all other aspects of the teaching-learning process. Now, psychology is in the saddle, and it dictates to philosophy what it must believe. This psychology is naturalistic and deterministic. With the advent of the Skinnerian approach, this revision marks a very serious approach toward a totally irrational view of man and his ability to learn. Man is exalted only to be debased.

With this school of psychology deeply entrenched in the American educational scheme, it was simply a matter of time until the professional hierarchy would demand that the curricular offerings in the public schools, as well as the professional centers of teacher training, should be modified accordingly. This drastic change is now in effect. It did not come overnight, and neither did it take place at the same pace in every part of the nation, but the creation of the Department of Health, Education and Welfare, the standardization of textbooks, and the standardization of the training process have resulted in a virtually complete victory for this anti-intellectual and irrational approach to education throughout the nation.[88]

The total impact of this psychology (or philosophy) is the denial of truth. Education is no longer concerned with transmitting truth—because there is no truth to transmit. There are no values to offer to young people because an empirical psychology (or philosophy) does not support the concept of values or leave any room for their presentation in the classroom.

A perusal of those textbooks dealing with the sociological foundations of education reveals the profound changes which have taken place in the thinking of educators in regard to the goals of education and the means for achieving them.

Over the years the nature of the curriculum offered in the public schools has changed drastically. The evidence suggests that four-year colleges today offer substantially what the better high schools offered in 1900; and, that the high schools offer today a seriously modified version of what the grammar schools offered 75 years ago.[89] Even the graduate schools have

88. This statement does not imply that all teachers have fallen into this mold. There are many older teachers who refuse to accept this view of the teaching process, and a large number of those who go through the humiliating process of certification are aware of what is involved. Once in the profession they refuse to bow to what they have been taught.

89. It is true that the offerings in science do not follow this pattern because of the advances made since that day. But a systematic study of textbooks then and now is most revealing and disheartening.

not been able to escape the pull of this downward trend except possibly in the areas of physics, chemistry, and related disciplines.

Contemporary texts tend to minimize the role of the schools in the transmission of knowledge. In fact, knowledge as such is relegated to a secondary role in favor of a major emphasis upon the encouragement of the achievement of a social awareness and creation of social values. Just how social values can be created in a philosophical atmosphere which is hostile to the idea of absolute truth and binding moral values is not mentioned. The dichotomy at this point is painfully evident. Along with the depreciation of knowledge there comes a similar disdain for teaching traditional moral values of the American heritage.

It never seems to dawn on these architects of the "New Education" that these social values are built on sand, and in the light of the pragmatic philosophy in which they were framed they are susceptible to interprctations which are very different from those intended.

As a result of this entire trend the schools have become the breeding places for sexual immorality, the use of drugs and alcohol, and other crimes of a serious nature. The retreat from learning has become a veritable rout, and many teachers have become the objects of violence on the part of their unruly and criminally inclined prisoners in their classrooms or offices. Teaching in the large cities has become a hazardous occupation. The more dedicated young teachers lose heart and leave the profession to those who are more hardened and who frequently are teaching just for the money, with little or no concern for the high professional requirements which their calling once demanded.

Textbook publishers have eagerly adapted to the new educational psychology and produce textbooks which meet its demands. History texts have been re-worked to be little more than social science surveys with a few facts included to reenforce the social theories advanced between their covers.[90]

Textbooks not only fail miserably as instruments by which the knowledge of the truth is transmitted, but they have become, in part, the purveyors of immorality and even pornography. An interesting and important case in point is the recent West Virginia textbook controversy. This controversy received national attention in the newspapers, on television, and

90. The author recently saw a rather widely used text in history, designed for use in senior high school, which proudly announced in its Introduction that it was not intended to convey facts, but to raise questions in the minds of the students. It admittedly fulfilled its first purpose but, by the same token, failed completely in the second. Without the foundation furnished by a factual approach to history, it is difficult to understand how a student can be induced to ask meaningful questions.

by way of radio. The coverage which it received was very misleading, and it is difficult to escape the conclusion that the deception was deliberate.[91]

In the field of education we see the fruits of the irrationalism of contemporary thought enshrined in the training of young people in our nation. Through its introduction into the schools this irrational view of God, truth, man, and the purposes of education have gained a footing which enables the architects of this educational philosophy to have a popularity which neither philosophers, political thinkers, sociologists, nor economists could ever gain for it.

This philosophy has become the frame of reference for most of the people of the nation. In gaining such a strategic victory it has paralyzed their ability to think clearly and to act in regard to this penetrating poison. The programs on television, the music on records, the novels that become the best sellers, the various religious cults which are able to claim such large followings among so many unenlightened people—all testify to the breakdown of the American heritage and the irrational nature of the intellectual and cultural activities of our day.

Historians and the Interpretation of the Western Heritage

Along with political science, psychology, and economics, the study and writing of history reflects the debasement which has taken place in Western thought. The close alliance between philosophical and historical thought which became apparent with Kant and Hegel has become even more close since their day. In the twentieth century the irrational trend in contemporary philosophy has cast its heavy shadow over historical scholarship until there is hardly a school of philosophy which does not have its counterpart among historians.

As a result, historical scholarship has ebbed and flowed between determinism and sheer chance in its choices as the basic factors in human affairs, between economic and environmental determinism, between a belief that facts speak for themselves and the more current schools which hold that history can never attain a knowledge of the facts as they really

---

91. The author had the privilege of personally investigating some of the material in this dispute. There is no doubt that it is pornographic, communistic, and designed to break down the American family as well as the moral fiber of the students who used it. The material was so obscene that to quote from it in a radio or television program would have given just cause for action leading to the withdrawal of the license of the broadcasting station guilty of allowing it to be used on the air. Yet it was believed that this was fit material to be used in the fifth, sixth, seventh, and eighth grades of the public schools.

happened. It has alternated between the conviction that there is meaning to be found in the flow of events and the equally strong conviction that the stream of history is without meaning except that meaning which the historian himself confers upon it. In a similar manner it has fluctuated between those who espouse communism and the New Left and those who are addicted to an existential approach to the interpretation of historical events.[92] As a generalization we may conclude that the writing and interpretation of history has veered sharply from the optimism of the early 1900s to a thinly disguised pessimism in more recent years, and that the study of history today is verging on chaos as a result of its subjection to the contemporary philosophical currents which have brought the Western mind to the verge of meaninglessness and despair.[93] However, at the same time, because of the importance of its role in human affairs, this loss of identity for history as a worthwhile study and academic discipline has had the very unfortunate effect of accelerating the debasement of Western culture. Western culture has reached the place where it can no longer understand itself or its present dilemma because it no longer understands or appreciates its own heritage and the roots from which it sprang. The deprecation of history as a necessary discipline and area of human knowledge can only accelerate the decline of the West and speed it on its way to oblivion and destruction.

We have seen that the irrational approach to the study of history had its roots in the philosophies of Kant and Hegel. The positive reaction to this approach, however, deepened the sense of futility and confusion among those historians who clung to the belief that it was still their task to ascertain the facts and then draw meaningful and valid conclusions from their investigations which could then be regarded as historical truths.

The frustrations of twentieth-century historical scholarship are actually the continuation of the confusion of the nineteenth. This called forth the efforts of Collingwood and Croce in Europe and Beard, Becker, and others in this country to find a new approach which would avoid the errors inherent in the various nineteenth-century attempts to formulate a philosophy of history. Both positivism and idealism had failed to achieve their goals.

The bankruptcy of present historical scholarship is found in R. G. Collongwood's philosophical approach to the meaning of history in England

92. There have been some intrepid historians who have even tried to use Freudian principles in their interpretation of such great characters as Martin Luther.

93. It is for this reason that the study of history has been brought into question in many colleges and universities and has given rise to the trend to integrate with the other disciplines into a hazy collection of courses known as "the social sciences."

and to the application of this type of thinking in the works of Charles Beard and Carl Becker in this country.

R. G. Collingwood (1889–1943), the Oxford philosopher, was an important figure in twentieth-century English academic circles. Defending the study of history as an autonomous branch of human knowledge, he argued for its acceptance and respectability in philosophical circles. But for this recognition he forced historical scholarship to pay a heavy price, which was nothing less than the forfeiture of its claim to intellectual respectability, a claim which he felt that he had made secure. In his essay, "The Historical Imagination," first published in 1935 and then later included in his *Idea of History,* Collingwood repudiated not only the positivist approach to historical investigation, but all those schools of interpretation which insist that facts have an objectivity of their own apart from the mind of the historians, and that historians can recapture past events in some way by recourse to the scientific methodology.

As a replacement for these rejected approaches, Collingwood offered one of his own and insisted that the historian must come to the realization that he is his own authority and that his own thought is both autonomous and self-authorizing. Thus, the criterion of historical truth cannot be the fact that some statement is made by an authority, simply because it is the truthfulness and information of the so-called authority which is in question. The historian must answer the question for himself on his own authority.[94] Even if the historian accepts what the authorities say, he does not because they say it, but because what they say satisfies his own criterion of historical truth.

For Collingwood, then, what is the criterion of historical truth? If it is not to be found in an agreement of authorities and the sources, where can the historian turn in his quest for historical certainty? Collingwood found the answer to this question in what he called the web of imagination, by which he meant the historian's own *a priori* imagination. This *a priori* furnishes the historian with a picture of the past which, in turn, justifies the sources which the historian uses in its construction. He gives credence to the sources only because they are justified in such a manner. This *a priori* imagination enables the historian to judge whether the picture of the past to which the evidence leads is a coherent and continuous picture; in short, whether it makes sense or not.

Collingwood assigned to the *a priori* imagination the task of evaluating

---

94. R. G. Collingwood, *The Idea of History* (Oxford: Oxford University Press, 1959), pp. 236-238.

the data which it also uses at the same time in constructing its picture of the past. In such an approach, what constitutes evidence?

The issue is very acute, for Collingwood denied that evidence is historical knowledge "to be swallowed and regurgitated by the historian." The historian must do something to the facts presented to him. In sweeping terms Collingwood insisted that everything is evidence which the historian can use as evidence. The entire perceptible world is potentially, and in principle, the evidence which the historian may use. But to use it he must come to it with the proper kind of historical knowledge. Evidence exists only when someone contemplates it historically. Otherwise, it is only perceived fact and "historically dumb."

His conclusion is that historical knowledge can arise only from historical knowledge or insight. If this is the case, how does this knowledge begin at all? His answer to this question is found in his assumption that historical thinking is an original and fundamental activity of the human mind, by which he seems to mean that the idea of the past is a kind of innate idea. Thus, historical thinking is that activity of the imagination by which we seek to provide this innate idea with a detailed content. We do this by using the present as the evidence for its own past. Collingwood thus taught that every present has a past of its own. Thus any imaginative reconstruction of the past aims at reconstructing the past of this particular present. But the perceptible present can never be perceived or interpreted in its entirety. Consequently, in the writing of history no achievement and no interpretation can be final. Collingwood extended this dictum to all areas of human intellectual activity.

He thus plunged the study of history into a morass of skepticism. Since every generation must rewrite history in its own way, younger historians must not be content with giving new answers to old questions. They must actually reverse the questions. He viewed history as a river into which no man can step twice. It must not be assumed that he was unaware of the latent skepticism in this concept, and he quickly repudiated such a possibility by declaring that what appears to be an inherent skepticism is only "the discovery of a second dimension of historical thought; the history of history; the discovery that the historian himself, together with the here-and-now which formed the total body of evidence available to him, is a part of the process he is studying, has its own place in that process, and can see it only from the point of view which at this moment he occupies within it."[95]

---

95. Ibid., p. 84.

Collingwood's efforts to correct the errors of nineteenth-century history were utterly futile. His extreme subjectivism could only mean the negation of any objective truth in history and therefore must lead to the conclusion that history possesses no objectively discernible purpose or meaning. The historian creates them for himself. Collingwood banished the theistic view of history to the sidelines of human intellectual activity and substituted a concept of historical truth in which autonomous man is the sole judge of truth. It is little wonder that contemporary historical study is a jungle of conflicting claims and interpretations and that today history has as many meanings as there are scholars and laymen who seek to interpret it. Historical scholarship has floundered on the shoals of humanism and is struggling with despair and a deep sense of futility.

Arnold Toynbee

Among European interpreters of history during the twentieth century, Arthur Spengler gained a temporary influence in his *Decline of the West,* in which he set forth a deterministic and cyclical view of history reminiscent of Veco. In relating the pattern of history to the seasons of the year he painted a hopeless picture of the human scene which denied both meaning and purpose to history. In relying upon a highly rationalistic interpretation of human events he gave a philosophy of history which was as irrational as it was pessimistic. His influence declined almost as rapidly as it had emerged, and today he is seldom read or given serious consideration.

Of far greater importance and lasting influence is the massive effort of Arnold Toynbee to rescue history from the grip of philosophical determinism and to offer some hope to the world that was reeling from the blows it had received at the hands of Hitler, Stalin, and Mussolini and from the wounds that it had received from World War II.[96]

Although many of Toynbee's critics, as well as more than a few of his admirers, have compared him to Augustine, there is no real basis for such a comparison. The similarities are superficial and the differences so great as to create an impossible cleavage. It is difficult to explain how any scholar who understands Augustine could arrive at such a conclusion. Although Toynbee, unlike Spengler, frequently mentions Christianity and the Scriptures, and seemingly gives to the church a vital role in his interpretation of history, it is also clear that Toynbee's God is not the God of Scriptures. In fact, Toynbee frankly admitted that he was in debt to

96. Arnold Toynbee, *A Study of History,* 12 vols. (Oxford and New York: Oxford University Press, 1934–1961).

Edward Gibbon, Carl Jung, Plato, John Stuart Mill, Goethe, and Hume. The influence of Bergson is also very evident in Toynbee's concept of challenge and response, which bears a strong resemblance to Bergson's *élan vitale.* In his own personal religious thinking he virtually repudiated Christianity.

Although Toynbee made a strenuous effort to avoid the determinism which was so dominant in Spengler's *Decline of the West,* a careful reading of his works brings the conclusion that he was not able to do so; thus this massive and scholarly effort to give a meaningful and authoritative answer to the problems of human history was, at best, only partially successful, for his philosophy denied the great biblical doctrines without which history must remain a hopeless riddle.

Although he valiantly strove to escape the snares which beset Hegel, Marx, and Spengler, his effort ended in ultimate failure "because he refused to see that the sovereign God alone has given meaning to His creation and to all history, over which He is the Lord. Once again the attempt to find the meaning from within has ended in failure."[97]

Historical writing in America in the early decades of the present century was heavily influenced by the optimism engendered by the popularity of the Darwinian theories and by the tremendous technological developments which the nation was enjoying. Darwinism was the prophetic voice of the American future. Scientific and technological advances constituted the prophetic voice, giving added authority to the dogmatic pronouncements of scientists and their political allies. This unbridled and unallayed optimism concerning the future of the nation and the human race reached a new high in the oratory which characterized the election of 1912. Historical scholarship was not immune to the contagion, even though some historians were adding words of caution and caustic criticism of American political and economic institutions. Even their cynicism was tempered and fortified by an underlying devotion to Darwinian principles.

In his early works Charles Beard appeared as the champion of economic determinism as the key to the understanding of American history.[98] In these works it was his intention to strip away earlier interpretations which glorified the Washington-Jefferson era and set forth the view that these earlier patriots were largely motivated by economic considerations as they

97. C. Gregg Singer, *Toynbee* (Philadelphia: Presbyterian and Reformed, 1968), p. 76.

98. Charles Beard, *An Economic Interpretation of the Constitution of the United States* (New York, 1913), and *Economic Origins of Jeffersonian Democracy* (New York, 1915).

framed the Constitution and established the new nation. In these works, Beard managed to combine his cynical concepts of human nature with Darwinian hope for the future. He did not disregard our national past, but in his economic interpretations he not only wrote for the purpose of exposing what he regarded as the errors of former historians, but for his own great purpose of proving that under the impact of Darwinism in the social realm the nation had passed beyond the assumptions of 1787 to higher ground. By attacking these institutions, particularly the Constitution, for the purpose of undermining their popular authority, it was his hope to prepare the way for an even greater evolutionary development of American society toward a true democracy, a collectivist society, freed from the shackles of eighteenth- and early nineteenth-century political theory.

Since the Constitution of 1787 was the most significant embodiment of the traditional philosophy of law and government from which he wished to free the American people, this document became the object of his attacks. His weapon was the economic interpretation of history which he derived largely from the work of Frederick Jackson Turner in his famous "frontier thesis" concerning the origins and development of American democracy.[99] This approach to American history was frankly deterministic, and Beard reshaped this deterministic approach into a doctrine of economic determinism. In essence, this approach to the understanding of history rests upon a major premise that, since the existence of man depends upon his ability to sustain himself, the economic aspects of life are therefore the determining facts in human activity. Although this statement is not as materialistic as that found in Marx, it partakes of the Marxian assumptions and must be regarded as irrational in content and implications.[100]

Beard's irrationalism appeared in another and no less dangerous form in his rather famous presidential address delivered to the American Historical Association in 1933, entitled "Written History As an Act of Faith."[101] This address was an attack on the use of the scientific method in historical scholarship. He maintained its use is impossible because every historian is a product of his age, and his work must necessarily reflect the

99. He also acknowledged his indebtedness to Edwin R. A. Seligman's *Economic Interpretation of History* (New York, 1902).

100. Even if it is granted that Beard underwent a major change in his outlook on history in his later writings, and particularly in his *President Roosevelt and the Coming War in 1941*, there is no convincing evidence that he ever forsook his basic assumptions proclaimed in 1913.

101. *American Historical Review* XXXIX, 2 (January, 1934), 219-229.

spirit of the times, of a nation, of a race, a group, class, or section.[102]

In his discussion of the nature of history and what he felt was the proper methodology, Beard reaffirmed the views of Benedetto Croce that history is essentially contemporary thought about the past. Thus history, as a discipline, is really what the historian thinks about the past actuality as he reconstructs it in terms of his own philosophical outlook. All historians reflect their own predilections in their choice of areas of history for investigation and in regard to the facts which they will present in their works. For Beard, then, the term "history" means history as thought about past actuality and not of the actuality itself, or even specific knowledge about that past.

Beard was equally insistent that the historian must cast off his servitude to the assumptions of natural science. He clearly saw that the intellectual operations which historians have borrowed from both the physical and biological sciences have greatly restricted their activities. He indicted historians for borrowing from the methodology of the physical sciences on the assumption of causation. He charged that under the hypothesis that it is necessary to imitate the natural scientists, historians have been arranging events in neat little chains of causation which explain why succeeding events take place.

With equal fervor Beard also rejected the approach to history of those scholars like Spengler who, relying on Darwin, conceived of history as a succession of cultural organisms rising, growing, maturing, and declining. Darwinism could not possibly furnish an answer to the problem of the meaning of history.

This rejection of looking to the methodology of science for the answer posed a serious dilemma for Beard, which he was quick to recognize. Having broken with the tyranny of the scientific method, historiography was in danger of coming to the conclusion that all written history is merely relative to time and circumstances and therefore a passing shadow, or an illusion.

Beard's remedy lay in his affirmation that, as all absolutes in history are to be rejected, the absolute of relativity must also be rejected. So Beard could argue that "as actuality moves forward into the future, the concept of relativity will also pass as previous conceptions and interpretations of events have passed." Thus for Beard there existed the happy possibility that, according to the doctrine of relativity, the skepticism involved in

102. Charles A. Beard, *The Philosophy of History in Our Time,* reprinted in Hans Meyerhoff, op. cit., pp. 140-151.

this doctrine will also pass away. But is not this hope based on a subtle reintroduction of the absolute of an unconscious reliance on Darwin, a reliance which he had already repudiated as an integral part of historical methodology? He was also aware of this dilemma and offered the hope that when the historian accepts none of the assumptions of theology, philosophy, physics, or biology, "when he passes out from the fleeting shadow of relativity, he confronts the absolute in his field—the absolute totality of all historical occurrences, past, present, and becoming to the end of all things."[103]

When the historian arrives at this point in his quest for meaning, he has but three choices to accept: the idea that history as a total actuality is chaos; that history as actuality is part of some order and revolves in cycles eternally; or, that history is moving in some direction away from the low level of primitive beginnings on an upward gradient toward a more ideal order of some kind. Beard admitted that there was evidence for each of these possible approaches. Nevertheless he insisted that "all the available evidence will not fit any one of them." But if the evidence does not fit any of these three possible choices, what choice is left to the historian?

Beard's answer to this query reveals only the hopelessness inherent in his position. He voiced his hope for historiography in the idea that written history is an act of faith, by which he meant the conviction that something true can be known about the movement of history. This conviction is a subjective decision and is not based upon objective evidence. His dilemma remained. He was still unwilling to casually dismiss the scientific method as of no value. He wrote: ". . . nor is the empirical or scientific method to be abandoned. It is the only method that can be employed in obtaining accurate knowledge of historical facts, personalities, situations and movements. It alone can disclose conditions that made possible what happened. It has a value in itself—a value high in the hierarchy of values indispensable to the life of a democracy." Beard dismissed the scientific methodology in historical studies only to bring it in again by the back door.

He apparently did not realize the scientific methodology cannot yield value (by definition) and that it cannot give rise to values indispensable for the life of a democracy. He was indulging in a vain hope. Beard's assumption that written history is an act of faith was betrayed by his own philosophy. If it is an act of faith, a faith in what? For this question he had no answer.

---

103. Ibid., p. 148.

After affirming his conviction that history in some mysterious way is moving forward to the emergence of a collectivistic democracy, he offered his final testimony:

> History is chaos and every attempt to interpret it otherwise is an illu--sion. History moves around in a kind of cycle. History moves in a line straight or spiral, and in some direction. The historian may seek to escape these issues by silence or by a confession of avoidance or he may face them boldly, aware of the intellectual and moral perils inherent in any decision—in his act of faith.[104]

As we sadly draw the curtain on Beard's philosophy of history, we are forced to the conclusion that, for him, written history could not be an act of faith, because he had no real faith in the knowability of historical facts. At best, his faith was faith in man the historian. But for that man, history, as such, must ever remain in hopeless puzzle and the quest for historical knowledge an endless futility. For Beard history was essentially irrational. To him it reveals no guiding purpose or meaning because it is divorced from the control of a sovereign God.

This irrationality and meaninglessness of history is starkly revealed in another prominent and influential American historian, Carl Lotus Becker (1873–1945). In his works he also relied on the relativism of R. G. Collingwood. Becker offered a clear and concise statement of his philosophy of history in a series of essays, the most important of which are "Everyman His Own Historian" and "What are Historical Facts?"[105] Like Collingwood, Becker was very critical of the positivist insistence that the historian must allow the facts to speak for themselves. He denied the positivist contention that the simple historical fact is a hard, cold something with a clear outline and measurable. Becker was correct in his assertion that it is utterly impossible for the facts of history to speak through the historians. The nature of these facts does not make it possible for them to be treated in this manner. However, Becker was not content to stop at this point. Using it as a springboard, he then insisted that the historian cannot deal with historical events themselves but only with the statements that the facts did occur. The historian can deal only with the affirmation that something is true. Becker drew what he felt was a very important distinction between the ephemeral events which disappear and the affirmation about those same events which persists. For him the his-

---

104. Presidential address delivered to the American Historical Association, December 29, 1931, and found in a book under the same title (New York, 1935).

105. *Western Political Quarterly* VIII, 3 (1955), 327-340. Reprinted in Meyerhoff, op. cit., pp. 120-137.

torical fact is not the event itself, but a symbol which enables the historian to recreate it imaginatively. He argued that it is dangerous to maintain that the symbol is either false or true. The most that a historian can claim for a symbol is that it is more or less appropriate. Appropriate for what? He did not deal with this most important question.

In keeping with this basic approach to the nature of historical facts, Becker then went on to discuss the question of the location of these historical facts or symbols. With more than a touch of dogmatism, he insisted that these historical facts must be in someone's mind or they are nowhere. As an illustration he selected the assassination of Lincoln, which took place on April 14, 1865. This was an actual event. But we now speak of it as a historical fact. "The event was, but is no longer. It is only the affirmed fact about the event that now is, that persists, and will persist until we discover that our affirmation is wrong or inadequate."[106]

This distinction led Becker to the admission that there are two histories—the actual series of events and the ideal series which we affirm and hold in memory. The first is absolute and unchanging, while the second is relative and always changing. He tried to avoid a dilemma at this point by announcing that the two usually correspond as much as possible. In brief, the task confronting the historian, according to him, is to arrange that the relative and changing correspond with the absolute and unchanging. Just how the historian was to accomplish this impossible task he never explained.

Becker then proceeded to discuss the question: What is the historical fact for? In his analysis of this question his subject and relative analysis is more pronounced. His theory was that if the historical fact is present imaginatively in someone's mind, then it must be part of the present. Thus, he presented himself and his colleagues with another dilemma. Since the present is a very slippery thing and an indefinite point in time, the image or the idea which the historian has present in his mind slips instantly into the past.

Becker ended his discussion with a confession of bankruptcy: "In truth the actual past is gone, and the world of history is an intangible world recreated imaginatively and present in our minds." This admission brings with it the logical conclusion that this living history, the ideal series of events which he historian holds in memory, is in a state of flux. It cannot be precisely the same for all historians at any given time or the same for one generation as for another. Thus, every generation rewrites the history

---

106. Carl L. Becker, *Every Man His Own Historian* (Chicago, 1966), p. 234.

of its own part to suit its own needs. Becker closed his essay, "Everyman His Own Historian," with the observation that however accurately we may determine the facts of history, "the facts themselves and our interpretation of our interpretations will be seen in a different perspective or a less vivid light as mankind moves into the unknown future."[107]

The entire thrust of Becker's interpretation militates against any possibility of the discovery of an objective meaning and purpose in the human past. Yet, for the greater part of his professional career, he was able to synthesize in his own thinking this relativism with the conviction that the triumph of democracy was the key to human history and the hope for the future. Not until the closing years of his life did he surrender this allegiance to the eventual triumph of democracy and yield to the pessimism inherent in his philosophy. His frustration and even despair became evident in his last major work on modern democracy.

Conclusion

This rather brief survey of contemporary Western life and thought can only bring with it the conclusion that it is a cut-flower civilization, living off the fast-dwindling reserves bequeathed to it by its theistic forebears, and that unless these reservoirs are replenished by the rich truths of Christian theism, our civilization will disappear as have its many predecessors. No civilization can live in the light of a philosophy which denies that it has meaning and purpose. Deprived of the inspiration of its biblical foundation, such a civilization soon loses the will to survive and fulfill its cultural mandate. Many observers believe that Western culture has reached this stage in its history.

107. Ibid., pp. 254-255.

Chapter 14
Conclusion: The Recovery of Christian Theism

In the preceding chapters we have traced the results of the departure from biblical theism in the life of Western culture from the Renaissance to the present day. The gradual disintegration of the rationalism of the early forms of humanism into the irrationalism of the twentieth century has been the major theme of this work. This disintegration has not been confined to the world of thought alone, but has made itself manifest in every aspect of modern culture, to such an extent that we hardly dare to describe the modern scene in any terminology which has been used to describe previous cultures and their accompanying civilizations. Some historians and theologians have preferred to use the term "post-Christian" to define the contemporary situation. Such a description, of course, fails to satisfy those scholars who refuse to believe that there can be such an entity as a culture which is under the influence of Christian orthodoxy to such an extent that it possesses a theistic character. Furthermore, they are also unwilling to accept the concept as a post-Christian culture because of its connotations that this culture is somehow inherently inferior to a Christian culture. Such an admission, in their eyes, constitutes a negation of their belief in the doctrine of cultural evolution, to which they cling with desperation.

Nevertheless, the descent of the rationalistic humanism of the Renaissance into the intellectual and theological wastelands has been the major theme of this study, we have traced the continuing failure of rationalistic philosophy to offer satisfactory answers to the questions which have confronted it. This rationalism for the last five centuries has had as its correlative an inescapable irrationalism which has haunted all modern humanistic and scientific thought from that period even until the twentieth century.

The empirical epistemology of Locke and his followers was no more successful than the rationalism which it replaced. Its major contribution to Western culture was to enhance the emergence of a secularism thoroughly embedded in materialism, a materialism which characterized the French Revolution and which ultimately produced Marxian communism and its philosophical satellites.

We have seen that this departure from Christian theism, involving an arduous journey through rationalism, empiricism, idealism, utilitarianism, pragmatism, scientific naturalism, and existentialism, brought with it a secularization of every aspect of modern civilization. Beginning with the revolt from historic Christian theology, it took its toll in political, social, and economic thought and practice, in education, and in the fine arts. Its impact left no elements of Western culture untouched or unaffected with its virus. Not only has this development left the Christian church and Christian theism outside the mainstream of modern culture, without influence and acceptance, but it has also placed contemporary man in the position of being ignorant of both the past and future, which he can neither know nor understand, and in the midst of an existential present which can only horrify him and destroy his confidence in all human institutions. He has thus been brought to the very depths of despair. With no heritage to guide him in the present and no future to beckon him to further cultural accomplishments, modern man has become the prisoner of his own irrationalism.

We have traced the decline of philosophy from the rationalism of Descartes through empiricism to existentialism. But this journey which philosophy took into the realm of the irrational was shared by theology, which, forsaking the heritage of both the Roman Catholic Church and the Reformers, found an abode in this same dark cavern.

Since theology shapes all of human thought, in either a positive or negative manner, Western culture has traversed the same rocky path. By 1900 political thought was steering its course toward modern totalitarianism through the route provided by Hegel and Nietzsche or by an equally dangerous pathway prepared by Hegel, Marx, Lenin, Stalin, and contemporary Marxist thought and practice. In both cases Darwinism added a powerful incentive for the creation of an absolutism out of the remains of European liberalism. In short, all contemporary political philosophies and forms of political government have either already ended in the embrace of some form of despotism or are headed in this direction. Those who have placed their faith in socialism as a safe form of collectivism which will also act as a safeguard in the defense of human rights have been sorely disappointed to find that socialism can lead only to absolutism, the absolutism of a controlled majority. Those who have placed their faith and their hope for the future in democracy are likewise doomed to disappointment. Contemporary events loudly proclaim the solemn lament that humanism, whatever form it may take in the political realm, is not only no defense against totalitarianism, but actually becomes an invitation for its formation and a vestibule through which it enters into already established governments and changes them into absolutisms of the most uncontrolled and uncontrollable kind.

This ironic development should not come as a surprise to those who understand the basic assumptions of modern liberalism. The classical view of human freedom, shared by empiricists and rationalists alike, by liberals and conservatives was, and is, in no way prepared to offer a meaningful and sustaining defense of human freedom.

Liberals have traditionally relied upon the seventeenth- and eighteenth-century doctrine of natural rights for the formulation of their political philosophy. All too often conservatives have placed their faith in the same doctrine, not realizing that they could not win the battle against liberalism if they chose these same weapons for their warfare.

This doctrine of natural rights, allied with the Declaration of Independence and other liberal documents, seemingly affirmed a grand and irrefutable plan of government. Such is not the case. Liberalism, with its belief in the autonomy of the rational man and his inherent goodness, found itself in the position of constantly demanding an increase in the powers of government to force man to be good and to prevent him from engaging in evil acts. Thus contemporary liberalism has become the dominant factor in the tremendous expansion of the powers of government to such a degree that they are willing to create a democratic dictatorship to offset the inherent weaknesses of their own liberal outlook.

Conservatives are not free from such a dilemma, for many of them have adopted the same basic liberal political philosophy. Their own defense against the liberal demand for increased governmental powers has been a pragmatic answer that the powers desired by the liberals are not workable or go too far. Neither of these arguments is a valid approach to the problem. Who is to say that any given power or policy will not work if a majority within a democratic society has decreed that it will, and who is to say an act of Congress or the President, or a decision of the Supreme Court goes too far if the majority of the citizens support the action?

Neither American liberalism nor conservatism has been willing to look to the scriptural basis for government and restrict its functions to those given to it by the Bible. With no anchor in the Word of God, modern government drifts with the ebb and flow of popular opinion, and the general current has been steadily in the direction of an absolutist or totalitarian regime arising out of the ruins of the democratic state, which has already cast the Constitution aside as a viable form of government for contemporary man.

This development, which has taken place over the last 75 years and which has gained much momentum during the past 40 years, is a direct result of the insistence that man is autonomous and not subject to a sovereign God. When any state denies the sovereignty of God in the management of its political, economic, and social affairs, it finds it necessary to erect a human sovereignty as a substitute. Then the question arises: Where is the source and home of this human sovereignty? History has repeatedly proved that it cannot be located in the people at large and that some elitist group will emerge to assume a sovereign role and run the state accordingly. Statism, in all of its forms, is the logical result of autonomous man attempting to govern himself.

The determinism in this Natural Law philosophy produced a relativism not only in the prevailing philosophy of government, but, as we have seen, also brought relativism into the meaning of law. Law has become a relative concept, framed in terms of what the community regards as socially useful, or harmful, at any given time, rather than a reflection of the law of God in regard to human conduct. Modern sociology and psychology have contributed to this flexible concept of the nature of law and added to the legal confusion of the day. As a result, our courts, for the most part, no longer dispense justice, but rather state the prevailing attitude of the community on moral, social, and political issues. For this reason abortion, the women's liberation movement, the increasing acceptance of the use of drugs, and sex before and without the benefit of marriage, along with homosexuality, have gained a legal acceptance which has no standing of any kind in the law of God, and which is contrary to the plain statements of the Scriptures in regard to human conduct. Pragmatism reigns almost unchallenged in the realm of the administration of justice and the popular conception of law. Conservatives, as well as liberals, have fallen victim to this interpretation of the moral law. The result has been the triumph of irrationalism in human and social relations. The autonomy of the rational man has degenerated into the autonomy of an irrational society.

In the realm of economic thought and practice a similar development (or degeneration) has taken place. The biblical view of the nature and rightful possession and use of wealth has given way to an unbiblical insistence that the wealth of a nation should benefit and be used ostensibly for the purpose of realizing an economic equality within a democratic society. Thus society through the use of government has endeavored to devise many means of achieving this goal. Some of these devious ways have been the use of the graduated income tax, the social security system, and welfare programs. These efforts have extended the powers of modern government far beyond their proper limits and have brought this nation, and most of the nations of the Western world, to the brink of an uncontrollable inflation and national bankruptcy.[1] The net result of this type of spending program has not brought the economic equality which the liberals have promised to the American people, but rather have they endangered the fiscal stability of the nation and of the security programs which form the foundation of this entire liberal political and economic establishment.[2]

Thoughtful liberals, with their conservative colleagues in both government and business, are extremely disturbed by the steady growth of the national debt and the ensuing inflation. The liberals and radicals in both the executive and the legislative branches of the government are caught in a web of their own making and are afraid to reveal to the electorate the depths of their campaign deception and their inability to fulfill the promises which they so easily made with little thought as to how they would be fulfilled.

The social life of the nation is facing the results of a similar deterioration in the moral structure of the American people. The Puritan heritage has lost its momentum, and even its memory is fading from the national scene. Psychology, sociology, liberal theology, and the media have engaged in a conspiracy to produce moral chaos in this country. Their efforts have met with unbelievable success. Abortion, homosexuality, and illicit sex in all its forms have become an accepted way of life for many Americans. "Doing one's own thing" has become the only moral standard which has any validity in the eyes of millions who have lost the moral perspective found in the Scriptures.

In this frontal attack on Christian morality as the foundation for social life and relations, the liberals have again created their own trap. The Watergate scandal and other outbursts of "anti-social" conduct on the part of government leaders created a tremendous outburst of disapproval

1. At the present writing the national debt of the United States has approached the 700-billion-dollar mark, and the total of future national commitments to over $500 trillion. Such sums stagger the imagination; yet, presidents and other allegedly responsible officials assure us that the budget can and must be budgeted and that we should not be alarmed by such figures, since we only owe this debt to ourselves.

2. At present writing the Social Security system is in serious plight, and many economists are thoroughly alarmed and are in grave doubt as to whether it can survive in its present form.

in Congress, the press, and the people at large. But why should it have created such an uproar? This anarchistic moral theory knows no limits and attacks every segment of society. The liberals who preached moral relativity in the realm of individual morality were totally unprepared for its invasion of the public domain and exuded great indignation at this unwarranted development.

Although it is unwarranted to conclude that all men in public life and holding public office are infected with the moral degradation which has gripped the nation, it is fair to conclude that it is far more rampant in these circles than is generally known. The revelations concerning Watergate, while probably necessary, were in a real sense politically inspired and were artfully conceived to turn the attention of the voters away from other and more serious moral problems which were lurking just beneath the surface of life in Washington.

This moral corruption is a direct result of the social philosophies which have gained the ascendancy in the life of the American people. They are the result of the assertion of human autonomy and the negation of the sovereignty of God in national as well as the individual life. This immorality is part of the irrationality now resident in our national and individual affairs to an alarming degree.

Likewise, this same irrationalism has gripped our educational thought and practice and has reduced the public schools and many colleges and universities to a level which is far below that of 40 or 50 years ago. The public schools are being used for purposes which are not the legitimate role for educational institutions. Colleges and universities have become nurseries for the demoralization of their students and the destruction of any belief in the American tradition or historic Christianity. In place of solid scholarship based upon scriptural presuppositions they have, to a great extent, substituted a thoroughly humanistic pagan philosophy of education which, in turn, has guided the content of the curriculum along similar channels, introducing methods of presentation in harmony with these irrational purposes which have been widely adopted by most of our educational institutions. If manipulation of the younger students has been the unannounced aim of public education on the elementary and secondary levels, this same purpose occupies an important place in the thought of the leaders in higher education. While this may, seemingly, take different forms which appear to be harmless and even legitimate, the general conclusion must be that our educational institutions of higher learning are one of the major factors in the decline of the Western mind and the breakdown of contemporary civilization.

The breakdown of the Western mind into irrationalism could result only in the decline of the civilization to which it had given birth, and as a result the remnants of that civilization which still survive can well be called a "cut-flower civilization." Living on the heritage of a past, the roots of which have been severed, this civilization faces disaster of a magnitude which must stagger the human mind. The closest parallel to that which is now taking place was the fall of the Roman Empire, a disaster which has no equal in the annals of the history of the West. We know the traumatic effects which that event had on the people who lived through it and were the unwilling witnesses of the destruction of that magnificent state with its magnificent political structure. The task of reconstruction took seven centuries; some historians would set the figure closer to a thousand years. They take the position that it was not until about 1400 that it could be said that Europe had recovered and rebuilt a civilization equivalent to that which was lost in the fall of Rome. The lesson is easily discerned that rebuilding takes a long time and is not easily achieved.

The difficulty in rebuilding Western civilization is compounded today and presents a greater and more formidable challenge than that which faced the Christian leaders of the early Middle Ages. They did not have the difficult task of rebuilding on the foundations of a culture which had turned its face away from its historical Christian heritage. Their problem was rather to build a Christian culture and civilization on the ruins of a classical civilization which had lost its nerve and its faith in paganism, whether it be Stoic, Aristotelian, or Platonic in its philosophy, and for whom the gods of antiquity had lost virtually all meaning.

Even the rebuilding of a declining medieval civilization, as difficult as it proved to be, was tempered by the fact that under the crust of a rationalism inherent in the post-Thomistic thought and in the humanism of the Renaissance there was a solid foundation of Augustinian theology and philosophy which was not forgotten and which was still able to claim a loyal following in the midst of the revival of classical thought of Renaissance humanism.

Even though today there is a very solid and devoted evangelical community planted within the context of a Western civilization now dying, the collapse of modern Western civilization can be traced directly to a deliberate repudiation of its Christian heritage. This repudiation has been prompted by a deep hatred of this legacy. The leaders of modern philosophical, theological, and cultural endeavor have, for the most part, deliberately spurned the foundation out of which the living waters of a great culture have flowed to bless the world in which we live and make its material progress a reality. This factor, never present before in the history of the West, raises a very serious question for which there is no available positive answer. It also raises the question as to whether there is a remedy and yet another. Would the preferred remedy be accepted?

An important aspect is that historic Christian theism must not be used as a utilitarian philosophy to be accepted merely for the sake of recovering a lost or dying civilization. God must never be sought simply for man's material advantage or enhancement. To seek and endeavor to restore a Christian civilization for its own sake and not for the glory of God is a serious distortion and misuse of the Scriptures and a utilitarian approach to God's plan for redemption.[3]

With this important consideration firmly in mind, we may proceed in answering the question: Is there a remedy for man's cultural predicament? Can the aimless drift of the modern mind into the uncharted seas of irrationalism and meaninglessness be checked? Can the intellectual and cultural activities of our society be given a new sense of purpose and direction? These are the most pressing questions of the day. Until they are answered, all efforts to revive the economy, bring inflationary pressures under control, erect a meaningful and sensible policy of conserving our national resources, remove the blight of homosexuality and abortion from the social scene, and restore a Christian ethic to our national economic, social, and political life will remain unattainable. We will continue to founder and drift from crisis to crisis until the ship of state wrecks itself upon the rocks of the realities of the present, which the political leaders and the multitude of the people have refused to face.

The Remedy

Historic orthodox Christianity, as it emerged in the works of the Reformers, is the one answer for the intellectual and moral issues of the day. A reliance upon a vague form of evangelical thought, or even a more formal theology which bears the marks of a syncretism with humanism or naturalistic elements, will not be sufficient to meet the cultural crisis now confronting us. The only sufficient answer for this crisis is a Christian theism which rests upon the whole counsel of God, not merely upon some segments of the biblical revelation, however important such segments may be in their own right.

For its most effective presentation, biblical truth demands and rests upon

3. For the biblical basis for this, see II Chronicles 7.

a systematic statement of all its aspects. In the same vein we must also conclude that biblical theism in its greatest richness and fulness likewise depends upon a systematic doctrinal formulation if it is to help man fulfill his cultural mandate in all aspects of his life. In short, Christian theism at its best rests upon a Reformed theology.[4]

The remedy, then, is to be found in a Christian theism which offers a full-orbed world and life view.[5] This biblical world and life view commits the Christian to a well-defined, specific intellectual position in regard to his concept of God, the nature and destiny of man, the origin and meaning of sin, the nature of redemption, the meaning of the living of the Christian life, and the meaning and purpose of human history. Christianity differs from all non-Christian systems of thought because their basic assumptions differ. Christianity is not the completion of human philosophy nor the extension of the religious consciousness of man to a higher plane of insight in regard to these vital issues. It rests upon a totally different set of presuppositions, the basic one being the revelation of the one true triune God as He comes to man in the infallible Scriptures.

In opposition to this world and life view stand all humanistic approaches to truth. Van Til has stated the case decisively: "If one does not make human knowledge wholly dependent upon the original self-knowledge and consequent revelation of God to man, then man will have to seek the knowledge within himself as the final reference point." Then man will have to seek and obtain an exhaustive knowledge of reality. This he cannot obtain, and as a result he will be forced to the conclusion that he has no true knowledge of anything at all. Van Til holds that this is the dilemma which confronts every form of non-Christian epistemology.[6]

At this point we come face to face with the solution to the basic

4. We are not implying that those theologies which fall short of Calvinism do not convey a meaningful statement of salvation which the sovereign God uses for the redemption of lost men. Nor are we saying that these theologies are not Christian, or that those who hold them are not Christian. This statement implies that the Reformed theology, as it is contained in the Westminster and other Reformed creeds, is the theology which most closely approximates that taught in the Scriptures and presents more closely the whole counsel of God as it is revealed in the Scriptures.

5. For the purposes of this chapter, divine inspiration and infallibility of the Scriptures as the basis for this world and life view will not be argued, but will be the basic presupposition for all that follows. This is the historic position of Christianity, without which no Christian culture is ultimately possible, and without which Western civilization must fall. For an incisive statement of the necessity and meaning of this basic presupposition, the reader is referred to Van Til, *A Christian Theory of Knowledge,* pp. 25-40.

6. Ibid., p. 17.

epistemological issue which has haunted philosophy throughout its history and for which it has no answer. Biblical theism in its fullest expression and development offers the only answer. It presupposes God as He is revealed in the Scriptures, but in so doing it does not seek a common ground with non-Christian thought at any point. It holds that if God is not presupposed, reason is a pure abstraction which has no contact with fact; and fact is also a pure abstraction which also has not contact with reason. It then follows that reason and fact cannot be brought into any fruitful contact with each other except upon the presupposition of God and His control over the universe.[7] Apart from this theistic world and life view man cannot actually know the meaning of the term "reason" and the concept of fact.

This statement by no means negates or denies the doctrine of general revelation and common grace, but they are not to be interpreted in such a way as to mean that they provide a common ground on which Christian believers and non-believers may meet. On the other hand, it is also true that God created man in His own image and that this image was not effaced by the fall into sin. Rather was the image so distorted in every aspect that since the fall unregenerate mankind is not capable of thinking God's thoughts after Him or doing His will as He requires of His creatures. In the fall man became a covenant breaker, and what truth he dimly sees he suppresses and holds in error. Thus, non-believers do not, and cannot understand the facts of the universe in the light of the system of truth revealed in the Scriptures or in the light of some other system of philosophy which men might imagine that they possess. It is for this reason that Van Til insists that "all the facts of the universe are either what they are because of their relation to the system of truth set forth in the Scriptures or they are not."[8] It is in the light of this point that the relation of the Scriptures to the facts of science and history are to be ultimately understood.

Some will now raise the question: What is the role of logic in this epistemology? Does it have a place? The answer lies in the insistence that logic as a branch of knowledge must also yield to the revelation of God in the Scriptures. When the theist speaks of the idea of truth as it is found in the Scriptures, he does not mean that this system is a logically penetrable system. Only God knows Himself and the created universe exhaustively. Even though He has revealed Himself to man infallibly, this revelation is not exhaustive. He has not revealed Himself exhaustively in either His creation or the Scriptures. Through the use of logic the natural

7. Ibid., p. 18.

8. Ibid., p. 17.

or unregenerate mind cannot arrive at a true knowledge of God. The laws of logic as philosophers have enunciated them are not independent reals standing apart from the biblical revelation. God is not subject to them for He is their Author. To the extent to which these logical formulations are valid, they derive their validity from the fact that they correctly reflect the nature of creation in all of its aspects. The law of non-contradiction is to be considered in this light. It is not an independent real to which God is subject, as even some Christian theologians and philosophers have maintained. Thus, Christians and non-Christians cannot regard it as a common meeting ground on the basis of which they may argue the value and validity of their respective positions. This law, like the others of formal logic, derives its authority from the sovereign God revealed in the Scriptures. There are no laws of logic above the God of the Scriptures "according to which He must measure His own internal consistency."[9]

According to the basic principles of a consistent biblical theism man's consciousness of himself and of the objective reality in which he lives presupposes for their intelligibility the consciousness of God. The basic issue is the final point of reference in the interpretation of reality and a consistent biblical theism finds it in the self-contained ontological Trinity. "By His counsel the triune God controls whatsoever comes to pass. If then, human consciousness must, in the nature of the case, always be the approximate starting point, it remains true that God is always the basic, and therefore, the ultimate or final reference in human interpretation."[10]

Equally important in this Christian approach to knowledge and the problem of culture is the fact of human sin. Man is a creature, a sinful creature, and when he became a sinner he made himself rather than God the ultimate or final point of reference.[11] "And it is precisely this presupposition, as it controls without exception all forms of non-Christian philosophy, that must be brought into question. If this presupposition is left unquestioned in any field all the facts and arguments presented to the unbeliever will be made over by him according to his pattern."[12]

Because of his sinful nature the unregenerate unbeliever is both unwilling and incapable of thinking God's thoughts after Him and of fulfilling His cultural mandate. Unable to escape the facts of the world in which he lives, he re-fashions them and confers upon them a meaning of

9. Ibid., p. 41.
10. Cornelius Van Til, *The Defense of the Faith* (Nutley, N. J.: Presbyterian and Reformed, 1963), p. 77.
11. Ibid.
12. Ibid.

his own according to his own particular frame of reference. Thus, unbelievers are covenant-breakers, holding the truth of God in falsehood. As a covenant-breaker the unbelieving man seeks to attach to all aspects of created reality that meaning which he desires to give to them rather than that meaning which God gave to His creation as its sovereign Creator. This revolt of the unbeliever against God's interpretation of the facts of creation constitutes the essence of his rebellion against God and, in the name of "rationalism," brings with it as its correlative, irrationalism. As this revolt against Christian theism has swept over the Western mind, so has it brought with it an equally extensive irrationalism which now threatens to engulf Western culture.

The sinner can never correctly read the meaning and truth found in God's general revelation, lacking both the ability and the desire to do so. Van Til presents a cogent argument for this theistic system of apologetics and approach to all knowledge. There is but one system of reality (that found in God), His creation of the universe and man, His providential government of His creation, the fall of man, and his subsequent sin.

> Thus there is one system of reality of which all that exists forms a part. And any individual fact of this system is what it is in this system. It is therefore a contradiction in terms to speak of presenting certain facts to man unless one presents them as a part of this system. The very factness of any individual fact of history is precisely what it is because of God and what He is. It is God's counsel that is the principle of individuation for the Christian man. God makes the facts to be what they are.[13]

For the Christian, then, there cannot be systems of selectivity but only *the* system, that system which reflects and is based upon the divine order of creation. It is in this factness of the system that facts obtain their meaning. Because they are in the system, they become knowable to the knowing mind, and for no other reason. However, not only the facts within the system, but the system itself receives its meaning from God.

> It is natural that only the supernatural revelation of God can inform man about such a system as that. For this system is of a nature quite different from the systems of which the natural man speaks. The natural man virtually attributes to himself that which a true Christian theology attributes to the self-contained God. The battle, therefore, is beween the absolutely self-contained God of Christianity and the would-be wholly contained mind of the natural man. Between them there can be no compromise.[14]

13. Ibid., p. 147.

14. Ibid., p. 148.

Here we see the answer to the riddle of how man knows himself and the universe in which he lives, how he receives a world and life view which confers meaning and purpose upon this total reality and upon man himself. Man cannot confer meaning upon his world or his own existence. Only the sovereign God who created the world and man can confer these attributes upon His creation. In the Scriptures He has been pleased to reveal to man what man cannot obtain for himself. In this revelation God has made available to man a rational comprehension of reality which, while not exhaustive, is true. Any attempt on the part of man to find another meaning and purpose to this reality can yield only the fruit of irrationalism, for it is nothing less than an effort to substitute for God's meaning another which man would place upon this created reality. All human philosophies have failed and will continue to fail as they seek another solution to the problem of knowledge. Although the quest is futile, philosophy continues to pursue its search for meaning in the maze of the systems of thought which have made it a veritable jungle of irrationalism.

In the light of these basic considerations it follows that only on the foundations of a consistent Christian theism can a meaningful and enduring culture be erected. Only within the limits of such a frame of reference can man think God's thoughts after Him and do His will. Only as he is regenerated, empowered by the Holy Spirit, and guided by the Scriptures can man fulfill a cultural mandate.

Philosophy

To come to terms with the mandates of Scripture the Christian must come to a new perspective and understanding of the role of philosophy in Christian scholarship. He must realize that the limited understanding which philosophers through the ages have gained concerning the nature of created reality is held in error and seen through the darkness of human sin. While we admit that through common grace fragments of philosophical and scientific truth have been granted to unbelievers, they have, at the same time, attempted to suppress it and to deny its divine authorship and claim it as their own invention.

Does this continuing failure of philosophy to achieve its goals and to find truth lead to the conclusion that the Christian should not pursue this discipline for its own sake but merely study it as it relates to the history of Christian thought? Should we pursue it simply because we recognize that throughout the history of the church it has had a pernicious, if not lethal, influence on Christian thought? Should we seek to understand philosophy so that the church should be alerted to the fact that most of the heresies which have beset it throughout its history have had their origin in the various efforts to achieve an accommodation between the Scriptures and the various philosophical currents? Or, is philosophy a valid and proper role for Christian scholars to embrace?

Obviously it is a proper function to alert the church to the dangers inherent in any effort to find a common ground with all philosophical systems. At best, this could be regarded as a negative justification for such endeavor on the part of Christian thinkers. To present to Christians the inherent incompatibility between philosophy and historic Christian orthodoxy is a necessary activity, and today it is more important than ever. Neo-evangelicalism, liberalism, and other schools within Christendom have tacitly accepted the principle of accommodation with contemporary currents of philosophic thought to the great detriment of pure doctrine.

But there is a more positive attitude for the Christian scholar to adopt, namely, that philosophy is a proper study if we are to claim all of human intellectual activity for Christ and make it subject to His will. The twentieth century has witnessed the rise of many orthodox theologians who see the issues presented by philosophy and who have made strenuous efforts to erect a system of apologetics which is thoroughly biblical and, by virtue of this fact, offer a sound defense of the faith once delivered to the saints. The most notable of these efforts is found in the many writings of Cornelius Van Til, who for 47 years occupied the chair of apologetics in Westminster Theological Seminary in Philadelphia.[15]

Philosophy must be captured and made subject to the claims of Christ. It is a legitimate and even profitable field of investigation for the Christian scholar. If it is studied in the light of the biblical world and life view, as that view has been formulated by Reformed theology, we may well speak of the possibility of a Christian philosophy and regard it as a useful ally in throwing further light on some important aspects of created reality. If it is studied and used with such a world and life view as its frame of reference, it does not come under the condemnation which the Bible places upon vain speculation as Paul presents it in I Corinthians. Philosophy becomes a dangerous weapon only when it is removed from this theistic context and is used as an end in itself. When it is so misused, we must take heed to the words of an early American statesman who uttered strong words of warning to the American people of his day:

> We may think wrongly upon right principles, but forever do so upon

15. For a comprehensive list of these works, see the Bibliography.

> wrong ones for how can the stream flow pure when the source of truth is polluted.[16]

To capture philosophy for the cause of Christ is to capture the modern mind for His service in the broadest sense of the word. It is to capture political, social, and economic thought; it is to lay claim to educational thought and practice and to provide a new frame of reference for the cultural activities of modern man in literature, art, architecture, and music in the spirit of Bach, Rembrandt, and many other great thinkers who laid the foundation of a culture which would truly reflect the great doctrinal affirmations of the Reformation.

Reconstruction in Political Thought and Practice

The loss of freedom in the modern world has been one of the most amazing phenomena of the present century. Two major wars have been fought to save it. Various political platforms have been put forth as panaceas to cure the sickness of Western political thought and practice and to restore health to the political systems of the West. All these efforts have failed. In the eyes of the average citizen the most frightening failure has been the failure of nerve which has gripped the democracies of the West and made them an easy prey to the totalitarian thought and which has engulfed much of the world.

It is obvious that a thorough reconstruction of our political thought and practice is absolutely necessary if the West is to be saved from conquest by the totalitarian forces now threatening it. How can this reconstruction be achieved? The history of the past three hundred years proves conclusively that it cannot be accomplished in terms of the political philosophies which are called upon to save us from the mighty abyss which yawns before us. The solutions offered by Hobbes, Locke, the French Revolution, the American Revolution, the Declaration of Independence, the rise of Jacksonian democracy, and social and political Darwinism have all failed. Leading statesmen throughout our history have foreseen this failure. The danger of replacing the republic created by the Constitution in 1787 with a democracy was clearly seen by those who were members of the Philadelphia Convention, and they uttered warnings that have been forgotten or unheeded. On numerous occasions these warnings have been repeated by national political leaders. During the nineteenth century voices were raised in protest against the eroding effects of the democratic

16. Charles Pinckney, *Three Addresses to the Citizens of South Carolina* (Philadelphia, 1783), p. lxi.

philosophy as it arose in American political life. Writing under the influence of Dr. James H. Thornwell, John C. Calhoun in his *Disquisition on Government* and *Discourse on the Government and the Constitution* portrayed with almost uncanny accuracy the nature of the next one hundred years of our history if the forces of democracy should be allowed to replace the Constitution as the guiding light in the political life of the nation.[17]

The secularism and ensuing irrationalism inherent in the eighteenth-century democratic philosophy received new impetus during the period from 1830 to 1860, in which Transcendentalism became the dominant philosophy. The rise of Darwinism after 1865, providing the underlying assumptions of American political, economic, and social thought with scientific support, gave an even greater momentum to the growth of irrationalism in American affairs until it became a veritable flood in the twentieth century.

What, then, is the remedy for the irrationalism which has the political life of this nation in its grip? Many like to think that it lies in a return to a simpler form of government, without any reformation of political thought. But such is not a remedy, for it does not deal with the cause of the disease. A change of political parties in control cannot produce a miracle for the needed change. There must be a complete change in political philosophy regarding the conduct of our local, state, and national affairs. Apart from such a development the nation will continue its headlong rush into some form of political absolutism. The exact form will largely be the result of the nature of that crisis which brings in its wake the final departure from even the most superficial allegiance to the constitutional tradition and plunges the nation into the arms of totalitarianism.

The basis for our political reconstruction must be a return to the political philosophy which gave to us our constitutional republic. This means that once again the Scriptures must become the source of political outlook. We must abandon the maxim of the democratic philosophy that we are a government of, by, and for the people and once again realize that we were intended to be a government under God, by Him and for His glory. We must conduct our political activities in the light of the transcending fact that God is sovereign and that nations have their origin in His will and derive their just powers from Him, not from the people. It must be understood that government is ordained of God for the realization of His will under common grace in the life of mankind. Government is not a necessary evil,

---

17. Richard Kralle, ed., *The Works of John C. Calhoun* (New York, 1863), vol. I.

as Rousseau would have us believe, but a positive good, made necessary by sin, but not evil in itself. The state is ordained of God with those just powers necessary for the maintenance of civil order at home, and for the defense of the nation from enemies abroad.

What, then, are these just and necessary powers? Obviously, the civil ruler (the magistrate) in the biblical scheme of government must have the power to enforce justice through a system of courts. Likewise, he must have the power of capital punishment, for he is responsible to God for the conduct of government. He has the power to wage just war, and to raise money through taxation to carry out these just and necessary powers. In short, his role is described in Romans 13:1-8.

The realization that the ruler, whether a president, chancellor, king, or prime minister, is responsible for carrying out the will of God in common grace for the people entrusted to his stewardship is basic to good government. The will of God for government is primarily contained in the Ten Commandments, and thus they become the basic source of human positive law. The function of the legislative body is to apply to particular circumstances the law of God. The legislature, in all of its concerns, must be guided by this fundamental moral law. Accordingly, in matters of social, economic, and political concern it must be guided by these and other equally important standards set in the Bible. In all deliberations concerning capital punishment, the legality of abortion, the nature and extent of taxation, the necessity of declaring war, and hundreds of similar matters, our legislative bodies must look to the Scriptures for basic guidelines for their legislative activities.

As the Scriptures confer upon government certain positive duties such as national defense and maintaining justice and civil order within their established boundaries, so do they place restraints upon the extent of governmental power. The Scriptures are very clear that government must not intervene between its citizens and those primary duties which they owe to God in the form of proper worship and moral living.

Modern totalitarianism, in its democratic form, has come to power largely through the constant urge in democratic societies to extend the power of government beyond its biblical limits and to claim for government functions which do not belong to it. This has been true of many Western countries where the concept of the welfare state has been integrated with the democratic philosophy. As a result, our federal government and those of the various states have intruded into fields where they have no right and have claimed for themselves more and more power. Throughout our national history, and more particularly since 1840, reformers, often well intentioned and poorly informed, have been eager and willing to give greater power to the federal government in many areas and have created a monstrous bureaucracy which threatens to destroy the very liberties these liberal leaders have sought to extend or protect. History—biblical and secular—clearly proves that when the people of a nation seek to extend the power of their government beyond its biblical limits to achieve goals clearly not in accord with the Scriptures, they lose the liberties they possessed when they accepted the will of God for their political conduct. For this reason political liberalism has become the death knell for human liberty, replacing the sovereignty of God with the humanistic concept of the sovereignty of man.

The biblical view of government also brings with it the problem of the nature of law. The Bible clearly declares that all power and just law has its origin in the revealed will of God for mankind and not in nature or some human consensus. By its very nature law cannot be the pronouncement of the democratic majority, for that majority denies the sovereignty of the God of the Scriptures in human affairs. The courts must not listen to the pronouncements of humanistic sociologists or psychologists in formulating their legal decisions, but must look to the Scriptures for guidance.

The recent decisions of the Supreme Court in regard to the death penalty, the "right" of abortion, religion in the schools, and other social issues clearly indicate the irrationality of much of our judicial thinking. These decisions completely depart from the biblical norm. The Court, all too frequently, arrives at its decisions after exploring what the popular opinion is on the issue rather than looking to past decisions of the Court in the times of its greatness or to the plain statements and limitations contained in the Constitution. We could recover much of our legal heritage if we could look to the original Constitution for the guidelines for legal pronouncements, quitting the opinions of sociologists and psychologists who have been schooled in the psychological principles of Freud, Dewey, or B. F. Skinner.[18] Our courts must once again accept the biblical doctrine of sin and its nature if they are to become centers of true justice rather than purveyors of a pernicious humanism which sacrifices victims of crime for the restoration of the criminal.

The Reconstruction of Economic Life

Can the economic life of the nation be saved from the present irration-

---

18. If this principle were followed, biblical principles as to what constitutes crime and its punishment would be in order rather than the present great concern for the criminal to the negation of justice in our legal system.

alism by which it is being conducted, and can a biblical system of freedom be restored to our economic activity? These are questions which Christians and non-Christians ask daily. Men of all persuasions—conservative and liberal, unbeliever and believer—all are concerned and feel these questions to be of supreme importance. All are seeking for answers which only Christian theism can answer. Modern man has tried every other solution and found all of them wanting. Yet the unbeliever, the humanistic liberal, remains unwilling to turn to Christianity for the one possible solution.

The current picture of economic thought and activity in the Western nations is an unintelligible patchwork of governmental policies, usually contradictory and in conflict. The result is that private initiative has been minimized and inflation has become the dominant threat. The acceptance of naturalism and other forms of economic determinism came with the advent of the New Deal under Franklin Roosevelt, though the roots of this economic thought had been sown in the fertile soil of the thought of the latter part of the nineteenth century. The New Deal enshrined it as the epitome of modern economic thought and practice. The nation is still under its sway.

The election of 1932 was, as David Lawrence observed, a permanent change of direction in the political and economic history of the United States. There has been no retreat. The great majority of the voting public was so engrossed in the immediate problems of the Great Depression that they did not look beyond the confines of their immediate present to see what lay ahead for the republic. Only gradually did the meaning of the election of 1932 and the coming of the New Deal become clear to many who had accepted Roosevelt's assurance that it was essentially a temporary program to meet the crisis which confronted them.

The New Deal was based upon the liberalism inherited from the reform movements of the latter nineteenth century, embodying many of the principles of Popularism, of the Progressive movement of the early years of the twentieth century, and of the radicalism which gained a foothold in American thought after World War I. Its anti-theistic character was concealed from the public, but there was a strong stratum of anti-Christian thinking in evidence just below the surface of the political and social oratory of the period.

At many points it involved a flagrant denial of the biblical principles of economic conduct. As a result, it produced currents in the economic life of the nation which continue to baffle every succeeding administration. The most prominent of these is the problem of inflation, a thinly concealed form of theft through governmental policy, which so cheapens the purchasing power of the dollar that the savings of millions have been radically affected. Government spending, the cause of the inflation, has a popular appeal which softens the stinging effects of inflation in the thinking of many voters who do not look far into the future. They do not realize that their pensions, social security benefits, and other forms of accumulated savings have been depleted because of the tremendous loss of purchasing power of the dollar. Inflation is an irrational approach to the solution of the national ills, and thoroughly immoral because it is deceptive as well as constituting a form of legalized theft.

Taxation is another illustration of the irrational character of the present economic system. Not only is the federal debt the largest known to history, but it has passed beyond the bounds of control. The debt can never be paid, and it constitutes a permanent mortgage on the economic welfare of the present and future generations. Taxation is a form of our economic irrationalism, for it constitutes an illicit method of redistributing the wealth of the citizenry under the pretext of aiding the unfortunate. This is a modern "Robin Hood" approach to the problem of poverty. The moral behind this type of taxation lies in the argument that it is legitimate to tax the wealthy to aid the poor by a program of confiscatory taxation. This use of such a tax means that the government obtains funds to carry out programs and achieve objectives which are not sanctioned by the Scriptures.

This is not the end of the story, however. Federal regulation of business, large and small, has long since passed beyond the biblical concept of the proper role of governmental action. This extension of governmental activity is a thinly disguised attempt to use government as the agency for the creation of a socialistic dictatorship in the interests of achieving an economic millennium.

Socialism in all of its forms rests on the same basic assumptions as does Marxian and other forms of communism. Therefore, it must be regarded as equally unbiblical. Though the methods may be different, and many socialists may claim to abhor violence as the means of achieving their goals, the goals they seek to achieve are no less anti-Christian than are those of their communist allies. Both philosophies reject the biblical doctrines of the sovereignty of God, the creation of man in His image, total depravity, redemption through Jesus Christ alone, the Christian ethic, and the biblical eschatology. They have substituted, in place of these essential doctrines of the Christian faith, a materialistic counterpart. This has, of necessity, caused the socialists to replace the sovereign God with a sovereign state which cannot be subject to any higher power.

This socialistic ideal has permeated the federal government and its various bureaus, particularly the Department of Health, Education and Welfare, and the thinking of most economists teaching in our colleges and universities. Because this economic philosophy is so thoroughly entrenched in our national life, many conservatives are at a loss to know how to combat it, largely because they share the same basic assumption on which socialism rests. Many share the same basic rejection of historic Christian orthodoxy, and in doing so have deprived themselves of the very weapon they need to combat the growing tyranny of the federal government in economic affairs. Much of the economic conservatism, along with the political, thus rests upon a faulty non-biblical foundation, lacking a firm Christian theism. The result of this weakness is that many who decry the trend toward socialism and call for a return to free enterprise, do so upon a faulty premise. Their position is not founded upon a biblical conception of freedom, nor is their philosophy of freedom too different from that of their socialist opponents.

The return to rationality and sanity in our economic life must, therefore, rest upon a sound biblical basis, and the economic role of man must be carefully studied in the light of the whole counsel of God. The Scriptures have much to say on this aspect of Christian stewardship, and it is our neglect of these great truths, as a nation, which has brought us to the present impasse. As a people, we must recapture the biblical view of freedom in our economic and political activity. We must realize that in all areas of life our freedom is found in our subjection to the will of God, that he is most truly free who is most truly a slave to Jesus Christ. This is a lost note in modern thought.

But what does this return to Christian theism mean? First of all, it means that in our private and public economic activities we are stewards of a sovereign God and that our wealth is His. We do not possess it in fee simple, but only as His stewards, and in our acquisition and use of that wealth we are responsible to Him who has created us in His image, the world, and its wealth which He has entrusted to us. This also means that we must sweep aside all the economic philosophies which have emerged out of the Renaissance and the Enlightenment. It means that if we are to recover a sane biblical rationalism in economic affairs, we must ignore all the theories derived from Adam Smith and the Enlightenment, the Manchester school of English thought, Karl Marx, the Christian socialism of nineteenth-century England, and its more modern derivatives, the American version of the Social Gospel movement, the New Deal, the Fair Deal, the New Frontier, the Great Society, and all other programs which are unbiblical in their origins and aims.

An economic philosophy which looks to the Scriptures for man's role in creation as prophet, priest, and king will emphasize the right use of wealth as well as the proper biblical means for its acquisition. Like political freedom, economic freedom finds its basis in the law of God. Any other foundation but produces a spurious doctrine of freedom which cannot withstand the stress and storms of contemporary economic activity. Economic freedom is freedom under law, the revealed law of God rather than the law of nature.[19]

More specifically, the biblical teaching on economic theory and practice distinctly provides for the private ownership of property. This form of ownership alone provides man with the means by which he may exercise his stewardship in a manner pleasing to God. Furthermore, the more modern concept of free enterprise must also be regarded as thoroughly biblical and that the state exists to protect this right of private property and its exercise through modern forms of business enterprise. Socialism is morally wrong, for it contravenes the will of God for man in his dominion over creation and places the state in the position where God must be. Socialism and its companion, communism, place the state (or the proletariat) where God rightfully belongs, allowing the human institutions to demand from men that service which they owe to God alone. This truth does not mean that the state has no power of regulating private free enterprise, but it does mean that such regulation must be in accord with the teaching of the Bible; that the state must not use its rightful power of regulation in such a way that regulation becomes the power for the illegal confiscation of wealth or an unjust restriction of the right of the individual, or individuals, in a corporation to carry on their economic activities in a manner allowed by the Scriptures.

For the state to infringe upon the right of private property and free enterprise in an unbiblical manner is to invite the tyranny which must result from this union of the economic with the political power. In such a union freedom must vanish, and in the use of his wealth the Christian finds himself at the mercy of a secular state which pays no attention to the biblical injunction in regard to the functions of the state and the rights of the individual to life, liberty, and property. When economic freedom is destroyed, the other liberties soon find themselves in the same grave. These God-given rights are so fundamentally related that to deny one is to deny the others. For this reason socialism becomes an octopus which captures

19. For an excellent discussion of the biblical teaching in regard to economic activity, see Gary North, *An Introduction to Christian Economics* (Nutley, N. J.: Craig Press), 1973.

to itself all human rights under the guise of providing a regulation of property for the welfare of the state.

We should listen to the words of caution uttered by Max Weber, who, as we have seen, was no friend to Christian theism, but who also admitted that pure socialism is irrational.

> Where a Planned Economy is radically carried out it must further accept the inevitable reduction in formal rationality of calculation which would result from the elimination of money and capital accounting. This is merely an example of the fact that substantive and formal rationality are largely opposed. This fundamental, and, in the last analysis unavoidable, element of irrationality in economic systems is one of the most important sources of all the problems of social polity, above all, the problems of socialism.[20]

There is in much of contemporary thought a lurking irrationalism as described by Weber. But Weber's own solution is also irrational. It is of great importance to notice that in this passage Weber was showing his awareness of the intellectual chaos resulting from the Kantian dualism, but his suggested remedy proves to be no remedy at all.

There is, therefore, no middle ground between the totalitarian state based on some form of socialism or communism on the one hand, and an economic system based upon a frame of reference found in biblical theism, on the other.

All contemporary efforts to create some kind of mixed economy, an economy providing for both governmental ownership and private ownership of the means of the production and distribution of goods, is a type of marriage based upon expediency. The result is a pragmatic approach to economic problems which possesses ultimate safeguards against further government encroachments upon the right of private ownership of property. The result is some kind of a compromise which usually accepts the dictum that the government will own and control those components of an economic system in order to provide those services which private enterprise is either unable or unwilling to provide more cheaply and efficiently. In any case, the solution is pragmatic and not founded upon governmental activities. This kind of reasoning places no limits on political activity, and as a result governments have expanded their economic activities and services and restricted the role of private enterprise. This union of power in the hands of any government creates a monopoly of far greater power than any

20. Max Weber, *The Theory of Social and Economic Organization,* ed. Talcott Parsons (New York, 1964), p. 279, quoted by Gary North, "Max Weber: Rationalism, Irrationalism, and the Bureaucrtic Cage," in *Foundations of Christian Scholarship,* ed. Gary North (Vallecito, Calif.: Ross House Books, 1976), p. 144.

corporation in the hands of private individuals, no matter how great its power may seem to be to the public. Not only is the resulting colossus unbiblical, but it is also contrary to the best interests of the people at large. But they see this too late. The political leviathan has already been created and is most unwilling to surrender its power.

To achieve the necessary reconstruction in the economic realm presents a Herculean task to Christian scholarship. Economic thought has been non-Christian in its presuppositions for several centuries. Hence the tradition in this field is thoroughly secular and has alternated between various forms of naturalistic frames of reference and those which are humanistic in their outlook in the search for the solution to economic issues. In spite of their philosophical differences, these various schools of thought have come to very similar conclusions. Conservative economists used very similar philosophic assumptions to oppose the radical and liberal economic philosophies. For this reason they have been unable to stem the rising tide of economic radicalism and the trend toward collectivism as it appears under the guise of democratic collectivism.

Collectivism is despotic in nature, whatever the name under which it appears. Collectivism depends upon a basic irrationalism which is a direct repudiation of the economic principles found in the Scriptures.

There is a Christian alternative to socialism in all its forms, to communism and the other economic philosophies of our day. Its roots and contents are found in the framework of a consistent Christian theism. The Reformers of the sixteenth century were fully aware of this aspect of the whole counsel of God and paid much attention to it in their writings. Their followers, unfortunately, have failed to follow them and assert the economic principles found within the Reformed heritage. The modern world has suffered as a result.[21]

As with political thought, so in economic thought the doctrine of creation looms as the most important concept in a theistic economic philosophy. It declares that man in his economic life, in his stewardship over the earth and the animal kingdom, is responsible to a sovereign God. Thus in all his economic activity he must act as a steward. In the use of his property and in his economic freedom he is bound by the commands of God. Furthermore, in his economic pursuits he must seek to give God the glory.

---

21. For a more thorough treatment of the economic thought of the Reformers, see Albert Hyma, *Renaissance to Reformation* (Grand Rapids, 1951), and C. Gregg Singer, *John Calvin: His Roots and Fruits* (Nutley, N. J.: Presbyterian and Reformed, 1976), pp. 45-51.

Such an outlook on economic affairs has some very practical and important ramifications for our national life in the twentieth century. First and foremost is that it creates a firm foundation for a doctrine of economic freedom. This form of freedom, like other freedoms, finds its origin in man's duty which he owes to God as a steward of his material wealth. This doctrine received much attention from John Calvin and the other Reformers. The biblical doctrine of the freedom of the will as it is set forth in historic orthodoxy has a very meaningful application in the economic realm of human life. Man has a freedom to do the will of God by the fact of creation. But by the fact of the fall he lost that original freedom and became a slave to sin. However, the fall did not relieve him of the responsibility he owed to God, even though it destroyed his ability to carry out that duty in the manner assigned to him. The regenerated Christian regains, to a certain degree, this ability. But this new freedom is not that of the autonomous human will; rather is it that servitude in, and by which, man wills to do what God has willed for him to do in fulfillment of the duties incumbent upon him as a created being.

Perhaps there is no more enlightening comment on the economic life which the Christian should pursue than that which was penned by John Calvin. He insisted that the pursuit of wealth and economic gain is both honorable and legitimate. Calvin also reminded his readers that there is a duty incumbent upon them which they must not forget or avoid.

> All the rich when they have property with which they can be of service to others, are just as magistrates or officers of God, to what seems to them proper, that is, to assist their neighbors. Those to whom God has given much grain and wine, are to offer part of these goods to those who are in need of the same. . . . God commands that those who have an abundance of possessions always keep their hands open for helping the poor. . . . But the latter must be patient and they have no right to pillage the wealthy, even though the government is slow to punish them. . . . If the rich do not acquit them themselves of their duty, they will have to give an account of their inhuman actions, but this will be before the Heavenly Judge. . . . God has distributed this world's goods as He has seen fit and even the richest of all people, no matter how bad they may be, shall not be robbed of their possessions by those in direct need.[22]

This passage is extremely important for the understanding of the biblical principles for human economic activity and the stewardship of wealth. Property is within the protection of the divine law, for it is an integral part

22. John Calvin, *Opera, Corpus Reformatorum,* ed. G. Baum, *et al.* (Brunsgave, 1863–1900), pp. 199-200.

of the divinely ordained economy for man. God gives more material possessions to some than to others in accordance with His providence and wisdom.[23]

Equality of goods is not the biblical standard, but rather is inequality the norm for human social and economic life which greets us as we give serious attention to the teachings of the Bible on economic issues.

This inequality of wealth, however, is a divinely appointed opportunity for those who have been blessed with a great amount of material possessions to exercise the stewardship of their wealth. The wealthy stand as magistrates in the economic arena and have the same duty of stewardship as do those who hold political office.[24]

On the other hand Calvin in the passage referred to above has some stern reminders for those who are less blessed with economic wealth. These reminders have just as much force as do the warnings to thc wealthy.

> "It is not within the province of the poor to undertake to redistribute wealth of the society in which they live for the purpose of achieving an equality which the Lord did not see fit to create. Those who are poor are to bear their poverty in patience for it is the will of God." However, Calvin did not mean that they should not utilize their talents with industry and ambition for the improvement of their worldly lot. This was the divinely appointed way to achieve economic gain.[25]

It becomes quite clear that Calvin meant that the poor were not to engage in any form of political or economic rebellion for the achievement of an economic equality. Thus all schemes of liberals and socialists to achieve a kind of economic equality through confiscatory taxation of wealth are inherently indulging in a species of rebellion against the will of God, and Christians must not engage in such activities.

It is also true that Calvin did not rally to the defense of those who acquired their wealth by illegal means and who used it without any regard for their obligations to the poor. "Both the wealthy and the poor are subject to the divine pattern of society and are therefore subject to a strict accounting for their stewardship by the Righteous Judge."

Thus the Christian engages in economic enterprise (free enterprise) in the light of this biblical doctrine of freedom, rather than in the light of that spurious doctrine which the Western world has inherited from John Locke and the French Revolution.

---

23. Singer, *John Calvin: His Roots and Fruits,* p. 46.
24. Ibid., p. 47.
25. Ibid.

This concept will guide the Christian to a proper means of acquiring and using wealth. He will obey the law of God in acquiring it and will use it as a good steward, not only in the sense that he will give to God his tithes and offerings, but that he will also use what remains in a manner pleasing to God. This means that he will treat the laborer as one who is worthy of his hire, that he will sell his goods in an honest manner, not endeavoring to over-persuade the public to buy what they do not need, or charge more than what would bring a legitimate profit to him or his corporation. It means that he will have a proper regard for truth in his advertising and in the way he treats the public.

For the Christian employee this concept of free enterprise has an equally binding meaning. The worker must be worthy of his hire; he must give an honest day's work for the wages he receives. These comments may seem trivial and unnecessary. But a closer scrutiny will reveal that our national failure to honor these scriptural injunctions has done much to our nation to bring it to its present economic impasse. It may also seem that they have been overly simplified and that modern economic life is so complicated that it is virtually impossible to realize these biblical injunctions in the business and, indeed, in the life of the nation. There is a sense in which such an assumption might be true. Our economic life is complicated, but to a great extent this is true because of our failure to accept the biblical position, and this in itself has created these complex conditions under which the system is operating.

The failure to deal justly with employees in the nineteenth century gave rise to the formation of the labor unions. Often the lawless manipulations of large corporations, heady with their new-found power and importance, led to a strong demand for the Sherman Anti-Trust Act of 1890, the Interstate Commerce Act of 1887, and the similar acts passed during the present century. The result has been a series of acts creating a network of regulations which are confusing in their contradictions, time consuming and costly in their demands, and they have led to the creation of a bureaucratic federal government which is equally guilty of violating the biblical principles of government and of freedom.

The American people have increasingly demanded of government the regulation of free enterprise and a host of services which have no place in the biblical scheme of government. These demands are, in turn, the result of widespread neglect and open disobedience of the law of God dealing with our economic conduct. Centralization, whether it leads to a monopolistic power in the hands of labor, business, or government, has no place in the biblical scheme of life, and each one of these forms of monopolistic power is an effort to avoid the consequences of our previous neglect of that same law of God in human affairs.

The Reconstruction of Psychology and Sociology

The reconstruction of contemporary thought and practice in the closely allied fields of psychology and sociology is perhaps the most formidable task facing Christian scholarship today. Darwinism, naturalism, existentialism, and behaviorism have forged an unholy alliance in these two areas for the express purpose of dehumanizing man and reducing him to the status of being an animal for the express purpose of rendering him as an object of manipulation by the social and political planners who wish to create a collectivist society. The planners would have this collectivist society void of any shred of Christian morality or outlook, a society in which man would worship himself without let or hindrance, subject only to those restraints which the manipulators would place upon him for the realization of their own purposes.

It is hardly necessary to point out to thoughtful people that modern psychology with its naturalistic outlook has been a failure, a devastating failure in education, in the treatment of criminals, and in counseling. This failure is not evident to those who have been thoroughly schooled in contemporary psychological thought.[26]

Even more than the fields of political science and economics these two disciplines have raised the flag of revolt against historic Christian orthodoxy, and their irrationality has wrought havoc in the modern mind.

Reconstruction, therefore, would take the form of complete eradication of those theories which have become so ingrained in the thinking of most psychologists and sociologists, and nothing less than major surgery could reclaim these disciplines for Christian theism and save them from the irrationalism which now has them as its prisoners.

The Reconstruction of Education

Unlike the fields of psychology and sociology, there is a rich heritage for the reconstruction of education to be found in and adapted to the needs of the twentieth century. We have moved far from the foundation on which

26. This is not to imply that there is no place for a discipline of psychology which is thoroughly anchored in the biblical view of God, man, and sin. In the confusion of our society there is a tremendous need for psychologists who are able to apply biblical insights in the treatment of mental and emotional problems. A real breakthrough has come in the work of Dr. Jay Adams, formerly on the faculty of Westminster Theological Seminary in Philadelphia, but now working with a clinic near Macon, Georgia.

our system of schools was once based, but there is a foundation and there is a rich legacy of literature to guide us in the task. Not only will it serves as a guide, but it has been used in Europe and America effectively in realizing the great ends which God ordained education to fulfill in the lives of His creatures.

Such a reconstruction will not be easily achieved. Education, as an institution, has fallen victim to modern psychology and sociology and has become dominated by the behaviorists, who have seen in the school system the key for the creation of the society which they have in view. In league with the federal agencies involved in financing and directing educational activity today, notably the Department of Health, Education and Welfare, the educational hierarchy has gone a long way toward realizing its goal of a collectivist society by manipulating the minds of young Americans. The chief architects of this society are B. F. Skinner and his associates. This is no idle dream in which they have been indulging, but a very present threat which should arouse the fears and unfaltering opposition of all American parents who truly love their children and take their parental responsibility seriously.

Education today is a house divided: divided between its professions of announced aims and its actual purposes; a house divided between its theological heritage and its opposition to Christian orthodoxy; a house divided between its announced allegiance to the enhancement and transference of knowledge to the rising generation, and its departure from any true loyalty to intellectual excellence and achievement; a house divided in its publicly stated allegiance to the American political and economic heritage, and its support of political, social, and economic radicalism in its actual practices; a house divided in its alleged support of Christian morality and its open endorsement of immorality, and accepting a situational ethics.

Many trenchant criticisms have been leveled against contemporary education, public and private, for its inability and unwillingness to turn out educated young people to take their place in society. Important voices have been raised in protest. The criticisms voiced by Admiral Rickover were so devastating that many educators felt compelled to rush to the defense of their vested monopoly over American thought. They came forth with graphs and charts to prove that Johnny can read, but to no avail. Johnny still cannot read. His reading and other abilities are in a much worse state than that which moved Rickover, Mortimer Smith, and other critics to direct their broadsides against this well-entrenched monopoly over the American mind. The criticisms are well founded, the attempted defense less than impressive in its answers to the accusations. It must also be admitted that these attacks were largely aimed at the symptoms of the disease and often missed the real cause of the malady.

The basic cause of the disease from which education is suffering is theological in nature. Modern educational philosophy, to the extent to which it may be called that, is a curious combination of evolutionary thought, Dewey's pragmatism, progressivism, and Skinner's manipulative behaviorism. Under the impact of these irrational, anti-Christian philosophies, as they have been implanted in the public and some private schools, implemented by the prodding of the Department of Health, Education and Welfare, contemporary educational thought and practice are largely anti-intellectual, anti-patriotic, and anti-Christian. The widely advertised neutrality of public education is a myth accepted only by the gullible who have never taken the trouble to acquaint themselves with what is actually being taught in the schools which their children attend.

This repudiation of evangelical Christian doctrine by the public schools, however, is not a recent innovation and dates back to the inception of the public school movement in 1830 and the emergence of Horace Mann and others as leaders in the field of American education. As a result, the task of the reconstruction of education involves two approaches. The first is virtually an unattainable goal—the Christianization of the public schools. It is so idealistic that it may be dismissed as a viable remedy. The forces of unbelief are too well entrenched in the educational hierarchy to allow such a development to take place; they can also call upon the courts of the land to prevent it from taking place. It is true that in a few cases Christians have won partial victories such as in those cases in which courts have ruled that evolution must be taught only as a theory and that the biblical doctrine of creation must also be presented. This development is good, but at best only a partial victory, and its evaluation must be tempered by the sober realization that the evolutionary theory permeates nearly every subject which is taught in American public schools and in every public university as well. This theory also holds sway in most private colleges and universities. The presentation of the evolutionary hypothesis as a proven fact in the teaching of sociology, psychology, economics, anthropology, political science, and history, as well as literature and religious courses, more than offsets a requirement that the biblical account of creation be given some attention in science courses dealing with the origins of the earth and man. It is probably too much to hope that a great popular uprising against this teaching could sweep away from the public schools this pernicious influence.

The acceptance of this reality makes it necessary for orthodox Christians to accept the alternative—namely, to create a system of excellent elementary and secondary schools along with the creation of more sound colleges, and even universities, which will rest their wide curricular offerings upon the historic Christian faith. Christian parents can no longer trust the intellectual, moral, or social development of their young people to secularists in the public schools, nor should they rely upon state-supported colleges and universities to complete the educational process for them.

It is necessary that these Christian schools, at every level, be truly Christian in concept and teaching, and not in name only. They must be Christian in the sense that their curricula, their methods of instruction, and their discipline rest upon biblical principles. An educational philosophy and practice that is truly theistic must proceed upon the foundation of those principles which are inherent in the doctrine of creation.

> In the first place, Christian theism maintains that the subject of knowledge owes its existence to God. Accordingly all its interpretative powers are from God and must therefore be reinterpretative powers. In the second place, when the subject of knowledge is to come into contact with the object of knowledge, the connection is possible only because God has laid it there. . . . In addition to this, Christian theism maintains that since sin has come into the world, no subject of knowledge can really come into contact with any object of knowledge, in the sense of interpreting it properly, unless the Scriptures give the required light and unless the regeneration by the Spirit gives a new power of sight.[27]

Basic to a biblical view of education is the recognition of the supremacy of the Scriptures as the infallible rule of faith and practice—as the infallible guide as to what man must think in regard to God, himself, and the rest of creation, over which he rules as God's vice-regent. The Scriptures are the guide to the meaning of the universe, and, with the enlightening power of the Holy Spirit to aid him in his quest, the regenerated man may gain some correct understanding of the nature of created reality.

Because of his sinful condition, the unbeliever will never be able to discover the ultimate truth lying behind creation, even though he may discover scientific and other facts under common grace which are useful and true within themselves. But the meaning of what he discovers must ever remain an unfathomable mystery. It is for this person that modern psychology, sociology, and psychiatry have come to the conclusion that man is nothing but an animal, to be treated as such by other animals, and that philosophy has virtually abandoned the quest for truth and contented itself with the refuse of existentialism.

---

27. Cornelius Van Til, *A Survey of Christian Epistemology,* p. 184.

For this same reason the study of history has run aground on the rocks of conviction that it is meaningless, without purpose or direction. Christian theism supplies the only corrective to this defeatist and despairing view of the history of man. Both history and science must be interpreted in the light of God's revelation to man through the Scriptures. The emptiness and futility which predominates in so much of modern scholarship has its roots in man's endeavor to interpret himself and the world in which he lives in the light of basic postulates of his own making. As Rushdoony so clearly points out, God is the inescapable premise of human thought.

> Man either faces a world of total chance and brute factuality, a world in which no fact has meaning and no fact has relationship to any other fact, or else he accepts the world of God's creation and sovereign law.[28]

Only a self-consistent Christian theism can banish from the modern mind its sense of despair and futility as it seeks to work in a world composed of brute facts which seem to have no relationship to each other and all are equally devoid of purpose. Van Til is quite correct when he insist that science is impossible on the non-Christian principle.[29] But we extend this principle to include the whole field of human intellectual endeavor. The attempt to carry on education and all intellectual and cultural endeavor on the basis of humanistic presuppositions ultimately brings despair in its wake. Christian theism supplies the answer to the whole dilemma.

> We believe the facts of the universe are unaccountable except upon the Christian theistic basis. In other words, facts and interpretations of facts cannot be separated. It is impossible even to discuss any particular event except in some relation to some principle of interpretation. The real question about facts is, therefore, what kind of universal can give the best account of the facts. Or rather, the real question is which universal can state or give meaning to any fact.[30]

Thus true scholarship must not, and cannot, be content with the mere acquisition of facts, for the acquisition of facts cannot be separated from the interpretation of the facts which are acquired. Thus a teacher must deal with both universal and particular facts, no matter what subject matter he may be presenting. He cannot emphasize one at the expense of the other, for both are of importance in the divine economy of knowledge. The importance of both the facts and the universals must be regarded in the

28. R. J. Rushdoony, *The Mythology of Science* (Nutley, N. J.: Presbyterian and Reformed, 1967), p. 42.
29. Cornelius Van Til, *The Dilemma of Education,* p. 285.
30. Cornelius Van Til, *Christian Theistic Evidences* (Philadelphia, 1961), p. 1.

light of God's creation. The realization of the importance of both universals and particulars and their relationship to each other, as well as their role in creation, gives to teaching its reason and impetus for being; it also brings with it the proper mode, or methodology, for teaching.

Progressive education developed not only a concept of the importance of facts in relationshp to its basic aims, but it also placed great stress on a methodology designed to realize these aims. But the purposes of education for the progressives were, and remain, thoroughly humanistic. This must not be the case for the Christian teacher or professor.

In Christian theism, as it has been set forth by Van Til, we find the basis for a methodology of teaching consistent with the goals of education as those goals are found in the Scriptures.

> It is the notion of the ontological Trinity that ultimately controls a truly Christian methodology. . . . Christian methodology is therefore based upon presuppositions that are quite the opposite of those of the non-Christian. It is claimed to be the very essence of any non-Christian form of methodology that it cannot be determined in advance to what conclusions it must lead.[31]

On this principle then we can, with Van Til, come to the conclusion in regard to the reconstruction of education.

> Whatever is in accord with Scripture is educative; whatever is not in accord with Scripture is miseducative. Difficult as it may be for both the teacher and the pupil to make out in individual instances how to apply this criterion, the criterion is plain and simple enough.[32]

In these basic presuppositions we find the foundation on which education can and must be reconstructed. Leaders in the field must shed themselves of the heritage derived from Dewey which has gained such a monopoly in contemporary educational thought and practice. Educators must once again view the young people entrusted to them as created in the image of God to think His thoughts after Him and to do His will accordingly. All the postulates of the evolutionary psychology and philosophy of education must be cast aside in favor of the biblical view. In short, educators must once again approach their task with the realization that man is God's vice-regent in history. The most important aspect of education is to realize this great truth and to develop a program which will enable those in the schools to fulfill their mandate under this vice-regency. Van Til has argued this point most cogently.

> The most important aspect of this program is surely that man should realize himself as God's vice-regent in history. Man was created as

31. Cornelius Van Til, *Apologetics* (Philadelphia, 1961), pp. 61-62.
32. Van Til, *The Dilemma of Education*, p. 33.

God's vice-regent and he must realize himself as God's vice-regent. There is no contradiction between these two statements. Man was created a character and yet he had to make himself even more of a character. And so we may say that man was created a king in order that he might become more of a king than he was.[33]

Thus the aim of education must be to bring to students this great realization. It cannot emphasize such goals as self-expression for its own sake, doing one's own thing, learning to be good citizens, learning a trade, learning to adjust to one's environment, and so on. An education which is Christian may well produce some of these results as by-products. A good Christian should be a good citizen; he may well feel called to learn a trade, and he may well learn the art of adjusting to various situations as a Christian. On the other hand, learning to do one's own thing or to express oneself is a very dangerous ideal to put in the minds of students if such a goal means that the will of God is nothing more than an impediment to its realization.

Conclusion

We have traversed the arena of Western thought from the later Middle Ages through the Renaissance, the Reformation, and the Enlightenment to our own era. We have seen that the single thread running throughout these seven hundred years of Western intellectual activity has been the recurring expression of irrationalism and that this irrationalism has been, without exception, the correlative of philosophic rationalism. The concessions which St. Thomas Aquinas made to the Arestotelian thought of his day allowed rationalism to reappear in the philosophical thought of the West as little more than a trickle. This trickle became a stream during the Renaissance. The fact that it was Platonic rather than Aristotelian in nature in no way sets aside the fact that the rationalism of Platonic thought during this era brought in its wake a reinforced irrationalism.

Although the Reformation stayed the development of rationalism as a major philosophic movement during the sixteenth century, it was not able to capture the mind of Europe to the extent necessary to capture philosophy for Jesus Christ, not even in those lands such as Germany where Lutheranism became a major, if not a dominant, influence.

In France the Reformation ultimately lost out even though it gained a semblance of a political victory with the issuance of the Edict of Nantes in 1598. The majority of the French were untouched by both Calvinism and Lutheranism. Descartes sent French thought in a new direction in which

33. Ibid., p. 32.

it paid less and less attention to any Christian theology. The Cartesian rationalism brought in its wake a new irrationalism which, in turn, undercut the whole body of French intellectual endeavor. By the eighteenth century French philosophy, reinforced by Locke and the empiricists, had become the prisoner of deism and an equally irrational skepticism. Indeed, in their development Kant felt that he heard the tolling of the death knell for European philosophy. His majestic endeavors to rescue Western thought from this grave which the eighteenth-century thinkers had unwittingly prepared for it, were a vain and and feeble effort. Just beneath his system there lurked the same irrationalism which had haunted the efforts of his predecessors. The quest for philosophic certainty was once again stymied by the failure of Kant to answer the unanswered questions posed by both the Rationalist and Emipirist schools. Kant once again gave a new direction for philosophic endeavor, but the path he charted for his successors in idealism was as rocky and dangerous as that from which he had rescued his own generation. With Kant irrationalism became more strident and dangerous in all of its forms: more strident because philosophers were giving a wider hearing than generally had been the case; more dangerous because idealism, to a far greater degree than previously, affected and infected the political, economic, social, and educational thought of the era. It influenced to an alarming degree the theology of the churches of Europe and America.

Thus in both nineteenth-century cultural activities and theology, idealism contributed greatly to irrationalism as it found expression in the political life of the nineteenth century.

Likewise, we have seen that the culture of both Europe and America during the twentieth century has given rise to a new outburst of irrationalism in all areas of modern life which threatens to destroy Western civilization.

What, then, can be done to change the direction of our civilization? Is it doomed, or is there hope? There is hope if modern man is willing to forsake his intellectual and theological ways and return to biblical principles.

Reconstruction of society will not be an easy task in either Europe or America. It will be a long and difficult process if it is done at all. To reconstitute the thinking of our day and direct it into biblical patterns of thought is a tremendous challenge for the most dedicated leadership possessed of the talents and wisdom necessary for the realization of such a goal. But it must be accomplished if Western man is to carry out the divine mandate to build a Christian culture. To aspire to less is to be found unfaithful in the totality of our stewardship. To Christians of the West comes such a challenge and so great an opportunity.

Bibliography

Acton, H. B., ed. *Kant's Moral Philosophy*. New York: St. Martin Press, 1970.

Acton, Lord. *The Study of History*. London and New York: Macmillan, 1895.

———. *Essays on Freedom and Power*. New York: World Publishing Co., 1948.

Adams, Henry. *The Degradation of the Democratic Dogma*. New York: Peter Smith, 1949.

Adams, H. P. *The Life and Writings of Vico*. London: Allen, 1935.

Albee, Ernest. *A History of English Utilitarianism*. New York: Macmillan, 1902.

Alexander, Samuel. *Space, Time and Deity*. New York, 1918.

Allen, E. L. *Existentialism from Within*. New York: Greenwood, 1953.

———. *Freedom in God: A Guide to the Thought of Nicholas Berdyaev*. Westport, Conn.: Greenwood, 1975.

Allers, Rudolf. *The Successful Error*. New York: Norwood, 1940.

Andrews, Samuel J. *Christianity and Anti-Christianity in Their Final Conflict*. Chicago: Putnam, 1898.

Antoni, Carlo. *From History to Sociology*, tr. H. V. White. Greenwood, 1959.

Arendt, Hannah. *Between Past and Future*. New York: Penguin, 1961.

———. *The Human Condition: A Study of the Dilemma Facing Modern Man*. Chicago: University of Chicago Press, 1959.

———. *The Origins of Totalitarianism*. Oxford University Press, 1942.

Aron, Raymond. *Introduction to the Study of the Philosophy of History*. Boston: Greenwood, 1948.

———. *Main Currents of Sociological Thought*, vol. 1, *Montesquieu, Marx, Tocqueville and the Sociologists of the Revolution of 1848*, tr. R. H. Ward. New York: Doubleday, 1969.

———. *The Opium of the Intellectuals*, tr. Terence Kilmartin. New York: Norton, 1962.

Ashton, E. B. *The Fascist, His State and His Mind*. New York: Putnam, 1937.

Bachelard, Suzanne. *A Study of Husserl's Form and Transcendental Logic.* Evanston, Ill.: Northwestern University Press, 1960.

Baillie, John. *The Belief in Progress.* New York: Oxford University Press, 1951.

Baker, Herschel. *Image of God in Man: A Study of the Idea of Human Dignity in Classical Antiquity; The Middle Ages and the Renaissance.* New York: Peter Smith, 1961.

Bales, James D. *Communism: Its Faith and Fallacies.* Grand Rapids: Wm. B. Eerdmans, 1959.

Barrett, William. *Irrational Man.* New York: Doubleday, 1958.

———. *What Is Existentialism?* New York: Grove Press, 1964.

Barth, Karl. *Church Dogmatics,* tr. G. T. Thomson. Edinburgh: T. & T. Clark, 1965.

———. *Commentary on Romans.* London: Oxford University Press, 1933.

———. *Protestant Thought from Rousseau to Ritschl,* tr. Brian Couzens. New York: Harper, 1959.

———. *The Word of God and the Word of Man,* tr. Douglas Horton. Boston: The Pilgrim Press, 1957.

Barzun, Jacques. *Darwin, Marx and Wagner: Critique of a Heritage.* Boston: Little, Brown and Co., 1946.

———. *The House of Intellect.* Chicago: University of Chicago Press, 1975.

Beard, Charles A. *An Economic Interpretation of the Constitution of the United States.* New York: Macmillan, 1913.

———. *Economic Origins of Jeffersonian Democracy.* New York: Macmillan, 1916.

Becker, Carl. *Every Man His Own Historian.* Chicago: Quadrangle Books, 1966.

———. *The Heavenly City of the Eighteenth Century Philosophers.* New Haven: Yale University Press, 1932.

Beecher, Henry Ward. *Evolution and Religion.* New York: Harvard and Fullbeck, 1893.

Bellamy, Edward. *Looking Backward: 2000–1887* Boston: Harvard University Press, 1967.

Berdyaev, Nicholas. *The Fate of Man in the Modern World,* tr. D. A. Lowrie. London: Morehouse, 1933.

Bergson, Henri. *Creative Evolution,* 2nd ed. Paris, 1905.

———. *Introduction to Metaphysics.* 1903.

———. *Matter and Memory.* 1896.

———. *Time and Free Will.* Paris, 1889.

———. *Two Sources of Morality and Religion.* Macmillan, 1932.

Berkeley, Bishop. *An Essay Toward a New Theory of Vision,* ed. David Armstrong. New York: E. P. Dutton, 1965.

———. *Principles of Human Knowledge: Philosophical Writings,* ed. David Armstrong. New York: Peter Smith, 1965.

Berlin, Isaiah. *Historical Inevitability.* London: Oxford University Press, 1954.

———. *Two Concepts of Liberty.* Oxford Press, 1958.

Bernstein, R. J. *John Dewey.* New York, 1968.

Besterman, Theodore. *Voltaire,* 3rd ed. Chicago: University of Chicago Press, 1977.

Bestor, Arthur. *The Educational Wastelands.* Urbana, Ill.: University of Illinois Press, 1953.

Bewkes, Eugene B. *The Western Heritage of Faith and Reason,* rev., ed. J. Calvin Kennedy. New York: Harper and Row, 1963.

Bingham, June. *Courage to Change: An Introduction to the Life and Thought of Reinhold Niebuhr.* New York: Scribner's, 1961.

Blackham, H. L. J. *Six Existential Thinkers.* London: Kegan and Paul, 1967.

Blake, Nelson Manfred. *A History of American Life and Thought.* New York: McGraw-Hill, 1963.

Bober, M. N. *Karl Marx Interpretation of History,* 2nd ed., rev. Cambridge, Mass.: Harvard University Press, 1948.

Boller, Paul. *American Thought in Transition: The Impact of Evolutionary Materialism, 1865–1900.* Chicago: Rand McNally, 1969.

Borkenau, F. *Pareto.* London: Chapman, 1936.

Borning, Bernard C. *The Political and Social Thought of Charles A. Beard.* Seattle: University of Washington Press, 1962.

Bossenbrook, W. J. *The German Mind.* Detroit: Wayne University Press, 1961.

Bredvold, Louis. *The Brave New World of the Enlightenment.* Ann Arbor: University of Michigan Press, 1961.

Breisach, Ernst. *Introduction to Modern Existentialism from Kierkegaard to Sartre.* New York: Grove Press, 1962.

Bretall, R. W., and Kegley, C. V., eds. *Reinhold Niebuhr: His Religious, Social and Political Thought.* New York: Macmillan, 1962.

Brightman, Edgar. *A Philosophy of Religion.* New York: Prentice-Hall, 1940.

——. *Religious Values.* New York: Prentice-Hall, 1947.

Brinton, Crane. *The Anatomy of Revolution.* New York: Vintage Books, 1965.

———. *Ideas and Men.* New York: Prentice-Hall, 1964.

———. *Nietzsche.* Cambridge, Mass.: Harvard University Press, 1941.

———. *The Shaping of Modern Thought.* New York: Prentice-Hall, 1963.

Brogan, Dennis. *The American Character.* New York: A. A. Knopf, 1944.

Bronowski, J. *The Ascent of Man.* Boston: Little, Brown, 1973.

Bronowski, J., and Mazlish, Bruce. *The Western Intellectual Tradition.* New York: Harper, 1960.

Brunner, Emile. *Christianity and Civilization.* New York: Scribner's, 1948.

———. *The Divine Imperative.* Philadelphia: Westminster Press, 1947.

———. *Dogmatics.* London: Lutterworth Press, 1949.

———. *Justice and the Social Order.* New York: Harper, 1945.

———. *Man in Revolt.* Philadelphia: Westminster Press, 1948.

———. *The Mediator.* New York: Macmillan, 1934.

Buber, Martin. *Eclipse of God: Studies in the Relation Between Religion and Philosophy.* New York: Harper, 1957.

———. *I and Thou,* tr. Walter Kaufmann. New York: Scribner's, 1970.

Bultmann, Rudolph. *Existence and Faith.* New York: Meridian Books, 1960.

———. *Faith and Understanding: Jesus Christ and Myth.* New York: Harper and Rowe, 1969.

———. *Kerygma and Myth.* New York: Harper and Row, 1943.

Burckhardt, Jacob. *Force and Freedom.* New York: Pantheon Books, 1943.

Burnham, James. *The Machiavellians.* New York: Putnam, 1943.

———. *Suicide of the West.* New York: Arlington House, 1964.

Butler, Bishop. *Analogy of Religion, Revealed and Natural.* London, 1900.

Calvin, John. *On God and Political Duty,* ed. John T. McNeill, Library of Christian Classics. Philadelphia: Westminster Press, 1959.

———. *The Institutes of the Christian Religion.* Philadelphia: Westminster Press, 1960.

Calvinistic Action Committee. *God-Centered Living, or, Calvinism in Action: A Symposium.* Grand Rapids: Baker Book House, 1951.

Camus, Albert. *The Fall.* New York: Knopf, 1961.

———. *The Myth of Sisyphus and Other Essays,* tr. Justin O'Brien. New York: Knopf, 1961.

———. *The Rebel.* New York: Knopf, 1956.

———. *Resistance, Rebellion and Death,* tr. Justin O'Brien. New York: Knopf, 1961.

———. *The Stranger,* tr. Gilbert Stuart. New York: Knopf., 1973.

Capaldi, Nicholas. *The Enlightenment and the Proper Study of Mankind.* New York: Capricorn Books, 1968.

Carew-Hunt, R. N. *The Theory and Practice of Communism.* New York: Penguin, 1964.

Carter, Paul. *The Idea of Progress in Most Recent Protestant Thought, 1930–1960, Church History,* XXII (1963), pp. 75-86.

Cassirer, Ernst. *An Essay on Man: An Introduction to the Philosophy of Human Culture.* New Haven: Yale University Press, 1944.

———. *The Myth of the State.* New Haven: Yale University Press, 1946.

———. *The Philosophy of the Enlightenment,* tr. C. A. Fritz and P. Pettegrove. Princeton, N. J.: Princeton University Press, 1961.

———. *The Platonic Renaissance in England.* Austin, Texas: Austin University Press, 1953.

———. *The Problem of Knowledge: Philosophy, Science, and History Since Hegel.* New Haven: Yale University Press, 1950.

Cauthen, Wilfred Kenneth. *The Impact of American Religious Liberalism.* New York: Harper, 1962.

———. *Types of American Liberalism, 1930–1935.* Ann Arbor: University of Michigan Press, 1957.

Chamberlain, Houston Stewart. *Foundations of the Nineteenth Century.* London: Lane, 1910.

Chesterton, Gilbert. *Orthodoxy.* New York: Doubleday, 1947.

Childs, John. *American Pragmatism and Education.* New York: Holt, 1956.

Chomsky, Noam. *Language and Mind.* New York: Harcourt-Brace, 1958.

———. *Problems of Knowledge and Freedom.* New York: Random House, 1971.

Chugerman, Frank. *Lester Frank Ward, the American Aristotle.* Durham, N. C.: Durham University Press, 1939.

Clark, Gordon. *A Christian View of Education.* Grand Rapids: Wm. B. Eerdmans, 1952.

———. *A Christian View of Men and Things.* Philadelphia: Presbyterian and Reformed, 1960.

———. *Dewey*. International Library of Philosophy and Theology. Nutley, N. J.: Presbyterian and Reformed, 1971.

———. *Historiography: Secular and Religious*. Philadelphia: Presbyterian and Reformed, 1960.

Clayton, John P. *Ernst Troelsch and the Future of Theology*. Cambridge, University Press, 1976.

Coates, Wilson H., and White, Hayden V. *The Emergence of Modern Humanism*. New York: McGraw-Hill, 1966.

———. *The Ordeal of Liberal Humanism*. New York: McGraw-Hill, 1970.

Cochrane, Charles Norris. *Christianity and Classical Culture*. London and New York: Oxford University Press, 1944.

Cohen, John. *Humanistic Psychology*. New York: Collier Books, 1962.

Cohen, Morris R. *The Faith of a Liberal*. New York: Henry Holt, 1946.

———. *The Meaning of Human History*. La Salle, Ill.: Open Court, 1971.

———. *Reason and Nature: An Inquiry into the Meaning of the Scientific Mind*, 2nd ed. Glencoe, Ill.: Free Press.

Collins, James. *The Mind of Kierkegaard*. Chicago: Regnery, 1953.

Commager, Henry Steele. *The American Mind: An Interpretation of American Thought and Character Since 1890*. New Haven: Yale University Press, 1950.

Comte, August. *A General View of Positivism*, tr. J. Bridges. London, 1865.

———. *Positive Philosophy*, 4 vols. New York, 1874.

Condorcet, Jean Marie. *Outlines of an Historical View of the Progress of the Human Mind*. London, 1795.

Connally, James M. *Human History and the Word of God: The Christian Meaning of History in Contemporary Thought*. New York: Harper, 1953.

Conner, James E., ed. *Lenin: Selected Writings in Politics and Revolution*. Indianapolis: Pegasus, 1968.

Cousins, Norman. *Modern Man Is Obsolete*. New York: Viking Press, 1945.

Cragg, G. R. *From Puritanism to the Age of Reason*. Cambridge University Press, 1950.

Cresson, A. *Bergson*. Paris, 1956.

Crespy, Georges. *From Science to Theology: An Essay on Teilhard de Chardin*. Nashville: Abingdon Press, 1968.

Croce, Benedetto. *History: Its Theory and Practice*. New York: Russell and Russell, 1960.

Crocker, Lester. *An Age of Crisis: Man and the World in Eighteenth Century French Thought.* Baltimore: Johns Hopkins University Press, 1959.

———. *Diderot, the Embattled Phiolospher.* New York: Macmillan, 1966.

———. *Jean Jacques Rousseau.* New York: Macmillan, 1968.

———. *Nature and Culture: Ethical Thought in the French Enlightenment.* Baltimore: Johns Hopkins University Press, 1963.

Crowley, Herbert. *The Promise of American Life.* Cambridge, Mass.: Harvard University Press, 1965.

Crumin, Lawrence, *The Transformation of the School: Progressivism in American Education, 1876–1937.* New York: Knopf, 1961.

Curti, Merle. *The Growth of American Thought.* New York: Harper, 1943.

———. *The Social Views of American Educators.* New York: Pageant Books, 1963.

Danielow, S. J. *The Lord of History: Reflections on the Inner Meaning of History.* Chicago: Regnery, 1966.

D'Arcy, S. J. M. C. *The Meaning and Matter of History: A Christian View.* New York: Farrar and Sheed, 1959.

Darwin, Charles. *The Origin of Species.* New York, 1877.

———. *Descent of Man and Selection in Relation to Sex,* 2 vols. New York, 1871.

Davis, H. W. C. *The Political Thought of Heinrich Von Trietschke.* London, 1914.

Dawson, Christopher. *Progress and Religion.* London: Longmans, 1945.

———. *Religion and the Rise of Western Culture.* London: Longmans, 1950.

DeKoster, Lester. *Communism and the Christian Faith.* Grand Rapids: Wm. B. Eerdmans, 1956.

Demant, A. *Theology of Society.* London, 1947.

Dennis, Lawrence. *The Coming American Fascism.* New York: Harper, 1936.

Descartes, René. *Dialogue on Method.* New York: Penguin, 1976.

Dewey, John. *Art as Experience.* New York: Capricorn Books, 1934.

———. *A Common Faith.* New Haven: Yale University Press, 1944.

———. *Democracy and Education.* New York: Macmillan, 1966.

———. *Essays in Experimental Logic.* New York: Dover, 1953.

———. *Experience and Education.* New York: Macmillan, 1938.

———. *Freedom and Culture*. New York: G. P. Putnam, 1939.

———. *Human Nature and Conduct: An Introduction to Social Psychology*. New York: Henry Holt, 1922.

———. *Moral Principles in Education*. Boston: Houghton-Mifflin, 1909.

———. *On Experience, Nature and Freedom*. Indianapolis: Bobbs-Merrill, 1960.

———. *The Structure of Experience*, ed. by John J. McDermott. New York: Putnam, 1973.

———. *Liberalism and Sound Action*. New York: Capricorn Books, 1963.

———. *The Quest for Certainty*. New York: Mintor Books, 1929.

———. *Reconstruction of Philosophy*. Boston: Beacon Press, 1957.

———. *The Study of Ethics. A Syllabus*. New York: Gordon Press, 1976.

De Wolf, L. H. *The Religious Revolt Against Reason*. New York: Greenwood Press, 1949.

Diderot. *Dialogues to Frances Burell*. New York, 1971.

Dillard, Dudley. *The Economics of John Maynard Keynes: The Theory of a Money Economy*. Englewood Cliffs, N. J.: Prentice-Hall, 1948.

Dooyeweerd, Herman. *The Christian Idea of the State*. Grand Rapids: Wm. B. Eerdmans, 1965.

———. *The Idea of a Christian Philosophy*. Grand Rapids: Wm. B. Eerdmans, 1965.

———. *In the Twilight of Western Thought*. Nutley, N. J.: Presbyterian and Reformed, 1960.

———. *A New Critique of Theoretical Thought*, 4 vols. Nutley, N. J.: Presbyterian and Reformed, 1959.

———. *The Secularization of Science*. n.d.

———. *The Sociology of Law and Its Philosophic Foundations*.

———. *Transcendental Problems of Philosophic Thought*. Grand Rapids: Wm. B. Eerdmans, 1968.

Drucker, Peter. *The End of Economic Man: A Study of the New Totalitarianism*. New York: Heinemann, 1939.

Dunning, William E. *A Survey of Political Theories: From Luther to Montesquieu*. New York: Macmillan, 1938.

Durkheim, Emile. *The Division of Labor in Modern Society*. 1893.

———. *Elementary Forms of Religious Life: A Study in Religious Sociology*, tr. Joseph Ward Swaim. Glenco, Ill.: Free Press, 1954.

———. *Moral Education: A Study in Its Theory and Application of the*

Sociology of Education, tr. Everett Wilson. Glencoe, Ill.: Free Press, 1961.

———. *Rules of Sociological Method,* tr. Sarah Soloway. Glencoe, Ill.: Free Press, 1950.

———. *Selected Writings,* tr. and ed. Antony Gidden. Cambridge University Press, 1972.

———. *Sociology and Philosophy.* Glencoe, Ill.: Free Press, 1953.

———. *Suicide,* tr. John A. Spaulding and George Simpson. Glencoe, Ill.: Free Press, 1950.

Edman, Irving. *John Dewey: His Contribution to the American Tradition.* New York: Columbia University Press, 1968.

Edmunds, Palmer. *Law and Civilization.* Washington, D. C.: Public Affairs Press, 1959.

Einstein, Albert. *Relativity.* Princeton University Press, 1938.

Einstein, Albert, and Infeld, Leupold, *The Evolution of Physics: The Growth of Ideas from the Early Concepts in Relativity and Quanta.* New York: Simon and Schuster, 1938.

Elliott, W. Y. *The Pragmatic Revolt in Politics.* New York: Macmillan, 1928.

Ellul, Jacques. *The Technological Society.* New York: Random House, 1964.

Engels, Friederich. *Feuerbach: The Roots of Socialist Philosophy.* Chicago, 1900.

———. *The Origins of the Family, Private Property and the State.* London, 1935.

———. *Socialism, Utopian and Scientific.* Chicago, 1900.

Esslinger, William. *Politics and Science.* New York: Philosophical Library, 1955.

Evans, M. Stanton. *The Future of Conservatism.* New York: Doubleday, 1968.

Ferguson, Wallace K. *Europe in Transition, 1300–1520.* Boston: Houghton-Mifflin, 1948.

———. *The Renaissance in Historical Thought.* Boston: Houghton-Mifflin, 1948.

———. *Renaissance Studies.* London, Ontario, 1963.

Feuerbach, Ludwig. *The Essence of Christianity.* New York: Harper, 1957.

Fichte, J. G. *Addresses to the German Nation,* tr. Jones and Trumbull. Chicago: Open Court, 1922.

Fichte, Johann Gottlieb. *The Science of Knowledge.* London, 1889.

———. *The Science of Rights.* London, 1889.

Figgis, J. N. *The Will to Freedom, or, The Gospel of Nietzsche and the Gospel of Christ.* New York: Scribner, 1917.

Fiske, John. *Darwinism and Other Essays.* Boston: Houghton-Mifflin, 1913.

———. *The Idea of God.* Boston: Houghton-Mifflin, 1888.

———. *Outlines of Cosmic Philosophy.* New York: Johnson Reprints, 1974.

———. *The Idea of Good as Affected by Modern Knowledge,* 3rd ed. Boston: Houghton-Mifflin, 1888.

Flewelling, Ralph. *The Survival of Western Culture.* New York, 1943.

Flint, Robert. *Anti-Theistic Theories.* London, 1879.

———. *The Philosophy of Law in France and Germany.* Edinburgh, 1877.

Forcy, Charles S. *Cross Roads of Liberalism: Croly, Weyland and Lippman, and the Progressive Era, 1900–1925.* New York: Oxford University Press, 1961.

Foster, M. B. *The Political Philosophies of Plato and Hegel.* Oxford University Press, 1935.

Frank, Jerome. *Law and the Modern World.* New York, 1930.

Franklin, Julian H. *Jean Bodin and the Sixteenth Century Revolution in the Methodology of Law and History.* New York: Columbia University Press, 1963.

Freud, Ernst L. *Letters of Sigmund Freud.* New York: Basic Books, 1960.

Freud, Sigmund. *Collected Papers,* 5 vols., ed. Ernest Jones. New York: Basic Books, 1959.

———. *The Future of an Illusion.* New York: Norton, 1960.

———. *Moses and Monotheism,* ed. Katherine Jones. New York: Random House, 1955.

———. *An Outline of Psychoanalysis: The Ego and the Id,* tr. Joan Riviere. New York: Norton, 1960.

Freund, Peter, and Denise, C. T. *Contemporary Philosophy and Its Origins.* Princeton, N. J.: Princeton University Press, 1967.

Friedell, Egon. *A Cultural History of the Modern Age,* 6 vols. New York: A. A. Knopf, 1964.

Fromm, Erich. *Escape from Freedom.* New York: Farrar and Rinehart, 1945.

———. *Marx's Concept of Man.* New York: Ungar, 1964.

Fromm, Erich, ed. *Socialism and Humanism: An International Symposium.* New York: Doubleday, 1966.

Frothingham, O. B. *Transcendentalism in New England.* New York: Harper, 1959.

Gabriel, Ralph. *The Course of American Democratic Thought.* New York: Ronald Press, 1940.

Gay, Peter. *The Dilemma of Democratic Socialism: Edward Bernstein to Karl Marx.* New York: Octagon, 1962.

———. *The Enlightenment: An Interpretation, The Rise of Modern Paganism,* vol. 1. New York: A. A. Knopf, 1966.

———. *The Enlightenment: The Science of Freedom,* vol. 2. New York: A. A. Knopf, 1969.

———. *John Locke on Education.* New York: Columbia University Press, 1964.

———. *The Party of Humanity.* New York: Norton, 1964.

Geehan, Edward, ed. *Jerusalem and Athens.* Nutley, N. J.: Presbyterian and Reformed, 1971.

Gerth, H. H., and Mills, C. Wright, eds. *From Max Weber: Essays on Sociology.* New York: Oxford University Press, 1947.

Gilkey, Langdon. *Maker of Heaven and Earth.* Garden City, N. Y.: Doubleday, 1966.

Girvets, Harry R. *The Evolution of Liberalism.* New York: Harper, 1966.

Gooch, G. P. *Democratice Ideas in the Nineteenth Century.* New York: Harper, 1959.

———. *History and Historians in the Nineteenth Century.* New York: Longmans, 1913.

Grabowsky, Stanislaus. *The Church: An Introduction to the Theology of St. Augustine.* London: Lutterworth, 1951.

Grader, P. *The Principles of Christian Art.* London, 1928.

Greeley, Andrew. *The Unsecular Man: The Persistence of Religion.* New York: Shocken, 1972.

Greene, John C. *Darwin and the Modern World.* Baton Rouge: Louisiana University Press, 1961.

———. *The Death of Adam: Evolution and Its Impact on Western Thought.* University of Iowa Press, 1959.

Grimsley, Ronald. *Existential Thought.* University of Cardiff Wales, 1967.

Grisez, Germain. *Beyond the New Morality: The Responsibilities of Freedom.* South Bend, Ind.: University of Notre Dame Press, 1974.

Gunn, James A. *Modern French Philosophy: A Study Since Comte.* New York, 1922.

Haeckel, Ernst. *The Riddle of the Universe at the Close of the Nineteenth Century*. St. Clare Shores, Mich., 1907.

Halevy, Elie. *The Growth of Philosophical Radicalism,* tr. Mary Morris. New York: Macmillan, 1928.

Hall, A. R. *The Scientific Revolution, 1500–1800: The Foundations of the Modern Scientific Attitude*. Boston: Beacon Press, 1956.

Hallowell, John R. *The Decline of Liberalism as an Ideology,* vol. 1, University of California Publications in Political Science. Berkeley, 1971.

———. *Main Currents in Modern Political Thought*. New York: Henry Holt, 1950.

Hamburgher, Michawl. *Intellectuals in Politics: John Stuart Mill and the Philosophic Radicals*. New Haven: Yale University Press, 1965.

Hanson, Alvin. *A Guide to Keynes*. New York and London: McGraw-Hill, 1953.

Harbison, E. Harris. *Christianity and History*. Princeton, N. J.: Princeton University Press, 1964.

Hare, Richard M. *Freedom and Reason*. New York: Oxford University Press, 1953.

Harries, Karsten. *The Meaning of Modern Art: A Philosophical Interpretation*. Evanston, Ill.: Northwestern University Press, 1968.

Hartshorne, C. *The Divine Relativity*. New Haven: Yale University Press, 1948.

Hartz, Louis. *The Liberal Tradition in America*. New York: Harcourt-Brace, 1955.

Hayek, Frederick. *The Constitution of Liberty*. Chicago: University of Chicago, 1960.

———. *The Counter-Revolution of Science*. Glencoe, Ill.: Free Press, 1952.

Hazlitt, Henry. *The Failure of the "New Economics."* New York: Van Nostrand, 1959.

Hearnshaw, F. J. C. *The Social and Political Ideas of Some Representative Thinkers of the Age of Reaction and Reconstruction*. New York: Barnes and Noble, 1949.

———. *The Social and Political Ideas of Some Great French Thinkers of the Age of Reason*. New York: Barns and Noble, 1967.

———. *The Social and Political Ideas of Some Representative Thinkers of the Renaissance and Reformation*. New York: Barnes and Noble, 1967.

———. *Social and Political Ideas of Some Representative Thinkers of the Revolutionary Era*. New York: Barnes and Noble, 1950.

Hegel, G. W. F. *History of Philosophy,* tr. E. S. Haldance and Frances Simpson. New York: Humanities Press, 1968.

———. *On Christianity: Early Theological Writings,* tr . T. M. Knox. New York: Harper, 1961.

———. *The Phenomenology of Mind,* tr. J. B. Baillie, 2nd ed., rev. London: Allen and Unwin, 1964.

———. *The Philosophy of History,* tr. J. Sibree. Chicago: Colonial Press, 1899.

———. *The Philosophy of Mind.* Oxford University Press, 1894.

———. *The Philosophy of Right,* tr. J. M. Knox. Chicago: Encyclopedia Britannica, 1955.

Heidegger, Martin. *Sein und Zeit.* New York: Harper, 1962.

Heilmann, Robert S. *The Ghost on the Ramparts and Other Essays in the Humanities.* Athens, Ga.: University of Georgia Press, 1973.

———. *Existentialism and the Modern Predicament.*

Heinshon, A. G. *The United States 1932–1960: An Anthology of Conservative Writings in the United States, 1932–1960.* Chicago: Regnery, 1962.

Henderson, Lawrence J. *Pareto's Sociology.* Cambridge, Mass.: Harvard University Press, 1935.

Henderson, Ian. *Bultmann.* Richmond, Va.: John Knox Press, 1966.

Hendry, Derek P., ed. *Conditioned Reenforcement.* Chicago: Dorsey Press, 1961.

Henry, Carl F. H. *The Drift of Western Thought.* Grand Rapids: Wm. B. Eerdmans, 1951.

———. *Notes on the Doctrine of God.* Holleston, Mass.: Wilde, 1953.

———. *Remaking the Modern Mind.* Grand Rapids: Wm. B. Eerdmans, 1946.

Himmerfarb, Gertrude. *Darwin and the Darwinian Revolution,* Norton Library. 1959.

Hitler, Adolf. *Mein Kampf,* tr. and ed. E. T. S. Digdale. Boston: Houghton-Mifflin, 1937.

Hocking, W. E. *The Meaning of God in Human Experience.* New Haven: Yale University Press, 1926.

———. *Present State of the Philosophy of Law and Right.* New Haven: Yale University Press, 1926.

———. *Science and the Idea of God.* Chapel Hill: University of North Carolina Press, 1944.

Hodge, Charles. *What Is Evolution?* New York, 1874.

Hofstadter, Richard. *Social Darwinism in American Thought, 1860–1915*. New York: Oxford University Press, 1945.

———. *Anti-Intellectualism in American Life*. New York: Knopf, 1963.

Holbach, Baron Paul H. *D' System of Nature,* ed. H. D. Robinson. New York: Clearwater, 1970.

Holmes, Oliver Wendell. *The Common Law*. Boston, 1881.

Homans, George C., and Curtis, Charles P. *An Introduction to Pareto*. New York: Knopf, 1934.

Hook, Sidney. *John Dewey, Philosopher of Science and Freedom*. New York: Greenwood Press, 1962.

———. *From Hegel to Marx: Studies in the Intellectual Development of Karl Marx*. Ann Arbor: University of Michigan Press, 1970.

———. *Toward an Understanding of Marx*. New York: Gollancz, 1933.

Hopkins, C. H. *The Rise of the Social Gospel in American Protestantism, 1866–1915*. New Haven: Yale University Press, 1940.

Hudson, W. D. *Ludwig Wittgenstein: The Bearing of His Philosophy on Religious Belief*. New York: St. Martin Press, 1975.

Hughes, Stuart. *Consciousness and Society: The Reorientation of European Social Thought, 1890–1930*. New York: Vintage Books, 1958.

Huizinga, J. *Varieties of History*. London, 1957.

Hull, Carl. *Philosophy of the Biological Sciences*. Englewood Cliffs, N. J.: Prentice-Hall, 1974.

Hume, David. *Dialogues Concerning Natural Religion*. London, 1907.

———. *A Treatise on Human Nature,* 2 vols. New York: Collier Books, 1964.

Husserl, Edmund. *The Crisis of European Science and Transcendental Phenomenology: An Introduction to Phenomenological Philosophy*. Chicago: Northwestern University Press, 1970.

———. *Formal and Transcendental Logic,* ed. David. The Hague, 1969.

Hutchinson, William. *The Modernistic Impulse in American Protestantism*. Cambridge, Mass.: Harvard University Press, 1976.

Huxley, Aldous. *Brave New World*. New York: Harper and Row, 1950.

———. *Brave New World Revisited*. New York: Harper and Row, 1958.

———. *The Perennial Philosophy*. New York: Harper and Row, 1945.

Huxley, Julian. *Evolution: The Modern Synthesis,* 2nd ed. New York: Wiley, 1964.

Huxley, Thomas. *On the Origin of Species*. Ann Arbor: University of Michigan Press, 1968.

———. *Man's place in Nature and Other Essays*. New York, 1908.

Ingram, T. Robert. *The World Under God's Law.* Houston, Tex.: St. Thomas Press, 1962.

Jaarsma, Cornelius. *The Educational Philosophy of Herman Bavinck.* Grand Rapids: Wm. B. Eerdmans, 1953.

Jacobs, Margaret C. *The Newtonian and the English Revolution of 1689–1720.* Ithaca, N. Y.: Cornell University Press, 1976.

James, William. *Pragmatism.* London and New York: Longmans, 1928.

———. *Some Problems of Philosophy: A Beginning of an Introduction to Philosophy.* New York: Greenwood, 1968.

———. *Varieties of Religious Experience: A Study in Human Nature.* New York: Longmans, 1929.

———. *The Will to Believe.* New York: Dover, 1960.

Jaspers, Karl: *Philosophical Faith and Revelation.* New York: Colliers, 1967.

———. *Reason and Existence.* New York: Longmans, 1955.

Jessop, T. E. *The Christian Understanding of Man.* London: Willett, 1938.

Johnson, H. A., and Niels Thulstrup. *A Kierkegaard Critique.* Chicago: Henry Regnery, 1967.

Jones, D. Gareth. *Teilhard de Chardin: An Analysis and Assessment.* Downers Grove, Ill.: InterVarsity Press, 1970.

Jones, W. T. *A History of Western Thought.* New York: Harcourt-Brace, 1959.

Jung, Carl. *Collected Works,* ed. Adler-Getal, 2nd ed. Princeton, N. J.: Princeton University Press, 1970.

———. *Psychology and Religion.* New Haven: Yale University Press, 1938.

———. *Psychology of the Unconscious,* tr. Beatrice Hinkle. New York: Dodd Mead, 1947.

Kamenka, Eugene. *The Ethical Foundations of Marxism,* rev. ed. Boston: Routledge and Kegan, 1972.

Kant, Immanuel. *Critique of Judgment,* tr. J. H. Bernard. London, 1892.

———. *Critique of Practical Reason,* tr. Lewis White Beck. New York: Bobbs-Merrill, 1956.

———. *The Critique of Pure Reason,* tr. Norman Kemp Smith. New York: St. Martin Press, 1965.

———. *Groundwork of Metaphysics of Morals.* New York: Harper and Row, 1969.

———. *On History,* tr. Lewis White Beck. Indianapolis: Bobbs-Merrill, 1963.

———. *Perpetual Peace.* New York: Garland Publishers, 1939.

———. *Principles of Politics.* Edinburgh, 1891.

Kariel, H. D. *In Search of Authority: Twentieth Century Political Thought.* New York: Free Press, 1964.

Keeling, S. V. *Descartes.* London: Oxford University Press, 1936.

Kellen, Horace M. *The Liberal Spirit.* Ithaca, N. Y.: Cornell University Press, 1948.

Keen, Samuel. *Gabriel Marcel.* Richmond, Va.: John Knox Press, 1967.

Kegley, Charles W., and Bretall, Robert W., eds. *The Theology of Paul Tillich.* New York: Macmillan, 1957.

Keynes, John Maynard. *The General Theory of Employment, Interest and Money.* New York: Macmillan, 1936.

Kidd, Benjamin. *Social Evolution.* New York: Macmillan, 1894.

Kierkegaard, Søren. *On Authority and Revelation.* New York: Gannon, 1966.

———. *Concept of Dread.* Princeton, N. J.: Princeton University Press, 1944.

———. *Concluding Unscientific Postscript,* tr. Walter Lowrie. Princeton, N. J.: Princeton University Press, 1941.

———. *Fear and Trembling,* and *The Sickness unto Death,* tr. Walter Lowrie. New York: Princeton University Press, 1954.

———. *Philosophical Fragments.* Princeton, N. J.: Princeton University Press, 1952.

Koch, Adrienne. *The American Enlightenment.* New York: Braziller, 1965.

———. *Power, Morals and the Founding Fathers: Essays in the Interpretation of the American Enlightenment.* Ithaca, N. Y.: Cornell University Press, 1961.

Koestenbaum, Peter. *The Vitality of Death: Essays in Existential Psychology and Philosophy.* Westport, Conn.: Greenwood, 1944.

Kohn, Hans. *The Idea of Nationalism.* New York: Macmillan, 1944.

Krieger, Leonard. *The German Idea of Freedom.* Boston: The Beacon Press, 1957.

Krikorian, Yervent. *Naturalism and the Human Spirit.* New York: Columbia University Press, 1964.

Kristeller, Paul O. *Renaissance Thought: The Classical and Humanistic Strains.* New York: Macmillan, 1961.

Kristeller, Paul O., and Randall, John H., eds. *The Renaissance Philosophy of Man.* Chicago: University of Chicago Press, 1948.

Kroner, Richard. *Culture and Faith.* University of Chicago Press, 1937.

———. *Speculation to Revelation in the History of Philosophical Thought,* 3 vols. Philadelphia: Westminster Press, 1956.

Krutch, Joseph Wood. *The Measure of Man's Mind.* Minneapolis: University of Minnesota Press, 1954.

Kuhn, Thomas S. *The Structure of Scientific Revolutions.* Chicago: University of Chicago Press, 1964.

Kuiper, R. B. *Christian Liberty.* Grand Rapids: Wm. B. Eerdmans, 1914.

Kuyper, Abraham. *Lectures on Calvinism.* Grand Rapids: Wm. B. Eerdmans, 1962.

Kuyper, Hermann. *Calvinism and Common Grace.* Grand Rapids: Wm. B. Eerdmans, 1929.

La Mettrie, Jules Offray. *Collected Works.* New York: Open Court, 1970.

Lamprecht, S. P. *The Moral and Political Philosophy of John Locke.* New York: Columbia University Press, 1918.

Laski, Harold. *The Foundations of Sovereignty.* New York: Arno, 1968.

———. *Political Thought in England from Locke to Bentham.* New York: Greenwood, 1961.

———. *The Rise of European Liberalism.* New York: Harper, 1936.

Latta, Robert. *The Monadology of Leibniz.* New York: Oxford University Press, 1965.

Lecky, W. E. H. *History of the Rise and Influence of the Spirit of Rationalism in Europe.* New York: Braziller, 1955.

———. *Democracy and Liberty.* London: Longmans, 1896.

Lee, Francis Nigel. *A Christian Introduction to the History of Philosophy.* Nutley, N. J.: Presbyterian and Reformed, 1969.

———. *Communist Eschatology.* Nutley, N. J.: Presbyterian and Reformed, 1974.

———. *The Origin and Destiny of Man* Nutley, N. J.: Presbyterian and Reformed, 1974.

Leibniz, Gottfried. *Discourses on Metaphysics.* Manchester, England: University of Manchester Press, 1953.

———. *New Essays Concerning Human Understanding.* LaSalle, Ill.: Open Court, 1916.

Leighton, Joseph. *Social Philosophies in Conflict.* New York: D. Appleton, 1937.

Lenin, V. I. *Collected Works: The Teachings of Karl Marx.* International Publishing Co., 1964.

———. *What Is to Be Done.* New York: Oxford University Press, 1963.

Lewis, C. S. *The Abolition of Man.* New York: Macmillan, 1947, 1965.

Lindsay, A. D. *Kant.* London: Oxford University Press, 1934.

Lingren, Henry. *Educational Psychology in the Class Room,* 4th ed. New York: McGraw-Hill, 1972.

Lippmann, Walter. *An Inquiry into the Principles of the Good Society.* Boston: Little, Brown, 1943.

———. *A Preface to Morals.* New York: Macmillan, 1929.

———. *A Preface to Politics.* New York: Macmillan, 1933.

Locke, John. *Essay Concerning Human Understanding,* 2 vols. Oxford University Press, 1894.

———. *Some Thoughts Concerning Education, Works,* 12th ed., 9 vols. London, 1824.

Lovejoy, A. O. *Essays in the History of Ideas.* Baltimore: Johns Hopkins Press, 1948.

———. *The Reason, the Understanding and Time.* Baltimore: Johns Hopkins Press, 1961.

Lovejoy, Arthur. *The Great Chain of Being.* Cambridge, Mass: Harvard University Press, 1936.

Lowe, Victor. *Understanding Whitehead.* Baltimore: Johns Hopkins Press, 1962.

Lowith, Carl. *From Hegel to Nietzsche.* Chicago: University of Chicago Press, 1949.

Lowrie, Walter. *Kierkegaard.* New York, 1963, 1976.

McIntyre, John. *The Christian Doctrine of History.* Grand Rapids: Wm. B. Eerdmans, 1957.

Machen, J. Gresham. *The Christian View of Man.* New York: Macmillan, 1937.

———. *Christianity and Liberalism.* Grand Rapids: Wm. B. Eerdmans, 1923.

———. *Christianity in the Modern World.* New York: Macmillan, 1936.

———. *What Is Christianity?* Grand Rapids: Wm. B. Eerdmans, 1951.

———. *What Is Faith?* Grand Rapids: Wm. B. Eerdmans, 1962.

Machiavelli, *The Prince,* tr. Ninian Hall Thomson, 2nd. ed., rev. Oxford University Press, 1907.

McIlwain, Charles H. *The Growth of Political Thought in the West.* New York: Macmillan, 1932.

Madge, John. *The Origins of Scientific Sociology.* Glenco, Ill.: Free Press, 1962.

Malreaux, Andre. *The Temptation of the West,* tr. Robert Hollander. New York: Random House, 1974.

———. *Man's Fate,* tr. Haakon Chevalier. New York: Random House, 1934.

———. *The Psychology of Art.* London, 1959.

———. *The Royal Way,* tr. Gilbert Stuart. London, 1954.

———. *The Voices of Science,* tr. Gilbert Stuart. New York: Doubleday, 1959.

Mannheim, Karl. *Ideology and Utopia: An Introduction to the Sociology of Knowledge.* New York: Harcourt Brace, 1936.

Manser, A. R. "The Concept of Evolution," *Philosophy.* January, 1965.

Manson, Grant. *Frank Lloyd Wright.* New York: Chapman, 1958.

Marcel, Gabriel. *Man Against Humanity.* Harbille Press, 1952.

———. *The Mystery of Being.* Harbille Press, 1950.

———. *The Philosophy of Existence.* Harbille Press, 1948.

Marcuse, Herbert. *Eros and Civilization: A Philosophical Inquiry into Freud.* Boston: Beacon Press, 1966.

———. *Reason and Revolution: Hegel and the Rise of Social Theory,* 2nd ed. Boston: Beacon Press, 1966.

Maritain, Jacques. *The Range of Reason.* New York: Scribner's, 1952.

———. *The Social and Political Philosophy of Jacques Maritain,* ed. Joseph Adams and Leo R. Ward. New York: Scribner's, 1955.

Martin, Kingsley. *French Liberal Thought in the Eighteenth Century.* New York: New York Times Press, 1953.

Marvin, D. F. S. *Comte: The Founder of Sociology.* New York: Chapman, 1936.

Marx, Karl. *Capital.* Chicago: Modern Library, 1952.

———. *The Holy Family.* New York, 1965.

———. *Value, Price and Profit.* Chicago: Allen Union.

Mason, Stephen F. *A History of Science.* New York: Macmillan, 1966.

Meerloo, S. *The Rape of the Mind: The Psychology of Thought Control, Menticide and Brainwashing.* New York: Grossett and Dunlop, 1971.

Meerz, J. T. *A History of European Thought in the Nineteenth Century.* Edinburgh and London, 1921–1923.

Mendelbaum, Maurice. *History, Man and Reason: A Study in Nineteenth Century Thought.* Baltimore: Johns Hopkins University Press, 1971.

Methven, Eugene H. *The Rise of Radicalism.* New Rochelle, N. Y.: Arlington House, 1973.

Meyerhoff, Hans. *The Philosophy of History in Our Time.* New York: Doubleday, 1959.

Micklin, F. A. *The Secular and the Sacred: An Inquiry into the Principles of a Christian Civilization.* London: Lutterworth, 1948.

Mill, John Stuart. *Essays on Positivism and Culture,* ed. Gertrude Himmerfarb. London, 1948.

———. *The Positive Philosophy of August Comte.* New York: Scholarly Books, 1973.

———. *A System of Logic,* 8th ed. New York, 1890.

———. *Unitarian Liberty and Representative Government.* New York: Dutton, 1951.

Miller, Perry. *The Life of the Mind in America: From the Revolution to the Civil War.* New York: Harcourt Brace, 1965.

———. *The New England Mind: The Seventeenth Century.* Cambridge, Mass.: Harvard University Press, 1954.

Mink, Louis O. *Mind, History and Dialectic: The Philosophy of R. G. Collingwood.* Bloomington, Ind.: Indiana University Press, 1969.

Mollina, Fernando. *The Sources of Existentialism as a Philosophy.* Englewood Cliffs, N. J.: Prentice-Hall, 1964.

Montague, Ashley. *Culture and the Evolution of Man.* New York: Oxford University Press, 1962.

———. *Man in Process.* New York: New American Library, 1962.

Montesquieu, Baron Charles Secondat dem. *The Spirit of Laws,* tr. Thomas Nugent. Chicago: University of Chicago Press, 1962.

Montgomery, John W. *The Shape of the Past.* Ann Arbor: University of Michigan Press, 1962.

Moore, Edward C. *American Pragmatism: Pierce, James and Dewey.* New York: Oxford University Press, 1961.

Moore, Edward Caldwell. *An Outline of the History of Christian Thought Since Kant.* New York: Scribner's, 1913.

Morais, Herbert. *Deism in Eighteenth Century America.* New York: Columbia University Press, 1934.

Moret, Daniel. *French Thought in the Seventeenth Century,* tr. M. Levin. Englewood Cliffs, N. J.: Prentice-Hall, 1929.

Morgenthau, Hans J. *The Decline of Democratic Politics.* Chicago: University of Chicago Press, 1969.

———. *Scientific Man vs. Power Politics.* Chicago: University of Chicago Press, 1946.

Morris, Herbert. *Freedom and Responsibility: Readings in Philosophy and Law.* Stanford University Press, 1961.

Mosier, Richard. *The American Temper: Patterns of our Intellectual Heritage*. Berkeley: University of California Press, 1952.

Mowrer, Hobart. *The Crisis in Psychiatry and Religion*. New York: Van Nostrum, 1961.

———. *Morality and Mental Health*. Chicago: Rand McNally, 1967.

Mumford, Lewis. *The Condition of Man*. New York: Harcourt Brace, 1944.

Munly, D. L. *The Ideal of a Secular Society and Its Significance for Christians*. Oxford University Press, 1963.

Murphy, Gardner. *Psychological Thought from Pythagoras to Freud*. New York: Harcourt Brace, 1968.

Murphy, Gardner, and Kovak, Joseph K. *Historical Introduction to Modern Psychology*, 3rd ed. New York: Harcourt Brace, 1972.

Murray, Michael. *The Thought of Teilhard de Chardin: An Informal Introduction*. New York: Seabury, 1966.

Nash, Arnold. *American Protestant Thought in the Twentieth Century*. New York: Macmillan, 1951.

Nash, George, ed. *The Conservative Intellectual Movement in America Since 1945*. New Rochelle, N. Y.: Arlington House, 1977.

Nash, Ronald, ed. *The Philosophy of Gordon Clark*. Nutley, N. J.: Presbyterian and Reformed, 1968.

Nef, John U. *A Search for Civilization*. Chicago: University of Chicago Press, 1962.

Neff, Frederick C. *Philosophy and American Education*. New York: Center for Applied Research, 1966.

Nelson, Benjamin. *Freud and the Twentieth Century*. New York: Peter Smith, 1957.

Niebuhr, Reinhold. *Beyond Tragedy: Essays in the Christian Interpretation of History*. New York: Scribner's, 1937.

———. *The Children of Light and the Children of Darkness*. New York: Scribner's, 1945.

———. *Faith and History*. New York: Scribner's, 1948.

———. *Moral Man in Immoral Society*. New York: Scribner's, 1932.

———. *The Nature and Destiny of Man*. New York: Scribner's, 1941–1943.

———. *The Self and the Drama of History*. New York: Scribner's, 1955.

Nietzsche, Frederick. *Beyond Good and Evil*. New York: Gordon Press, 1973.

———. *The Birth of Tragedy*. Chicago: University of Chicago Press, 1945.

———. *The Genealogy of Morals.* New York: Modern Library, 1927.

———. *The Use and Abuse of History.* New York: Oxford University Press, 1949.

———. *Thus Spake Zarathustra,* tr. Thomas Common. Modern Library, New York, n.d

———. *Will to Power,* tr. Walter Kaufman. New York: Random House, 1968.

Nisbet, Robert A. *The Degradation of the Academic Dogma.* New York: Basic Books, 1971.

———. *Social Change and History.* New York: Oxford University Press, 1969.

———. *The Sociological Tradition.* New York: Basic Books, 1966.

Noble, David. *The Paradox of Progressive Thought.* Minneapolis: University of Minnesota Press, 1958.

———. *The Progressive Mind, 1890–1917.* Chicago: Rand McNally, 1970.

North, Gary, ed. *Foundations of Christian Scholarship.* Vallecito, Calif.: Ross House Books, 1976.

———. *An Introduction to Christian Economics.* Nutley, N. J.: Presbyterian and Reformed, 1973.

———. *Marx's Religion of Revolution.* Nutley, N. J.: Presbyterian and Reformed, 1968.

Northrop, F. S. C. *Man, Nature and God.* New York: Greenwood, 1962.

———. *The Meeting of the East and the West.* New York: Macmillan, 1947.

Nutter, Warren. *Central Planning, Visible Hand.* New York, 1976.

Oates, Whitney J. *Basic Writings of St. Augustine.* New York: Random House, 1948.

Olson, Robert G. *An Introduction to Existentialism.* New York: Dover, 1961.

Orr, Linda. *Jules Michelet: Nature, History and Language.* Ithaca, N. Y.: Cornell University Press, 1976.

Ortega y Gasset, Jose. *The Deterioration of Art.* Princeton, N. J.: Princeton University Press, 1972.

———. *History as a System.* New York: Norton, 1941.

———. *The Modern Theme.* New York: W. W. Norton, 1951.

———. *The Revolt of the Masses.* New York: W. W. Norton, 1932.

———. *What Is Philosophy?* New York: Norton, 1960.

Orton, W. A. *The Liberal Tradition.* New Haven: Yale University Press, 1945.

Owen, O. R. G. *Scientific Man and Religion.* Philadelphia: Westminster Press, 1952.

Palmer, R. *The Age of Democratic Revolution.* New Haven: Yale University Press, 1959.

Pareto, Vilfredo. *The Mind and Society,* 4 vols. New York: Harcourt Brace, 1935.

———. *Sociological Writings,* ed. and tr. Finer and Derick Mirfin. New York: Prager, 1966.

Parker, Charles. *The Moral Basis of Burke's Political Theory.* Cambridge University Press, 1966.

Parrington, Vernon L. *Main Currents in American Thought,* 3 vols. New York: Harcourt Brace, 1954.

Parsons, Talcott. *The Structure of Social Action.* Glencoe, Ill.: Free Press, 1949.

Pauck, Wilhelm, and Pauck, Maria. *Paul Tillich, His Life and Thoughts.* The Grammar of Science. London and New York: Harper and Row, 1937, 1976.

Pelikan, Jaroslav. *The Finality of Jesus Christ in an Age of Universal History.* London: Longmans, 1965.

Perry, Ralph Barton. *General Theory of Value.* New York: Longmans, 1926.

———. *The Humanity of Man.* New York: Longman's, 1936.

———. *The Philosophy of the Recent Past.* New York: Scribner's, 1925.

———. *The New Realism.* New York: Longmans, 1912.

———. *Present Philosophical Tendencies: A Critical Survey of Naturalism, Idealism, Pragmatism and Realism.* New York: Longmans, 1912.

———. *The Thought and Character of William James.* Cambridge, Mass.: Harvard University Press, 1948.

Persons, Stowe. *American Minds: A History of Ideas.* New York: Henry Holt, 1958.

———. *Evolutionary Thought in America.* Princeton University Press, 1950.

Petry, Ray C. *Christian Eschatology and Social Thought.* New York: Abingdon, 1956.

Picard, Max. *Hitler in Ourselves.* Chicago: Regnery, 1947.

Piper, Otto. *God in History.* New York: Macmillan, 1939.

Polman, A. C. R. *Karl Barth.* Philadelphia: Presbyterian and Reformed, 1960.

Popper, Karl. *Objective Knowledge*. Oxford University Press, 1972.

———. *The Open Society and Its Enemies*. Princeton, N. J.: Princeton University Press, 1966.

———. *The Poverty of Historicism*. London: Routledge, 1957.

Pound, Roscoe. *An Introduction to the Philosophy of Law*. New Haven: Yale University Press, 1954.

———. *Fact and Fiction in B. F. Skinner's Science and Utopia*. Warren Green, Publishers, 1974.

Rachlin, Howard. *Behavior and Learning: An Introduction to Modern Behaviorism*. San Francisco: W. Freeman, 1976.

Randall, John Herman. *The Career of Philosophy—From the Middle Ages to the Enlightenment*. New York: Columbia University Press, 1962.

———. *How Philosophy Uses Its Past*. New York: Columbia University Press, 1965.

———. *The Making of the Modern Mind: A Survey of the Intellectual Background of the Modern Age*. Boston: Houghton Mifflin, 1926.

Raphael, Robert. *Richard Wagner*. n.d.

Ratner, Joseph, ed. *The Philosophy of Spinoza*. New York, n.d.

Rauschenbusch, Walter. *Christianity and the Social Crisis*. New York: Macmillan, 1907.

———. *Christianizing the Social Order*. New York: Macmillan, 1912.

———. *A Theology for the Social Gospel*. New York: Macmillan, 1917.

Read, Herbert. *The Philosophy of Modern Art*. Folcroft, Pa.: Faber and Faber, 1973.

Reese, Michael. *The Philosophy of Biology*. Hutchinson, Kan., 1964.

Reinhardt, Kurt. *The Existentialist Revolt*. New York: Ungar, 1960.

Rewald, John. *The History of Impressionism,* 4th ed., rev. Museum of Modern Art, New York, 1973.

Richardson, Edgar. *Painting in America from 1502 to the present*. New York: Crowell, 1965.

Riley, I. E. *American Thought from Puritanism to Pragmatism and Beyond,* 2nd ed. New York: Peter Smith, 1941.

Ritter, Alan. *The Political Thought of Pierre Joseph Proudhon*. Princeton, N. J.: Princeton University Press, 1969.

Roberts, T. A. *History and Christian Apologetics*. London: SPCK, 1960.

Robertson, J. M. *The Meaning of Liberalism*. London: Macmillan, 1912.

Rogers, A. K. *A Student's History of Philosophy*. New York: Macmillan, 1949.

Rogers, James A. "Darwinism and Social Darwinism," *Journal of the History of Ideas* 33 (1972), 265-288.

Rookmaaker, H. R.. *Modern Art and the Death of a Culture.* Downers Grove, Ill.: InterVarsity Press, 1970.

Rousseau, Jacques. *Social Contrat and Discourses.* New York: Regnery, 1954.

Royce, Josiah. *Spirit of Modern Philosophy.* Boston: Houghton Mifflin, 1899.

———. *The Social Philosophy of Josiah Royce,* ed. Stuart Brown. Syracuse, N. Y.: Syracuse University Press, 1950.

———. *The World and the Individual,* 2 vols. New York: Macmillan, 1904.

Ruggerio, Guido de. *The History of European Liberalism,* tr. R. G. Collingwood. Boston: Beacon Press, 1969.

———. *Modern Philosophy.* New York: Macmillan, 1921.

Rushdoony, R. J. *The Biblical Philosophy of History.* Nutley, N. J.: Presbyterian and Reformed, 1969.

———. *By What Standard?* Nutley, N. J.: Presbyterian and Reformed, 1959.

———. *Freud.* International Library of Theology and Philosophy. Philadelphia: Presbyterian and Reformed, 1965.

———. *Intellectual Schizophrenia.* Philadelphia: Presbyterian and Reformed, 1961.

———. *The Institutes of Biblical Law.* Nutley, N. J.: Presbyterian and Reformed, 1974.

———. *The Messianic Character of American Education.* Nutley, N. J.: Presbyterian and Reformed, 1965.

———. *The Methodology of Science.* Nutley, N. J.: Presbyterian and Reformed, 1967.

———. *The One and the Many: Studies in the Philosophy of Order and Ultimacy.* Nutley, N. J.: Presbyterian and Reformed, 1971.

———. *Van Til.* Nutley, N. J.: Presbyterian and Reformed, 1960.

Russell, Bertrand. *The ABC of Relativity,* rev. ed. New York: Allen and Unwin, 1935.

———. *A Critical Exposition of the Philosophy of Leibniz,* 2nd ed., London: Allen and Unwin, 1958.

———. *The History of Western Philosophy.* New York: Simon and Schuster, 1946.

———. *Human Knowledge: Its Scope and Limits.* New York: Simon and Schuster, 1967.

———. *Inquiry into the Meaning of Truth.* Allen and Unwin, 1940.

———. *Problems of Philosophy.* Oxford Press, 1959.

———. *Religion and Science.* New York: Oxford University Press, 1961.

———. *The Philosophy of Bergson,* reprint. Folcroft (1914).

———. *The Scientific Outlook.* New York: Norton, 1962.

Rust, Eric. *The Christian Understanding of History.* London: Oxford University Press, 1942.

Sabine, George H. *A History of Political Theory,* 3rd ed. New York: Henry Holt, 1961.

Sartre, Jean Paul. *Being and Nothingness: An Essay on Phenomenological Ontology,* tr. Hazel Barnes. New York: Philosophical Library, 1956.

———. *Existentialism.* New York: Philosophical Library, 1947.

———. *Nausea.* Paris: New Directions Press, 1939.

Savigny, Frederick. *On the Vocation of Our Age for Legislation and Jurisprudence.* London, 1931.

Schaeffer, Francis A. *The God Who Is There.* Downers Grove, Ill.: Inter-Varsity Press, 1969.

———. *How Shall We Then Live?* Old Tappan, N. J.: Fleming H. Revell, 1976.

Schapiro, J. Salwyn. *Jean Marie Condorcet and the Rise of Liberalism.* New York: Octagon, 1969.

———. *Liberalism and the Challenge of Fascism.* New York: McGraw-Hill, 1949.

———. *The World in Crisis: Political Movements in the Twentieth Century.* New York: McGraw-Hill, 1950.

Schilp, P. Z. *The Philosophy of John Dewey.* Evanston, Ill.: Northwestern University Press, 1939.

Schneider, Herbert W. *A History of American Philosophy.* New York: Columbia University Press, 1946.

———. "The Influence of Darwin and Spengler on American Philosophical Theology," *Journal of the History of Ideas* 6 (1945), 3-18.

———. *Making the Fascist State.* New York: Henry Holt, 1928.

Schopenhauer, Arthur. *The World as Will and Idea,* 3 vols. London, 1883.

Schragg, Calvin. *Existence and Freedom.* Evanston, Ill.: Northwestern University Press, 1961.

Scott, Nathan A. *Reinhold Niebuhr.* University of Minnesota Press, 1963.

Scott, Otto J. *Robespierre, the Voice of Virtue.* New York, 1976.

Seidenburg, Roderick. *Anatomy of the Future*. Chapel Hill, N. C.: University of North Carolina Press, 1961.

———. *Post-Historic Man: An Inquiry*. Chapel Hill, N. C.: University of North Carolina Press, 1959.

Seligman, Ben. *Molders of Modern Thought*. Chicago: Quadrangle Books, 1970.

Seligman, R. Z. *The Economic Interpretation of History*. New York: Macmillan, 1907.

Schills, E. A., and Finch, H. Z. *Max Weber, on the Methodology of the Social Sciences*. Glencoe, Ill.: Free Press, 1949.

Simpson, George. *August Comte, Sire of Sociology*. New York: Crowell, 1969.

Simpson, George Gaylord. *This View of Life: The World of an Evolutionist*. New York: Harcourt Brace, 1961.

Singer, Charles Gregg. *John Calvin: His Roots and Fruits*. Nutley, N. J.: Presbyterian and Reformed, 1967.

Singer, C. Gregg. *A Theological Interpretation of American History*. Nutley, N. J.: Presbyterian and Reformed, 1964.

———. *The Unholy Alliance*. New Rochelle N. Y.: Arlington House, 1975.

———. *Toynbee. Modern Thinkers Series*. Nutley, N. J.: Presbyterian and Reformed, 1967.

Skinner, B. F. *Behavior of Organisms*. New York, 1941.

———. *Beyond Freedom and Dignity*. New York: Knopf, 1971.

———. *Science and Human Behavior*. Englewood Cliffs, N. J.: Prentice-Hall, 1953.

———. *Verbal Behavior*. Englewood Cliffs, N. J.: Prentice-Hall, 1957.

———. *Walden Two*. New York: Macmillan, 1975.

Smith, Norman Kemp. *A Commentary on Kant's Critique of Pure Reason*. New York: Humanities Press, 1967.

———. *The Philosophy of David Hume*. New York: St. Martins Press, 1964.

Smith, Preserved. *A History of Modern Culture*, 2 vols. New York: Henry Holt, 1930.

Somerville, John. *The Philosophy of Marxism: An Exposition*. New York: Random House, 1967.

Sorokin, Pitirim. *Contemporary Sociological Theories*. New York: Harper, 1928.

———. *The Crisis of Our Age*. New York: E. P. Dutton, 1941.

———. *Social and Cultural Dynamics,* 6 vols. New York: American Books, 1937–1941.

———. *Sociological Theories of Today.* New York: Harper and Row, 1966.

Spencer, Herbert. *Essays: Scientific, Political and Speculative.* London, 1958.

———. *The Evolution of Society.* Chicago: University of Chicago Press, 1967.

———. *First Principles.* London and New York: Appleton, 1899.

———. *Principles of Sociology.* Hamden, Conn.: Greenwood, 1969.

———. *Social Statics.* New York, 1916.

Spier, J. M. *Christianity and Existentialism.* Nutley, N. J.: Presbyterian and Reformed, 1953.

———. *What Is Christian Philosophy?* tr. Fred Klooster. Grand Rapids: Wm. B. Eerdmans, 1935.

Spinks, Matthew. *Christian Thought from Erasmus to Berdyaev.* Englewood Cliffs, N. J.: Prentice-Hall, 1962.

Spilker, Robert. *Literary History of the United States,* 3rd ed., 2 vols. New York, 1963.

Stace, W. T. *The Philosophy of Hegel.* London, 1924.

Stent, Guenthern. *The Coming of the Golden Ages: A View of the End of Progress.* Garden City, N. Y.: Doubleday, 1969.

Stephen, Leslie. *History of English Thought in the Eighteenth Century.* New York: Peter Smith, 1949.

Stern, Fritz. *The Politics of Cultural Despair: A Study of the Rise of German Ideology.* Berkeley: University of California Press, 1961.

Stob, Ralph. *Christianity and Classical Civilization.* Grand Rapids: Wm. B. Eerdmans, 1950.

Stott, Leland. *The Psychology of Human Development.* New York: Holt, 1974.

Strauss, David. *The Old Faith and the New.* New York, 1872.

Sumner, William Graham. *The Challenge of the State and Other Essays.* New Haven: Yale University Press, 1914.

———. *Folkways.* Boston: Ginn and Co., 1906.

Sumner, William Graham, and Keller, Albert G. *The Science of Society.* London: Oxford University Press, 1927.

———. *Social Darwinism.* Englewood Cliffs, N. J.: Prentice-Hall, 1963.

Teggart, F. J. *The Idea of Progress.* Berkeley: University of California Press, 1949.

Tawney, R. H. *Religion and the Rise of Capitalism.* Glouster, Mass.: Peter Smith, 1930.

Taylor, E. L. Hebden. *The Christian Philosophy of Law, Politics and the State.* Nutley, N. J.: Presbyterian and Reformed, 1963.

———. *Reformation or Revolution.* Nutley, N. J.: Presbyterian and Reformed, 1969.

Thelen, May F. *Man as Sinner in Contemporary Realistic Theology.* New York: Oxford University Press, 1947.

Thody, Philip. *Albert Camus: A Study of His Work.* London: Macmillan 1957.

Thompson, Kenneth. *Whitehead's Philosophy of Religion.* The Hague and Paris, 1971.

Thompson, Robert Ellis. *The Divine Order of Human Society.* Philadelphia: Presbyterian Board Sabbath School Work, 1891.

Thornwell, James H. *Discourses on Truth.* New York: Robert Carter, 1859.

Tillich, Paul. *Biblical Religion and the Search for Ultimate Meaning.* Chicago: University of Chicago Press, 1955.

———. *The Courage to Be.* New Haven: Yale University Press, 1968.

———. *Dynamics of Faith.* New York: Harper, 1957.

———. *History of Culture.* New York: Oxford University Press, 1959.

———. *The New Being.* New York: Scribner's, 1955.

———. *Systematic Theology,* 3 vols. Chicago: University of Chicago Press, 1951–1963.

Torry, N. L. *The Spirit of Voltaire.* New York: Oxford University Press, 1938.

Toynbee, Arnold. *Civilization on Trial.* London: Oxford University Press, 1948.

———. *Study of History,* 12 vols. London and New York: Oxford University Press, 1934–1961.

———. *War and Civilization.* New York: Oxford University Press, 1950.

———. *The World and the West.* New York: Oxford University Press, 1950.

Trietschke, Heinrich von. *Politics,* 2 vols. New York: Harcourt Brace 1963.

Tyler, Alice Felt. *Freedom's Ferment.* Minneapolis: University of Minnesota Press, 1944.

Ussher, Arland. *Journey Through Dread: A Study of Kierkegaard, Heidegger, and Sartre.* New York: Bible and Tanner, 1968.

Vacca, Robert, *The Coming Dark Age*. New York, 1973.

Van Prinsterer, Groen. *Unbelief and Revolution*. The Hague, 1847.

Van Reissen, H. *Nietzsche*. Philadelphia: Presbyterian and Reformed, 1960.

———. *The Society of the Future*. Presbyterian and Reformed, 1953.

Van Tassel, D. D. *American Thought in the Twentieth Century*. New York: Crowell, 1967.

Van Til, Cornelius. *The Case for Calvinism*. Nutley, N. J.: Presbyterian and Reformed, 1964.

———. *Christian Theistic Ethics*. Class syllabus. Westminster Theological Seminary, 1964.

———. *A Christian Theory of Knowledge*. Nutley, N. J.: Presbyterian and Reformed, 1969.

———. *Christianity and Barthianism*. Philadelphia: Presbyterian and Reformed, 1965.

———. *Christianity in Conflict*. Class syllabus. Westminster Theological Seminary, 1964.

———. *Christianity and Idealism*. Nutley, N. J.: Presbyterian and Reformed, 1955.

———. *Chrisitanity and Modern Theology*. Philadelphia: Presbyterian and Reformed, 1955.

———. *The Defense of the Faith*, rev. ed. Philadelphia: Presbyterian and Reformed, 1967.

———. *The Dilemma of Education*. Philadelphia: Presbyterian and Reformed, 1956.

———. *An Introduction to Systematic Theology*, class syllabus. Westminster Theological Seminary, 1966.

———. *The Scale of Being*, class syllabus. Westminster Theological Seminary, n.d.

———. *The Sovereignty of Grace*. Nutley, N. J.: Presbyterian and Reformed, 1969.

Van Til, Henry. *The Calvinistic Concept of Culture*. Grand Rapids: Wm. B. Eerdmans, 1959.

Vico, Gambattista. *The New Science*. Ithaca, N. Y.: Cornell University Press, 1968.

Vogelein, Eric. *From the Enlightenment to Revolution*, ed. John Hallowell. Durham, N. C: Duke University Press, 1975.

———. *Order and History*, 3 vols. Baton Rouge: Louisiana State University, 1956.

Von Mises, Ludwig. *Epistemological Problems of Economics.* Princeton, N. J.: Princeton University Press, 1960.

———. *Human Action,* 3rd ed. New Haven: Yale University Press, 1966.

Wagar, C. Warren, ed. *Idea of Progress Since the Renaissance.* New York: Wiley, 1969.

Walsh, William H. *Philosophy of History: An Introduction.* New York: Harper, 1961.

Ward, Lester Frank. *Applied Sociology.* New York: Appleton, 1906.

———. *Outlines of Sociology.* New York: Macmillan, 1907.

———. *Pure Sociology.* New York: Macmillan, 1903.

———. *The Psychic Factors in Civilization.* Boston: Ginn and Co., 1893.

Warren, Frank. *Liberalism and Communism.* Bloomington, Ind.: University of Indiana Press, 1966.

Watkins, F. M. *The Political Tradition of the West: A Study of the Development of Modern Liberalism.* Cambridge, Mass.: Harvard University Press, 1948.

Watson, J. B. *An Introduction to Comparative Psychology.* New York: Henry Holt, 1913.

Webb, C. C. *Studies in the History of Natural Theology.* London: Oxford University Press, 1915.

———. *Kant's Philosophy of Religion.* London: Oxford University Press, 1926.

Weber, Max. *Basic Concepts of Sociology,* tr. H. F. Sacher. New York: Greenwood, 1969.

———. *Economy and Society: An Outline of Interpretative Sociology.* Berkeley: University of California Press, 1956.

———. *On the Methodology of the Social Sciences.* Glencoe, Ill.: Glencoe Free Press, 1949.

———. *Politics and Vocation.* New York, 1919.

———. *The Protestant Ethic and the Spirit of Capitalism,* tr. Talcott Parsons. New York and London: Macmillan, 1956.

———. *The Sociology of True Religion.* Boston: Beacon Press, 1964.

Weldon, T. D. *Introduction to Kant's Critique of Pure Reason.* London: Oxford University Press, 1945.

Werkmeister, H. W. *A History of Philosophical Ideas in America.* New York: Ronald Press, 1949.

Whitehead, Alfred North. *Anthology,* selected by F. S. C. Northrip and W. G. Mason. New York, 1953.

———. *Adventures in Ideas.* New York: Macmillan, 1933.

———. *Dialogues,* as recorded by Lucian Price. Boston: Little, Brown, 1954.

———. *The Function of Reason.* Princeton, N. J.: Princeton University Press, 1929.

———. *Modes of Thought.* New York: Macmillan, 1938.

———. *Philosophy of Alfred North Whitehead,* ed. by Ralph Schilp, 2nd ed., rev. New York: Tudor, 1951.

———. *Process and Reality.* London and New York: Macmillan, 1929.

———. *Religion in the Making.* New York: Macmillan, 1926.

———. *Science and the Modern World.* New York: Macmillan, 1925.

Wiener, Philip, and Noland, Aron. *Roots of Scientific Thought.* New Brunswick, N. J.: Rutgers University Press, 1962.

———. *Evolution and the Founders of Pragmatism.* Philadelphia: University of Pennsylvania Press, 1972.

Wightman, E. D. P. *The Growth of Scientific Ideas.* London: Oxford University Press, 1950.

Williamson, Rene de Visme. *Independence and Involvement.* Baton Rouge: Louisiana State University Press, 1964.

———. *Political and Protestant Theology: An Interpretation of Tillich, Barth, Bonhoeffer and Brunner.* Baton Rouge: Louisiana State University Press, 1976.

Wilson, R. J. *Darwinism and the Intellectual.* Homewood, Ill.: Dorsey Press, 1967.

Windleband, Wilhelm. *History of Philosophy,* 2nd ed., rev. New York: Harper, 1957.

Wood, H. G. *Freedom and Necessity in History.* London: Lutterworth, 1957.

Wright, B. F. *American Interpretations of Natural Law.* Cambridge: Harvard University Press, 1931.

Wright, E. H. *The Meaning of Rousseau.* London: Oxford University Press, 1929.

Young, William. *Towards a Reformed Philosophy: The Development of a Protestant Theology in Dutch Calvinist's Thought Since the Time of Kuyper.* Grand Rapids: Wm. B. Eerdmans, 1952.

Znaniecki, Florian. *Humanistic Sociology: Selected Papers.* Chicago: University of Chicago Press, 1969.

Zeitlein, Irving. *Ideology in the Development of Sociological Theory.* Englewood Cliffs, N. J.: Prentice-Hall, 1968.

———. *Rethinking Society: A Critique of Contemporary Sociological Theory.* New York: Prentice Hall, 1973.

Index of Persons

Index of Subjects